Mastering CMake
Version 3.1

**Ken
Martin** & **Bill
Hoffman**

With contributions from:

Andy Cedilnik, David Cole, Marcus Hanwell, Julien Jomier, Brad King, Robert Maynard, Alex Neundorf

Published by Kitware Inc.

Join the CMake community at www.cmake.org

Contributors to this work include those listed on the title page as well as:
Cover Design: Steve Jordan
Technical Contributors: World-Wide CMake Developer Community at www.cmake.org.

All product names mentioned herein are the trademarks of their respective owners.

Printed and produced in the United States
ISBN: 978-1-930934-31-3

1 Why CMake?   **1**
   1.1 The History of CMake   2

2 Getting Started   **5**
   2.1 Getting and Installing CMake on Your Computer   5
   2.2 Building CMake Yourself   5
   2.3 Basic CMake Usage and Syntax   6
   2.4 Hello World for CMake   7
   2.5 How to Run CMake?   8
   2.6 Editing CMakeLists Files 15
   2.7 Setting Initial Values for CMake 15
   2.8 Building Your Project 16

3 Key Concepts   **19**
   3.1 Main Structures 19
   3.2 Targets 22
   3.3 Source Files 23
   3.4 Directories, Generators, Tests, and Properties 23
   3.5 Variables and Cache Entries 24
   3.6 Build Configurations 28

4 Writing CMakeLists Files   **29**
   4.1 CMake Language 29
   4.2 Basic Commands 29
   4.3 Flow Control 30
   4.4 Regular Expressions 35
   4.5 Checking Versions of CMake 37
   4.6 Using Modules 37
   4.7 Policies 41
   4.8 Advanced Linking 48
   4.9 Object Libraries 49
   4.10 Shared Libraries and Loadable Modules 50

	4.11	Shared Library Versioning	54
	4.12	Installing Files	55
	4.13	Advanced Commands	68

5 System Inspection — **71**

	5.1	Using Header Files and Libraries	71
	5.2	System Properties	73
	5.3	Finding Packages	77
	5.4	Built-in Find Modules	78
	5.5	How to Pass Parameters to a Compilation	79
	5.6	How to Configure a Header File	80
	5.7	Creating CMake Package Configuration Files	82
	5.8	CMake Package Registry	84

6 Custom Commands And Targets — **87**

	6.1	Portable Custom Commands	87
	6.2	Using add_custom_command on a Target	88
	6.3	Using add_custom_command to Generate a File	89
	6.4	Adding a Custom Target	91
	6.5	Specifying Dependencies and Outputs	93
	6.6	When There Isn't One Rule For One Output	94

7 Converting Existing Systems To CMake — **95**

	7.1	Source Code Directory Structures	95
	7.2	Build Directories	96
	7.3	Useful CMake Commands When Converting Projects	98
	7.4	Converting UNIX Makefiles	99
	7.5	Converting Autoconf Based Projects	100
	7.6	Converting Windows Based Workspaces	101

8 Cross Compiling With CMake — **103**

	8.1	Toolchain Files	103
	8.2	Finding External Libraries, Programs and Other Files	105
	8.3	System Inspection	107
	8.4	Running Executables Built in the Project	109
	8.5	Cross-Compiling Hello World	112
	8.6	Cross-Compiling for a Microcontroller	115
	8.7	Cross Compiling an Existing Project	118
	8.8	Cross-Compiling a Complex Project - VTK	119
	8.9	Some Tips and Tricks	121

9 Packaging With CPack — **123**

	9.1	CPack Basics	123
	9.2	CPack Source Packages	127
	9.3	CPack Installer Commands	127
	9.4	CPack for Windows Installer NSIS	128

9.5	CPack for Cygwin Setup	145
9.6	CPack for Mac OS X PackageMaker	147
9.7	CPack for Mac OS X Drag and Drop	151
9.8	CPack for Mac OS X X11 Applications	151
9.9	CPack for Debian Packages	154
9.10	CPack for RPM	155
9.11	CPack Files	155

10 Automation & Testing With CMake   **157**

10.1	Testing with CMake, CTest, and CDash	157
10.2	How Does CMake Facilitate Testing?	158
10.3	Additional Test Properties	159
10.4	Testing Using CTest	160
10.5	Using CTest to Drive Complex Tests	162
10.6	Handling a Large Number of Tests	163
10.7	Managing Test Data	164
10.8	Producing Test Dashboards	166
10.9	Customizing Dashboards for a Project	174
10.10	Setting up Automated Dashboard Clients	177
10.11	Advanced CTest Scripting	183
10.12	Setting up a Dashboard Server	187

11 Porting CMake to New Platforms and Languages   **211**

11.1	The Determine System Process	211
11.2	The Enable Language Process	212
11.3	Porting to a New Platform	214
11.4	Adding a New Language	215
11.5	Rule Variable Listing	216
11.6	Compiler and Platform Examples	217
11.7	Extending CMake	218

12 Tutorials   **223**

12.1	A Basic Starting Point (Step 1)	223
12.2	Adding a Library (Step 2)	225
12.3	Installing and Testing (Step 3)	227
12.4	Adding System Introspection (Step 4)	228
12.5	Adding a Generated File and Generator (Step 5)	229
12.6	Building an Installer (Step 6)	233
12.7	Adding Support for a Dashboard (Step 7)	234

A Command-Line Tools   **235**

A.1	cmake(1)	235
A.2	ctest(1)	240
A.3	cpack(1)	257

B Interactive Dialogs   **261**

B.1   cmake-gui(1) 261
B.2   ccmake(1)   264

C   Reference Manuals   **269**
C.1   cmake-commands(7) 269
C.2   cmake-generator-expressions(7) 356
C.3   cmake-generators(7) 360
C.4   cmake-modules(7) 366
C.5   cmake-policies(7) 537
C.6   cmake-properties(7) 559
C.7   cmake-variables(7) 623

Index   **685**

WHY CMAKE?

If you have ever maintained the build and installation process for a software package, you will be interested in CMake. CMake is an open-source build manager for software projects that allows developers to specify build parameters in a simple, portable, text file format. This file is then used by CMake to generate project files for native build tools including Integrated Development Environments such as Microsoft Visual Studio or Apple's Xcode, as well as UNIX, Linux, NMake, Ninja, and Borland style Makefiles. CMake handles the difficult aspects of building software such as cross-platform builds, system introspection, and user customized builds, in a simple manner that allows users to easily tailor builds for complex hardware and software systems.

For any project, and especially cross-platform projects, there is a need for a unified build system. Many non CMake-based projects ship with both a UNIX Makefile (or Makefile.in) and a Microsoft Visual Studio workspace. This requires that developers constantly try to keep both build systems up-to-date and consistent with each other. To target additional build systems, such as Xcode, requires even more custom copies of these files, creating an even bigger problem. This problem is compounded if you try to support optional components, such as including JPEG support if libjpeg is available on the system. CMake solves this by consolidating these different operations into one simple, easy-to-understand file format.

If you have multiple developers working on a project, or multiple target platforms, then the software will have to be built on more than one computer. Given the wide range of installed software and custom options that are involved with setting up a modern computer, the chances are that two computers running the same OS will be slightly different. CMake provides many benefits for single platform, multi-machine development environments including:

- The ability to automatically search for programs, libraries, and header files that may be required by the software being built. This includes the ability to consider environment variables and Window's registry settings when searching.

- The ability to build in a directory tree outside of the source tree. This is a useful feature found on many UNIX platforms; CMake provides this feature on Windows as well. This allows a developer to remove an entire build directory without fear of removing source files.

- The ability to create complex, custom commands for automatically generated files such as Qt's moc (qt.nokia.com) or SWIG (www.swig.org) wrapper generators. These commands are used to generate new source files during the build process that are in turn compiled into the software.

- The ability to select optional components at configuration time. For example, several of VTK's (www.vtk.org) libraries are optional, and CMake provides an easy way for users to select which libraries are built.

- The ability to automatically generate workspaces and projects from a simple text file. This can be very handy for systems that have many programs or test cases, each of which requires a separate project file, typically a tedious manual process to create using an IDE.

- The ability to easily switch between static and shared builds. CMake knows how to create shared libraries and modules on all platforms supported. Complicated platform-specific linker flags are handled, and advanced features like built-in run time search paths for shared libraries are supported on many UNIX systems.

- Automatic generation of file dependencies and support for parallel builds on most platforms.

When developing cross-platform software, CMake provides a number of additional features:

- The ability to test for machine byte order and other hardware-specific characteristics.

- A single set of build configuration files that work on all platforms. This avoids the problem of developers having to maintain the same information in several different formats inside a project.

- Support for building shared libraries on all platforms that support it.

- The ability to configure files with system-dependent information, such as the location of data files and other information. CMake can create header files that contain information such as paths to data files and other information in the form of #define macros. System specific flags can also be placed in configured header files. This has advantages over command line -D options to the compiler, because it allows other build systems to use the CMake built library without having to specify the exact same command line options used during the build.

1.1 The History of CMake

CMake development began in 1999 as part of the Insight Toolkit (ITK, www.itk.org), funded by the U.S. National Library of Medicine. ITK is a large software project that works on many platforms and can interact with many other software packages. To support this, a powerful, yet easy-to-use build tool was required. Having worked with build systems for large projects in the past, the developers designed CMake to address these needs. Since then CMake has continuously grown in popularity, with many projects and developers adopting it for its ease-of-use and flexibility. Since 1999, CMake has been under active development and has matured to the point where it is a proven solution for a wide range of build issues. The most telling example of this is the successful adoption of CMake as the build system of the K Desktop Environment (KDE), arguably the largest open-source software project in existence.

CMake also includes software testing support in the form of CTest. Part of the process of testing software involves building the software, possibly installing it, and determining what parts of the software are appropriate for the current system. This makes CTest a logical extension of CMake as it already has most of this information. In a similar vein, CMake contains CPack, which is designed to support cross-platform distribution of software. It provides a cross-platform approach to creating native installations for your software, making use of existing popular packages such as NSIS, RPM, Cygwin, and PackageMaker.

CMake continues to track and support popular build tools as they become available. CMake has quickly provided support for new versions of Microsofts's Visual Studio and Apple's Xcode IDE. In addition, support for the new build tool Ninja from Google has been added to CMake. With CMake, once you write your input files you get support for new compilers and build systems for free because the support for them is built into new releases of CMake and not tied to your software distribution. CMake also has ongoing support for cross-compiling to other operating systems or embedded devices. Most commands in CMake properly handle the differences between the host system and the target platform when cross-compiling.

1.1.1 Why Not Use Autoconf?

Before developing CMake, its authors had experience with the existing set of available build tools. Autoconf combined with Automake provides some of the same functionality as CMake, but to use these tools on a Windows platform requires the installation of many additional tools not found natively on a Windows box. In addition to requiring a host of tools, autoconf can be difficult to use or extend, and impossible for performing some tasks that are easy in CMake. Even if you do get autoconf and its required environment running on your system, it generates Makefiles that will force users to the command line. CMake on the other hand, provides a choice, allowing developers to generate project files that can be used directly from the IDE to which Windows and Xcode developers are accustomed.

While autoconf supports user-specified options, it does not support dependent options where one option depends on another property or selection. For example, in CMake you could have a user option to have multithreading be dependent on first determining if the user's system has multithreading support. CMake provides an interactive user interface, making it easy for the user to see which options are available and how to set them.

For UNIX users, CMake also provides automated dependency generation that is not done directly by autoconf. CMake's simple input format is also easier to read and maintain than a combination of Makefile.in and configure.in files. The ability of CMake to remember and chain library dependency information has no equivalent in autoconf/automake.

1.1.2 Why Not Use JAM, qmake, SCons, or ANT?

Other tools such as ANT, qmake, SCons, and JAM have taken different approaches to solving these problems and they have helped us to shape CMake. Of the four, qmake is the most similar to CMake, although it lacks much of the system interrogation that CMake provides. Qmake's input format is more closely related to a traditional Makefile. ANT, JAM, and SCons are also cross-platform although they do not support generating native project files. They do break away from the traditional Makefile-oriented input with ANT using XML; JAM using its own language; and SCons using Python. A number of these tools run the compiler directly, as opposed to letting the system's build process perform that task. Many of these tools require other tools such as Python or Java to be installed before they will work.

1.1.3 Why Not Script It Yourself?

Some projects use existing scripting languages such as Perl or Python to configure build processes. Although similar functionality can be achieved with systems like this, over-use of these tools can make the build process more of an Easter egg hunt than a simple-to-use build system. When building your software package, users are forced to find and install version 4.3.2 of this and 3.2.4 of that before they can even start the build process. To avoid that problem, it was decided that CMake would require no more tools than the software it was being used to build would require. At a minimum, using CMake requires a C compiler, that compiler's native build tools, and a CMake executable. CMake was written in C++, requires only a C++ compiler to build, and precompiled binaries are available for most systems. Scripting it yourself also typically means you will not be generating native Xcode or Visual Studio workspaces, making Mac and Windows builds limited.

1.1.4 On What Platforms Does CMake Run?

CMake runs on a wide variety of platforms including Microsoft Windows, Apple Mac OS X, and most UNIX or UNIX-like platforms. At the time of the writing of this book, CMake was tested nightly on the following platforms: Windows 98/2000/XP/Vista/7, AIX, HPUX, IRIX, Linux, Mac OS X, Solaris, OSF, QNX, CYGWIN, MinGW, and FreeBSD. You can check www.cmake.org for a current list of tested platforms.

Likewise, CMake supports most common compilers. It supports the GNU compiler on all CMake-supported platforms. Other tested compilers include Visual Studio 6 through 11, Intel C, SGI CC, Mips Pro, Borland, Sun CC, and HP aCC. CMake should work for most UNIX-style compilers out-of-the-box. If the compiler takes arguments in a strange way, then see the section Porting CMake to New Platform for information on how to customize CMake for a new compiler.

1.1.5 How Stable is CMake?

Before adopting any new technology or tool for a project, a developer will want to know how well supported and popular the tool is. Over the past 12 years, CMake has grown in popularity as a build tool. Both the developer and user communities continue to grow. The website ohlo (http://www.ohloh.net) reports that there are over 8,000,000 lines of CMake code in existence. CMake has continued to develop support for new build technologies and tools as they become available. The CMake development team has a strong commitment to backwards compatibility. If CMake can build your project once, it should always be able to build your project. Also, since CMake is an open-source project, the source code is always available for a project to edit and patch as needed.

GETTING STARTED

2.1 Getting and Installing CMake on Your Computer

Before using CMake, you will need to install or build the CMake binaries on your system. On many systems, you may find that CMake is already installed or is available for install with the standard package manager tool for the system. Cygwin, Debian, FreeBSD, OS X MacPorts, Mac OS X Fink, and many others all have CMake distributions. If your system does not have a CMake package, you can find CMake precompiled for many common architectures at www.cmake.org. If you do not find precompiled binaries for your system, then you can build CMake from source. To build CMake, you will need a modern C++ compiler.

2.1.1 UNIX and Mac Binary Installations

If your system provides CMake as one of its standard packages, follow your system's package installation instructions. If your system does not have CMake, or has an out-of-date version of CMake, you can download precompiled binaries from www.cmake.org. The binaries from www.cmake.org come in the form of a compressed .tar file. To install, simply extract the compressed .tar file into a destination directory such as `/usr/local`. Any directory is allowed, so CMake does not require root privileges for installation.

2.1.2 Windows Binary Installation

For Windows, CMake provides an installer executable available for download from www.cmake.org. To install this file, simply run the executable on the Windows machine where you want to install CMake. You will be able to run CMake from the Start Menu or from the command line after it is installed.

2.2 Building CMake Yourself

If binaries are not available for your system, or if binaries are not available for the version of CMake you wish to use, you can build CMake from the source code. You can obtain the CMake source code from the www.cmake.org download page. Once you have the source code, it can be built in two different ways. If you have a version of CMake on your system, you can use it to build other versions of CMake. The current development version of CMake can generally be built from the previous release of CMake. This is how new versions of CMake are built on most Windows systems.

The second way to build CMake is by running its bootstrap build script. To do this, change directory into your CMake source directory and type:

```
./bootstrap
make
make install
```

The make install step is optional since CMake can run directly from the build directory if desired. On UNIX, if you are not using the system's C++ compiler, you need to tell the bootstrap script which compiler you want to use. This is done by setting the environment variable CXX before running bootstrap. If you need to use any special flags with your compiler, set the CXXFLAGS environment variable. For example, on the SGI with the 7.3X compiler, you would build CMake like this:

```
cd CMake
(setenv CXX CC; setenv CXXFLAGS "-LANG:std"; ./bootstrap)
make
make install
```

2.3 Basic CMake Usage and Syntax

Using CMake is simple. The build process is controlled by creating one-or-more CMakeLists files (actually CMakeLists.txt but this guide will leave off the extension in most cases) in each of the directories that make up a project. The CMakeLists files contain the project description in CMake's simple language. The language is expressed as a series of comments and commands. Comments start with # and run to the end of the line. Commands have the form

```
command (args...)
```

where command is the name of the command, and args is a whitespace-separated list of arguments. Each command is evaluated in the order that it appears in the CMakeLists file. CMake is no longer case insensitive to command names as of version 2.2, so where you see command, you could use COMMAND or Command instead. Older versions of CMake only accepted uppercase commands.

CMake command arguments may be either quoted or unquoted. A quoted argument starts and ends in a double quote (") and always represents exactly one argument. Any double quotes contained inside the value must be escaped with a backslash (\"). An unquoted argument starts in any character other than a double quote (later double quotes are literal) and is automatically expanded into zero-or-more arguments by separating on semicolons within the value. For example:

```
command ("")          # 1 quoted argument
command ("a b c")     # 1 quoted argument
command ("a;b;c")     # 1 quoted argument
command ("a" "b" "c") # 3 quoted arguments
```

```
command (a b c)      # 3 unquoted arguments
command (a;b;c)      # 1 unquoted argument expands to 3
```

CMake supports simple variables storing strings. Use the set () (page 330) command to set variable values. In its simplest form, the first argument to set is the name of the variable and the rest of the arguments are the values. Multiple value arguments are packed into a semicolon-separated list and stored in the variable as a string. For example:

```
set (Foo "")       # 1 quoted arg -> value is ""
set (Foo a)        # 1 unquoted arg -> value is "a"
set (Foo "a b c")  # 1 quoted arg -> value is "a b c"
set (Foo a b c)    # 3 unquoted args -> value is "a;b;c"
```

Variables may be referenced in command arguments using syntax ${VAR} where VAR is the variable name. If the named variable is not defined, the reference is replaced with an empty string; otherwise it is replaced by the value of the variable. Replacement is performed prior to the expansion of unquoted arguments, so variable values containing semicolons are split into zero-or-more arguments in place of the original unquoted argument. For example:

```
set (Foo a b c)       # 3 unquoted args -> value is "a;b;c"
command(${Foo})       # unquoted arg replaced by a;b;c
                      # and expands to three arguments
command("${Foo}")     # quoted arg value is "a;b;c"
set (Foo "")          # 1 quoted arg -> value is empty string
command(${Foo})       # unquoted arg replaced by empty string
                      # and expands to zero arguments
command("${Foo}")     # quoted arg value is empty string
```

System environment variables and Windows registry values can be accessed directly in CMake. To access system environment variables, use the syntax $ENV{VAR}. CMake can also reference registry entries in many commands using a syntax of the form [HKEY_CURRENT_USER\\Software\\path1\\path2;key], where the paths are built from the registry tree and key.

2.4 Hello World for CMake

For starters, let us consider the simplest possible CMakeLists file. To compile an executable from one source file, the CMakeLists file would contain two lines:

```
project (Hello)
add_executable (Hello Hello.c)
```

To build the Hello executable, follow the process described in Running CMake (See section 0) to generate the build files. The project() (page 327) command indicates what the name of the resulting workspace should be and the add_executable() (page 273) command adds an executable target to the build process. That's all there is to it for this simple example. If your project requires a few files, it is also quite easy to modify with the add_executable line as shown below.

```
add_executable (Hello Hello.c File2.c File3.c File4.c)
```

`add_executable` is just one of many commands available in CMake. Consider the more complicated example below.

```
cmake_minimum_required (2.6)
project (HELLO)

set (HELLO_SRCS Hello.c File2.c File3.c)

if (WIN32)
  set(HELLO_SRCS ${HELLO_SRCS} WinSupport.c)
else ()
  set(HELLO_SRCS ${HELLO_SRCS} UnixSupport.c)
endif ()

add_executable (Hello ${HELLO_SRCS})

# look for the Tcl library
find_library (TCL_LIBRARY
  NAMES tcl tcl84 tcl83 tcl82 tcl80
  PATHS /opt/TclTk/lib c:/TclTk/lib
  )

if (TCL_LIBRARY)
  target_link_library (Hello ${TCL_LIBRARY})
endif ()
```

In this example, the `set()` (page 330) command is used to group together source files into a list. The `if()` (page 313) command is used to add either WinSupport.c or UnixSupport.c to this list based on whether or not CMake is running on Windows. Finally, the `add_executable()` (page 273) command is used to build the executable with the files listed in the variable `HELLO_SRCS`. The `find_library()` (page 294) command looks for the Tcl library under a few different names and in a few different paths. An if command checks if the `TCL_LIBRARY` was found, and if so, adds it to the link line for the Hello executable target.

2.5 How to Run CMake?

Once CMake has been installed on your system, using it to build a project is easy. There are two main directories CMake uses when building a project: the source directory and the binary directory. The source directory is where the source code for your project is located. This is also where the CMakeLists files will be found. The binary directory is where you want CMake to put the resulting object files, libraries, and executables. CMake will not write any files to the source directory, only to the binary directory. We encourage use of "out-of-source" builds in which the source and binary directories are different, but one may also perform "in-source" builds in which the source and binary directories are the same.

CMake supports both in-source and out-of-source builds on all operating systems. This means that you can configure your build to be completely outside of the source code tree, which makes it very easy to remove all of the files generated by a build. Having the build tree differ from the source tree also makes it easy to support having multiple builds of a single source tree. This is useful when you want to have multiple builds with different options but just one copy of the source code. Now let us consider the specifics of running CMake using its Qt-based GUI and command line interfaces.

2.5.1 Running CMake's Qt Interface

CMake includes a Qt-based user interface that can be used on most platforms, including UNIX, Mac OS X, and Windows. This interface is included in the CMake source code, but you will need an installation of Qt on your system in order to build it.

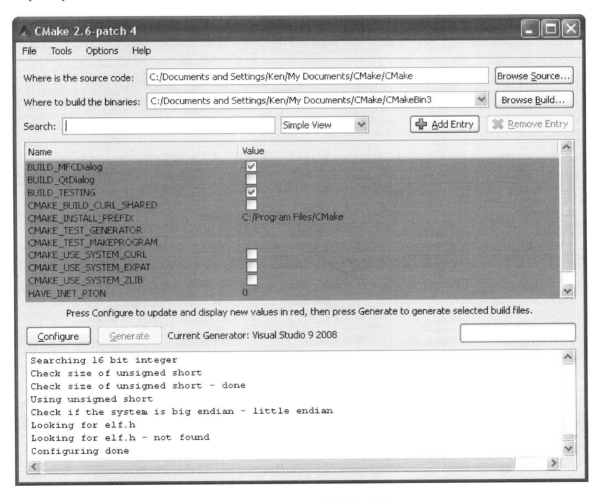

Figure 2.1: Qt based CMake GUI

On Windows, the executable is named `cmake-gui.exe` and it should be in your Start menu under Program Files. There may also be a shortcut on your desktop, or if you built CMake from the source, it will be in the build directory. For UNIX and Mac users, the executable is named cmake-gui and it can be found where you installed the CMake executables. A GUI will appear similar to what is shown in Figure 2.1. The top two fields are the source code and binary directories. They allow you to specify where the source code is located for what you want to compile, and where the resulting binaries should be placed. You should set these two values first. If the binary directory you specify does not exist, it will be created for you. If the binary directory has been configured by CMake before, it will then automatically set the source tree.

The middle area is where you can specify different options for the build process. More obscure variables may be hidden, but can be seen if you select "Advanced View" from the view pulldown. You can search for values in the middle area by typing all or part of the name into the search box. This can be handy for finding specific settings or options in a large project. The bottom area of the window includes the Configure and Generate buttons as well as a progress bar and scrollable output window.

Once you have specified the source code and binary directories, click the Configure button. This will cause CMake to read in the CMakeLists files from the source code directory and update the cache area to display any new options for the project. If you are running cmake-gui for the first time on this binary directory it will prompt you to determine which generator you wish to use, as shown in Figure 2.2. This dialog also presents options for customizing and tweaking the compilers you wish to use for the build.

After the first configure, you can adjust the cache settings if desired and click the Configure button again. New values that were created by the configure process will be colored red. To be sure you have seen all possible values, click Configure until none of the values are red and you are happy with all the settings. Once you are done configuring, click the Generate button to produce the appropriate files.

It is important that you make sure that your environment is suitable for running cmake-gui. If you are using an IDE such as Visual Studio, your environment will be setup correctly. If you are using NMake or MinGW, make sure that the compiler can run from your environment. You can either directly set the required environment variables for your compiler or use a shell in which they are already set. For example, Microsoft Visual Studio has an option on the start menu for creating a Visual Studio Command Prompt. This opens up a command prompt window that has its environment already setup for Visual Studio. You should run cmake-gui from this command prompt if you want to use NMake Makefiles. The same approach applies to MinGW; you should run cmake-gui from a MinGW shell that has a working compiler in its path.

When cmake-gui finishes, it will have generated the build files in the binary directory you specified. If Visual Studio was selected as the generator, a MSVC workspace (or solution) file is created. This file's name is based on the name of the project you specified in the `project()` (page 327) command at the beginning of your CMakeLists file. For many other generator types, Makefiles are generated. The next step in this process is to open the workspace with MSVC. Once open, the project can be built in the normal manner of Microsoft Visual C++. The ALL_BUILD target can be used to build all of the libraries and executables in the package. If you are using a Makefile build type, then you would build by running make or nmake on the resulting Makefiles.

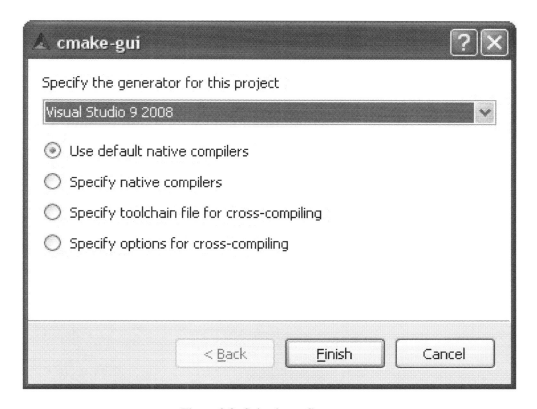

Figure 2.2: Selecting a Generator

2.5.2 Running the ccmake Curses Interface

On most UNIX platforms, if the curses library is supported, CMake provides an executable called ccmake. This interface is a terminal-based text application that is very similar to the Qt-based GUI. To run ccmake, change directory (cd) to the directory where you want the binaries to be placed. This can be the same directory as the source code for what we call in-source builds, or it can be a new directory you create. Then run ccmake with the path to the source directory on the command line. For in-source builds, use "." for the source directory. This will start the text interface as shown in Figure 2.3 (in this case, the cache variables are from VTK and most are set automatically).

Figure 2.3: ccmake running on UNIX

Brief instructions are displayed in the bottom of the window. If you hit the "c" key, it will configure the project. You should always configure after changing values in the cache. To change values, use the arrow keys to select cache entries, and hit the enter key to edit them. Boolean values will toggle with the enter key. Once you have set all the values as you like, you can hit the "g" key to generate the Makefiles and exit. You can also hit "h" for help, "q" to quit, and "t" to toggle the viewing of advanced cache entries. Two examples of CMake usage on the UNIX platform follow for a hello world project called Hello. In the first example, an in-source build is performed.

```
cd Hello
ccmake .
make
```

In the second example, an out-of-source build is performed.

```
mkdir Hello-Linux
cd Hello-Linux
ccmake ../Hello
make
```

2.5.3 Running CMake from the Command Line

From the command line, CMake can be run as an interactive question-and-answer session or as a non-interactive program. To run in interactive mode, just pass the "-i" option to CMake. This will cause CMake to ask you for a value for each entry in the cache file for the project. CMake will provide reasonable defaults, just like it does in the GUI and curses-based interfaces. The process stops when there are no longer any more questions to ask. An example of using the interactive mode of CMake is provided below.

```
$ cmake -i -G "NMake Makefiles" ../CMake
Would you like to see advanced options? [No]:
Please wait while cmake processes CMakeLists.txt files....

Variable Name: BUILD_TESTING
Description: Build the testing tree.
Current Value: ON
New Value (Enter to keep current value):

Variable Name: CMAKE_INSTALL_PREFIX
Description: Install path prefix, prepended onto install directories.
Current Value: C:/Program Files/CMake
New Value (Enter to keep current value):

Please wait while cmake processes CMakeLists.txt files....

CMake complete, run make to build project.
```

Using CMake to build a project in non-interactive mode is a simple process if the project has few or no options. For larger projects like VTK, using ccmake, cmake -i, or cmake-gui is recommended. To build a project with a non-interactive CMake, first change directory to where you want the binaries to be placed. For an in-source build, run cmake. and pass in any options using the -D flag. For out-of-source builds, the process is the same except you run cmake and also provide the path to the source code as its argument. Then type make and your project should compile. Some projects will have install targets as well and you can type make install to install them.

2.5.4 Specifying the Compiler to CMake

On some systems, you may have more than one compiler to choose from or your compiler may be in a non-standard place. In these cases, you will need to specify to CMake where your desired compiler is located. There are three ways to specify this: the generator can specify the compiler; an environment variable can be set; or a cache entry can be set. Some generators are tied to a specific compiler; for example, the Visual Studio 8 generator always uses the Microsoft Visual Studio 8 compiler. For Makefile-based generators, CMake will try a list of usual compilers until it finds a working one. The list can be found in the files:

```
Modules/CMakeDeterminCCompiler.cmake and
Modules/CMakeDetermineCXXCompiler.cmake
```

The lists can be preempted with environment variables that can be set before CMake is run. The CC environment variable specifies the C compiler, while CXX specifies the C++ compiler. You can specify the compilers directly on the command line by using -DCMAKE_CXX_COMPILER=cl for example.

Once CMake has been run and picked a compiler, you can change the selection by changing the cache entries CMAKE_CXX_COMPILER and CMAKE_C_COMPILER, although this is not recommended. The problem with doing this is that the project you are configuring may have already run some tests on the compiler to determine what it supports. Changing the compiler does not normally cause these tests to be rerun, which can lead to incorrect results. If you must change the compiler, start over with an empty binary directory. The flags for the compiler and the linker can also be changed by setting environment variables. Setting LDFLAGS will initialize the cache values for link flags, while CXXFLAGS and CFLAGS will initialize CMAKE_CXX_FLAGS and CMAKE_C_FLAGS respectively.

2.5.5 Dependency Analysis

CMake has powerful, built-in implicit dependency (#include) analysis capabilities for C, C++, and Fortran source code files. CMake also has limited support for Java dependencies. Since Integrated Development Environments (IDEs) support and maintain their own dependency information, CMake skips this step for those build systems. However, Makefiles with a make program do not know how to automatically compute and keep dependency information up-to-date. For these builds, CMake automatically computes dependency information for C, C++, and Fortran files. Both the generation and maintenance of these dependencies are automatically done by CMake. Once a project is initially configured by CMake, users only need to run make, and CMake does the rest of the work. CMake's dependencies fully support parallel builds for multiprocessor systems.

Although users do not need to know how CMake does this work, it may be useful to look at the dependency information files for a project. The information for each target is stored in four files called depend.make, flags.make, build.make, and DependInfo.cmake. depend.make stores the depend information for all the object files in the directory. flags.make contains the compile flags used for the source files of this target. If they change then the files will be recompiled. DependInfo.cmake is used to keep the dependency information up-to-date and contains information about which files are part of the project and the languages they are in. Finally, the rules for building the dependencies are stored in build.make. If a dependency is out-of-date then all of the dependencies for that target will be recomputed, keeping the dependency information current.

2.6 Editing CMakeLists Files

CMakeLists files can be edited in almost any text editor. Some editors, such as Notepad++, come with CMake syntax highlighting and indentation support built-in. For editors such as Emacs or Vim, CMake includes indentation and syntax highlighting modes. These can be found in the `Auxiliary` directory of the source distribution, or downloaded from the CMake web site. The file `cmake-mode.el` is the Emacs mode, and `cmake-indent.vim` and `cmake-syntax.vim` are used by Vim. Within Visual Studio, CMakeLists files are listed as part of the project and you can edit them simply by double-clicking on them. Within any of the supported generators (Makefiles, Visual Studio, etc.), if you edit a CMakeLists file and rebuild, there are rules that will automatically invoke CMake to update the generated files (e.g. Makefiles or project files) as required. This helps to assure that your generated files are always in sync with your CMakeLists files.

Since CMake computes and maintains dependency information, CMake executables must always be available (though they don't have to be in your PATH) when make or an IDE is being run on CMake-generated files. This means that if a CMake input file changes on disk, your build system will automatically re-run CMake and produce up-to-date build files. For this reason, you generally should not generate Makefiles or projects with CMake and move them to another machine that does not have CMake installed.

2.7 Setting Initial Values for CMake

While CMake works well in an interactive mode, sometimes you will need to set up cache entries without running a GUI. This is common when setting up nightly dashboards, or if you will be creating many build trees with the same cache values. In these cases, the CMake cache can be initialized in two different ways. The first way is to pass the cache values on the CMake command line using `-DCACHE_VAR:TYPE=VALUE` arguments. For example, consider the following nightly dashboard script for a UNIX machine:

```
#!/bin/tcsh

cd ${HOME}

# wipe out the old binary tree and then create it again
rm -rf Foo-Linux
mkdir Foo-Linux
cd Foo-Linux

# run cmake to setup the cache
cmake   DBUILD_TESTING:BOOL=ON <etc...> ../Foo

# generate the dashboard
ctest -D Nightly
```

The same idea can be used with a batch file on Windows. The second way is to create a file to be loaded using CMake's `-C` option. In this case, instead of setting up the cache with `-D` options, it is done though a file that is parsed by CMake. The syntax for this file is the standard CMakeLists syntax, which is typically a series of `set()` (page 330) commands such as:

```
#Build the vtkHybrid kit.
set (VTK_USE_HYBRID ON CACHE BOOL "doc string")
```

In some cases there might be an existing cache, and you want to force the cache values to be set a certain way. For example, say you want to turn Hybrid on even if the user has previously run CMake and turned it off. Then you can do

```
#Build the vtkHybrid kit always.
set (VTK_USE_HYBRID ON CACHE BOOL "doc" FORCE)
```

Another option is that you want to set and then hide options so the user will not be tempted to adjust them later on. This can be done using the following commands

```
#Build the vtkHybrid kit always and don't distract
#the user by showing the option.
set (VTK_USE_HYBRID ON CACHE INTERNAL "doc" FORCE)
mark_as_advanced (VTK_USE_HYBRID)
```

You might be tempted to edit the cache file directly, or to "initialize" a project by giving it an initial cache file. This may not work and could cause additional problems in the future. First, the syntax of the CMake cache is subject to change. Second, cache files contain full paths which make them unsuitable for moving between binary trees. If you want to initialize a cache file, use one of the two standard methods described above.

2.8 Building Your Project

After you have run CMake, your project will be ready to be built. If your target generator is based on Makefiles then you can build your project by changing the directory to your binary tree and typing make (or gmake or nmake as appropriate). If you generated files for an IDE such as Visual Studio, you can start your IDE, load the project files into it, and build as you normally would.

Another option is to use CMake's ``--build`` option from the command line. This option is simply a convenience that allows you to build your project from the command line, even if that requires launching an IDE. The command line options for ``--build`` include:

```
Usage: cmake --build <dir> [options] [-- [native-options]]
Options:
  <dir>          = Project binary directory to be built.
  --target <tgt> = Build <tgt> instead of default targets.
  --config <cfg> = For multi-configuration tools, choose <cfg>.
  --clean-first  = Build target 'clean' first, then build.
                 = (To clean only, use --target 'clean'.)
  --            = Pass remaining options to the native tool.
```

Even if you are using Visual Studio as your generator, type the following to build your project from the command line if you wish:

```
cmake --build <your binary dir>
```

That is all there is to installing and running CMake for simple projects. In the following chapters, we will consider CMake in more detail and explain how to use it on more complex software projects.

KEY CONCEPTS

3.1 Main Structures

This chapter provides an introduction to CMake's key concepts. As you start working with CMake, you will run into a variety of concepts such as targets, generators, and commands. In CMake, these concepts are implemented as C++ classes and are referenced in many of CMake's commands. Understanding these concepts will provide you with the working knowledge you need to create effective CMakeLists files.

Before going into detail about CMake's classes, it is worth understanding their basic relationships. At the lowest level are source files; these correspond to typical C or C++ source code files. Source files are combined into targets. A target is typically an executable or library. A directory represents a directory in the source tree and typically has a CMakeLists file and one-or-more targets associated with it. Every directory has a local generator that is responsible for generating the Makefiles or project files for that directory. All of the local generators share a common global generator that oversees the build process. Finally, the global generator is created and driven by the cmake class itself.

Figure 3.1 shows the basic class structure of CMake. We will now consider CMake's concepts in a bit more detail. CMake's execution begins by creating an instance of the cmake class and passing command line arguments to it. This class manages the overall configuration process and holds information that is global to the build process, such as the cache values. One of the first things the cmake class does is to create the correct global generator based on the user's selection of which generator to use (such as Visual Studio 10, Borland Makefiles, or UNIX Makefiles). At this point, the cmake class passes control to the global generator it created by invoking the configure and generate methods.

The global generator is responsible for managing the configuration and generation of all of the Makefiles (or project files) for a project. In practice, most of the work is actually done by local generators that are created by the global generator. One local generator is created for each directory of the project that is processed. So while a project will have only one global generator, it may have many local generators. For example, under Visual Studio 7, the global generator creates a solution file for the entire project while the local generators create a project file for each target in their directory.

In the case of the "Unix Makefiles" generator, the local generators create most of the Makefiles and the global generator simply orchestrates the process and creates the main top-level Makefile. Implementation

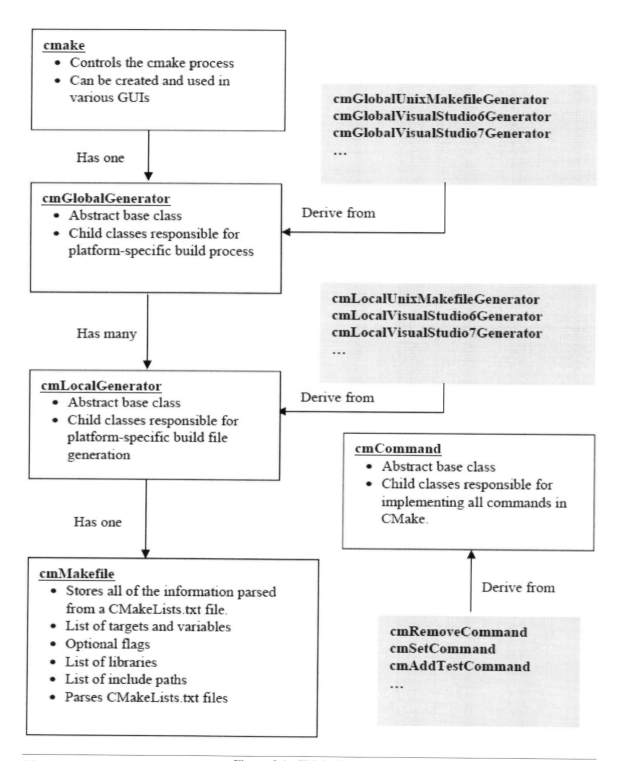

Figure 3.1: CMake Internals **Chapter 3. Key Concepts**

details vary widely among generators. Visual Studio 6 generators make use of .dsp and .dsw file templates and perform variable replacements on them. The generators for Visual Studio 7 and later directly generate the XML output without using any file templates. The Makefile generators including UNIX, NMake, Borland, etc. use a set of rule templates and replacements to generate their Makefiles.

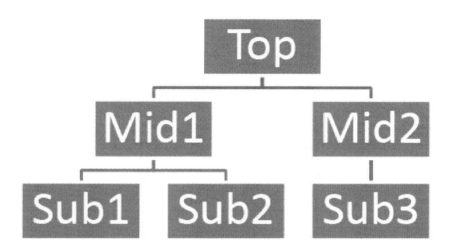

Figure 3.2: Sample Directory Tree

Each local generator has an instance of the class cmMakefile, which is where the results of parsing the CMakeLists files are stored. For each directory in a project there will be a single cmMakefile instance, which is why the cmMakefile class is often referred to as the directory. This is clearer for build systems that do not use Makefiles. That instance will hold all of the information from parsing that directory's CMakeLists file (see Figure 3.1). One way to think of the cmMakefile class is as a structure that starts out initialized with a few variables from its parent directory, and is then filled in as the CMakeLists file is processed. Reading in the CMakeLists file is simply a matter of CMake executing the commands it finds in the order it encounters them.

Each command in CMake is implemented as a separate C++ class, and has two main parts. The first part of a command is the InitialPass method, which receives the arguments and the cmMakefile instance for the directory currently being processed and performs its operations. The set command processes its arguments and if the arguments are correct, it calls a method on the cmMakefile to set the variable. The results of the command are always stored in the cmMakefile instance; information is never stored in a command. The last part of a command is the FinalPass. The FinalPass of a command is executed after all commands (for the entire CMake project) have had their InitialPass invoked. Most commands do not have a FinalPass, but in some rare cases a command must do something with global information that may not be available during the initial pass.

Once all of the CMakeLists files have been processed, the generators use the information collected into the cmMakefile instances to produce the appropriate files for the target build system (such as Makefiles).

3.2 Targets

Now that we have discussed the overall process of CMake, let us consider some of the key items stored in the `cmMakefile` instance. Probably the most important item is targets. Targets represent executables, libraries, and utilities built by CMake. Every `add_library()` (page 274), `add_executable()` (page 273), and `ADD_CUSTOM_TARGET()` (page 272) command creates a target. For example, the following command will create a target named "foo" that is a static library, with `foo1.c` and `foo2.c` as source files.

```
add_library (foo STATIC foo1.c foo2.c)
```

The name "foo" is now available for use as a library name everywhere else in the project, and CMake will know how to expand the name into the library when needed. Libraries can be declared as a particular type such as `STATIC`, `SHARED`, `MODULE`, or left undeclared. `STATIC` indicates that the library must be built as a static library. Likewise, `SHARED` indicates it must be built as a shared library. `MODULE` indicates that the library must be created so that it can be dynamically-loaded into an executable. Module libraries are implemented as shared libraries on many platforms, but not all. Therefore, CMake does not allow other targets to link to modules. If none of these options are specified, it indicates that the library could be built as either shared or static. In that case, CMake uses the setting of the variable `BUILD_SHARED_LIBS` to determine if the library should be `SHARED` or `STATIC`. If it is not set, then CMake defaults to building static libraries.

Likewise, executables have some options. By default, an executable will be a traditional console application that has a main entry point. One may specify a `WIN32` option to request a WinMain entry point on Windows systems, while retaining main on non-Windows systems.

In addition to storing their type, targets also keep track of general properties. These properties can be set and retrieved using the `set_target_properties()` (page 332) and `get_target_property()` (page 312) commands, or the more general `set_property()` (page 329) and `get_property()` (page 311) commands. One useful property is `LINK_FLAGS` (page 598), which is used to specify additional link flags for a specific target. Targets store a list of libraries that they link against, which are set using the `target_link_libraries()` (page 340) command. Names passed into this command can be libraries, full paths to libraries, or the name of a library from an `add_library()` (page 274) command. Targets also store the link directories to use when linking, and custom commands to execute after building.

For each library or executable CMake creates, it tracks of all the libraries on which that target depends. Since static libraries do not actually link to the libraries on which they depend, it is important for CMake to keep track of their dependencies so they can be specified when other targets link to the static library. For example:

```
add_library (foo foo.cxx)
target_link_libraries (foo bar)

add_executable (foobar foobar.cxx)
target_link_libraries (foobar foo)
```

will link the libraries "foo" and "bar" into the executable "foobar" even though only "foo" was explicitly specified for it. This is required when linking to static libraries. Since the foo library uses symbols from the bar library, foobar will most likely also need bar since it uses foo.

In some cases, such as when using external libraries, or when reducing the overlinking when creating dynamic libraries you want only a subset of your link dependencies to be propagated to targets that link to you. These advanced use cases are covered in the AdvancedLinking section of the Linking Chapter.

3.3 Source Files

The source file structure is in many ways similar to a target. It stores the filename, extension, and a number of general properties related to a source file. Like targets, you can set and get properties using `set_source_files_properties` and `get_source_file_property`, or the more generic versions. Available properties include:

COMPILE_FLAGS Compile flags specific to this source file. These can include source specific -D and -I flags.

GENERATED The `GENERATED` property indicates that the source file is generated as part of the build process. It tells CMake not to complain if the source file does not exist prior to building. This is set automatically by `add_custom_command` for its output.

OBJECT_DEPENDS Adds additional files on which this source file should depend. CMake automatically performs dependency analysis to determine the usual C, C++, and Fortran dependencies. This parameter is used rarely in cases where there is an unconventional dependency or if the source files do not exist at dependency analysis time.

3.4 Directories, Generators, Tests, and Properties

In addition to targets and source files, you may find yourself occasionally working with other classes such as directories, generators, and tests. Normally such interactions take the shape of setting or getting properties from these objects. All of these classes have properties associated with them, as do source files and targets. A property is a key-value pair attached to a specific object such as a target. The most generic way to access properties is through the `set_property()` (page 329) and `get_property()` (page 311) commands. These commands allow you to set or get a property from any class in CMake that has properties. Some of the properties for targets and source files have already been covered. Some useful properties for a directory include:

ADDITIONAL_MAKE_CLEAN_FILES' This property specifies a list of additional files that will be cleaned as a part of the "make clean" stage. CMake will clean up any generated files that it knows about by default, but your build process may use other tools that leave files behind. This property can be set to a list of those files so that they also will be properly cleaned up.

EXCLUDE_FROM_ALL This property indicates if all the targets in this directory and all sub-directories should be excluded from the default build target. If it is not, then with a Makefile, for example, typing make will cause these targets to be built as well. The same concept applies to the default build of other generators.

LISTFILE_STACK This property is mainly useful when trying to debug errors in your CMake scripts. It returns a list of which list files are currently being processed, in order. So if one CMakeLists file does an `include` command, it is effectively pushing the included CMakeLists file onto the stack.

A full list of properties supported in CMake can be obtained by running `cmake` with the `--help-property-list` option. The generators and directories are automatically created for you as CMake processes your source tree.

3.5 Variables and Cache Entries

CMakeLists files use variables much like any programming language. As discussed in Chapter 2 variables hold string values for later use. A number of useful variables are automatically defined by CMake and are discussed in the `cmake-variables(7)` (page 623) manual.

Variables in CMake are referenced using a `${VARIABLE}` notation, and are defined in the order of the execution of set commands. Consider the following example:

```
# FOO is undefined

set (FOO 1)
# FOO is now set to 1

set (FOO 0)
# FOO is now set to 0
```

This may seem straightforward, but consider the following example:

```
set (FOO 1)

if (${FOO} LESS 2)
  set (FOO 2)
else (${FOO} LESS 2)
  set (FOO 3)
endif (${FOO} LESS 2)
```

Clearly the if statement is true, which means that the body of the if statement will be executed. That will set the variable FOO to 2, and so when the `else` statement is encountered FOO will have a value of 2. Normally in CMake the new value of FOO would be used, but the `else` statement is a rare exception to the rule and always refers back to the value of the variable when the `if` statement was executed. In this case, the body of the `else` clause will not be executed. To further understand the scope of variables, consider this example:

```
set (foo 1)

# process the dir1  subdirectory
add_subdirectory (dir1)

# include and process the commands in file1.cmake
include (file1.cmake)

set (bar 2)
```

```
# process the dir2 subdirectory
add_subdirectory (dir2)

# include and process the commands in file2.cmake
include (file2.cmake)
```

In this example, because the variable foo is defined at the beginning, it will be defined while processing both dir1 and dir2. In contrast, bar will only be defined when processing dir2. Likewise, foo will be defined when processing both file1.cmake and file2.cmake, whereas bar will only be defined while processing file2.cmake.

Variables in CMake have a scope that is a little different from most languages. When you set a variable, it is visible to the current CMakeLists file or function and any subdirectory's CMakeLists files, any functions or macros that are invoked, and any files that are included using the INCLUDE() (page 317) command. When a new subdirectory is processed (or a function called), a new variable scope is created and initialized with the current value of all variables in the calling scope. Any new variables created in the child scope, or changes made to existing variables, will not impact the parent scope. Consider the following example:

```
function (foo)
  message (${test}) # test is 1 here
  set (test 2)
  message (${test}) # test is 2 here, but only in this scope
endfunction()

set (test 1)
foo()
message (${test}) # test will still be 1 here
```

In some cases, you might want a function or subdirectory to set a variable in its parent's scope. This is one way for CMake to return a value from a function, and it can be done by using the PARENT_SCOPE option with the set() (page 330) command. We can modify the prior example so that the function foo changes the value of test in its parent's scope as follows:

```
function (foo)
  message (${test}) # test is 1 here
  set (test 2 PARENT_SCOPE)
  message (${test}) # test still 1 in this scope
endfunction()

set (test 1)
foo()
message (${test}) # test will now be 2 here
```

Variables can also represent a list of values. In these cases when the variable is expanded it will be expanded into multiple values. Consider the following example:

```
# set a list of items
set (items_to_buy apple orange pear beer)
```

```
# loop over the items
foreach (item ${items_to_buy})
  message ( "Don't forget to buy one ${item}" )
endforeach ()
```

In some cases, you might want to allow the user building your project to set a variable from the CMake user interface. In that case, the variable must be a cache entry. Whenever CMake is run, it produces a cache file in the directory where the binary files are to be written. The values of this cache file are displayed by the CMake user interface. There are a few purposes of this cache. The first is to store the user's selections and choices, so that if they should run CMake again they will not need to reenter that information. For example, the option() (page 327) command creates a Boolean variable and stores it in the cache.

```
option (USE_JPEG "Do you want to use the jpeg library")
```

The above line would create a variable called USE_JPEG and put it into the cache. That way the user can set that variable from the user interface and its value will remain in case the user should run CMake again in the future. To create a variable in the cache, use commands like option, find_file() (page 292), or the standard set command with the CACHE option.

```
set (USE_JPEG ON CACHE BOOL "include jpeg support?")
```

When you use the cache option, also provide the type of the variable and a documentation string. The type of the variable is used by the GUI to control how that variable is set and displayed, but the value is always a string. Variable types include BOOL, PATH, FILEPATH, and STRING. The documentation string is used by the GUI to provide online help.

Another purpose of the cache is to persistently store values between CMake runs. These entries may not be visible or adjustable by the user. Typically these values are system-dependent variables such as CMAKE_WORDS_BIGENDIAN, which require CMake to compile and run a program to determine their value. Once these values have been determined, they are stored in the cache to avoid having to recompute them every time CMake is run. CMake generally tries to limit these variables to properties that should never change (such as the byte order of the machine you are on). If you significantly change your computer, either by changing the operating system or switching to a different compiler, you will need to delete the cache file (and probably all of your binary tree's object files, libraries, and executables).

Variables that are in the cache also have a property indicating if they are advanced or not. By default, when a CMake GUI is run (such as ccmake or cmake-gui), the advanced cache entries are not displayed. This is so the user can focus on the cache entries that they should consider changing. The advanced cache entries are other options that the user can modify, but typically will not. It is not unusual for a large software project to have fifty or more options, and the advanced property lets a software project divide them into key options for most users and advanced options for advanced users. Depending on the project, there may not be any non-advanced cache entries. To make a cache entry advanced, the mark_as_advanced() (page 325) command is used with the name of the variable (a.k.a. cache entry).

In some cases, you might want to restrict a cache entry to a limited set of predefined options. You can do this by setting the STRINGS (page 621) property on the cache entry. The following CMakeLists code illustrates this by creating a property named CRYPTOBACKEND as usual, and then setting the STRINGS property on it to a set of three options.

```
set (CRYPTOBACKEND "OpenSSL" CACHE STRING
     "Select a cryptography backend")
set_property (CACHE CRYPTOBACKEND PROPERTY STRINGS
              "OpenSSL" "LibTomCrypt" "LibDES")
```

When cmake-gui is run and the user selects the CRYPTOBACKEND cache entry, they will be presented with a pulldown to select which option they want, as shown in Figure 3.3.

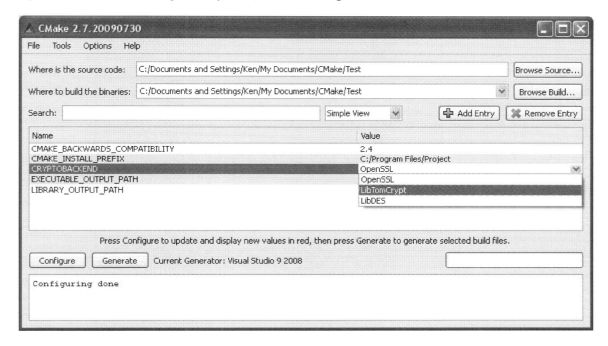

Figure 3.3: Cache Value Options in cmake-gui

A few final points should be made concerning variables and their interaction with the cache. If a variable is in the cache, it can still be overridden in a CMakeLists file using the set command without the CACHE option. Cache values are checked when a referenced variable is not defined in the current scope. The set command will define a variable for the current scope without changing the value in the cache.

```
# assume that FOO is set to ON in the cache

set (FOO OFF)
# sets foo to OFF for processing this CMakeLists file
# and subdirectories; the value in the cache stays ON
```

Once a variable is in the cache, its "cache" value cannot normally be modified from a CMakeLists file. The reasoning behind this is that once CMake has put the variable into the cache with its initial value, the user may then modify that value from the GUI. If the next invocation of CMake overwrote their change back to the set value, the user would never be able to make a change that CMake wouldn't overwrite. A set (FOO

ON CACHE BOOL "doc") command will typically only do something when the cache doesn't have the variable in it. Once the variable is in the cache, that command will have no effect.

In the rare event that you really want to change a cached variable's value, use the FORCE option in combination with the CACHE option to the set command. The FORCE option will cause the set command to override and change the cache value of a variable.

3.6 Build Configurations

Build configurations allow a project to be built in different ways for debug, optimized, or any other special set of flags. CMake supports, by default, Debug, Release, MinSizeRel, and RelWithDebInfo configurations. Debug has the basic debug flags turned on. Release has the basic optimizations turned on. MinSizeRel has flags that produce the smallest object code, but not necessarily the fastest code. RelWithDebInfo builds an optimized build with debug information as well.

CMake handles the configurations in slightly different ways depending on the generator being used. The conventions of the native build system are followed when possible. This means that configurations impact the build in different ways when using Makefiles versus using Visual Studio project files.

The Visual Studio IDE supports the notion of Build Configurations. A default project in Visual Studio usually has Debug and Release configurations. From the IDE you can select build Debug, and the files will be built with Debug flags. The IDE puts all of the binary files into directories with the name of the active configuration. This brings about an extra complexity for projects that build programs that need to be run as part of the build process from custom commands. See the CMAKE_CFG_INTDIR (page 625) variable and the custom commands section for more information about how to handle this issue. The variable CMAKE_CONFIGURATION_TYPES (page 640) is used to tell CMake which configurations to put in the workspace.

With Makefile-based generators, only one configuration can be active at the time CMake is run, and it is specified with the CMAKE_BUILD_TYPE (page 639) variable. If the variable is empty then no flags are added to the build. If the variable is set to the name of a configuration, then the appropriate variables and rules (such as CMAKE_CXX_FLAGS_<ConfigName>) are added to the compile lines. Makefiles do not use special configuration subdirectories for object files. To build both debug and release trees, the user is expected to create multiple build directories using the out-of-source build feature of CMake, and set the CMAKE_BUILD_TYPE to the desired selection for each build. For example:

```
# With source code in the directory MyProject
# to build MyProject-debug create that directory, cd into it and
(ccmake ../MyProject -DCMAKE_BUILD_TYPE=Debug)
# the same idea is used for the release tree MyProject-release
(ccmake ../MyProject -DCMAKE_BUILD_TYPE=Release)
```

WRITING CMAKELISTS FILES

This chapter will cover the basics of writing effective CMakeLists files for your software. It will cover the basic commands and issues you will need to handle most projects. It will also discuss how to convert existing UNIX or Windows projects into CMakeLists files. While CMake can handle extremely complex projects, for most projects you will find this chapter's contents will tell you all you need to know. CMake is driven by the CMakeLists.txt files written for a software project. The CMakeLists files determine everything from which options to present to users, to which source files to compile. In addition to discussing how to write a CMakeLists file, this chapter will also cover how to make them robust and maintainable. The basic syntax of a CMakeLists.txt file and key concepts of CMake have already been discussed in chapters 2 and 3. This chapter will expand on those concepts and introduce a few new ones.

4.1 CMake Language

As discussed in Chapter 2, CMakeLists files follow a simple syntax consisting of comments, commands, and whitespace. A comment is indicated using the # character and runs from that character until the end of the line. A command consists of the command name, opening parenthesis, whitespace-separated arguments, and a closing parenthesis. All whitespace (spaces, line feeds, tabs) is ignored except to separate arguments. Anything within a set of double quotes is treated as one argument, as is typical for most languages. The backslash can be used to escape characters, preventing the normal interpretation of them. The subsequent examples in this chapter will help to clear up some of these syntactic issues. You might wonder why CMake decided to have its own language instead of using an existing one such as Python, Java, or Tcl. The main reason is that we did not want to make CMake require an additional tool to run. By requiring one of these other languages, all users of CMake would be required to have that language installed, and potentially a specific version of that language. This is on top of the language extensions that would be required to do some of the CMake work, for both performance and capability reasons.

4.2 Basic Commands

While the previous chapters have already introduced many of the basic commands for CMakeLists files, this chapter will review and expand on them. The top-level CMakeLists file should call the PROJECT()

(page 327) command. This command both names the project and optionally specifies which languages will be used by it:

```
project (projectname [C] [CXX] [Fortran] [NONE])
```

If no languages are specified then CMake defaults to supporting C and C++. If the NONE language is passed then CMake does not include language-specific support.

For each directory in a project where the CMakeLists.txt file invokes the project command, CMake generates a top-level IDE project file. The project will contain all targets that are in the CMakeLists.txt file and any subdirectories, as specified by the add_subdirectory() (page 277) command. If the EXCLUDE_FROM_ALL (page 569) option is used in the add_subdirectory command, the generated project will not appear in the top-level Makefile or IDE project file; this is useful for generating sub-projects that do not make sense as part of the main build process. Consider that a project with a number of examples could use this feature to generate the build files for each example with one run of CMake, but not have the examples built as part of the normal build process.

The set and unset commands manipulate variables and entries in the persistent cache. The string() (page 335), list() (page 323), remove() (page 349), and separate_arguments() (page 329) commands offer basic manipulation of strings and lists.

The add_executable() (page 273) and add_library() (page 274) commands are the main commands for defining the libraries and executables to build, and which source files comprise them. For Visual Studio projects, the source files will show up in the IDE as usual, but any header files the project uses will not be. To have the header files show up, simply add them to the list of source files for the executable or library; this can be done for all generators. Any generators that do not use the header files directly (such as Makefile based generators) will simply ignore them.

4.3 Flow Control

The CMake language provides three flow control constructs:

- Conditional statements (e.g. if() (page 313))

- Looping constructs (e.g. foreach() (page 309) and while() (page 345))

- Procedure definitions (e.g. macro() (page 324) and function() (page 309))

First we will consider the if command. In many ways, the if command in CMake is just like the if command in any other language. It evaluates its expression and uses it to execute the code in its body or optionally the code in the else() (page 284) clause. For example:

```
if (FOO)
  # do something here
else ()
  # do something else
endif ()
```

The condition in the if statement may optionally be repeated in the else and endif() (page 285) clauses:

```
if (FOO)
   # do something here
else (FOO)
   # do something else
endif (FOO)
```

In this book, you will see examples of both styles. When you include conditionals in the `else` and `endif` clause then they must exactly match the original conditional of the `if` statement. The following code would not work:

```
set (FOO 1)
if (${FOO})
   # do something
endif (1)
# ERROR, it doesn't match the original if conditional
```

CMake provides verbose error messages in cases where an if statement is not properly matched with an `endif`.

CMake also supports `elseif()` (page 284) to help sequentially test for multiple conditions. For example:

```
if (MSVC80)
   # do something here
elseif (MSVC90)
   # do something else
elseif (APPLE)
   # do something else
endif ()
```

The `if` command documents the many conditions it can test. Some of the more common conditions include:

if (constant) True if the constant is 1, ON, YES, TRUE, Y, or a non-zero number. False if the constant is 0, OFF, NO, FALSE, N, IGNORE; is an empty string, or ends in the suffix "-NOTFOUND." Named boolean constants are case-insensitive. If the argument is not one of these constants then it is treated as a variable.

if (variable) True if the variable is defined to a value that is not a false constant.

if (NOT <expression>) True if the expression is not true.

if (<expr1> AND <expr2>) True if both expressions would be considered true individually.

if (<expr1> OR <expr2>) True if either expression would be considered true individually.

if (DEFINED variable) True if the given variable has been set, regardless of what value it was set to.

if (<variable|string> MATCHES regex) True if the given string or variable's value matches the regular given expression.

Additional binary test operators include `EQUAL`, `LESS`, and `GREATER` for numeric comparisons; `STRLESS`, `STREQUAL`, and `STRGREATER` for lexicographic comparisons; and `VERSION_LESS`, `VERSION_EQUAL`, and `VERSION_GREATER` to compare versions of the form `major[.minor[.patch[.tweak]]]`.

The OR test has the lowest precedence, followed by AND, then NOT, and then any other test. Tests of the same precedence are performed from left-to-right. Expressions may be enclosed in parentheses to adjust precedence. For example, consider the following conditionals

```
if ((1 LESS 2) AND (3 LESS 4))
  message ("sequence of numbers")
endif ()

if (1 AND 3 AND 4)
  message ("series of true values")
endif (1 AND 3 AND 4)

if (NOT 0 AND 3 AND 4)
  message ("a false value")
endif (NOT 0 AND 3 AND 4)

if (0 OR 3 AND 4)
  message ("or statements")
endif (0 OR 3 AND 4)

if (EXISTS ${PROJECT_SOURCE_DIR}/Help.txt AND COMMAND IF)
  message ("Help exists")
endif (EXISTS ${PROJECT_SOURCE_DIR}/Help.txt AND COMMAND IF)

set (fooba 0)

if (NOT DEFINED foobar)
  message ("foobar is not defined")
endif (NOT DEFINED foobar)

if (NOT DEFINED fooba)
  message ("fooba not defined")
endif (NOT DEFINED fooba)

if (NOT 0 AND 0)
  message ("This line is never executed")
endif (NOT 0 AND 0)
if (NOT (0 AND 0))
  message ("This line is always executed")
endif (NOT (0 AND 0))
```

Now let us consider the other flow control commands. The `foreach`, `while`, `macro`, and `function` commands are the best way to reduce the size of your CMakeLists files and keep them maintainable. The `foreach()` (page 309) command enables you to execute a group of CMake commands repeatedly on the members of a list. Consider the following example adapted from VTK

```
foreach (tfile
        TestAnisotropicDiffusion2D
        TestButterworthLowPass
        TestButterworthHighPass
```

```
         TestCityBlockDistance
         TestConvolve
         )
 add_test(${tfile}-image ${VTK_EXECUTABLE}
   ${VTK_SOURCE_DIR}/Tests/rtImageTest.tcl
   ${VTK_SOURCE_DIR}/Tests/${tfile}.tcl
   -D ${VTK_DATA_ROOT}
   -V Baseline/Imaging/${tfile}.png
   -A ${VTK_SOURCE_DIR}/Wrapping/Tcl
   )
endforeach ( tfile )
```

The first argument of the foreach command is the name of the variable that will take on a different value with each iteration of the loop; the remaining arguments are the list of values over which to loop. In this example, the body of the foreach loop is just one CMake command, add_test. In the body of the foreach loop, each time the loop variable (tfile in this example) is referenced will be replaced with the current value from the list. In the first iteration, occurrences of ${tfile} will be replaced with TestAnisotropicDiffusion2D. In the next iteration, ${tfile} will be replaced with TestButterworthLowPass. The foreach loop will continue to loop until all of the arguments have been processed.

It is worth mentioning that foreach loops can be nested, and that the loop variable is replaced prior to any other variable expansion. This means that in the body of a foreach loop, you can construct variable names using the loop variable. In the code below, the loop variable tfile is expanded, and then concatenated with _TEST_RESULT. The new variable name is then expanded and tested to see if it matches FAILED.

```
if (${${tfile}}_TEST_RESULT} MATCHES FAILED)
  message ("Test ${tfile} failed.")
endif ()
```

The while() (page 345) command provides looping based on a test condition. The format for the test expression in the while command is the same as it is for the if command, as described earlier. Consider the following example, which is used by CTest. Note that CTest updates the value of CTEST_ELAPSED_TIME internally.

```
##########################################################
# run paraview and ctest test dashboards for 6 hours
#
while (${CTEST_ELAPSED_TIME} LESS 36000)
  set (START_TIME ${CTEST_ELAPSED_TIME})
  ctest_run_script ( "dash1_ParaView_vs71continuous.cmake" )
  ctest_run_script ( "dash1_cmake_vs71continuous.cmake" )
endwhile ()
```

The foreach and while commands allow you to handle repetitive tasks that occur in sequence, whereas the macro and function commands support repetitive tasks that may be scattered throughout your CMakeLists files. Once a macro or function is defined, it can be used by any CMakeLists files processed after its definition.

A function in CMake is very much like a function in C or C++. You can pass arguments into it, and they become variables within the function. Likewise, some standard variables such as ARGC, ARGV, ARGN, and ARGV0, ARGV1, etc. are defined. Function calls have a dynamic scope. Within a function you are in a new variable scope; this is like how you drop into a subdirectory using the add_subdirectory() (page 277) command and are in a new variable scope. All the variables that were defined when the function was called remain defined, but any changes to variables or new variables only exist within the function. When the function returns, those variables will go away. Put more simply: when you invoke a function, a new variable scope is pushed; when it returns, that variable scope is popped.

The function() (page 309) command defines a new function. The first argument is the name of the function to define; all additional arguments are formal parameters to the function.

```
function(DetermineTime _time)
  # pass the result up to whatever invoked this
  set (${_time} "1:23:45" PARENT_SCOPE)
endfunction()

# now use the function we just defined
DetermineTime( current_time )

if( DEFINED current_time )
  message(STATUS "The time is now: ${current_time}")
endif()
```

Note that in this example, _time is used to pass the name of the return variable. The set() (page 330) command is invoked with the value of _time, which will be current_time. Finally, the set command uses the PARENT_SCOPE option to set the variable in the caller's scope instead of the local scope.

Macros are defined and called in the same manner as functions. The main differences are that a macro does not push and pop a new variable scope, and that the arguments to a macro are not treated as variables but as strings replaced prior to execution. This is very much like the differences between a macro and a function in C or C++. The first argument is the name of the macro to create; all additional arguments are formal parameters to the macro.

```
# define a simple macro
macro (assert TEST COMMENT)
  if (NOT ${TEST})
    message ("Assertion failed: ${COMMENT}")
  endif (NOT ${TEST})
endmacro (assert)

# use the macro
find_library (FOO_LIB foo /usr/local/lib)
assert ( ${FOO_LIB} "Unable to find library foo" )
```

The simple example above creates a macro called assert. The macro is defined into two arguments; the first is a value to test and the second is a comment to print out if the test fails. The body of the macro is a simple if() (page 313) command with a message() (page 326) command inside of it. The macro body ends when the endmacro() (page 285) command is found. The macro can be invoked simply by using its name as if it were a command. In the above example, if FOO_LIB was not found then a message would be displayed indicating the error condition.

The macro command also supports defining macros that take variable argument lists. This can be useful if you want to define a macro that has optional arguments or multiple signatures. Variable arguments can be referenced using ARGC and ARGV0, ARGV1, etc., instead of the formal parameters. ARGV0 represents the first argument to the macro; ARGV1 represents the next, and so forth. You can also use a mixture of formal arguments and variable arguments, as shown in the example below.

```
# define a macro that takes at least two arguments
# (the formal arguments) plus an optional third argument
macro (assert TEST COMMENT)
  if (NOT ${TEST})
    message ("Assertion failed: ${COMMENT}")

    # if called with three arguments then also write the
    # message to a file specified as the third argument
    if (${ARGC} MATCHES 3)
      file (APPEND ${ARGV2} "Assertion failed: ${COMMENT}")
    endif (${ARGC} MATCHES 3)

  endif (NOT ${TEST})
endmacro (assertASSERT)

# use the macro
find_library (FOO_LIB foo /usr/local/lib)
assert ( ${FOO_LIB} "Unable to find library foo" )
```

In this example, the two required arguments are TEST and COMMENT. These required arguments can be referenced by name, as they are in this example, or by referencing ARGV0 and ARGV1. If you want to process the arguments as a list, use the ARGV and ARGN variables. ARGV (as opposed to ARGV0, ARGV1, etc) is a list of all the arguments to the macro, while ARGN is a list of all the arguments after the formal arguments. Inside your macro, you can use the foreach command to iterate over ARGV or ARGN as desired.

CMake has two commands for interrupting the processing flow. The break() (page 279) command breaks out of a foreach or while loop before it would normally end. The return() (page 328) command returns from a function or listfile before the function or listfile has reached its end.

4.4 Regular Expressions

A few CMake commands, such as if() (page 313) and string() (page 335), make use of regular expressions or can take a regular expression as an argument. In its simplest form, a regular expression is a sequence of characters used to search for exact character matches. However, many times the exact sequence to be found is unknown, or only a match at the beginning or end of a string is desired. Since there are several different conventions for specifying regular expressions, CMake's standard is described below. The description is based on the open source regular expression class from Texas Instruments, which is used by CMake for parsing regular expressions.

Regular expressions can be specified by using combinations of standard alphanumeric characters and the following regular expression meta-characters:

^ Matches at the beginning of a line or string.

$ Matches at the end of a line or string.

. Matches any single character other than a new line.

[ ] Matches any character(s) inside the brackets.

[^] Matches any character(s) not inside the brackets.

[−] Matches any character in range on either side of a dash.

★ Matches the preceding pattern zero-or more-times.

+ Matches the preceding pattern one-or-more times.

? Matches the preceding pattern zero times or once only.

() Saves a matched expression and uses it in a later replacement.

(|) Matches either the left-or-right side of the bar.

Note that more than one of these meta-characters can be used in a single regular expression in order to create complex search patterns. For example, the pattern [^ab1-9] says to match any character sequence that does not begin with the characters "a" or "b" or numbers in the series one through nine. The following examples may help clarify regular expression usage:

- The regular expression "^hello" matches a "hello" only at the beginning of a search string. It would match "hello there," but not "hi,nhello there."

- The regular expression "long$" matches a "long" only at the end of a search string. It would match "so long," but not "long ago."

- The regular expression "t..t..g" will match anything that has a "t" and any two characters, followed by another "t," and any two characters, and then a "g." It would match "testing" or "test again," but would not match "toasting."

- The regular expression "[1-9ab]" matches any number one-through-nine, and the characters "a" and "b". It would match "hello 1" or "begin", but would not match "no-match".

- The regular expression "[^1-9ab]" matches any character that is not a number one-through-nine, or an "a" or "b." It would NOT match "1ab2" or "b2345a," but would match "no-match."

- The regular expression "br* " matches something that begins with a "b" and is followed by zero-or more "r"s, and ends in a space. It would match "brrrrr" and "b," but would not match "brrh."

- The regular expression "br+" matche s something that begins with a "b" and is followed by one or more "r"s, and ends in a space. It would match "brrrrr," and "br," but would not match "b " or "brrh."

- The regular expression "br?" matches something that begins with a "b," is followed by zero-or-one "r"s, and ends in a space. It would match "br," and "b ," but would not match "brrr" or "brrh."

- The regular expression "(..p)b" matches something ending with pb and beginning with the two characters before the first "p" encountered in the line. For example, it would find "repb" in "rep drepaqrepb." The regular expression "(..p)a" would find "repa qrepb" in "rep drepa qrepb."

- The regular expression "d(..p)" matches something ending with "p," beginning with "d," and having two characters in-between that are the same as the two characters before the first "p" encountered in the line. It would match "drepa qrepb" in "rep drepa qrepb."

4.5 Checking Versions of CMake

CMake is an evolving program and as new versions are released, new features or commands are introduced. As a result, there may be instances where you might want to use a command that is in a current version of CMake but not in previous versions. There are a couple of ways to handle this; one option is to use the `if()` (page 313) command to check whether a new command exists. For example:

```
# test if the command exists
if (COMMAND some_new_command)
  # use the command
  some_new_command ( ARGS...)
endif ()
```

Alternatively, one may test against the actual version of CMake that is being run by evaluating the `CMAKE_VERSION` (page 634) variable:

```
# look for newer versions of CMake
if (${CMAKE_VERSION} VERSION_GREATER 2.6.3)
  # do something special here
endif ()
```

When writing your CMakeLists files, you may decide that you do not want to support old versions of CMake. To do this, place the following command at the top of your CMakeLists file

```
cmake_minimum_required (VERSION 2.6.3)
```

This indicates that the person running CMake must have at least version 2.6.3. If they are running an older version of CMake, an error message will be displayed telling them that the project requires at least the specified version of CMake.

Finally, some new releases of CMake might no longer support some behavior you were using (although we try to avoid this). In these cases, use CMake policies, as discussed in the `cmake-policies(7)` (page 537) manual.

4.6 Using Modules

Code reuse is a valuable technique in software development and CMake has been designed to support it. Allowing CMakeLists files to make use of reusable modules enables the entire community to share reusable sections of code. For CMake, these sections are called modules and can be found in the Modules subdirectory of your installation. Modules are simply sections of CMake commands put into a file; they can then be included into other CMakeLists files using the `include()` (page 317) command. For example, the following commands will include the `CheckTypeSize` module from CMake and then use the macro it defines.

```
include (CheckTypeSize)
check_type_size(long SIZEOF_LONG)
```

A module's location can be specified using the full path to the module file, or by letting CMake find the module by itself. CMake will look for modules in the directories specified by `CMAKE_MODULE_PATH` (page 646); if it cannot find it there, it will look in the Modules subdirectory. This way projects can override modules that CMake provides and customize them for their needs. Modules can be broken into a few main categories:

Find Modules These modules support the `find_package()` (page 297) command to determine the location of software elements, such as header files or libraries, that belong to a given package. Do not include them directly. Use the `find_package()` (page 297) command. Each module comes with documentation describing the package it finds and the variables in which it provides results. Conventions used in Find modules are covered in more detail in Chapter 5.

System Introspection Modules These modules test the system to provide information about the target platform or compiler, such as the size of a float or support for ANSI C++ streams. Many of these modules have names prefixed with `Test` or `Check`, such as `TestBigEndian` and `CheckTypeSize`. Some of them try to compile code in order to determine the correct result. In these cases, the source code is typically named the same as the module, but with a `.c` or `.cxx` extension. System introspection modules are covered in more detail in Chapter 12.

Utility Modules These modules provide useful macros and functions implemented in the CMake language and intended for specific, common use cases. See documentation of each module for details.

4.6.1 Using CMake with SWIG

One example of how modules can be used is to look at wrapping your C/C++ code in another language using Simplified Wrapper and Interface Generator (SWIG; www.swig.org). SWIG is a tool that reads annotated C/C++ header files and creates wrapper code (glue code) to make the corresponding C/C++ libraries available to other programming languages such as Tcl, Python, or Java. CMake supports SWIG with the `find_package()` (page 297) command. Although it can be used from CMake with custom commands, the SWIG package provides several macros that make building SWIG projects with CMake simpler. To use the SWIG macros, you must first call the `find_package` command with the name SWIG. Then, include the file referenced by the variable `SWIG_USE_FILE`. This will define several macros and set up CMake to easily build SWIG-based projects.

Two very useful macros are `SWIG_ADD_MODULE` and `SWIG_LINK_LIBRARIES`. `SWIG_ADD_MODULE` works much like the `add_library()` (page 274) command in CMake. The command is invoked like this:

```
SWIG_ADD_MODULE (module_name language source1 source2 ... sourceN)
```

The first argument is the name of the module being created. The next argument is the target language SWIG is producing a wrapper for. The rest of the arguments consist of a list of source files used to create the shared module. The big difference is that SWIG .i interface files can be used directly as sources. The macro will create the correct custom commands to run SWIG, and generate the C or C++ wrapper code from the SWIG interface files. The sources can also be regular C or C++ files that need to be compiled in with the wrappers.

The SWIG_LINK_LIBRARIES macro is used to link support libraries to the module. This macro is used because depending on the language being wrapped by SWIG, the name of the module may be different. The actual name of the module is stored in a variable called SWIG_MODULE_${name}_REAL_NAME where ${name} is the name passed into the SWIG_ADD_MODULE macro. For example, SWIG_ADD_MODULE(foo tcl foo.i) creates a variable called SWIG_MODULE_foo_REAL_NAME, which contains the name of the actual module created.

Now consider the following example that uses the example found in SWIG under Examples/python/class.

```
# Find SWIG and include the use swig file
find_package (SWIG REQUIRED)
include (${SWIG_USE_FILE})

# Find python library and add include path for python headers
find_package (PythonLibs)
include_directories (${PYTHON_INCLUDE_PATH})

# set the global swig flags to empty
set (CMAKE_SWIG_FLAGS "")

# let swig know that example.i is c++ and add the -includeall
# flag to swig
set_source_files_properties (example.i PROPERTIES CPLUSPLUS ON)
set_source_files_properties (example.i
                             PROPERTIES SWIG_FLAGS "-includeall")

# Create the swig module called example
# using the example.i source and example.cxx
# swig will be used to create wrap_example.cxx from example.i
SWIG_ADD_MODULE (example python example.i example.cxx)
SWIG_LINK_LIBRARIES (example ${PYTHON_LIBRARIES})
```

This example first uses find_package to locate SWIG, and includes the SWIG_USE_FILE defining the SWIG CMake macros. It then finds the Python libraries and sets up CMake to build with the Python library. Notice that the SWIG input file "example.i" is used like any other source file in CMake, and the properties are set on the file telling SWIG that the file is C++ and that the SWIG flag -includeall should be used when running SWIG on that source file. The module is created by telling SWIG the name of the module, the target language, and the list of source files. Finally, the Python libraries are linked to the module.

4.6.2 Using CMake with Qt

Projects using the popular widget toolkit Qt from Nokia (qt.nokia.com) can be built with CMake. CMake supports multiple versions of Qt, including versions 3 and 4. The first step is to tell CMake which version(s) of Qt to look for. Many Qt applications are designed to work with Qt3 or Qt4, but not both. If your application is designed for Qt4, use the FindQt4 module; for Qt3, use the FindQt3 module. If your project can work with either version of Qt then use the generic FindQt module. All of the modules provide helpful tools for building Qt projects. The following is a simple example of building a project that uses Qt4.

```
find_package ( Qt4 REQUIRED)

include (${QT_USE_FILE})

# what are our ui files?
set (QTUI_SRCS qtwrapping.ui)
QT4_WRAP_UI (QTUI_H_SRCS ${QTUI_SRCS})
QT4_WRAP_CPP (QT_MOC_SRCS TestMoc.h)

add_library (myqtlib ${QTUI_H_SRCS} ${QT_MOC_SRCS})
target_link_libraries (myqtlib ${QT_LIBRARIES} )

add_executable (qtwrapping qtwrappingmain.cxx)
target_link_libraries (qtwrapping myqtlib)
```

In addition to explicitly listing Qt MOC sources. CMake also has a feature called automoc which automatically scan all source files for moc contructs and runs moc accordingly. To change the above example to use automoc, simply turn the automoc property on for the library and remove the `QT4_WRAP_CPP(QT_MOC_SRCS TestMoc.h)` line.

```
set_target_properties(foo myqtlib PROPERTIES AUTOMOC TRUE)
```

For more information about automoc, see the documentation in the variables section about variables with _AUTOMOC_ in them.

4.6.3 Using CMake with FLTK

CMake also supports the The Fast Light Toolkit (FLTK) with special commands. The `FLTK_WRAP_UI` command is used to run the FLTK fluid program on a .fl file and produce a C++ source file as part of the build. The following example shows how to use FLTK with CMake.

```
find_package (FLTK)
if (FLTK_FOUND)
  set (FLTK_SRCS
       fltk1.fl
       )
  fltk_wrap_ui (wraplibFLTK ${FLTK_SRCS})
  add_library (wraplibFLTK ${wraplibFLTK_UI_SRCS} )
endif (FLTK_FOUND)
```

4.7 Policies

Occasionally a new feature or change is made to CMake that is not fully backwards compatible with older versions. This can create problems when someone tries to use an old CMakeLists file with a new version of CMake. To help both end users and developers through such issues, we have introduced policies. Policies are a mechanism for helping improve backwards compatibility and tracking compatibility issues between different versions of CMake.

4.7.1 Design Goals

There were four main design goals for the CMake policy mechanism:

1. Existing projects should build with newer versions of CMake than that used by the project authors.

   - Users should not need to edit code to get the projects to build.

   - Warnings may be issued but the projects should build.

2. Correctness of new interfaces or bug fixes in old interfaces should not be inhibited by compatibility requirements. Any reduction in correctness of the latest interface is not fair on new projects.

3. Every change made to CMake that may require changes to a project's CMakeLists files should be documented.

   - Each change should also have a unique identifier that can be referenced with warning and error messages.

   - The new behavior is enabled only when the project has somehow indicated it is supported.

4. We must be able to eventually remove code that implements compatibility with ancient CMake versions.

   - Such removal is necessary to keep the code clean and to allow for internal refactoring.

   - After such removal, attempts at building projects written for ancient versions must fail with an informative message.

All policies in CMake are assigned a name in the form CMPNNNN where NNNN is an integer value. Policies typically support both an old behavior that preserves compatibility with earlier versions of CMake, and a new behavior that is considered correct and preferred for use by new projects. Every policy has documentation detailing the motivation for the change, and the old and new behaviors.

4.7.2 Setting Policies

Projects may configure the setting of each policy to request old or new behaviors. When CMake encounters user code that may be affected by a particular policy, it checks to see whether the project has set the policy. If the policy has been set (to OLD or NEW) then CMake follows the behavior specified. If the policy has not been set then the old behavior is used, but a warning is issued telling the project author to set the policy.

There are a couple ways to set the behavior of a policy. The quickest way is to set all policies to a version that corresponds to the release version of CMake the project was written in. Setting the policy version requests the new behavior for all policies introduced in the corresponding version of CMake or earlier. Policies introduced in later versions are marked as "not set" in order to produce proper warning messages. The policy version is set using the `cmake_policy()` (page 280) command's `VERSION` signature. For example, the code

```
cmake_policy (VERSION 2.6)
```

will request the new behavior for all policies introduced in CMake 2.6 or earlier. The `cmake_minimum_required()` (page 280) command will also set the policy version, which is convenient for use at the top of projects. A project should typically begin with the lines

```
cmake_minimum_required (VERSION 2.6)
project (MyProject)
# ...code using CMake 2.6 policies
```

Of course, one should replace "2.6" with the version of CMake you are currently writing to. You can also set each policy individually if you wish; this is sometimes helpful for project authors who want to incrementally convert their projects to use a new behavior, or silence warnings about dependence on an old behavior. The `cmake_policy` command's `SET` option may be used to explicitly request old or new behavior for a particular policy.

For example, CMake 2.6 introduced the policy `CMP0002` (page 538), which requires all logical target names to be globally unique (duplicate target names previously worked by accident in some cases, but were not diagnosed). Projects using duplicate target names and working accidentally will receive warnings referencing the policy. The warnings may be silenced with the code

```
cmake_policy (SET CMP0002 OLD)
```

which explicitly tells CMake to use the old behavior for the policy (silently accepting duplicate target names). Another option is to use the code

```
cmake_policy (SET CMP0002 NEW)
```

to explicitly tell CMake to use new behavior and produce an error when a duplicate target is created. Once this is added to the project, it will not build until the author removes any duplicate target names.

When a new version of CMake is released, it introduces new policies that can still build old projects, because by default they do not request NEW behavior for any of the new policies. When starting a new project, one should always specify the most recent release of CMake to be supported as the policy version level. This will ensure that the project is written to work using policies from that version of CMake and not using any old behavior. If no policy version is set, CMake will warn and assume a policy version of 2.4. This allows existing projects that do not specify `cmake_minimum_required` to build as they would have with CMake 2.4.

4.7.3 The Policy Stack

Policy settings are scoped using a stack. A new level of the stack is pushed when entering a new subdirectory of the project (with `add_subdirectory()` (page 277)) and popped when leaving it. Therefore, setting a policy in one directory of a project will not affect parent or sibling directories, but it will affect subdirectories.

This is useful when a project contains subprojects that are maintained separately yet built inside the tree. The top-level CMakeLists file in a project may write

```
cmake_policy (VERSION 2.6)
project (MyProject)
add_subdirectory (OtherProject)
# ... code requiring new behavior as of CMake 2.6 ...
```

while the `OtherProject/CMakeLists.txt` file contains

```
cmake_policy (VERSION 2.4)
project (OtherProject)
# ... code that builds with CMake 2.4 ...
```

This allows a project to be updated to CMake 2.6 while subprojects, modules, and included files continue to build with CMake 2.4 until their maintainers update them.

User code may use the `cmake_policy` command to push and pop its own stack levels as long as every push is paired with a pop. This is useful when temporarily requesting different behavior for a small section of code. For example, policy `CMP0003` (page 539) removes extra link directories that used to be included when new behavior is used. When incrementally updating a project, it may be difficult to build a particular target with the remaining targets being OK. The code

```
cmake_policy (PUSH)
cmake_policy (SET CMP0003 OLD) # use old-style link for now
add_executable (myexe ...)
cmake_policy (POP)
```

will silence the warning and use the old behavior for that target. You can get a list of policies and help on specific policies by running CMake from the command line as follows

```
cmake --help-command cmake_policy
cmake --help-policies
cmake --help-policy CMP0003
```

4.7.4 Updating a Project For a New Version of CMake

When a CMake release introduces new policies, it may generate warnings for some existing projects. These warnings indicate that changes to a project may be necessary for dealing with the new policies. While old releases of a project can continue to build with the warnings, the project development tree should be updated to take the new policies into account. There are two approaches to updating a tree: one-shot and incremental. The question of which one is easier depends on the size of the project and which new policies produce warnings.

The One-Shot Approach

The simplest approach to updating a project for a new version of CMake is simply to change the policy version which is set at the top of the project. Then, try building with the new CMake version to fix problems.

For example, to update a project to build with CMake 2.8, one might write

```
cmake_minimum_required (VERSION 2.8)
```

at the beginning of the top-level CMakeLists file. This tells CMake to use the new behavior for every policy introduced in CMake 2.8 and below. When building this project with CMake 2.8, no warnings will be produced regarding policies because it knows that no policies were introduced in later versions. However, if the project was depending on the old policy behavior, it may not build since CMake is now using the new behavior without warning. It is up to the project author who added the policy version line to fix these issues.

The Incremental Approach

Another approach to updating a project for a new version of CMake is to deal with each warning one-by-one. One advantage of this approach is that the project will continue to build throughout the process, so the changes can be made incrementally.

When CMake encounters a situation where it needs to know whether to use the old or new behavior for a policy, it checks whether the project has set the policy. If the policy is set, CMake silently uses the corresponding behavior. If the policy is not set, CMake uses the old behavior but warns the author that the policy is not set.

In many cases, a warning message will point to the exact line of code in the CMakeLists files that caused the warning. In some cases, the situation cannot be diagnosed until CMake is generating the native build system rules for the project, so the warning will not include explicit context information. In these cases, CMake will try to provide some information about where code may need to be changed. The documentation for these "generation-time" policies should indicate the point in the project code where the policy should be set to take effect.

In order to incrementally update a project, one warning should be addressed at a time. Several cases may occur, as described below.

Silence a Warning When the Code is Correct

Many policy warnings may be produced simply because the project has not set the policy even though the project may work correctly with the new behavior (there is no way for CMake to know the difference). For a warning about some policy, CMP<NNNN>, you can check whether this is the case by adding

```
cmake_policy (SET CMP<NNNN> NEW)
```

to the top of the project and trying to build it. If the project builds correctly with the new behavior, move on to the next policy warning. If the project does not build correctly, one of the other cases may apply.

Silence a Warning Without Updating the Code

Users can suppress all instances of a warning CMP<NNNN> by adding

```
cmake_policy (SET CMP<NNNN> OLD)
```

to the top of a project. However, we encourage project authors to update their code to work with the new behavior for all policies. This is especially important because versions of CMake in the (distant) future may remove support for old behaviors and produce an error for projects requesting them (which tells the user to get an older versions of CMake to build the project).

Silence a Warning by Updating Code

When a project does not work correctly with the NEW behaviors for a policy, the code needs to be updated. In order to deal with a warning for some policy CMP<NNNN>,add

```
cmake_policy (SET CMP<NNNN> NEW)
```

to the top of the project and then fix the code to work with the NEW behavior.

If many instances of the warning occur fixing all of them simultaneously may be too difficult: instead, a developer may fix them one at a time by using the PUSH/POP signatures of the cmake_policy command:

```
cmake_policy (PUSH)
cmake_policy (SET CMP<NNNN> NEW)
# ... code updated for new policy behavior ...
cmake_policy (POP)
```

This will request the new behavior for a small region of code that has been fixed. Other instances of the policy warning may still appear and must be fixed separately.

Updating the Project Policy Version

After addressing all policy warnings and getting the project to build cleanly with the new CMake version one step remains. The policy version set at the top of the project should now be updated to match the new CMake version, just as in the one-shot approach described above. For example, after updating a project to build cleanly with CMake 2.8, users may update the top of the project with the line

```
cmake_minimum_required(VERSION 2.8)
```

This will set all policies introduced in CMake 2.8 or below to use the new behavior. Then users may sweep through the rest of the code and remove the calls that use the cmake_policy command to request the new behavior incrementally. The end result should look the same as the one-shot approach, but could be attained step-by-step.

Supporting Multiple CMake Versions

Some projects might want to support a few releases of CMake simultaneously. The goal is to build with an older version, while also working with newer versions without warnings. In order to support both CMake 2.4 and 2.6, one may write code like

```
cmake_minimum_required (VERSION 2.4)
if (COMMAND cmake_policy)
  # policy settings ...
  cmake_policy (SET CMP0003 NEW)
endif (COMMAND cmake_policy)
```

This will set the policies to build with CMake 2.6 and to ignore them for CMake 2.4. In order to support both CMake 2.6 and some policies of CMake 2.8, one may write code like:

```
cmake_minimum_required (VERSION 2.6)
if (POLICY CMP1234)
  # policies not known to CMake 2.6 ...
  cmake_policy (SET CMP1234 NEW)
endif (POLICY CMP1234)
```

This will set the policies to build with CMake 2.8 and to ignore them for CMake 2.6. If it is known that the project builds with both CMake 2.6 and CMake 2.8's new policies users may write:

```
cmake_minimum_required (VERSION 2.6)
if (NOT ${CMAKE_VERSION} VERSION_LESS 2.8)
   cmake_policy (VERSION 2.8)
endif ()
```

Linking Libraries

In CMake 2.6 and later, a new approach to generating link lines for targets has been implemented. Consider these libraries:

```
/path/to/libfoo.a
/path/to/libfoo.so
```

Previously, if someone wrote

```
target_link_libraries (myexe /path/to/libfoo.a)
```

CMake would generate this code to link it:

```
... -L/path/to -Wl,-Bstatic -lfoo -Wl,-Bdynamic ...
```

This worked most of the time, but some platforms (such as Mac OS X) do not support the -Bstatic or equivalent flag. This made it impossible to link to the static version of a library without creating a symlink in another directory and using that one instead. Now CMake will generate this code:

```
... /path/to/libfoo.a ...
```

This guarantees that the correct library is chosen. However, there are some caveats to keep in mind. In the past, a project could write this (incorrect) code and it would work by accident

```
add_executable (myexe myexe.c)
target_link_libraries (myexe /path/to/libA.so B)
```

Here B is meant to link /path/to/libB.so. This code is incorrect because it asks CMake to link to B, but does not provide the proper linker search path for it. It used to work by accident because the -L/path/to would get added as part of the implementation of linking to A. The correct code would be either

```
link_directories (/path/to)
add_executable (myexe myexe.c)
target_link_libraries (myexe /path/to/libA.so B)
```

or even better

```
add_executable (myexe myexe.c)
target_link_libraries (myexe /path/to/libA.so /path/to/libB.so)
```

Linking to System Libraries

System libraries on UNIX-like systems are typically provided in /usr/lib or /lib. These directories are considered implicit linker search paths because linkers automatically search these locations, even without a flag like -L/usr/lib. Consider the code

```
find_library (M_LIB m)
target_link_libraries (myexe ${M_LIB})
```

Typically the find_library command would find the math library /usr/lib/libm.so, but some platforms provide multiple versions of libraries correesponding to different architectures. For example, on an IRIX machine one might find the libraries

```
/usr/lib/libm.so          (ELF o32)
/usr/lib32/libm.so        (ELF n32)
/usr/lib64/libm.so        (ELF 64)
```

On a Solaris machine one might find:

```
/usr/lib/libm.so            (sparcv8 architecture)
/usr/lib/sparcv9/libm.so    (sparcv9 architecture)
```

Unfortunately, find_library may not know about all of the architecture-specific system search paths used by the linker. In fact, when it finds /usr/lib/libm.so, it may be finding a library with the incorrect architecture. If the link computation were to produce the line

```
... /usr/lib/libm.so ...
```

the linker might complain if /usr/lib/libm.so does not match the architecture it wants. One solution to this problem is to have the link computation recognize that the library is in a system directory and ask the linker to search for the library. It could produce the link line

```
... -lm ...
```

and the linker would search through its architecture-specific implicit link directories to find the correct library. Unfortunately, this solution suffers from the original problem of distinguishing between static and shared versions. In order to ask the linker to find a static system library with the correct architecture, it must produce the link line

```
... -Wl,-Bstatic -lm ... -Wl,-Bshared ...
```

Since not all platforms support such flags, CMake compromises. Libraries that are not in implicit system locations are linked by passing the full library path to the linker. Libraries that are in implicit system locations (such as /usr/lib) are linked by passing the -l option if a flag like -Bstatic is available, and by passing the full library path to the linker otherwise.

4.7.5 Specifying Optimized or Debug Libraries with a Target

On Windows platforms, users are often required to link debug libraries with debug libraries, and optimized libraries with optimized libraries. CMake helps satisfy this requirement with the target_link_libraries() (page 340) command, which accepts an optional flag labeled as debug or optimized. If a library is preceded with either debug or optimized, then that library will only be linked in with the appropriate configuration type. For example

```
add_executable (foo foo.c)
target_link_libraries (foo debug libdebug optimized libopt)
```

In this case, foo will be linked against libdebug if a debug build was selected, or against libopt if an optimized build was selected.

4.8 Advanced Linking

In CMake library dependencies are transitive by default no matter if they are dynamic or static. When a target is linked with another target it will inherit all the libraries linked to this target, and they will appear on the link line for the other target too.

This behavior can be changed by setting a targets LINK_INTERFACE_LIBRARIES (page 598) property. If set, only targets listed in LINK_INTERFACE_LIBRARIES will used as the set of transitive link dependencies for a target. CMake provides two convenient ways to set the LINK_INTERFACE_LIBRARIES

```
target_link_libraries(<target> LINK_INTERFACE_LIBRARIES
                      [[debug|optimized|general] <lib>] ...)
```

The LINK_INTERFACE_LIBRARIES mode appends the libraries to the LINK_INTERFACE_LIBRARIES and its per-configuration equivalent target properties instead of using them for linking. Libraries specified as "debug" are appended to the LINK_INTERFACE_LIBRARIES_DEBUG property (or to the properties corresponding to configurations listed in the DEBUG_CONFIGURATIONS (page 563) global property if it is set). Libraries specified as "optimized" are appended to the LINK_INTERFACE_LIBRARIES property. Libraries specified as "general" (or without any keyword) are treated as if specified for both "debug" and "optimized".

```
target_link_libraries(<target>
                <LINK_PRIVATE|LINK_PUBLIC>
                  [[debug|optimized|general] <lib>] ...
                [<LINK_PRIVATE|LINK_PUBLIC>
                  [[debug|optimized|general] <lib>] ...])
```

The LINK_PUBLIC and LINK_PRIVATE modes can be used to specify both the link dependencies and the link interface in one command. Libraries and targets following LINK_PUBLIC are linked to, and are made part of the LINK_INTERFACE_LIBRARIES. Libraries and targets following LINK_PRIVATE are linked to, but are not made part of the LINK_INTERFACE_LIBRARIES. Using LINK_PUBLIC and LINK_PRIVATE causes all other libraries (before and after) linked to a target to be private unless they are explicitly stated to be LINK_PUBLIC.

CMake will also propagate "usage requirements" from linked library targets. Usage requirements affect compilation of sources in the <target>. They are specified by properties defined on linked targets. During generation of the build system, CMake integrates usage requirement property values with the corresponding build properties for <target>:

INTERFACE_COMPILE_DEFINITIONS (page 592): Appends to COMPILE_DEFINITIONS (page 616)

INTERFACE_INCLUDE_DIRECTORIES (page 593): Appends to INCLUDE_DIRECTORIES (page 570)

INTERFACE_POSITION_INDEPENDENT_CODE (page 594): Sets:prop_tgt:
POSITION_INDEPENDENT_CODE or checked for consistency with existing value

For example to specify include directories that are required when linking to a library you would can do the following

```
add_library(foo foo.cxx)
set_property(TARGET foo APPEND PROPERTY
INTERFACE_INCLUDE_DIRECTORIES "${CMAKE_CURRENT_BINARY_DIR}"
"${CMAKE_CURRENT_SOURCE_DIR}")
```

Now anything that links to the target foo will automatically have foo's binary and source as include directories. The order of the include directories brought in through "usage requirements" will match the order of the targets in the target_link_libraries call.

4.9 Object Libraries

Before version 2.8.8, CMake had no way to encapsulate numerous libraries into one combined library. Previously you would have to compile each individual library and the combined library. This is okay if the compilation time was low and each library used the same preprocessor definitions, include directories, and flags.

However, large projects typically organize their source files into groups, often in separate subdirectories, that each need different include directories and preprocessor definitions. For this use case CMake has developed the concept of Object Libraries. An Object Library is a collection of source files compiled into an object file which is not linked into a library file or made into an archive.

Instead other targets created by add_library or add_executable may reference the objects using an expression of the form $<TARGET_OBJECTS:name> as a source, where "name" is the target created by the add_library() (page 274) call. For example:

```
add_library(A OBJECT a.cpp )
add_library(B OBJECT b.cpp )
add_library(Combined $<TARGET_OBJECTS:A> $<TARGET_OBJECTS:B> )
```

will include A and B object files in a library called Combined. Object libraries may contain only sources (and headers) that compile to object files.

4.10 Shared Libraries and Loadable Modules

Shared libraries and loadable modules are very powerful tools for software developers. They can be used to create extension modules or plugins for off-the-shelf software, and can be used to decrease the compile/link/run cycles for C and C++ programs. However, despite years of use, the cross-platform creation of shared libraries and modules remains a dark art understood by only a few developers. CMake has the ability to aid developers in the creation of shared libraries and modules. CMake knows the correct tools and flags to use in order to produce shared libraries for most modern operating systems that support them. Unfortunately, CMake cannot do all the work, and developers must sometimes alter source code and understand the basic concepts and common pitfalls associated with shared libraries before they can be used effectively. This section will describe many of the considerations required for taking advantage of shared libraries and loadable modules.

A shared library should be thought of more like an executable than a static library; on most systems they actually require executable permissions to be set on the shared library file. This means that shared libraries can link to other shared libraries when they are created in the same way as an executable. Unlike a static library where the atomic unit is the object file, for shared libraries, the entire library is the atomic unit. This can cause some unexpected linker errors when converting from static to shared libraries. If an object file is part of a static library but the executable linking to the library does not use any of the symbols in that object file, then the file is simply excluded from the final linked executable. With shared libraries, all the object files that make up the library and all of the dependencies that they require come as one unit. For example, suppose you had a library with an object file defining the function DisplayOnXWindow(), which required the X11 library. If you linked an executable to that library, but did not call the DisplayOnXWindow() function, the static library version would not require X11; but the shared library version would require the X11 library. This is because a shared library has to be taken as one unit, and a static library is only an archive of object files from which linkers can choose the objects needed. This means that static linked executables can be smaller, as they only contain the object code actually used.

Another difference between shared and static libraries is library order. With static libraries the order on the link line can make a difference; this is because most linkers only use the symbols that are needed in a single pass over all the given libraries. So, the library order should go from the library that uses the most other libraries to the library that does not use any other libraries. CMake will preserve and remember the order of libraries and library dependencies in a project. This means that each library in a project should use the `target_link_libraries()` (page 340) command to specify all of the libraries that it directly depends on. The libraries will be linked with each other for shared builds, but not static builds; however, the link information is used in static builds when executables are linked. An executable that only links library libA will get libA plus libB and libC, as long as libA's dependency on libB and libC was properly specified using `target_link_libraries (libA libB libC)`.

At this point, one might wonder why shared libraries would be preferred over static libraries. There are several reasons. First, shared libraries can decrease the compile/link/run cycle time because the linker does not have to do as much work as there are fewer decisions to be made about which object files to keep. Often times, the executable does not even need to be re-linked after the shared library is rebuilt; therefore developers can work on a library by compiling and linking only the small part of the program that is currently being developed, and then re-running the executable after each build of the shared library. Also, if a library is used by many different executables on a system, then there only needs to be one copy of the library on disk and often in memory too.

In addition to the concept of a software library, shared libraries can also be used on many systems as run time loadable modules. This means that at run time, a program can load and execute object code that was not part of the original software. This allows developers to create software that is both open and closed. (For more information, see Object-Oriented Software Construction by Bertrand Meyer.) Closed software is that which cannot be modified. It has been through a testing cycle and can be certified to perform specific tasks with regression tests. However, a seemingly opposite goal is sought after by developers of object-oriented software as Open software can be extended by future developers. This can be done via inheritance and polymorphism with object systems. Shared libraries that can be loaded at run time allow for these seemingly opposing goals to be achieved in the same software package. Many common applications support the idea of plugins; the most common of these applications is the web browser. Internet Explorer uses plugins to support video over the web and 3D visualization. In addition to plugins, loadable factories can be used to replace C++ objects at run time, as is done in the Visualization Toolkit (VTK).

Once it is decided that shared libraries or loadable modules are the right choice for a particular project, there are a few issues that developers need to be aware of. The first question that must be answered is "which symbols are exported by the shared library?" This may sound like a simple question, but the answer is different for each platform. On many but not all UNIX systems, the default behavior is to export all the symbols much like a static library. However, on Windows systems, developers must explicitly tell the linker and compiler which symbols are to be exported and imported from shared libraries. This is often a big problem for UNIX developers moving to Windows. There are two ways to tell the compiler/linker which symbols to export/import on Windows. The most common approach is to decorate the code with a Microsoft C/C++ language extension. An alternative is to create an extra file called a .def file, which is a simple ASCII file containing the names of all the symbols to be exported from a library.

The Microsoft extension uses the `__declspec` directive. If a symbol has `__declspec( dllexport )` in front of it, it will be exported; if it has `__declspec( dllimport )`, it will be imported. Since the same file may be shared during the creation and use of a library, it must be both exported and imported in the same source file. This can only be done with the preprocessor. The developer can create a macro called `LIBRARY_EXPORT` which is defined to `dllexport` when building the library, and `dllimport` when using the library. CMake helps this process by automatically defining `${LIBNAME}_EXPORTS` when building a DLL (dynamic link library, a.k.a. a shared library) on Windows.

4.10. Shared Libraries and Loadable Modules   **51**

The following code snippet is from the VTK library, vtkCommon, and is included by all files in the vtkCommon library:

```
if defined(WIN32)

if defined(vtkCommon_EXPORTS)
define VTK_COMMON_EXPORT __declspec( dllexport )
else
define VTK_COMMON_EXPORT __declspec( dllimport )
endif
else
define VTK_COMMON_EXPORT
endif
```

The example checks for Windows and for the `vtkCommon_EXPORTS` macro provided by CMake. So, on UNIX , `VTK_COMMON_EXPORT` is defined to nothing; on Windows during the building of vtkCommon.dll, it is defined as `__declspec(dllexport)`; and when the file is being used by another file, it is defined to `__declspec(dllimport)`.

More recently, Linux and other Unix systems have added linker options that allow symbols to be explicitly exported in a similar manner as Windows. CMake has a module that will allow you to use explicit symbol exports on all systems that support them. The module is GenerateExportHeader.cmake, and contains the function `generate_export_header`. The function will modify the CXX and C flags to turn on explicit symbol exports for the system. It will also generate a header file much like the handwritten one above, which works for Windows only. For more information, see `generate_export_header` in the appendix.

The second approach on Windows requires a .def file to specify the symbols to be exported. This file could be created by hand, but for a large and changing C++ library, that could be time consuming and error-prone. CMake's custom commands can be used to run a pre-link program which will create a .def file from the compiled object files automatically. In the following example, a Perl script called `makedef.pl` is used; the script runs the `DUMPBIN` program on the .obj files, extracts all of the exportable symbols, and writes a .def file with the correct exports for all the symbols in the library mylib.

```
----CMakeLists.txt-----

cmake_minimum_required (VERSION 2.6)
project (myexe)

set (SOURCES mylib.cxx mylib2.cxx)

# create a list of all the object files
string (REGEX REPLACE "\\.cxx" ".obj" OBJECTS "${SOURCES}")

# create a shared library with the .def file
add_library (mylib SHARED ${SOURCES}
  ${CMAKE_CURRENT_BINARY_DIR}/mylib.def
  )
# set the .def file as generated
set_source_files_properties (
  ${CMAKE_CURRENT_BINARY_DIR}/mylib.def
```

```
  PROPERTIES GENERATED 1
  )

# create an executable
add_executable (myexe myexe.cxx)

# link the executable to the dll
target_link_libraries(myexe mylib)

#convert to windows slashes
set (OUTDIR
 ${CMAKE_CURRENT_BINARY_DIR}/${CMAKE_CFG_INTDIR}
 )

string (REGEX REPLACE "/" "\\\\" OUTDIR ${OUTDIR})

# create a custom pre link command that runs
# a perl script to create a .def file using dumpbin
add_custom_command (
  TARGET mylib PRE_LINK
  COMMAND perl
  ARGS ${CMAKE_CURRENT_SOURCE_DIR}/makedef.pl
  ${CMAKE_CURRENT_BINARY_DIR}\\mylib.def mylib
  ${OUTDIR} ${OBJECTS}
  COMMENT "Create .def file"
  )

::

---myexe.cxx----
#include <iostream>
#include "mylib.h"
int main()
{
  std::cout << myTen() << "\n";
  std::cout << myEight() << "\n";
}

---mylib.cxx--
int myTen()
{
  return 10;
}

--mylib2.cxx---
int myEight()
{
  return 8;
}
```

There is a significant difference between Windows and the default linker options on UNIX systems with respect to the requirements of symbols. DLLs on Windows are required to be fully resolved, meaning that they must link every symbol at creation. UNIX systems allow shared libraries to get symbols from the executable or other shared libraries at run time . On UNIX systems that support this feature, CMake will compile with the flags that allow executable symbols to be used by shared libraries. This small difference can cause large problems. A common but hard to track with DLLs occurs with C++ template classes and static members. In these instances, two DLLs can end up with separate copies of what is supposed to be a single, global static member of a class. There are also problems with this approach on most UNIX systems; the start-up time for large applications with many symbols can be long since much of the linking is deferred to run time.

Another common pitfall occurs with C++ global objects. These objects require constructors to be called before they can be used. The main that links or loads C++ shared libraries MUST be linked with the C++ compiler, or globals like cout may not be initialized before they are used, causing strange crashes at start up time.

Since executables that link to shared libraries must be able to find the libraries at run time, special environment variables and linker flags must be used. There are tools that can be used to show which libraries an executable is actually using. On many UNIX systems there is a tool called `ldd` (`otool -L` on Mac OS X), which shows which libraries are used by an executable. On Windows, a program called `depends` can be used to find the same type of information. On many UNIX systems, there are also environment variables like `LD_LIBRARY_PATH` that tell the program where to find the libraries at run time. Where supported CMake will add run time library path information into the linked executables, so that `LD_LIBRARY_PATH` is not required. This feature can be turned off by setting the cache entry `CMAKE_SKIP_RPATH` (page 633) to false; this may be desirable for installed software that should not be looking in the build tree for shared libraries. On Windows, there is only one `PATH` environment variable that is used for both DLLs and finding executables.

4.11 Shared Library Versioning

When an executable is linked to a shared library, it is important that the copy of the shared library loaded at run time matches that expected by the executable. On some UNIX systems, a shared library has an associated "soname" intended to solve this problem. When an executable links against the library, its soname is copied into the executable. At run time, the dynamic linker uses this name from the executable to search for the library.

Consider a hypothetical shared library "foo" providing a few C functions that implement some functionality. The interface to foo is called an Application Programming Interface (API). If the implementation of these C functions change in a new version of foo, but the API remains the same, then executables linked against foo will still run correctly. When the API changes, old executables will no longer run with a new copy of foo; a new API version number must be associated with foo.

This can be implemented by creating the original version of foo with a soname and file name such as `libfoo.so.1`. A symbolic link such as `libfoo.so -> libfoo.so.1` will allow standard linkers to work with the library and create executables. The new version of foo can be called `libfoo.so.2` and the symbolic link updated so that new executables use the new library. When an old executable runs, the dynamic linker will look for libfoo.so.1, find the old copy of the library, and run correctly. When a new executable runs, the dynamic linker will look for libfoo.so.2 and correctly load the new version.

This scheme can be expanded to handle the case of changes to foo that do not modify the API. We introduce a second set of version numbers that is totally independent of the first, which corresponds to the software version providing foo. For example, a larger project may have introduced the existence of the library foo starting in version 3.4. In this case, the file name for foo might be libfoo.so.3.4, but the soname would still be libfoo.so.1 because the API for foo is still on its first version. A symbolic link from libfoo.so.1 -> libfoo.so.3.4 will allow executables linked against the library to run. When a bug is fixed in the software without changing the API to foo, then the new library file name might be libfoo.so.3.5, and the symbolic link can be updated to allow existing executables to run.

CMake supports this soname-based version number encoding on platforms supporting soname natively. A target property for the shared library named VERSION (page 609) specifies the version number used to create the file name for the library. This version should correspond to that of the software package providing foo. On Windows, the VERSION property is used to set the binary image number using major.minor format. Another target property named SOVERSION (page 608) specifies the version number used to create the soname for the library. This version should correspond to the API version number for foo. These target properties are ignored on platforms where CMake does not support this scheme.

The following CMake code configures the version numbers of the shared library foo

```
set_target_properties (foo PROPERTIES VERSION 1.2 SOVERSION 4)
```

This results in the following library and symbolic links:

```
libfoo.so.1.2
libfoo.so.4 -> libfoo.so.1.2
libfoo.so -> libfoo.so.4
```

If only one of the two properties is specified, the other defaults to its value automatically. For example, the code

```
set_target_properties (foo PROPERTIES VERSION 1.2)
```

results in the following shared library and symbolic link:

```
libfoo.so.1.2
libfoo.so -> libfoo.so.1.2
```

CMake makes no attempt to enforce sensible version numbers. It is up to the programmer to utilize this feature in a productive manner.

4.12 Installing Files

Software is typically installed into a directory separate from the source and build trees. This allows it to be distributed in a clean form and isolates users from the details of the build process. CMake provides the install() (page 317) command to specify how a project is to be installed. This command is invoked by a project in the CMakeLists file and tells CMake how to generate installation scripts. The scripts are executed at install time to perform the actual installation of files. For Makefile generators (UNIX, NMake, Borland, MinGW, etc.), the user simply runs `make install` (or `nmake install`) and the make tool will invoke CMake's installation module. With GUI based systems (Visual Studio, Xcode, etc.), the user simply builds the target called `INSTALL`.

Each call to the `install` command defines some installation rules. Within one CMakeLists file (source directory), these rules will be evaluated in the order that the corresponding commands are invoked. The order across multiple directories is not specified.

The `install` command has several signatures designed for common installation use cases. A particular invocation of the command specifies the signature as the first argument. The signatures are `TARGETS`, `FILES`, `PROGRAMS`, `DIRECTORY`, `SCRIPT`, and `CODE`.

install (TARGETS ...) Installs the binary files corresponding to targets built inside the project.

install (FILES ...) General-purpose file installation, which is typically used for header files, documentation, and data files required by your software.

install (PROGRAMS ...) Installs executable files not built by the project, such as shell scripts. This argument is identical to `install (FILES)` except that the default permissions of the installed file include the executable bit.'

install (DIRECTORY ...) This argument installs an entire directory tree. It may be used for installing directories with resources, such as icons and images.

install (SCRIPT ...) Specifies a user-provided CMake script file to be executed during installation. This is typically used to define pre-install or post-install actions for other rules.

install (CODE ...) Specifies user-provided CMake code to be executed during the installation. This is similar to `install (SCRIPT)` but the code is provided inline in the call as a string. The `TARGETS`, `FILES`, `PROGRAMS`, `DIRECTORY` signatures are all meant to create install rules for files. The targets, files, or directories to be installed are listed immediately after the signature name argument. Additional details can be specified using keyword arguments followed by corresponding values. Keyword arguments provided by most of the signatures are as follows.

DESTINATION This argument specifies the location where the installation rule will place files, and must be followed by a directory path indicating the location. If the directory is specified as a full path, it will be evaluated at install time as an absolute path. If the directory is specified as a relative path, it will be evaluated at install time relative to the installation prefix. The prefix may be set by the user through the cache variable `CMAKE_INSTALL_PREFIX` (page 645). A platform-specific default is provided by CMake: `/usr/local` on UNIX, and "<SystemDrive>/`Program Files`/<ProjectName>" on Windows, where SystemDrive is along the lines of `C:` and ProjectName is the name given to the topmost `PROJECT()` (page 327) command.

PERMISSIONS This argument specifies file permissions to be set on the installed files. This option is needed only to override the default permissions selected by a particular `INSTALL` command signature. Valid permissions are `OWNER_READ`, `OWNER_WRITE`, `OWNER_EXECUTE`, `GROUP_READ`, `GROUP_WRITE`, `GROUP_EXECUTE`, `WORLD_READ`, `WORLD_WRITE`, `WORLD_EXECUTE`, `SETUID`, and `SETGID`. Some platforms do not support all of these permissions; on such platforms those permission names are ignored.

CONFIGURATIONS This argument specifies a list of build configurations for which an installation rule applies (Debug, Release, etc.). For Makefile generators, the build configuration is specified by the CMAKE_BUILD_TYPE cache variable. For Visual Studio and Xcode generators, the configuration is selected when the INSTALL target is built. An installation rule will be evaluated only if the current install configuration matches an entry in the list provided to this argument. Configuration name comparison is case-insensitive.

COMPONENT This argument specifies the installation component for which the installation rule applies. Some projects divide their installations into multiple components for separate packaging. For example, a project may define a Runtime component that contains the files needed to run a tool; a Development component containing the files needed to build extensions to the tool; and a Documentation component containing the manual pages and other help files. The project may then package each component separately for distribution by installing only one component at a time. By default, all components are installed. Component-specific installation is an advanced feature intended for use by package maintainers. It requires manual invocation of the installation scripts with an argument defining the COMPONENT variable to name the desired component. Note that component names are not defined by CMake. Each project may define its own set of components.

OPTIONAL This argument specifies that it is not an error if the input file to be installed does not exist. If the input file exists, it will be installed as requested. If it does not exist, it will be silently not installed.

Projects typically install some of the library and executable files created during their build process. The install command provides the TARGETS signature for this purpose:

```
install (TARGETS targets...
       [[ARCHIVE|LIBRARY|RUNTIME|FRAMEWORK|BUNDLE|
        PRIVATE_HEADER|PUBLIC_HEADER|RESOURCE]
        [DESTINATION <dir>]
        [PERMISSIONS permissions...]
        [CONFIGURATIONS [Debug|Release|...]]
        [COMPONENT <component>]
        [OPTIONAL]
           [EXPORT <export name>]
           [NAMELINK_ONLY|NAMELINK_SKIP]
      ] [...])
```

The TARGETS keyword is immediately followed by a list of the targets created using add_executable() (page 273) or add_library() (page 274), which are to be installed. One or more files corresponding to each target will be installed.

Files installed with this signature may be divided into three categories: ARCHIVE, LIBRARY, and RUNTIME. These categories are designed to group target files by typical installation destination. The corresponding keyword arguments are optional, but if present, specify that other arguments following them apply only to target files of that type. Target files are categorized as follows:

executables - "RUNTIME" Created by add_executable (.exe on Windows, no extension on UNIX)

loadable modules - "LIBRARY" Created by add_library with the MODULE option (.dll on Windows, .so on UNIX)

shared libraries - "LIBRARY" Created by `add_library` with the `SHARED` option on UNIX-like platforms (.so on most UNIX, .dylib on Mac)

dynamic-link libraries - "RUNTIME" Created by `add_library` with the `SHARED` option on Windows platforms (.dll)

import libraries - "ARCHIVE" A linkable file created by a dynamic-link library that exports symbols (.lib on most Windows, .dll.a on Cygwin and MinGW).

static libraries - "ARCHIVE" Created by `add_library` with the `STATIC` option (.lib on Windows, .a on UNIX, Cygwin, and MinGW)

Consider a project that defines an executable, `myExecutable`, which links to a shared library `mySharedLib`. It also provides a static library `myStaticLib` and a plugin module to the executable called `myPlugin` that also links to the shared library. The executable, static library, and plugin file may be installed individually using the commands

```
install (TARGETS myExecutable DESTINATION bin)
install (TARGETS myStaticLib DESTINATION lib/myproject)
install (TARGETS myPlugin DESTINATION lib)
```

The executable will not be able to run from the installed location until the shared library to it links to is also installed. Installation of the library requires a bit more care in order to support all platforms. It must be installed in a location searched by the dynamic linker on each platform. On UNIX-like platforms, the library is typically installed to `lib`, while on Windows it should be placed next to the executable in `bin`. An additional challenge is that the import library associated with the shared library on Windows should be treated like the static library, and installed to `lib/myproject`. In other words, we have three different kinds of files created with a single target name that must be installed to three different destinations! Fortunately, this problem can be solved using the category keyword arguments. The shared library may be installed using the command:

```
install (TARGETS mySharedLib
         RUNTIME DESTINATION bin
         LIBRARY DESTINATION lib
         ARCHIVE DESTINATION lib/myproject)
```

This tells CMake that the `RUNTIME` file (.dll) should be installed to `bin`, the `LIBRARY` file (.so) should be installed to `lib`, and the `ARCHIVE` (.lib) file should be installed to `lib/myproject`. On UNIX, the `LIBRARY` file will be installed; on Windows, the `RUNTIME` and `ARCHIVE` files will be installed.

If the above sample project is to be packaged into separate run time and development components, we must assign the appropriate component to each target file installed. The executable, shared library, and plugin are required in order to run the application, so they belong in a `Runtime` component. Meanwhile, the import library (corresponding to the shared library on Windows) and the static library are only required to develop extensions to the application, and therefore belong in a `Development` component.

Component assignments may be specified by adding the `COMPONENT` argument to each of the commands above. You may also combine all of the installation rules into a single command invocation, which is equivalent to all of the above commands with components added. The files generated by each target are installed using the rule for their category.

```
install (TARGETS myExecutable mySharedLib myStaticLib myPlugin
         RUNTIME DESTINATION bin              COMPONENT Runtime
         LIBRARY DESTINATION lib              COMPONENT Runtime
         ARCHIVE DESTINATION lib/myproject COMPONENT Development)
```

Either NAMELINK_ONLY or NAMELINK_SKIP may be specified as a LIBRARY option. On some platforms, a versioned shared library has a symbolic link such as

```
lib<name>.so -> lib<name>.so.1
```

where lib<name>.so.1 is the soname of the library, and lib<name>.so is a "namelink" that helps
linkers to find the library when given -l<name>. The NAMELINK_ONLY option results in installation of
only the namelink when a library target is installed. The NAMELINK_SKIP option causes installation of
library files other than the namelink when a library target is installed. When neither option is given, both
portions are installed. On platforms where versioned shared libraries do not have namelinks, or when a
library is not versioned, the NAMELINK_SKIP option installs the library and the NAMELINK_ONLY option
installs nothing. See the VERSION and SOVERSION target properties for details on creating versioned,
shared libraries.

Projects may install files other than those that are created with add_executable or add_library, such
as header files or documentation. General-purpose installation of files is specified using the FILES signature:

```
install (FILES files... DESTINATION <dir>
         [PERMISSIONS permissions...]
         [CONFIGURATIONS [Debug|Release|...]]
         [COMPONENT <component>]
         [RENAME <name>] [OPTIONAL])
```

The FILES keyword is immediately followed by a list of files to be installed. Relative paths are evaluated
with respect to the current source directory. Files will be installed to the given DESTINATION directory. For
example, the command

```
install (FILES my-api.h ${CMAKE_CURRENT_BINARY_DIR}/my-config.h
         DESTINATION include)
```

installs the file my-api.h from the source tree, and the file my-config.h from the build tree into
the include directory under the installation prefix. By default installed files are given the permissions
OWNER_WRITE, OWNER_READ, GROUP_READ, and WORLD_READ, but this may be overridden by specifying the PERMISSIONS option. Consider cases in which users would want to install a global configuration
file on a UNIX system that is readable only by its owner (such as root). We accomplish this with the command

```
install (FILES my-rc DESTINATION /etc
         PERMISSIONS OWNER_WRITE OWNER_READ)
```

which installs the file my-rc with owner read/write permission into the absolute path /etc.

The RENAME argument specifies a name for an installed file that may be different from the original file.
Renaming is allowed only when a single file is installed by the command. For example, the command

```
install(FILES version.h DESTINATION include RENAME my-version.h)
```

will install the file `version.h` from the source directory to `include/my-version.h` under the installation prefix.

Projects may also install helper programs, such as shell scripts or Python scripts that are not actually compiled as targets. These may be installed with the `FILES` signature using the `PERMISSIONS` option to add execute permission. However, this case is common enough to justify a simpler interface. CMake provides the `PROGRAMS` signature for this purpose:

```
install (PROGRAMS files... DESTINATION <dir>
        [PERMISSIONS permissions...]
        [CONFIGURATIONS [Debug|Release|...]]
        [COMPONENT <component>]
        [RENAME <name>] [OPTIONAL])
```

The `PROGRAMS` keyword is immediately followed by a list of scripts to be installed. This command is identical to the `FILES` signature, except that the default permissions additionally include `OWNER_EXECUTE`, `GROUP_EXECUTE`, and `WORLD_EXECUTE`. For example, we may install a Python utility script with the command

```
install (PROGRAMS my-util.py DESTINATION bin)
```

which installs `my-util.py` to the `bin` directory under the installation prefix and gives it owner, group, world read and execute permissions, plus owner write.

Projects may also provide an entire directory full of resource files, such as icons or html documentation. An entire directory may be installed using the `DIRECTORY` signature:

```
install (DIRECTORY dirs... DESTINATION <dir>
        [FILE_PERMISSIONS permissions...]
        [DIRECTORY_PERMISSIONS permissions...]
        [USE_SOURCE_PERMISSIONS]
        [CONFIGURATIONS [Debug|Release|...]]
        [COMPONENT <component>]
        [[PATTERN <pattern> | REGEX <regex>]
        [EXCLUDE] [PERMISSIONS permissions...]] [...])
```

The `DIRECTORY` keyword is immediately followed by a list of directories to be installed. Relative paths are evaluated with respect to the current source directory. Each named directory is installed to the destination directory. The last component of each input directory name is appended to the destination directory as that directory is copied. For example, the command

```
install (DIRECTORY data/icons DESTINATION share/myproject)
```

will install the `data/icons` directory from the source tree into `share/myproject/icons` under the installation prefix. A trailing slash will leave the last component empty and install the contents of the input directory to the destination. The command

```
install (DIRECTORY doc/html/ DESTINATION doc/myproject)
```

installs the contents of `doc/html` from the source directory into `doc/myproject` under the installation prefix. If no input directory names are given, as in

```
install (DIRECTORY DESTINATION share/myproject/user)
```

the destination directory will be created but nothing will be installed into it.

Files installed by the `DIRECTORY` signature are given the same default permissions as the `FILES` signature. Directories installed by the `DIRECTORY` signature are given the same default permissions as the `PROGRAMS` signature. The `FILE_PERMISSIONS` and `DIRECTORY_PERMISSIONS` options may be used to override these defaults. Consider a case in which a directory full of example shell scripts is to be installed into a directory that is both owner and group writable. We may use the command

```
install (DIRECTORY data/scripts DESTINATION share/myproject
        FILE_PERMISSIONS
          OWNER_READ OWNER_EXECUTE OWNER_WRITE
          GROUP_READ GROUP_EXECUTE
          WORLD_READ WORLD_EXECUTE
        DIRECTORY_PERMISSIONS
          OWNER_READ OWNER_EXECUTE OWNER_WRITE
          GROUP_READ GROUP_EXECUTE GROUP_WRITE
          WORLD_READ WORLD_EXECUTE)
```

which installs the directory `data/scripts` into `share/myproject/scripts` and sets the desired permissions. In some cases, a fully-prepared input directory created by the project may have the desired permissions already set. The `USE_SOURCE_PERMISSIONS` option tells CMake to use the file and directory permissions from the input directory during installation. If in the previous example the input directory were to have already been prepared with correct permissions, the following command may have been used instead:

```
install (DIRECTORY data/scripts DESTINATION share/myproject
        USE_SOURCE_PERMISSIONS)
```

If the input directory to be installed is under source management, such as CVS, there may be extra subdirectories in the input that you do not wish to install. There may also be specific files that should not be installed or be installed with different permissions, while most files get the defaults. The `PATTERN` and `REGEX` options may be used for this purpose. A `PATTERN` option is followed first by a globbing pattern and then by an `EXCLUDE` or `PERMISSIONS` option. A `REGEX` option is followed first by a regular expression and then by `EXCLUDE` or `PERMISSIONS`. The `EXCLUDE` option skips installation of those files or directories matching the preceding pattern or expression, while the `PERMISSIONS` option assigns specific permissions to them.

Each input file and directory is tested against the pattern or regular expression as a full path with forward slashes. A pattern will match only complete file or directory names occurring at the end of the full path, while a regular expression may match any portion. For example, the pattern `foo*` will match `.../foo.txt` but not `.../myfoo.txt` or `.../foo/bar.txt`; however, the regular expression `foo` will match all of them.

Returning to the above example of installing an icons directory, consider the case in which the input directory is managed by CVS and also contains some extra text files that we do not want to install. The command

```
install (DIRECTORY data/icons DESTINATION share/myproject
         PATTERN "CVS" EXCLUDE
         PATTERN "*.txt" EXCLUDE)
```

installs the icons directory while ignoring any CVS directory or text file contained. The equivalent command using the REGEX option is

```
install (DIRECTORY data/icons DESTINATION share/myproject
         REGEX "/CVS$" EXCLUDE
         REGEX "/[^/]*.txt$" EXCLUDE)
```

which uses '/' and '$' to constrain the match in the same way as the patterns. Consider a similar case in which the input directory contains shell scripts and text files that we wish to install with different permissions than the other files. The command

```
install (DIRECTORY data/other/ DESTINATION share/myproject
         PATTERN "CVS" EXCLUDE
         PATTERN "*.txt"
           PERMISSIONS OWNER_READ OWNER_WRITE
         PATTERN "*.sh"
           PERMISSIONS OWNER_READ OWNER_WRITE OWNER_EXECUTE)
```

will install the contents of data/other from the source directory to share/myproject while ignoring CVS directories and giving specific permissions to .txt and .sh files.

Project installations may need to perform tasks other than just placing files in the installation tree. Third-party packages may provide their own mechanisms for registering new plugins that must be invoked during project installation. The SCRIPT signature is provided for this purpose:

```
install (SCRIPT <file>)
```

The SCRIPT keyword is immediately followed by the name of a CMake script. CMake will execute the script during installation. If the file name given is a relative path, it will be evaluated with respect to the current source directory. A simple use case is printing a message during installation. We first write a message.cmake file containing the code

```
message ("Installing My Project")
```

and then reference this script using the command:

```
install (SCRIPT message.cmake)
```

Custom installation scripts are not executed during the main CMakeLists file processing; they are executed during the installation process itself. Variables and macros defined in the code containing the install (SCRIPT) call will not be accessible from the script. However, there are a few variables defined during the script execution that may be used to get information about the installation. The variable CMAKE_INSTALL_PREFIX (page 645) is set to the actual installation prefix. This may be different from the corresponding cache variable value, because the installation scripts may be executed by a packaging tool that uses a different prefix. An environment variable ENV{DESTDIR} may be set by the user or packaging tool. Its value is prepended to the installation prefix and to absolute installation paths to determine the location where files are installed. In order to reference an install location on disk, custom script may use `$ENV{DESTDIR}${CMAKE_INSTALL_PREFIX}` as the top portion of the path. The variable `CMAKE_INSTALL_CONFIG_NAME` is set to the name of the build configuration currently being installed (Debug, Release, etc.). During component-specific installation, the variable `CMAKE_INSTALL_COMPONENT` is set to the name of the current component.

Custom installation scripts, as simple as the message above, are more easily created with the script code placed inline in the call to the `INSTALL` command. The `CODE` signature is provided for this purpose:

```
install (CODE "<code>")
```

The `CODE` keyword is immediately followed by a string containing the code to place in the installation script. An install-time message may be created using the command

```
install (CODE "MESSAGE(\"Installing My Project\")")
```

which has the same effect as the `message.cmake` script but contains the code inline.

4.12.1 Installing Prerequisite Shared Libraries

Executables are frequently built using shared libraries as building blocks. When you install such an executable, you must also install its prerequisite shared libraries, called "prerequisites" because the executable requires their presence in order to load and run properly. The three main sources of shared libraries are the operating system itself, the build products of your own project, and third party libraries belonging to an external project. The ones from the operating system may be relied upon to be present without installing anything: they are on the base platform where your executable runs. The build products in your own project presumably have add_library build rules in the CMakeLists files, and so it should be straightforward to create CMake install rules for them. It is the third party libraries that frequently become a high maintenance item when there are more than a handful of them, or when the set of them fluctuates from version-to-version of the third party project. Libraries may be added, code may be reorganized, and the third party shared libraries themselves may actually have additional prerequisites that are not obvious at first glance.

CMake provides two modules to make it easier to deal with required shared libraries. The first module, GetPrerequisites.cmake, provides the `get_prerequisites` function to analyze and classify the prerequisite shared libraries upon which an executable depends. Given an executable file as input, it will produce a list of the shared libraries required to run that executable, including any prerequisites of the discovered shared libraries themselves. It uses native tools on the various underlying platforms to perform this analysis: dumpbin (Windows), otool (Mac), and ldd (Linux). The second module, BundleUtilities.cmake, provides the `fixup_bundle` function to copy and fix prerequisite shared libraries using well-defined locations relative to the executable. For Mac bundle applications, it embeds the libraries inside the bundle, fixing them with `install_name_tool` to make a self-contained unit. On Windows, it copies the libraries into the same directory with the executable since executables will search in their own directories for their required DLLs.

The `fixup_bundle` function helps you create relocatable install trees. Mac users appreciate self-contained bundle applications: you can drag them anywhere, double click them, and they still work. They do not rely on anything being installed in a certain location other than the operating system itself. Similarly, Windows users without administrative privileges appreciate a relocatable install tree where an executable and all required

DLLs are installed in the same directory, so that it works no matter where you install it. You can even move things around after installing them and it will still work.

To use `fixup_bundle`, first install one of your executable targets. Then, configure a CMake script that can be called at install time. Inside the configured CMake script, simply include BundleUtilities and call the `fixup_bundle` function with appropriate arguments.

In CMakeLists.txt

```
install (TARGETS myExecutable DESTINATION bin)

# To install, for example, MSVC runtime libraries:
include (InstallRequiredSystemLibraries)

# To install other/non-system 3rd party required libraries:
configure_file (
  ${CMAKE_CURRENT_SOURCE_DIR}/FixBundle.cmake.in
  ${CMAKE_CURRENT_BINARY_DIR}/FixBundle.cmake
  @ONLY
  )

install (SCRIPT ${CMAKE_CURRENT_BINARY_DIR}/FixBundle.cmake)
```

In FixBundle.cmake.in:

```
include (BundleUtilities)

# Set bundle to the full path name of the executable already
# existing in the install tree:
set (bundle
"${CMAKE_INSTALL_PREFIX}/myExecutable@CMAKE_EXECUTABLE_SUFFIX@")

# Set other_libs to a list of full path names to additional
# libraries that cannot be reached by dependency analysis.
# (Dynamically loaded PlugIns, for example.)
set (other_libs "")

# Set dirs to a list of directories where prerequisite libraries
# may be found:
set (dirs
  "@CMAKE_RUNTIME_OUTPUT_DIRECTORY@"
  "@CMAKE_LIBRARY_OUTPUT_DIRECTORY@"
  )

fixup_bundle ("${bundle}" "${other_libs}" "${dirs}")
```

You are responsible for verifying that you have permission to copy and distribute the prerequisite shared libraries for your executable. Some libraries may have restrictive software licenses that prohibit making copies a la `fixup_bundle`.

4.12.2 Exporting and Importing Targets

CMake 2.6 introduced support for exporting targets from one CMake-based project and importing them into another. The main feature allowing this functionality is the notion of an IMPORTED target. Here we present imported targets and then show how CMake files may be generated by a project to export its targets for use by other projects.

4.12.3 Importing Targets

Imported targets are used to convert files outside of the project on disk into logical targets inside a CMake project. They are created using the IMPORTED (page 590) option to the add_executable() (page 273) and add_library() (page 274) commands. No build files are generated for imported targets. They are used simply for convenient, flexible reference to outside executables and libraries. Consider the following example which creates and uses an IMPORTED executable target

```
add_executable (generator IMPORTED)                     # 1
set_property (TARGET generator PROPERTY
              IMPORTED_LOCATION "/path/to/some_generator") # 2

add_custom_command (OUTPUT generated.c
                COMMAND generator generated.c)          # 3

add_executable (myexe src1.c src2.c generated.c)
```

Line #1 creates a new CMake target called generator. Line #2 tells CMake the location of the target on disk to import. Line #3 references the target in a custom command. Once CMake is run, the generated build system will contain a command line such as

```
/path/to/some_generator /project/binary/dir/generated.c
```

in the rule to generate the source file. In a similar manner, libraries from other projects may be used through IMPORTED targets

```
add_library (foo IMPORTED)
set_property (TARGET foo PROPERTY
              IMPORTED_LOCATION "/path/to/libfoo.a")
add_executable (myexe src1.c src2.c)
target_link_libraries (myexe foo)
```

On Windows, a .dll and its .lib import library may be imported together:

```
add_library (bar IMPORTED)
set_property (TARGET bar PROPERTY
              IMPORTED_LOCATION "c:/path/to/bar.dll")
set_property (TARGET bar PROPERTY
              IMPORTED_IMPLIB "c:/path/to/bar.lib")
add_executable (myexe src1.c src2.c)
target_link_libraries (myexe bar)
```

A library with multiple configurations may be imported with a single target:

```
add_library (foo IMPORTED)
set_property (TARGET foo PROPERTY
             IMPORTED_LOCATION_RELEASE "c:/path/to/foo.lib")
set_property (TARGET foo PROPERTY
             IMPORTED_LOCATION_DEBUG "c:/path/to/foo_d.lib")
add_executable (myexe src1.c src2.c)
target_link_libraries (myexe foo)
```

The generated build system will link `myexe` to `foo.lib` when it is built in the release configuration, and `foo_d.lib` when built in the debug configuration.

4.12.4 Exporting Targets

Imported targets on their own are useful, but they still require the project that imports them to know the locations of the target files on disk. The real power of imported targets is when the project providing the target files also provides a file to help import them.

The `install(TARGETS)` and `install(EXPORT)` commands work together to install both a target and a CMake file to help import it. For example, the code

```
add_executable (generator generator.c)
install (TARGETS generator DESTINATION lib/myproj/generators
         EXPORT myproj-targets)
install (EXPORT myproj-targets DESTINATION lib/myproj)
```

will install the two files

```
<prefix>/lib/myproj/generators/generator
<prefix>/lib/myproj/myproj-targets.cmake
```

The first is the regular executable named `generator`. The second file, `myproj-targets.cmake`, is a CMake file designed to make it easy to import `generator`. This file contains code such as

```
get_filename_component (_self "${CMAKE_CURRENT_LIST_FILE}" PATH)
get_filename_component (PREFIX "${_self}/../.." ABSOLUTE)
add_executable (generator IMPORTED)
set_property (TARGET generator PROPERTY
  IMPORTED_LOCATION "${PREFIX}/lib/myproj/generators/generator")
```

(note that `${PREFIX}` is computed relative to the file location). An outside project may now use generator as follows

```
include (${PREFIX}/lib/myproj/myproj-targets.cmake) # 1
add_custom_command (OUTPUT generated.c
                    COMMAND generator generated.c)   # 2
add_executable (myexe src1.c src2.c generated.c)
```

Line #1 loads the target import script (see section 0 to make this automatic). The script may import any number of targets. Their locations are computed relative to the script location so the install tree may be easily moved. Line #2 references the generator executable in a custom command. The resulting build system will run the executable from its installed location. Libraries may also be exported and imported

```
add_library (foo STATIC foo1.c)
install (TARGETS foo DESTINATION lib EXPORTS myproj-targets)
install (EXPORT myproj-targets DESTINATION lib/myproj)
```

This installs the library and an import file referencing it. Outside projects may simply write

```
include (${PREFIX}/lib/myproj/myproj-targets.cmake)
add_executable (myexe src1.c)
target_link_libraries (myexe foo)
```

and the executable will be linked to the library `foo`, exported, and installed by the original project.

Any number of target installations may be associated with the same export name. Export names are considered global so any directory may contribute a target installation. Only the one for calling to the `install (EXPORT)` command is needed to install an import file that references all targets. Both of the examples above may be combined into a single export file, even if they are in different subdirectories of the project, as shown in the code below.

```
# A/CMakeLists.txt
add_executable (generator generator.c)
install (TARGETS generator DESTINATION lib/myproj/generators
         EXPORT myproj-targets)

# B/CMakeLists.txt
add_library (foo STATIC foo1.c)
install (TARGETS foo DESTINATION lib EXPORTS myproj-targets)

# Top CMakeLists.txt
add_subdirectory (A)
add_subdirectory (B)
install (EXPORT myproj-targets DESTINATION lib/myproj)
```

Typically projects are built and installed before being used by an outside project. However, in some cases, it is desirable to export targets directly from a build tree. The targets may then be used by an outside project that references the build tree with no installation involved. The `export()` (page 287) command is used to generate a file exporting targets from a project build tree. For example, the code

```
add_executable (generator generator.c)
export (TARGETS generator FILE myproj-exports.cmake)
```

will create a file in the project build tree called `myproj-exports.cmake`, which contains the required code to import the target. This file may be loaded by an outside project that is aware of the project build tree, in order to use the executable to generate a source file. An example application of this feature is for building a generator executable on a host platform when cross-compiling. The project containing the generator executable may be built on the host platform and then the project that is being cross-compiled for another platform may load it.

4.13 Advanced Commands

There are a few commands that can be very useful, but are not typically used in writing CMakeLists files. This section will discuss a few of these commands and when they are useful. First, consider the `add_dependencies()` (page 273) command which creates a dependency between two targets. CMake automatically creates dependencies between targets when it can determine them. For example, CMake will automatically create a dependency for an executable target that depends on a library target. The `add_dependencies` command is typically used to specify inter target dependencies between targets where at least one of the targets is a custom target (see Chapter 6 for more information on custom targets).

The `include_regular_expression()` (page 316) command also relates to dependencies. This command controls the regular expression that is used for tracing source code dependencies. By default, CMake will trace all the dependencies for a source file including system files such as `stdio.h`. If you specify a regular expression with the `include_regular_expression` command, that regular expression will be used to limit which include files are processed. For example; if your software project's include files all started with the prefix foo (e.g. `fooMain.c fooStruct.h`, etc), you could specify a regular expression of `^foo.*$` to limit the dependency checking to just the files of your project.

Occasionally you might want to get a listing of all the source files that another source file depends on. This is useful when you have a program that uses pieces of a large library, but are unsure which pieces it is using. The `output_required_files()` (page 349) command will take a source file and produce a list of all the other source files it depends on. You could then use this list to produce a reduced version of the library that only contains the necessary files for your program.

Some tools, such as Rational Purify on the Sun platform, are run by inserting an extra command before the final link step. So, instead of

```
CC foo.o -o foo
```

The link step would be

```
purify CC foo.o -o foo
```

It is possible to do this with CMake. To run an extra program in front of the link line, change the rule variables `CMAKE_CXX_LINK_EXECUTABLE` and `CMAKE_C_LINK_EXECUTABLE`. Rule variables are described in Chapter 11. The values for these variables are contained in the file `Modules/CMakeDefaultMakeRuleVariables.cmake`, and they are sometimes redefined in `Modules/Platform/*.cmake`. Make sure it is set after the `PROJECT()` (page 327) command in the CMakeLists file. Here is a small example of using purify to link a program called foo

```
project (foo)

set (CMAKE_CXX_LINK_EXECUTABLE
```

```
    "purify ${CMAKE_CXX_LINK_EXECUTABLE}")
add_executable (foo foo.cxx)
```

Of course, for a generic CMakeLists file, you should have some `if` checks for the correct platform. This will only work for the Makefile generators because the rule variables are not used by the IDE generators. Another option would be to use `$(PURIFY)` instead of plain purify. This would pass through CMake into the Makefile and be a make variable. The variable could be defined on the command line like this: make PURIFY=purify. If not specified then it would just use the regular rule for linking a C++ executable as PURIFY would be expanded by make to nothing.

SYSTEM INSPECTION

This chapter will describe how to use CMake to inspect the environment of the system where the software is being built. This is a critical factor in creating cross-platform applications or libraries. It covers how to find and use system and user installed header files and libraries. It also covers some of the more advanced features of CMake, including the `try_compile()` (page 343) and `try_run()` (page 344) commands. These commands are extremely powerful tools for determining the capabilities of the system and compiler that is hosting your software.

This chapter also describes how to generate configured files and how to cross compile with CMake. Finally, the steps required to enable a project for the `find_package()` (page 297) command are covered, explaining how to create a `<Package>Config.cmake` file and other required files.

5.1 Using Header Files and Libraries

Many C and C++ programs depend on external libraries; however, when it comes to the practical aspects of compiling and linking a project, taking advantage of existing libraries can be difficult for both developers and users. Problems typically show up as soon as the software is built on a system other than the one on which it was developed. Assumptions regarding where libraries and header files are located become obvious when they are not installed in the same place on the new computer and the build system is unable to find them. CMake has many features to aid developers in the integration of external software libraries into a project.

The CMake commands that are most relevant to this type of integration are the `find_file()` (page 292), `find_library()` (page 294), `find_path()` (page 303), `find_program()` (page 306), and `find_package()` (page 297) commands. For most C and C++ libraries, a combination of `find_library` and `find_path` will be enough to compile and link with an installed library. The command `find_library` can be used to locate, or allow a user to locate a library, and `find_path` can be used to find the path to a representative include file from the project. For example, if you wanted to link to the tiff library, you could use the following commands in your CMakeLists.txt file

```
# find libtiff, looking in some standard places
find_library (TIFF_LIBRARY
              NAMES tiff tiff2
              PATHS /usr/local/lib /usr/lib
              )
```

```
# find tiff.h looking in some standard places
find_path (TIFF_INCLUDES tiff.h
          /usr/local/include
          /usr/include
          )

include_directories (${TIFF_INCLUDES})

add_executable (mytiff mytiff.c )

target_link_libraries (myprogram ${TIFF_LIBRARY})
```

The first command used is `find_library`, which in this case, will look for a library with the name tiff or tiff2. The `find_library` command only requires the base name of the library without any platform-specific prefixes or suffixes, such as lib and .dll. The appropriate prefixes and suffixes for the system running CMake will be added to the library name automatically when CMake attempts to find it. All the `FIND_*` commands will look in the `PATH` environment variable. In addition, the commands allow the specification of additional search paths as arguments to be listed after the `PATHS` marker argument. In addition to supporting standard paths, windows registry entries and environment variables can be used to construct search paths. The syntax for registry entries is the following:

```
[HKEY_CURRENT_USER\\Software\\Kitware\\Path;Build1]
```

Since software can be installed in many different places, it is impossible for CMake to find the library every time, but most standard installations should be covered. The `find_*` commands automatically create a cache variable so that users can override or specify the location from the CMake GUI. This way, if CMake is unable to locate the files it is looking for, users will still have an opportunity to specify them. If CMake does not find a file, the value is set to `VAR-NOTFOUND`; this value tells CMake that it should continue looking each time CMake's configure step is run. Note that in if statements, values of `VAR-NOTFOUND` will evaluate as false.

The next command used is `find_path`, a general purpose command that, in this example, is used to locate a header file from the library. Header files and libraries are often installed in different locations, and both locations are required to compile and link programs that use them. The use of `find_path` is similar to `find_library`, although it only supports one name, a list of search paths.

The next part of the CMakeLists file uses the variables created by the `find_*` commands. The variables can be used without checking for valid values, as CMake will print an error message notifying the user if any of the required variables have not been set. The user can then set the cache values and reconfigure until the message goes away. Optionally, a CMakeLists file could use the if command to use alternative libraries or options to build the project without the library if it cannot be found.

From the above example you can see how using the `find_*` commands can help your software compile on a variety of systems. It is worth noting that the `find_*` commands search for a match starting with the first argument and first path, so when listing paths and library names, list your preferred paths and names first. If there are multiple versions of a library and you would prefer tiff over tiff2, make sure they are listed in that order.

5.2 System Properties

Although it is a common practice in C and C++ code to add platform-specific code inside preprocessor `ifdef` directives, for maximum portability this should be avoided. Software should not be tuned to specific platforms with `ifdefs`, but rather to a canonical system consisting of a set of features. Coding to specific systems makes the software less portable, because systems and the features they support change with time, and even from system to system. A feature that may not have worked on a platform in the past may be a required feature for the platform in the future. The following code fragments illustrate the difference between coding to a canonical system and a specific system:

```
// coding to a feature
#ifdef HAS_FOOBAR_CALL
  foobar();
#else
  myfoobar();
#endif

// coding to specific platforms
#if defined(SUN) && defined(HPUX) && !defined(GNUC)
  foobar();
#else
  myfoobar();
#endif
```

The problem with the second approach is that the code will have to be modified for each new platform on which the software is compiled. For example, a future version of SUN may no longer have the foobar call. Using the `HAS_FOOBAR_CALL` approach, the software will work as long as `HAS_FOOBAR_CALL` is defined correctly, and this is where CMake can help. CMake can be used to define `HAS_FOOBAR_CALL` correctly and automatically by making use of the `try_compile()` (page 343) and `try_run()` (page 344) commands. These commands can be used to compile and run small test programs during the CMake configure step. The test programs will be sent to the compiler that will be used to build the project, and if errors occur, the feature can be disabled. These commands require that you write a small C or C++ program to test the feature. For example, to test if the `foobar` call is provided on the system, try compiling a simple program that uses `foobar`. First write the simple test program (testNeedFoobar.c in this example) and then add the CMake calls to the CMakeLists file to try compiling that code. If the compilation works then `HAS_FOOBAR_CALL` will be set to true.

```
--- testNeedFoobar.c -----

#include <foobar.h>
main()
{
  foobar();
}

--- testNeedFoobar.cmake ---

try_compile (HAS_FOOBAR_CALL
```

```
${CMAKE_BINARY_DIR}
${PROJECT_SOURCE_DIR}/testNeedFoobar.c
)
```

Now that HAS_FOOBAR_CALL is set correctly in CMake, you can use it in your source code through either the add_definitions() (page 273) command or by configuring a header file. We recommend configuring a header file as that file can be used by other projects that depend on your library. This is discussed further in the section called 'How To Configure a Header File'.

Sometimes compiling a test program is not enough. In some cases, you may actually want to compile and run a program to get its output. A good example of this is testing the byte order of a machine. The following example shows how to write a small program that CMake will compile and run to determine the byte order of a machine.

```
---- TestByteOrder.c ------

int main () {
  /* Are we most significant byte first or last */
  union
  {
    long l;
    char c[sizeof (long)];
  } u;
  u.l = 1;
  exit (u.c[sizeof (long) - 1] == 1);
}


----- TestByteOrder.cmake-----

try_run (RUN_RESULT_VAR
  COMPILE_RESULT_VAR
  ${CMAKE_BINARY_DIR}
  ${PROJECT_SOURCE_DIR}/Modules/TestByteOrder.c
  OUTPUT_VARIABLE OUTPUT
  )
```

The return result of the run will go into RUN_RESULT_VAR, the result of the compile will go into COMPILE_RESULT_VAR, and any output from the run will go into OUTPUT. You can use these variables to report debug information to the users of your project.

For small test programs the file() (page 287) command with the WRITE option can be used to create the source file from the CMakeLists file. The following example tests the C compiler to verify that it can be run.

```
file (WRITE
  ${CMAKE_BINARY_DIR}/CMakeTmp/testCCompiler.c
  "int main(){return 0;}"
  )

try_compile (CMAKE_C_COMPILER_WORKS
  ${CMAKE_BINARY_DIR}
```

```
${CMAKE_BINARY_DIR}/CMakeTmp/testCCompiler.c
OUTPUT_VARIABLE OUTPUT
)
```

There are several predefined try-run and try-compile macros in the `CMake/Modules` directory, some of which are listed below. These macros allow some common checks to be performed without having to create a source file for each test. For detailed documentation or to see how these macros work, look at the implementation files for them in the `CMake/Modules directory` of your installation. Many of these macros will look at the current value of the `CMAKE_REQUIRED_FLAGS` and `CMAKE_REQUIRED_LIBRARIES` variables to add additional compile flags or link libraries to the test.

CheckFunctionExists.cmake This macro checks to see if a C function is on a system by taking two arguments with the first being the name of the function to check for and the second being the variable to store the result into. This macro uses `CMAKE_REQUIRED_FLAGS` and `CMAKE_REQUIRED_LIBRARIES` if they are set.

CheckIncludeFile.cmake This macro checks for an include file on a system by taking two arguments with first being the include file to look for and the second being the variable to store the result into. Additional CFlags can be passed in as a third argument or by setting `CMAKE_REQUIRED_FLAGS`.

CheckIncludeFileCXX.cmake This macro checks for an include file in a C++ program by taking two arguments with the first being the include file to look for and the second being the variable to store the result into. Additional CFlags can be passed in as a third argument.

CheckIncludeFiles.cmake This macros checks for a group of include files by taking two arguments with the first being the include files to look for and the second being the variable to store the result into. This macro uses `CMAKE_REQUIRED_FLAGS` if it is set, and is useful when a header file you are interested in checking for is dependent on including another header file first.

CheckLibraryExists.cmake This macro checks to see if a library exists by taking four arguments with the first being the name of the library to check for; the second being the name of a function that should be in that library; the third argument being the location of where the library should be found; and the fourth argument being a variable to store the result into. This macro uses `CMAKE_REQUIRED_FLAGS` and `CMAKE_REQUIRED_LIBRARIES` if they are set.

CheckSymbolExists.cmake This macro checks to see if a symbol is defined in a header file by taking three arguments with the first being the symbol to look for; the second argument being a list of header files to try including; and the third argument being where the result is stored. This macro uses `CMAKE_REQUIRED_FLAGS` and `CMAKE_REQUIRED_LIBRARIES` if they are set.

CheckTypeSize.cmake This macro determines the size in bytes of a variable type by taking two arguments with the first argument being the type to evaluate, and the second argument being where the result is stored. Both `CMAKE_REQUIRED_FLAGS` and `CMAKE_REQUIRED_LIBRARIES` are used if they are set.

CheckVariableExists.cmake This macro checks to see if a global variable exists by taking two arguments with the first being the variable to look for, and the second argument being the variable to store the result in. This macro will prototype the named variable and then try to use it. If the test program compiles then the variable exists. This will only work for C variables. This macro uses `CMAKE_REQUIRED_FLAGS` and `CMAKE_REQUIRED_LIBRARIES` if they are set.

Consider the following example which shows a variety of these modules being used to compute properties of the platform. At the beginning of the example four modules are loaded from CMake. The remainder of the example uses the macros defined in those modules to test for header files, libraries, symbols, and type sizes respectively.

```
# Include all the necessary files for macros
include (CheckIncludeFiles)
include (CheckLibraryExists)
include (CheckSymbolExists)
include (CheckTypeSize)

# Check for header files
set (INCLUDES "")
CHECK_INCLUDE_FILES ("${INCLUDES};winsock.h" HAVE_WINSOCK_H)

if (HAVE_WINSOCK_H)
  set (INCLUDES ${INCLUDES} winsock.h)
endif (HAVE_WINSOCK_H)

CHECK_INCLUDE_FILES ("${INCLUDES};io.h" HAVE_IO_H)
if (HAVE_IO_H)
  set (INCLUDES ${INCLUDES} io.h)
endif (HAVE_IO_H)

# Check for all needed libraries
set (LIBS "")
CHECK_LIBRARY_EXISTS ("dl;${LIBS}" dlopen "" HAVE_LIBDL)
if (HAVE_LIBDL)
  set (LIBS ${LIBS} dl)
endif (HAVE_LIBDL)

CHECK_LIBRARY_EXISTS ("ucb;${LIBS}" gethostname "" HAVE_LIBUCB)
if (HAVE_LIBUCB)
  set (LIBS ${LIBS} ucb)
endif (HAVE_LIBUCB)

# Add the libraries we found to the libraries to use when
# looking for symbols with the CHECK_SYMBOL_EXISTS macro
set (CMAKE_REQUIRED_LIBRARIES ${LIBS})

# Check for some functions that are used
CHECK_SYMBOL_EXISTS (socket   "${INCLUDES}" HAVE_SOCKET)
CHECK_SYMBOL_EXISTS (poll     "${INCLUDES}" HAVE_POLL)

# Various type sizes
CHECK_TYPE_SIZE (int      SIZEOF_INT)
CHECK_TYPE_SIZE (size_t   SIZEOF_SIZE_T)
```

For more advanced `try_compile` and `try_run` operations, it may be desirable to pass flags to the compiler or to CMake. Both commands support the optional arguments `CMAKE_FLAGS` and

COMPILE_DEFINITIONS. CMAKE_FLAGS can be used to pass -DVAR:TYPE=VALUE flags to CMake. The value of COMPILE_DEFINITIONS is passed directly to the compiler command line.

5.3 Finding Packages

Many software projects provide tools and libraries that are meant as building blocks for other projects and applications. CMake projects that depend on outside packages locate their dependencies using the find_package() (page 297) command. A typical invocation is of the form:

```
find_package(<Package> [version])
```

where <Package> is the name of the package to be found, and [version] is an optional version request (of the form major[.minor.[patch]]). The command's notion of a package is distinct from that of CPack, which is meant for creating source and binary distributions and installers.

The command operates in two modes: Module mode and Config mode. In Module mode, the command searches for a find-module: a file named Find<Package>.cmake. It looks first in the CMAKE_MODULE_PATH (page 646) and then in the CMake installation. If a find-module is found, it is loaded to search for individual components of the package. Find-modules contain package-specific knowledge of the libraries and other files they expect to find, and internally use commands like find_library() (page 294) to locate them. CMake provides find-modules for many common packages; see the cmake-modules(7) (page 366) manual. Find-modules are tedious and difficult to write and maintain because they need very specific knowledge of every version of the package to be found.

The Config mode of find_package() (page 297) provides a powerful alternative through cooperation with the package to be found. It enters this mode after failing to locate a find-module or when explicitly requested by the caller. In Config mode the command searches for a package configuration file: a file named <Package>Config.cmake or <package>-config.cmake which is provided by the package to be found. Given the name of a package, the find_package command knows how to search deep inside installation prefixes for locations like:

```
<prefix>/lib/<package>/<package>-config.cmake
```

(see documentation of the find_package command for a complete list of locations). CMake creates a cache entry called <Package>_DIR to store the location found or allow the user to set it. Since a package configuration file comes with an installation of its package, it knows exactly where to find everything provided by the installation. Once the find_package command locates the file it provides the locations of package components without any additional searching.

The [version] option asks find_package to locate a particular version of the package. In Module mode, the command passes the request on to the find-module. In Config mode the command looks next to each candidate package configuration file for a package version file: a file named <Package>ConfigVersion.cmake or <package>-config-<version>.cmake. The version file is loaded to test whether the package version is an acceptable match for the version requested (see documentation of find_package for the version file API specification). If the version file claims compatibility, the configuration file is accepted, or is otherwise ignored. This approach allows each project to define its own rules for version compatibility.

5.4 Built-in Find Modules

CMake has many predefined modules that can be found in the Modules subdirectory of CMake. The modules can find many common software packages. See the `cmake-modules(7)` (page 366) manual for a detailed list.

Each `Find<XX>.cmake` module defines a set of variables that will allow a project to use the software package once it is found. Those variables all start with the name of the software being found <XX>. With CMake we have tried to establish a convention for naming these variables, but you should read the comments at the top of the module for a more definitive answer. The following variables are used by convention when needed:

<XX>_INCLUDE_DIRS Where to find the package's header files, typically <XX>.h, etc.

<XX>_LIBRARIES The libraries to link against to use <XX>. These include full paths.

<XX>_DEFINITIONS Preprocessor definitions to use when compiling code that uses <XX>.

<XX>_EXECUTABLE Where to find the <XX> tool that is part of the package.

<XX>_<YY>_EXECUTABLE Where to find the <YY> tool that comes with <XX>.

<XX>_ROOT_DIR Where to find the base directory of the installation of <XX>. This is useful for large packages where you want to reference many files relative to a common base (or root) directory.

<XX>_VERSION_<YY> Version <YY> of the package was found if true. Authors of find modules should make sure at most one of these is ever true. For example TCL_VERSION_84.

<XX>_<YY>_FOUND If false, then the optional <YY> part of <XX> package is unavailable.

<XX>_FOUND Set to false or undefined if we haven't found or don't want to use <XX>.

Not all of the variables are present in each of the `FindXX.cmake files`. However, the `<XX>_FOUND` should exist under most circumstances. If <XX> is a library, then `<XX>_LIBRARIES` should also be defined, and `<XX>_INCLUDE_DIR` should usually be defined.

Modules can be included in a project either with the `include` command or the `find_package()` (page 297) command.

```
find_package(OpenGL)
```

is equivalent to:

```
include(${CMAKE_ROOT}/Modules/FindOpenGL.cmake)
```

and

```
include(FindOpenGL)
```

If the project converts over to CMake for its build system, the `find_package` will still work if the package provides a `<XX>Config.cmake` file. How to create a CMake package is described later in this chapter.

5.5 How to Pass Parameters to a Compilation

Once you have determined the features of the system in which you are interested, it is time to configure the software based on what has been found. There are two common ways to pass this information to the compiler: on the compile line, or using a preconfigured header. The first way is to pass definitions on the compile line. A preprocessor definition can be passed to the compiler from a CMakeLists file with the `add_definitions()` (page 273) command. For example, a common practice in C code is to have the ability to selectively compile in/out debug statements.

```
#ifdef DEBUG_BUILD
  printf("the value of v is %d", v);
#endif
```

A CMake variable could be used to turn on or off debug builds using the `option()` (page 327) command:

```
option (DEBUG_BUILD
       "Build with extra debug print messages.")

if (DEBUG_BUILD)
  add_definitions (-DDEBUG_BUILD)
endif (DEBUG_BUILD)
```

Another example would be to tell the compiler the result of the previous HAS_FOOBAR_CALL test that was discussed earlier in this chapter. You could do this with the following:

```
if (HAS_FOOBAR_CALL)
  add_definitions (-DHAS_FOOBAR_CALL)
endif (HAS_FOOBAR_CALL)
```

If you want to pass preprocessor definitions at a finer level of granularity, you can use the COMPILE_DEFINITIONS property that is defined for directories, targets, and source files. For example, the code

```
add_library (mylib src1.c src2.c)
add_executable (myexe main1.c)
set_property (
   DIRECTORY
   PROPERTY COMPILE_DEFINITIONS A AV=1
   )
set_property (
   TARGET mylib
   PROPERTY COMPILE_DEFINITIONS B BV=2
   )
set_property (
   SOURCE src1.c
   PROPERTY COMPILE_DEFINITIONS C CV=3
   )
```

will build the source files with these definitions:

```
src1.c:    -DA -DAV=1 -DB -DBV=2 -DC -DCV=3
src2.c:    -DA -DAV=1 -DB -DBV=2
main2.c:   -DA -DAV=1
```

When the `add_definitions` command is called with flags like `-DX`, the definitions are extracted and added to the current directory's `COMPILE_DEFINITIONS` (page 568) property. When a new subdirectory is created with `add_subdirectory()` (page 277), the current state of the directory-level property is used to initialize the same property in the subdirectory.

Note in the above example that the `set_property` command will actually set the property and replace any existing value. The command provides the `APPEND` option to add more definitions without removing existing ones. For example, the code

```
set_property (
   SOURCE src1.c
   APPEND PROPERTY COMPILE_DEFINITIONS D DV=4
   )
```

will add the definitions `-DD -DDV=4` when building `src1.c`. Definitions may also be added on a per-configuration basis using the `COMPILE_DEFINITIONS_<CONFIG>` property. For example, the code

```
set_property (
   TARGET mylib
   PROPERTY COMPILE_DEFINITIONS_DEBUG MYLIB_DEBUG_MODE
   )
```

will build sources in mylib with `-DMYLIB_DEBUG_MODE` only when compiling in a Debug configuration.

The second approach for passing definitions to the source code is to configure a header file. For maximum portability of a toolkit, it is recommended that `-D` options are not required for the compiler command line. Instead of command line options, CMake can be used to configure a header file that applications can include. The header file will include all of the `#define` macros needed to build the project. The problem with using compile line definitions can be seen when building an application that uses a library. If building the library correctly relies on compile line definitions, then chances are that an application that uses the library will also require the exact same set of compile line definitions; this puts a large burden on the application writer to make sure they add the correct flags to match the library. If instead the library's build process configures a header file with all of the required definitions, any application that uses the library will automatically get the correct definitions when that header file is included. A definition can often change the size of a structure or class, and if the macros are not exactly the same during the build process of the library and the application linking to the library, the application may reference the "wrong part" of a class or struct and crash unexpectedly.

5.6 How to Configure a Header File

Configured header files are the right choice for most software projects. To configure a file with CMake, the `configure_file` command is used. This command requires an input file that is parsed by CMake to produce an output file with all variables expanded or replaced. There are three ways to specify a variable in an input file for `configure_file`.

```
#cmakedefine VARIABLE
```

If VARIABLE is true, then the result will be:

```
#define VARIABLE
```

If VARIABLE is false, then the result will be:

```
/* #undef VARIABLE */
```

${VARIABLE} This is simply replaced by the value of VARIABLE.

@VARIABLE@ This is simply replaced by the value of VARIABLE.

Since the ${} syntax is commonly used by other languages, users can tell the `configure_file` command to only expand variables using the @var@ syntax by passing the @ONLY option to the command; this is useful if you are configuring a script that may contain ${var} strings that you want to preserve. This is important because CMake will replace all occurrences of ${var} with the empty string if var is not defined in CMake.

The following example configures a .h file for a project that contains preprocessor variables. The first definition indicates if the FOOBAR call exists in the library, and the next one contains the path to the build tree.

```
---- CMakeLists.txt file-----

# Configure a file from the source tree
# called projectConfigure.h.in and put
# the resulting configured file in the build
# tree and call it projectConfigure.h
configure_file (
  ${PROJECT_SOURCE_DIR}/projectConfigure.h.in
  ${PROJECT_BINARY_DIR}/projectConfigure.h)
```

```
-----projectConfigure.h.in file------
/* define a variable to tell the code if the */
/* foobar call is available on this system */
#cmakedefine HAS_FOOBAR_CALL

/* define a variable with the path to the */
/* build directory */
#define PROJECT_BINARY_DIR "${PROJECT_BINARY_DIR}"
```

It is important to configure files into the binary tree, not the source tree. A single source tree may be shared by multiple build trees or platforms. By configuring files into the binary tree the differences between builds or platforms will be kept isolated in the build tree and will not corrupt other builds. This means that you will need to include the directory of the build tree where you configured the header file into the project's list of include directories using the `include_directories` command.

5.7 Creating CMake Package Configuration Files

Projects must provide package configuration files so that outside applications can find them. Consider a simple project "Gromit" providing an executable to generate source code and a library against which the generated code must link. The `CMakeLists.txt` file might start with:

```
cmake_minimum_required (VERSION 2.6.3)
project (Gromit C)
set (version 1.0)

# Create library and executable.
add_library (gromit STATIC gromit.c gromit.h)
add_executable (gromit-gen gromit-gen.c)
```

In order to install Gromit and export its targets for use by outside projects, add the code:

```
# Install and export the targets.
install (FILES gromit.h DESTINATION include/gromit-${version})
install (TARGETS gromit gromit-gen
         DESTINATION lib/gromit-${version}
         EXPORT gromit-targets)
install (EXPORT gromit-targets
         DESTINATION lib/gromit-${version})
```

as described in Section 4.11. Finally, Gromit must provide a package configuration file in its installation tree so that outside projects can locate it with `find_package`:

```
# Create and install package configuration and version files.
configure_file (
    ${Gromit_SOURCE_DIR}/pkg/gromit-config.cmake.in
    ${Gromit_BINARY_DIR}/pkg/gromit-config.cmake @ONLY)

configure_file (
    ${Gromit_SOURCE_DIR}/gromit-config-version.cmake.in
    ${Gromit_BINARY_DIR}/gromit-config-version.cmake @ONLY)

install (FILES ${Gromit_BINARY_DIR}/pkg/gromit-config.cmake
         ${Gromit_BINARY_DIR}/gromit-config-version.cmake
         DESTINATION lib/gromit-${version})
```

This code configures and installs the package configuration file and a corresponding package version file. The package configuration input file `gromit-config.cmake.in` has the code:

```
# Compute installation prefix relative to this file.
get_filename_component (_dir "${CMAKE_CURRENT_LIST_FILE}" PATH)
get_filename_component (_prefix "${_dir}/../.." ABSOLUTE)

# Import the targets.
include ("${_prefix}/lib/gromit-@version@/gromit-targets.cmake")
```

```
# Report other information.
set (gromit_INCLUDE_DIRS "${_prefix}/include/gromit-@version@")
```

After installation, the configured package configuration file `gromit-config.cmake` knows the locations of other installed files relative to itself. The corresponding package version file is configured from its input file `gromit-config-version.cmake.in`, which contains code such as:

```
set (PACKAGE_VERSION "@version@")
if (NOT "${PACKAGE_FIND_VERSION}" VERSION_GREATER "@version@")
  set (PACKAGE_VERSION_COMPATIBLE 1) # compatible with older
  if ("${PACKAGE_FIND_VERSION}" VERSION_EQUAL "@version@")
    set (PACKAGE_VERSION_EXACT 1) # exact match for this version
  endif ()
endif ()
```

An application that uses the Gromit package might create a CMake file that looks like this:

```
cmake_minimum_required (VERSION 2.6.3)
project (MyProject C)

find_package (gromit 1.0 REQUIRED)
include_directories (${gromit_INCLUDE_DIRS})
# run imported executable
add_custom_command (OUTPUT generated.c
                    COMMAND gromit-gen generated.c)
add_executable (myexe generated.c)
target_link_libraries (myexe gromit) # link to imported library
```

The call to `find_package` locates an installation of Gromit or terminates with an error message if none can be found (due to `REQUIRED`). After the command succeeds, the Gromit package configuration file `gromit-config.cmake` has been loaded, so Gromit targets have been imported and variables like `gromit_INCLUDE_DIRS` have been defined.

The above example creates a package configuration file and places it in the `install` tree. One may also create a package configuration file in the `build` tree to allow applications to use the project without installation. In order to do this, one extends Gromit's CMake file with the code:

```
# Make project usable from build tree.
export (TARGETS gromit gromit-gen FILE gromit-targets.cmake)
configure_file (${Gromit_SOURCE_DIR}/gromit-config.cmake.in
               ${Gromit_BINARY_DIR}/gromit-config.cmake @ONLY)
```

This `configure_file` call uses a different input file, `gromit-config.cmake.in`, containing:

```
# Import the targets.
include("@Gromit_BINARY_DIR@/gromit-targets.cmake")

# Report other information.
set(gromit_INCLUDE_DIRS "@Gromit_SOURCE_DIR@")
```

The package configuration file `gromit-config.cmake` placed in the build tree provides the same information to an outside project as that in the install tree, but refers to files in the source and build trees. It shares an identical package version file `gromit-config-version.cmake` which is placed in the install tree.

5.8 CMake Package Registry

CMake 2.8.5 and later provide two central locations to register packages that have been built or installed anywhere on a system: a *User Package Registry* and a *System Package Registry*. The `find_package` command searches the two package registries as two of the search steps specified in its documentation. The registries are especially useful for helping projects find packages in non-standard install locations or directly in the package build trees. A project may populate either the user or system registry (using its own means) to refer to its location. In either case, the package should store a package configuration file at the registered location and optionally a package version file as discussed in the Finding Packages section.

The *User Package Registry* is stored in a platform-specific, per-user location. On Windows it is stored in the Windows registry under a key in `HKEY_CURRENT_USER`. A `<package>` may appear under registry key

```
HKEY_CURRENT_USER\Software\Kitware\CMake\Packages\<package>
```

as a `REG_SZ` value with arbitrary name that specifies the directory containing the package configuration file. On UNIX platforms, the user package registry is stored in the user home directory under `~/.cmake/packages`. A `<package>` may appear under the directory

```
~/.cmake/packages/<package>
```

as a file with arbitrary name whose content specifies the directory containing the package configuration file. The `export(PACKAGE)` command may be used to register a project build tree in the user package registry. CMake does not currently provide an interface to add install trees to the user package registry; installers must be manually taught to register their packages if desired.

The *System Package Registry* is stored in a platform-specific, system-wide location. On Windows it is stored in the Windows registry under a key in `HKEY_LOCAL_MACHINE`. A `<package>` may appear under registry key

```
HKEY_LOCAL_MACHINE\Software\Kitware\CMake\Packages\<package>
```

as a `REG_SZ` value with arbitrary name that specifies the directory containing the package configuration file. There is no system package registry on non-Windows platforms. CMake does not provide an interface to add to the system package registry; installers must be manually taught to register their packages if desired.

Package registry entries are individually owned by the project installations that they reference. A package installer is responsible for adding its own entry and the corresponding uninstaller is responsible for removing it. However, in order to keep the registries clean, the `find_package` command automatically removes stale package registry entries it encounters if it has sufficient permissions. An entry is considered stale if it refers to a directory that does not exist or does not contain a matching package configuration file. This is particularly useful for user package registry entries created by the `export(PACKAGE)` command for build trees which have no uninstall event and are simply deleted by developers.

Package registry entries may have arbitrary name. A simple convention for naming them is to use content hashes, as they are deterministic and unlikely to collide. The `export(PACKAGE)` command uses this approach. The name of an entry referencing a specific directory is simply the content hash of the directory path itself. For example, a project may create package registry entries such as

```
> reg query HKCU\Software\Kitware\CMake\Packages\MyPackage
HKEY_CURRENT_USER\Software\Kitware\CMake\Packages\MyPackage
 45e7d55f13b87179bb12f907c8de6fc4
                        REG_SZ      c:/Users/Me/Work/lib/cmake/MyPackage
 7b4a9844f681c80ce93190d4e3185db9
                        REG_SZ      c:/Users/Me/Work/MyPackage-build
```

on Windows, or

```
$ cat ~/.cmake/packages/MyPackage/7d1fb77e07ce59a81bed093bbee945bd
/home/me/work/lib/cmake/MyPackage
$ cat ~/.cmake/packages/MyPackage/f92c1db873a1937f3100706657c63e07
/home/me/work/MyPackage-build
```

on UNIX. The command `find_package(MyPackage)` will search the registered locations for package configuration files. The search order among package registry entries for a single package is unspecified. Registered locations may contain package version files to tell `find_package` whether a specific location is suitable for the version requested.

CUSTOM COMMANDS AND TARGETS

Frequently the build process for a software project goes beyond simply compiling libraries and executables. In many cases, additional tasks may be required during or after the build process. Common examples include: compiling documentation using a documentation package; generating source files by running another executable; generating files using tools for which CMake doesn't have rules (such as lex and yacc); moving the resulting executables; post processing the executable, etc. CMake supports these additional tasks using both custom commands and targets. This chapter will describe how to use custom commands and targets to perform complex tasks that CMake does not inherently support.

6.1 Portable Custom Commands

Before going into detail on how to use custom commands, we will discuss how to deal with some of their portability issues. Custom commands typically involve running programs with files as inputs or outputs. Even a simple command, such as copying a file, can be tricky to do in a cross-platform way. For example, copying a file on UNIX is done with the cp command, while on Windows it is done with the copy command. To make matters worse, frequently the names of files will change on different platforms. Executables on Windows end with .exe, while on UNIX they do not. Even between UNIX implementations there are differences, such as which extensions are used for shared libraries; .so, .sl, .dylib, etc.

CMake provides three main tools for handling these differences. The first is the −E option (short for execute) to cmake. When the cmake executable is passed the −E option, it acts as a general purpose, cross-platform utility command. The arguments following the −E option indicate what cmake should do. Some options include:

chdir dir command args Changes the current directory to dir and then executes the command with the provided arguments.

copy file destination Copies a file from one directory or filename to another.

copy_if_different in-file out-file copy_if_different first checks to see if the files are different before copying them. This is critical in many rules since the build process is based on file modification times. If the copied file is used as the input to another build rule, then copy_if_different can eliminate unnecessary recompilations.

copy_directory source destination This option copies the source directory including any subdirectories to the destination directory.

remove file1 file2 ... Removes the listed files from the disk.

echo string Echos a string to the console. This is useful for providing output during the build process.

time command args Runs the command and times its execution.

These options provide a platform-independent way to perform a few common tasks. The cmake executable can be referenced by using the CMAKE_COMMAND (page 625) variable in your CMakeLists files, as later examples will show.

Of course, CMake doesn't limit you to using cmake −E in all your commands. You can use any command that you like, though it's important to consider portability issues when doing it. A common practice is to use find_program() (page 306) to find an executable (Perl, for example), and then use that executable in your custom commands.

The second tool that CMake provides to address portability issues is a number of variables describing the characteristics of the platform. The cmake-variables(7) (page 623) manual lists many variables that are useful for custom commands that need to reference files with platform-dependent names. These include CMAKE_EXECUTABLE_SUFFIX (page 627), CMAKE_SHARED_LIBRARY_PREFIX (page 632), etc. which describe file naming conventions.

Finally, CMake 2.8.4 and later support "generator expressions" in custom commands. These are expressions that use the special syntax $<...>; they are evaluated by the generator of the native build files. Please see the cmake-generator-expressions(7) (page 356) manual for further details. They may appear anywhere in a custom command line. Supported expressions include:

$<CONFIGURATION> Build configuration name, such as "Debug" or "Release".

$<TARGET_FILE:tgt> The main file on disk associated with named target "*tgt*" (.exe, .so.1.2, .a).

Generator expressions are not evaluated while processing CMake input files, but are instead delayed until generation of the final build system. Therefore, the values substituted for them know all the details of their evaluation context, including the current build configuration and all build properties associated with a target.

6.2 Using add_custom_command on a Target

Now we will consider the signature for add_custom_command. In Makefile terminology, add_custom_command adds a rule to a Makefile. For those more familiar with Visual Studio, it adds a custom build step to a file. add_custom_command has two main signatures: one for adding a custom command to a target and one for adding a custom command to build a file. When adding a custom command to a target the signature is as follows:

```
add_custom_command (
  TARGET target
  PRE_BUILD | PRE_LINK | POST_BUILD
  COMMAND command [ARGS arg1 arg2 arg3 ...]
```

```
[COMMAND command [ARGS arg1 arg2 arg3 ...] ...]
[COMMENT comment]
)
```

The target is the name of a CMake target (executable, library, or custom) to which you want to add the custom command. There is a choice of when the custom command should be executed. PRE_BUILD indicates that the command should be executed before any other dependencies for the target are built. PRE_LINK indicates that the command should be executed after all the dependencies are built, but before the actual link command. POST_BUILD indicates that the custom command should be executed after the target has been built. The COMMAND argument is the command (executable) to run, and ARGS provides an optional list of arguments to the command. Finally, the COMMENT argument can be used to provide a quoted string to be used as output when this custom command is run. This is useful if you want to provide some feedback or documentation on what is happening during the build. You can specify as many commands as you want for a custom command. They will be executed in the order specified.

6.2.1 How to Copy an Executable Once it is Built?

Now let us consider a simple custom command for copying an executable once it has been built.

```
# first define the executable target as usual
add_executable (Foo bar.c)

# then add the custom command to copy it
add_custom_command (
  TARGET Foo
  POST_BUILD
  COMMAND ${CMAKE_COMMAND}
  ARGS -E copy $<TARGET_FILE:Foo> /testing_department/files
  )
```

The first command in this example is the standard command for creating an executable from a list of source files. In this cases, an executable named Foo is created from the source file bar.c. Next is the add_custom_command invocation. Here the target is simply Foo and we are adding a post build command. The command to execute is cmake which has its full path specified in the CMAKE_COMMAND variable. Its arguments are -E copy and the source and destination locations. In this case, it will copy the Foo executable from where it was built into the /testing_department/files directory. Note that the TARGET parameter accepts a CMake target (Foo in this example), but arguments specified to the COMMAND parameter normally require full paths. In this case, we pass to cmake -E copy, the full path to the executable referenced via the $<TARGET_FILE:...> generator expression.

6.3 Using add_custom_command to Generate a File

The second use for add_custom_command() (page 269) is to add a rule for how to build an output file. Here the rule provided will replace any current rules for building that file. The signature is as follows:

```
add_custom_command (OUTPUT output1 [output2 ...]
  COMMAND command [ARGS [args...]]
  [COMMAND command [ARGS arg1 arg2 arg3 ...] ...]
  [MAIN_DEPENDENCY depend]
  [DEPENDS [depends...]]
  [COMMENT comment]
  )
```

The OUTPUT is the file (or files) that will result from running this custom command. The COMMAND and ARGS parameters are the command to execute and the arguments to pass to it. As with the prior signature you can have as many commands as you wish. The DEPENDS are files or executables that depend on this custom command. If any of these dependencies change, this custom command will re-execute. The MAIN_DEPENDENCY is an optional argument that acts as a regular dependency; under Visual Studio, it provides a suggestion for what file to hang this custom command onto. If the MAIN_DEPENDENCY is not specified, CMake will create one automatically. The MAIN_DEPENDENCY should not be a regular .c or .cxx file since the custom command will override the default build rule for the file. Finally, the optional COMMENT is a comment that may be used by some generators to provide additional information during the build process.

6.3.1 Using an Executable to Build a Source File

Sometimes a software project builds an executable that is then used for generating source files, which are used to build other executables or libraries. This may sound like an odd case, but it occurs quite frequently. One example is the build process for the TIFF library, which creates an executable that is then run to generate a source file that has system specific information in it. This file is then used as a source file in building the main TIFF library. Another example is the Visualization Toolkit (VTK), which builds an executable called vtkWrapTcl that wraps C++ classes into Tcl. The executable is built and then used to create more source files for the build process.

```
#####################################################
# Test using a compiled program to create a file
#####################################################

# add the executable that will create the file
# build creator executable from creator.cxx
add_executable (creator creator.cxx)

# add the custom command to produce created.c
add_custom_command (
  OUTPUT ${PROJECT_BINARY_DIR}/created.c
  DEPENDS creator
  COMMAND creator ${PROJECT_BINARY_DIR}/created.c
  )

# add an executable that uses created.c
add_executable (Foo ${PROJECT_BINARY_DIR}/created.c)
```

The first part of this example produces the creator executable from the source file creator.cxx. The custom command then sets up a rule for producing the source file `created.c` by running the executable `creator`. The custom command depends on the `creator` target and writes its result into the output tree (`PROJECT_BINARY_DIR`). Finally, an executable target called `Foo` is added, which is built using the `created.c` source file. CMake will create all the required rules in the Makefile (or Visual Studio workspace) so that when you build the project, the `creator` executable will be built, and run to create `created.c`, which will then be used to build the `Foo` executable.

6.4 Adding a Custom Target

In the discussion so far, CMake targets have generally referred to executables and libraries. CMake supports a more general notion of targets, called custom targets, which can be used whenever you want the notion of a target but without the end product being a library or an executable. Examples of custom targets include targets to build documentation, run tests, or update web pages. To add a custom target, use the `ADD_CUSTOM_TARGET` command with the following signature:

```
ADD_CUSTOM_TARGET ( name [ALL]
  [command arg arg arg ... ]
  [DEPENDS depend depend depend ... ]
  )
```

The name specified will be the name given to the target. You can use that name to specifically build that target with Makefiles (make name) or Visual Studio (right-click on the target and then select Build). If the optional `ALL` argument is specified, this target will be included in the ALL_BUILD target and will automatically be built whenever the Makefile or Project is built. The command and arguments are optional; if specified, they will be added to the target as a post-build command. For custom targets that will only execute a command this is all you will need. More complex custom targets may depend on other files, in these cases the `DEPENDS` arguments are used to list which files this target depends on. We will consider examples of both cases. First, let us look at a custom target that has no dependencies:

```
ADD_CUSTOM_TARGET ( FooJAR ALL
  ${JAR} -cvf "\"${PROJECT_BINARY_DIR}/Foo.jar\""
            "\"${PROJECT_SOURCE_DIR}/Java\""
  )
```

With the above definition, whenever the `FooJAR` target is built, it will run Java's Archiver (jar) to create the `Foo.jar` file from java classes in the `${PROJECT_SOURCE_DIR}/Java` directory. In essence, this type of custom target allows the developer to tie a command to a target so that it can be conveniently invoked during the build process. Now let us consider a more complex example that roughly models the generation of PDF files from LaTeX. In this case, the custom target depends on other generated files (mainly the end product .pdf files)

```
# Add the rule to build the .dvi file from the .tex
# file. This relies on LATEX being set correctly
#
add_custom_command(
  OUTPUT  ${PROJECT_BINARY_DIR}/doc1.dvi
```

```
      DEPENDS ${PROJECT_SOURCE_DIR}/doc1.tex
      COMMAND ${LATEX} ${PROJECT_SOURCE_DIR}/doc1.tex
      )

# Add the rule to produce the .pdf file from the .dvi
# file. This relies on DVIPDF being set correctly
#
add_custom_command(
   OUTPUT  ${PROJECT_BINARY_DIR}/doc1.pdf
   DEPENDS ${PROJECT_BINARY_DIR}/doc1.dvi
   COMMAND ${DVIPDF} ${PROJECT_BINARY_DIR}/doc1.dvi
   )

# finally add the custom target that when invoked
# will cause the generation of the pdf file
#
ADD_CUSTOM_TARGET ( TDocument ALL
   DEPENDS ${PROJECT_BINARY_DIR}/doc1.pdf
   )
```

This example makes use of both `add_custom_command` and `ADD_CUSTOM_TARGET`. The two `add_custom_command` invocations are used to specify the rules for producing a .pdf file from a .tex file. In this case, there are two steps and two custom commands. First a .dvi file is produced from the .tex file by running LaTeX, then the .dvi file is processed to produce the desired .pdf file. Finally, a custom target is added called TDocument. Its command simply echoes out what it is doing, while the real work is done by the two custom commands. The `DEPENDS` argument sets up a dependency between the custom target and the custom commands. When TDocument is built, it will first look to see if all of its dependencies are built. If any are not built, it will invoke the appropriate custom commands to build them. This example can be shortened by combining the two custom commands into one custom command, as shown in the following example:

```
# Add the rule to build the .pdf file from the .tex
# file. This relies on LATEX and DVIPDF being set correctly
#
add_custom_command(
   OUTPUT  ${PROJECT_BINARY_DIR}/doc1.pdf
   DEPENDS ${PROJECT_SOURCE_DIR}/doc1.tex
   COMMAND ${LATEX}  ${PROJECT_SOURCE_DIR}/doc1.tex
   COMMAND ${DVIPDF} ${PROJECT_BINARY_DIR}/doc1.dvi
   )

# finally add the custom target that when invoked
# will cause the generation of the pdf file
#
ADD_CUSTOM_TARGET ( TDocument ALL
   DEPENDS ${PROJECT_BINARY_DIR}/doc1.pdf
   )
```

Now consider a case where the documentation consists of multiple files. The above example can be modified to handle many files by using a list of inputs and a foreach loop. For example

```
# set the list of documents to process
set (DOCS doc1 doc2 doc3)

# add the custom commands for each document
foreach (DOC ${DOCS})

  add_custom_command (
    OUTPUT  ${PROJECT_BINARY_DIR}/${DOC}.pdf
    DEPENDS ${PROJECT_SOURCE_DIR}/${DOC}.tex
    COMMAND ${LATEX} ${PROJECT_SOURCE_DIR}/${DOC}.tex
    COMMAND ${DVIPDF} ${PROJECT_BINARY_DIR}/${DOC}.dvi
    )

  # build a list of all the results
  list (APPEND DOC_RESULTS ${PROJECT_BINARY_DIR}/${DOC}.pdf)

endforeach (DOC)

# finally add the custom target that when invoked
# will cause the generation of the pdf file
#
ADD_CUSTOM_TARGET ( TDocument ALL
  DEPENDS ${DOC_RESULTS}
  )
```

In this example, building the custom target TDocument will cause all of the specified .pdf files to be generated. Adding a new document to the list is simply a matter of adding its filename to the DOCS variable at the top of the example.

6.5 Specifying Dependencies and Outputs

When using custom commands and custom targets you will often be specifying dependencies. When you specify a dependency or the output of a custom command, you should always specify the full path. For example, if the command produces foo.h in the binary tree then its output should be something like ${PROJECT_BINARY_DIR}/foo.h. CMake will try to determine the correct path for the file if it is not specified; complex projects frequently end up using files in both the source and build trees, this can eventually lead to errors if the full paths are not specified.

When specifying a target as a dependency, you can leave off the full path and executable extension, referencing it simply by its name. Consider the specification of the generator target as an add_custom_command dependency in the example earlier in this chapter. CMake recognizes creator as matching an existing target and properly handles the dependencies.

6.6 When There Isn't One Rule For One Output

There are a couple of unusual cases that can arise when using custom commands that warrant further explanation. The first is a case where one command (or executable) can create multiple outputs, and the second is when multiple commands can be used to create a single output.

6.6.1 A Single Command Producing Multiple Outputs

In CMake, a custom command can produce multiple outputs simply by listing multiple outputs after the OUTPUT keyword. CMake will create the correct rules for your build system so that no matter which output is required for a target, the right rules will be run. If the executable happens to produce a few outputs but the build process is only using one of them, then you can simply ignore the other outputs when creating your custom command. Say that the executable produces a source file that is used in the build process, and also an execution log that is not used. The custom command should specify the source file as the output and ignore the fact that a log file is also generated.

Another case of having one command with multiple outputs is when the command is the same but the arguments to it change. This is effectively the same as having a different command, and each case should have its own custom command. An example of this was the documentation example on page 112, where a custom command was added for each .tex file. The command is the same but the arguments passed to it change each time.

6.6.2 Having One Output That Can Be Generated By Different Commands

In rare cases, you may find that you have more than one command that you can use to generate an output. Most build systems, such as make and Visual Studio, do not support this and likewise CMake does not. There are two common approaches that can be used to resolve this. If you truly have two different commands that produce the same output and no other significant outputs, then you can simply pick one of them and create a custom command for it.

In more complex cases there are multiple commands with multiple outputs; for example:

```
Command1 produces foo.h and bar.h
Command2 produces widget.h and bar.h
```

There are a few approaches that can be used in this case. You might consider combining both commands and all three outputs into a single custom command, so that whenever one output is required, all three are built at the same time. You could also create three custom commands, one for each unique output. The custom command for foo.h would invoke Command1, while the one for widget.h would invoke Command2. When specifying the custom command for bar.h, you could choose either Command1 or Command2.

CONVERTING EXISTING SYSTEMS TO CMAKE

For many people, the first thing they will do with CMake is convert an existing project from using an older build system to use CMake. This can be a fairly easy process, but there are a few issues to consider. This section will address those issues and provide some suggestions for effectively converting a project over to CMake. The first issue to consider when converting to CMake is the project's directory structure.

7.1 Source Code Directory Structures

Most small projects will have their source code in either the top level directory or in a directory named `src` or `source`. Even if all of the source code is in a subdirectory, we highly recommend creating a CMakeLists file for the top level directory. There are two reasons for this. First, it can be confusing to some people that they must run CMake on the subdirectory of the project, instead of the main directory. Second, you may want to install documentation or other support files from the other directories. By having a CMakeLists file at the top of the project, you can use the `add_subdirectory()` (page 277) command to step down into the documentation directory where its CMakeLists file can install the documentation (you can have a CMakeLists file for a documentation directory with no targets or source code).

For projects that have source code in multiple directories, there are a few options. One option that many Makefile-based projects use is to have a single Makefile at the top-level directory that lists all the source files to compile in their subdirectories. For example:

```
SOURCES=\
  subdir1/foo.cxx \
  subdir1/foo2.cxx \
  subdir2/gah.cxx \
  subdir2/bar.cxx
```

This approach works just as well with CMake using a similar syntax:

```
set (SOURCES
  subdir1/foo.cxx
  subdir1/foo2.cxx
  subdir1/gah.cxx
```

```
subdir2/bar.cxx
  )
```

Another option is to have each subdirectory build a library or libraries that can then be linked into the executables. In those cases, each subdirectory would define its own list of source files and add the appropriate targets. A third option is a mixture of the first two; each subdirectory can have a CMakeLists file that lists its sources, but the top-level CMakeLists file will not use the add_subdirectory command to step into the subdirectories. Instead, the top-level CMakeLists file will use the include() (page 317) command to include each of the subdirectory's CMakeLists files. For example, a top-level CMakeLists file might include the following code

```
# collect the files for subdir1
include (subdir1/CMakeLists.txt)
foreach (FILE ${FILES})
  set (subdir1Files ${subdir1Files} subdir1/${FILE})
endforeach (FILE)

# collect the files for subdir2
include (subdir2/CMakeLists.txt)
foreach (FILE ${FILES})
  set (subdir2Files ${subdir2Files} subdir2/${FILE})
endforeach (FILE)

# add the source files to the executable
add_executable (foo ${subdir1Files} ${subdir2Files})
```

While the CMakeLists files in the subdirectories might look like the following:

```
# list the source files for this directory
set (FILES
  foo1.cxx
  foo2.cxx
  )
```

The approach you use is entirely up to you. For large projects, having multiple shared libraries can certainly improve build times when changes are made. For smaller projects, the other two approaches have their advantages. The main suggestion here is to choose a strategy and stick with it.

7.2 Build Directories

The next issue to consider is where to put the resulting object files, libraries, and executables. There are a few different, commonly used approaches, and some work better with CMake than others. Probably the most common approach is to produce the binary files in the same directory as the source files. For some Windows generators, such as Visual Studio, they are actually kept in a subdirectory matching the selected configuration; e.g. debug, release, etc. CMake supports this approach by default. A closely-related approach is to put the binary files into a separate tree that has the same structure as the source tree. For example, if the source tree looked like the following:

```
foo/
  subdir1
  subdir2
```

the binary tree might look like:

```
foobin/
  subdir1
  subdir2
```

CMake also supports this structure by default. Switching between in-source builds and out-of-source builds is simply a matter of changing the binary directory when you run CMake (see 'How to Run CMake?' in Chapter 2). Note that if you have already done an in-source build and want to switch to an out of source build, you should start with a fresh copy of the source tree. If you need to support multiple architectures from one source tree, we highly recommend a directory structure like the following:

```
projectfoo/
  foo/
    subdir1
    subdir2
  foo-linux/
    subdir1
    subdir2
  foo-osx/
    subdir1
    subdir2
  foo-solaris/
    subdir1
    subdir2
```

That way, each architecture has its own build directory and will not interfere with any other architecture. Remember that not only are the object files kept in the binary directories, but also any configured files that are typically written to the binary tree. Another tree structure found primarily on UNIX projects is one where the binary files for different architectures are kept in subdirectories of the source tree (see below). CMake does not work well with this structure, so we recommend switching to the separate build tree structure shown above.

```
foo/
  subdir1/
    linux
    solaris
    hpux
  subdir2/
    linux
    solaris
    hpux
```

CMake provides three variables for controlling where binary targets are written. They are the CMAKE_RUNTIME_OUTPUT_DIRECTORY (page 664), CMAKE_LIBRARY_OUTPUT_DIRECTORY (page 660), and CMAKE_ARCHIVE_OUTPUT_DIRECTORY (page 657) variables. These variables are used to initialize properties of libraries and executables to control where they will be written. Setting these enables a project to place all the libraries and executables into a single directory. For projects with many subdirectories, this can be a real time saver. A typical implementation is shown below:

```
# Setup output directories.
set(CMAKE_RUNTIME_OUTPUT_DIRECTORY ${PROJECT_BINARY_DIR}/bin)
set(CMAKE_LIBRARY_OUTPUT_DIRECTORY ${PROJECT_BINARY_DIR}/lib)
set(CMAKE_ARCHIVE_OUTPUT_DIRECTORY ${PROJECT_BINARY_DIR}/lib)
```

In this example, all the "runtime" binaries will be written to the bin subdirectory of the project's binary tree, including executable files on all platforms and DLLs on Windows. Other binaries will be written to the lib directory. This approach is very useful for projects that make use of shared libraries (DLLs) because it collects all of the shared libraries into one directory. If the executables are placed in the same directory, then they can find the required shared libraries more easily when run on Windows.

One final note on directory structures: with CMake, it is perfectly acceptable to have a project within a project. For example, within the Visualization Toolkit's source tree is a directory that contains a complete copy of the zlib compression library. In writing the CMakeLists file for that library, we use the PROJECT command to create a project named VTKZLIB even though it is within the VTK source tree and project. This has no real impact on VTK, but it does allow us to build zlib independent of VTK without having to modify its CMakeLists file.

7.3 Useful CMake Commands When Converting Projects

There are a few CMake commands that can make the job of converting an existing project easier and faster. The file() (page 287) command with the GLOB argument allows you to quickly set a variable containing a list of all the files that match the glob expression. For example:

```
# collect up the source files
file (GLOB SRC_FILES "*.cxx")

# create the executable
add_executable (foo ${SRC_FILES})
```

will set the SRC_FILES variable to a list of all the .cxx files in the current source directory. It will then create an executable using those source files. Windows developers should be aware that glob matches are case sensitive.

Two other useful commands are make_directory() (page 349) and exec_program() (page 346). By default, CMake will create all the output directories it needs for the object files, libraries, and executables. With existing projects there may be some part of the build process that creates directories that CMake would not normally create. In these cases, the make_directory command can be used. As soon as CMake executes that command, it will create the directory specified if it does not already exist. The exec_program command will execute a program when it is encountered by CMake. This is useful if you want to quickly convert a UNIX autoconf configured header file to CMake. Instead of doing the full conversion to CMake, you could run configure from an exec_program command to generate the configured header file (on UNIX only, of course).

7.4 Converting UNIX Makefiles

If your project is currently based on standard UNIX Makefiles (not autoconf and Makefile.in or imake) then their conversion to CMake should be fairly straightforward. Essentially, for every directory in your project that has a Makefile, you will create a matching CMakeLists file. How you handle multiple Makefiles in a directory depends on their function. If the additional Makefiles (or Makefile type files) are simply included in the main Makefile, you can create matching CMake syntax files and include them into your main CMakeLists file in a similar manner. If the different Makefiles are meant to be invoked on the command line for different situations, consider creating a main CMakeLists file that uses some logic to choose which one to include() (page 317) based on a CMake option.

Converting the Makefile syntax to CMake is fairly easy. Frequently Makefiles have a list of object files to compile. These can be converted to CMake variables as follows:

```
OBJS= \
  foo1.o \
  foo2.o \
  foo3.o
```

becomes

```
set (SOURCES
  foo1.c
  foo2.c
  foo3.c
)
```

While the object files are typically listed in a Makefile, in CMake the focus is on the source files. If you used conditional statements in your Makefiles, they can be converted over to CMake if commands. Since CMake handles generating dependencies, most dependencies or rules to generate dependencies can be eliminated. Where you have rules to build libraries or executables, replace them with add_library() (page 274) or add_executable() (page 273) commands. Some UNIX build systems (and source code) make heavy use of the system architecture to determine which files to compile or what flags to use. Typically this information is stored in a Makefile variable called ARCH or UNAME.

The first choice in these cases is to replace the architecture-specific code with a more generic test. For example, instead of switching your handling of byte order based on operating system, make the decision based on the results of a byte order test such as CheckBigEndian.cmake. With some software packages, there is too much architecture specific code for such a change to be reasonable, or you may want to make decisions based on architecture for other reasons. In those cases, you can use the variables defined in the CMakeDetermineSystem module. They provide fairly detailed information on the operating system and version of the host computer.

7.5 Converting Autoconf Based Projects

Autoconf-based projects primarily consist of three key pieces. The first is the configure.in file which drives the process. The second is Makefile.in which will become the resulting Makefile, and the third piece is the remaining configured files that result from running configure. In converting an autoconf based project to CMake, start with the configure.in and Makefile.in files.

The Makefile.in file can be converted to CMake syntax as explained in the preceding section on converting UNIX Makefiles. Once this has been done, convert the configure.in file into CMake syntax. Most functions (macros) in autoconf have corresponding commands in CMake. A short table of some of the basic conversions is listed below:

AC_ARG_WITH Use the `option()` (page 327) command.

AC_CHECK_HEADER Use the `CHECK_INCLUDE_FILE` macro from the `CheckIncludeFile` module.

AC_MSG_CHECKING Use the message command with the `STATUS` argument.

AC_SUBST Done automatically when using the `configure_file()` (page 282) command.

AC_CHECK_LIB Use the `CHECK_LIBRARY_EXISTS` macro from the `CheckLibraryExists` module.

AC_CONFIG_SUBDIRS Use the `add_subdirectory()` (page 277) command.

AC_OUTPUT Use the `configure_file()` (page 282) command.

AC_TRY_COMPILE Use the `try_compile()` (page 343) command.

If your configure script performs test compilations using `AC_TRY_COMPILE`, you can use the same code for CMake. Either put it directly into your CMakeLists file if it is short, or preferably put it into a source code file for your project. We typically put such files into a CMake subdirectory for large projects that require such testing.

Where you are relying on autoconf to configure files, you can use CMake's `configure_file` command. The basic approach is the same and we typically name input files to be configured with a `.in` extension just as autoconf does. This command replaces any variables in the input file referenced as `${VAR}` or `@VAR@` with their values as determined by CMake. If a variable is not defined, it will be replaced with nothing. Optionally, only variables of the form `@VAR@` will be replaced and `${VAR}` will be ignored. This is useful for configuring files for languages that use `${VAR}` as a syntax for evaluating variables. You can also conditionally define variables using the C pre processor by using `#cmakedefine VAR`. If the variable is defined then `configure_file` will convert the `#cmakedefine` into a `#define`; if it is not defined, it will become a commented out `#undef`. For example:

```
/* what byte order is this system */
#cmakedefine CMAKE_WORDS_BIGENDIAN

/* what size is an INT */
#cmakedefine SIZEOF_INT @SIZEOF_INT@
```

7.6 Converting Windows Based Workspaces

To convert a Visual Studio workspace (or solution for Visual Studio .Net) to CMake involves a few steps. First you will need to create a CMakeLists file at the top of your source code directory. This file should start with a `project()` (page 327) command that defines the name of the project. This will become the name of the resulting workspace (or solution for Visual Studio .Net). Next, add all of your source files into CMake variables. For large projects that have multiple directories, create a CMakeLists file in each directory as described in the section on source directory structures at the beginning of this chapter. You will then add your libraries and executables using `add_library()` (page 274) and `add_executable()` (page 273). By default, `add_executable` assumes that your executable is a console application. Adding the `WIN32` argument to `add_executable` indicates that it is a Windows application (using WinMain instead of main).

There are a few nice features that Visual Studio supports and CMake can take advantage of. One is support for class browsing. Typically in CMake, only source files are added to a target, not header files. If you add header files to a target, they will show up in the workspace and then you will be able to browse them as usual. Visual Studio also supports the notion of groups of files. By default, CMake creates groups for source files and header files. Using the `source_group()` (page 334) command, you can create your own groups and assign files to them. If you have any custom build steps in your workspace, these can be added to your CMakeLists files using the `add_custom_command()` (page 269) command. Custom targets (Utility Targets) in Visual Studio can be added with the `add_custom_target()` (page 272) command.

CROSS COMPILING WITH CMAKE

Cross-compiling a piece of software means that the software is built on one system, but is intended to run on a different system. The system used to build the software will be called the "build host," and the system for which the software is built will be called the "target system" or "target platform." The target system usually runs a different operating system (or none at all) and/or runs on different hardware. A typical use case is in software development for embedded devices like network switches, mobile phones, or engine control units. In these cases, the target platform doesn't have or is not able to run the required software development environment.

Starting with CMake 2.6.0, cross-compiling is fully supported by CMake, ranging from cross-compiling from Linux to Windows; cross-compiling for supercomputers, through to cross-compiling for small embedded devices without an operating system (OS).

Cross-compiling has several consequences for CMake:

- CMake cannot automatically detect the target platform.

- CMake cannot find libraries and headers in the default system directories.

- Executables built during cross compiling cannot be executed.

Cross-compiling support doesn't mean that all CMake-based projects can be magically cross-compiled out-of-the-box (some are), but that CMake separates between information about the build platform and target platform and gives the user mechanisms to solve cross-compiling issues without additional requirements such as running virtual machines, etc.

To support cross-compiling for a specific software project, CMake must to be told about the target platform via a toolchain file. The CMakeLists.txt may have to be adjusted so they are aware that the build platform may have different properties than the target platform, and it has to deal with the instances where a compiled executable tries to execute on the build host.

8.1 Toolchain Files

In order to use CMake for cross-compiling, a CMake file that describes the target platform has to be created, called the "toolchain file," This file tells CMake everything it needs to know about the target platform. Here is an example that uses the MinGW cross-compiler for Windows under Linux; the contents will be explained line-by-line afterwards

```
# the name of the target operating system
set (CMAKE_SYSTEM_NAME Windows)

# which compilers to use for C and C++
set (CMAKE_C_COMPILER   i586-mingw32msvc-gcc )
set (CMAKE_CXX_COMPILER i586-mingw32msvc-g++ )

# where is the target environment located
set (CMAKE_FIND_ROOT_PATH  /usr/i586-mingw32msvc
    /home/alex/mingw-install )

# adjust the default behavior of the FIND_XXX() commands:
# search programs in the host environment
set (CMAKE_FIND_ROOT_PATH_MODE_PROGRAM NEVER)

# search headers and libraries in the target environment
set (CMAKE_FIND_ROOT_PATH_MODE_LIBRARY ONLY)
set (CMAKE_FIND_ROOT_PATH_MODE_INCLUDE ONLY)
```

Assuming that this file is saved with the name TC-mingw.cmake in your home directory, you instruct CMake to use this file by setting the CMAKE_TOOLCHAIN_FILE (page 633) variable:

```
~/src$ cd build
~/src/build$ cmake -DCMAKE_TOOLCHAIN_FILE=~/TC-mingw.cmake ..
...
```

CMAKE_TOOLCHAIN_FILE has to be specified only on the initial CMake run; after that, the results are reused from the CMake cache. You don't need to write a separate toolchain file for every piece of software you want to build. The toolchain files are per target platform; i.e. if you are building several software packages for the same target platform, you only have to write one toolchain file that can be used for all packages. What do the settings in the toolchain file mean? We will examine them one-by-one. Since CMake cannot guess the target operating system or hardware, you have to set the following CMake variables:

CMAKE_SYSTEM_NAME (page 653) This variable is mandatory; it sets the name of the target system, i.e. to the same value as CMAKE_SYSTEM_NAME would have if CMake were run on the target system. Typical examples are "Linux" and "Windows." It is used for constructing the file names of the platform files like Linux.cmake or Windows-gcc.cmake. If your target is an embedded system without an OS, set CMAKE_SYSTEM_NAME to "Generic." Presetting CMAKE_SYSTEM_NAME this way instead of being detected, automatically causes CMake to consider the build a cross-compiling build and the CMake variable CMAKE_CROSSCOMPILING (page 626) will be set to TRUE. CMAKE_CROSSCOMPILING is the variable that should be tested in CMake files to determine whether the current build is a cross-compiled build or not.

CMAKE_SYSTEM_VERSION (page 653) This variable is optional; it sets the version of your target system. CMake does not currently use CMAKE_SYSTEM_VERSION.

CMAKE_SYSTEM_PROCESSOR (page 653) This variable is optional; it sets the processor or hardware name of the target system. It is used in CMake for one purpose, to load the

```
${CMAKE_SYSTEM_NAME}-COMPILER_ID-${CMAKE_SYSTEM_PROCESSOR}.cmake
```

file. This file can be used to modify settings such as compiler flags for the target. You should only have to set this variable if you are using a cross-compiler where each target needs special build settings. The value can be chosen freely, so it could be, for example, i386, IntelPXA255, or MyControlBoardRev42.

In CMake code, the CMAKE_SYSTEM_XXX variables always describe the target platform. The same is true for the short WIN32, UNIX, APPLE variables. These variables can be used to test the properties of the target. If it is necessary to test the build host system, there is a corresponding set of variables: CMAKE_HOST_SYSTEM (page 651), CMAKE_HOST_SYSTEM_NAME (page 651),:variable:*CMAKE_HOST_SYSTEM_VERSION*, CMAKE_HOST_SYSTEM_PROCESSOR (page 651); and also the short forms: CMAKE_HOST_WIN32 (page 652), CMAKE_HOST_UNIX (page 652) and CMAKE_HOST_APPLE (page 651).

Since CMake cannot guess the target system, it cannot guess which compiler it should use. Setting the following variables defines what compilers to use for the target system.

CMAKE_C_COMPILER This specifies the C compiler executable as either a full path or just the filename. If it is specified with full path, then this path will be preferred when searching for the C++ compiler and the other tools (binutils, linker, etc.). If the compiler is a GNU cross-compiler with a prefixed name (e.g. "arm-elf-gcc"), CMake will detect this and automatically find the corresponding C++ compiler (i.e. "arm-elf-c++"). The compiler can also be set via the CC environment variable. Setting CMAKE_C_COMPILER directly in a toolchain file has the advantage that the information about the target system is completely contained in this file, and it does not depend on environment variables.

CMAKE_CXX_COMPILER This specifies the C++ compiler executable as either a full path or just the filename. It is handled the same way as CMAKE_C_COMPILER. If the toolchain is a GNU toolchain, it should suffice to set only CMAKE_C_COMPILER; CMake should find the corresponding C++ compiler automatically. As for CMAKE_C_COMPILER, also for C++ the compiler can be set via the CXX environment variable.

Once the system and the compiler are determined by CMake, it will load the corresponding files in the order described in Chapter 11 in the section called The Enable Language Process.

8.2 Finding External Libraries, Programs and Other Files

Most non-trivial projects make use of external libraries or tools. CMake offers the find_program, find_library, find_file, find_path, and find_package commands for this purpose. They search the file system in common places for these files and return the results. find_package is a bit different in that it does not actually search itself, but executes Find<*>.cmake modules, which in turn call the find_program, find_library, find_file, and find_path commands.

When cross-compiling, these commands become more complicated. For example, when cross-compiling to Windows on a Linux system, getting /usr/lib/libjpeg.so as the result of the command find_package(JPEG) would be useless, since this would be the JPEG library for the host system and not the target system. In some cases, you want to find files that are meant for the target platform; in other cases you will want to find files for the build host. The following variables are designed to give you the flexibility to change how the typical find commands in CMake work, so that you can find both build host and target files as necessary.

The toolchain will come with its own set of libraries and headers for the target platform, which are usually installed under a common prefix. It is a good idea to set up a directory where all the software that is built for the target platform will be installed, so that the software packages don't get mixed up with the libraries that come with the toolchain.

The `find_program()` (page 306) command is typically used to find a program that will be executed during the build, so this should still search in the host file system, and not in the environment of the target platform. find_library is normally used to find a library that is then used for linking purposes, so this command should only search in the target environment. For `find_path()` (page 303) and `find_file()` (page 292), it is not so obvious; in many cases, they are used to search for headers, so by default they should only search in the target environment. The following CMake variables can be set to adjust the behavior of the find commands for cross-compiling.

CMAKE_FIND_ROOT_PATH (page 643) This is a list of the directories that contain the target environment. Each of the directories listed here will be prepended to each of the search directories of every find command. Assuming your target environment is installed under /opt/eldk/ppc_74xx and your installation for that target platform goes to ~/install-eldk-ppc74xx, set `CMAKE_FIND_ROOT_PATH` to these two directories. Then find_library (JPEG_LIB jpeg) will search in /opt/eldk/ppc_74xx/lib, /opt/eldk/ppc_74xx/usr/lib, ~/install-eldk-ppc74xx/lib, ~/install-eldk-ppc74xx/usr/lib, and should result in /opt/eldk/ppc_74xx/usr/lib/libjpeg.so.

By default, `CMAKE_FIND_ROOT_PATH` is empty. If set, first the directories prefixed with the path given in `CMAKE_FIND_ROOT_PATH` will be searched, and then the unprefixed versions of the same directories will be searched.

By setting this variable, you are basically adding a new set of search prefixes to all of the find commands in CMake, but for some find commands you may not want to search the target or host directories. You can control how each find command invocation works by passing in one of the three following options `NO_CMAKE_FIND_ROOT_PATH`, `ONLY_CMAKE_FIND_ROOT_PATH`, or `CMAKE_FIND_ROOT_PATH_BOTH` when you call it. You can also control how the find commands work using the following three variables.

CMAKE_FIND_ROOT_PATH_MODE_PROGRAM (page 644) This sets the default behavior for the find_program command. It can be set to NEVER, ONLY, or BOTH. The default setting is BOTH. When set to NEVER, `CMAKE_FIND_ROOT_PATH` will not be used for find_program calls except where it is enabled explicitly. If set to ONLY, only the search directories with the prefixes coming from `CMAKE_FIND_ROOT_PATH` will be used by find_program. The default is BOTH, which means that first the prefixed directories and then the unprefixed directories, will be searched.

In most cases, `find_program()` (page 306) is used to search for an executable which will then be executed, e.g. using `execute_process()` (page 285) or `add_custom_command()` (page 269). So in most cases an executable from the build host is required, so setting `CMAKE_FIND_ROOT_PATH_MODE_PROGRAM` to NEVER is normally preferred.

CMAKE_FIND_ROOT_PATH_MODE_LIBRARY (page 643) This is the same as above, but for the find_library command. In most cases this is used to find a library which will then be used for linking, so a library for the target is required. In most cases, it should be set to ONLY.

CMAKE_FIND_ROOT_PATH_MODE_INCLUDE (page 643) This is the same as above and used for both find_path and find_file. In most cases, this is used for finding include directories, so the target environment should be searched. In most cases, it should be set to ONLY. If you also need to find files in the file system of the build host (e.g. some data files that will be processed during the build); you may need to adjust the behavior for those find_path or find_file calls using the NO_CMAKE_FIND_ROOT_PATH, ONLY_CMAKE_FIND_ROOT_PATH and CMAKE_FIND_ROOT_PATH_BOTH options.

With a toolchain file set up as described, CMake now knows how to handle the target platform and the cross-compiler. We should now able to build software for the target platform. For complex projects, there are more issues that must to be taken care of.

8.3 System Inspection

Most portable software projects have a set of system inspection tests for determining the properties of the (target) system. The simplest way to check for a system feature with CMake is by testing variables. For this purpose, CMake provides the variables UNIX (page 655), WIN32 (page 656), and APPLE (page 650). When cross-compiling, these variables apply to the target platform, for testing the build host platform there are corresponding variables CMAKE_HOST_UNIX (page 652), CMAKE_HOST_WIN32 (page 652), and CMAKE_HOST_APPLE (page 651).

If this granularity is too coarse, the variables CMAKE_SYSTEM_NAME (page 653), CMAKE_SYSTEM (page 653), CMAKE_SYSTEM_VERSION (page 653), and CMAKE_SYSTEM_PROCESSOR (page 653) can be tested, along with their counterparts CMAKE_HOST_SYSTEM_NAME (page 651), CMAKE_HOST_SYSTEM (page 651), CMAKE_HOST_SYSTEM_VERSION (page 652), and CMAKE_HOST_SYSTEM_PROCESSOR (page 651), which contain the same information, but for the build host and not for the target system.

```
if (CMAKE_SYSTEM MATCHES Windows)
   message (STATUS "Target system is Windows")
endif ()

if (CMAKE_HOST_SYSTEM MATCHES Linux)
   message (STATUS "Build host runs Linux")
endif ()
```

8.3.1 Using Compile Checks

In CMake, there are macros such as CHECK_INCLUDE_FILES and CHECK_C_SOURCE_RUNS that are used to test the properties of the platform. Most of these macros internally use either the try_compile() (page 343) or the try_run() (page 344) commands. The try_compile command works as expected when cross-compiling; it tries to compile the piece of code with the cross-compiling toolchain, which will give the expected result.

All tests using try_run will not work since the created executables cannot normally run on the build host. In some cases, this might be possible (e.g. using virtual machines, emulation layers like Wine or interfaces to the actual target) as CMake does not depend on such mechanisms. Depending on emulators during the build process would introduce a new set of potential problems; they may have a different view on the file system, use other line endings, require special hardware or software, etc.

If `try_run` is invoked when cross-compiling, it will first try to compile the software, which will work the same way as when not cross compiling. If this succeeds, it will check the variable CMAKE_CROSSCOMPILING (page 626) to determine whether the resulting executable can be executed or not. If it cannot, it will create two cache variables, which then have to be set by the user or via the CMake cache. Assume the command looks like this:

```
try_run (SHARED_LIBRARY_PATH_TYPE
        SHARED_LIBRARY_PATH_INFO_COMPILED
        ${PROJECT_BINARY_DIR}/CMakeTmp
        ${PROJECT_SOURCE_DIR}/CMake/SharedLibraryPathInfo.cxx
        OUTPUT_VARIABLE OUTPUT
        ARGS "LDPATH"
        )
```

In this example, the source file `SharedLibraryPathInfo.cxx` will be compiled and if that succeeds, the resulting executable should be executed. The variable SHARED_LIBRARY_PATH_INFO_COMPILED will be set to the result of the build, i.e. TRUE or FALSE. CMake will create a cache variable SHARED_LIBRARY_PATH_TYPE and preset it to PLEASE_FILL_OUT-FAILED_TO_RUN. This variable must be set to what the exit code of the executable would have been if it had been executed on the target. Additionally, CMake will create a cache variable SHARED_LIBRARY_PATH_TYPE__TRYRUN_OUTPUT and preset it to PLEASE_FILL_OUT-NOTFOUND. This variable should be set to the output that the executable prints to stdout and stderr if it were executed on the target. This variable is only created if the `try_run` command was used with the RUN_OUTPUT_VARIABLE or the OUTPUT_VARIABLE argument. You have to fill in the appropriate values for these variables. To help you with this CMake tries its best to give you useful information. To accomplish this CMake creates a file `${CMAKE_BINARY_DIR}/TryRunResults.cmake`, which you can see an example of here:

```
# SHARED_LIBRARY_PATH_TYPE
#    indicates whether the executable would have been able to run
#    on its target platform. If so, set SHARED_LIBRARY_PATH_TYPE
#    to the exit code (in many cases 0 for success), otherwise
#    enter "FAILED_TO_RUN".
# SHARED_LIBRARY_PATH_TYPE__TRYRUN_OUTPUT
#    contains the text the executable would have printed on
#    stdout and stderr. If the executable would not have been
#    able to run, set SHARED_LIBRARY_PATH_TYPE__TRYRUN_OUTPUT
#    empty. Otherwise check if the output is evaluated by the
#    calling CMake code. If so, check what the source file would
#    have printed when called with the given arguments.
# The SHARED_LIBRARY_PATH_INFO_COMPILED variable holds the build
# result for this TRY_RUN().
#
# Source file: ~/src/SharedLibraryPathInfo.cxx
# Executable : ~/build/cmTryCompileExec-SHARED_LIBRARY_PATH_TYPE
# Run arguments:  LDPATH
```

```
#      Called from: [1]    ~/src/CMakeLists.cmake

set (SHARED_LIBRARY_PATH_TYPE
     "0"
     CACHE STRING "Result from TRY_RUN" FORCE)

set (SHARED_LIBRARY_PATH_TYPE__TRYRUN_OUTPUT
     ""
     CACHE STRING "Output from TRY_RUN" FORCE)
```

You can find all of the variables that CMake could not determine, from which CMake file they were called, the source file, the arguments for the executable, and the path to the executable. CMake will also copy the executables to the build directory; they have the names `cmTryCompileExec-<name of the variable>`, e.g. in this case `cmTryCompileExec-SHARED_LIBRARY_PATH_TYPE`. You can then try to run this executable manually on the actual target platform and check the results.

Once you have these results, they have to be put into the CMake cache. This can be done by using ccmake/cmake-gui/"make edit_cache" and editing the variables directly in the cache. It is not possible to reuse these changes in another build directory or if CMakeCache.txt is removed.

The recommended approach is to use the TryRunResults.cmake file created by CMake. You should copy it to a safe location (i.e. where it will not be removed if the build directory is deleted) and give it a useful name, e.g. TryRunResults-MyProject-eldk-ppc.cmake. The contents of this file have to be edited so that the set commands set the required variables to the appropriate values for the target system. This file can then be used to preload the CMake cache by using the -C option of cmake:

```
src/build/ $ cmake -C ~/TryRunResults-MyProject-eldk-ppc.cmake .
```

You do not have to use the other CMake options again as they are now in the cache. This way you can use MyProjectTryRunResults-eldk-ppc.cmake in multiple build trees, and it can be distributed with your project so that it is easier for other users to cross compile it.

8.4 Running Executables Built in the Project

In some cases it is necessary that during a build, an executable is invoked that was built earlier in the same build; this is usually the case for code generators and similar tools. This does not work when cross compiling, as the executables are built for the target platform and cannot run on the build host (without the use of virtual machines, compatibility layers, emulators, etc.). With CMake, these programs are created using add_executable, and executed with `add_custom_command()` (page 269) or `add_custom_target()` (page 272). The following three options can be used to support these executables with CMake. The old version of the CMake code could look something like this

```
add_executable (mygen gen.c)
get_target_property (mygenLocation mygen LOCATION)
add_custom_command (
  OUTPUT "${CMAKE_CURRENT_BINARY_DIR}/generated.h"
```

```
COMMAND ${mygenLocation}
    -o "${CMAKE_CURRENT_BINARY_DIR}/generated.h" )
```

Now we will show how this file can be modified so that it works when cross-compiling. The basic idea is that the executable is built only when doing a native build for the build host, and is then exported as an executable target to a CMake script file. This file is then included when cross-compiling, and the executable target for the executable mygen will be loaded. An imported target with the same name as the original target will be created. Since CMake 2.6 add_custom_command recognizes target names as executables, so for the command in add_custom_command, simply the target name can be used; it is not necessary to use the LOCATION property to obtain the path of the executable:

```
if (CMAKE_CROSSCOMPILING)
    find_package (MyGen)
endif ()

if (NOT CMAKE_CROSSCOMPILING)
    add_executable (mygen gen.c)
    export (TARGETS mygen FILE
            "${CMAKE_BINARY_DIR}/MyGenConfig.cmake")
endif ()

add_custom_command (
  OUTPUT "${CMAKE_CURRENT_BINARY_DIR}/generated.h"
  COMMAND mygen -o "${CMAKE_CURRENT_BINARY_DIR}/generated.h" )
```

With the CMakeLists.txt modified like this, the project can be cross-compiled. First, a native build has to be done in order to create the necessary mygen executable. After that, the cross-compiling build can begin. The build directory of the native build has to be given to the cross-compiling build as the location of the MyGen package, so that find_package(MyGen) can find it:

```
mkdir build-native; cd build-native
cmake ..
make
cd ..
mkdir build-cross; cd build-cross
cmake -DCMAKE_TOOLCHAIN_FILE=MyToolchain.cmake \
      -DMyGen_DIR=~/src/build-native/ ..
make
```

This code works, but CMake versions prior to 2.6 will not be able to process it, as they do not know the export command or recognize the target name mygen in add_custom_command. A compatible version that works with CMake 2.4 looks like this:

```
if (CMAKE_CROSSCOMPILING)
    find_package (MyGen)
endif (CMAKE_CROSSCOMPILING)

if (NOT CMAKE_CROSSCOMPILING)
    add_executable (mygen gen.c)
```

```
    if (COMMAND EXPORT)
      export (TARGETS mygen FILE
             "${CMAKE_BINARY_DIR}/MyGenConfig.cmake")
    endif (COMMAND EXPORT)
endif (NOT CMAKE_CROSSCOMPILING)

get_target_property (mygenLocation mygen LOCATION)

add_custom_command (
  OUTPUT "${CMAKE_CURRENT_BINARY_DIR}/generated.h"
  COMMAND ${mygenLocation}
    -o "${CMAKE_CURRENT_BINARY_DIR}/generated.h" )
```

In this case, the target is only exported if the export command exists and the location of the executable is retrieved using the LOCATION target property.

```
mkdir build-native; cd build-native
cmake ..
make
cd ..
mkdir build-cross; cd build-cross
cmake -DCMAKE_TOOLCHAIN_FILE=MyToolchain.cmake \
      -DMyGen_DIR=~/src/build-native/ ..
make
```

The "old" CMake code could also be using the utility_source command:

```
subdirs (mygen)
utility_source (MYGEN_LOCATION mygen mygen gen.c)
add_custom_command (
    OUTPUT "${CMAKE_CURRENT_BINARY_DIR}/generated.h"
    COMMAND ${MYGEN_LOCATION}
      -o "${CMAKE_CURRENT_BINARY_DIR}/generated.h" )
```

In this case, the CMake script doesn't have to be changed, but the invocation of CMake is more complicated, as each executable location has to be specified manually:

```
mkdir build-native; cd build-native
cmake ..
make
cd ..
mkdir build-cross; cd build-cross
cmake -DCMAKE_TOOLCHAIN_FILE=MyToolchain.cmake
      -DMYGEN_LOCATION=~/src/build-native/bin/mygen ..
make
```

8.5 Cross-Compiling Hello World

Now let's actually start with the cross-compiling. The first step is to install a cross-compiling toolchain. If this is already installed, you can skip the next paragraph.

There are many different approaches and projects that deal with cross-compiling for Linux, ranging from free software projects working on Linux-based PDAs to commercial embedded Linux vendors. Most of these projects come with their own way to build and use the respective toolchain. Any of these toolchains can be used with CMake; the only requirement is that it works in the normal file system and does not expect a "sandboxed" environment, like for example the Scratchbox project.

An easy-to-use toolchain with a relatively complete target environment is the Embedded Linux Development Toolkit (http://www.denx.de/wiki/DULG/ELDK). It supports ARM, PowerPC, and MIPS as target platforms. ELDK can be downloaded from ftp://ftp.sunet.se/pub/Linux/distributions/eldk/. The easiest way is to download the ISOs, mount them, and then install them:

```
mkdir mount-iso/
sudo mount -tiso9660 mips-2007-01-21.iso mount-iso/ -o loop
cd mount-iso/
./install -d /home/alex/eldk-mips/
...
Preparing...            ############################################# [100%]
   1:appWeb-mips_4KCle ############################################# [100%]
Done
ls /opt/eldk-mips/
bin  eldk_init  etc  mips_4KC  mips_4KCle  usr  var  version
```

ELDK (and other toolchains) can be installed anywhere, either in the home directory or system-wide if there are more users working with them. In this example, the toolchain will now be located in /home/alex/eldk-mips/usr/bin/ and the target environment is in /home/alex/eldk-mips/mips_4KC/.

Now that a cross-compiling toolchain is installed, CMake has to be set up to use it. As already described, this is done by creating a toolchain file for CMake. In this example, the toolchain file looks like this:

```
# the name of the target operating system
set (CMAKE_SYSTEM_NAME Linux)

# which C and C++ compiler to use
set (CMAKE_C_COMPILER /home/alex/eldk-mips/usr/bin/mips_4KC-gcc)
set (CMAKE_CXX_COMPILER
     /home/alex/eldk-mips/usr/bin/mips_4KC-g++)

# location of the target environment
set (CMAKE_FIND_ROOT_PATH /home/alex/eldk-mips/mips_4KC
                          /home/alex/eldk-mips-extra-install )

# adjust the default behavior of the FIND_XXX() commands:
# search for headers and libraries in the target environment,
# search for programs in the host environment
```

```
set (CMAKE_FIND_ROOT_PATH_MODE_PROGRAM NEVER)
set (CMAKE_FIND_ROOT_PATH_MODE_LIBRARY ONLY)
set (CMAKE_FIND_ROOT_PATH_MODE_INCLUDE ONLY)
```

The toolchain files can be located anywhere, but it is a good idea to put them in a central place so that they can be reused in multiple projects. We will save this file as ~/Toolchains/Toolchain-eldk-mips4K.cmake. The variables mentioned above are set here: CMAKE_SYSTEM_NAME, the C/C++ compilers, and CMAKE_FIND_ROOT_PATH to specify where libraries and headers for the target environment are located. The find modes are also set up so that libraries and headers are searched for in the target environment only, whereas programs are searched for in the host environment only. Now we will cross-compile the hello world project from Chapter 2

```
project (Hello)
add_executable (Hello Hello.c)
```

Run CMake, this time telling it to use the toolchain file from above:

```
mkdir Hello-eldk-mips
cd Hello-eldk-mips
cmake -DCMAKE_TOOLCHAIN_FILE=~/Toolchains/Toolchain-eldk-mips4K.cmake ..
make VERBOSE=1
```

This should give you an executable that can run on the target platform. Thanks to the VERBOSE=1 option, you should see that the cross-compiler is used. Now we will make the example a bit more sophisticated by adding system inspection and install rules. We will build and install a shared library named Tools, and then build the Hello application which links to the Tools library.

```
include (CheckIncludeFiles)
check_include_files (stdio.h HAVE_STDIO_H)

set (VERSION_MAJOR 2)
set (VERSION_MINOR 6)
set (VERSION_PATCH 0)

configure_file (config.h.in ${CMAKE_BINARY_DIR}/config.h)

add_library (Tools  SHARED  tools.cxx)
set_target_properties (Tools PROPERTIES
    VERSION ${VERSION_MAJOR}.${VERSION_MINOR}.${VERSION_PATCH}
    SOVERSION ${VERSION_MAJOR})

install (FILES tools.h DESTINATION include)
install (TARGETS Tools DESTINATION lib)
```

There is no difference in a normal CMakeLists.txt; no special prerequisites are required for cross-compiling. The CMakeLists.txt checks that the header stdio.h is available and sets the version number for the Tools library. These are configured into config.h, which is then used in tools.cxx. The version number is also used to set the version number of the Tools library. The library and headers are installed to ${CMAKE_INSTALL_PREFIX (page 645)}/lib and ${CMAKE_INSTALL_PREFIX}/include respectively.

Running CMake gives this result:

```
mkdir build-eldk-mips
cd build-eldk-mips
cmake -DCMAKE_TOOLCHAIN_FILE=~/Toolchains/Toolchain-eldk-mips4K.cmake \
      -DCMAKE_INSTALL_PREFIX=~/eldk-mips-extra-install ..
-- The C compiler identification is GNU
-- The CXX compiler identification is GNU
-- Check for working C compiler: /home/alex/eldk-mips/usr/bin/mips_4KC-gcc
-- Check for working C compiler:
   /home/alex/eldk-mips/usr/bin/mips_4KC-gcc -- works
-- Check size of void*
-- Check size of void* - done
-- Check for working CXX compiler: /home/alex/eldk-mips/usr/bin/mips_4KC-g++
-- Check for working CXX compiler:
   /home/alex/eldk-mips/usr/bin/mips_4KC-g++ -- works
-- Looking for include files HAVE_STDIO_H
-- Looking for include files HAVE_STDIO_H - found
-- Configuring done
-- Generating done
-- Build files have been written to: /home/alex/src/tests/Tools/build-mips
make install
Scanning dependencies of target Tools
[100%] Building CXX object CMakeFiles/Tools.dir/tools.o
Linking CXX shared library libTools.so
[100%] Built target Tools
Install the project...
-- Install configuration: ""
-- Installing /home/alex/eldk-mips-extra-install/include/tools.h
-- Installing /home/alex/eldk-mips-extra-install/lib/libTools.so
```

As can be seen in the output above, CMake detected the correct compiler, found the stdio.h header for the target platform, and successfully generated the Makefiles. The make command was invoked, which then successfully built and installed the library in the specified installation directory. Now we can build an executable that uses the Tools library and does some system inspection

```
project (HelloTools)

find_package (ZLIB REQUIRED)

find_library (TOOLS_LIBRARY Tools)
find_path (TOOLS_INCLUDE_DIR tools.h)

if (NOT TOOLS_LIBRARY OR NOT TOOLS_INCLUDE_DIR)
  message (FATAL_ERROR "Tools library not found")
endif (NOT TOOLS_LIBRARY OR NOT TOOLS_INCLUDE_DIR)

set (CMAKE_INCLUDE_CURRENT_DIR TRUE)
set (CMAKE_INCLUDE_DIRECTORIES_PROJECT_BEFORE TRUE)
include_directories ("${TOOLS_INCLUDE_DIR}"
```

```
                          "${ZLIB_INCLUDE_DIR}")

add_executable (HelloTools main.cpp)
target_link_libraries (HelloTools ${TOOLS_LIBRARY}
                       ${ZLIB_LIBRARIES})
set_target_properties (HelloTools PROPERTIES
                       INSTALL_RPATH_USE_LINK_PATH TRUE)

install (TARGETS HelloTools DESTINATION bin)
```

Building works in the same way as with the library; the toolchain file has to be used and then it should just work:

```
cmake -DCMAKE_TOOLCHAIN_FILE=~/Toolchains/Toolchain-eldk-mips4K.cmake \
      -DCMAKE_INSTALL_PREFIX=~/eldk-mips-extra-install ..
-- The C compiler identification is GNU
-- The CXX compiler identification is GNU
-- Check for working C compiler: /home/alex/denx-mips/usr/bin/mips_4KC-gcc
-- Check for working C compiler:
   /home/alex/denx-mips/usr/bin/mips_4KC-gcc -- works
-- Check size of void*
-- Check size of void* - done
-- Check for working CXX compiler: /home/alex/denx-mips/usr/bin/mips_4KC-g++
-- Check for working CXX compiler:
   /home/alex/denx-mips/usr/bin/mips_4KC-g++ -- works
-- Found ZLIB: /home/alex/denx-mips/mips_4KC/usr/lib/libz.so
-- Found Tools library: /home/alex/denx-mips-extra-install/lib/libTools.so
-- Configuring done
-- Generating done
-- Build files have been written to:
   /home/alex/src/tests/HelloTools/build-eldk-mips
make
[100%] Building CXX object CMakeFiles/HelloTools.dir/main.o
Linking CXX executable HelloTools
[100%] Built target HelloTools
```

Obviously CMake found the correct zlib and also libTools.so, which had been installed in the previous step.

8.6 Cross-Compiling for a Microcontroller

CMake can be used for more than cross-compiling to targets with operating systems, it is also possible to use it in development for deeply-embedded devices with small microcontrollers and no operating system at all. As an example, we will use the Small Devices C Compiler (http://sdcc.sourceforge.net), which runs under Windows, Linux, and Mac OS X, and supports 8 and 16 Bit microcontrollers. For driving the build, we will use MS NMake under Windows. As before, the first step is to write a toolchain file so that CMake knows about the target platform. For sdcc, it should look something like this

---

```
set (CMAKE_SYSTEM_NAME Generic)
set (CMAKE_C_COMPILER "c:/Program Files/SDCC/bin/sdcc.exe")
```

The system name for targets that do not have an operating system, "Generic," should be used as the
CMAKE_SYSTEM_NAME (page 653). The CMake platform file for "Generic" doesn't set up any specific
features. All that it assumes is that the target platform does not support shared libraries, and so all properties
will depend on the compiler and CMAKE_SYSTEM_PROCESSOR (page 653). The toolchain file above does
not set the FIND-related variables. As long as none of the find commands is used in the CMake commands,
this is fine. In many projects for small microcontrollers, this will be the case. The CMakeLists.txt should
look like the following

```
project (Blink C)

add_library (blink blink.c)

add_executable (hello main.c)
target_link_libraries (hello blink)
```

There are no major differences in other CMakeLists.txt files. One important point is that the language "C" is
enabled explicitly using the PROJECT command. If this is not done, CMake will also try to enable support
for C++, which will fail as sdcc only has support for C. Running CMake and building the project should work
as usual:

```
cmake -G"NMake Makefiles" \
      -DCMAKE_TOOLCHAIN_FILE=c:/Toolchains/Toolchain-sdcc.cmake ..
-- The C compiler identification is SDCC
-- Check for working C compiler: c:/program files/sdcc/bin/sdcc.exe
-- Check for working C compiler: c:/program files/sdcc/bin/sdcc.exe -- works
-- Check size of void*
-- Check size of void* - done
-- Configuring done
-- Generating done
-- Build files have been written to: C:/src/tests/blink/build

nmake
Microsoft (R) Program Maintenance Utility Version 7.10.3077
Copyright (C) Microsoft Corporation.  All rights reserved.

Scanning dependencies of target blink
[ 50%] Building C object CMakeFiles/blink.dir/blink.rel
Linking C static library blink.lib
[ 50%] Built target blink
Scanning dependencies of target hello
[100%] Building C object CMakeFiles/hello.dir/main.rel
Linking C executable hello.ihx
[100%] Built target hello
```

This was a simple example using NMake with sdcc with the default settings of sdcc. Of course, more
sophisticated project layouts are possible. For this kind of project, it is also a good idea to set up an install

directory where reusable libraries can be installed, so it is easier to use them in multiple projects. It is normally necessary to choose the correct target platform for sdcc; not everybody uses i8051, which is the default for sdcc. The recommended way to do this is via setting CMAKE_SYSTEM_PROCESSOR.

This will cause CMake to search for and load the platform file Platform/Generic-SDCC-C-${CMAKE_SYSTEM_PROCESSOR}.cmake. As this happens, right before loading Platform/Generic-SDCC-C.cmake, it can be used to set up the compiler and linker flags for the specific target hardware and project. Therefore, a slightly more complex toolchain file is required

```
get_filename_component (_ownDir
                    "${CMAKE_CURRENT_LIST_FILE}" PATH)
set (CMAKE_MODULE_PATH "${_ownDir}/Modules" ${CMAKE_MODULE_PATH})

set (CMAKE_SYSTEM_NAME Generic)
set (CMAKE_C_COMPILER "c:/Program Files/SDCC/bin/sdcc.exe")
set (CMAKE_SYSTEM_PROCESSOR "Test_DS80C400_Rev_1")

# here is the target environment located
set (CMAKE_FIND_ROOT_PATH  "c:/Program Files/SDCC"
                        "c:/ds80c400-install" )

# adjust the default behavior of the FIND_XXX() commands:
# search for headers and libraries in the target environment
# search for programs in the host environment
set (CMAKE_FIND_ROOT_PATH_MODE_PROGRAM NEVER)
set (CMAKE_FIND_ROOT_PATH_MODE_LIBRARY ONLY)
set (CMAKE_FIND_ROOT_PATH_MODE_INCLUDE ONLY)
```

This toolchain file contains a few new settings; it is also about the most complicated toolchain file you should ever need. CMAKE_SYSTEM_PROCESSOR is set to Test_DS80C400_Rev_1, an identifier for the specific target hardware. This has the effect that CMake will try to load Platform/Generic-SDCC-C-Test_DS80C400_Rev_1.cmake. As this file does not exist in the CMake system module directory, the CMake variable CMAKE_MODULE_PATH (page 646) has to be adjusted so that this file can be found. If this toolchain file is saved to c:/Toolchains/sdcc-ds400.cmake, the hardware-specific file should be saved in c:/Toolchains/Modules/Platform/. An example of this is shown below:

```
set (CMAKE_C_FLAGS_INIT "-mds390 --use-accelerator")
set (CMAKE_EXE_LINKER_FLAGS_INIT "")
```

This will select the DS80C390 as the target platform and add the –use-accelerator argument to the default compile flags. In this example the "NMake Makefiles" generator was used. In the same way e.g. the "MinGW Makefiles" generator could be used for a GNU make from MinGW, or another Windows version of GNU make, are available. At least version 3.78 is required, or the "Unix Makefiles" generator under UNIX. Also, any Makefile-based, IDE-project generators could be used; e.g. the Eclipse, CodeBlocks, or the KDevelop3 generator.

8.7 Cross Compiling an Existing Project

Existing CMake-based projects may need some work so that they can be cross-compiled; other projects may work without any modifications. One such project is FLTK, the Fast Lightweight Toolkit. We will compile FLTK on a Linux machine using the MinGW cross-compiler for Windows.

The first step is to install the MinGW cross-compiler. For some Linux distributions, there are ready-to-use binary packages. For Debian, the package name is mingw32. Once this is installed, set up a toolchain file as described above. It should look something like this

```
# the name of the target operating system
set (CMAKE_SYSTEM_NAME Windows)

# which compiler to use
set (CMAKE_C_COMPILER i586-mingw32msvc-gcc)
set (CMAKE_CXX_COMPILER i586-mingw32msvc-g++)

# where are the target libraries and headers installed ?
set (CMAKE_FIND_ROOT_PATH /usr/i586-mingw32msvc
                          /home/alex/mingw-install )

# find_program() should by default NEVER search the target tree
# adjust the default behavior of the FIND_XX() commands:
# search for headers and libraries in the target environment
# search for programs in the host environment
set (CMAKE_FIND_ROOT_MODE_PROGRAM NEVER)
set (CMAKE_FIND_ROOT_MODE_LIBRARY ONLY)
set (CMAKE_FIND_ROOT_MODE_INCLUDE ONLY)
```

Once this is working, run CMake with the appropriate options on FLTK:

```
mkdir build-mingw
cd build-mingw
cmake -DCMAKE_TOOLCHAIN_FILE=~/Toolchains/Toolchain-mingw32.cmake \
     -DCMAKE_INSTALL_PREFIX=~/mingw-install ..
-- The C compiler identification is GNU
-- The CXX compiler identification is GNU
-- Check for working C compiler: /usr/bin/i586-mingw32msvc-gcc
-- Check for working C compiler: /usr/bin/i586-mingw32msvc-gcc -- works
...
```

In FLTK, the `utility_source` command is used to build the executable fluid, whose location is put into the CMake variable `FLUID_COMMAND`. If you intend to run this executable, you need to preload the cache with the full path to a version of that program that can be run on the build host.

```
-- Configuring done
-- Generating done
-- Build files have been written to:
   /home/alex/src/fltk-1.1.x-r5940/build-mingw
```

Below you can see a warning from CMake about the use of the `utility_source()` (page 350) command. To find out more, CMake offers the `--debug-output` argument:

```
rm -rf *
cmake -DCMAKE_TOOLCHAIN_FILE=~/Toolchains/Toolchain-mingw32.cmake \
      -DCMAKE_INSTALL_PREFIX=~/mingw-install .. --debug-output
...
UTILITY_SOURCE is used in cross compiling mode for
FLUID_COMMAND. If your intention is to run this executable, you
need to preload the cache with the full path to a version of
that program, which runs on this build machine.
Called from: [1] /home/alex/src/fltk-1.1.x-r5940/CMakeLists.txt
```

This tells us that `utility_source` has been called from /home/alex/src/fltk-1.1.x-r5940/CMakeLists.txt, then CMake processed some more directories, and finally created Makefiles in each subdirectory. Examining the top-level CMakeLists.txt shows the following:

```
# Set the fluid executable path
utility_source (FLUID_COMMAND fluid fluid fluid.cxx)
set (FLUID_COMMAND "${FLUID_COMMAND}" CACHE INTERNAL "" FORCE)
```

`FLUID_COMMAND` is used to hold the path for the executable fluid, which is built by the project. Fluid is used during the build to generate code, so the cross-compiled executable will not work, and instead a native fluid has to be used. In the following example, the variable `FLUID_COMMAND` is set to the location of a fluid executable for the build host, which is then used in the cross-compiling build to generate code that will be compiled for the target system:

```
cmake . -DFLUID_COMMAND=/.../fltk-1.1.x-r5940/build-native/bin/fluid
...
-- Configuring done
-- Generating done
make
Scanning dependencies of target fltk_zlib
[  0%] Building C object zlib/CMakeFiles/fltk_zlib.dir/adler32.obj
[  0%] Building C object zlib/CMakeFiles/fltk_zlib.dir/compress.obj
...
Scanning dependencies of target valuators
[100%] Building CXX object test/CMakeFiles/valuators.dir/valuators.obj
Linking CXX executable ../bin/valuators.exe
[100%] Built target valuators
```

That's it, the executables are now in `mingw-bin/`, and can be run via wine or by copying them to a Windows system.

8.8 Cross-Compiling a Complex Project - VTK

Building a complex project is a multi-step process. Complex in this case means that the project uses tests that run executables, and that it builds executables which are used later in the build to generate code (or something similar). One such project is VTK, which uses several `try_run()` (page 344) tests and creates several code generators. When running CMake on the project, every `try_run` command will produce an error message; at the end there will be a `TryRunResults.cmake` file in the build directory. You need to go through all of the entries of this file and fill in the appropriate values. If you are uncertain about the correct result, you can also try to execute the test binaries on the real target platform, where they are saved in the binary directory.

VTK contains several code generators, one of which is ProcessShader. These code generators are added using `add_executable()` (page 273); get_target_property(LOCATION)'' is used to get the locations of the resulting binaries, which are then used in `add_custom_command()` (page 269) or `add_custom_target()` (page 272) commands. Since the cross-compiled executables cannot be executed during the build, the `add_executable()` (page 273) calls are surrounded by `if (NOT CMAKE_CROSSCOMPILING)` commands and the executable targets are imported into the project using the `add_executable` command with the `IMPORTED` option. These import statements are in the file `VTKCompileToolsConfig.cmake`, which does not have to be created manually, but it is created by a native build of VTK.

In order to cross-compile VTK, you need to:

- Install a toolchain and create a toolchain file for CMake.
- Build VTK natively for the build host.
- Run CMake for the target platform.
- Complete `TryRunResults.cmake`.
- Use the `VTKCompileToolsConfig.cmake` file from the native build.
- Build.

So first, build a native VTK for the build host using the standard procedure.

```
cvs -d :pserver:anonymous@public.kitware.com:/cvsroot/VTK co VTK
cd VTK
mkdir build-native; cd build-native
ccmake ..
make
```

Ensure that all required options are enabled using ccmake; e.g. if you need Python wrapping for the target platform, you must enable Python wrapping in `build-native/`. Once this build has finished, there will be a `VTKCompileToolsConfig.cmake` file in `build-native/`. If this succeeded, we can continue to cross compiling the project, in this example for an IBM BlueGene supercomputer.

```
cd VTK
mkdir build-bgl-gcc
cd build-bgl-gcc
cmake -DCMAKE_TOOLCHAIN_FILE=~/Toolchains/Toolchain-BlueGeneL-gcc.cmake \
      -DVTKCompileTools_DIR=~/VTK/build-native/ ..
```

This will finish with an error message for each `try_run` and a `TryRunResults.cmake file`, that you have to complete as described above. You should save the file to a safe location, or it will be overwritten on the next CMake run.

```
cp TryRunResults.cmake ../TryRunResults-VTK-BlueGeneL-gcc.cmake
ccmake -C ../TryRunResults-VTK-BlueGeneL-gcc.cmake .
...
make
```

On the second run of ccmake, all the other arguments can be skipped as they are now in the cache. It is possible to point CMake to the build directory that contains a CMakeCache.txt, so CMake will figure out that this is the build directory.

8.9 Some Tips and Tricks

8.9.1 Dealing with try_run tests

In order to make cross compiling your project easier, try to avoid `try_run()` (page 344) tests and use other methods to test something instead. For examples of how this can be done, consider the tests for endianess in `CMake/Modules/TestBigEndian.cmake`, and the test for the compiler id using the source file `CMake/Modules/CMakeCCompilerId.c`. In both, `try_compile()` (page 343) is used to compile the source file into an executable, where the desired information is encoded into a text string. Using the `COPY_FILE` option of `try_compile`, this executable is copied to a temporary location and then all strings are extracted from this file using `file()` (page 287) (STRINGS). The test result is obtained using regular expressions to get the information from the string.

If you cannot avoid `try_run` tests, try to use only the exit code from the run and not the output of the process. That way it will not be necessary to set both the exit code and the stdout and stderr variables for the `try_run` test when cross-compiling. This allows the `OUTPUT_VARIABLE` or the `RUN_OUTPUT_VARIABLE` options for `try_run` to be omitted.

If you have done that, created and completed a correct `TryRunResults.cmake` file for the target platform, you might consider adding this file to the sources of the project, so that it can be reused by others. These files are per-target, per-toolchain.

8.9.2 Target platform and toolchain issues

If your toolchain is unable to build a simple program without special arguments, like e.g. a linker script file or a memory layout file, the tests CMake does initially will fail. To make it work the CMake module CMakeForceCompiler offers the following macros:

```
CMAKE_FORCE_SYSTEM (name version processor),
CMAKE_FORCE_C_COMPILER (compiler compiler_id sizeof_void_p)
CMAKE_FORCE_CXX_COMPILER (compiler compiler_id).
```

These macros can be used in a toolchain file so that the required variables will be preset and the CMake tests avoided.

8.9.3 RPATH handling under UNIX

For native builds, CMake builds executables and libraries by default with RPATH. In the build tree, the RPATH is set so that the executables can be run from the build tree; i.e. the RPATH points into the build tree. When installing the project, CMake links the executables again, this time with the RPATH for the install tree, which is empty by default.

When cross-compiling you probably want to set up RPATH handling differently. As the executable cannot run on the build host, it makes more sense to build it with the install RPATH right from the start. There are several CMake variables and target properties for adjusting RPATH handling.

```
set (CMAKE_BUILD_WITH_INSTALL_RPATH TRUE)
set (CMAKE_INSTALL_RPATH "<whatever you need>")
```

With these two settings, the targets will be built with the install RPATH instead of the build RPATH, which avoids the need to link them again when installing. If you don't need RPATH support in your project, you don't need to set CMAKE_INSTALL_RPATH (page 660); it is empty by default.

Setting CMAKE_INSTALL_RPATH_USE_LINK_PATH (page 660) to TRUE is useful for native builds, since it automatically collects the RPATH from all libraries against which a targets links. For cross-compiling it should be left at the default setting of FALSE, because on the target the automatically generated RPATH will be wrong in most cases; it will probably have a different file system layout than the build host.

PACKAGING WITH CPACK

CPack is a powerful, easy to use, cross-platform software packaging tool distributed with CMake since version 2.4.2. It uses the generators concept from CMake to abstract package generation on specific platforms. It can be used with or without CMake, but it may depend on some software being installed on the system. Using a simple configuration file, or using a CMake module, the author of a project can package a complex project into a simple installer. This chapter will describe how to apply CPack to a CMake project.

9.1 CPack Basics

Users of your software may not always want to, or be able to, build the software in order to install it. The software may be closed source, or it may take a long time to compile, or in the case of an end user application, the users may not have the skill or the tools to build the application. For these cases, what is needed is a way to build the software on one machine, and then move the install tree to a different machine. The most basic way to do this is to use the DESTDIR environment variable to install the software into a temporary location, then to tar or zip up that directory and move it to another machine. However, the DESTDIR approach falls short on Windows, simply because path names typically start with a drive letter (C:/) and you cannot simply prefix one full path with another and get a valid path name. Another more powerful approach is to use CPack, included in CMake.

CPack is a tool included with CMake, it can be used to create installers and packages for projects. CPack can create two basic types of packages, source and binary. CPack works in much the same way as CMake does for building software. It does not aim to replace native packaging tools, rather it provides a single interface to a variety of tools. Currently CPack supports the creation of Windows installers using NullSoft installer NSIS, Mac OS X PackageMaker tool, OS X Drag and Drop, OS X X11 Drag and Drop, Cygwin Setup packages, Debian packages, RPMs, .tar.gz, .sh (self extracting .tar.gz files), and .zip compressed files. The implementation of CPack works in a similar way to CMake. For each type of packaging tool supported, there is a CPack generator written in C++ that is used to run the native tool and create the package. For simple tar based packages, CPack includes a library version of tar and does not require tar to be installed on the system. For many of the other installers, native tools must be present for CPack to function.

With source packages, CPack makes a copy of the source tree and creates a zip or tar file. For binary packages, the use of CPack is tied to the install commands working correctly for a project. When setting up install commands, the first step is to make sure the files go into the correct directory structure with the correct permissions. The next step is to make sure the software is relocatable and can run in an installed tree. This may require changing the software itself, and there are many techniques to do that for different environments that go beyond the scope of this book. Basically, executables should be able to find data or other files using relative paths to the location of where it is installed. CPack installs the software into a temporary directory, and copies the install tree into the format of the native packaging tool. Once the install commands have been added to a project, enabling CPack in the simplest case is done by including the CPack.cmake file into the project.

9.1.1 Simple Example

The most basic CPack project would look like this

```
project(CoolStuff)
add_executable(coolstuff coolstuff.cxx)
install(TARGETS coolstuff RUNTIME DESTINATION bin)
include(CPack)
```

In the CoolStuff project, an executable is created and installed into the directory bin. Then the CPack file is included by the project. At this point project CoolStuff will have CPack enabled. To run CPack for a CoolStuff, you would first build the project as you would any other CMake project. CPack adds several targets to the generated project. These targets in Makefiles are package and package_source, and PACKAGE in Visual Studio and Xcode. For example, to build a source and binary package for CoolStuff using a Makefile generator you would run the following commands:

```
mkdir build
cd build
cmake ../CoolStuff
make
make package
make package_source
```

This would create a source zip file called `CoolStuff-0.1.1-Source.zip`, a NSIS installer called `CoolStuff-0.1.1-win32.exe`, and a binary zip file `CoolStuff-0.1.1-win32.zip`. The same thing could be done using the CPack command line.

```
cd build
cpack -C CPackConfig.cmake
cpack -C CPackSourceConfig.cmake
```

9.1.2 What Happens When CPack.cmake Is Included?

When the `include(CPack)` command is executed, the `CPack.cmake` file is included into the project. By default this will use the `configure_file` command to create `CPackConfig.cmake` and `CPackSourceConfig.cmake` in the binary tree of the project. These files contain a series of set commands that set variables for use when CPack is run during the packaging step. The names of the files that are configured by the `CPack.cmake` file can be customized with these two variables; `CPACK_OUTPUT_CONFIG_FILE` which defaults to `CPackConfig.cmake` and `CPACK_SOURCE_OUTPUT_CONFIG_FILE` which defaults to `CPackSourceConfig.cmake`.

The source for these files can be found in the `Templates/CPackConfig.cmake.in`. This file contains some comments, and a single variable that is set by `CPack.cmake`. The file contains this line of CMake code:

```
@_CPACK_OTHER_VARIABLES_@
```

If the project contains the file `CPackConfig.cmake.in` in the top level of the source tree, that file will be used instead of the file in the Templates directory. If the project contains the file `CPackSourceConfig.cmake.in`, then that file will be used for the creation of `CPackSourceConfig.cmake`.

The configuration files created by `CPack.cmake` will contain all the variables that begin with "CPACK_" in the current project. This is done using the command

```
get_cmake_property(res VARIABLES)
```

The above command gets all variables defined for the current CMake project. Some CMake code then looks for all variables starting with "CPACK_", and each variable found is configured into the two configuration files as CMake code. For example, if you had a variable set like this in your CMake project

```
set(CPACK_PACKAGE_NAME "CoolStuff")
```

`CPackConfig.cmake` and `CPackSourceConfig.cmake` would have the same thing in them:

```
set(CPACK_PACKAGE_NAME "CoolStuff")
```

It is important to keep in mind that CPack is run after CMake on the project. CPack uses the same parser as CMake, but will not have the same variable values as the CMake project. It will only have the variables that start with CPACK_, and these variables will be configured into a configuration file by CMake. This can cause some errors and confusion if the values of the variables use escape characters. Since they are getting parsed twice by the CMake language, they will need double the level of escaping. For example, if you had the following in your CMake project:

```
set(CPACK_PACKAGE_VENDOR "Cool \"Company\"")
```

The resulting CPack files would have this:

```
set(CPACK_PACKAGE_VENDOR "Cool "Company"")
```

That would not be exactly what you would want or expect. In fact, it just wouldn't work. To get around this problem, there are two solutions. The first is to add an additional level of escapes to the original set command like this:

```
set(CPACK_PACKAGE_VENDOR "Cool \\\"Company\\\"")
```

This would result in the correct `set` command which would look like this:

```
set(CPACK_PACKAGE_VENDOR "Cool \"Company\"")
```

The second solution to the escaping problem is to use a CPack project config file, explained in the next section.

9.1.3 Adding Custom CPack Options

To avoid the escaping problem a project specific CPack configure file can be specified. This file will be loaded by CPack after CPackConfig.cmake or CPackSourceConfig.cmake is loaded, and CPACK_GENERATOR will be set to the CPack generator being run. Variables set in this file only require one level of CMake escapes. This file can be configured or not, and contains regular CMake code. In the example above, you could move CPACK_FOOBAR into a file MyCPackOptions.cmake.in and configure that file into the build tree of the project. Then set the project configuration file path like this:

```
configure_file ("${PROJECT_SOURCE_DIR}/MyCPackOptions.cmake.in"
                "${PROJECT_BINARY_DIR}/MyCPackOptions.cmake"
                @ONLY)
set (CPACK_PROJECT_CONFIG_FILE
    "${PROJECT_BINARY_DIR}/CMakeCPackOptions.cmake")
```

Where MyCPackOptions.cmake.in contained:

```
set(CPACK_PACKAGE_VENDOR "Cool \"Company\"")
```

The CPACK_PROJECT_CONFIG_FILE variable should contain the full path to the CPack config file for the project, as seen in the above example. This has the added advantage that the CMake code can contain if statements based on the CPACK_GENERATOR value, so that packager specific values can be set for a project. For example, the CMake project sets the icon for the installer in this file:

```
set (CPACK_NSIS_MUI_ICON
    "@CMake_SOURCE_DIR@/Utilities/Release\\CMakeLogo.ico")
```

Note that the path has forward slashes except for the last part which has an escaped as the path separator. As of the writing of this book, NSIS needed the last part of the path to have a Windows style slash. If you do not do this, you may get the following error:

```
File: ".../Release/CMakeLogo.ico" -> no files found.
Usage: File [/nonfatal] [/a] ([/r] [/x filespec [...]]
       filespec [...] | /oname=outfile one_file_only)
```

9.1.4 Options Added by CPack

In addition to creating the two configuration files, CPack.cmake will add some advanced options to your project. The options added depend on the environment and OS that CMake is running on, and control the default packages that are created by CPack. These options are of the form CPACK_<CPack Generator Name>, where generator names available on each platform can be found in the following table:

Windows	Cygwin	Linux/UNIX	Mac OS X
NSIS	CYGWIN_BINARY	DEB	PACKAGEMAKER
ZIP	SOURCE_CYGWIN	RPM	DRAGANDROP
SOURCE_ZIP		STGZ	BUNDLE
		TBZ2	OSXX11
		TGZ	
		TZ	
		SOURCE_TGZ	
		SOURCE_TZ	

Turning these options on or off affects the packages that are created when running CPack with no options. If the option is off in the CMakeCache.txt file for the project, you can still build that package type by specifying the -G option to the CPack command line.

9.2 CPack Source Packages

Source packages in CPack simply copy the entire source tree for a project into a package file, and no install rules are used as they are in the case of binary packages. Out of source builds should be used to avoid having extra binary stuff polluting the source package. If you have files or directories in your source tree that are not wanted in the source package, you can use the variable CPACK_SOURCE_IGNORE_FILES to exclude things from the package. This variable contains a list of regular expressions. Any file or directory that matches a regular expression in that list will be excluded from the sources. The default setting is as follows:

```
"/CVS/;/\\\\\\\.svn/;\\\\\\\.swp$;\\\\\\\.#;/#"
```

There are many levels of escapes used in the default value as this variable is parsed by CMake once and CPack again. It is important to realize that the source tree will not use any install commands, it will simply copy the entire source tree minus the files it is told to ignore into the package. To avoid the multiple levels of escape, the file referenced by CPACK_PROJECT_CONFIG_FILE should be used to set this variable. The expression is a regular expression and not a wild card statement, see Chapter 4 for more information about CMake regular expressions.

9.3 CPack Installer Commands

Since binary packages require CPack to interact with the install rules of the project being packaged, this section will cover some of the options CPack provides to interact with the install rules of a project. CPack can work with CMake's install scripts or with external install commands.

9.3.1 CPack and CMake install commands

In most CMake projects, using the CMake install rules will be sufficient to create the desired package. By default CPack will run the install rule for the current project. However, if you have a more complicated project, you can specify sub-projects and install directories with the variable

CPACK_INSTALL_CMAKE_PROJECTS. This variable should hold quadruplets of install directory, install project name, install component, and install subdirectory. For example, if you had a project with a sub project called MySub that was compiled into a directory called SubProject, and you wanted to install all of its components, you would have this:

```
SET(CPACK_INSTALL_CMAKE_PROJECTS   "SubProject;MySub;ALL;/")
```

9.3.2 CPack and DESTDIR

By default CPack does not use the DESTDIR option during the installation phase. Instead it sets the CMAKE_INSTALL_PREFIX to the full path of the temporary directory being used by CPack to stage the install package. This can be changed by setting CPACK_SET_DESTDIR (page 682) to on. If the CPACK_SET_DESTDIR option is on, CPack will use the project's cache value for CPACK_INSTALL_PREFIX, and set DESTDIR to the temporary staging area. This allows absolute paths to be installed under the temporary directory. Relative paths are installed into DESTDIR/${project's CMAKE_INSTALL_PREFIX} where DESTDIR is set to the temporary staging area.

As noted earlier, the DESTDIR approach does not work when the install rules reference files by Windows full paths beginning with drive letters (C:/).

When doing a non-DESTDIR install for packaging, which is the default, any absolute paths are installed into absolute directories, and not into the package. Therefore, projects that do not use the DESTDIR option, must not use any absolute paths in install rules. Conversely, projects that use absolute paths, must use the DESTDIR option.

One other variable can be used to control the root path projects are installed into, the CPACK_PACKAGING_INSTALL_PREFIX (page 682). By default many of the generators install into the directory /usr. That variable can be used to change that to any directory, including just /.

9.3.3 CPack and other installed directories

It is possible to run other install rules if the project is not CMake based. This can be done by using the variables CPACK_INSTALL_COMMANDS, and CPACK_INSTALLED_DIRECTORIES. CPACK_INSTALL_COMMANDS are commands that will be run during the installation phase of the packaging. CPACK_INSTALLED_DIRECTORIES should contain pairs of directory and subdirectory. The subdirectory can be '.' to be installed in the top-level directory of the installation. The files in each directory will be copied to the corresponding subdirectory of the CPack staging directory and packaged with the rest of the files.

9.4 CPack for Windows Installer NSIS

To create Windows style wizard based installer programs, CPack uses NSIS (NullSoft Scriptable Install System). More information about NSIS can be found at the NSIS home page: http://nsis.sourceforge.net/

NSIS is a powerful tool with a scripting language used to create professional Windows installers. To create Windows installers with CPack, you will need NSIS installed on your machine.

CPack uses configured template files to control NSIS. There are two files configured by CPack during the creation of a NSIS installer. Both files are found in the CMake Modules directory. `Modules/NSIS.template.in` is the template for the NSIS script, and `Modules/NSIS.InstallOptions.ini.in` is the template for the modern user interface or MUI used by NSIS. The install options file contains the information about the pages used in the install wizard. This section will describe how to configure CPack to create an NSIS install wizard.

9.4.1 CPack Variables Used by CMake for NSIS

This section contains screen captures from the CMake NSIS install wizard. For each part of the installer that can be changed or controlled from CPack, the variables and values used are given.

The first thing that a user will see of the installer in Windows is the icon for the installer executable itself. By default the installer will have the Null Soft Installer icon, as seen in Figure 9.1 for the 20071023 CMake installer. This icon can be changed by setting the variable `CPACK_NSIS_MUI_ICON`. The installer for 20071025 in the same figure shows the CMake icon being used for the installer.

cmake-2.5.20071023-win32-x86.exe	6,290 KB	Application
cmake-2.5.20071025-win32-x86.exe	6,324 KB	Application

Figure 9.1: Icon for installer in Windows Explorer

The last thing a users will see of the installer in Windows is the icon for the uninstall executable, as seen in Figure 9.2. This option can be set with the `CPACK_NSIS_MUI_UNIICON` variable. Both the install and uninstall icons must be the same size and format, a valid windows .ico file usable by Windows Explorer. The icons are set like this:

```
# set the install/uninstall icon used for the installer itself
set (CPACK_NSIS_MUI_ICON
    "${CMake_SOURCE_DIR}/Utilities/Release\\CMakeLogo.ico")
set (CPACK_NSIS_MUI_UNIICON
    "${CMake_SOURCE_DIR}/Utilities/Release\\CMakeLogo.ico")
```

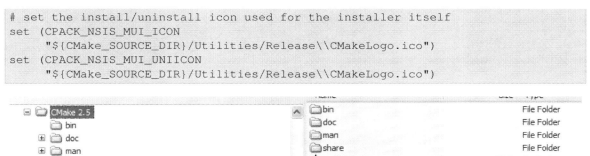

Figure 9.2: Uninstall Icon for NSIS installer

On Windows, programs can also be removed using the Add or Remove Programs tool from the control panel as seen in Figure 9.3. The icon for this should be embedded in one of the installed executables. This can be set like this:

```
# set the add/remove programs icon using an installed executable
SET(CPACK_NSIS_INSTALLED_ICON_NAME "bin\\cmake-gui.exe")
```

🔺 CMake 2.4 a cross-platform, open-source build system   Size   10.02MB

Figure 9.3: Add or Remove Programs Entry

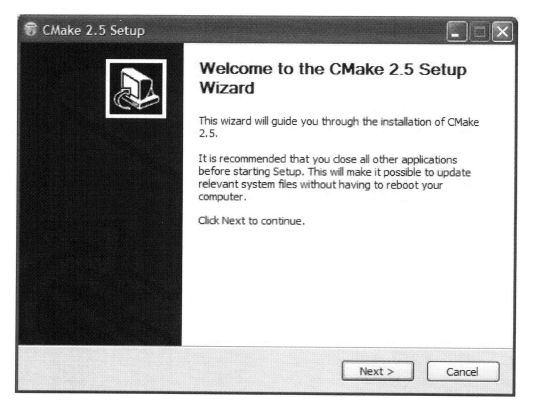

Figure 9.4: First Screen of Install Wizard

When running the installer, the first screen of the wizard will look like Figure 9.4. In this screen you can control the name of the project that shows up in two places on the screen. The name used for the project is controlled by the variable CPACK_PACKAGE_INSTALL_DIRECTORY or CPACK_NSIS_PACKAGE_NAME. In this example, it was set to "CMake 2.5" like this:

```
set (CPACK_PACKAGE_INSTALL_DIRECTORY "CMake
    ${CMake_VERSION_MAJOR}.${CMake_VERSION_MINOR}")
```

or this:

```
set (CPACK_NSIS_PACKAGE_NAME "CMake
    ${CMake_VERSION_MAJOR}.${CMake_VERSION_MINOR}")
```

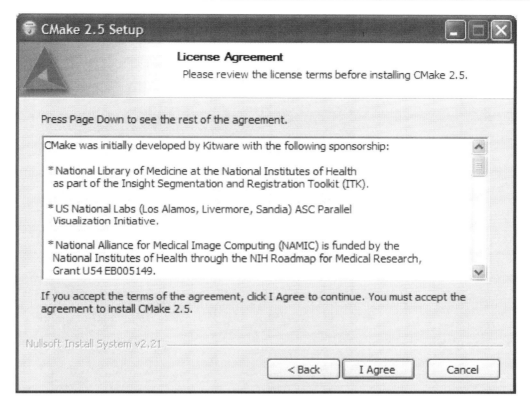

Figure 9.5: Second Screen of Install Wizard

The second page of the install wizard can be seen in Figure 9.5. This screen contains the license agreement and there are several things that can be configured on this page. The banner bitmap to the left of the "License Agreement" label is controlled by the variable CPACK_PACKAGE_ICON like this:

```
set (CPACK_PACKAGE_ICON
    "${CMake_SOURCE_DIR}/Utilities/Release\\CMakeInstall.bmp")
```

CPACK_PACKAGE_INSTALL_DIRECTORY is used again on this page everywhere you see the text "CMake 2.5". The text of the license agreement is set to the contents of the file specified in the CPACK_RESOURCE_FILE_LICENSE variable. CMake does the following:

```
set (CPACK_RESOURCE_FILE_LICENSE
    "${CMAKE_CURRENT_SOURCE_DIR}/Copyright.txt")
```

The third page of the installer can be seen in Figure 9.6. This page will only show up if CPACK_NSIS_MODIFY_PATH is set to on. If you check the Create "name" Desktop Icon button, and you

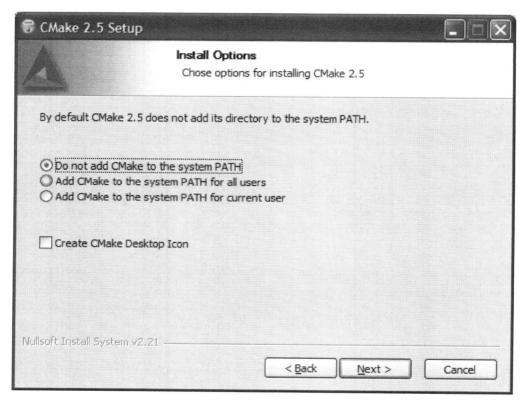

Figure 9.6: Third page of installer wizard

put executable names in the variable CPACK_CREATE_DESKTOP_LINKS, then a desktop icon for those executables will be created. For example, to create a desktop icon for the cmake-gui program of CMake, the following is done:

```
set (CPACK_CREATE_DESKTOP_LINKS cmake-gui)
```

Multiple desktop links can be created if your application contains more than one executable. The link will be created to the Start Menu entry, so CPACK_PACKAGE_EXECUTABLES, which is described later in this section, must also contain the application in order for a desktop link to be created.

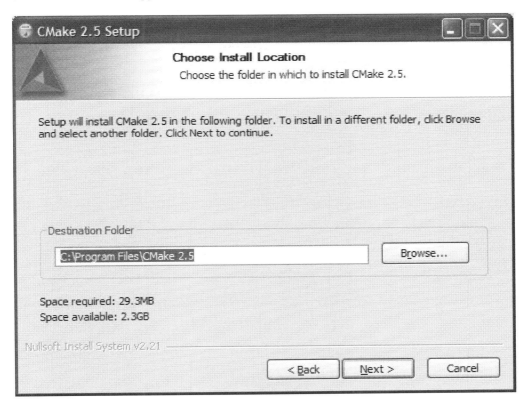

Figure 9.7: Fourth page of installer wizard

The fourth page of the installer seen in Figure 9.7 uses the variable CPACK_PACKAGE_INSTALL_DIRECTORY to specify the default destination folder in Program Files. The following CMake code was used to set that default:

```
set (CPACK_PACKAGE_INSTALL_DIRECTORY "CMake
     ${CMake_VERSION_MAJOR}.${CMake_VERSION_MINOR}")
```

The remaining pages of the installer wizard do not use any additional CPack variables, and are not included in this section. Another important option that can be set by the NSIS CPack generator is the registry key used.

There are several CPack variables that control the default key used. The key is defined in the NSIS.template.in file as follows:

```
!define MUI_STARTMENUPAGE_REGISTRY_KEY
    "Software\@CPACK_PACKAGE_VENDOR@\@CPACK_PACKAGE_INSTALL_REGISTRY_KEY@"
```

Where the CPACK_PACKAGE_VENDOR value defaults to Humanity, and CPACK_PACKAGE_INSTALL_REGISTRY_KEY defaults to ${CPACK_PACKAGE_NAME} ${CPACK_PACKAGE_VERSION}

So for CMake 2.5.20071025 the registry key would look like this:

```
HKEY_LOCAL_MACHINE\SOFTWARE\Kitware\CMake 2.5.20071025
```

9.4.2 Creating Windows Short Cuts in the Start Menu

There are two variables that control the short cuts that are created in the Windows Start menu by NSIS. The variables contain lists of pairs, and must have an even number of elements to work correctly. The first is CPACK_PACKAGE_EXECUTABLES, it should contain the name of the executable file followed by the name of the shortcut text. For example in the case of CMake, the executable is called cmake-gui, but the shortcut is named "CMake". CMake does the following to create that shortcut:

```
set (CPACK_PACKAGE_EXECUTABLES "cmake-gui" "CMake" )
```

The second is CPACK_NSIS_MENU_LINKS. This variable contains arbitrary links into the install tree, or to external web pages. The first of the pair is always the existing source file or location, and the second is the name that will show up in the Start menu. To add a link to the help file for cmake-gui and a link to the CMake web page add the following:

```
set (CPACK_NSIS_MENU_LINKS
    "doc/cmake-${VERSION_MAJOR}.${VERSION_MINOR}/cmake-gui.html"
    "cmake-gui Help" "http://www.cmake.org" "CMake Web Site")
```

9.4.3 Advanced NSIS CPack Options

In addition to the variables already discussed, CPack provides a few additional variables that are directly configured into the NSIS script file. These can be used to add NSIS script fragments to the final NSIS script used to create the installer. They are as follows:

CPACK_NSIS_EXTRA_INSTALL_COMMANDS Extra commands used during install.

CPACK_NSIS_EXTRA_UNINSTALL_COMMANDS Extra commands used during uninstall.

CPACK_NSIS_CREATE_ICONS_EXTRA Extra NSIS commands in the icon section of the script.

CPACK_NSIS_DELETE_ICONS_EXTRA Extra NSIS commands in the delete icons section of the script.

When using these variables the NSIS documentation should be referenced, and the author should look at the NSIS.template.in file for the exact placement of the variables.

9.4.4 Setting File Extension Associations With NSIS

One example of a useful thing that can be done with the extra install commands is to create associations from file extensions to the installed application. For example, if you had an application CoolStuff that could open files with the extension `.cool`, you would set the following extra install and uninstall commands:

```
set (CPACK_NSIS_EXTRA_INSTALL_COMMANDS "
    WriteRegStr HKCR '.cool' '' 'CoolFile'
    WriteRegStr HKCR 'CoolFile' '' 'Cool Stuff File'
    WriteRegStr HKCR 'CoolFile\\shell' '' 'open'
    WriteRegStr HKCR 'CoolFile\\DefaultIcon' \\
                '' '$INSTDIR\\bin\\coolstuff.exe,0'
    WriteRegStr HKCR 'CoolFile\\shell\\open\\command' \\
                '' '$INSTDIR\\bin\\coolstuff.exe \"%1\"'
    WriteRegStr HKCR \"CoolFile\\shell\\edit' \\
                '' 'Edit Cool File'
    WriteRegStr HKCR 'CoolFile\\shell\\edit\\command' \\
                '' '$INSTDIR\\bin\\coolstuff.exe \"%1\"'
    System::Call \\
      'Shell32::SHChangeNotify(i 0x8000000, i 0, i 0, i 0)'
    ")

set (CPACK_NSIS_EXTRA_UNINSTALL_COMMANDS "
    DeleteRegKey HKCR '.cool'
    DeleteRegKey HKCR 'CoolFile'
    ")
```

This creates a Windows file association to all files ending in `.cool`, so that when a user double clicks on a `.cool` file, `coolstuff.exe` is run with the full path to the file as an argument. This also sets up an association for editing the file from the windows right-click menu to the same `coolstuff.exe` program. The Windows explorer icon for the file is set to the icon found in the `coolstuff.exe` executable. When it is uninstalled, the registry keys are removed. Since the double quotes and Windows path separators must be escaped, it is best to put this code into the `CPACK_PROJECT_CONFIG_FILE` for the project.

```
configure_file(
  ${CoolStuff_SOURCE_DIR}/CoolStuffCPackOptions.cmake.in
  ${CoolStuff_BINARY_DIR}/CoolStuffCPackOptions.cmake @ONLY)

set (CPACK_PROJECT_CONFIG_FILE
  ${CoolStuff_BINARY_DIR}/CoolStuffCPackOptions.cmake)
include (CPack)
```

9.4.5 Installing Microsoft Run Time Libraries

Although not strictly an NSIS CPack command, if you are creating applications on Windows with the Microsoft compiler you will most likely want to distribute the run time libraries from Microsoft alongside your project. In CMake, all you need to do is the following:

```
include (InstallRequiredSystemLibraries)
```

This will add the compiler run time libraries as install files that will go into the bin directory of your application. If you do not want the libraries to go into the bin directory, you would do this:

```
set (CMAKE_INSTALL_SYSTEM_RUNTIME_LIBS_SKIP TRUE)
include (InstallRequiredSystemLibraries)
install (PROGRAMS ${CMAKE_INSTALL_SYSTEM_RUNTIME_LIBS}
         DESTINATION mydir)
```

It is important to note that the run time libraries must be right next to the executables of your package in order for Windows to find them. With Visual Studio 2005 and 2008, side by side manifest files are also required to be installed with your application when distributing the run time libraries. If you want to package a debug version of your software you will need to set CMAKE_INSTALL_DEBUG_LIBRARIES to ON prior to the include. Be aware, however, that the license terms may prohibit you from re-distributing the debug libraries. Double check the licensing terms for the version of Visual Studio you're using before deciding to set CMAKE_INSTALL_DEBUG_LIBRARIES to ON.

9.4.6 CPack Component Install Support

By default, CPack's installers consider all of the files installed by a project as a single, monolithic unit: either the whole set of files is installed, or none of the files are installed. However, with many projects it makes sense for the installation to be subdivided into distinct, user-selectable components. Some users may want to install only the comand-line tools for a project, while other users might want the GUI or the header files.

This section describes how to configure CPack to generate component-based installers that allow users to select the set of project components that they wish to install. As an example, a simple installer will be created for a library that has three components: a library binary, a sample application, and a C++ header file. When finished the resulting installers for Windows and Mac OS X look like the ones in Figure 9.8.

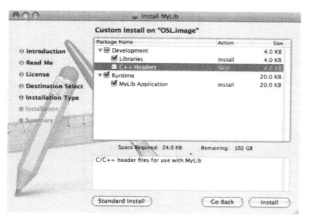
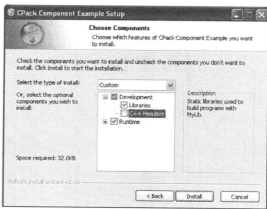

Figure 9.8: Mac and Windows Component Installers

The simple example we will be working with is as follows; it has a library and an executable. CPack commands that have already been covered are used.

```
cmake_minimum_required(VERSION 2.6.0 FATAL_ERROR)
project(MyLib)

add_library(mylib mylib.cpp)

add_executable(mylibapp mylibapp.cpp)
target_link_libraries(mylibapp mylib)

install(TARGETS mylib ARCHIVE DESTINATION lib)
install(TARGETS mylibapp RUNTIME DESTINATION bin)
install(FILES mylib.h DESTINATION include)
# add CPack to project
set(CPACK_PACKAGE_NAME "MyLib")
set(CPACK_PACKAGE_VENDOR "CMake.org")
set(CPACK_PACKAGE_DESCRIPTION_SUMMARY
    "MyLib - CPack Component Installation Example")
set(CPACK_PACKAGE_VERSION "1.0.0")
set(CPACK_PACKAGE_VERSION_MAJOR "1")
set(CPACK_PACKAGE_VERSION_MINOR "0")
set(CPACK_PACKAGE_VERSION_PATCH "0")
set(CPACK_PACKAGE_INSTALL_DIRECTORY "CPack Component Example")

# This must always be after all CPACK\_\* variables are defined
include(CPack)
```

Specifying Components

The first step in building a component-based installation is to identify the set of installable components. In this example, three components will be created: the library binary, the application, and the header file. This decision is arbitrary and project-specific, but be sure to identify the components that correspond to units of functionality important to your user, rather than basing the components on the internal structure of your program.

For each of these components, we need to identify which component each of the installed files belong in. For each INSTALL command in CMakeLists.txt, add an appropriate COMPONENT argument stating which component the installed files will be associated with:

```
install(TARGETS mylib
  ARCHIVE
  DESTINATION lib
  COMPONENT libraries)
install(TARGETS mylibapp
  RUNTIME
  DESTINATION bin
  COMPONENT applications)
```

```
install(FILES mylib.h
  DESTINATION include
  COMPONENT headers)
```

Note that the COMPONENT argument to the INSTALL command is not new; it has been a part of CMake's INSTALL command to allow installation of only part of a project. If you are using any of the older installation commands (INSTALL_TARGETS, INSTALL_FILES, etc.), you will need to convert them to INSTALL commands in order to use components.

The next step is to notify CPack of the names of all of the components in your project by calling the cpack_add_component function for each component of the package:

```
cpack_add_component(applications)
cpack_add_component(libraries)
cpack_add_component(headers)
```

At this point you can build a component-based installer with CPack that will allow one to independently install the applications, libraries, and headers of MyLib. The Windows and Mac OS X installers will look like the ones shown in Figure 9.9.

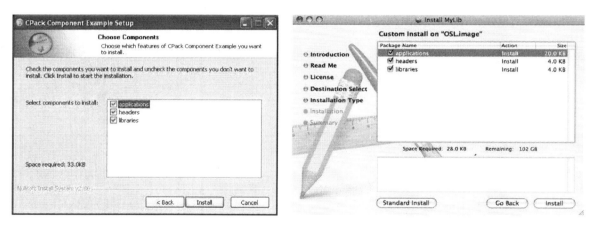

Figure 9.9: Windows and Mac OS X Component Installer First Page

Naming Components

At this point, you may have noted that the names of the actual components in the installer are not very descriptive: they just say "applications," "libraries," or "headers," as specified in the component names. These names can be improved by using the DISPLAY_NAME option in the cpack_add_component function:

```
cpack_add_component(applications DISPLAY_NAME
"MyLib Application")
```

```
cpack_add_component(libraries DISPLAY_NAME "Libraries")
cpack_add_component(headers DISPLAY_NAME "C++ Headers")
```

Any macro prefixed with CPACK_COMPONENT_${COMPNAME}, where ${COMPNAME} is the uppercase name of a component, is used to set a particular property of that component in the installer. Here, we set the DISPLAY_NAME property of each of our components so that we get human-readable names. These names will be listed in the selection box rather than the internal component names "applications," "libraries," "headers."

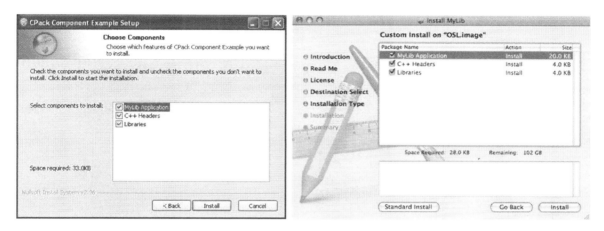

Figure 9.10: Windows and Mac OS X Installers with named components

Adding Component Descriptions

There are several other properties associated with components, including the ability to make a component hidden, required, or disabled by default, that provide additional descriptive information. Of particular note is the DESCRIPTION property, which provides some descriptive text for the component. This descriptive text will show up in a separate "description" box in the installer, and will be updated either when the user's mouse hovers over the name of the corresponding component (Windows), or when the user clicks on a component (Mac OS X). We will add a description for each of our components below:

```
cpack_add_component(applications DISPLAY_NAME "MyLib Application"
  DESCRIPTION
  "An extremely useful application that makes use of MyLib"
  )
cpack_add_component(libraries DISPLAY_NAME "Libraries"
  DESCRIPTION
  "Static libraries used to build programs with MyLib"
  )
cpack_add_component(headers DISPLAY_NAME "C++ Headers"
  DESCRIPTION "C/C++ header files for use with MyLib"
  )
```

Generally, descriptions should provide enough information for the user to make a decision on whether to install the component, but should not themselves be more than a few lines long (the "Description" box in the installers tends to be small). Figure 9.11 shows the description display for both the Windows and Mac OS X installers.

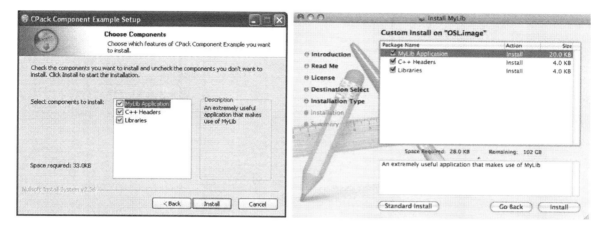

Figure 9.11: Component Installers with descriptions

Component Interdependencies

With most projects the various components are not completely independent. For example, an application component may depend on the shared libraries in another component to execute properly, such that installing the application component without the corresponding shared libraries would result in an unusable installation. CPack allows you to express the dependencies between components, so that a component will only be installed if all of the other components it depends on are also installed.

To illustrate component dependencies we will place a simple restriction on our component-based installer. Since we do not provide source code in our installer, the C++ header files we distribute can only actually be used if the user also installs the library binary to link their program against. Thus, the "headers" component depends on the availability of the "libraries" component. We can express this notion by setting the DEPENDS property for the HEADERS component as such:

```
cpack_add_component(headers DISPLAY_NAME "C++ Headers"
  DESCRIPTION
  "C/C++ header files for use with MyLib"
  DEPENDS libraries
  )
```

The DEPENDS property for a component is actually a list, as such a component can depend on several other components. By expressing all of the component dependencies in this manner you can ensure that users will not be able to select an incomplete set of components at installation time.

Grouping Components

When the number of components in your project grows large, you may need to provide additional organization for the list of components. To help with this organization, CPack includes the notion of component groups. A component group is simply a way to provide a name for a group of related components. Within the user interface a component group has its own name, and underneath that group are the names of all of the components in that group. Users will have the option to (de-)select the installation of all components in the group with a single click, or expand the group to select individual components.

We will expand our example by categorizing its three components, "applications," "libraries," and "headers," into "Runtime" and "Development" groups. We can place a component into a group by using the GROUP option to the cpack_add_component function as follows:

```
cpack_add_component(applications
  DISPLAY_NAME "MyLib Application"
  DESCRIPTION
    "An extremely useful application that makes use of MyLib"
  GROUP Runtime)
cpack_add_component(libraries
  DISPLAY_NAME "Libraries"
  DESCRIPTION
  "Static libraries used to build programs with MyLib"
  GROUP Development)
cpack_add_component(headers
  DISPLAY_NAME "C++ Headers"
  DESCRIPTION "C/C++ header files for use with MyLib"
  GROUP Development
  DEPENDS libraries
  )
```

Like components, component groups have various properties that can be customized, including the DISPLAY_NAME and DESCRIPTION. For example, the following code adds an expanded description to the "Development" group:

```
cpack_add_component_group(Development
 EXPANDED
 DESCRIPTION
"All of the tools you'll ever need to develop software")
```

Once you have customized the component groups to your liking, rebuild the binary installer to see the new organization: the MyLib application will show up under the new "Runtime" group, while the MyLib library and C++ header will show up under the new "Development" group. One can easily turn on/off all of the components within a group using the installer's GUI. This can be seen in Figure 9.12.

Installation Types (NSIS Only)

When a project contains a large number of components, it is common for a Windows installer to provide pre-selected sets of components based on specific user needs. For example, a user wanting to develop software

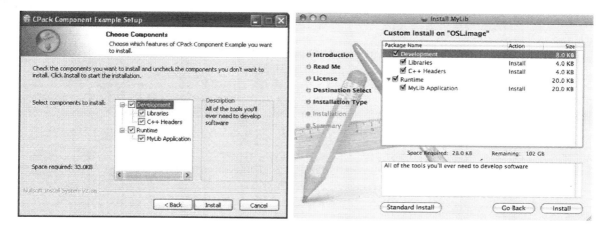

Figure 9.12: Component Grouping

against a library will want one set of components, while an end user might use an entirely different set. CPack supports this notion of pre-selected component sets via installation types. An installation type is simply a set of components. When the user selects an installation type, exactly that set of components is selected. Then the user is permitted to further customize their installation as desired. Currently this is only supported by the NSIS generator.

For our simple example, we will create two installation types: a "Full" installation type that contains all of the components, and a "Developer" installation type that includes only the libraries and headers. To do this we use the function `cpack_add_install_type` to add the types.

```
cpack_add_install_type(Full DISPLAY_NAME "Everything")
cpack_add_install_type(Developer)
```

Next, we set the `INSTALL_TYPES` property of each component to state which installation types will include that component. This is done with the INSTALL_TYPES option to the `cpack_add_component` function.

```
cpack_add_component(libraries DISPLAY_NAME "Libraries"
  DESCRIPTION
    "Static libraries used to build programs with MyLib"
  GROUP Development
  INSTALL_TYPES Developer Full)
cpack_add_component(applications
  DISPLAY_NAME "MyLib Application"
  DESCRIPTION
    "An extremely useful application that makes use of MyLib"
  GROUP Runtime
  INSTALL_TYPES Full)
cpack_add_component(headers
  DISPLAY_NAME "C++ Headers"
  DESCRIPTION "C/C++ header files for use with MyLib"
  GROUP Development
```

```
      DEPENDS libraries
      INSTALL_TYPES Developer Full)
```

Components can be listed under any number of installation types. If you rebuild the Windows installer, the components page will contain a combo box that allows you to select the installation type, and therefore its corresponding set of components as shown in Figure 9.13.

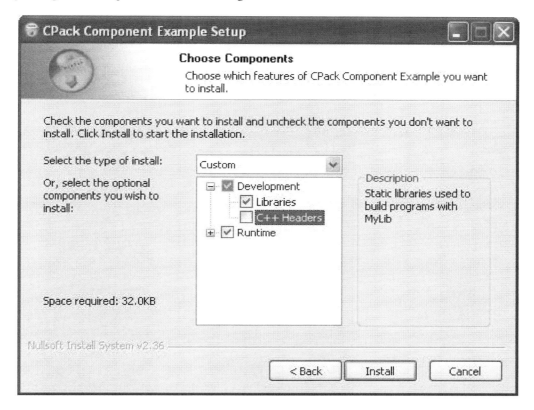

Figure 9.13: NSIS Installation Types

Variables that control CPack components

The functions `cpack_add_install_type`, `cpack_add_component_group`, and `cpack_add_component` just set `CPACK_` variables. Those variables are described in the following list:

CPACK_COMPONENTS_ALL This is a list containing the names of all components that should be installed by CPack. The presence of this macro indicates that CPack should build a component-based installer. Files associated with any components not listed here or any installation commands not associated with any component will not be installed.

CPACK_COMPONENT_${COMPNAME}_DISPLAY_NAME The displayed name of the component ${COMPNAME}, used in graphical installers to display the component name. This value can be any string.

CPACK_COMPONENT_${COMPNAME}_DESCRIPTION An extended description of the component ${COMPNAME}, used in graphical installers to give the user additional information about the component. Descriptions can span multiple lines using "n" as the line separator.

CPACK_COMPONENT_${COMPNAME}_HIDDEN A flag that indicates that this component will be hidden in the graphical installer, and therefore cannot be selected or installed. Only available with NSIS.

CPACK_COMPONENT_${COMPNAME}_REQUIRED A flag that indicates that this component is required, and therefore will always be installed. It will be visible in the graphical installer but it cannot be unselected.

CPACK_COMPONENT_${COMPNAME}_DISABLED A flag that indicates that this component should be disabled (unselected) by default. The user is free to select this component for installation.

CPACK_COMPONENT_${COMPNAME}_DEPENDS Lists the components on which this component depends. If this component is selected, then each of the components listed must also be selected.

CPACK_COMPONENT_${COMPNAME}_GROUP Names a component group that this component is a part of. If not provided, the component will be a standalone component, not part of any component group.

CPACK_COMPONENT_${COMPNAME}_INSTALL_TYPES Lists the installation types that this component is a part of. When one of these installations types is selected, this component will automatically be selected. Only available with NSIS.

CPACK_COMPONENT_GROUP_${GROUPNAME}_DISPLAY_NAME The displayed name of the component group ${GROUPNAME}, used in graphical installers to display the component group name. This value can be any string.

CPACK_COMPONENT_GROUP_${GROUPNAME}_DESCRIPTION An extended description of the component group ${GROUPNAME}, used in graphical installers to give the user additional information about the components contained within this group. Descriptions can span multiple lines using "n" as the line separator.

CPACK_COMPONENT_GROUP_${GROUPNAME}_BOLD_TITLE A flag indicating whether the group title should be in bold. Only available with NSIS.

CPACK_COMPONENT_GROUP_${GROUPNAME}_EXPANDED A flag indicating whether the group should start out "expanded", showing its components. Otherwise only the group name itself will be shown until the user clicks on the group. Only available with NSIS.

CPACK_INSTALL_TYPE_${INSTNAME}_DISPLAY_NAME The displayed name of the installation type. This value can be any string.

9.5 CPack for Cygwin Setup

Cygwin (http://www.cygwin.com/) is a Linux-like environment for Windows that consists of a run time DLL and a collection of tools. To add tools to the official cygwin, the cygwin setup program is used. The setup tool has very specific layouts for the source and binary trees that are to be included. CPack can create the source and binary tar files and correctly bzip them so that they can be uploaded to the cygwin mirror sites. You must of course have your package accepted by the cygwin community before that is done. Since the layout of the package is more restrictive than other packaging tools, you may have to change some of the install options for your project.

The cygwin setup program requires that all files be installed into /usr/bin, /usr/share/package-version, /usr/share/man and /usr/share/doc/package-version. The cygwin CPack generator will automatically add the /usr to the install directory for the project. The project must install things into share and bin, and CPack will add the /usr prefix automatically.

Cygwin also requires that you provide a shell script that can be used to create the package from the sources. Any cygwin specific patches that are required for the package must also be provided in a diff file. CMake's configure_file command can be used to create both of these files for a project. Since CMake is a cygwin package, the CMake code used to configure CMake for the cygwin CPack generators is as follows

```
set (CPACK_PACKAGE_NAME CMake)

# setup the name of the package for cygwin
set (CPACK_PACKAGE_FILE_NAME
    "${CPACK_PACKAGE_NAME}-${CMake_VERSION}")

# the source has the same name as the binary
set (CPACK_SOURCE_PACKAGE_FILE_NAME ${CPACK_PACKAGE_FILE_NAME})

# Create a cygwin version number in case there are changes
# for cygwin that are not reflected upstream in CMake
set (CPACK_CYGWIN_PATCH_NUMBER 1)

# if we are on cygwin and have cpack, then force the
# doc, data and man dirs to conform to cygwin style directories
set (CMAKE_DOC_DIR "/share/doc/${CPACK_PACKAGE_FILE_NAME}")
set (CMAKE_DATA_DIR "/share/${CPACK_PACKAGE_FILE_NAME}")
set (CMAKE_MAN_DIR "/share/man")

# These files are required by the cmCPackCygwinSourceGenerator and
# the files put into the release tar files.
set (CPACK_CYGWIN_BUILD_SCRIPT
    "${CMake_BINARY_DIR}/@CPACK_PACKAGE_FILE_NAME@-
       @CPACK_CYGWIN_PATCH_NUMBER@.sh")
set (CPACK_CYGWIN_PATCH_FILE
     "${CMake_BINARY_DIR}/@CPACK_PACKAGE_FILE_NAME@-
        @CPACK_CYGWIN_PATCH_NUMBER@.patch")
```

```
# include the sub directory for cygwin releases
include (Utilities/Release/Cygwin/CMakeLists.txt)

# when packaging source make sure to exclude the .build directory
set (CPACK_SOURCE_IGNORE_FILES
  "/CVS/" "/\\\\.build/" "/\\\\.svn/" "\\\\.swp$" "\\\\.#" "/#" "~$")
```

Utilities/Release/Cygwin/CMakeLists.txt:

```
# create the setup.hint file for cygwin
configure_file (
 "${CMake_SOURCE_DIR}/Utilities/Release/Cygwin/cygwin-setup.hint.in"
 "${CMake_BINARY_DIR}/setup.hint")

configure_file (
 "${CMake_SOURCE_DIR}/Utilities/Release/Cygwin/README.cygwin.in"
 "${CMake_BINARY_DIR}/Docs/@CPACK_PACKAGE_FILE_NAME@-
    @CPACK_CYGWIN_PATCH_NUMBER@.README")

install_files (/share/doc/Cygwin FILES
    ${CMake_BINARY_DIR}/Docs/@CPACK_PACKAGE_FILE_NAME@-
       @CPACK_CYGWIN_PATCH_NUMBER@.README)

# create the shell script that can build the project
configure_file (
"${CMake_SOURCE_DIR}/Utilities/Release/Cygwin/cygwin-package.sh.in"
 ${CPACK_CYGWIN_BUILD_SCRIPT})

# Create the patch required for cygwin for the project
configure_file (
"${CMake_SOURCE_DIR}/Utilities/Release/Cygwin/cygwin-patch.diff.in"
 ${CPACK_CYGWIN_PATCH_FILE})
```

The file `Utilities/Release/Cygwin/cygwin-package.sh.in` can be found in the CMake source tree. It is a shell script that can be used to re-create the cygwin package from source. For other projects, there is a template install script that can be found in `Templates/cygwin-package.sh.in`. This script should be able to configure and package any cygwin based CPack project, and it is required for all official cygwin packages.

Another important file for cygwin binaries is `share/doc/Cygwin/package-version.README`. This file should contain the information required by cygwin about the project. In the case of CMake, the file is configured so that it can contain the correct version information. For example, part of that file for CMake looks like this:

```
Build instructions:
  unpack CMake-2.5.20071029-1-src.tar.bz2
    if you use setup to install this src package, it will be
        unpacked under /usr/src automatically
  cd /usr/src
```

```
./CMake-2.5.20071029-1.sh all
This will create:
  /usr/src/CMake-2.5.20071029.tar.bz2
  /usr/src/CMake-2.5.20071029-1-src.tar.bz2
```

9.6 CPack for Mac OS X PackageMaker

On the Apple Mac OS X operating system, CPack provides the ability to use the system PackageMaker tool. This section will show the CMake application install screens users will see when installing the CMake package on OS X. The CPack variables set to change the text in the installer will be given for each screen of the installer.

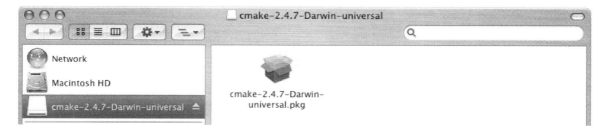

Figure 9.14: Mac Package inside .dmg

In Figure 9.14, the `.pkg` file found inside the `.dmg` disk image created by the CPack package maker for Mac OS X is seen. The name of this file is controlled by the CPACK_PACKAGE_FILE_NAME variable. If this is not set, CPack will use a default name based on the package name and version settings.

When the `.pkg` file is run, the package wizard starts with the screen seen in Figure 9.15. The text in this window is controlled by the file pointed to by the CPACK_RESOURCE_FILE_WELCOME variable.

The figure above shows the read me section of the package wizard. The text for this window is customized by using the CPACK_RESOURCE_FILE_README variable. It should contain a path to the file containing the text that should be displayed on this screen.

This figure contains the license text for the package. Users must accept the license for the installation process to continue. The text for the license comes from the file pointed to by the CPACK_RESOURCE_FILE_LICENSE variable.

The other screens in the installation process are not customizable from CPack. To change more advanced features of this installer, there are two CPack templates that you can modify, Modules/CPack.Info.plist.in and Modules/CPack.Description.plist.in. These files can be replaced by using the CMAKE_MODULE_PATH variable to point to a directory in your project containing a modified copy of either or both.

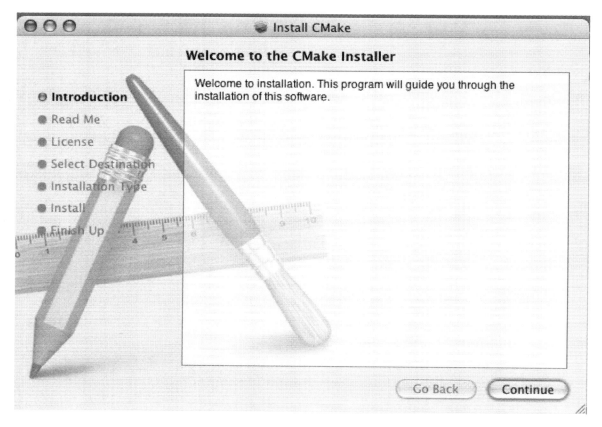

Figure 9.15: Introduction Screen Mac PackageMaker

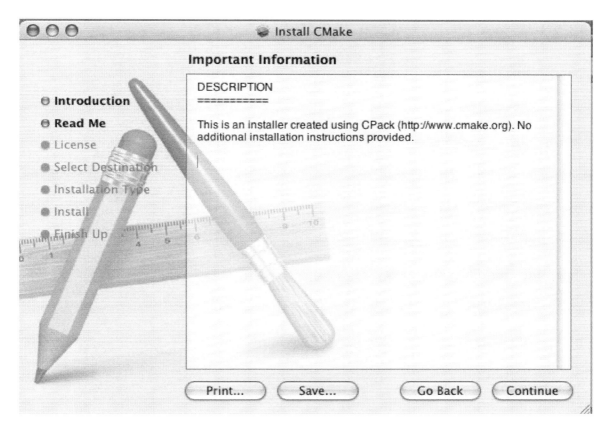

Figure 9.16: Readme section of Mac package wizard

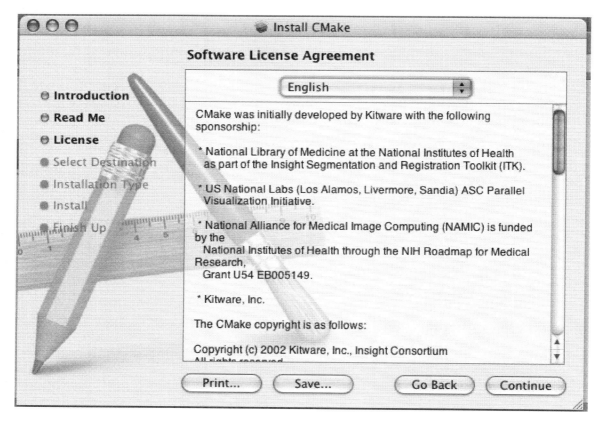

Figure 9.17: License screen Mac packager

9.7 CPack for Mac OS X Drag and Drop

CPack also supports the creation of a Drag and Drop installer for the Mac. In this case a .dmg disk image is created. The image contains both a symbolic link to the /Applications directory and a copy of the project's install tree. In this case it is best to use a Mac application bundle or a single folder containing your relocatable installation as the only install target for the project. The variable CPACK_PACKAGE_EXECUTABLES is used to point to the application bundle for the project.

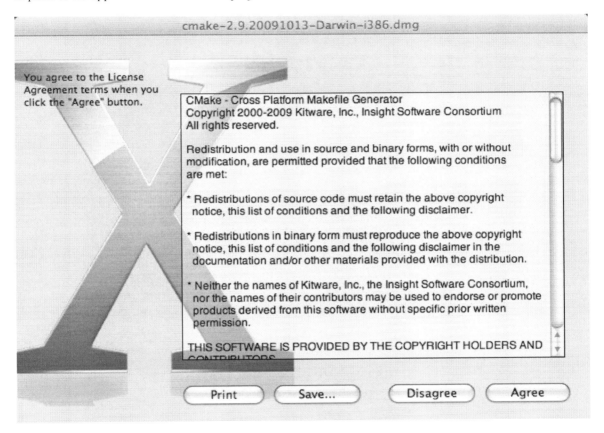

Figure 9.18: Drag and Drop License dialog

9.8 CPack for Mac OS X X11 Applications

CPack also includes an OS X X11 package maker generator. This can be used to package X11 based applications, as well as make them act more like native OS X applications by wrapping them with a script that will allow users to run them as they would any native OS X application. Much like the OS X PackageMaker

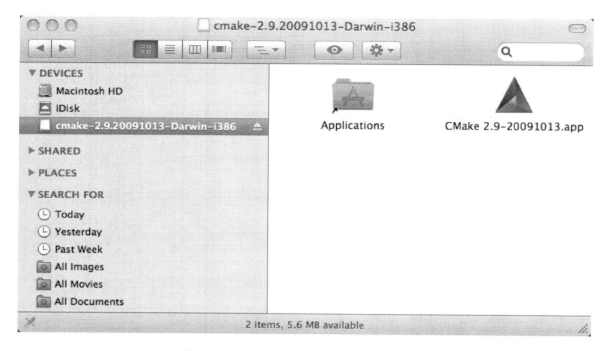

Figure 9.19: Resulting Drag and Drop folders

generator, the OS X X11 generator creates a disk image `.dmg` file. In this example, an X11 application called KWPolygonalObjectViewerExample is packaged with the OS X X11 CPack generator.

Figure 9.20: Mac OS X X11 package disk image

This figure shows the disk image created. In this case the CPACK_PACKAGE_NAME was set to KWPolygonalObjectViewerExample, and the version information was left with the CPack default of 0.1.1. The variable CPACK_PACKAGE_EXECUTABLES was set to the pair KWPolygonalObjectViewerExample and KWPolygonalObjectViewerExample, the installed X11 application is called KWPolygonalObjectViewerExample.

The above figure shows what a user would see after clicking on the `.dmg` file created by CPack. Mac OS X is mounting this disk image as a disk

This figure shows the mounted disk image. It will contain a symbolic link to the /Applications

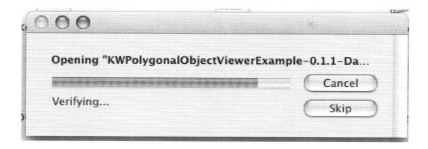

Figure 9.21: Opening OS X X11 disk image

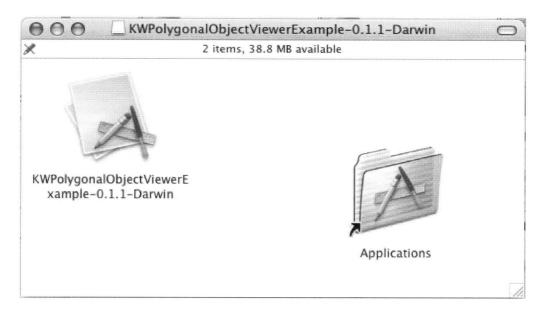

Figure 9.22: Mounted .dmg disk image

directory for the system, and it will contain an application bundle for each executable found in CPACK_PACKAGE_EXECUTABLES. The users can then drag and drop the applications into the Applications folder as seen in the figure below.

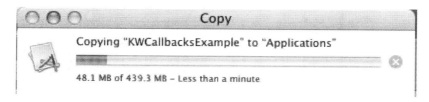

Figure 9.23: Drag and drop application to Applications

CPack actually provides a C++ based executable that can run an X11 application via the Apple scripting language. The application bundle installed will run that forwarding application when the user double clicks on KWPolygonalObjectViewerExample. This script will make sure that the X11 server is started. The script that is run can be found in CMake/Modules/CPack.RuntimeScript.in. The source for the script launcher C++ program can be found in Source/CPack/OSXScriptLauncher.cxx.

9.9 CPack for Debian Packages

A Debian package .deb is simply an "ar" archive. CPack includes the code for the BSD style ar that is required by Debian packages. The Debian packager uses the standard set of CPack variables to initialize a set of Debian specific variables. These can be overridden in the CPACK_PROJECT_CONFIG_FILE; the name of the generator is "DEB". The variables used by the DEB generator are as follows:

CPACK_DEBIAN_PACKAGE_NAME

defaults to lower case of CPACK_PACKAGE_NAME.

CPACK_DEBIAN_PACKAGE_ARCHITECTURE

defaults to i386.

CPACK_DEBIAN_PACKAGE_DEPENDS

This must be set to other packages that this package depends on, and if empty a warning is emitted.

CPACK_DEBIAN_PACKAGE_MAINTAINER

defaults to value of CPACK_PACKAGE_CONTACT

CPACK_DEBIAN_PACKAGE_DESCRIPTION

defaults to value of CPACK_PACKAGE_DESCRIPTION_SUMMARY

CPACK_DEBIAN_PACKAGE_SECTION

defaults to devl

CPACK_DEBIAN_PACKAGE_PRIORITY

> defaults to `optional`

9.10 CPack for RPM

CPack has support for creating Linux RPM files. The name of the generator as set in `CPACK_GENERATOR` is "RPM". The RPM package capability requires that rpmbuild is installed on the machine and is in PATH. The RPM packager uses the standard set of CPack variables to initialize RPM specific variables. The RPM specific variables are as follows:

CPACK_RPM_PACKAGE_SUMMARY

> defaults to value of `CPACK_PACKAGE_DESCRIPTION_SUMMARY`

CPACK_RPM_PACKAGE_NAME

> defaults to lower case of `CPACK_PACKAGE_NAME`

CPACK_RPM_PACKAGE_VERSION

> defaults to value of `CPACK_PACKAGE_VERSION`.

CPACK_RPM_PACKAGE_ARCHITECTURE

> defaults to `i386`

CPACK_RPM_PACKAGE_RELEASE

> defaults to `1`. This is the version of the RPM file, not the version of the software being packaged.

CPACK_RPM_PACKAGE_GROUP

> defaults to `none`.

CPACK_RPM_PACKAGE_VENDOR

> defaults to value of `CPACK_PACKAGE_VENDOR`

9.11 CPack Files

There are a number of files that are used by CPack that can be useful for learning more about how CPack works and what options you can set. These files can also be used as the starting point for other generators for CPack. These files can mostly be found in the Modules and Templates directories of CMake and typically start with the prefix CPack. As of version 2.8.8, you may also refer to `cpack --help-variable-list` and `cpack --help-variable` for the full set of documented `CPACK_*` variables.

## TEN

AUTOMATION & TESTING WITH CMAKE

10.1 Testing with CMake, CTest, and CDash

Testing is a key tool for producing and maintaining robust, valid software. This chapter will examine the tools that are part of CMake to support software testing. We will begin with a brief discussion of testing approaches, and then discuss how to add tests to your software project using CMake. Finally we will look at additional tools that support creating centralized software status dashboards.

The tests for a software package may take a number of forms. At the most basic level there are smoke tests, such as one that simply verifies that the software compiles. While this may seem like a simple test, with the wide variety of platforms and configurations available, smoke tests catch more problems than any other type of test. Another form of smoke test is to verify that a test runs without crashing. This can be handy for situations where the developer does not want to spend the time creating more complex tests, but is willing to run some simple tests. Most of the time these simple tests can be small example programs. Running them verifies not only that the build was successful, but that any required shared libraries can be loaded (for projects that use them), and that at least some of the code can be executed without crashing.

Moving beyond basic smoke tests leads to more specific tests such as regression, black-, and white-box testing. Each of these has its strengths. Regression testing verifies that the results of a test do not change over time or platform. This is very useful when performed frequently, as it provides a quick check that the behavior and results of the software have not changed. When a regression test fails, a quick look at recent code changes can usually identify the culprit. Unfortunately, regression tests typically require more effort to create than other tests.

White- and black-box testing refer to tests written to exercise units of code (at various levels of integration), with and without knowledge of how those units are implemented respectively. White-box testing is designed to stress potential failure points in the code knowing how that code was written, and hence its weaknesses. As with regression testing, this can take a substantial amount of effort to create good tests. Black-box testing typically knows little or nothing about the implementation of the software other than its public API. Black-box testing can provide a lot of code coverage without too much effort in developing the tests. This is especially true for libraries of object oriented software where the APIs are well defined. A black-box test can be written to go through and invoke a number of typical methods on all the classes in the software.

The final type of testing we will discuss is software standard compliance testing. While the other test types we have discussed are focused on determining if the code works properly, compliance testing tries to determine if the code adheres to the coding standards of the software project. This could be a check to verify that all classes have implemented some key method, or that all functions have a common prefix. The options for this type of test are limitless and there are a number of ways to perform such testing. There are software analysis tools that can be used, or specialized test programs (maybe python scripts etc) could be written. The key point to realize is that the tests do not necessarily have to involve running some part of the software. The tests might run some other tool on the source code itself.

There are a number of reasons why it helps to have testing support integrated into the build process. First, complex software projects may have a number of configuration or platform-dependent options. The build system knows what options can be enabled and can then enable the appropriate tests for those options. For example, the Visualization Toolkit (VTK) includes support for a parallel processing library called MPI. If VTK is built with MPI support then additional tests are enabled that make use of MPI and verify that the MPI-specific code in VTK works as expected. Secondly, the build system knows where the executables will be placed, and it has tools for finding other required executables (such as perl, python etc). The third reason is that with UNIX Makefiles it is common to have a test target in the Makefile so that developers can type make test and have the test(s) run. In order for this to work, the build system must have some knowledge of the testing process.

10.2 How Does CMake Facilitate Testing?

CMake facilitates testing your software through special testing commands and the CTest executable. First, we will discuss the key testing commands in CMake. To add testing to a CMake-based project, simply include(CTest) (page 317) and use the add_test() (page 277) command. The add_test command has a simple syntax as follows:

```
add_test (NAME TestName COMMAND ExecutableToRun arg1 arg2 ...)
```

The first argument is simply a string name for the test. This is the name that will be displayed by testing programs. The second argument is the executable to run. The executable can be built as part of the project or it can be a standalone executable such as python, perl, etc. The remaining arguments will be passed to the running executable. A typical example of testing using the add_test command would look like this:

```
add_executable (TestInstantiator TestInstantiator.cxx)
target_link_libraries (TestInstantiator vtkCommon)
add_test (NAME TestInstantiator
          COMMAND TestInstantiator)
```

The add_test command is typically placed in the CMakeLists file for the directory that has the test in it. For large projects, there may be multiple CMakeLists files with add_test commands in them. Once the add_test commands are present in the project, the user can run the tests by invoking the "test" target of Makefile, or the RUN_TESTS target of Visual Studio or Xcode. An example of running tests on the CMake tests using the Makefile generator on Linux would be:

```
$ make test
Running tests...
Test project
```

```
      Start 2: kwsys.testEncode
1/20 Test  #2: kwsys.testEncode .........    Passed    0.02 sec
      Start 3: kwsys.testTerminal
2/20 Test  #3: kwsys.testTerminal .......    Passed    0.02 sec
      Start 4: kwsys.testAutoPtr
3/20 Test  #4: kwsys.testAutoPtr ........    Passed    0.02 sec
```

10.3 Additional Test Properties

By default a test passes if all of the following conditions are true:

- The test executable was found
- The test ran without exception
- The test exited with return code 0

That said, these behaviors can be modified using the set_property() (page 329) command:

```
set_property (TEST test_name
              PROPERTY prop1 value1 value2 ...)
```

This command will set additional properties for the specified tests. Example properties are:

ENVIRONMENT Specifies environment variables that should be defined for running a test. If set to a list of environment variables and values of the form MYVAR=value, those environment variables will be defined while the test is running. The environment is restored to its previous state after the test is done.

LABELS Specifies a list of text labels associated with a test. These labels can be used to group tests together based on what they test. For example, you could add a label of MPI to all tests that exercise MPI code.

WILL_FAIL If this option is set to true, then the test will pass if the return code is not 0, and fail if it is. This reverses the third condition of the pass requirements.

PASS_REGULAR_EXPRESSION If this option is specified, then the output of the test is checked against the regular expression provided (a list of regular expressions may be passed in as well). If none of the regular expressions match, then the test will fail. If at least one of them matches, then the test will pass.

FAIL_REGULAR_EXPRESSION If this option is specified, then the output of the test is checked against the regular expression provided (a list of regular expressions may be passed in as well). If none of the regular expressions match, then the test will pass. If at least one of them matches, then the test will fail.

If both PASS_REGULAR_EXPRESSION (page 614) and FAIL_REGULAR_EXPRESSION (page 613) are specified, then the FAIL_REGULAR_EXPRESSION takes precedence. The following example illustrates using the PASS_REGULAR_EXPRESSION and FAIL_REGULAR_EXPRESSION:

```
add_test (NAME outputTest COMMAND outputTest)

set (passRegex "^Test passed"  "^All ok")
set (failRegex "Error" "Fail")
```

```
set_property (TEST outputTest
              PROPERTY PASS_REGULAR_EXPRESSION "${passRegex}")
set_property (TEST outputTest
              PROPERTY FAIL_REGULAR_EXPRESSION "${failRegex}")
```

10.4 Testing Using CTest

When you run the tests from your build environment, what really happens is that the build environment runs CTest. CTest is an executable that comes with CMake; it handles running the tests for the project. While CTest works well with CMake, you do not have to use CMake in order to use CTest. The main input file for CTest is called CTestTestfile.cmake. This file will be created in each directory that was processed by CMake (typically every directory with a CMakeLists file). The syntax of CTestTestfile.cmake is like the regular CMake syntax, with a subset of the commands available. If CMake is used to generate testing files, they will list any subdirectories that need to be processed as well as any add_test() (page 277) calls. The subdirectories are those that were added by subdirs() (page 350) or add_subdirectory() (page 277) commands. CTest can then parse these files to determine what tests to run. An example of such a file is shown below:

```
# CMake generated Testfile for
#        Source directory: C:/CMake
#        Build directory: C:/CMakeBin
#
# This file includes the relevent testing commands required
# for testing this directory and lists subdirectories to
# be tested as well.

ADD_TEST (SystemInformationNew ...)

SUBDIRS (Source/kwsys)
SUBDIRS (Utilities/cmzlib)
...
```

When CTest parses the CTestTestfile.cmake files, it will extract the list of tests from them. These tests will be run, and for each test CTest will display the name of the test and its status. Consider the following sample output:

```
$ ctest
Test project C:/CMake-build26
        Start 1: SystemInformationNew
 1/21 Test  #1: SystemInformationNew ......    Passed    5.78 sec
        Start 2: kwsys.testEncode
 2/21 Test  #2: kwsys.testEncode .........    Passed    0.02 sec
        Start 3: kwsys.testTerminal
 3/21 Test  #3: kwsys.testTerminal .......    Passed    0.00 sec
        Start 4: kwsys.testAutoPtr
 4/21 Test  #4: kwsys.testAutoPtr ........    Passed    0.02 sec
```

Chapter 10. Automation & Testing With CMake

```
      Start 5: kwsys.testHashSTL
 5/21 Test  #5: kwsys.testHashSTL ........   Passed    0.02 sec
...
100% tests passed, 0 tests failed out of 21
Total Test time (real) =  59.22 sec
```

CTest is run from within your build tree. It will run all the tests found in the current directory as well as any subdirectories listed in the CTestTestfile.cmake. For each test that is run CTest will report if the test passed and how long it took to run the test.

The CTest executable includes some handy command line options to make testing a little easier. We will start by looking at the options you would typically use from the command line.

```
-R <regex>              Run tests matching regular expression
-E <regex>              Exclude tests matching regular expression
-L <regex>              Run tests with labels matching the regex
-LE <regex>             Run tests with labels not matching regexp
-C <config>             Choose the configuration to test
-V,--verbose            Enable verbose output from tests.
-N,--show-only          Disable actual execution of tests.
-I [Start,End,Stride,test#,test#|Test file]
                        Run specific tests by range and number.
-H                                     Display a help message
```

The -R option is probably the most commonly used. It allows you to specify a regular expression; only the tests with names matching the regular expression will be run. Using the -R option with the name (or part of the name) of a test is a quick way to run a single test. The -E option is similar except that it excludes all tests matching the regular expression. The -L and -LE options are similar to -R and -E, except that they apply to test labels that were set using the set_property() (page 329) command as described in section 0. The -C option is mainly for IDE builds where you might have multiple configurations, such as Release and Debug in the same tree. The argument following the -C determines which configuration will be tested. The -V argument is useful when you are trying to determine why a test is failing. With -V, CTest will print out the command line used to run the test, as well as any output from the test itself. The -V option can be used with any invocation of CTest to provide more verbose output. The -N option is useful if you want to see what tests CTest would run without actually running them.

Running the tests and making sure they all pass before committing any changes to the software is a sure-fire way to improve your software quality and development process. Unfortunately, for large projects the number of tests and the time required to run them may be prohibitive. In these situations the -I option of CTest can be used. The -I option allows you to flexibly specify a subset of the tests to run. For example, the following invocation of CTest will run every seventh test.

```
ctest -I ,,7
```

While this is not as good as running every test, it is better than not running any and it may be a more practical solution for many developers. Note that if the start and end arguments are not specified, as in this example, then they will default to the first and last tests. In another example, assume that you always want to run a few tests plus a subset of the others. In this case you can explicitly add those tests to the end of the arguments for -I. For example:

```
ctest -I ,,5,1,2,3,10
```

will run tests 1, 2, 3, and 10, plus every fifth test. You can pass as many test numbers as you want after the stride argument.

10.5 Using CTest to Drive Complex Tests

Sometimes to properly test a project you need to actually compile code during the testing phase. There are several reasons for this. First, if test programs are compiled as part of the main project, they can end up taking up a significant amount of the build time. Also, if a test fails to build, the main build should not fail as well. Finally, IDE projects can quickly become too large to load and work with. The CTest command supports a group of command line options that allow it to be used as the test executable to run. When used as the test executable, CTest can run CMake, run the compile step, and finally run a compiled test. We will now look at the command line options to CTest that support building and running tests.

```
--build-and-test  src_directory build_directory
Run cmake on the given source directory using the specified build directory.
--test-command         Name of the program to run.
--build-target         Specify a specific target to build.
--build-nocmake        Run the build without running cmake first.
--build-run-dir        Specify directory to run programs from.
--build-two-config     Run cmake twice before the build.
--build-exe-dir        Specify the directory for the executable.
--build-generator      Specify the generator to use.
--build-project        Specify the name of the project to build.
--build-makeprogram    Specify the make program to use.
--build-noclean        Skip the make clean step.
--build-options        Add extra options to the build step.
```

For an example, consider the following add_test() (page 277) command taken from the CMakeLists.txt file of CMake itself. It shows how CTest can be used both to compile and run a test.

```
add_test (simple ${CMAKE_CTEST_COMMAND}
   --build-and-test "${CMAKE_SOURCE_DIR}/Tests/Simple"
                    "${CMAKE_BINARY_DIR}/Tests/Simple"
   --build-generator ${CMAKE_GENERATOR}
   --build-makeprogram ${CMAKE_MAKE_PROGRAM}
   --build-project Simple
   --test-command simple)
```

In this example, the add_test command is first passed the name of the test, "simple". After the name of the test, the command to be run is specified. In this case, the test command to be run is CTest. The CTest command is referenced via the CMAKE_CTEST_COMMAND (page 626) variable. This variable is always set by CMake to the CTest command that came from the CMake installation used to build the project. Next, the source and binary directories are specified. The next options to CTest are the –build-generator and –build-makeprogram options. These are specified using the CMake variables CMAKE_MAKE_PROGRAM (page 630) and `CMAKE_GENERATOR` (page 628). Both `CMAKE_MAKE_PROGRAM` and `CMAKE_GENERATOR` are defined by CMake. This is an important step as it makes sure that the same generator is used for building the test as was used for building the project itself. The –build-project option is passed `Simple`, which corresponds to the `project()` (page 327) command used in the Simple test. The final argument is the –test-command which tells CTest the command to run once it gets a successful build, and should be the name of the executable that will be compiled by the test.

10.6 Handling a Large Number of Tests

When a large number of tests exist in a single project, it is cumbersome to have individual executables available for each test. That said, the developer of the project should not be required to create tests with complex argument parsing. This is why CMake provides a convenience command for creating a test driver program. This command is called `create_test_sourcelist()` (page 282). A test driver is a program that links together many small tests into a single executable. This is useful when building static executables with large libraries to shrink the total required size. The signature for `create_test_sourcelist` is as follows:

```
create_test_sourcelist (SourceListName
                        DriverName
                        test1 test2 test3
                        EXTRA_INCLUDE include.h
                        FUNCTION function
                        )
```

The first argument is the variable which will contain the list of source files that must be compiled to make the test executable. The DriverName is the name of the test driver program (e.g. the name of the resulting executable). The rest of the arguments consist of a list of test source files. Each test source file should have a function in it that has the same name as the file with no extension (`foo.cxx` should have `int foo(argc, argv);`). The resulting executable will be able to invoke each of the tests by name on the command line. The `EXTRA_INCLUDE` and `FUNCTION` arguments support additional customization of the test driver program. Consider the following CMakeLists file fragment to see how this command can be used:

```
# create the testing file and list of tests
create_test_sourcelist (Tests
  CommonCxxTests.cxx
  ObjectFactory.cxx
  otherArrays.cxx
  otherEmptyCell.cxx
  TestSmartPointer.cxx
  SystemInformation.cxx
  ...
  )

# add the executable
add_executable (CommonCxxTests ${Tests})
```

```
# remove the test driver source file
set (TestsToRun ${Tests})
remove (TestsToRun CommonCxxTests.cxx)

# Add all the ADD_TEST for each test
foreach (test ${TestsToRun})
  get_filename_component (TName ${test} NAME_WE)
  add_test (NAME ${TName} COMMAND CommonCxxTests ${TName})
endforeach ()
```

The `create_test_sourcelist` command is invoked to create a test driver. In this case it creates and writes `CommonCxxTests.cxx` into the binary tree of the project, using the rest of the arguments to determine its contents. Next, the `add_executable()` (page 273) command is used to add that executable to the build. Then a new variable called `TestsToRun` is created with an initial value of the sources required for the test driver. The `remove()` (page 349) command is used to remove the driver program itself from the list. Then, a `foreach()` (page 309) command is used to loop over the remaining sources. For each source, its name without a file extension is extracted and put in the variable `TName`, then a new test is added for `TName`. The end result is that for each source file in the `create_test_sourcelist` an `add_test` command is called with the name of the test. As more tests are added to the `create_test_sourcelist` command, the `foreach` loop will automatically call `add_test` for each one.

10.7 Managing Test Data

In addition to handling large numbers of tests, CMake contains a system for managing test data. It is encapsulated in an ExternalData CMake module, downloads large data on an as-needed basis, retains version information, and allows distributed storage.

The design of the ExternalData follows that of distributed version control systems using hash-based file identifiers and object stores, but it also takes advantage of the presence of a dependency-based build system. The figure below illustrates the approach. Source trees contain lighweight "content links" referencing data in remote storage by hashes of their content. The ExternalData module produces build rules to download the data to local stores and reference them from build trees by symbolic links (copies on Windows).

A content link is a small, plain text file containing a hash of the real data. Its name is the same as its data file, with an additional extension identifying the hash algorithm e.g. img.png.md5. Content links always take the same (small) amount of space in the source tree regardless of the real data size. The CMakeLists.txt CMake configuration files refer to data using a DATA{} syntax inside calls to the ExternalData module API. For example, DATA{img.png} tells the ExternalData module to make img.png available in the build tree even if only a img.png.md5 content link appears in the source tree.

The ExternalData module implements a flexible system to prevent duplication of content fetching and storage. Objects are retrieved from a list of (possibly redundant) local and remote locations specified in the ExternalData CMake configuration as a list of "URL templates". The only requirement of remote storage systems is the ability to fetch from a URL that locates content through specification of the hash algorithm and hash value. Local or networked file systems, an Apache FTP server or a Midas[1] server , for example, all

---

[1] http://www.midasplatform.org

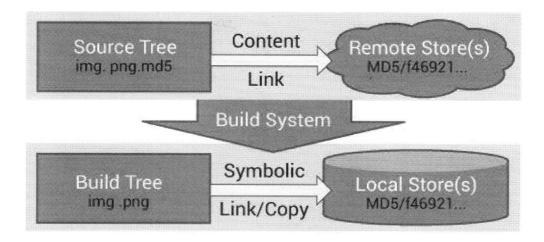

Figure 10.1: ExternalData module flow chart

have this capability. Each URL template has %(algo) and %(hash) placeholders for ExternalData to replace with values from a content link.

A persistent local object store can cache downloaded content to share among build trees by setting the ExternalData_OBJECT_STORES CMake build configuration variable. This is helpful to de-duplicate content for multiple build trees. It also resolves an important pragmatic concern in a regression testing context; when many machines simultaneously start a nightly dashboard build, they can use their local object store instead of overloading the data servers and flooding network traffic.

Retrieval is integrated with a dependency-based build system, so resources are fetched only when needed. For example, if the system is used to retrieve testing data and BUILD_TESTING is OFF, the data are not retrieved unnecessarily. When the source tree is updated and a content link changes, the build system fetches the new data as needed.

Since all references leaving the source tree go through hashes, they do not depend on any external state. Remote and local object stores can be relocated without invalidating content links in older versions of the source code. Content links within a source tree can be relocated or renamed without modifying the object stores. Duplicate content links can exist in a source tree, but download will only occur once. Multiple versions of data with the same source tree file name in a project's history are uniquely identified in the object stores.

Hash-based systems allow the use of untrusted connections to remote resources because downloaded content is verified after it is retrieved. Configuration of the URL templates list improves robustness by allowing multiple redundant remote storage resources. Storage resources can also change over time on an as-needed basis. If a project's remote storage moves over time, a build of older source code versions is always possible by adjusting the URL templates configured for the build tree or by manually populating a local object store.

A simple application of the ExternalData module looks like the following:

```
include(ExternalData)
set(midas "http://midas.kitware.com/MyProject")


# Add standard remote object stores to user's
# configuration.
list(APPEND ExternalData_URL_TEMPLATES
 "${midas}?algorithm=%(algo)&hash=%(hash)"
 "ftp://myproject.org/files/%(algo)/%(hash)"
 )
# Add a test referencing data.
ExternalData_Add_Test(MyProjectData
 NAME SmoothingTest
 COMMAND SmoothingExe DATA{Input/Image.png}
                      SmoothedImage.png
 )
# Add a build target to populate the real data.
ExternalData_Add_Target(MyProjectData)
```

The ExternalData_Add_Test function is a wrapper around CMake's add_test command. The source tree is probed for a Input/Image.png.md5 content link containing the data's MD5 hash. After checking the local object store, a request is made sequentially to each URL in the ExternalData_URL_TEMPLATES list with the data's hash. Once found, a symlink is created in the build tree. The DATA{Input/Image.png} path will expand to the build tree path in the test command line. Data are retrieved when the MyProjectData target is built.

10.8 Producing Test Dashboards

As your project's testing needs grow, keeping track of the test results can become overwhelming. This is especially true for projects that are tested nightly on a number of different platforms. In these cases, we recommend using a test dashboard to summarize the test results. (see Figure 10.2)

A test dashboard summarizes the results for many tests on many platforms, and its hyperlinks allow people to drill down into additional levels of detail quickly. The CTest executable includes support for producing test dashboards. When run with the correct options, CTest will produce XML-based output recording the build and test results, and post them to a dashboard server. The dashboard server runs an open source software package called CDash. CDash collects the XML results and produces HTML web pages from them.

Before discussing how to use CTest to produce a dashboard, let us consider the main parts of a testing dashboard. Each night at a specified time, the dashboard server will open up a new dashboard so each day there is a new web page showing the results of tests for that twenty-four hour period. There are links on the main page that allow you to quickly navigate through different days. Looking at the main page for a project (such as CMake's dashboard off of www.cmake.org), you will see that it is divided into a few main components. Near the top you will find a set of links that allow you to step to previous dashboards, as well as links to project pages such as the bug tracker, documentation, etc.

Below that, you will find groups of results. Typically groups that you will find include Nightly, Experimental,

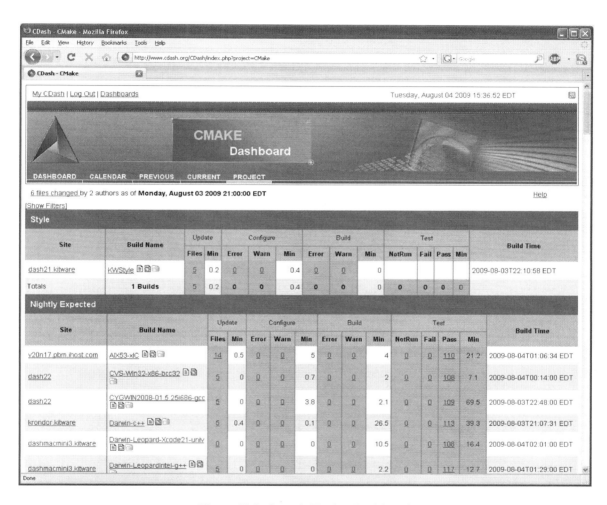

Figure 10.2: Sample Testing Dashboard

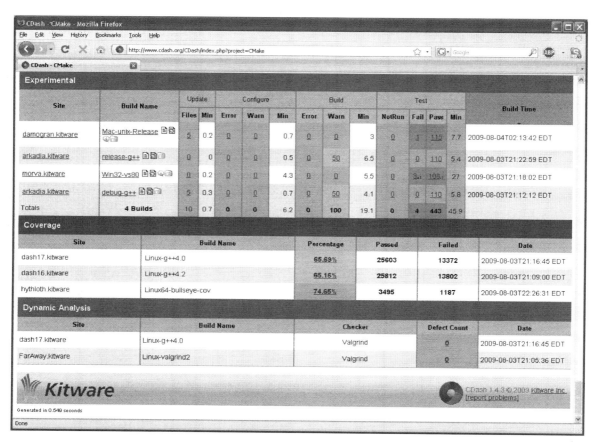

Figure 10.3: Experimental, Coverage, and Dynamic Analysis Results

Continuous, Coverage, and Dynamic Analysis (see Figure 10.3). The category into which a dashboard entry will be placed depends on how it was generated. The simplest are Experimental entries which represent dashboard results for someone's current copy of the project's source code. With an experimental dashboard, the source code is not guaranteed to be up to date. In contrast a Nightly dashboard entry is one where CTest tries to update the source code to a specific date and time. The expectation is that all nightly dashboard entries for a given day should be based on the same source code.

A continuous dashboard entry is one that is designed to run every time new files are checked in. Depending on how frequently new files are checked in a single day's dashboard could have many continuous entries. Continuous dashboards are particularly helpful for cross platform projects where a problem may only show up on some platforms. In those cases a developer can commit a change that works for them on their platform and then another platform running a continuous build could catch the error, allowing the developer to correct the problem promptly.

Dynamic Analysis and Coverage dashboards are designed to test the memory safety and code coverage of a project. A Dynamic Analysis dashboard entry is one where all the tests are run with a memory access/leak checking program enabled. Any resulting errors or warnings are parsed, summarized and displayed. This is important to verify that your software is not leaking memory, or reading from uninitialized memory. Coverage dashboard entries are similar in that all the tests are run, but as they are the lines of code being executed are tracked. When all the tests have been run, a listing of how many times each line of code was executed is produced and displayed on the dashboard.

10.8.1 Adding CDash Dashboard Support to a Project

In this section we show how to submit results to the CDash dashboard. You can either use the Kitware CDash servers at my.cdash.org or you can setup your own CDash server as described in section 10.11. If you are using my.cdash.org, you can click on the "Start My Project" button which will ask you to create an account (or login if you already have one), and then bring you to a page to start creating your project. If you have installed your own CDash server, then you should login to your CDash server as administrator and select "Create New Project" from the administration panel. Regardless of which approach you use, the next few steps will be to fill in information about your project as shown in Figure 10.4. Many of the items below are optional, so do not be concerned if you do not have a value for them; just leave them empty if they don't apply.

Name: what you want to call the project.

Description: description of the project to be shown on the first page.

Home URL: home URL of the project to appear in the main menu of the dashboard.

Bug Tracker URL: URL to the bug tracker. Currently CDash supports Mantis[2], and if a bug is entered in the repository with the message "BUG: 132456", CDash will automatically link to the appropriate bug.

Documentation URL: URL to where the project's documentation is kept. This will appear in the main menu of the dashboard.

[2]http://www.mantisbt.org/

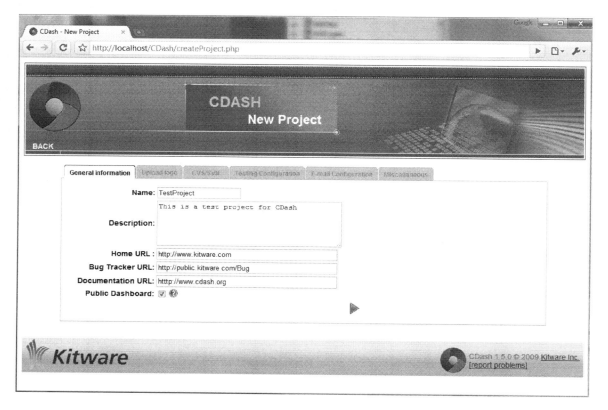

Figure 10.4: Creating a new project in CDash

Public Dashboard: if checked, the dashboard is public and anybody can see the results of the dashboard. If unchecked, only users assigned to this project can access the dashboard.

Logo: logo of the project to be displayed on the main dashboard. Optimal size for a logo is 100x100 pixels. Transparent GIFs work best as they can blend in with the CDash background.

Repository Viewer URL: URL of the web repository browser. CDash currently supports: ViewCVS, Trac, Fisheye, ViewVC, WebSVN, Loggerhead, GitHub, gitweb, hgweb, and others. Some example URLs are: * http://public.kitware.com/cgi-bin/viewcvs.cgi/?cvsroot=CMake (for ViewVC) * https://www.kitware.com/websvn/listing.php?repname=MyRepository (for WebSVN)

Repositories: in order to display the daily updates, CDash gets a diff version of the modified files. Current CDash supports only anonymous repository access. A typical URL is `:pserver:anoncvs@myproject.org:/cvsroot/MyProject`.

Nightly Start Time: CDash displays the current dashboard using a 24 hour window. The nightly start time defines the beginning of this window. Note that the start time is expressed in the form HH:MM:SS TZ, e.g. 01:00:00 UTC. It is recommended to express the nightly start time in UTC to keep operations running smoothly across the boundaries of local time changes, like moving to or from daylight saving time.

Coverage Threshold: CDash marks that coverage has passed (green) if the global coverage for a build or specific files is above this threshold. It is recommended to set the coverage threshold to a high value and decrease it as you focus on improving your coverage.

Enable Test Timing: enable/disable test timing for this project. See "Test timing" in the next section for more information.

Test Time Standard Deviation: set a multiplier for the standard deviation of a test time. If the time for a test is higher than the mean + multiplier*standard deviation, the test time status is marked as failed. The default value is 4 if not specified. Note that changing this value does not affect previous builds; only builds submitted after the modification.

Test Time Standard Deviation Threshold: set a minimum standard deviation for a test time. If the current standard deviation for a test is lower than this threshold, then the threshold is used instead. This is particularly important for tests that have a very low standard deviation, but still some variability. The default threshold is set to 2 if not specified. Note that changing this value does not affect previous builds, only builds submitted after the modification.

Test Time # Max Failures Before Flag: some tests might take longer from one day to another depending on the client machine load. This variable defines the number of times a test should fail because of timing issues before being flagged.

Email Submission Failures: enable/disable sending email when a build fails (configure, error, warnings, update, and test failings) for this project. This is a general feature.

Email Redundant Failure: by default CDash does not send email for the same failures. For instance, if a build continues to fail over time, only one email would be sent. If the email redundant failures is checked, then CDash will send an email every time a build has a failure.

Email Administrator: enable/disable sending email when submission to CDash is invalid. This can help tracking down misconfigured clients. This is particularly useful when CTest is not used to submit to

CDash.

Email Build Missing: enable/disable sending email when a build has not submitted.

Email Low Coverage: enable/disable sending email when the coverage for files is lower than the default threshold value specified above.

Email Test Timing Changed: enable/disable sending email when a test's timing has changed.

Maximum Number of Items in Email: dictates how many failures should be sent in an email.

Maximum Number of Characters in Email: dictates how many characters from the log should be sent in the email.

Google Analytics Tracker: CDash supports visitor tracking through Google analytics.   See "Adding Google Analytics" for more information.

Show Site IP Addresses: enable/disable the display of IP addresses of the sites submitting to this project.

Display Labels: as of CDash 1.4, and CTest 2.8, labels can be attached to various build and test results. If checked, these labels are displayed on applicable CDash pages.

AutoRemove Timeframe: set the number of days to retain results for this project. If the timeframe is less than 2 days, CDash will not remove any builds.

AutoRemove Max Builds: set the maximum number of builds to remove when performing the auto-removal of builds.

After providing this information, you can click on "Create Project" to create the project in CDash. At this point the server is ready to accept dashboard submissions. The next step is to provide the dashboard server information to your software project. This information is kept in a file named CTestConfig.cmake at the top level of your source tree. You can download this file by clicking on the "Edit Project" button for your dashboard (it looks like a pie chart with a wrench underneath it), then clicking on the miscellaneous tab and selecting "Download CTestConfig", and then saving the CTestConfig.cmake in your source tree. In the next section, we review this file in more detail.

10.8.2 Client Setup

To support dashboards in your project you need to include the CTest module as follows.

```
# Include CDash dashboard testing module
include (CTest)
```

The CTest module will then read settings from the CTestConfig.cmake file you downloaded from CDash. If you have added add_test() (page 277) command calls to your project creating a dashboard entry is as simple as running:

```
ctest -D Experimental
```

The -D option tells CTest to create a dashboard entry. The next argument indicates what type of dashboard entry to create. Creating a dashboard entry involves quite a few steps that can be run independently, or as one command. In this example, the Experimental argument will cause CTest to perform a number of different steps as one command. The different steps of creating a dashboard entry are summarized below.

Start Prepare a new dashboard entry. This creates a `Testing` subdirectory in the build directory. The `Testing` subdirectory will contain a subdirectory for the dashboard results with a name that corresponds to the dashboard time. The `Testing` subdirectory will also contain a subdirectory for the temporary testing results called `Temporary`.

Update Perform a source control update of the source code (typically used for nightly or continuous runs). Currently CTest supports Concurrent Versions System (CVS), Subversion, Git, Mercurial, and Bazaar.

Configure Run CMake on the project to make sure the Makefiles or project files are up to date.

Build Build the software using the specified generator.

Test Run all the tests and record the results.

MemoryCheck Perform memory checks using Purify or valgrind.

Coverage Collect source code coverage information using gcov or Bullseye.

Submit Submit the testing results as a dashboard entry to the server.

Each of these steps can be run independently for a Nightly or Experimental entry using the following syntax:

```
ctest -D NightlyStart
ctest -D NightlyBuild
ctest -D NightlyCoverage -D NightlySubmit
```

or

```
ctest -D ExperimentalStart
ctest -D ExperimentalConfigure
ctest -D ExperimentalCoverage -D ExperimentalSubmit
```

Alternatively, you can use shortcuts that perform the most common combinations all at once. The shortcuts that CTest has defined include:

ctest -D Experimental performs the start, configure, build, test, coverage, and submit commands.

ctest -D Nightly performs the start, update, configure, build, test, coverage, and submit commands.

ctest -D Continuous performs the start, update, configure, build, test, coverage, and submit commands.

ctest -D MemoryCheck performs the start, configure, build, memorycheck, coverage, and submit commands.

When first setting up a dashboard it is often useful to combine the −D option with the −V option. This will allow you to see the output of all the different stages of the dashboard process. Likewise, CTest maintains log files in the `Testing/Temporary` directory it creates in your binary tree. There you will find log files for the most recent dashboard run. The dashboard results (XML files) are stored in the `Testing` directory as well.

10.9 Customizing Dashboards for a Project

CTest has a few options that can be used to control how it processes a project. If, when CTest runs a dashboard, it finds `CTestCustom.ctest` files in the binary tree, it will load these files and use the settings from them to control its behavior. The syntax of a CTestCustom file is the same as regular CMake syntax. That said, only set commands are normally used in this file. These commands specify properties that CTest will consider when performing the testing.

10.9.1 Dashboard Submissions Settings

A number of the basic dashboard settings are provided in the file that you download from CDash. You can edit these initial values and provide additional values if you wish. The first value that is set is the nightly start time. This is the time that dashboards all around the world will use for checking out their copy of the nightly source code. This time also controls how dashboard submissions will be grouped together. All submissions from the nightly start time until the next nightly start time will be included on the same "day".

```
# Dashboard is opened for submissions for a 24 hour period
# starting at the specified NIGHTLY_START_TIME. Time is
# specified in 24 hour format.
set (CTEST_NIGHTLY_START_TIME "01:00:00 UTC")
```

The next group of settings control where to submit the testing results. This is the location of the CDash server.

```
# CDash server to submit results (used by client)
set (CTEST_DROP_METHOD http)
set (CTEST_DROP_SITE "my.cdash.org")
set (CTEST_DROP_LOCATION "/submit.php?project=KensTest")
set (CTEST_DROP_SITE_CDASH TRUE)
```

The `CTEST_DROP_SITE` (page 678) specifies the location of the CDash server. Build and test results generated by CDash clients are sent to this location. The `CTEST_DROP_LOCATION` (page 678) is the directory or the HTTP URL on the server where CDash clients leave their build and test reports. The `CTEST_DROP_SITE_CDASH` (page 678) specifies that the current server is CDash, which prevents CTest from trying to "trigger" the submission (this is still done if this variable is not set to allow for backwards compatibility with Dart and Dart 2).

Currently CDash supports only the HTTP drop submission method; however CTest supports other submission types. The `CTEST_DROP_METHOD` (page 678) specifies the method used to submit testing results. The most common setting for this will be HTTP which uses the Hyper Text Transfer Protocol (HTTP) to transfer the test data to the server. Other drop methods are supported for special cases such as FTP and SCP. In the example below, clients that are submitting their results using the HTTP protocol use a web address as their drop site. If the submission is via FTP, this location is relative to where the `CTEST_DROP_SITE_USER` (page 678) will log in by default. The CTEST_DROP_SITE_USER specifies the FTP username the client will use on the server. For FTP submissions this user will typically be "anonymous". However, any username that can communicate with the server can be used. For FTP servers that require a password, it can be stored in the `CTEST_DROP_SITE_PASSWORD` (page 678) variable. The `CTEST_DROP_SITE_MODE` (not used in this example) is an optional variable that you can use to specify the FTP mode. Most FTP servers will handle the default passive mode, but you can set the mode explicitly to active if your server does not.

CTest can also be run from behind a firewall. If the firewall allows FTP or HTTP traffic, then no additional settings are required. If the firewall requires an FTP/HTTP proxy or uses a SOCKS4 or SOCKS5 type proxy, some environment variables need to be set. HTTP_PROXY and FTP_PROXY specify the servers that service HTTP and FTP proxy requests. HTTP_PROXY_PORT and FTP_PROXY_PORT specify the port on which the HTTP and FTP proxies reside. HTTP_PROXY_TYPE specifies the type of the HTTP proxy used. The three different types of proxies supported are the default, which includes a generic HTTP/FTP proxy, "SOCKS4", and "SOCKS5", which specify SOCKS4 and SOCKS5 compatible proxies.

10.9.2 Filtering Errors and Warnings

By default, CTest has a list of regular expressions that it matches for finding the errors and warnings from the output of the build process. You can override these settings in your `CTestCustom.ctest` files using several variables as shown below.

```
set (CTEST_CUSTOM_WARNING_MATCH
  ${CTEST_CUSTOM_WARNING_MATCH}
  "{standard input}:[0-9][0-9]*: Warning: "
  )

set (CTEST_CUSTOM_WARNING_EXCEPTION
  ${CTEST_CUSTOM_WARNING_EXCEPTION}
  "tk8.4.5/[^/]+/[^/]+.c[:\"]"
  "xtree.[0-9]+. : warning C4702: unreachable code"
  "warning LNK4221"
  "variable .var_args[2]*. is used before its value is set"
  "jobserver unavailable"
  )
```

Another useful feature of the CTestCustom files is that you can use it to limit the tests that are run for memory checking dashboards. Memory checking using purify or valgrind is a CPU intensive process that can take twenty hours for a dashboard that normally takes one hour. To help alleviate this problem, CTest allows you to exclude some of the tests from the memory checking process as follows:

```
set (CTEST_CUSTOM_MEMCHECK_IGNORE
     ${CTEST_CUSTOM_MEMCHECK_IGNORE}
  TestSetGet
  otherPrint-ParaView
  Example-vtkLocal
  Example-vtkMy
  )
```

The format for excluding tests is simply a list of test names as specified when the tests were added in your CMakeLists file with `add_test()` (page 277).

In addition to the demonstrated settings, such as `CTEST_CUSTOM_WARNING_MATCH`, `CTEST_CUSTOM_WARNING_EXCEPTION`, and `CTEST_CUSTOM_MEMCHECK_IGNORE`, CTest also checks several other variables.

CTEST_CUSTOM_ERROR_MATCH Additional regular expressions to consider a build line as an error line

CTEST_CUSTOM_ERROR_EXCEPTION Additional regular expressions to consider a build line not as an error line

CTEST_CUSTOM_WARNING_MATCH Additional regular expressions to consider a build line as a warning line

CTEST_CUSTOM_WARNING_EXCEPTION Additional regular expressions to consider a build line not as a warning line

CTEST_CUSTOM_MAXIMUM_NUMBER_OF_ERRORS Maximum number of errors before CTest stops reporting errors (default 50)

CTEST_CUSTOM_MAXIMUM_NUMBER_OF_WARNINGS Maximum number of warnings before CTest stops reporting warnings (default 50)

CTEST_CUSTOM_COVERAGE_EXCLUDE Regular expressions for files to be excluded from the coverage analysis

CTEST_CUSTOM_PRE_MEMCHECK List of commands to execute before performing memory checking

CTEST_CUSTOM_POST_MEMCHECK List of commands to execute after performing memory checking

CTEST_CUSTOM_MEMCHECK_IGNORE List of tests to exclude from the memory checking step

CTEST_CUSTOM_PRE_TEST List of commands to execute before performing testing

CTEST_CUSTOM_POST_TEST List of commands to execute after performing testing

CTEST_CUSTOM_TESTS_IGNORE List of tests to exclude from the testing step

CTEST_CUSTOM_MAXIMUM_PASSED_TEST_OUTPUT_SIZE Maximum size of test output for the passed test (default 1k)

CTEST_CUSTOM_MAXIMUM_FAILED_TEST_OUTPUT_SIZE Maximum size of test output for the failed test (default 300k)

Commands specified in `CTEST_CUSTOM_PRE_TEST` and `CTEST_CUSTOM_POST_TEST`, as well as the equivalent memory checking ones, are executed once per CTest run. These commands can be used, for example, if all tests require some initial setup and some final cleanup to be performed.

10.9.3 Adding Notes to a Dashboard

CTest and CDash support adding note files to a dashboard submission. These will appear on the dashboard as a clickable icon that links to the text of all the files. To add notes, call CTest with the -A option followed by a semicolon-separated list of filenames. The contents of these files will be submitted as notes for the dashboard. For example:

```
ctest -D Continuous -A C:/MyNotes.txt;C:/OtherNotes.txt
```

Another way to submit notes with a dashboard is to copy or write the notes as files into a Notes directory under the `Testing` directory of your binary tree. Any files found there when CTest submits a dashboard will also be uploaded as notes.

10.10 Setting up Automated Dashboard Clients

IMPORTANT: This section is obsolete, and left in only for reference. To setup new dashboards, please skip ahead to the next section, and write an "advanced ctest script" instead of following the directions in this section.

CTest has a built-in scripting mode to help make the process of setting up dashboard clients even easier. CTest scripts will handle most of the common tasks and options that CTest -D Nightly does not. The dashboard script is written using CMake syntax and mainly involves setting up different variables or options, or creating an elaborate procedure, depending on the complexity of testing. Once you have written the script you can run the nightly dashboard as follows:

```
ctest -S myScript.cmake
```

First we will consider the most basic script you can use, and then we will cover the different options you can make use of. There are four variables that you must always set in your scripts. The first two variables are the names of the source and binary directories on disk, CTEST_SOURCE_DIRECTORY (page 680) and CTEST_BINARY_DIRECTORY (page 675). These should be fully specified paths. The next variable, CTEST_COMMAND, specifies which CTest command to use for running the dashboard. This may seem a bit confusing at first. The -S option of CTest is provided to do all the setup and customization for a dashboard, but the actual running of the dashboard is done with another invocation of CTest -D. Basically once the CTest script has done what it needs to do to setup the dashboard, it invokes CTest -D to actually generate the results. You can adjust the value of CTEST_COMMAND to control what type of dashboard to generate (Nightly, Experimental, Continuous), as well as to pass other options to the internal CTest process such as -I ,,7 to run every 7th test. To refer to the CTest that is running the script, use the variable: CTEST_EXECUTABLE_NAME. The last required variable is CTEST_CMAKE_COMMAND, which specifies the full path to the cmake executable that will be used to configure the dashboard. To refer to the CMake command that corresponds to the CTest command running the script, use the variable: CMAKE_EXECUTABLE_NAME. The CTest script does an initial configuration with cmake in order to generate the CTestConfig.cmake file that CTest will use for the dashboard. The following example demonstrates the use of these four variables and is an example of the simplest script you can have.

```
# these are the source and binary directories on disk
set (CTEST_SOURCE_DIRECTORY C:/martink/test/CMake)
set (CTEST_BINARY_DIRECTORY C:/martink/test/CMakeBin)

# which CTest command to use for running the dashboard
set (CTEST_COMMAND
  "\"${CTEST_EXECUTABLE_NAME}\" -D Nightly"
  )
```

```
# what CMake command to use for configuring this dashboard
set (CTEST_CMAKE_COMMAND
  "\"${CMAKE_EXECUTABLE_NAME}\""
  )
```

The script above is not that different to running CTest -D from the command line yourself. All it adds is that it verifies that the binary directory exists and creates it if it does not. Where CTest scripting really shines is in the optional features it supports. We will consider these options one by one, starting with one of the most commonly used options CTEST_START_WITH_EMPTY_BINARY_DIRECTORY. When this variable is set to true, it will delete the binary directory and then recreate it as an empty directory prior to running the dashboard. This guarantees that you are testing a clean build every time the dashboard is run. To use this option you simply set it in your script. In the example above we would simply add the following lines:

```
# should CTest wipe the binary tree before running
set (CTEST_START_WITH_EMPTY_BINARY_DIRECTORY TRUE)
```

Another commonly used option is the CTEST_INITIAL_CACHE variable. Whatever values you set this to will be written into the CMakeCache file prior to running the dashboard. This is an effective and simple way to initialize a cache with some preset values. The syntax is the same as what is in the cache with the exception that you must escape any quotes. Consider the following example:

```
# this is the initial cache to use for the binary tree, be
# careful to escape any quotes inside of this string
set (CTEST_INITIAL_CACHE "

//Command used to build entire project from the command line.
MAKECOMMAND:STRING=\"devenv.com\" CMake.sln /build Debug /project ALL_BUILD

//make program
CMAKE_MAKE_PROGRAM:FILEPATH=C:/PROGRA~1/MICROS~1.NET/Common7/IDE/devenv.com

//Name of generator.
CMAKE_GENERATOR:INTERNAL=Visual Studio 7 .NET 2003

//Path to a program.
CVSCOMMAND:FILEPATH=C:/cygwin/bin/cvs.exe

//Name of the build
BUILDNAME:STRING=Win32-vs71

//Name of the computer/site where compile is being run
SITE:STRING=DASH1.kitware

")
```

Note that the above code is basically just one set() (page 330) command setting the value of CTEST_INITIAL_CACHE to a multiline string value. For Windows builds, these are the most common cache entries that need to be set prior to running the dashboard. The first three values control what compiler will be used to build this dashboard (Visual Studio 7.1 in this example). CVSCOMMAND might be found automatically, but if not it can be set here. The last two cache entries are the names that will be used to identify this dashboard submission on the dashboard.

The next two variables work together to support additional directories and projects. For example, imagine that you had a separate data directory that you needed to keep up-to-date with your source directory. Setting the variables CTEST_CVS_COMMAND (page 677) and CTEST_EXTRA_UPDATES_1 tells CTest to perform a cvs update on the specified directory, with the specified arguments prior to running the dashboard. For example:

```
# what cvs command to use for configuring this dashboard
set (CTEST_CVS_COMMAND "C:/cygwin/bin/cvs.exe")

# set any extra directories to do an update on
set (CTEST_EXTRA_UPDATES_1
    "C:/Dashboards/My Tests/VTKData" "-dAP")
```

If you have more than one directory that needs to be updated you can use CTEST_EXTRA_UPDATES_2 through CTEST_EXTRA_UPDATES_9 in the same manner. The next variable you can set is called CTEST_ENVIRONMENT. This variable consolidates several set commands into a single command. Setting this variable allows you to set environment variables that will be used by the process running the dashboards. You can set as many environment variables as you want using the syntax shown below.

```
# set any extra environment variables here
set (CTEST_ENVIRONMENT
  "DISPLAY=:0"
  "USE_GCC_MALLOC=1"
)
# is the same as
set (ENV{DISPLAY} ":0")
set (ENV{USE_GCC_MALLOC} "1")
```

The final general purpose option we will discuss is CTest's support for restoring a bad dashboard. In some cases, you might want to make sure that you always have a working build of the software. In other instances, you might use the resulting executables or libraries from one dashboard in the build process of another dashboard. If the first dashboard fails in either of these situations, it is best to drop back to the last previously working dashboard. You can do this in CTest by setting CTEST_BACKUP_AND_RESTORE to true. When this is set to true, CTest will first backup the source and binary directories. It will then check out a new source directory and create a new binary directory. After that, it will run a full dashboard. If the dashboard is successful the backup directories are removed, if for some reason the new dashboard fails the new directories will be removed and the old directories restored. To make this work, you must also set the CTEST_CVS_CHECKOUT (page 677) variable. This should be set to the command required to check out your source tree. This doesn't actually have to be cvs, but it must result in a source tree in the correct location. Consider the following example:

```
# do a backup and should the build fail restore,
# if this is true you must set the CTEST_CVS_CHECKOUT
# variable below.
set (CTEST_BACKUP_AND_RESTORE TRUE)
```

```
# this is the full cvs command to checkout the source dir
# this will be run from the directory above the source dir
set (CTEST_CVS_CHECKOUT
  "/usr/bin/cvs -d /cvsroot/FOO co -d FOO FOO"
)
```

Note that whatever checkout command you specify will be run from the directory above the source directory. A typical nightly dashboard client script will look like this:

```
set (CTEST_SOURCE_NAME CMake)
set (CTEST_BINARY_NAME CMake-gcc)
set (CTEST_DASHBOARD_ROOT "$ENV{HOME}/Dashboards/My Tests")

set (CTEST_SOURCE_DIRECTORY
    "${CTEST_DASHBOARD_ROOT}/${CTEST_SOURCE_NAME}")
set (CTEST_BINARY_DIRECTORY
    "${CTEST_DASHBOARD_ROOT}/${CTEST_BINARY_NAME}")

# which ctest command to use for running the dashboard
set (CTEST_COMMAND
  "\"${CTEST_EXECUTABLE_NAME}\"
  -D Nightly
  -A \"${CTEST_SCRIPT_DIRECTORY}/${CTEST_SCRIPT_NAME}\"")

# what CMake command to use for configuring this dashboard
set (CTEST_CMAKE_COMMAND "\"${CMAKE_EXECUTABLE_NAME}\"")

# should ctest wipe the binary tree before running
set (CTEST_START_WITH_EMPTY_BINARY_DIRECTORY TRUE)
# this is the initial cache to use for the binary tree
set (CTEST_INITIAL_CACHE "
SITE:STRING=midworld.kitware
BUILDNAME:STRING=DarwinG5-g++
MAKECOMMAND:STRING=make -i -j2
")

# set any extra environment variables here
set (CTEST_ENVIRONMENT
        "CC=gcc"
        "CXX=g++"
  )
```

10.10.1 Settings for Continuous Dashboards

The next three variables are used for setting up continuous dashboards. As mentioned earlier a continuous dashboard is designed to run continuously throughout the day, providing quick feedback on the state of the software. If you are doing a continuous dashboard you can use CTEST_CONTINUOUS_DURATION and CTEST_CONTINUOUS_MINIMUM_INTERVAL to run the continuous repeatedly. The duration controls how long the script should run continuous dashboards, and the minimum interval specifies the shortest allowed time between continuous dashboards. For example, say that you want to run a continuous dashboard from 9AM until 7PM and that you want no more than one dashboard every twenty minutes. To do this you would set the duration to 600 minutes (ten hours) and the minimum interval to 20 minutes. If you run the test script at 9AM it will start a continuous dashboard. When that dashboard finishes it will check to see how much time has elapsed. If less than 20 minutes has elapsed CTest will sleep until the 20 minutes are up. If 20 or more minutes have elapsed then it will immediately start another continuous dashboard. Do not be concerned that you will end up with 30 dashboards a day (10 hours * three times an hour). If there have been no changes to the source code, CTest will not build and submit a dashboard. It will instead start waiting until the next interval is up and then check again. Using this feature just involves setting the following variables to the values you desire.

```
set (CTEST_CONTINUOUS_DURATION 600)
set (CTEST_CONTINUOUS_MINIMUM_INTERVAL 20)
```

Earlier, we introduced the CTEST_START_WITH_EMPTY_BINARY_DIRECTORY variable that can be set to start the dashboards with an empty binary directory. If this is set to true for a continuous dashboard then every continuous where there has been a change in the source code will result in a complete build from scratch. For larger projects this can significantly limit the number of continuous dashboards that can be generated in a day, while not using it can result in build errors or omissions because it is not a clean build. Fortunately there is a compromise: if you set CTEST_START_WITH_EMPTY_BINARY_DIRECTORY_ONCE to true, CTest will start with a clean binary directory for the first continuous build but not subsequent ones. Based on your settings for the duration this is an easy way to start with a clean build every morning, but use existing builds for the rest of the day.

Another helpful feature to use with a continuous dashboard is the -I option. A large project may have so many tests that running all the tests limits how frequently a continuous dashboard can be generated. By adding -I „7 (or -I „5 etc) to the CTEST_COMMAND value, the continuous dashboard will only run every seventh test, significantly reducing the time required between continuous dashboards. For example:

```
# which ctest command to use for running the dashboard
set (CTEST_COMMAND
  "\"${CTEST_EXECUTABLE_NAME}\" -D Continuous -I ,,7"
  )
```

As you can imagine, there is a compromise to be made between the coverage of the continuous dashboard and the frequency of its updates. Depending on the size of your project and the computing resources at your disposal, these variables can be used to fine tune a continuous dashboard to meet your needs. An example of a CTest script for a continuous dashboard looks like this

```
# these are the names of the source and binary directories
set (CTEST_SOURCE_NAME CMake-cont)
set (CTEST_BINARY_NAME CMakeBCC-cont)
set (CTEST_DASHBOARD_ROOT "c:/Dashboards/My Tests")
set (CTEST_SOURCE_DIRECTORY
     "${CTEST_DASHBOARD_ROOT}/${CTEST_SOURCE_NAME}")
set (CTEST_BINARY_DIRECTORY
     "${CTEST_DASHBOARD_ROOT}/${CTEST_BINARY_NAME}")
```

10.10. Setting up Automated Dashboard Clients

```
# which ctest command to use for running the dashboard
set (CTEST_COMMAND
    "\"${CTEST_EXECUTABLE_NAME}\"
    -D Continuous
    -A \"${CTEST_SCRIPT_DIRECTORY}/${CTEST_SCRIPT_NAME}\"")

# what CMake command to use for configuring this dashboard
set (CTEST_CMAKE_COMMAND "\"${CMAKE_EXECUTABLE_NAME}\"")

# this is the initial cache to use for the binary tree
set (CTEST_INITIAL_CACHE "
SITE:STRING=dash14.kitware
BUILDNAME:STRING=Win32-bcc5.6
CMAKE_GENERATOR:INTERNAL=Borland Makefiles
CVSCOMMAND:FILEPATH=C:/Program Files/TortoiseCVS/cvs.exe
CMAKE_CXX_FLAGS:STRING=-w- -whid -waus -wpar -tWM
CMAKE_C_FLAGS:STRING=-w- -whid -waus -tWM
")

# set any extra environment variables here
set (ENV{PATH} "C:/Program
Files/Borland/CBuilder6/Bin\;C:/Program
Files/Borland/CBuilder6/Projects/Bpl"
)
```

10.10.2 Variables Available in CTest Scripts

There are a few variables that will be set before your script executes. The first two variables are the directory the script is in, CTEST_SCRIPT_DIRECTORY, and name of the script itself CTEST_SCRIPT_NAME. These two variables can be used to make your scripts more portable. For example, if you wanted to include the script itself as a note for the dashboard you could do the following:

```
set (CTEST_COMMAND
  "\"${CTEST_EXECUTABLE_NAME}\" -D Continuous
    -A \"${CTEST_SCRIPT_DIRECTORY}/${CTEST_SCRIPT_NAME}\""
  )
```

Another variable you can use is CTEST_SCRIPT_ARG. This variable can be set by providing a comma separated argument after the script name when invoking CTest -S. For example CTest -S foo.cmake,21 would result in CTEST_SCRIPT_ARG being set to 21.

10.10.3 Limitations of Traditional CTest Scripting

The traditional CTest scripting described in this section has some limitations. The first is that the dashboard will always fail if the Configure step fails. The reason for that is that the input files for CTest are actually generated by the Configure step. To make things worse, the update step will not happen and the dashboard will be stuck. To prevent this, an additional update step is necessary. This can be achieved by adding CTEST_EXTRA_UPDATES_1 variable with "-D yesterday" or similar flag. This will update the repository prior to doing a dashboard. Since it will update to yesterday's time stamp, the actual update step of CTest will find the files that were modified since the previous day.

The second limitation of traditional CTest scripting is that it is not actually scripting. We only have control over what happens before the actual CTest run, but not what happens during or after. For example, if we want to run the testing and then move the binaries somewhere, or if we want to build the project, do some extra tasks and then run tests or something similar, we need to perform several complicated tasks, such as run CMake with -P option as a part of CTEST_COMMAND.

10.11 Advanced CTest Scripting

The CTest scripting described in the previous section is still valid and will still work. This section describes how to write command-based CTest scripts that allow the maintainer to have much more fine-grained control over the individual steps of a dashboard.

10.11.1 Extended CTest Scripting

To overcome the limitations of traditional CTest scripting, CTest provides an extended scripting mode. In this mode, the dashboard maintainer has access to individual CTest command functions, such as ctest_configure and ctest_build. By running these functions individually, the user can flexibly develop custom testing schemes. Here's an example of an extended CTest script

```
cmake_minimum_required (VERSION 2.2)

set (CTEST_SITE          "andoria.kitware")
set (CTEST_BUILD_NAME    "Linux-g++")
set (CTEST_NOTES_FILES
     "${CTEST_SCRIPT_DIRECTORY}/${CTEST_SCRIPT_NAME}")

set (CTEST_DASHBOARD_ROOT   "$ENV{HOME}/Dashboards/My Tests")
set (CTEST_SOURCE_DIRECTORY "${CTEST_DASHBOARD_ROOT}/CMake")
set (CTEST_BINARY_DIRECTORY "${CTEST_DASHBOARD_ROOT}/CMake-gcc ")

set (CTEST_UPDATE_COMMAND    "/usr/bin/cvs")
set (CTEST_CONFIGURE_COMMAND
     "\"${CTEST_SOURCE_DIRECTORY}/bootstrap\"")
set (CTEST_BUILD_COMMAND     "/usr/bin/make -j 2")


ctest_empty_binary_directory (${CTEST_BINARY_DIRECTORY})

ctest_start (Nightly)
ctest_update (SOURCE "${CTEST_SOURCE_DIRECTORY}")
ctest_configure (BUILD "${CTEST_BINARY_DIRECTORY}")
```

```
ctest_build (BUILD "${CTEST_BINARY_DIRECTORY}")
ctest_test  (BUILD "${CTEST_BINARY_DIRECTORY}")
ctest_submit ()
```

The first line is there to make sure an appropriate version of CTest is used. The advanced scripting was introduced in CTest 2.2. The CMake parser is used, and so all scriptable commands from CMake are available. This includes the CMake_minimum_required command:

```
cmake_minimum_required (VERSION 2.2)
```

Overall, the layout of the rest of this script is similar to a traditional one. There are several settings that CTest will use to perform its tasks. Then, unlike with traditional CTest, there are the actual tasks that CTest will perform. Instead of providing information in the project's CMake cache, in this scripting mode all the information is provided to CTest. For compatibility reasons we may choose to write the information to the cache, but that is up to the dashboard maintainer. The first block contains the variables about the submission.

```
set (CTEST_SITE              "andoria.kitware")
set (CTEST_BUILD_NAME        "Linux-g++")
set (CTEST_NOTES_FILES
    "${CTEST_SCRIPT_DIRECTORY}/${CTEST_SCRIPT_NAME}")
```

These variables serve the same role as the SITE and BUILD_NAME cache variables. They are used to identify the system once it submits the results to the dashboard. CTEST_NOTES_FILES is a list of files that should be submitted as the notes of the dashboard submission. This variable corresponds to the -A flag of CTest.

The second block describes the information that CTest functions will use to perform the tasks:

```
set (CTEST_DASHBOARD_ROOT    "$ENV{HOME}/Dashboards/My Tests")
set (CTEST_SOURCE_DIRECTORY "${CTEST_DASHBOARD_ROOT}/CMake")
set (CTEST_BINARY_DIRECTORY "${CTEST_DASHBOARD_ROOT}/CMake-gcc ")
set (CTEST_UPDATE_COMMAND    "/usr/bin/cvs")
set (CTEST_CONFIGURE_COMMAND
    "\"${CTEST_SOURCE_DIRECTORY}/bootstrap\"")
set (CTEST_BUILD_COMMAND     "/usr/bin/make -j 2")
```

The CTEST_SOURCE_DIRECTORY and CTEST_BINARY_DIRECTORY serve the same purpose as in the traditional CTest script. The only difference is that we will be able to override these variables later on when calling the CTest functions, if necessary. The CTEST_UPDATE_COMMAND is the path to the command used to update the source directory from the repository. Currently CTest supports Concurrent Versions System (CVS), Subversion, Git, Mercurial, and Bazaar.

Both the configure and build handlers support two modes. One mode is to provide the full command that will be invoked during that stage. This is designed to support projects that do not use CMake as their configuration or build tool. In this case, you specify the full command lines to configure and build your project by setting the CTEST_CONFIGURE_COMMAND and CTEST_BUILD_COMMAND variables respectively. This is similar to specifying CTEST_CMAKE_COMMAND in the traditional CTest scripting.

For projects that use CMake for their configuration and build steps you do not need to specify the command lines for configuring and building your project. Instead, you will specify the CMake generator to use by setting the CTEST_CMAKE_GENERATOR variable. This way CMake will be run with the appropriate generator. One example of this is:

```
set (CTEST_CMAKE_GENERATOR "Visual Studio 8 2005")
```

For the build step you should also set the variables CTEST_PROJECT_NAME and CTEST_BUILD_CONFIGURATION, to specify how to build the project. In this case CTEST_PROJECT_NAME will match the top level CMakeLists file's PROJECT command, and therefore also match the name of the generated Visual Studio *.sln file. The CTEST_BUILD_CONFIGURATION should be one of Release, Debug, MinSizeRel, or RelWithDebInfo. Additionally, CTEST_BUILD_FLAGS can be provided as a hint to the build command. An example of testing for a CMake based project would be:

```
set (CTEST_CMAKE_GENERATOR "Visual Studio 8 2005")
set (CTEST_PROJECT_NAME "Grommit")
set (CTEST_BUILD_CONFIGURATION "Debug")
```

The final block performs the actual testing and submission:

```
ctest_empty_binary_directory (${CTEST_BINARY_DIRECTORY})

ctest_start (Nightly)

ctest_update (SOURCE
              "${CTEST_SOURCE_DIRECTORY}" RETURN_VALUE res)
ctest_configure (BUILD
                 "${CTEST_BINARY_DIRECTORY}" RETURN_VALUE res)
ctest_build (BUILD "${CTEST_BINARY_DIRECTORY}" RETURN_VALUE res)
ctest_test (BUILD "${CTEST_BINARY_DIRECTORY}" RETURN_VALUE res)
ctest_submit (RETURN_VALUE res)
```

The ctest_empty_binary_directory command empties the directory and all subdirectories. Please note that this command has a safety measure built in, which is that it will only remove the directory if there is a CMakeCache.txt file in the top level directory. This was intended to prevent CTest from mistakenly removing a non-build directory.

The rest of the block contains the calls to the actual CTest functions. Each of them corresponds to a CTest -D option. For example, instead of:

```
ctest -D ExperimentalBuild
```

the script would contain:

```
ctest_start (Experimental)
ctest_build (BUILD "${CTEST_BINARY_DIRECTORY}" RETURN_VALUE res)
```

Each step yields a return value, which indicates if the step was successful. For example, the return value of the Update stage can be used in a continuous dashboard to determine if the rest of the dashboard should be run.

To demonstrate some advantages of using extended CTest scripting, let us examine a more advanced CTest script. This script drives testing of an application called Slicer. Slicer uses CMake internally, but it drives the build process through a series of Tcl scripts. One of the problems of this approach is that it does not support out-of-source builds. Also, on Windows certain modules come pre-built, so they have to be copied to the build directory. To test a project like that, we would use a script like this:

```
cmake_minimum_required (VERSION 2.2)

# set the dashboard specific variables -- name and notes
set (CTEST_SITE              "dash11.kitware")
set (CTEST_BUILD_NAME        "Win32-VS71")
set (CTEST_NOTES_FILES
    "${CTEST_SCRIPT_DIRECTORY}/${CTEST_SCRIPT_NAME}")

# do not let any single test run for more than 1500 seconds
set (CTEST_TIMEOUT "1500")

# set the source and binary directories
set (CTEST_SOURCE_DIRECTORY  "C:/Dashboards/MyTests/slicer2")
set (CTEST_BINARY_DIRECTORY  "${CTEST_SOURCE_DIRECTORY}-build")

set (SLICER_SUPPORT
    "//Dash11/Shared/Support/SlicerSupport/Lib")
set (TCLSH   "${SLICER_SUPPORT}/win32/bin/tclsh84.exe")
# set the complete update, configure and build commands
set (CTEST_UPDATE_COMMAND
    "C:/Program Files/TortoiseCVS/cvs.exe")
set (CTEST_CONFIGURE_COMMAND
    "\"${TCLSH}\"
    \"${CTEST_BINARY_DIRECTORY}/Scripts/genlib.tcl\"")
set (CTEST_BUILD_COMMAND
    "\"${TCLSH}\"
    \"${CTEST_BINARY_DIRECTORY}/Scripts/cmaker.tcl\"")

# clear out the binary tree
file (WRITE "${CTEST_BINARY_DIRECTORY}/CMakeCache.txt"
      "// Dummy cache just so that ctest will wipe binary dir")
ctest_empty_binary_directory (${CTEST_BINARY_DIRECTORY})

# special variables for the Slicer build process
set (ENV{MSVC6}              "0")
set (ENV{GENERATOR}          "Visual Studio 7 .NET 2003")
set (ENV{MAKE}              "devenv.exe ")
set (ENV{COMPILER_PATH}
    "C:/Program Files/Microsoft Visual Studio .NET
2003/Common7/Vc7/bin")
set (ENV{CVS}                "${CTEST_UPDATE_COMMAND}")

# start and update the dashboard
ctest_start (Nightly)
ctest_update (SOURCE "${CTEST_SOURCE_DIRECTORY}")
```

```
# define a macro to copy a directory
macro (COPY_DIR srcdir destdir)
  exec_program ("${CMAKE_EXECUTABLE_NAME}" ARGS
            "-E copy_directory \"${srcdir}\" \"${destdir}\"")
endmacro ()


# Slicer does not support out of source builds so we
# first copy the source directory to the binary directory
# and then build it
copy_dir ("${CTEST_SOURCE_DIRECTORY}"
          "${CTEST_BINARY_DIRECTORY}")


# copy support libraries that slicer needs into the binary tree
copy_dir ("${SLICER_SUPPORT}"
          "${CTEST_BINARY_DIRECTORY}/Lib")


# finally do the configure, build, test and submit steps
ctest_configure (BUILD "${CTEST_BINARY_DIRECTORY}")
ctest_build (BUILD "${CTEST_BINARY_DIRECTORY}")
ctest_test (BUILD "${CTEST_BINARY_DIRECTORY}")
ctest_submit ()
```

With extended CTest scripting we have full control over the flow, so we can perform arbitrary commands at any point. For example, after performing an update of the project, the script copies the source tree into the build directory. This allows it to do an "out-of-source" build.

10.12 Setting up a Dashboard Server

For many projects, using Kitware's my.cdash.org dashboard hosting will be sufficient. If that is the case for you, then you can skip this section. If you wish to setup your own server, then this section will walk you through the process. There are a few options for what to run on the server to process the dashboard results. The preferred option is to use CDash, a dashboard server based on PHP, MySQL, CSS, and XSLT. Predecessors to CDash such as DART 1 and DART 2 can also be used. Information on the DART systems can be found at http://www.itk.org/Dart/HTML/Index.shtml.

10.12.1 CDash Server

CDash is a dashboard server developed by Kitware that is based on the common "LAMP stack." It makes use of PHP, CSS, XSL, MySQL/PostgreSQL, and of course your web server (normally Apache). CDash takes the dashboard submissions as XML and stores them in an SQL database (currently MySQL and PostgreSQL are supported). When the web server receives requests for pages, the PHP scripts extract the relevant data from the database and produce XML that is sent to XSL templates, that in turn convert it into HTML. CSS is used to provide the overall look and feel for the pages. CDash can handle large projects, and has been hosting up to 30 projects on a reasonable web-server, with just over 200 million records and about 89 Gigabytes in the database, stored on a separate database-server machine.

Server requirements

- MySQL (5.x and higher) or PostgreSQL (8.3 and higher)
- PHP (5.0 recommended)
- XSL module for PHP (apt-get install php5-xsl)
- cURL module for PHP
- GD module for PHP

Gettting CDash

You can get CDash from the www.cdash.org website, or you can get the latest code from SVN using the following command:

```
svn co https://www.kitware.com/svn/CDash/trunk CDash
```

Quick installation

1. Unzip or checkout CDash in your webroot directory on the server. Make sure the web server has read permission to the files

2. Create a `cdash/config.local.php` and add the following lines, adapted for your server configuration:

```
// Hostname of the database server
$CDASH_DB_HOST = 'localhost';
// Login for database access
$CDASH_DB_LOGIN = 'root';
// Password for database access
$CDASH_DB_PASS = '';
// Name of the database
$CDASH_DB_NAME = 'cdash';
// Database type
$CDASH_DB_TYPE = 'mysql';
```

3. Point your web browser to the `install.php` script:

```
http://mywebsite.com/CDash/install.php
```

4. Follow the installation instructions

5. When the installation is done, add the following line in the `config.local.php` to ensure the installation script is no longer accessible

```
$CDASH_PRODUCTION_MODE = true;
```

Testing the installation

In order to test the installation of the CDash server, you can download a small test project and test the submission to CDash by following these steps:

1. Download and unzip the test project at:

```
http://www.cdash.org/download/CDashTest.zip
```

2. Create a CDash project named "test" on your CDash server (see 10.7 Producing Test Dashboards)

3. Download the `CTestConfig.cmake` file from the CDash server, replacing the existing one in CDashTest with the one from your server

4. Run CMake on CDashTest to configure the project

5. Run:

```
make Experimental
```

6. Go to the dashboard page for the "test" project, you should see the submission in the Experimental section.

10.12.2 Advanced Server Management

Project Roles: CDash supports three role levels for users:

- Normal users are regular users with read and/or write access to the project's code repository.

- Site maintainers are responsible for periodic submissions to CDash.

- Project administrators have reserved privileges to administer the project in CDash.

The first two levels can be defined by the users themselves. Project administrator access must be granted by another administrator of the project, or a CDash server administrator.

In order to change the current role for a user:

1. Select [Manage project roles] in the administration section

2. If you have more than one project, select the appropriate project

3. In the "current users" section, change the role for a user

4. Click "update" to update the current role

5. In order to completely remove a user from a project, click "remove"

6. If the CVS login is not correct it can be changed from this page. Note that users can also change their CVS login manually from their profile

In order to add a current role for a user:

1. Select [Manage project roles] in the administration section

2. Then, if you have more than one project, select the appropriate project

3. In the "Add new user" section type the first letters of the first name, last name, or email address of the user you want to add. Or type '%' in order to show all the users registered in CDash

4. Select the appropriate user's role

5. Optionally enter the user's CVS login

6. Click on "add user"

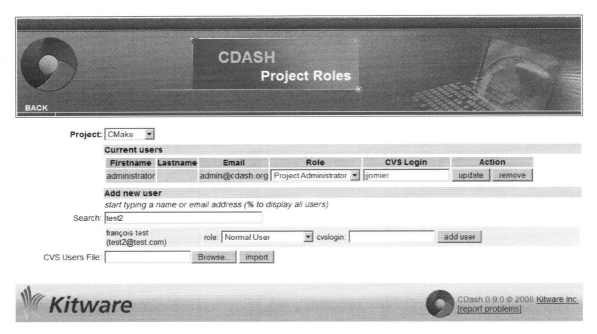

Figure 10.5: Project Role management page in CDash

Importing users: to batch import a list of current users for a given project

1. Click on [manage project role] in the administration section

2. Select the appropriate project

3. Click "Browse" to select a CVS users file.

4. The file should be formatted as follows:

```
cvsuser:email:first_name last_name
```

5. Click "import"

6. Make sure the reported names and email addresses are correct; deselect any that should not be imported

7. Click on "Register and send email". This will automatically register the users, set a random password and send a registration request to the appropriate email addresses.

Google Analytics

Usage statistics of the CDash server can be assessed using Google Analytics. In order to setup google analytics:

1. Go to http://www.google.com/analytics/index.html

2. Setup an account, if necessary

3. Add a website project

4. Login into CDash as the administrator of a project

5. Click on "Edit Project"

6. Add the code from Google into the Google Analytics Tracker (i.e. UA-43XXXX-X) for your project

Submission backup

CDash backups all the incoming XML submissions and places them in the `backup` directory by default. The default timeframe is 48 hours. The timeframe can be changed in the `config.local.php` as follows:

```
$CDASH_BACKUP_TIMEFRAME=72;
```

If projects are private it is recommended to set the backup directory outside of the apache root directory to make sure that nobody can access the XML files, or to add the following lines to the .htaccess in the backup directory:

```
<Files *>
order allow,deny
deny from all
</Files>
```

Note that the backup directory is emptied only when a new submission arrives. If necessary, CDash can also import builds from the backup directory.

1. Log into CDash as administrator

2. Click on [Import from backups] in the administration section

3. Click on "Import backups"

10.12.3 Build Groups

Builds can be organized by groups. In CDash, three groups are defined automatically and cannot be removed: `Nightly`, `Continuous` and `Experimental`. These groups are the same as the ones imposed by CTest. Each group has an associated description that is displayed when clicking on the name of the group on the main dashboard.

To add a new group:

1. Click on [manage project groups] in the administration section

2. Select the appropriate project

3. Under the "create new group" section enter the name of the new group

4. Click on "create group". The newly created group appears at the bottom of the current dashboard

To order groups:

1. Click on [manage project groups] in the administration section

2. Select the appropriate project

3. Under the "Current Groups" section, click on the [up] or [down] links. The order displayed in this page is exactly the same as the order on the dashboard

To update group description:

1. Click on [manage project groups] in the administration section

2. Select the appropriate project

3. Under the "Current Groups" section, update or add a description in the field next to the [up]/[down] links

4. Click "Update Description" in order to commit your changes

By default, a build belongs to the group associated with the build type defined by CTest, i.e. a nightly build will go in the nightly section. CDash matches a build by its name, site, and build type. For instance, a nightly build named "Linux-gcc-4.3" from the site "midworld.kitware will be moved to the nightly section unless a rule on "Linux-gcc-4.3"-"midworld.kitware"-"Nightly" is defined. There are two ways to move a build into a given group by defining a rule: Global Move and Single Move.

Global move allows moving builds in batch.

1. Click on [manage project groups] in the administration section .

2. Select the appropriate project (if more than one) .

3. Under "Global Move" you will see a list of the builds submitted in the past 7 days (without duplicates). Note that expected builds are also shown, even if they have not been submitting for the past 7 days.

4. You can narrow your search by selecting a specific group (default is All).

5. Select the builds to move. Hold "shift" in order to select multiple builds.

6. Select the target group. This is mandatory.

7. Optionally check the "expected" box if you expect the builds to be submitted on a daily basis. For more information on expected builds, see the "Expected builds" section below.

8. Click "Move Selected Builds to Group" to move the groups.

Single move allows modifying only a particular build.

If logged in as an administrator of the project, a small folder icon is displayed next to each build on the main dashboard page. Clicking on the icon shows some options for each build. In particular, project administrators can mark a build as expected, move a build to a specific group, or delete a bogus build.

Expected builds: Project administrators can mark certain builds as expected. That means builds are expected to submit daily. This allows you to quickly check if a build has not been submitting on today's dashboard, or to quickly assess how long the build has been missing by clicking on the info icon on the main dashboard.

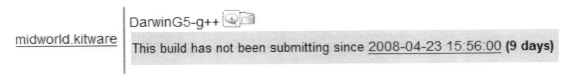

Figure 10.6: Information regarding a build from the main dashboard page

If an expected build was not submited the previous day and the option "Email Build Missing" is checked for the project, an email will be sent to the site maintainer and project administrator to alert them (see the Sites section for more information).

10.12.4 Email

CDash sends email to developers and project administrators when a failure occurs for a given build. The configuration of the email feature is located in three places: the `config.local.php` file, the project administration section, and the project's groups section.

In the `config.local.php`, two variables are defined to specify the email address from which email is sent and the reply address. Note that the SMTP server cannot be defined in the current version of CDash, it is assumed that a local email server is running on the machine.

```
$CDASH_EMAIL_FROM = 'admin@mywebsite.com';
$CDASH_EMAIL_REPLY = 'noreply@mywebsite.com';
```

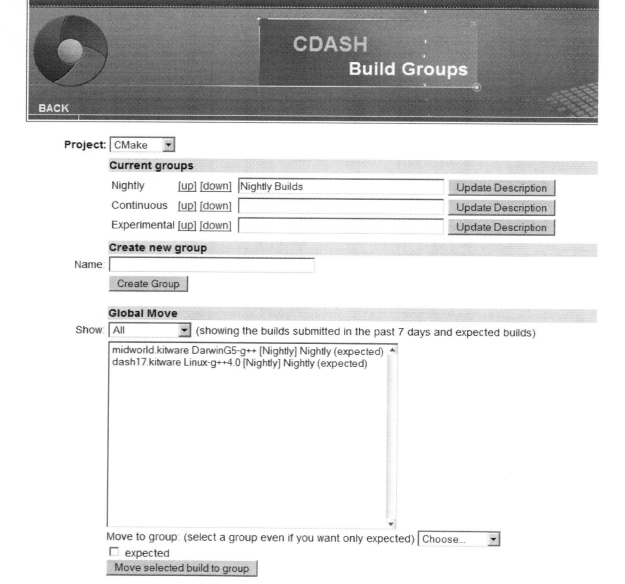

Figure 10.7: Build Group Configuration Page

In the email configuration section of the project, several parameters can be tuned to control the email feature. These parameters were described in the previous section, "Adding CDash Support to a Project".

In the "build groups" administration section of a project, an administrator can decide if emails are sent to a specific group, or if only a summary email should be sent. The summary email is sent for a given group when at least one build is failing on the current day.

10.12.5 Sites

CDash refers to a site as an individual machine submitting at least one build to a given project. A site might submit multiple builds (e.g. nightly and continuous) to multiple projects stored in CDash.

In order to see the site description, click on the name of the site from the main dashboard page for a project. The description of a site includes information regarding the processor type and speed, as well as the amount of memory available on the given machine. The description of a site is automatically sent by CTest, however in some cases it might be required to manually edit it. Moreover, if the machine is upgraded, i.e. the memory is upgraded; CDash keeps track of the history of the description, allowing users to compare performance before and after the upgrade.

Sites usually belong to one maintainer, responsible for the submissions to CDash. It is important for site maintainers to be warned when a site is not submitting as it could be related to a configuration issue. In order to claim a site, a maintainer should

1. Log into CDash
2. Click on a dashboard containing at least one build for the site
3. Click on the site name to open the description of the site
4. Click on [claim this site]

Once a site is claimed, its maintainer will receive emails if the client machine does not submit for an unknown reason, assuming that the site is expected to submit nightly. Furthermore, the site will appear in the "My Sites" section of the maintainer's profile, facilitating a quick check of the site's status.

Another feature of the site page is the pie chart showing the load of the machine. Assuming that a site submits to multiple projects, it is usually useful to know if the machine has room for other submissions to CDash. The pie chart gives an overview of the machine submission time for each project.

10.12.6 Graphs

CDash curently plots three types of graph. The graphs are generated dynamically from the database records, and are interactive.

The build time graph displays the time required to build a project over time. In order to display the graph you need to:

1. Go to the main dashboard for the project.
2. Click on the build name you want to track.

Time spent per project (computed from data collected in the past 24h):

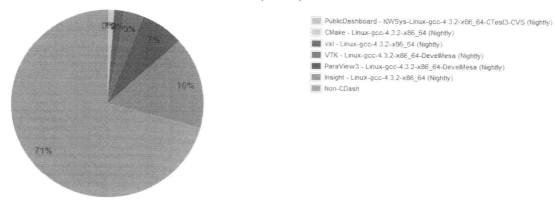

Figure 10.8: Pie chart showing how much time is spent by a given site on building CDash projects

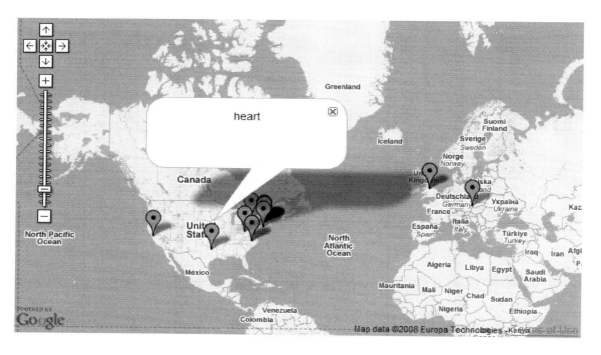

Figure 10.9: Map showing the location of the different sites building a project

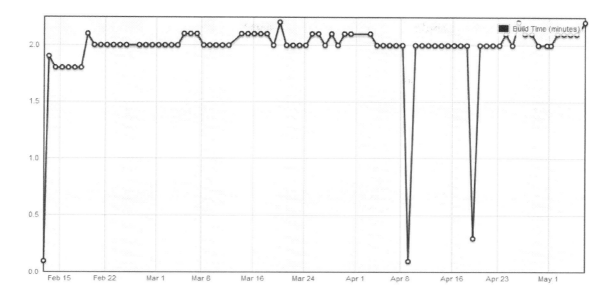

Figure 10.10: Example of build time over time

3. On the build summary page, click on [Show Build Time Graph].

The test time graphs display the time to run a specific test as well as its status (passed/failed) over time. To display it:

1. Go to the main dashboard for a project.

2. Click on the number of test passed or failed.

3. From the list of tests, click on the status of the test.

4. Click on [Show Test Time Graph] and/or [Show Failing/Passing Graph].

10.12.7 Adding Notes to a Build

In some cases, it is useful to inform other developers that someone is currently looking at the errors for a build. CDash implements a simple note mechanism for that purpose:

1. Login to CDash.

2. On the dashboard project page, click on the build name that you would like to add the note to.

3. Click on the [Add a Note to this Build] link, located next to the current build matrix (see thumbnail).

4. Enter a short message that will be added as a note.

5. Select the status of the note: Simple note, Fix in progress, Fixed.

6. Click on "Add Note".

10.12.8 Logging

CDash supports an internal logging mechanism using the error_log() PHP function. Any critical SQL errors are logged. By default, the CDash log file is located in the backup directory under the name `cdash.log`. The location of the log file can be modified by changing the variable in the `config.local.php` configuration file.

```
$CDASH_BACKUP_DIRECTORY='/var/temp/cdashbackup/log';
```

The log file can be accessed directly from CDash if the log file is in the standard location:

1. Log into CDash as administrator.

2. Click on [CDash logs] in the administration section.

3. Click on cdash.log to see the log file.

CDash 2.0 introduced a log file rotation feature.

10.12.9 Test Timing

CDash supports checks on the duration of tests. CDash keeps the current weighted average of the mean and standard deviation for the time each test takes to run in the database. In order to keep the computation as efficient as possible the following formula is used, which only involves the previous build.

```
// alpha is the current "window" for the computation
// By default, alpha is 0.3
newMean = (1-alpha)*oldMean + alpha*currentTime

newSD = sqrt((1-alpha)*SD*SD +
  alpha*(currentTime-newMean)*(currentTime-newMean)
```

A test is defined as having failed timing based on the following logic:

```
if previousSD < thresholdSD then previousSD = thresholdSD
if currentTime > previousMean+multiplier*previousSD then fail
```

10.12.10 Mobile Support

Since CDash is written using template layers via XSLT, developing new layouts is as simple as adding new rendering templates. As a demonstration, an iPhone web template is provided with the current version of CDash.

```
http://mycdashserver/CDash/iphone
```

The main page shows a list of the public projects hosted on the server. Clicking on the name of a project loads its current dashboard. In the same manner, clicking on a given build displays more detailed information about that build. As of this writing, the ability to login and to access private sections of CDash are not supported with this layout.

10.12.11 Backing up CDash

All of the data (except the logs) used by CDash is stored in its database. It is important to backup the database regularly, especially so before performing a CDash upgrade. There are a couple of ways to backup a MySQL database. The easiest is to use the mysqldump[3] command:

```
mysqldump -r cdashbackup.sql cdash
```

If you are using MyISAM tables exclusively, you can copy the CDash directory in your MySQL data directory. Note that you need to shutdown MySQL before doing the copy so that no file could be changed during the copy. Similarly to MySQL, PostGreSQL has a pg_dump utility:

```
pg_dump -U posgreSQL_user cdash > cdashbackup.sql
```

10.12.12 Upgrading CDash

When a new version of CDash is released or if you decide to update from the SVN repository, CDash will warn you on the front page if the current database needs to be upgraded. When upgrading to a new release version the following steps should be taken:

1. Backup your SQL database (see previous section).

2. Backup your `config.local.php` (or `config.php`) configuration files.

3. Replace your current cdash directory with the latest version and copy the `config.local.php` in the cdash directory.

4. Navigate your browser to your CDash page. (e.g. http://localhost/CDash).

5. Note the version number on the main page, it should match the version that you are upgrading to.

6. The following message may appear: "The current database shema doesn't match the version of CDash you are running, upgrade your database structure in the Administration panel of CDash." This is a helpful reminder to perform the following steps.

7. Login to CDash as administrator.

8. In the 'Administration' section, click on '[CDash Maintenance]'.

9. Click on 'Upgrade CDash': this process might take some time depending on the size of your database (do not close your browser).

   • Progress messages may appear while CDash performs the upgrade.

---

[3]http://dev.mysql.com/doc/refman/5.1/en/mysqldump.html

Figure 10.11: Example of dashboard on the iPhone

- If the upgrade process takes too long you can check in the `backup/cdash.log` file to see where the process is taking a long time and/or failing.

- It has been reported that on some systems the spinning icon never turns into a check mark. Please check the `cdash.log` for the "Upgrade done." string if you feel that the upgrade is taking too long.

- On a 50GB database the upgrade might take up to 2 hours.

10. Some web browsers might have issues when upgrading (with some javascript variables not being passed correctly), in that case you can perform individual updates. For example, upgrading from CDash 1-2 to 1-4:

```
http://mywebsite.com/CDash/backwardCompatibilityTools.php?upgrade-1-4=1
```

10.12.13 CDash Maintenance

Database maintenance: we recommend that you perform database optimization (reindexing, purging, etc.) regularly to maintain a stable database. MySQL has a utility called `mysqlcheck`, and PostgreSQL has several utilities such as `vacuumdb`.

Deleting builds with incorrect dates: some builds might be submitted to CDash with the wrong date, either because the date in the XML file is incorrect or the timezone was not recognized by CDash (mainly by PHP). These builds will not show up in any dashboard because the start time is bogus. In order to remove these builds:

1. Login to CDash as administrator.

2. Click on [CDash maintenance] in the administration section.

3. Click on 'Delete builds with wrong start date'.

Recompute test timing: if you just upgraded CDash you might notice that the current submissions are showing a high number of failing test due to time defects. This is because CDash does not have enough sample points to compute the mean and standard deviation for each test, in particular the standard deviation might be very small (probably zero for the first few samples). You should turn the "enable test timing" off for about a week, or until you get enough build submissions and CDash has calculated an approximate mean and standard deviation for each test time.

The other option is to force CDash to compute the mean and standard deviation for each test for the past few days. Be warned that this process may take a long time, depending on the number of test and projects involved. In order to recompute the test timing:

1. Login to CDash as administrator.

2. Click on [CDash maintenance] in the administration section.

3. Specify the number of days (default is 4) to recompute the test timings for.

4. Click on "Compute test timing". When the process is done the new mean, standard deviation, and status should be updated for the tests submitted during this period.

Automatic build removal.

In order to keep the database at a reasonable size, CDash can automatically purge old builds. There are currently two ways to setup automatic removal of builds: without a cronjob, edit the `config.local.php` and add/edit the following line

```
$CDASH_AUTOREMOVE_BUILDS='1';
```

CDash will automatically remove builds on the first submission of the day. Note that removing builds might add an extra load on the database, or slow down the current submission process if your database is large and the number of submissions is high. If you can use a cronjob the PHP command line tool can be used to trigger build removals at a convenient time. For example, removing the builds for all the projects at 6am every Sunday:

```
0 6 * * 0 php5 /var/www/CDash/autoRemoveBuilds.php all
```

Note that the 'all' parameter can be changed to a specific project name in order to purge builds from a single project.

CDash XML Schema

The XML parsers in CDash can be easily extended to support new features. The current XML schemas generated by CTest, and their features as described in the book, are located at:

```
http://public.kitware.com/Wiki/CDash:XML
```

10.12.14 Subprojects

CDash (versions 1.4 and later) supports splitting projects into subprojects. Some of the subprojects may in turn depend on other subprojects. A typical real life project consists of libraries, executables, test suites, documentation, web pages, and installers. Organizing your project into well-defined subprojects and presenting the results of nightly builds on a CDash dashboard can help identify where the problems are at different levels of granularity.

A project with subprojects has a different view for its top level CDash page than a project without any. It contains a summary row for the project as a whole, and then one summary row for each subproject.

Organizing and defining subprojects

To add subproject organization to your project, you must: (1) define the subprojects for CDash, so that it knows how to display them properly and (2) use build scripts with CTest to submit subproject builds of your project. Some (re-)organization of your project's CMakeLists.txt files may also be necessary to allow building of your project by subprojects.

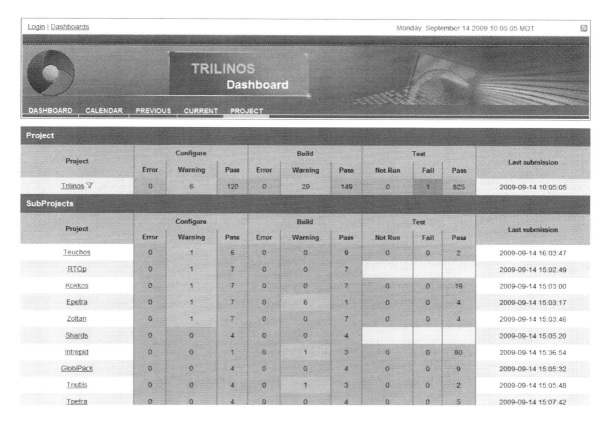

Figure 10.12: Main project page with subprojects

There are two ways to define subprojects and their dependencies: interactively in the CDash GUI when logged in as a project administrator, or by submitting a `Project.xml` file describing the subprojects and dependencies.

Adding Subprojects Interactively

As a project administrator, a "Manage subprojects" button will appear for each of your projects on the My CDash page. Clicking the Manage Subprojects button opens the manage subproject page, where you may add new subprojects or establish dependencies between existing subprojects for any project that you are an administrator of. There are two tabs on this page: one for viewing the current subprojects along with their dependencies, and one for creating new subprojects.

To add subprojects, for instance two subprojects called Exes and Libs, and to make Exes depend on Libs, the following steps are necessary:

- Click the "Add a subproject" tab.
- Type "Exes" in the "Add a subproject" edit field.
- Click the "Add subproject" button.
- Click the "Add a subproject" tab.
- Type "Libs" in the "Add a subproject" edit field.
- Click the "Add Subproject" button.
- In the "Exes" row of the "Current Subprojects" tab, choose "Libs" from the "Add dependency" drop down list and click the "Add dependency" button.

To remove a dependency or a subproject, click on the "X" next to the item you wish to delete.

Adding Subprojects Automatically

Another way to define CDash subprojects and their dependencies is to submit a "Project.xml" file along with the usual submission files that CTest sends when it submits a build to CDash. To define the same two subprojects as in the interactive example above (Exes and Libs) with the same dependency (Exes depend on Libs), the `Project.xml` file would look like the following example:

```
<Project name="Tutorial">
  <SubProject name="Libs"></SubProject>
  <SubProject name="Exes">
    <Dependency name="Libs">
  </SubProject>
</Project>
```

Once the `Project.xml` file is written or generated, it can be submitted to CDash from a ctest -S script using the new FILES argument to the `ctest_submit` command, or directly from the ctest command line in a build tree configured for dashboard submission.

From inside a ctest -S script:

```
ctest_submit(FILES "${CTEST_BINARY_DIRECTORY}/Project.xml")
```

From the command line:

```
cd ../Project-build
ctest --extra-submit Project.xml
```

CDash will automatically add subprojects and dependencies according to the Project.xml file. CDash will also remove any subprojects or dependencies not defined in the Project.xml file. Additionally, if the same Project.xml is submitted multiple times, the second and subsequent submissions will have no observable effect: the first submission adds/modifies the data, the second and later submissions send the same data, so no changes are necessary. CDash tracks changes to the subproject definitions over time to allow for projects to evolve. If you view dashboards from a past date, CDash will present the project/subproject views according to the subproject definitions in effect on that date.

10.12.15 Using ctest_submit with PARTS and FILES

In CTest version 2.8 and later, the ctest_submit() (page 354) command supports new PARTS and FILES arguments. With PARTS, you can send any subset of the xml files with each ctest_submit call. Previously, all parts would be sent with any call to ctest_submit. Typically, the script would wait until all dashboard stages were complete and then call ctest_submit once to send the results of all stages at the end of the run. Now, a script may call ctest_submit with PARTS to do partial submissions of subsets of the results. For example, you can submit configure results after ctest_configure() (page 352), build results after ctest_build() (page 351), and test results after ctest_test() (page 355). This allows for information to be posted as the builds progress.

With FILES, you can send arbitrary XML files to CDash. In addition to the standard build result XML files that CTest sends, CDash also handles the new Project.xml file that describes subprojects and dependencies. Prior to the addition of the ctest_submit PARTS handling, a typical dashboard script would contain a single ctest_submit() call on its last line

```
ctest_start (Experimental)
ctest_update (SOURCE "${CTEST_SOURCE_DIRECTORY}")
ctest_configure (BUILD "${CTEST_BINARY_DIRECTORY}")
ctest_build (BUILD "${CTEST_BINARY_DIRECTORY}")
ctest_test (BUILD "${CTEST_BINARY_DIRECTORY}")
ctest_submit ()
```

Now, submissions can occur incrementally, with each part of the submission sent piecemeal as it becomes available:

```
ctest_start (Experimental)
ctest_update (SOURCE "${CTEST_SOURCE_DIRECTORY}")
ctest_configure (BUILD "${CTEST_BINARY_DIRECTORY}")
ctest_submit (PARTS Update Configure Notes)
```

```
ctest_build (BUILD "${CTEST_BINARY_DIRECTORY}" APPEND)
ctest_submit (PARTS Build)

ctest_test (BUILD "${CTEST_BINARY_DIRECTORY}")
ctest_submit (PARTS Test)
```

Submitting incrementally by parts means that you can inspect the results of the configure stage live on the CDash dashboard while the build is still in progress. Likewise, you can inspect the results of the build stage live while the tests are still running. When submitting by parts, it's important to use the APPEND keyword in the ctest_build command. If you don't use APPEND, then CDash will erase any existing build with the same build name, site name, and build stamp when it receives the Build.xml file.

10.12.16 Splitting Your Project into Multiple Subprojects

One ctest_build() (page 351) invocation that builds everything, followed by one ctest_test() (page 355) invocation that tests everything is sufficient for a project that has no subprojects, but if you want to submit results on a per-subproject basis to CDash, you will have to make some changes to your project and test scripts. For your project you need to identify what targets are part of what sub-projects. If you organize your CMakeLists files such that you have a target to build for each subproject, and you can derive (or look up) the name of that target based on the subproject name, then revising your script to separate it into multiple smaller configure/build/test chunks should be relatively painless. To do this, you can modify your CMakeLists files in various ways depending on your needs. The most common changes are listed below.

CMakeLists.txt modifications

- Name targets the same as subprojects, base target names on subproject names, or provide a look up mechanism to map from subproject name to target name.

- Possibly add custom targets to aggregate existing targets into subprojects, using add_dependencies to say which existing targets the custom target depends on.

- Add the LABELS target property to targets with a value of the subproject name.

- Add the LABELS test property to tests with a value of the subproject name.

Next, you need to modify your CTest scripts that run your dashboards. To split your one large monolithic build into smaller subproject builds, you can use a foreach loop in your CTest driver script. To help you iterate over your subprojects, CDash provides a variable named CTEST_PROJECT_SUBPROJECTS in CTestConfig.cmake. Given the above example, CDash produces a variable like this:

```
set (CTEST_PROJECT_SUBPROJECTS Libs Exes)
```

CDash orders the elements in this list such that the independent subprojects (that do not depend on any other subprojects) are first, followed by subprojects that depend only on the independent subprojects, and after that subprojects that depend on those. The same logic continues until all subprojects are listed exactly once in this list in an order that makes sense for building them sequentially, one after the other.

To facilitate building just the targets associated with a subproject, use the variable named CTEST_BUILD_TARGET to tell:command:*ctest_build* what to build. To facilitate running just the tests associated with a subproject, assign the LABELS test property to your tests and use the new INCLUDE_LABEL argument to ctest_test() (page 355).

ctest driver script modifications

- Iterate over the subprojects in dependency order (from independent to most dependent...).

- Set the SubProject and Label global properties – CTest uses these properties to submit the results to the correct subproject on the CDash server.

- Build the target(s) for this subproject: compute the name of the target to build from the subproject name, set CTEST_BUILD_TARGET, call ctest_build.

- Run the tests for this subproject using the INCLUDE or INCLUDE_LABEL arguments to ctest_ctest.

- Use ctest_submit with the PARTS argument to submit partial results as they complete.

To illustrate this, the following example shows the changes required to split a build into smaller pieces. Assume that the subproject name is the same as the target name required to build the subproject's components. For example, here is a snippet from CMakeLists.txt, in the hypothetical Tutorial project. The only additions necessary (since the target names are the same as the subproject names) are the calls to set_property() (page 329) for each target and each test.

```
# "Libs" is the library name (therefore a target name) and
# the subproject name
add_library (Libs ...)
set_property (TARGET Libs PROPERTY LABELS Libs)
add_test (LibsTest1 ...)
add_test (LibsTest2 ...)
set_property (TEST LibsTest1 LibsTest2 PROPERTY LABELS Libs)

# "Exes" is the executable name (therefore a target name)
# and the subproject name
add_executable (Exes ...)
target_link_libraries (Exes Libs)
set_property (TARGET Exes PROPERTY LABELS Exes)
add_test (ExesTest1 ...)
add_test (ExesTest2 ...)
set_property (TEST ExesTest1 ExesTest2 PROPERTY LABELS Exes)
```

Here is an example of what the CTest driver script might look like before and after organizing this project into subprojects. Before the changes

```
ctest_start (Experimental)
ctest_update (SOURCE "${CTEST_SOURCE_DIRECTORY}")
ctest_configure (BUILD "${CTEST_BINARY_DIRECTORY}")
# builds *all* targets: Libs and Exes
ctest_build (BUILD "${CTEST_BINARY_DIRECTORY}")
```

```
# runs *all* tests
ctest_test (BUILD "${CTEST_BINARY_DIRECTORY}")
# submits everything all at once at the end
ctest_submit ()
```

After the changes:

```
ctest_start (Experimental)
ctest_update (SOURCE "${CTEST_SOURCE_DIRECTORY}")
ctest_submit (PARTS Update Notes)

# to get CTEST_PROJECT_SUBPROJECTS definition:
include ("${CTEST_SOURCE_DIRECTORY}/CTestConfig.cmake")

foreach (subproject ${CTEST_PROJECT_SUBPROJECTS})
  set_property (GLOBAL PROPERTY SubProject ${subproject})
  set_property (GLOBAL PROPERTY Label ${subproject})

  ctest_configure (BUILD "${CTEST_BINARY_DIRECTORY}")
  ctest_submit (PARTS Configure)

  set (CTEST_BUILD_TARGET "${subproject}")
  ctest_build (BUILD "${CTEST_BINARY_DIRECTORY}" APPEND)
    # builds target ${CTEST_BUILD_TARGET}
  ctest_submit (PARTS Build)

  ctest_test (BUILD "${CTEST_BINARY_DIRECTORY}"
    INCLUDE_LABEL "${subproject}"
  )
# runs only tests that have a LABELS property matching
# "${subproject}"
  ctest_submit (PARTS Test)
endforeach ()
```

In some projects, more than one ctest_build step may be required to build all the pieces of the subproject. For example, in Trilinos, each subproject builds the ${subproject}_libs target, and then builds the all target to build all the configured executables in the test suite. They also configure dependencies such that only the executables that need to be built for the currently configured packages build when the all target is built.

Normally, if you submit multiple Build.xml files to CDash with the same exact build stamp, it will delete the existing entry and add the new entry in its place. In the case where multiple ctest_build steps are required, each with their own ctest_submit(PARTS Build) call, use the APPEND keyword argument in all of the ctest_build calls that belong together. The APPEND flag tells CDash to accumulate the results from multiple submissions and display the aggregation of all of them in one row on the dashboard. From CDash's perspective, multiple ctest_build calls (with the same build stamp and subproject and APPEND turned on) result in a single CDash build.

Adopt some of these tips and techniques in your favorite CMake-based project:

- LABELS is a new CMake/CTest property that applies to source files, targets and tests. Labels are sent to CDash inside the resulting xml files.

- Use ctest_submit (PARTS ...) to do incremental submissions. Results are available for viewing on the dashboards sooner. Don't forget to use APPEND in your ctest_build calls when submitting by parts.

- Use INCLUDE_LABEL with ctest_test to run only the tests with labels that match the regular expression.

- Use CTEST_BUILD_TARGET to build your subprojects one at a time, submitting subproject dashboards along the way.

PORTING CMAKE TO NEW PLATFORMS AND LANGUAGES

In order to generate build files for a particular system, CMake needs to determine what system it is running on and what compiler tools to use for enabled languages. To do this CMake loads a series of files containing CMake code from the Modules directory. This all has to happen before the first try-compile or try-run is executed. To avoid having to re-compute all of this information for each try-compile and for subsequent runs of CMake, the discovered values are stored in several configured files that are read each time CMake is run. These files are also copied into the try-compile and try-run directories. This chapter will describe how this process of system and tool discovery works. An understanding of the process is necessary to extend CMake to run on new platforms, and to add support for new languages.

11.1 The Determine System Process

The first thing CMake needs to do is to determine what platform it is running on and what the target platform is. Except for when you are cross compiling, the host platform and the target platform are identical. The host platform is determined by loading the `CMakeDetermineSystem.cmake` file. On POSIX systems, "uname" is used to get the name of the system. `CMAKE_HOST_SYSTEM_NAME` (page 651) is set to the result of uname -s, and `CMAKE_HOST_SYSTEM_VERSION` (page 652) is set to the result of uname -r. On Windows systems, `CMAKE_HOST_SYSTEM_NAME` is set to Windows and `CMAKE_HOST_SYSTEM_VERSION` is set to the value returned by the system function GetVersionEx. The variable `CMAKE_HOST_SYSTEM` (page 651) is set to a combination of `CMAKE_HOST_SYSTEM_NAME` and `CMAKE_HOST_SYSTEM_VERSION` as follows:

```
${CMAKE_HOST_SYSTEM_NAME}-${CMAKE_HOST_SYSTEM_VERSION}
```

Additionally, CMake tries to figure out the processor of the host. On POSIX systems it uses uname -m or uname -p to retrieve this information, while on Windows it uses the environment variable `PROCESSOR_ARCHITECTURE`. `CMAKE_HOST_SYSTEM_PROCESSOR` (page 651) holds the value of the result.

Now that CMake has the information about the host that it is running on, it needs to find this information for the target platform. The results will be stored in the `CMAKE_SYSTEM_NAME` (page 653), `CMAKE_SYSTEM_VERSION` (page 653), `CMAKE_SYSTEM` (page 653), and `CMAKE_SYSTEM_PROCESSOR` (page 653) variables, corresponding to the `CMAKE_HOST_SYSTEM_*` variables described above. See the "Cross compiling with CMake" chapter on how this is done when cross compiling. In all other cases the CMAKE_SYSTEM_* variables will be set to the value of their corresponding CMAKE_HOST_SYSTEM_* variable.

Once the CMAKE_SYSTEM information has been determined, CMakeSystem.cmake.in is configured into ${CMAKE_BINARY_DIR}/CMakeFiles/CMakeSystem.cmake. CMake versions prior to 2.6.0 did not support cross compiling, and so only the CMAKE_SYSTEM_* set of variables was available.

11.2 The Enable Language Process

After the platform has been determined, the next step is to enable all languages specified in the project() (page 327) command. For each language specified, CMake loads CMakeDetermine(LANG)Compiler.cmake where LANG is the name of the language specified in the project() (page 327) command. For example with project (f Fortran), the file is called CMakeDetermineFortranCompiler.cmake. This file discovers the compiler and tools that will be used to compile files for the particular language. Starting with version 2.6.0 CMake tries to identify the compiler for C, C++ and Fortran not only by its filename, but by compiling some source code, which is named CMake(LANG)CompilerId.(LANG_SUFFIX). If this succeeds, it will return a unique id for every compiler supported by CMake. Once the compiler has been determined for a language, CMake configures the file CMake(LANG)Compiler.cmake.in into CMake(LANG)Compiler.cmake.

After the platform and compiler tools have been determined, CMake loads CMakeSystemSpecificInformation.cmake, which in turn will load ${CMAKE_SYSTEM_NAME}.cmake from the platform subdirectory of modules if it exists for the platform. An example would be SunOS.cmake. This file contains OS specific information about compiler flags, creation of executables, libraries, and object files.

Next, CMake loads CMake(LANG)Information.cmake for each LANG that was enabled, which loads ${CMAKE_SYSTEM_NAME}-${COMPILER_ID}-LANG-${CMAKE_SYSTEM_PROCESSOR}.cmake if it exists, and after that ${CMAKE_SYSTEM_NAME}-${COMPILER_ID}-LANG.cmake. In these file names COMPILER_ID references the compiler identification determined as described above. The CMake(LANG)Information.cmake file contains default rules for creating executables, libraries, and object files on most UNIX systems. The defaults can be overridden by setting values in either ${CMAKE_SYSTEM_NAME}.cmake or ${CMAKE_SYSTEM_NAME}-${COMPILER_ID}-LANG.cmake.

${CMAKE_SYSTEM_NAME}-${COMPILER_ID}-LANG-${CMAKE_SYSTEM_PROCESSOR}.cmake is intended to be used only for cross compiling, and is loaded before ${CMAKE_SYSTEM_NAME}-${COMPILER_ID}-LANG.cmake, so variables can be set up which can then be used in the rule variables.

In addition to the files with the COMPILER_ID in their name, CMake also supports these files using the COMPILER_BASE_NAME. COMPILER_BASE_NAME is the name of the compiler with no path information. For example, cl would be the COMPILER_BASE_NAME for the Microsoft Windows compiler, and Windows-cl.cmake would be loaded. If a COMPILER_ID exists, it will be preferred over the

COMPILER_BASE_NAME, since on one side the same compiler can have different names, but there can be also different compilers all with the same name. This means, if

```
${CMAKE_SYSTEM_NAME}-${COMPILER_ID}-LANG-${CMAKE_SYSTEM_PROCESSOR}.cmake
```

was not found, CMake tries

```
${CMAKE_SYSTEM_NAME}-${COMPILER_BASE_NAME}.cmake
```

and if

```
${CMAKE_SYSTEM_NAME}-${COMPILER_ID}-LANG.cmake
```

was not found, CMake tries

```
${CMAKE_SYSTEM_NAME}-${COMPILER_BASE_NAME}.cmake.
```

CMake(LANG)Information.cmake and associated Platform files define special CMake variables, called rule variables. A rule variable consists of a list of commands separated by spaces and each enclosed by quotes. In addition to the normal variable expansion performed by CMake, some special tag variables are expanded by the Makefile generator. Tag variables have the syntax of <NAME>, where NAME is the name of the variable. An example rule variable is CMAKE_CXX_CREATE_SHARED_LIBRARY, and the default setting is

```
set (CMAKE_CXX_CREATE_SHARED_LIBRARY
    "<CMAKE_CXX_COMPILER> <CMAKE_SHARED_LIBRARY_CXX_FLAGS>
     <LINK_FLAGS> <CMAKE_SHARED_LIBRARY_CREATE_CXX_FLAGS>
     <CMAKE_SHARED_LIBRARY_SONAME_CXX_FLAG><TARGET_SONAME> -o
     <TARGET> <OBJECTS> <LINK_LIBRARIES>")
```

At this point, CMake has determined the system it is running on, the tools it will be using to compile the enabled languages, and the rules to use the tools. This means there is enough information for CMake to perform a try-compile. CMake will now test the detected compilers for each enabled language by loading CMakeTest(LANG)Compiler.cmake. This file will usually run a try-compile on a simple source file for the given language to make sure the chosen compiler actually works.

Once the platform has been determined, and the compilers have been tested, CMake loads a few more files that can be used to change some of the computed values. The first file that is loaded is CMake(PROJECTNAME)Compatibility.cmake, where PROJECTNAME is the name given to the top level PROJECT command in the project. The project compatibility file is used to add backwards compatibility fixes into CMake. For example, if a new version of CMake fails to build a project that the previous version of CMake could build, then fixes can be added on a per project basis to CMake. The last file that is loaded is ${CMAKE_USER_MAKE_RULES_OVERRIDE}. This file is an optionally user supplied variable, that can allow a project to make very specific platform-based changes to the build rules.

11.3 Porting to a New Platform

Many common platforms are already supported by CMake. However, you may come across a compiler or platform that has not yet been used. If the compiler uses an Integrated Development Environment (IDE), then you will have to extend CMake from the C++ level. However, if the compiler supports a standard make program, then you can specify in CMake the rules to use to compile object code and build libraries by creating CMake configuration files. These files are written using the CMake language with a few special tags that are expanded when the Makefiles are created by CMake. If you run CMake on your system and get a message like the following, you will want to read how to create platform specific settings.

```
System is unknown to CMake, create:
Modules/Platform/MySystem.cmake
to use this system, please send your config file to
cmake@www.cmake.org so it can be added to CMake
```

At a minimum you will need to create the `Platform/${CMAKE_SYSTEM_NAME}.cmake` file for the new platform. Depending on the tools for the platform, you may also want to create `Platform/${CMAKE_SYSTEM_NAME}-${COMPILER_BASE_NAME}.cmake`. On most systems, there is a vendor compiler and the GNU compiler. The rules for both of these compilers can be put in `Platform/${CMAKE_SYSTEM_NAME}.cmake` instead of creating separate files for each of the compilers. For most new systems or compilers, if they follow the basic UNIX compiler flags you will only need to specify the system specific flags for shared library and module creation.

The following example is from `Platform/IRIX.cmake`. This file specifies several flags, and also one CMake rule variable. The rule variable tells CMake how to use the IRIX CC compiler to create a static library, which is required for template instantiation to work with IRIX CC.

```
# there is no -ldl required on this system
set (CMAKE_DL_LIBS "")

# Specify the flag to create a shared c library
set (CMAKE_SHARED_LIBRARY_CREATE_C_FLAGS
    "-shared -rdata_shared")

# Specify the flag to create a shared c++ library
set (CMAKE_SHARED_LIBRARY_CREATE_CXX_FLAGS
    "-shared -rdata_shared")

# specify the flag to specify run time paths for shared
# libraries -rpath
set (CMAKE_SHARED_LIBRARY_RUNTIME_C_FLAG "-Wl,-rpath,")

# specify a separator for paths on the -rpath, if empty
# then -rpath will be repeated.
set (CMAKE_SHARED_LIBRARY_RUNTIME_C_FLAG_SEP "")

# if the compiler is not GNU, then specify the initial flags
if (NOT CMAKE_COMPILER_IS_GNUCXX)
```

```
# use the CC compiler to create static library
set (CMAKE_CXX_CREATE_STATIC_LIBRARY
     "<CMAKE_CXX_COMPILER> -ar -o <TARGET> <OBJECTS>")

# initializes flags for the native compiler
set (CMAKE_CXX_FLAGS_INIT "")
set (CMAKE_CXX_FLAGS_DEBUG_INIT "-g")
set (CMAKE_CXX_FLAGS_MINSIZEREL_INIT "-O3 -DNDEBUG")
set (CMAKE_CXX_FLAGS_RELEASE_INIT "-O2 -DNDEBUG")
set (CMAKE_CXX_FLAGS_RELWITHDEBINFO_INIT "-O2")
endif (NOT CMAKE_COMPILER_IS_GNUCXX)
```

11.4 Adding a New Language

In addition to porting CMake to new platforms, a user may want to add a new language. This can be done either through the use of custom commands, or by defining a new language for CMake. Once a new language is defined, the standard add_library() (page 274) and add_executable() (page 273) commands can be used to create libraries and executables for the new language. To add a new language, you need to create four files. The name LANG has to match- in exact case- the name used in the PROJECT() (page 327) command to enable the language. For example, Fortran has the file CMakeDeterminFortranCompiler.cmake, and it is enabled with a call like this project (f Fortran). The four files are as follows:

CMakeDetermine(LANG)Compiler.cmake This file will find the path to the compiler for LANG and then configure CMake(LANG)Compiler.cmake.in.

CMake(LANG)Compiler.cmake.in This file should be used as input to a configure file call in the CMakeDetermine(LANG)Compiler.cmake file. It is used to store compiler information and is copied down into try-compile directories so that try compiles do not need to re-determine and test the LANG.

CMakeTest(LANG)Compiler.cmake This should make use of a try compile command to make sure the compiler and tools are working. If the tools are working, the following variable should be set in this way:

```
set (CMAKE_(LANG)_COMPILER_WORKS 1 CACHE INTERNAL "")
```

CMake(LANG)Information.cmake Set values for the following rule variables for LANG:

```
CMAKE_(LANG)_CREATE_SHARED_LIBRARY
CMAKE_(LANG)_CREATE_SHARED_MODULE
CMAKE_(LANG)_CREATE_STATIC_LIBRARY
CMAKE_(LANG)_COMPILE_OBJECT
CMAKE_(LANG)_LINK_EXECUTABLE
```

11.5 Rule Variable Listing

For each language that CMake supports, the following rule variables are expanded into build Makefiles at generation time. LANG is the name used in the PROJECT (name LANG) command. CMake currently supports CXX, C, Fortran, and Java as values for LANG.

11.5.1 General Tag Variables

The following set of variables will be expanded by CMake.

<TARGET> The name of the target being built (this may be a full path).

<TARGET_QUOTED> The name of the target being built (this may be a full path) double quoted.

<TARGET_BASE> This is replaced by the name of the target without a suffix.

<TARGET_SONAME> This is replaced by CMAKE_SHARED_LIBRARY_SONAME_(LANG)_FLAG

<OBJECTS> This is the list of object files to be linked into the target.

<OBJECTS_QUOTED> This is the list of object files to be linked into the target double quoted.

<OBJECT> This is the name of the object file to be built.

<LINK_LIBRARIES> This is the list of libraries that are linked into an executable or shared object.

<FLAGS> This contains the command line flags for the linker or compiler.

<LINK_FLAGS> These are the flags used at link time.

<SOURCE> The source file name.

11.5.2 Language Specific Information

The following set of variables related to the compiler tools will also be expanded.

<CMAKE_(LANG)_COMPILER> This is the (LANG) compiler command.

<CMAKE_SHARED_LIBRARY_CREATE_(LANG)_FLAGS> These are the flags used to create a shared library for (LANG) code.

<CMAKE_SHARED_MODULE_CREATE_(LANG)_FLAGS> These are the flags used to create a shared module for (LANG) code.

<CMAKE_(LANG)_LINK_FLAGS> These are the flags used to link a (LANG) program.

<CMAKE_AR> This is the command to create a .a archive file.

<CMAKE_RANLIB> This is the command to ranlib a .a archive file.

11.6 Compiler and Platform Examples

11.6.1 Como Compiler

A good example to look at is the como compiler on Linux, found in `Modules/Platforms/Linux-como.cmake`. This compiler requires several non-standard commands when creating libraries and executables in order to instantiate C++ templates.

```
# create a shared C++ library
set (CMAKE_CXX_CREATE_SHARED_LIBRARY
    "<CMAKE_CXX_COMPILER> --prelink_objects <OBJECTS>"
    "<CMAKE_CXX_COMPILER>
<CMAKE_SHARED_LIBRARY_CREATE_CXX_FLAGS> <LINK_FLAGS> -o <TARGET>
<OBJECTS> <LINK_LIBRARIES>")

# create a C++ static library
set (CMAKE_CXX_CREATE_STATIC_LIBRARY
    "<CMAKE_CXX_COMPILER> --prelink_objects <OBJECTS>"
    "<CMAKE_AR> cr <TARGET> <LINK_FLAGS> <OBJECTS> "
    "<CMAKE_RANLIB> <TARGET> ")

set (CMAKE_CXX_LINK_EXECUTABLE
    "<CMAKE_CXX_COMPILER> --prelink_objects <OBJECTS>"
    "<CMAKE_CXX_COMPILER> <CMAKE_CXX_LINK_FLAGS> <LINK_FLAGS>
<FLAGS> <OBJECTS> -o <TARGET> <LINK_LIBRARIES>")

set (CMAKE_SHARED_LIBRARY_RUNTIME_FLAG "")
set (CMAKE_SHARED_LIBRARY_C_FLAGS "")
set (CMAKE_SHARED_LIBRARY_LINK_FLAGS "")
```

This overrides the creation of libraries (shared and static), and the linking of executable C++ programs. You can see that the linking process of executables and shared libraries requires an extra command that calls the compiler with the flag `--prelink_objects`, and gets all of the object files passed to it.

11.6.2 Borland Compiler

The full Borland compiler rules can be found in `Platforms/Windows-bcc32.cmake`. The following code is an excerpt from that file, showing some of the features used to define rules for the Borland compiler set.

```
set (CMAKE_CXX_CREATE_SHARED_LIBRARY
    "<CMAKE_CXX_COMPILER> ${CMAKE_START_TEMP_FILE}-e<TARGET>
 -tWD  <LINK_FLAGS> -tWR <LINK_LIBRARIES> <OBJECTS>${CMAKE_END_TEMP_FILE}"
 "implib -c -w <TARGET_BASE>.lib <TARGET_BASE>.dll"
)

set (CMAKE_CXX_CREATE_SHARED_MODULE
```

```
        ${CMAKE_CXX_CREATE_SHARED_LIBRARY})

# create a C shared library
set (CMAKE_C_CREATE_SHARED_LIBRARY
 "<CMAKE_C_COMPILER> ${CMAKE_START_TEMP_FILE}-e<TARGET> -tWD
 <LINK_FLAGS> -tWR <LINK_LIBRARIES>
 <OBJECTS>${CMAKE_END_TEMP_FILE}"
 "implib -c -w <TARGET_BASE>.lib <TARGET_BASE>.dll"
)

# create a C++ static library
set (CMAKE_CXX_CREATE_STATIC_LIBRARY  "tlib
${CMAKE_START_TEMP_FILE}/p512 <LINK_FLAGS> /a <TARGET_QUOTED>
<OBJECTS_QUOTED>${CMAKE_END_TEMP_FILE}")

# compile a C++ file into an object file
set (CMAKE_CXX_COMPILE_OBJECT
    "<CMAKE_CXX_COMPILER>  ${CMAKE_START_TEMP_FILE}-DWIN32 -P
<FLAGS>   -o<OBJECT> -c <SOURCE>${CMAKE_END_TEMP_FILE}")
```

11.7 Extending CMake

Occasionally you will come across a situation where you want to do something during your build process that CMake cannot seem to handle. Examples of this include creating wrappers for C++ classes to make them available to other languages, or creating bindings for C++ classes to support runtime introspection. In these cases you may want to extend CMake by adding your own commands. CMake supports this capability through its C plugin API. Using this API, a project can extend CMake to add specialized commands to handle project-specific tasks.

A loaded command in CMake is essentially a C code plugin that is compiled into a shared library (a.k.a. DLL). This shared library can then be loaded into the running CMake to provide the functionality of the loaded command. Creating a loaded command is a two step process. You must first write the C code and CMakeLists file for the command, and then place it in your source tree. Next you must modify your project's CMakeLists file to compile the loaded command and load it. We will start by looking at writing the plugin. Before resorting to creating a loaded command, you should first see if you can accomplish what you want with a macro. With the commands in CMake a macro/function has almost the same level of flexibility as a loaded command, but does not require compilation or as much complexity. You can almost always, and should, use a macro/function instead of a loaded command.

11.7.1 Creating a Loaded Command

While CMake itself is written in C++, we suggest that you write your plugins using only C code. This avoids a number of portability and compiler issues that can plague C++ plugins being loaded into CMake executables. The API for a plugin is defined in the header file cmCPluginAPI.h. This file defines all of the CMake functions that you can invoke from your plugin. It also defines the cmLoadedCommandInfo structure that is passed to a plugin. Before going into detail about these functions, consider the following simple plugin:

```
#include "cmCPluginAPI.h"
static int InitialPass(void *inf, void *mf,
                       int argc, char *argv[])
{
  cmLoadedCommandInfo *info = (cmLoadedCommandInfo *)inf;
  info->CAPI->AddDefinition(mf, "FOO", "BAR");

  return 1;
}
void CM_PLUGIN_EXPORT
HELLO_WORLDInit(cmLoadedCommandInfo *info)
{
  info->InitialPass = InitialPass;
  info->Name = "HELLO_WORLD";
}
```

First this plugin includes the cmCPluginAPI.h file to get the definitions and structures required for a plugin. Next it defines a static function called InitialPass that will be called whenever this loaded command is invoked. This function is always passed four parameters: the cmLoadedCommandInfo structure, the Makefile, the number of arguments, and the list of arguments. Inside this function, we typecast the inf argument to its actual type and then use it to invoke the C API (CAPI) AddDefinition function. This function will set the variable FOO to the value of BAR in the current cmMakefile instance.

The second function is called HELLO_WORLDInit, and it will be called when the plugin is loaded. The name of this function must exactly match the name of the loaded command with Init appended. In this example the name of the command is HELLO_WORLD, so the function is named HELLO_WORLDInit. This function will be called as soon as your command is loaded. It is responsible for initializing the elements of the cmLoadedCommandInfo structure. In this example it sets the InitialPass member to the address of the InitialPass function defined above. It will then set the name of the command by setting the Name member to HELLO_WORLD.

11.7.2 Using a Loaded Command

Now let us consider how to use this new HELLO_WORLD command in a project. The basic process is that CMake will have to compile the plugin into a shared library and then dynamically load it. To do this you first create a subdirectory in your project's source tree called CMake or CMakeCommands (by convention, any name can be used). Place the source code to your plugin in that directory. We recommend naming the file with the prefix cm and then the name of the command. For example, cmHELLO_WORLD.c. Then you must create a simple CMakeLists.txt file for this directory that includes instructions to build the shared library. Typically this will be the following

```
project (HELLO_WORLD)

set (CMAKE_CXX_FLAGS "${CMAKE_CXX_FLAGS}"
  "${CMAKE_ANSI_CXXFLAGS}"
```

```
  )
set (CMAKE_C_FLAGS "${CMAKE_C_FLAGS}"
  "${CMAKE_ANSI_CFLAGS}"
  )
include_directories (${CMAKE_ROOT}/include
  ${CMAKE_ROOT}/Source
  )

add_library (cmHELLO_WORLD MODULE cmHELLO_WORLD.c)
```

It is critical that you name the library cm, followed by the name of the command as shown in the add_library call in the above example (e.g. cmHELLO_WORLD). When CMake loads a command it assumes that the command is in a library named using that pattern. The next step is to modify your project's main CMakeLists file to compile and load the plugin. This can be accomplished with the following code:

```
# if the command has not been loaded, compile and load it
if (NOT COMMAND HELLO_WORLD)

  # try compiling it first
  try_compile (COMPILE_OK
    ${PROJECT_BINARY_DIR}/CMake
    ${PROJECT_SOURCE_DIR}/CMake
    HELLO_WORLD
    )

  # if it compiled OK then load it
  if (COMPILE_OK)
    load_command (HELLO_WORLD
      ${PROJECT_BINARY_DIR}/CMake
      ${PROJECT_BINARY_DIR}/CMake/Debug
      )

  # if it did not compile OK, then display an error
  else (COMPILE_OK)
    message ("error compiling HELLO_WORLD extension")
  endif (COMPILE_OK)

endif (NOT COMMAND HELLO_WORLD)
```

In the above example you would simply replace HELLO_WORLD with the name of your command and replace ${PROJECT_SOURCE_DIR}/CMake with the actual name of the subdirectory where you placed your loaded command. Now, let us look at creating loaded commands in more detail. We will start by looking at the cmLoadedCommandInfo structure.

```
typedef const char* (*CM_DOC_FUNCTION)();

typedef int (*CM_INITIAL_PASS_FUNCTION)(
    void *info, void *mf, int argc, char *[]);
```

```
typedef void (*CM_FINAL_PASS_FUNCTION)(
    void *info, void *mf);
typedef void (*CM_DESTRUCTOR_FUNCTION)(void *info);

typedef struct {
    unsigned long reserved1;
    unsigned long reserved2;
    cmCAPI *CAPI;
    int m_Inherited;
    CM_INITIAL_PASS_FUNCTION InitialPass;
    CM_FINAL_PASS_FUNCTION FinalPass;
    CM_DESTRUCTOR_FUNCTION Destructor;
    CM_DOC_FUNCTION GetTerseDocumentation;
    CM_DOC_FUNCTION GetFullDocumentation;
    const char *Name;
    char *Error;
    void *ClientData;
} cmLoadedCommandInfo;
```

The first two entries of the structure are reserved for future use. The next entry, CAPI, is a pointer to a structure containing pointers to all the CMake functions you can invoke from a plugin. The m_Inherited member only applies to CMake versions 2.0 and earlier. It can be set to indicate if this command should be inherited by subdirectories or not. If you are creating a command that will work with versions of CMake prior to 2.2 then you probably want to set this to zero. The next five members are pointers to functions that your plugin may provide. The InitialPass function must be provided, and it is invoked whenever your loaded command is invoked from a CMakeLists file. The FinalPass function is optional, and is invoked after configuration but before generation of the output. The Destructor function is optional, and will be invoked when your command is destroyed by CMake (typically on exit). It can be used to clean up any memory that you have allocated in the InitialPass or FinalPass. The next two functions are optional, and are used to provide documentation for your command. The Name member is used to store the name of your command. This is what will be compared against when parsing a CMakeLists file. It should be in all caps in keeping with CMake's naming conventions. The Error and ClientData members are used internally by CMake; you should not directly access them. Instead you can use the CAPI functions to manipulate them.

Let us consider some of the common CAPI functions you will use from within a loaded command. First, we will consider some utility functions that are provided specifically for loaded commands. Since loaded commands use a C interface they will receive arguments as (int argc, char *argv[]). For convenience, you can call GetTotalArgumentSize(argc, argv), which will return the total length of all the arguments. Likewise, some CAPI methods will return an (argc,argv) pair that you will be responsible for freeing. The FreeArguments(argc, argv) function can be used to free such return values. If your loaded command has a FinalPass(), then you might want to pass data from the InitialPass() to the FinalPass() invocation. This can be accomplished using the SetClientData(void *info, void *data) and void *GetClientData(void *info) functions. Since the client data is passed as a void * argument, any client data larger than a pointer must be allocated and then finally freed in your Destructor() function. Be aware that CMake will create multiple instances of your loaded command so using global variables or static variables is not recommended. If you should encounter an error in executing your loaded command, you can call `SetError(void *info, const char *errorString)` to pass an error message on to the user.

Another group of CAPI functions worth noting are the `cmSourceFile` functions. `cmSourceFile` is a C++ object that represents information about a single file including its full path, file extension, special compiler flags, etc. Some loaded commands will need to either create or access `cmSourceFile` instances. This can be done using the `void *CreateSourceFile()` and `void * GetSource (void *mf, const char *sourceName)` functions. Both of these functions return a pointer to a `cmSourceFile` as a `void *` return value. This pointer can then be passed into other functions that manipulate `cmSourceFiles` such as `SourceFileGetProperty()` or `SourceFileSetProperty()`.

TUTORIALS

This chapter provides a step-by-step tutorial that covers common build system issues that CMake helps address. Many of these topics have been introduced in prior chapters as separate issues, but seeing how they all work together in an example project can be very helpful. This tutorial can be found in the Tests/Tutorial directory of the CMake source code tree. Each step has its own subdirectory containing a complete copy of the tutorial for that step.

12.1 A Basic Starting Point (Step 1)

The most basic project is an executable built from source code files. For simple projects, a two line CMake-Lists file is all that is required. This will be the starting point for our tutorial. The CMakeLists file looks like

```
cmake_minimum_required (2.6)
project (Tutorial)

add_executable(Tutorial tutorial.cxx)
```

Note that this example uses lower case commands in the CMakeLists file. Upper, lower, and mixed case commands are supported by CMake. The source code for `tutorial.cxx` will compute the square root of a number and the first version of it is very simple, as follows:

```
// A simple program that computes the square root of a number
#include <stdio.h>
#include <math.h>
int main (int argc, char *argv[])
{
  if (argc < 2)
    {
    fprintf(stdout,"Usage: %s number\n",argv[0]);
    return 1;
    }
  double inputValue = atof(argv[1]);
  double outputValue = sqrt(inputValue);
```

```
        fprintf(stdout,"The square root of %g is %g\n",
                inputValue, outputValue);
        return 0;
}
```

12.1.1 Adding a Version Number and Configured Header File

The first feature we will add is to provide our executable and project with a version number. While you can do this exclusively in the source code, doing it in the CMakeLists file provides more flexibility. To add a version number we modify the CMakeLists file as follows

```
cmake_minimum_required (2.6)
project (Tutorial)

# The version number.
set (Tutorial_VERSION_MAJOR 1)
set (Tutorial_VERSION_MINOR 0)

# configure a header file to pass some of the CMake settings
# to the source code
configure_file (
  "${PROJECT_SOURCE_DIR}/TutorialConfig.h.in"
  "${PROJECT_BINARY_DIR}/TutorialConfig.h"
  )

# add the binary tree to the search path for include files
# so that we will find TutorialConfig.h
include_directories("${PROJECT_BINARY_DIR}")

# add the executable
add_executable(Tutorial tutorial.cxx)
```

Since the configured file will be written into the binary tree, we must add that directory to the list of paths to search for include files. We then create a `TutorialConfig.h.in` file in the source tree with the following contents:

```
// the configured options and settings for Tutorial
#define Tutorial_VERSION_MAJOR @Tutorial_VERSION_MAJOR@
#define Tutorial_VERSION_MINOR @Tutorial_VERSION_MINOR@
```

When CMake configures this header file, the values for `@Tutorial_VERSION_MAJOR@` and `@Tutorial_VERSION_MINOR@` will be replaced by the values from the CMakeLists file. Next, we modify `tutorial.cxx` to include the configured header file and to make use of the version numbers. The resulting source code is listed below.

```
// A simple program that computes the square root of a number
#include <stdio.h>
#include <math.h>
```

```
#include "TutorialConfig.h"

int main (int argc, char *argv[])
{
  if (argc < 2)
    {
    fprintf(stdout,"%s Version %d.%d\n",
            argv[0],
            Tutorial_VERSION_MAJOR,
            Tutorial_VERSION_MINOR);
    fprintf(stdout,"Usage: %s number\n",argv[0]);
    return 1;
    }
  double inputValue = atof(argv[1]);
  double outputValue = sqrt(inputValue);
  fprintf(stdout,"The square root of %g is %g\n",
          inputValue, outputValue);
  return 0;
}
```

The main changes are the inclusion of the `TutorialConfig.h` header file and printing out a version number as part of the usage message.

12.2 Adding a Library (Step 2)

Now we will add a library to our project. This library will contain our own implementation for computing the square root of a number. The executable can then use this library instead of the standard square root function provided by the compiler. For this tutorial we will put the library into a subdirectory called MathFunctions. It will have the following one line CMakeLists file

```
add_library(MathFunctions mysqrt.cxx)
```

The source file `mysqrt.cxx` has one function called `mysqrt` that provides similar functionality to the compiler's `sqrt` function. To make use of the new library we add an `add_subdirectory()` (page 277) call in the top level CMakeLists file so that the library will get built. We also add another include directory so that the `MathFunctions/mysqrt.h` header file can be found for the function prototype. The last change is to add the new library to the executable. The last few lines of the top level CMakeLists file now look like

```
include_directories ("${PROJECT_SOURCE_DIR}/MathFunctions")
add_subdirectory (MathFunctions)

# add the executable
add_executable (Tutorial tutorial.cxx)
target_link_libraries (Tutorial MathFunctions)
```

Now, let us consider making the MathFunctions library optional. In this tutorial there really isn't any reason to do so, but with larger libraries or libraries that rely on third party code you might want to. The first step is to add an `option()` (page 327) to the top level CMakeLists file.

```
# should we use our own math functions?
option (USE_MYMATH
        "Use tutorial provided math implementation" ON)
```

This will show up in the CMake GUI with a default value of ON that the user can change as desired. This setting will be stored in the cache so that the user does not need to keep setting it each time they run CMake on this project. The next change is to make the build and linking of the MathFunctions library conditional. To do this we change the end of the top level CMakeLists file to look like the following

```
# add the MathFunctions library?
#
if (USE_MYMATH)
  include_directories ("${PROJECT_SOURCE_DIR}/MathFunctions")
  add_subdirectory (MathFunctions)
  set (EXTRA_LIBS ${EXTRA_LIBS} MathFunctions)
endif (USE_MYMATH)

# add the executable
add_executable (Tutorial tutorial.cxx)
target_link_libraries (Tutorial  ${EXTRA_LIBS})
```

This uses the setting of USE_MYMATH to determine if the MathFunctions should be compiled and used. Note the use of a variable (EXTRA_LIBS in this case) to collect up any optional libraries to later be linked into the executable. This is a common approach used to keep larger projects with many optional components clean. The corresponding changes to the source code are fairly straight forward and leave us with:

```
// A simple program that computes the square root of a number
#include <stdio.h>
#include <math.h>
#include "TutorialConfig.h"

#ifdef USE_MYMATH
#include "MathFunctions.h"
#endif

int main (int argc, char *argv[])
{
  if (argc < 2)
    {
    fprintf(stdout,"%s Version %d.%d\n", argv[0],
            Tutorial_VERSION_MAJOR,
            Tutorial_VERSION_MINOR);
    fprintf(stdout,"Usage: %s number\n",argv[0]);
    return 1;
    }

  double inputValue = atof(argv[1]);
```

```
#ifdef USE_MYMATH
  double outputValue = mysqrt(inputValue);
#else
  double outputValue = sqrt(inputValue);
#endif

  fprintf(stdout,"The square root of %g is %g\n",
          inputValue, outputValue);
  return 0;
}
```

In the source code we make use of USE_MYMATH as well. This is provided from CMake to the source code through the TutorialConfig.h.in configured file by adding the following line to it:

```
#cmakedefine USE_MYMATH
```

12.3 Installing and Testing (Step 3)

For the next step we will add install rules and testing support to our project. The install rules are fairly straight forward. For the MathFunctions library we setup the library and the header file to be installed by adding the following two lines to MathFunctions' CMakeLists file

```
install (TARGETS MathFunctions DESTINATION bin)
install (FILES MathFunctions.h DESTINATION include)
```

For the application, the following lines are added to the top level CMakeLists file to install the executable and the configured header file:

```
# add the install targets
install (TARGETS Tutorial DESTINATION bin)
install (FILES "${PROJECT_BINARY_DIR}/TutorialConfig.h"
         DESTINATION include)
```

That is all there is to it. At this point you should be able to build the tutorial, then type make install (or build the INSTALL target from an IDE), and it will install the appropriate header files, libraries, and executables. The CMake variable CMAKE_INSTALL_PREFIX is used to determine the root of where the files will be installed. Adding testing is also a fairly straight forward process. At the end of the top level CMakeLists file we can add a number of basic tests to verify that the application is working correctly.

```
# does the application run
add_test (TutorialRuns Tutorial 25)

# does it sqrt of 25
add_test (TutorialComp25 Tutorial 25)

set_tests_properties (TutorialComp25
  PROPERTIES PASS_REGULAR_EXPRESSION "25 is 5")
```

```
# does it handle negative numbers
add_test (TutorialNegative Tutorial -25)
set_tests_properties (TutorialNegative
  PROPERTIES PASS_REGULAR_EXPRESSION "-25 is 0")

# does it handle small numbers
add_test (TutorialSmall Tutorial 0.0001)
set_tests_properties (TutorialSmall
  PROPERTIES PASS_REGULAR_EXPRESSION "0.0001 is 0.01")

# does the usage message work?
add_test (TutorialUsage Tutorial)
set_tests_properties (TutorialUsage
  PROPERTIES
  PASS_REGULAR_EXPRESSION "Usage:.*number")
```

The first test simply verifies that the application runs, does not segfault or otherwise crash, and has a zero return value. This is the basic form of a CTest test. The next few tests all make use of the PASS_REGULAR_EXPRESSION test property to verify that the output of the test contains certain strings, in this case: verifying that the computed square root is what it should be and that the usage message is printed when an incorrect number of arguments are provided. If you wanted to add a lot of tests to test different input values you might consider creating a macro() (page 324) like the following:

```
#define a macro to simplify adding tests, then use it
macro (do_test arg result)
  add_test (TutorialComp${arg} Tutorial ${arg})
  set_tests_properties (TutorialComp${arg}
    PROPERTIES PASS_REGULAR_EXPRESSION ${result})
endmacro (do_test)

# do a bunch of result based tests
do_test (25 "25 is 5")
do_test (-25 "-25 is 0")
```

For each invocation of do_test, another test is added to the project with a name, input, and results based on the passed arguments.

12.4 Adding System Introspection (Step 4)

Next let us consider adding some code to our project that depends on features the target platform may not have. For this example we will add some code that depends on whether or not the target platform has the log and exp functions. Of course, almost every platform has these functions, but for this tutorial assume that they are less common. If the platform has log then we will use that to compute the square root in the mysqrt function. We first test for the availability of these functions using the CheckFunctionExists.cmake macro in the top level CMakeLists file as follows:

```
# does this system provide the log and exp functions?
include (CheckFunctionExists.cmake)
check_function_exists (log HAVE_LOG)
check_function_exists (exp HAVE_EXP)
```

Next we modify the `TutorialConfig.h.in` to define those values if CMake found them on the platform as follows:

```
// does the platform provide exp and log functions?
#cmakedefine HAVE_LOG
#cmakedefine HAVE_EXP
```

It is important that the tests for `log` and `exp` are done before the `configure_file()` (page 282) command for `TutorialConfig.h`. The `configure_file` command immediately configures the file using the current settings in CMake. Finally, in the `mysqrt` function we can provide an alternate implementation based on `log` and `exp` if they are available on the system using the following code:

```
// if we have both log and exp then use them
#if defined (HAVE_LOG) && defined (HAVE_EXP)
  result = exp(log(x)*0.5);
#else // otherwise use an iterative approach
  . . .
```

12.5 Adding a Generated File and Generator (Step 5)

In this section we will show how you can add a generated source file into the build process of an application. For this example, we will create a table of precomputed square roots as part of the build process, and then compile that table into our application. To accomplish this we first need a program that will generate the table. In the MathFunctions subdirectory a new source file named `MakeTable.cxx` will do just that.

```
// A simple program that builds a sqrt table
#include <stdio.h>
#include <math.h>

int main (int argc, char *argv[])
{
  int i;
  double result;

  // make sure we have enough arguments
  if (argc < 2)
    {
    return 1;
    }

  // open the output file
  FILE *fout = fopen(argv[1],"w");
```

```
if (!fout)
  {
  return 1;
  }

// create a source file with a table of square roots
fprintf(fout,"double sqrtTable[] = {\n");
for (i = 0; i < 10; ++i)
  {
  result = sqrt(static_cast<double>(i));
  fprintf(fout,"%g,\n",result);
  }

// close the table with a zero
fprintf(fout,"0};\n");
fclose(fout);
return 0;
}
```

Note that the table is produced as valid C++ code and that the name of the file to write the output to is passed in as an argument. The next step is to add the appropriate commands to MathFunctions' CMakeLists file to build the MakeTable executable, and then run it as part of the build process. A few commands are needed to accomplish this, as shown below.

```
# first we add the executable that generates the table
add_executable(MakeTable MakeTable.cxx)

# add the command to generate the source code
add_custom_command (
  OUTPUT ${CMAKE_CURRENT_BINARY_DIR}/Table.h
  COMMAND MakeTable ${CMAKE_CURRENT_BINARY_DIR}/Table.h
  DEPENDS MakeTable
  )

# add the binary tree directory to the search path for
# include files
include_directories( ${CMAKE_CURRENT_BINARY_DIR} )

# add the main library
add_library(MathFunctions mysqrt.cxx
${CMAKE_CURRENT_BINARY_DIR}/Table.h  )
```

First, the executable for MakeTable is added as any other executable would be added. Then we add a custom command that specifies how to produce Table.h by running MakeTable. Next, we have to let CMake know that mysqrt.cxx depends on the generated file Table.h. This is done by adding the generated Table.h to the list of sources for the library MathFunctions. We also have to add the current binary directory to the list of include directories so that Table.h can be found and included by mysqrt.cxx.

When this project is built, it will first build the MakeTable executable. It will then run MakeTable to produce `Table.h`. Finally, it will compile `mysqrt.cxx` which includes `Table.h` to produce the MathFunctions library.

At this point the top level CMakeLists file with all the features we have added looks like the following

```
cmake_minimum_required (2.6)
project (Tutorial)

# The version number.
set (Tutorial_VERSION_MAJOR 1)
set (Tutorial_VERSION_MINOR 0)

# does this system provide the log and exp functions?
include (${CMAKE_ROOT}/Modules/CheckFunctionExists.cmake)

check_function_exists (log HAVE_LOG)
check_function_exists (exp HAVE_EXP)

# should we use our own math functions
option(USE_MYMATH
  "Use tutorial provided math implementation" ON)

# configure a header file to pass some of the CMake settings
# to the source code
configure_file (
  "${PROJECT_SOURCE_DIR}/TutorialConfig.h.in"
  "${PROJECT_BINARY_DIR}/TutorialConfig.h"
  )

# add the binary tree to the search path for include files
# so that we will find TutorialConfig.h
include_directories ("${PROJECT_BINARY_DIR}")

# add the MathFunctions library?
if (USE_MYMATH)
  include_directories ("${PROJECT_SOURCE_DIR}/MathFunctions")
  add_subdirectory (MathFunctions)
  set (EXTRA_LIBS ${EXTRA_LIBS} MathFunctions)
endif (USE_MYMATH)

# add the executable
add_executable (Tutorial tutorial.cxx)
target_link_libraries (Tutorial  ${EXTRA_LIBS})

# add the install targets
install (TARGETS Tutorial DESTINATION bin)
install (FILES "${PROJECT_BINARY_DIR}/TutorialConfig.h"
         DESTINATION include)

# does the application run
```

12.5. Adding a Generated File and Generator (Step 5)   **231**

```
add_test (TutorialRuns Tutorial 25)

# does the usage message work?
add_test (TutorialUsage Tutorial)
set_tests_properties (TutorialUsage
  PROPERTIES
  PASS_REGULAR_EXPRESSION "Usage:.*number"
  )


#define a macro to simplify adding tests
macro (do_test arg result)
  add_test (TutorialComp${arg} Tutorial ${arg})
  set_tests_properties (TutorialComp${arg}
    PROPERTIES PASS_REGULAR_EXPRESSION ${result}
    )
endmacro (do_test)

# do a bunch of result based tests
do_test (4 "4 is 2")
do_test (9 "9 is 3")
do_test (5 "5 is 2.236")
do_test (7 "7 is 2.645")
do_test (25 "25 is 5")
do_test (-25 "-25 is 0")
do_test (0.0001 "0.0001 is 0.01")
```

TutorialConfig.h looks like:

```
// the configured options and settings for Tutorial
#define Tutorial_VERSION_MAJOR @Tutorial_VERSION_MAJOR@
#define Tutorial_VERSION_MINOR @Tutorial_VERSION_MINOR@
#cmakedefine USE_MYMATH

// does the platform provide exp and log functions?
#cmakedefine HAVE_LOG
#cmakedefine HAVE_EXP
```

and the CMakeLists file for MathFunctions looks like

```
# first we add the executable that generates the table
add_executable(MakeTable MakeTable.cxx)
# add the command to generate the source code
add_custom_command (
  OUTPUT ${CMAKE_CURRENT_BINARY_DIR}/Table.h
  DEPENDS MakeTable
  COMMAND MakeTable ${CMAKE_CURRENT_BINARY_DIR}/Table.h
  )
# add the binary tree directory to the search path
# for include files
```

```
include_directories( ${CMAKE_CURRENT_BINARY_DIR} )

# add the main library
add_library(MathFunctions mysqrt.cxx
${CMAKE_CURRENT_BINARY_DIR}/Table.h)

install (TARGETS MathFunctions DESTINATION bin)
install (FILES MathFunctions.h DESTINATION include)
```

12.6 Building an Installer (Step 6)

Next, suppose that we want to distribute our project to other people so that they can use it. We want to provide both binary and source distributions on a variety of platforms. This is a little different from the install we did previously in Installing and Testing (Step 3), where we were installing the binaries that we had built from the source code. In this example, we will be building installation packages that support binary installations and package management features as found in cygwin, debian, RPMs etc. To accomplish this we will use CPack to create platform specific installers as described in Chapter 9. Specifically, we need to add a few lines to the bottom of our toplevel CMakeLists.txt file.

```
# build a CPack driven installer package
include (InstallRequiredSystemLibraries)
set (CPACK_RESOURCE_FILE_LICENSE
     "${CMAKE_CURRENT_SOURCE_DIR}/License.txt")
set (CPACK_PACKAGE_VERSION_MAJOR "${Tutorial_VERSION_MAJOR}")
set (CPACK_PACKAGE_VERSION_MINOR "${Tutorial_VERSION_MINOR}")
include (CPack)
```

That is all there is to it. We start by including InstallRequiredSystemLibraries. This module will include any runtime libraries that are needed by the project for the current platform. Next, we set some CPack variables to where we have stored the license and version information for this project. The version information makes use of the variables we set earlier in this tutorial. Finally, we include the CPack module which will use these variables and some other properties of the system you are on to setup an installer.

The next step is to build the project in the usual manner and then run CPack on it. To build a binary distribution, you would run:

```
cpack -C CPackConfig.cmake
```

To create a source distribution, you would type

```
cpack -C CPackSourceConfig.cmake
```

12.7 Adding Support for a Dashboard (Step 7)

Adding support for submitting our test results to a dashboard is very easy. We already defined a number of tests for our project in the earlier steps of this tutorial. We just have to run those tests and submit them to a dashboard. To include support for dashboards, we include the CTest module in our toplevel CMakeLists file.

```
# enable dashboard scripting
include (CTest)
```

We also create a CTestConfig.cmake file where we can specify the name of this project for the dashboard.

```
set (CTEST_PROJECT_NAME "Tutorial")
```

CTest will read in this file when it runs. To create a simple dashboard you can run CMake on your project, change directory to the binary tree, and then run ctest -D Experimental. The results of your dashboard will be uploaded to Kitware's public dashboard at:

```
http://www.cdash.org/CDash/index.php?project=PublicDashboard
```

COMMAND-LINE TOOLS

A.1 cmake(1)

A.1.1 Synopsis

```
cmake [<options>] (<path-to-source> | <path-to-existing-build>)
cmake [(-D<var>=<value>)...] -P <cmake-script-file>
cmake --build <dir> [<options>] [-- <build-tool-options>...]
cmake -E <command> [<options>]
cmake --find-package <options>...
```

A.1.2 Description

The "cmake" executable is the CMake command-line interface. It may be used to configure projects in scripts. Project configuration settings may be specified on the command line with the -D option.

CMake is a cross-platform build system generator. Projects specify their build process with platform-independent CMake listfiles included in each directory of a source tree with the name CMakeLists.txt. Users build a project by using CMake to generate a build system for a native tool on their platform.

A.1.3 Options

-C <initial-cache> Pre-load a script to populate the cache.

> When cmake is first run in an empty build tree, it creates a CMakeCache.txt file and populates it with customizable settings for the project. This option may be used to specify a file from which to load cache entries before the first pass through the project's cmake listfiles. The loaded entries take priority over the project's default values. The given file should be a CMake script containing SET commands that use the CACHE option, not a cache-format file.

-D <var>:<type>=<value> Create a cmake cache entry.

When cmake is first run in an empty build tree, it creates a CMakeCache.txt file and populates it with customizable settings for the project. This option may be used to specify a setting that takes priority over the project's default value. The option may be repeated for as many cache entries as desired.

-U <globbing_expr> Remove matching entries from CMake cache.

This option may be used to remove one or more variables from the CMakeCache.txt file, globbing expressions using * and ? are supported. The option may be repeated for as many cache entries as desired.

Use with care, you can make your CMakeCache.txt non-working.

-G <generator-name> Specify a build system generator.

CMake may support multiple native build systems on certain platforms. A generator is responsible for generating a particular build system. Possible generator names are specified in the Generators section.

-T <toolset-name> Specify toolset name if supported by generator.

Some CMake generators support a toolset name to be given to the native build system to choose a compiler. This is supported only on specific generators:

```
Visual Studio >= 10
Xcode >= 3.0
```

See native build system documentation for allowed toolset names.

-A <platform-name> Specify platform name if supported by generator.

Some CMake generators support a platform name to be given to the native build system to choose a compiler or SDK. This is supported only on specific generators:

```
Visual Studio >= 8
```

See native build system documentation for allowed platform names.

-Wno-dev Suppress developer warnings.

Suppress warnings that are meant for the author of the CMakeLists.txt files.

-Wdev Enable developer warnings.

Enable warnings that are meant for the author of the CMakeLists.txt files.

-E CMake command mode.

For true platform independence, CMake provides a list of commands that can be used on all systems. Run with -E help for the usage information. Commands available are: chdir, compare_files, copy, copy_directory, copy_if_different, echo, echo_append, env, environment, make_directory, md5sum, remove, remove_directory, rename, sleep, tar, time, touch, touch_nocreate. In addition, some platform specific commands are available. On Windows: delete_regv, write_regv. On UNIX: create_symlink.

-L[A][H] List non-advanced cached variables.

List cache variables will run CMake and list all the variables from the CMake cache that are not marked as INTERNAL or ADVANCED. This will effectively display current CMake settings, which can then be changed with -D option. Changing some of the variables may result in more variables being created. If A is specified, then it will display also advanced variables. If H is specified, it will also display help for each variable.

--build <dir> Build a CMake-generated project binary tree.

This abstracts a native build tool's command-line interface with the following options:

```
    <dir>              = Project binary directory to be built.
    --target <tgt>   = Build <tgt> instead of default targets.
    --config <cfg>   = For multi-configuration tools, choose <cfg>.
    --clean-first    = Build target 'clean' first, then build.
                       (To clean only, use --target 'clean'.)
    --use-stderr     = Ignored.  Behavior is default in CMake >= 3.0.
    --               = Pass remaining options to the native tool.
```

Run cmake --build with no options for quick help.

-N View mode only.

Only load the cache. Do not actually run configure and generate steps.

-P <file> Process script mode.

Process the given cmake file as a script written in the CMake language. No configure or generate step is performed and the cache is not modified. If variables are defined using -D, this must be done before the -P argument.

--find-package Run in pkg-config like mode.

Search a package using find_package() and print the resulting flags to stdout. This can be used to use cmake instead of pkg-config to find installed libraries in plain Makefile-based projects or in autoconf-based projects (via share/aclocal/cmake.m4).

--graphviz=[file] Generate graphviz of dependencies, see CMakeGraphVizOptions.cmake for more.

Generate a graphviz input file that will contain all the library and executable dependencies in the project. See the documentation for CMakeGraphVizOptions.cmake for more details.

--system-information [file] Dump information about this system.

Dump a wide range of information about the current system. If run from the top of a binary tree for a CMake project it will dump additional information such as the cache, log files etc.

--debug-trycompile Do not delete the try_compile build tree. Only useful on one try_compile at a time.

Do not delete the files and directories created for try_compile calls. This is useful in debugging failed try_compiles. It may however change the results of the try-compiles as old junk from a previous try-compile may cause a different test to either pass or fail incorrectly. This option is best used for one try-compile at a time, and only when debugging.

--debug-output Put cmake in a debug mode.

Print extra stuff during the cmake run like stack traces with message(send_error) calls.

--trace Put cmake in trace mode.

Print a trace of all calls made and from where with message(send_error) calls.

--warn-uninitialized Warn about uninitialized values.

Print a warning when an uninitialized variable is used.

--warn-unused-vars Warn about unused variables.

Find variables that are declared or set, but not used.

--no-warn-unused-cli Don't warn about command line options.

Don't find variables that are declared on the command line, but not used.

--check-system-vars Find problems with variable usage in system files.

Normally, unused and uninitialized variables are searched for only in CMAKE_SOURCE_DIR and CMAKE_BINARY_DIR. This flag tells CMake to warn about other files as well.

--help,-help,-usage,-h,-H,/? Print usage information and exit.

Usage describes the basic command line interface and its options.

--version,-version,/V [<f>] Show program name/version banner and exit.

If a file is specified, the version is written into it. The help is printed to a named <f>ile if given.

--help-full [<f>] Print all help manuals and exit.

All manuals are printed in a human-readable text format. The help is printed to a named <f>ile if given.

--help-manual <man> [<f>] Print one help manual and exit.

The specified manual is printed in a human-readable text format. The help is printed to a named <f>ile if given.

--help-manual-list [<f>] List help manuals available and exit.

The list contains all manuals for which help may be obtained by using the --help-manual option followed by a manual name. The help is printed to a named <f>ile if given.

--help-command <cmd> [<f>] Print help for one command and exit.

The cmake-commands(7) (page 269) manual entry for <cmd> is printed in a human-readable text format. The help is printed to a named <f>ile if given.

--help-command-list [<f>] List commands with help available and exit.

The list contains all commands for which help may be obtained by using the --help-command option followed by a command name. The help is printed to a named <f>ile if given.

--help-commands [<f>] Print cmake-commands manual and exit.

The cmake-commands(7) (page 269) manual is printed in a human-readable text format. The help is printed to a named <f>ile if given.

--help-module <mod> [<f>] Print help for one module and exit.

The cmake-modules(7) (page 366) manual entry for <mod> is printed in a human-readable text format. The help is printed to a named <f>ile if given.

--help-module-list [<f>] List modules with help available and exit.

The list contains all modules for which help may be obtained by using the --help-module option followed by a module name. The help is printed to a named <f>ile if given.

--help-modules [<f>] Print cmake-modules manual and exit.

The cmake-modules(7) (page 366) manual is printed in a human-readable text format. The help is printed to a named <f>ile if given.

--help-policy <cmp> [<f>] Print help for one policy and exit.

The cmake-policies(7) (page 537) manual entry for <cmp> is printed in a human-readable text format. The help is printed to a named <f>ile if given.

--help-policy-list [<f>] List policies with help available and exit.

The list contains all policies for which help may be obtained by using the --help-policy option followed by a policy name. The help is printed to a named <f>ile if given.

--help-policies [<f>] Print cmake-policies manual and exit.

The cmake-policies(7) (page 537) manual is printed in a human-readable text format. The help is printed to a named <f>ile if given.

--help-property <prop> [<f>] Print help for one property and exit.

The cmake-properties(7) (page 559) manual entries for <prop> are printed in a human-readable text format. The help is printed to a named <f>ile if given.

--help-property-list [<f>] List properties with help available and exit.

The list contains all properties for which help may be obtained by using the --help-property option followed by a property name. The help is printed to a named <f>ile if given.

--help-properties [<f>] Print cmake-properties manual and exit.

The cmake-properties(7) (page 559) manual is printed in a human-readable text format. The help is printed to a named <f>ile if given.

--help-variable <var> [<f>] Print help for one variable and exit.

The cmake-variables(7) (page 623) manual entry for <var> is printed in a human-readable text format. The help is printed to a named <f>ile if given.

--help-variable-list [<f>] List variables with help available and exit.

The list contains all variables for which help may be obtained by using the --help-variable option followed by a variable name. The help is printed to a named <f>ile if given.

--help-variables [<f>] Print cmake-variables manual and exit.

> The cmake-variables(7) (page 623) manual is printed in a human-readable text format. The help is printed to a named <f>ile if given.

A.1.4 See Also

The following resources are available to get help using CMake:

Home Page http://www.cmake.org

> The primary starting point for learning about CMake.

Frequently Asked Questions http://www.cmake.org/Wiki/CMake_FAQ

> A Wiki is provided containing answers to frequently asked questions.

Online Documentation http://www.cmake.org/HTML/Documentation.html

> Links to available documentation may be found on this web page.

Mailing List http://www.cmake.org/HTML/MailingLists.html

> For help and discussion about using cmake, a mailing list is provided at cmake@cmake.org[1]. The list is member-post-only but one may sign up on the CMake web page. Please first read the full documentation at http://www.cmake.org before posting questions to the list.

A.2 ctest(1)

A.2.1 Synopsis

```
ctest [<options>]
```

A.2.2 Description

The "ctest" executable is the CMake test driver program. CMake-generated build trees created for projects that use the ENABLE_TESTING and ADD_TEST commands have testing support. This program will run the tests and report results.

A.2.3 Options

-C <cfg>, --build-config <cfg> Choose configuration to test.

---

[1] cmake@cmake.org

Some CMake-generated build trees can have multiple build configurations in the same tree. This option can be used to specify which one should be tested. Example configurations are "Debug" and "Release".

-V, --verbose Enable verbose output from tests.

Test output is normally suppressed and only summary information is displayed. This option will show all test output.

-VV, --extra-verbose Enable more verbose output from tests.

Test output is normally suppressed and only summary information is displayed. This option will show even more test output.

--debug Displaying more verbose internals of CTest.

This feature will result in a large number of output that is mostly useful for debugging dashboard problems.

--output-on-failure Output anything outputted by the test program if the test should fail. This option can also be enabled by setting the environment variable CTEST_OUTPUT_ON_FAILURE

-F Enable failover.

This option allows ctest to resume a test set execution that was previously interrupted. If no interruption occurred, the -F option will have no effect.

-j <jobs>, --parallel <jobs> Run the tests in parallel using the given number of jobs.

This option tells ctest to run the tests in parallel using given number of jobs. This option can also be set by setting the environment variable CTEST_PARALLEL_LEVEL.

-Q, --quiet Make ctest quiet.

This option will suppress all the output. The output log file will still be generated if the –output-log is specified. Options such as –verbose, –extra-verbose, and –debug are ignored if –quiet is specified.

-O <file>, --output-log <file> Output to log file

This option tells ctest to write all its output to a log file.

-N, --show-only Disable actual execution of tests.

This option tells ctest to list the tests that would be run but not actually run them. Useful in conjunction with the -R and -E options.

-L <regex>, --label-regex <regex> Run tests with labels matching regular expression.

This option tells ctest to run only the tests whose labels match the given regular expression.

-R <regex>, --tests-regex <regex> Run tests matching regular expression.

This option tells ctest to run only the tests whose names match the given regular expression.

-E <regex>, --exclude-regex <regex> Exclude tests matching regular expression.

This option tells ctest to NOT run the tests whose names match the given regular expression.

-LE <regex>, --label-exclude <regex> Exclude tests with labels matching regular expression.

This option tells ctest to NOT run the tests whose labels match the given regular expression.

-D <dashboard>, --dashboard <dashboard> Execute dashboard test

This option tells ctest to act as a CDash client and perform a dashboard test. All tests are <Mode><Test>, where Mode can be Experimental, Nightly, and Continuous, and Test can be Start, Update, Configure, Build, Test, Coverage, and Submit.

-D <var>:<type>=<value> Define a variable for script mode

Pass in variable values on the command line. Use in conjunction with -S to pass variable values to a dashboard script. Parsing -D arguments as variable values is only attempted if the value following -D does not match any of the known dashboard types.

-M <model>, --test-model <model> Sets the model for a dashboard

This option tells ctest to act as a CDash client where the TestModel can be Experimental, Nightly, and Continuous. Combining -M and -T is similar to -D

-T <action>, --test-action <action> Sets the dashboard action to perform

This option tells ctest to act as a CDash client and perform some action such as start, build, test etc. Combining -M and -T is similar to -D

--track <track> Specify the track to submit dashboard to

Submit dashboard to specified track instead of default one. By default, the dashboard is submitted to Nightly, Experimental, or Continuous track, but by specifying this option, the track can be arbitrary.

-S <script>, --script <script> Execute a dashboard for a configuration

This option tells ctest to load in a configuration script which sets a number of parameters such as the binary and source directories. Then ctest will do what is required to create and run a dashboard. This option basically sets up a dashboard and then runs ctest -D with the appropriate options.

-SP <script>, --script-new-process <script> Execute a dashboard for a configuration

This option does the same operations as -S but it will do them in a separate process. This is primarily useful in cases where the script may modify the environment and you do not want the modified environment to impact other -S scripts.

-A <file>, --add-notes <file> Add a notes file with submission

This option tells ctest to include a notes file when submitting dashboard.

-I [Start,End,Stride,test#,test#|Test file], --tests-information Run a specific number of tests by number.

This option causes ctest to run tests starting at number Start, ending at number End, and incrementing by Stride. Any additional numbers after Stride are considered individual test numbers. Start, End,or stride can be empty. Optionally a file can be given that contains the same syntax as the command line.

-U, --union Take the Union of -I and -R

When both -R and -I are specified by default the intersection of tests are run. By specifying -U the union of tests is run instead.

--rerun-failed Run only the tests that failed previously

This option tells ctest to perform only the tests that failed during its previous run. When this option is specified, ctest ignores all other options intended to modify the list of tests to run (-L, -R, -E, -LE, -I, etc). In the event that CTest runs and no tests fail, subsequent calls to ctest with the –rerun-failed option will run the set of tests that most recently failed (if any).

--max-width <width> Set the max width for a test name to output

Set the maximum width for each test name to show in the output. This allows the user to widen the output to avoid clipping the test name which can be very annoying.

--interactive-debug-mode [0|1] Set the interactive mode to 0 or 1.

This option causes ctest to run tests in either an interactive mode or a non-interactive mode. On Windows this means that in non-interactive mode, all system debug pop up windows are blocked. In dashboard mode (Experimental, Nightly, Continuous), the default is non-interactive. When just running tests not for a dashboard the default is to allow popups and interactive debugging.

--no-label-summary Disable timing summary information for labels.

This option tells ctest not to print summary information for each label associated with the tests run. If there are no labels on the tests, nothing extra is printed.

--build-and-test Configure, build and run a test.

This option tells ctest to configure (i.e. run cmake on), build, and or execute a test. The configure and test steps are optional. The arguments to this command line are the source and binary directories. By default this will run CMake on the Source/Bin directories specified unless –build-nocmake is specified. The –build-generator option *must* be provided to use –build-and-test. If –test-command is specified then that will be run after the build is complete. Other options that affect this mode are –build-target –build-nocmake, –build-run-dir, –build-two-config, –build-exe-dir, –build-project,–build-noclean, –build-options

--build-target Specify a specific target to build.

This option goes with the –build-and-test option, if left out the all target is built.

--build-nocmake Run the build without running cmake first.

Skip the cmake step.

--build-run-dir Specify directory to run programs from.

Directory where programs will be after it has been compiled.

--build-two-config Run CMake twice

--build-exe-dir Specify the directory for the executable.

--build-generator Specify the generator to use.

--build-generator-platform Specify the generator-specific platform.

--build-generator-toolset Specify the generator-specific toolset.

--build-project Specify the name of the project to build.

--build-makeprogram Override the make program chosen by CTest with a given one.

--build-noclean Skip the make clean step.

--build-config-sample A sample executable to use to determine the configuration

A sample executable to use to determine the configuration that should be used. e.g. Debug/Release/etc

--build-options Add extra options to the build step.

This option must be the last option with the exception of –test-command

--test-command The test to run with the –build-and-test option.

--test-timeout The time limit in seconds, internal use only.

--tomorrow-tag Nightly or experimental starts with next day tag.

This is useful if the build will not finish in one day.

--ctest-config The configuration file used to initialize CTest state when submitting dashboards.

This option tells CTest to use different initialization file instead of CTestConfiguration.tcl. This way multiple initialization files can be used for example to submit to multiple dashboards.

--overwrite Overwrite CTest configuration option.

By default ctest uses configuration options from configuration file. This option will overwrite the configuration option.

--extra-submit <file>[;<file>] Submit extra files to the dashboard.

This option will submit extra files to the dashboard.

--force-new-ctest-process Run child CTest instances as new processes

By default CTest will run child CTest instances within the same process. If this behavior is not desired, this argument will enforce new processes for child CTest processes.

--schedule-random Use a random order for scheduling tests

This option will run the tests in a random order. It is commonly used to detect implicit dependencies in a test suite.

--submit-index Legacy option for old Dart2 dashboard server feature. Do not use.

--timeout <seconds> Set a global timeout on all tests.

This option will set a global timeout on all tests that do not already have a timeout set on them.

--stop-time <time> Set a time at which all tests should stop running.

Set a real time of day at which all tests should timeout. Example: 7:00:00 -0400. Any time format understood by the curl date parser is accepted. Local time is assumed if no timezone is specified.

--http1.0 Submit using HTTP 1.0.

This option will force CTest to use HTTP 1.0 to submit files to the dashboard, instead of HTTP 1.1.

--no-compress-output Do not compress test output when submitting.

This flag will turn off automatic compression of test output. Use this to maintain compatibility with an older version of CDash which doesn't support compressed test output.

--print-labels Print all available test labels.

This option will not run any tests, it will simply print the list of all labels associated with the test set.

--help,-help,-usage,-h,-H,/? Print usage information and exit.

Usage describes the basic command line interface and its options.

--version,-version,/V [<f>] Show program name/version banner and exit.

If a file is specified, the version is written into it. The help is printed to a named <f>ile if given.

--help-full [<f>] Print all help manuals and exit.

All manuals are printed in a human-readable text format. The help is printed to a named <f>ile if given.

--help-manual <man> [<f>] Print one help manual and exit.

The specified manual is printed in a human-readable text format. The help is printed to a named <f>ile if given.

--help-manual-list [<f>] List help manuals available and exit.

The list contains all manuals for which help may be obtained by using the --help-manual option followed by a manual name. The help is printed to a named <f>ile if given.

--help-command <cmd> [<f>] Print help for one command and exit.

The cmake-commands(7) (page 269) manual entry for <cmd> is printed in a human-readable text format. The help is printed to a named <f>ile if given.

--help-command-list [<f>] List commands with help available and exit.

The list contains all commands for which help may be obtained by using the --help-command option followed by a command name. The help is printed to a named <f>ile if given.

--help-commands [<f>] Print cmake-commands manual and exit.

The cmake-commands(7) (page 269) manual is printed in a human-readable text format. The help is printed to a named <f>ile if given.

--help-module <mod> [<f>] Print help for one module and exit.

The cmake-modules(7) (page 366) manual entry for <mod> is printed in a human-readable text format. The help is printed to a named <f>ile if given.

`--help-module-list [<f>]` List modules with help available and exit.

The list contains all modules for which help may be obtained by using the `--help-module` option followed by a module name. The help is printed to a named <f>ile if given.

`--help-modules [<f>]` Print cmake-modules manual and exit.

The `cmake-modules`(7) (page 366) manual is printed in a human-readable text format. The help is printed to a named <f>ile if given.

`--help-policy <cmp> [<f>]` Print help for one policy and exit.

The `cmake-policies`(7) (page 537) manual entry for `<cmp>` is printed in a human-readable text format. The help is printed to a named <f>ile if given.

`--help-policy-list [<f>]` List policies with help available and exit.

The list contains all policies for which help may be obtained by using the `--help-policy` option followed by a policy name. The help is printed to a named <f>ile if given.

`--help-policies [<f>]` Print cmake-policies manual and exit.

The `cmake-policies`(7) (page 537) manual is printed in a human-readable text format. The help is printed to a named <f>ile if given.

`--help-property <prop> [<f>]` Print help for one property and exit.

The `cmake-properties`(7) (page 559) manual entries for `<prop>` are printed in a human-readable text format. The help is printed to a named <f>ile if given.

`--help-property-list [<f>]` List properties with help available and exit.

The list contains all properties for which help may be obtained by using the `--help-property` option followed by a property name. The help is printed to a named <f>ile if given.

`--help-properties [<f>]` Print cmake-properties manual and exit.

The `cmake-properties`(7) (page 559) manual is printed in a human-readable text format. The help is printed to a named <f>ile if given.

`--help-variable <var> [<f>]` Print help for one variable and exit.

The `cmake-variables`(7) (page 623) manual entry for `<var>` is printed in a human-readable text format. The help is printed to a named <f>ile if given.

`--help-variable-list [<f>]` List variables with help available and exit.

The list contains all variables for which help may be obtained by using the `--help-variable` option followed by a variable name. The help is printed to a named <f>ile if given.

`--help-variables [<f>]` Print cmake-variables manual and exit.

The `cmake-variables`(7) (page 623) manual is printed in a human-readable text format. The help is printed to a named <f>ile if given.

A.2.4 Dashboard Client

CTest can operate as a client for the CDash[2] software quality dashboard application. As a dashboard client, CTest performs a sequence of steps to configure, build, and test software, and then submits the results to a CDash[3] server.

Dashboard Client Steps

CTest defines an ordered list of testing steps of which some or all may be run as a dashboard client:

Start Start a new dashboard submission to be composed of results recorded by the following steps. See the CTest Start Step (page 249) section below.

Update Update the source tree from its version control repository. Record the old and new versions and the list of updated source files. See the CTest Update Step (page 249) section below.

Configure Configure the software by running a command in the build tree. Record the configuration output log. See the CTest Configure Step (page 252) section below.

Build Build the software by running a command in the build tree. Record the build output log and detect warnings and errors. See the CTest Build Step (page 252) section below.

Test Test the software by loading a `CTestTestfile.cmake` from the build tree and executing the defined tests. Record the output and result of each test. See the CTest Test Step (page 253) section below.

Coverage Compute coverage of the source code by running a coverage analysis tool and recording its output. See the CTest Coverage Step (page 253) section below.

MemCheck Run the software test suite through a memory check tool. Record the test output, results, and issues reported by the tool. See the CTest MemCheck Step (page 253) section below.

Submit Submit results recorded from other testing steps to the software quality dashboard server. See the CTest Submit Step (page 255) section below.

Dashboard Client Modes

CTest defines three modes of operation as a dashboard client:

Nightly This mode is intended to be invoked once per day, typically at night. It enables the `Start`, `Update`, `Configure`, `Build`, `Test`, `Coverage`, and `Submit` steps by default. Selected steps run even if the `Update` step reports no changes to the source tree.

Continuous This mode is intended to be invoked repeatedly throughout the day. It enables the `Start`, `Update`, `Configure`, `Build`, `Test`, `Coverage`, and `Submit` steps by default, but exits after the `Update` step if it reports no changes to the source tree.

---

[2] http://cdash.org/
[3] http://cdash.org/

Experimental This mode is intended to be invoked by a developer to test local changes. It enables the Start, Configure, Build, Test, Coverage, and Submit steps by default.

Dashboard Client via CTest Command-Line

CTest can perform testing on an already-generated build tree. Run the ctest command with the current working directory set to the build tree and use one of these signatures:

```
ctest -D <mode>[<step>]
ctest -M <mode> [ -T <step> ]...
```

The <mode> must be one of the above Dashboard Client Modes (page 247), and each <step> must be one of the above Dashboard Client Steps (page 247).

CTest reads the Dashboard Client Configuration (page 248) settings from a file in the build tree called either CTestConfiguration.ini or DartConfiguration.tcl (the names are historical). The format of the file is:

```
# Lines starting in '#' are comments.
# Other non-blank lines are key-value pairs.
<setting>: <value>
```

where <setting> is the setting name and <value> is the setting value.

In build trees generated by CMake, this configuration file is generated by the CTest (page 419) module if included by the project. The module uses variables to obtain a value for each setting as documented with the settings below.

Dashboard Client via CTest Script

CTest can perform testing driven by a cmake-language(7) script that creates and maintains the source and build tree as well as performing the testing steps. Run the ctest command with the current working directory set outside of any build tree and use one of these signatures:

```
ctest -S <script>
ctest -SP <script>
```

The <script> file must call *CTest Commands* (page 351) commands to run testing steps explicitly as documented below. The commands obtain Dashboard Client Configuration (page 248) settings from their arguments or from variables set in the script.

A.2.5 Dashboard Client Configuration

The Dashboard Client Steps (page 247) may be configured by named settings as documented in the following sections.

CTest Start Step

Start a new dashboard submission to be composed of results recorded by the following steps.

In a CTest Script (page 248), the `ctest_start()` (page 354) command runs this step. Arguments to the command may specify some of the step settings. The command first runs the command-line specified by the `CTEST_CHECKOUT_COMMAND` variable, if set, to initialize the source directory.

Configuration settings include:

BuildDirectory The full path to the project build tree.

  - CTest Script (page 248) variable: `CTEST_BINARY_DIRECTORY` (page 675)
  - `CTest` (page 419) module variable: `PROJECT_BINARY_DIR` (page 636)

SourceDirectory The full path to the project source tree.

  - CTest Script (page 248) variable: `CTEST_SOURCE_DIRECTORY` (page 680)
  - `CTest` (page 419) module variable: `PROJECT_SOURCE_DIR` (page 638)

CTest Update Step

In a CTest Script (page 248), the `ctest_update()` (page 355) command runs this step. Arguments to the command may specify some of the step settings.

Configuration settings to specify the version control tool include:

BZRCommand `bzr` command-line tool to use if source tree is managed by Bazaar.

  - CTest Script (page 248) variable: `CTEST_BZR_COMMAND` (page 676)
  - `CTest` (page 419) module variable: none

BZRUpdateOptions Command-line options to the `BZRCommand` when updating the source.

  - CTest Script (page 248) variable: `CTEST_BZR_UPDATE_OPTIONS` (page 676)
  - `CTest` (page 419) module variable: none

CVSCommand `cvs` command-line tool to use if source tree is managed by CVS.

  - CTest Script (page 248) variable: `CTEST_CVS_COMMAND` (page 677)
  - `CTest` (page 419) module variable: `CVSCOMMAND`

CVSUpdateOptions Command-line options to the `CVSCommand` when updating the source.

  - CTest Script (page 248) variable: `CTEST_CVS_UPDATE_OPTIONS` (page 677)
  - `CTest` (page 419) module variable: `CVS_UPDATE_OPTIONS`

GITCommand `git` command-line tool to use if source tree is managed by Git.

  - CTest Script (page 248) variable: `CTEST_GIT_COMMAND` (page 678)

- CTest (page 419) module variable: GITCOMMAND

GITUpdateCustom Specify a semicolon-separated list of custom command lines to run in the source tree (Git work tree) to update it instead of running the GITCommand.

- CTest Script (page 248) variable: CTEST_GIT_UPDATE_CUSTOM (page 678)
- CTest (page 419) module variable: CTEST_GIT_UPDATE_CUSTOM

GITUpdateOptions Command-line options to the GITCommand when updating the source.

- CTest Script (page 248) variable: CTEST_GIT_UPDATE_OPTIONS (page 678)
- CTest (page 419) module variable: GIT_UPDATE_OPTIONS

HGCommand hg command-line tool to use if source tree is managed by Mercurial.

- CTest Script (page 248) variable: CTEST_HG_COMMAND (page 678)
- CTest (page 419) module variable: none

HGUpdateOptions Command-line options to the HGCommand when updating the source.

- CTest Script (page 248) variable: CTEST_HG_UPDATE_OPTIONS (page 679)
- CTest (page 419) module variable: none

P4Client Value of the −c option to the P4Command.

- CTest Script (page 248) variable: CTEST_P4_CLIENT (page 679)
- CTest (page 419) module variable: CTEST_P4_CLIENT

P4Command p4 command-line tool to use if source tree is managed by Perforce.

- CTest Script (page 248) variable: CTEST_P4_COMMAND (page 679)
- CTest (page 419) module variable: P4COMMAND

P4Options Command-line options to the P4Command for all invocations.

- CTest Script (page 248) variable: CTEST_P4_OPTIONS (page 680)
- CTest (page 419) module variable: CTEST_P4_OPTIONS

P4UpdateCustom Specify a semicolon-separated list of custom command lines to run in the source tree (Perforce tree) to update it instead of running the P4Command.

- CTest Script (page 248) variable: none
- CTest (page 419) module variable: CTEST_P4_UPDATE_CUSTOM

P4UpdateOptions Command-line options to the P4Command when updating the source.

- CTest Script (page 248) variable: CTEST_P4_UPDATE_OPTIONS (page 680)
- CTest (page 419) module variable: CTEST_P4_UPDATE_OPTIONS

SVNCommand svn command-line tool to use if source tree is managed by Subversion.

- CTest Script (page 248) variable: CTEST_SVN_COMMAND (page 680)

- CTest (page 419) module variable: SVNCOMMAND

SVNOptions Command-line options to the SVNCommand for all invocations.

- CTest Script (page 248) variable: CTEST_SVN_OPTIONS (page 680)

- CTest (page 419) module variable: CTEST_SVN_OPTIONS

SVNUpdateOptions Command-line options to the SVNCommand when updating the source.

- CTest Script (page 248) variable: CTEST_SVN_UPDATE_OPTIONS (page 680)

- CTest (page 419) module variable: SVN_UPDATE_OPTIONS

UpdateCommand Specify the version-control command-line tool to use without detecting the VCS that manages the source tree.

- CTest Script (page 248) variable: CTEST_UPDATE_COMMAND (page 681)

- CTest (page 419) module variable: <VCS>COMMAND when UPDATE_TYPE is <vcs>, else UPDATE_COMMAND

UpdateOptions Command-line options to the UpdateCommand.

- CTest Script (page 248) variable: CTEST_UPDATE_OPTIONS (page 681)

- CTest (page 419) module variable: <VCS>_UPDATE_OPTIONS when UPDATE_TYPE is <vcs>, else UPDATE_OPTIONS

UpdateType Specify the version-control system that manages the source tree if it cannot be detected automatically. The value may be bzr, cvs, git, hg, p4, or svn.

- CTest Script (page 248) variable: none, detected from source tree

- CTest (page 419) module variable: UPDATE_TYPE if set, else CTEST_UPDATE_TYPE

UpdateVersionOnly Specify that you want the version control update command to only discover the current version that is checked out, and not to update to a different version.

- CTest Script (page 248) variable: CTEST_UPDATE_VERSION_ONLY (page 681)

Additional configuration settings include:

NightlyStartTime In the Nightly dashboard mode, specify the "nightly start time". With centralized version control systems (cvs and svn), the Update step checks out the version of the software as of this time so that multiple clients choose a common version to test. This is not well-defined in distributed version-control systems so the setting is ignored.

- CTest Script (page 248) variable: CTEST_NIGHTLY_START_TIME (page 679)

- CTest (page 419) module variable: NIGHTLY_START_TIME if set, else CTEST_NIGHTLY_START_TIME

CTest Configure Step

In a CTest Script (page 248), the `ctest_configure()` (page 352) command runs this step. Arguments to the command may specify some of the step settings.

Configuration settings include:

ConfigureCommand Command-line to launch the software configuration process. It will be executed in the location specified by the `BuildDirectory` setting.

- CTest Script (page 248) variable: `CTEST_CONFIGURE_COMMAND` (page 676)

- `CTest` (page 419) module variable: `CMAKE_COMMAND` (page 625) followed by `PROJECT_SOURCE_DIR` (page 638)

CTest Build Step

In a CTest Script (page 248), the `ctest_build()` (page 351) command runs this step. Arguments to the command may specify some of the step settings.

Configuration settings include:

DefaultCTestConfigurationType When the build system to be launched allows build-time selection of the configuration (e.g. `Debug`, `Release`), this specifies the default configuration to be built when no `-C` option is given to the `ctest` command. The value will be substituted into the value of `MakeCommand` to replace the literal string `${CTEST_CONFIGURATION_TYPE}` if it appears.

- CTest Script (page 248) variable: `CTEST_CONFIGURATION_TYPE` (page 676)

- `CTest` (page 419) module variable: `DEFAULT_CTEST_CONFIGURATION_TYPE`, initialized by the `CMAKE_CONFIG_TYPE` environment variable

MakeCommand Command-line to launch the software build process. It will be executed in the location specified by the `BuildDirectory` setting.

- CTest Script (page 248) variable: `CTEST_BUILD_COMMAND` (page 675)

- `CTest` (page 419) module variable: `MAKECOMMAND`, initialized by the `build_command()` (page 279) command

UseLaunchers For build trees generated by CMake using a Makefile generator or the `Ninja` (page 361) generator, specify whether the `CTEST_USE_LAUNCHERS` feature is enabled by the `CTestUseLaunchers` (page 420) module (also included by the `CTest` (page 419) module). When enabled, the generated build system wraps each invocation of the compiler, linker, or custom command line with a "launcher" that communicates with CTest via environment variables and files to report granular build warning and error information. Otherwise, CTest must "scrape" the build output log for diagnostics.

- CTest Script (page 248) variable: `CTEST_USE_LAUNCHERS` (page 681)

- `CTest` (page 419) module variable: `CTEST_USE_LAUNCHERS`

CTest Test Step

In a CTest Script (page 248), the `ctest_test()` (page 355) command runs this step. Arguments to the command may specify some of the step settings.

Configuration settings include:

TimeOut The default timeout for each test if not specified by the `TIMEOUT` (page 615) test property.

- CTest Script (page 248) variable: `CTEST_TEST_TIMEOUT` (page 680)
- `CTest` (page 419) module variable: `DART_TESTING_TIMEOUT`

CTest Coverage Step

In a CTest Script (page 248), the `ctest_coverage()` (page 352) command runs this step. Arguments to the command may specify some of the step settings.

Configuration settings include:

CoverageCommand Command-line tool to perform software coverage analysis. It will be executed in the location specified by the `BuildDirectory` setting.

- CTest Script (page 248) variable: `CTEST_COVERAGE_COMMAND` (page 676)
- `CTest` (page 419) module variable: `COVERAGE_COMMAND`

CoverageExtraFlags Specify command-line options to the `CoverageCommand` tool.

- CTest Script (page 248) variable: `CTEST_COVERAGE_EXTRA_FLAGS` (page 677)
- `CTest` (page 419) module variable: `COVERAGE_EXTRA_FLAGS`

CTest MemCheck Step

In a CTest Script (page 248), the `ctest_memcheck()` (page 353) command runs this step. Arguments to the command may specify some of the step settings.

Configuration settings include:

MemoryCheckCommand Command-line tool to perform dynamic analysis. Test command lines will be launched through this tool.

- CTest Script (page 248) variable: `CTEST_MEMORYCHECK_COMMAND` (page 679)
- `CTest` (page 419) module variable: `MEMORYCHECK_COMMAND`

MemoryCheckCommandOptions Specify command-line options to the `MemoryCheckCommand` tool. They will be placed prior to the test command line.

- CTest Script (page 248) variable: `CTEST_MEMORYCHECK_COMMAND_OPTIONS` (page 679)
- `CTest` (page 419) module variable: `MEMORYCHECK_COMMAND_OPTIONS`

MemoryCheckType Specify the type of memory checking to perform.

- CTest Script (page 248) variable: CTEST_MEMORYCHECK_TYPE (page 679)
- CTest (page 419) module variable: MEMORYCHECK_TYPE

MemoryCheckSanitizerOptions Specify options to sanitizers when running with a sanitize-enabled build.

- CTest Script (page 248) variable: CTEST_MEMORYCHECK_SANITIZER_OPTIONS (page 679)
- CTest (page 419) module variable: MEMORYCHECK_SANITIZER_OPTIONS

MemoryCheckSuppressionFile Specify a file containing suppression rules for the MemoryCheckCommand tool. It will be passed with options appropriate to the tool.

- CTest Script (page 248) variable: CTEST_MEMORYCHECK_SUPPRESSIONS_FILE (page 679)
- CTest (page 419) module variable: MEMORYCHECK_SUPPRESSIONS_FILE

Additional configuration settings include:

BoundsCheckerCommand Specify a MemoryCheckCommand that is known to be command-line compatible with Bounds Checker.

- CTest Script (page 248) variable: none
- CTest (page 419) module variable: none

PurifyCommand Specify a MemoryCheckCommand that is known to be command-line compatible with Purify.

- CTest Script (page 248) variable: none
- CTest (page 419) module variable: PURIFYCOMMAND

ValgrindCommand Specify a MemoryCheckCommand that is known to be command-line compatible with Valgrind.

- CTest Script (page 248) variable: none
- CTest (page 419) module variable: VALGRIND_COMMAND

ValgrindCommandOptions Specify command-line options to the ValgrindCommand tool. They will be placed prior to the test command line.

- CTest Script (page 248) variable: none
- CTest (page 419) module variable: VALGRIND_COMMAND_OPTIONS

CTest Submit Step

In a CTest Script (page 248), the `ctest_submit()` (page 354) command runs this step. Arguments to the command may specify some of the step settings.

Configuration settings include:

BuildName Describe the dashboard client platform with a short string. (Operating system, compiler, etc.)

- CTest Script (page 248) variable: `CTEST_BUILD_NAME` (page 675)
- `CTest` (page 419) module variable: `BUILDNAME`

CDashVersion Specify the version of CDash[4] on the server.

- CTest Script (page 248) variable: none, detected from server
- `CTest` (page 419) module variable: `CTEST_CDASH_VERSION`

CTestSubmitRetryCount Specify a number of attempts to retry submission on network failure.

- CTest Script (page 248) variable: none, use the `ctest_submit()` (page 354) `RETRY_COUNT` option.
- `CTest` (page 419) module variable: `CTEST_SUBMIT_RETRY_COUNT`

CTestSubmitRetryDelay Specify a delay before retrying submission on network failure.

- CTest Script (page 248) variable: none, use the `ctest_submit()` (page 354) `RETRY_DELAY` option.
- `CTest` (page 419) module variable: `CTEST_SUBMIT_RETRY_DELAY`

CurlOptions Specify a semicolon-separated list of options to control the Curl library that CTest uses internally to connect to the server. Possible options are `CURLOPT_SSL_VERIFYPEER_OFF` and `CURLOPT_SSL_VERIFYHOST_OFF`.

- CTest Script (page 248) variable: `CTEST_CURL_OPTIONS` (page 677)
- `CTest` (page 419) module variable: `CTEST_CURL_OPTIONS`

DropLocation The path on the dashboard server to send the submission.

- CTest Script (page 248) variable: `CTEST_DROP_LOCATION` (page 678)
- `CTest` (page 419) module variable: `DROP_LOCATION` if set, else `CTEST_DROP_LOCATION`

DropMethod Specify the method by which results should be submitted to the dashboard server. The value may be `cp`, `ftp`, `http`, `https`, `scp`, or `xmlrpc` (if CMake was built with support for it).

- CTest Script (page 248) variable: `CTEST_DROP_METHOD` (page 678)
- `CTest` (page 419) module variable: `DROP_METHOD` if set, else `CTEST_DROP_METHOD`

DropSite The dashboard server name (for `ftp`, `http`, and `https`, `scp`, and `xmlrpc`).

---

[4]http://cdash.org/

- CTest Script (page 248) variable: CTEST_DROP_SITE (page 678)
- CTest (page 419) module variable: DROP_SITE if set, else CTEST_DROP_SITE

DropSitePassword The dashboard server login password, if any (for ftp, http, and https).

- CTest Script (page 248) variable: CTEST_DROP_SITE_PASSWORD (page 678)
- CTest (page 419) module variable: DROP_SITE_PASSWORD if set, else CTEST_DROP_SITE_PASWORD

DropSiteUser The dashboard server login user name, if any (for ftp, http, and https).

- CTest Script (page 248) variable: CTEST_DROP_SITE_USER (page 678)
- CTest (page 419) module variable: DROP_SITE_USER if set, else CTEST_DROP_SITE_USER

IsCDash Specify whether the dashboard server is CDash[5] or an older dashboard server implementation requiring TriggerSite.

- CTest Script (page 248) variable: CTEST_DROP_SITE_CDASH (page 678)
- CTest (page 419) module variable: CTEST_DROP_SITE_CDASH

ScpCommand scp command-line tool to use when DropMethod is scp.

- CTest Script (page 248) variable: CTEST_SCP_COMMAND (page 680)
- CTest (page 419) module variable: SCPCOMMAND

Site Describe the dashboard client host site with a short string. (Hostname, domain, etc.)

- CTest Script (page 248) variable: CTEST_SITE (page 680)
- CTest (page 419) module variable: SITE, initialized by the site_name() (page 334) command

TriggerSite Legacy option to support older dashboard server implementations. Not used when IsCDash is true.

- CTest Script (page 248) variable: CTEST_TRIGGER_SITE (page 680)
- CTest (page 419) module variable: TRIGGER_SITE if set, else CTEST_TRIGGER_SITE

A.2.6 See Also

The following resources are available to get help using CMake:

Home Page http://www.cmake.org

The primary starting point for learning about CMake.

---

[5]http://cdash.org/

Frequently Asked Questions http://www.cmake.org/Wiki/CMake_FAQ

> A Wiki is provided containing answers to frequently asked questions.

Online Documentation http://www.cmake.org/HTML/Documentation.html

> Links to available documentation may be found on this web page.

Mailing List http://www.cmake.org/HTML/MailingLists.html

> For help and discussion about using cmake, a mailing list is provided at cmake@cmake.org[6]. The list is member-post-only but one may sign up on the CMake web page. Please first read the full documentation at http://www.cmake.org before posting questions to the list.

A.3 cpack(1)

A.3.1 Synopsis

```
cpack -G <generator> [<options>]
```

A.3.2 Description

The "cpack" executable is the CMake packaging program. CMake-generated build trees created for projects that use the INSTALL_* commands have packaging support. This program will generate the package.

CMake is a cross-platform build system generator. Projects specify their build process with platform-independent CMake listfiles included in each directory of a source tree with the name CMakeLists.txt. Users build a project by using CMake to generate a build system for a native tool on their platform.

A.3.3 Options

-G <generator> Use the specified generator to generate package.

> CPack may support multiple native packaging systems on certain platforms. A generator is responsible for generating input files for particular system and invoking that systems. Possible generator names are specified in the Generators section.

-C <Configuration> Specify the project configuration

> This option specifies the configuration that the project was build with, for example 'Debug', 'Release'.

-D <var>=<value> Set a CPack variable.

> Set a variable that can be used by the generator.

---

[6]cmake@cmake.org

--config <config file> Specify the config file.

Specify the config file to use to create the package. By default CPackConfig.cmake in the current directory will be used.

--verbose,-V enable verbose output

Run cpack with verbose output.

--debug enable debug output (for CPack developers)

Run cpack with debug output (for CPack developers).

-P <package name> override/define CPACK_PACKAGE_NAME

If the package name is not specified on cpack commmand line thenCPack.cmake defines it as CMAKE_PROJECT_NAME

-R <package version> override/define CPACK_PACKAGE_VERSION

If version is not specified on cpack command line thenCPack.cmake defines it from CPACK_PACKAGE_VERSION_[MAJOR|MINOR|PATCH]look into CPack.cmake for detail

-B <package directory> override/define CPACK_PACKAGE_DIRECTORY

The directory where CPack will be doing its packaging work.The resulting package will be found there. Inside this directoryCPack creates '_CPack_Packages' sub-directory which is theCPack temporary directory.

--vendor <vendor name> override/define CPACK_PACKAGE_VENDOR

If vendor is not specified on cpack command line (or inside CMakeLists.txt) thenCPack.cmake defines it with a default value

--help,-help,-usage,-h,-H,/? Print usage information and exit.

Usage describes the basic command line interface and its options.

--version,-version,/V [<f>] Show program name/version banner and exit.

If a file is specified, the version is written into it. The help is printed to a named <f>ile if given.

--help-full [<f>] Print all help manuals and exit.

All manuals are printed in a human-readable text format. The help is printed to a named <f>ile if given.

--help-manual <man> [<f>] Print one help manual and exit.

The specified manual is printed in a human-readable text format. The help is printed to a named <f>ile if given.

--help-manual-list [<f>] List help manuals available and exit.

The list contains all manuals for which help may be obtained by using the `--help-manual` option followed by a manual name. The help is printed to a named <f>ile if given.

--help-command <cmd> [<f>] Print help for one command and exit.

The cmake-commands(7) (page 269) manual entry for <cmd> is printed in a human-readable text format. The help is printed to a named <f>ile if given.

--help-command-list [<f>] List commands with help available and exit.

The list contains all commands for which help may be obtained by using the --help-command option followed by a command name. The help is printed to a named <f>ile if given.

--help-commands [<f>] Print cmake-commands manual and exit.

The cmake-commands(7) (page 269) manual is printed in a human-readable text format. The help is printed to a named <f>ile if given.

--help-module <mod> [<f>] Print help for one module and exit.

The cmake-modules(7) (page 366) manual entry for <mod> is printed in a human-readable text format. The help is printed to a named <f>ile if given.

--help-module-list [<f>] List modules with help available and exit.

The list contains all modules for which help may be obtained by using the --help-module option followed by a module name. The help is printed to a named <f>ile if given.

--help-modules [<f>] Print cmake-modules manual and exit.

The cmake-modules(7) (page 366) manual is printed in a human-readable text format. The help is printed to a named <f>ile if given.

--help-policy <cmp> [<f>] Print help for one policy and exit.

The cmake-policies(7) (page 537) manual entry for <cmp> is printed in a human-readable text format. The help is printed to a named <f>ile if given.

--help-policy-list [<f>] List policies with help available and exit.

The list contains all policies for which help may be obtained by using the --help-policy option followed by a policy name. The help is printed to a named <f>ile if given.

--help-policies [<f>] Print cmake-policies manual and exit.

The cmake-policies(7) (page 537) manual is printed in a human-readable text format. The help is printed to a named <f>ile if given.

--help-property <prop> [<f>] Print help for one property and exit.

The cmake-properties(7) (page 559) manual entries for <prop> are printed in a human-readable text format. The help is printed to a named <f>ile if given.

--help-property-list [<f>] List properties with help available and exit.

The list contains all properties for which help may be obtained by using the --help-property option followed by a property name. The help is printed to a named <f>ile if given.

--help-properties [<f>] Print cmake-properties manual and exit.

> The cmake-properties(7) (page 559) manual is printed in a human-readable text format. The help is printed to a named <f>ile if given.

--help-variable <var> [<f>] Print help for one variable and exit.

> The cmake-variables(7) (page 623) manual entry for <var> is printed in a human-readable text format. The help is printed to a named <f>ile if given.

--help-variable-list [<f>] List variables with help available and exit.

> The list contains all variables for which help may be obtained by using the --help-variable option followed by a variable name. The help is printed to a named <f>ile if given.

--help-variables [<f>] Print cmake-variables manual and exit.

> The cmake-variables(7) (page 623) manual is printed in a human-readable text format. The help is printed to a named <f>ile if given.

A.3.4 See Also

The following resources are available to get help using CMake:

Home Page http://www.cmake.org

> The primary starting point for learning about CMake.

Frequently Asked Questions http://www.cmake.org/Wiki/CMake_FAQ

> A Wiki is provided containing answers to frequently asked questions.

Online Documentation http://www.cmake.org/HTML/Documentation.html

> Links to available documentation may be found on this web page.

Mailing List http://www.cmake.org/HTML/MailingLists.html

> For help and discussion about using cmake, a mailing list is provided at cmake@cmake.org[7]. The list is member-post-only but one may sign up on the CMake web page. Please first read the full documentation at http://www.cmake.org before posting questions to the list.

---

[7]cmake@cmake.org

INTERACTIVE DIALOGS

B.1 cmake-gui(1)

B.1.1 Synopsis

```
cmake-gui [<options>]
cmake-gui [<options>] (<path-to-source> | <path-to-existing-build>)
```

B.1.2 Description

The "cmake-gui" executable is the CMake GUI. Project configuration settings may be specified interactively. Brief instructions are provided at the bottom of the window when the program is running.

CMake is a cross-platform build system generator. Projects specify their build process with platform-independent CMake listfiles included in each directory of a source tree with the name CMakeLists.txt. Users build a project by using CMake to generate a build system for a native tool on their platform.

B.1.3 Options

--help, -help, -usage, -h, -H, /? Print usage information and exit.

> Usage describes the basic command line interface and its options.

--version, -version, /V [<f>] Show program name/version banner and exit.

> If a file is specified, the version is written into it. The help is printed to a named <f>ile if given.

--help-full [<f>] Print all help manuals and exit.

> All manuals are printed in a human-readable text format. The help is printed to a named <f>ile if given.

--help-manual <man> [<f>] Print one help manual and exit.

> The specified manual is printed in a human-readable text format. The help is printed to a named <f>ile if given.

--help-manual-list **[<f>]** List help manuals available and exit.

The list contains all manuals for which help may be obtained by using the `--help-manual` option followed by a manual name. The help is printed to a named <f>ile if given.

--help-command **<cmd>** **[<f>]** Print help for one command and exit.

The `cmake-commands`(7) (page 269) manual entry for `<cmd>` is printed in a human-readable text format. The help is printed to a named <f>ile if given.

--help-command-list **[<f>]** List commands with help available and exit.

The list contains all commands for which help may be obtained by using the `--help-command` option followed by a command name. The help is printed to a named <f>ile if given.

--help-commands **[<f>]** Print cmake-commands manual and exit.

The `cmake-commands`(7) (page 269) manual is printed in a human-readable text format. The help is printed to a named <f>ile if given.

--help-module **<mod>** **[<f>]** Print help for one module and exit.

The `cmake-modules`(7) (page 366) manual entry for `<mod>` is printed in a human-readable text format. The help is printed to a named <f>ile if given.

--help-module-list **[<f>]** List modules with help available and exit.

The list contains all modules for which help may be obtained by using the `--help-module` option followed by a module name. The help is printed to a named <f>ile if given.

--help-modules **[<f>]** Print cmake-modules manual and exit.

The `cmake-modules`(7) (page 366) manual is printed in a human-readable text format. The help is printed to a named <f>ile if given.

--help-policy **<cmp>** **[<f>]** Print help for one policy and exit.

The `cmake-policies`(7) (page 537) manual entry for `<cmp>` is printed in a human-readable text format. The help is printed to a named <f>ile if given.

--help-policy-list **[<f>]** List policies with help available and exit.

The list contains all policies for which help may be obtained by using the `--help-policy` option followed by a policy name. The help is printed to a named <f>ile if given.

--help-policies **[<f>]** Print cmake-policies manual and exit.

The `cmake-policies`(7) (page 537) manual is printed in a human-readable text format. The help is printed to a named <f>ile if given.

--help-property **<prop>** **[<f>]** Print help for one property and exit.

The `cmake-properties`(7) (page 559) manual entries for `<prop>` are printed in a human-readable text format. The help is printed to a named <f>ile if given.

--help-property-list **[<f>]** List properties with help available and exit.

The list contains all properties for which help may be obtained by using the `--help-property` option followed by a property name. The help is printed to a named <f>ile if given.

--help-properties **[<f>]** Print cmake-properties manual and exit.

The `cmake-properties(7)` (page 559) manual is printed in a human-readable text format. The help is printed to a named <f>ile if given.

--help-variable **<var>** **[<f>]** Print help for one variable and exit.

The `cmake-variables(7)` (page 623) manual entry for `<var>` is printed in a human-readable text format. The help is printed to a named <f>ile if given.

--help-variable-list **[<f>]** List variables with help available and exit.

The list contains all variables for which help may be obtained by using the `--help-variable` option followed by a variable name. The help is printed to a named <f>ile if given.

--help-variables **[<f>]** Print cmake-variables manual and exit.

The `cmake-variables(7)` (page 623) manual is printed in a human-readable text format. The help is printed to a named <f>ile if given.

B.1.4 See Also

The following resources are available to get help using CMake:

Home Page http://www.cmake.org

The primary starting point for learning about CMake.

Frequently Asked Questions http://www.cmake.org/Wiki/CMake_FAQ

A Wiki is provided containing answers to frequently asked questions.

Online Documentation http://www.cmake.org/HTML/Documentation.html

Links to available documentation may be found on this web page.

Mailing List http://www.cmake.org/HTML/MailingLists.html

For help and discussion about using cmake, a mailing list is provided at cmake@cmake.org[1]. The list is member-post-only but one may sign up on the CMake web page. Please first read the full documentation at http://www.cmake.org before posting questions to the list.

---

[1]cmake@cmake.org

B.2 ccmake(1)

B.2.1 Synopsis

```
ccmake [<options>] (<path-to-source> | <path-to-existing-build>)
```

B.2.2 Description

The "ccmake" executable is the CMake curses interface. Project configuration settings may be specified interactively through this GUI. Brief instructions are provided at the bottom of the terminal when the program is running.

CMake is a cross-platform build system generator. Projects specify their build process with platform-independent CMake listfiles included in each directory of a source tree with the name CMakeLists.txt. Users build a project by using CMake to generate a build system for a native tool on their platform.

B.2.3 Options

-C <initial-cache> Pre-load a script to populate the cache.

> When cmake is first run in an empty build tree, it creates a CMakeCache.txt file and populates it with customizable settings for the project. This option may be used to specify a file from which to load cache entries before the first pass through the project's cmake listfiles. The loaded entries take priority over the project's default values. The given file should be a CMake script containing SET commands that use the CACHE option, not a cache-format file.

-D <var>:<type>=<value> Create a cmake cache entry.

> When cmake is first run in an empty build tree, it creates a CMakeCache.txt file and populates it with customizable settings for the project. This option may be used to specify a setting that takes priority over the project's default value. The option may be repeated for as many cache entries as desired.

-U <globbing_expr> Remove matching entries from CMake cache.

> This option may be used to remove one or more variables from the CMakeCache.txt file, globbing expressions using * and ? are supported. The option may be repeated for as many cache entries as desired.

> Use with care, you can make your CMakeCache.txt non-working.

-G <generator-name> Specify a build system generator.

> CMake may support multiple native build systems on certain platforms. A generator is responsible for generating a particular build system. Possible generator names are specified in the Generators section.

-T <toolset-name> Specify toolset name if supported by generator.

Some CMake generators support a toolset name to be given to the native build system to choose a compiler. This is supported only on specific generators:

```
Visual Studio >= 10
Xcode >= 3.0
```

See native build system documentation for allowed toolset names.

-A <platform-name> Specify platform name if supported by generator.

Some CMake generators support a platform name to be given to the native build system to choose a compiler or SDK. This is supported only on specific generators:

```
Visual Studio >= 8
```

See native build system documentation for allowed platform names.

-Wno-dev Suppress developer warnings.

Suppress warnings that are meant for the author of the CMakeLists.txt files.

-Wdev Enable developer warnings.

Enable warnings that are meant for the author of the CMakeLists.txt files.

--help, -help, -usage, -h, -H, /? Print usage information and exit.

Usage describes the basic command line interface and its options.

--version, -version, /V [<f>] Show program name/version banner and exit.

If a file is specified, the version is written into it. The help is printed to a named <f>ile if given.

--help-full [<f>] Print all help manuals and exit.

All manuals are printed in a human-readable text format. The help is printed to a named <f>ile if given.

--help-manual <man> [<f>] Print one help manual and exit.

The specified manual is printed in a human-readable text format. The help is printed to a named <f>ile if given.

--help-manual-list [<f>] List help manuals available and exit.

The list contains all manuals for which help may be obtained by using the --help-manual option followed by a manual name. The help is printed to a named <f>ile if given.

--help-command <cmd> [<f>] Print help for one command and exit.

The cmake-commands(7) (page 269) manual entry for <cmd> is printed in a human-readable text format. The help is printed to a named <f>ile if given.

--help-command-list [<f>] List commands with help available and exit.

The list contains all commands for which help may be obtained by using the --help-command option followed by a command name. The help is printed to a named <f>ile if given.

--help-commands [<f>] Print cmake-commands manual and exit.

The cmake-commands(7) (page 269) manual is printed in a human-readable text format. The help is printed to a named <f>ile if given.

--help-module <mod> [<f>] Print help for one module and exit.

The cmake-modules(7) (page 366) manual entry for <mod> is printed in a human-readable text format. The help is printed to a named <f>ile if given.

--help-module-list [<f>] List modules with help available and exit.

The list contains all modules for which help may be obtained by using the --help-module option followed by a module name. The help is printed to a named <f>ile if given.

--help-modules [<f>] Print cmake-modules manual and exit.

The cmake-modules(7) (page 366) manual is printed in a human-readable text format. The help is printed to a named <f>ile if given.

--help-policy <cmp> [<f>] Print help for one policy and exit.

The cmake-policies(7) (page 537) manual entry for <cmp> is printed in a human-readable text format. The help is printed to a named <f>ile if given.

--help-policy-list [<f>] List policies with help available and exit.

The list contains all policies for which help may be obtained by using the --help-policy option followed by a policy name. The help is printed to a named <f>ile if given.

--help-policies [<f>] Print cmake-policies manual and exit.

The cmake-policies(7) (page 537) manual is printed in a human-readable text format. The help is printed to a named <f>ile if given.

--help-property <prop> [<f>] Print help for one property and exit.

The cmake-properties(7) (page 559) manual entries for <prop> are printed in a human-readable text format. The help is printed to a named <f>ile if given.

--help-property-list [<f>] List properties with help available and exit.

The list contains all properties for which help may be obtained by using the --help-property option followed by a property name. The help is printed to a named <f>ile if given.

--help-properties [<f>] Print cmake-properties manual and exit.

The cmake-properties(7) (page 559) manual is printed in a human-readable text format. The help is printed to a named <f>ile if given.

--help-variable <var> [<f>] Print help for one variable and exit.

The cmake-variables(7) (page 623) manual entry for <var> is printed in a human-readable text format. The help is printed to a named <f>ile if given.

`--help-variable-list` `[<f>]` List variables with help available and exit.

> The list contains all variables for which help may be obtained by using the `--help-variable` option followed by a variable name. The help is printed to a named <f>ile if given.

`--help-variables` `[<f>]` Print cmake-variables manual and exit.

> The `cmake-variables(7)` (page 623) manual is printed in a human-readable text format. The help is printed to a named <f>ile if given.

B.2.4 See Also

The following resources are available to get help using CMake:

Home Page http://www.cmake.org

> The primary starting point for learning about CMake.

Frequently Asked Questions http://www.cmake.org/Wiki/CMake_FAQ

> A Wiki is provided containing answers to frequently asked questions.

Online Documentation http://www.cmake.org/HTML/Documentation.html

> Links to available documentation may be found on this web page.

Mailing List http://www.cmake.org/HTML/MailingLists.html

> For help and discussion about using cmake, a mailing list is provided at cmake@cmake.org[2]. The list is member-post-only but one may sign up on the CMake web page. Please first read the full documentation at http://www.cmake.org before posting questions to the list.

---

[2]cmake@cmake.org

REFERENCE MANUALS

C.1 cmake-commands(7)

C.1.1 Normal Commands

These commands may be used freely in CMake projects.

add_compile_options

Adds options to the compilation of source files.

```
add_compile_options(<option> ...)
```

Adds options to the compiler command line for targets in the current directory and below that are added after this command is invoked. See documentation of the `directory` (page 569) and `target` (page 581) `COMPILE_OPTIONS` properties.

This command can be used to add any options, but alternative commands exist to add preprocessor definitions (`target_compile_definitions()` (page 338) and `add_definitions()` (page 273)) or include directories (`target_include_directories()` (page 339) and `include_directories()` (page 316)).

Arguments to `add_compile_options` may use "generator expressions" with the syntax `$<...>`. See the `cmake-generator-expressions(7)` (page 356) manual for available expressions. See the `cmake-buildsystem(7)` manual for more on defining buildsystem properties.

add_custom_command

Add a custom build rule to the generated build system.

There are two main signatures for `add_custom_command`.

Generating Files

The first signature is for adding a custom command to produce an output:

```
add_custom_command(OUTPUT output1 [output2 ...]
                   COMMAND command1 [ARGS] [args1...]
                   [COMMAND command2 [ARGS] [args2...] ...]
                   [MAIN_DEPENDENCY depend]
                   [DEPENDS [depends...]]
                   [IMPLICIT_DEPENDS <lang1> depend1
                                    [<lang2> depend2] ...]
                   [WORKING_DIRECTORY dir]
                   [COMMENT comment] [VERBATIM] [APPEND])
```

This defines a command to generate specified OUTPUT file(s). A target created in the same directory (CMakeLists.txt file) that specifies any output of the custom command as a source file is given a rule to generate the file using the command at build time. Do not list the output in more than one independent target that may build in parallel or the two instances of the rule may conflict (instead use the add_custom_target() (page 272) command to drive the command and make the other targets depend on that one). In makefile terms this creates a new target in the following form:

```
OUTPUT: MAIN_DEPENDENCY DEPENDS
        COMMAND
```

The options are:

APPEND Append the COMMAND and DEPENDS option values to the custom command for the first output specified. There must have already been a previous call to this command with the same output. The COMMENT, MAIN_DEPENDENCY, and WORKING_DIRECTORY options are currently ignored when APPEND is given, but may be used in the future.

COMMAND Specify the command-line(s) to execute at build time. If more than one COMMAND is specified they will be executed in order, but *not* necessarily composed into a stateful shell or batch script. (To run a full script, use the configure_file() (page 282) command or the file(GENERATE) (page 287) command to create it, and then specify a COMMAND to launch it.) The optional ARGS argument is for backward compatibility and will be ignored.

If COMMAND specifies an executable target (created by the add_executable() (page 273) command) it will automatically be replaced by the location of the executable created at build time. Additionally a target-level dependency will be added so that the executable target will be built before any target using this custom command. However this does NOT add a file-level dependency that would cause the custom command to re-run whenever the executable is recompiled.

Arguments to COMMAND may use generator expressions (page 356). References to target names in generator expressions imply target-level dependencies, but NOT file-level dependencies. List target names with the DEPENDS option to add file-level dependencies.

COMMENT Display the given message before the commands are executed at build time.

DEPENDS Specify files on which the command depends. If any dependency is an OUTPUT of another custom command in the same directory (`CMakeLists.txt` file) CMake automatically brings the other custom command into the target in which this command is built. If `DEPENDS` is not specified the command will run whenever the `OUTPUT` is missing; if the command does not actually create the `OUTPUT` then the rule will always run. If `DEPENDS` specifies any target (created by the `add_custom_target()` (page 272), `add_executable()` (page 273), or `add_library()` (page 274) command) a target-level dependency is created to make sure the target is built before any target using this custom command. Additionally, if the target is an executable or library a file-level dependency is created to cause the custom command to re-run whenever the target is recompiled.

Arguments to `DEPENDS` may use `generator expressions` (page 356).

IMPLICIT_DEPENDS Request scanning of implicit dependencies of an input file. The language given specifies the programming language whose corresponding dependency scanner should be used. Currently only `C` and `CXX` language scanners are supported. The language has to be specified for every file in the `IMPLICIT_DEPENDS` list. Dependencies discovered from the scanning are added to those of the custom command at build time. Note that the `IMPLICIT_DEPENDS` option is currently supported only for Makefile generators and will be ignored by other generators.

MAIN_DEPENDENCY Specify the primary input source file to the command. This is treated just like any value given to the `DEPENDS` option but also suggests to Visual Studio generators where to hang the custom command.

OUTPUT Specify the output files the command is expected to produce. If an output name is a relative path it will be interpreted relative to the build tree directory corresponding to the current source directory. If the output of the custom command is not actually created as a file on disk it should be marked with the `SYMBOLIC` (page 619) source file property.

VERBATIM All arguments to the commands will be escaped properly for the build tool so that the invoked command receives each argument unchanged. Note that one level of escapes is still used by the CMake language processor before add_custom_command even sees the arguments. Use of `VERBATIM` is recommended as it enables correct behavior. When `VERBATIM` is not given the behavior is platform specific because there is no protection of tool-specific special characters.

WORKING_DIRECTORY Execute the command with the given current working directory. If it is a relative path it will be interpreted relative to the build tree directory corresponding to the current source directory.

Build Events

The second signature adds a custom command to a target such as a library or executable. This is useful for performing an operation before or after building the target. The command becomes part of the target and will only execute when the target itself is built. If the target is already built, the command will not execute.

```
add_custom_command(TARGET target
                   PRE_BUILD | PRE_LINK | POST_BUILD
                   COMMAND command1 [ARGS] [args1...]
                   [COMMAND command2 [ARGS] [args2...] ...]
```

```
                    [WORKING_DIRECTORY dir]
                    [COMMENT comment] [VERBATIM])
```

This defines a new command that will be associated with building the specified target. When the command will happen is determined by which of the following is specified:

PRE_BUILD Run before any other rules are executed within the target. This is supported only on Visual Studio 7 or later. For all other generators PRE_BUILD will be treated as PRE_LINK.

PRE_LINK Run after sources have been compiled but before linking the binary or running the librarian or archiver tool of a static library. This is not defined for targets created by the add_custom_target() (page 272) command.

POST_BUILD Run after all other rules within the target have been executed.

add_custom_target

Add a target with no output so it will always be built.

```
add_custom_target(Name [ALL] [command1 [args1...]]
                    [COMMAND command2 [args2...] ...]
                    [DEPENDS depend depend depend ... ]
                    [WORKING_DIRECTORY dir]
                    [COMMENT comment] [VERBATIM]
                    [SOURCES src1 [src2...]])
```

Adds a target with the given name that executes the given commands. The target has no output file and is ALWAYS CONSIDERED OUT OF DATE even if the commands try to create a file with the name of the target. Use ADD_CUSTOM_COMMAND to generate a file with dependencies. By default nothing depends on the custom target. Use ADD_DEPENDENCIES to add dependencies to or from other targets. If the ALL option is specified it indicates that this target should be added to the default build target so that it will be run every time (the command cannot be called ALL). The command and arguments are optional and if not specified an empty target will be created. If WORKING_DIRECTORY is set, then the command will be run in that directory. If it is a relative path it will be interpreted relative to the build tree directory corresponding to the current source directory. If COMMENT is set, the value will be displayed as a message before the commands are executed at build time. Dependencies listed with the DEPENDS argument may reference files and outputs of custom commands created with add_custom_command() in the same directory (CMakeLists.txt file).

If VERBATIM is given then all arguments to the commands will be escaped properly for the build tool so that the invoked command receives each argument unchanged. Note that one level of escapes is still used by the CMake language processor before add_custom_target even sees the arguments. Use of VERBATIM is recommended as it enables correct behavior. When VERBATIM is not given the behavior is platform specific because there is no protection of tool-specific special characters.

The SOURCES option specifies additional source files to be included in the custom target. Specified source files will be added to IDE project files for convenience in editing even if they have not build rules.

add_definitions

Adds -D define flags to the compilation of source files.

```
add_definitions(-DFOO -DBAR ...)
```

Adds definitions to the compiler command line for targets in the current directory and below (whether added before or after this command is invoked). This command can be used to add any flags, but it is intended to add preprocessor definitions (see the `add_compile_options()` (page 269) command to add other flags). Flags beginning in -D or /D that look like preprocessor definitions are automatically added to the `COMPILE_DEFINITIONS` (page 568) directory property for the current directory. Definitions with non-trivial values may be left in the set of flags instead of being converted for reasons of backwards compatibility. See documentation of the `directory` (page 568), `target` (page 580), `source file` (page 616) `COMPILE_DEFINITIONS` properties for details on adding preprocessor definitions to specific scopes and configurations.

See the `cmake-buildsystem(7)` manual for more on defining buildsystem properties.

add_dependencies

Add a dependency between top-level targets.

```
add_dependencies(<target> [<target-dependency>]...)
```

Make a top-level <target> depend on other top-level targets to ensure that they build before <target> does. A top-level target is one created by ADD_EXECUTABLE, ADD_LIBRARY, or ADD_CUSTOM_TARGET. Dependencies added to an IMPORTED target are followed transitively in its place since the target itself does not build.

See the DEPENDS option of ADD_CUSTOM_TARGET and ADD_CUSTOM_COMMAND for adding file-level dependencies in custom rules. See the OBJECT_DEPENDS option in SET_SOURCE_FILES_PROPERTIES to add file-level dependencies to object files.

add_executable

Add an executable to the project using the specified source files.

```
add_executable(<name> [WIN32] [MACOSX_BUNDLE]
               [EXCLUDE_FROM_ALL]
               source1 [source2 ...])
```

Adds an executable target called <name> to be built from the source files listed in the command invocation. The <name> corresponds to the logical target name and must be globally unique within a project. The actual file name of the executable built is constructed based on conventions of the native platform (such as <name>.exe or just <name>.

By default the executable file will be created in the build tree directory corresponding to the source tree directory in which the command was invoked. See documentation of the RUNTIME_OUTPUT_DIRECTORY (page 607) target property to change this location. See documentation of the OUTPUT_NAME (page 604) target property to change the <name> part of the final file name.

If WIN32 is given the property WIN32_EXECUTABLE (page 612) will be set on the target created. See documentation of that target property for details.

If MACOSX_BUNDLE is given the corresponding property will be set on the created target. See documentation of the MACOSX_BUNDLE (page 601) target property for details.

If EXCLUDE_FROM_ALL is given the corresponding property will be set on the created target. See documentation of the EXCLUDE_FROM_ALL (page 585) target property for details.

Source arguments to add_executable may use "generator expressions" with the syntax $<...>. See the cmake-generator-expressions(7) (page 356) manual for available expressions. See the cmake-buildsystem(7) manual for more on defining buildsystem properties.

```
add_executable(<name> IMPORTED [GLOBAL])
```

An *IMPORTED executable target* references an executable file located outside the project. No rules are generated to build it, and the IMPORTED (page 590) target property is True. The target name has scope in the directory in which it is created and below, but the GLOBAL option extends visibility. It may be referenced like any target built within the project. IMPORTED executables are useful for convenient reference from commands like add_custom_command() (page 269). Details about the imported executable are specified by setting properties whose names begin in IMPORTED_. The most important such property is IMPORTED_LOCATION (page 590) (and its per-configuration version IMPORTED_LOCATION_<CONFIG> (page 590)) which specifies the location of the main executable file on disk. See documentation of the IMPORTED_* properties for more information.

```
add_executable(<name> ALIAS <target>)
```

Creates an *Alias Target*, such that <name> can be used to refer to <target> in subsequent commands. The <name> does not appear in the generated buildsystem as a make target. The <target> may not be an *Imported Target* or an ALIAS. ALIAS targets can be used as targets to read properties from, executables for custom commands and custom targets. They can also be tested for existance with the regular if(TARGET) (page 313) subcommand. The <name> may not be used to modify properties of <target>, that is, it may not be used as the operand of set_property() (page 329), set_target_properties() (page 332), target_link_libraries() (page 340) etc. An ALIAS target may not be installed or exported.

add_library

Add a library to the project using the specified source files.

Normal Libraries

```
add_library(<name> [STATIC | SHARED | MODULE]
            [EXCLUDE_FROM_ALL]
            source1 [source2 ...])
```

Adds a library target called `<name>` to be built from the source files listed in the command invocation. The `<name>` corresponds to the logical target name and must be globally unique within a project. The actual file name of the library built is constructed based on conventions of the native platform (such as `lib<name>.a` or `<name>.lib`).

`STATIC`, `SHARED`, or `MODULE` may be given to specify the type of library to be created. `STATIC` libraries are archives of object files for use when linking other targets. `SHARED` libraries are linked dynamically and loaded at runtime. `MODULE` libraries are plugins that are not linked into other targets but may be loaded dynamically at runtime using dlopen-like functionality. If no type is given explicitly the type is `STATIC` or `SHARED` based on whether the current value of the variable `BUILD_SHARED_LIBS` (page 638) is `ON`. For `SHARED` and `MODULE` libraries the `POSITION_INDEPENDENT_CODE` (page 605) target property is set to `ON` automatically.

By default the library file will be created in the build tree directory corresponding to the source tree directory in which the command was invoked. See documentation of the `ARCHIVE_OUTPUT_DIRECTORY` (page 574), `LIBRARY_OUTPUT_DIRECTORY` (page 596), and `RUNTIME_OUTPUT_DIRECTORY` (page 607) target properties to change this location. See documentation of the `OUTPUT_NAME` (page 604) target property to change the `<name>` part of the final file name.

If `EXCLUDE_FROM_ALL` is given the corresponding property will be set on the created target. See documentation of the `EXCLUDE_FROM_ALL` (page 585) target property for details.

Source arguments to `add_library` may use "generator expressions" with the syntax `$<...>`. See the `cmake-generator-expressions(7)` (page 356) manual for available expressions. See the `cmake-buildsystem(7)` manual for more on defining buildsystem properties.

Imported Libraries

```
add_library(<name> <SHARED|STATIC|MODULE|UNKNOWN> IMPORTED
            [GLOBAL])
```

An *IMPORTED library target* references a library file located outside the project. No rules are generated to build it, and the `IMPORTED` (page 590) target property is `True`. The target name has scope in the directory in which it is created and below, but the `GLOBAL` option extends visibility. It may be referenced like any target built within the project. `IMPORTED` libraries are useful for convenient reference from commands like `target_link_libraries()` (page 340). Details about the imported library are specified by setting properties whose names begin in `IMPORTED_` and `INTERFACE_`. The most important such property is `IMPORTED_LOCATION` (page 590) (and its per-configuration variant `IMPORTED_LOCATION_<CONFIG>` (page 590)) which specifies the location of the main library file on disk. See documentation of the `IMPORTED_*` and `INTERFACE_*` properties for more information.

Object Libraries

```
add_library(<name> OBJECT <src>...)
```

Creates an *Object Library*. An object library compiles source files but does not archive or link their object files into a library. Instead other targets created by `add_library()` (page 274) or `add_executable()` (page 273) may reference the objects using an expression of the form `$<TARGET_OBJECTS:objlib>` as a source, where `objlib` is the object library name. For example:

```
add_library(... $<TARGET_OBJECTS:objlib> ...)
add_executable(... $<TARGET_OBJECTS:objlib> ...)
```

will include objlib's object files in a library and an executable along with those compiled from their own sources. Object libraries may contain only sources that compile, header files, and other files that would not affect linking of a normal library (e.g. `.txt`). They may contain custom commands generating such sources, but not `PRE_BUILD`, `PRE_LINK`, or `POST_BUILD` commands. Object libraries cannot be imported, exported, installed, or linked. Some native build systems may not like targets that have only object files, so consider adding at least one real source file to any target that references `$<TARGET_OBJECTS:objlib>`.

Alias Libraries

```
add_library(<name> ALIAS <target>)
```

Creates an *Alias Target*, such that `<name>` can be used to refer to `<target>` in subsequent commands. The `<name>` does not appear in the generatedbuildsystem as a make target. The `<target>` may not be an *Imported Target* or an `ALIAS`. `ALIAS` targets can be used as linkable targets and as targets to read properties from. They can also be tested for existance with the regular `if(TARGET)` (page 313) subcommand. The `<name>` may not be used to modify properties of `<target>`, that is, it may not be used as the operand of `set_property()` (page 329), `set_target_properties()` (page 332), `target_link_libraries()` (page 340) etc. An `ALIAS` target may not be installed or exported.

Interface Libraries

```
add_library(<name> INTERFACE [IMPORTED [GLOBAL]])
```

Creates an *Interface Library*. An `INTERFACE` library target does not directly create build output, though it may have properties set on it and it may be installed, exported and imported. Typically the `INTERFACE_*` properties are populated on the interface target using the commands:

- `set_property()` (page 329),
- `target_link_libraries(INTERFACE)` (page 340),
- `target_include_directories(INTERFACE)` (page 339),
- `target_compile_options(INTERFACE)` (page 339),

- target_compile_definitions(INTERFACE) (page 338), and

- target_sources(INTERFACE) (page 342),

and then it is used as an argument to target_link_libraries() (page 340) like any other target.

An INTERFACE *Imported Target* may also be created with this signature. An IMPORTED library target references a library defined outside the project. The target name has scope in the directory in which it is created and below, but the GLOBAL option extends visibility. It may be referenced like any target built within the project. IMPORTED libraries are useful for convenient reference from commands like target_link_libraries() (page 340).

add_subdirectory

Add a subdirectory to the build.

```
add_subdirectory(source_dir [binary_dir]
                 [EXCLUDE_FROM_ALL])
```

Add a subdirectory to the build. The source_dir specifies the directory in which the source CMakeLists.txt and code files are located. If it is a relative path it will be evaluated with respect to the current directory (the typical usage), but it may also be an absolute path. The binary_dir specifies the directory in which to place the output files. If it is a relative path it will be evaluated with respect to the current output directory, but it may also be an absolute path. If binary_dir is not specified, the value of source_dir, before expanding any relative path, will be used (the typical usage). The CMakeLists.txt file in the specified source directory will be processed immediately by CMake before processing in the current input file continues beyond this command.

If the EXCLUDE_FROM_ALL argument is provided then targets in the subdirectory will not be included in the ALL target of the parent directory by default, and will be excluded from IDE project files. Users must explicitly build targets in the subdirectory. This is meant for use when the subdirectory contains a separate part of the project that is useful but not necessary, such as a set of examples. Typically the subdirectory should contain its own project() command invocation so that a full build system will be generated in the subdirectory (such as a VS IDE solution file). Note that inter-target dependencies supercede this exclusion. If a target built by the parent project depends on a target in the subdirectory, the dependee target will be included in the parent project build system to satisfy the dependency.

add_test

Add a test to the project to be run by ctest(1) (page 240).

```
add_test(NAME <name> COMMAND <command> [<arg>...]
         [CONFIGURATIONS <config>...]
         [WORKING_DIRECTORY <dir>])
```

Add a test called <name>. The test name may not contain spaces, quotes, or other characters special in CMake syntax. The options are:

COMMAND Specify the test command-line. If `<command>` specifies an executable target (created by `add_executable()` (page 273)) it will automatically be replaced by the location of the executable created at build time.

CONFIGURATIONS Restrict execution of the test only to the named configurations.

WORKING_DIRECTORY Set the `WORKING_DIRECTORY` (page 615) test property to specify the working directory in which to execute the test. If not specified the test will be run with the current working directory set to the build directory corresponding to the current source directory.

The `COMMAND` and `WORKING_DIRECTORY` options may use "generator expressions" with the syntax `$<...>`. See the `cmake-generator-expressions(7)` (page 356) manual for available expressions.

Example usage:

```
add_test(NAME mytest
         COMMAND testDriver --config $<CONFIGURATION>
                            --exe $<TARGET_FILE:myexe>)
```

This creates a test `mytest` whose command runs a `testDriver` tool passing the configuration name and the full path to the executable file produced by target `myexe`.

Note: CMake will generate tests only if the `enable_testing()` (page 284) command has been invoked. The `CTest` (page 419) module invokes the command automatically when the `BUILD_TESTING` option is ON.

```
add_test(<name> <command> [<arg>...])
```

Add a test called `<name>` with the given command-line. Unlike the above `NAME` signature no transformation is performed on the command-line to support target names or generator expressions.

aux_source_directory

Find all source files in a directory.

```
aux_source_directory(<dir> <variable>)
```

Collects the names of all the source files in the specified directory and stores the list in the `<variable>` provided. This command is intended to be used by projects that use explicit template instantiation. Template instantiation files can be stored in a "Templates" subdirectory and collected automatically using this command to avoid manually listing all instantiations.

It is tempting to use this command to avoid writing the list of source files for a library or executable target. While this seems to work, there is no way for CMake to generate a build system that knows when a new source file has been added. Normally the generated build system knows when it needs to rerun CMake because the CMakeLists.txt file is modified to add a new source. When the source is just added to the directory without modifying this file, one would have to manually rerun CMake to generate a build system incorporating the new file.

break

Break from an enclosing foreach or while loop.

```
break()
```

Breaks from an enclosing foreach loop or while loop

build_command

Get a command line to build the current project. This is mainly intended for internal use by the CTest (page 419) module.

```
build_command(<variable>
              [CONFIGURATION <config>]
              [TARGET <target>]
              [PROJECT_NAME <projname>] # legacy, causes warning
             )
```

Sets the given <variable> to a command-line string of the form:

```
<cmake> --build . [--config <config>] [--target <target>] [-- -i]
```

where <cmake> is the location of the cmake(1) (page 235) command-line tool, and <config> and <target> are the values provided to the CONFIGURATION and TARGET options, if any. The trailing ---i option is added for Makefile generators.

When invoked, this cmake --build command line will launch the underlying build system tool.

```
build_command(<cachevariable> <makecommand>)
```

This second signature is deprecated, but still available for backwards compatibility. Use the first signature instead.

It sets the given <cachevariable> to a command-line string as above but without the --config or --target options. The <makecommand> is ignored but should be the full path to msdev, devenv, nmake, make or one of the end user build tools for legacy invocations.

Note: In CMake versions prior to 3.0 this command returned a command line that directly invokes the native build tool for the current generator. Their implementation of the PROJECT_NAME option had no useful effects, so CMake now warns on use of the option.

---

cmake_host_system_information

Query host system specific information.

```
cmake_host_system_information(RESULT <variable> QUERY <key> ...)
```

Queries system information of the host system on which cmake runs. One or more <key> can be provided to select the information to be queried. The list of queried values is stored in <variable>.

<key> can be one of the following values:

```
NUMBER_OF_LOGICAL_CORES    = Number of logical cores.
NUMBER_OF_PHYSICAL_CORES   = Number of physical cores.
HOSTNAME                   = Hostname.
FQDN                       = Fully qualified domain name.
TOTAL_VIRTUAL_MEMORY       = Total virtual memory in megabytes.
AVAILABLE_VIRTUAL_MEMORY   = Available virtual memory in megabytes.
TOTAL_PHYSICAL_MEMORY      = Total physical memory in megabytes.
AVAILABLE_PHYSICAL_MEMORY  = Available physical memory in megabytes.
```

cmake_minimum_required

Set the minimum required version of cmake for a project.

```
cmake_minimum_required(VERSION major[.minor[.patch[.tweak]]]
                       [FATAL_ERROR])
```

If the current version of CMake is lower than that required it will stop processing the project and report an error. When a version higher than 2.4 is specified the command implicitly invokes

```
cmake_policy(VERSION major[.minor[.patch[.tweak]]])
```

which sets the cmake policy version level to the version specified. When version 2.4 or lower is given the command implicitly invokes

```
cmake_policy(VERSION 2.4)
```

which enables compatibility features for CMake 2.4 and lower.

The FATAL_ERROR option is accepted but ignored by CMake 2.6 and higher. It should be specified so CMake versions 2.4 and lower fail with an error instead of just a warning.

cmake_policy

Manage CMake Policy settings. See the cmake-policies(7) (page 537) manual for defined policies.

As CMake evolves it is sometimes necessary to change existing behavior in order to fix bugs or improve implementations of existing features. The CMake Policy mechanism is designed to help keep existing projects building as new versions of CMake introduce changes in behavior. Each new policy (behavioral change) is given an identifier of the form CMP<NNNN> where <NNNN> is an integer index. Documentation associated with each policy describes the OLD and NEW behavior and the reason the policy was introduced. Projects may set each policy to select the desired behavior. When CMake needs to know which behavior to use it checks for a setting specified by the project. If no setting is available the OLD behavior is assumed and a warning is produced requesting that the policy be set.

Setting Policies by CMake Version

The `cmake_policy` command is used to set policies to `OLD` or `NEW` behavior. While setting policies individually is supported, we encourage projects to set policies based on CMake versions:

```
cmake_policy(VERSION major.minor[.patch[.tweak]])
```

Specify that the current CMake code is written for the given version of CMake. All policies introduced in the specified version or earlier will be set to use `NEW` behavior. All policies introduced after the specified version will be unset (unless the `CMAKE_POLICY_DEFAULT_CMP<NNNN>` (page 647) variable sets a default). This effectively requests behavior preferred as of a given CMake version and tells newer CMake versions to warn about their new policies. The policy version specified must be at least 2.4 or the command will report an error.

Note that the `cmake_minimum_required(VERSION)` (page 280) command implicitly calls `cmake_policy(VERSION)` too.

Setting Policies Explicitly

```
cmake_policy(SET CMP<NNNN> NEW)
cmake_policy(SET CMP<NNNN> OLD)
```

Tell CMake to use the `OLD` or `NEW` behavior for a given policy. Projects depending on the old behavior of a given policy may silence a policy warning by setting the policy state to `OLD`. Alternatively one may fix the project to work with the new behavior and set the policy state to `NEW`.

Checking Policy Settings

```
cmake_policy(GET CMP<NNNN> <variable>)
```

Check whether a given policy is set to `OLD` or `NEW` behavior. The output `<variable>` value will be `OLD` or `NEW` if the policy is set, and empty otherwise.

CMake Policy Stack

CMake keeps policy settings on a stack, so changes made by the cmake_policy command affect only the top of the stack. A new entry on the policy stack is managed automatically for each subdirectory to protect its parents and siblings. CMake also manages a new entry for scripts loaded by `include()` (page 317) and `find_package()` (page 297) commands except when invoked with the `NO_POLICY_SCOPE` option (see also policy `CMP0011` (page 543)). The `cmake_policy` command provides an interface to manage custom entries on the policy stack:

```
cmake_policy(PUSH)
cmake_policy(POP)
```

Each PUSH must have a matching POP to erase any changes. This is useful to make temporary changes to policy settings. Calls to the cmake_minimum_required(VERSION) (page 280), cmake_policy(VERSION), or cmake_policy(SET) commands influence only the current top of the policy stack.

Commands created by the function() (page 309) and macro() (page 324) commands record policy settings when they are created and use the pre-record policies when they are invoked. If the function or macro implementation sets policies, the changes automatically propagate up through callers until they reach the closest nested policy stack entry.

configure_file

Copy a file to another location and modify its contents.

```
configure_file(<input> <output>
               [COPYONLY] [ESCAPE_QUOTES] [@ONLY]
               [NEWLINE_STYLE [UNIX|DOS|WIN32|LF|CRLF] ])
```

Copies a file <input> to file <output> and substitutes variable values referenced in the file content. If <input> is a relative path it is evaluated with respect to the current source directory. The <input> must be a file, not a directory. If <output> is a relative path it is evaluated with respect to the current binary directory. If <output> names an existing directory the input file is placed in that directory with its original name.

If the <input> file is modified the build system will re-run CMake to re-configure the file and generate the build system again.

This command replaces any variables in the input file referenced as ${VAR} or @VAR@ with their values as determined by CMake. If a variable is not defined, it will be replaced with nothing. If COPYONLY is specified, then no variable expansion will take place. If ESCAPE_QUOTES is specified then any substituted quotes will be C-style escaped. The file will be configured with the current values of CMake variables. If @ONLY is specified, only variables of the form @VAR@ will be replaced and ${VAR} will be ignored. This is useful for configuring scripts that use ${VAR}.

Input file lines of the form "#cmakedefine VAR ..." will be replaced with either "#define VAR ..." or /* #undef VAR */ depending on whether VAR is set in CMake to any value not considered a false constant by the if() command. (Content of "...", if any, is processed as above.) Input file lines of the form "#cmakedefine01 VAR" will be replaced with either "#define VAR 1" or "#define VAR 0" similarly.

With NEWLINE_STYLE the line ending could be adjusted:

```
'UNIX' or 'LF' for \n, 'DOS', 'WIN32' or 'CRLF' for \r\n.
```

COPYONLY must not be used with NEWLINE_STYLE.

create_test_sourcelist

Create a test driver and source list for building test programs.

```
create_test_sourcelist(sourceListName driverName
                       test1 test2 test3
                       EXTRA_INCLUDE include.h
                       FUNCTION function)
```

A test driver is a program that links together many small tests into a single executable. This is useful when building static executables with large libraries to shrink the total required size. The list of source files needed to build the test driver will be in sourceListName. DriverName is the name of the test driver program. The rest of the arguments consist of a list of test source files, can be semicolon separated. Each test source file should have a function in it that is the same name as the file with no extension (foo.cxx should have int foo(int, char*[]);) DriverName will be able to call each of the tests by name on the command line. If EXTRA_INCLUDE is specified, then the next argument is included into the generated file. If FUNCTION is specified, then the next argument is taken as a function name that is passed a pointer to ac and av. This can be used to add extra command line processing to each test. The cmake variable CMAKE_TESTDRIVER_BEFORE_TESTMAIN can be set to have code that will be placed directly before calling the test main function. CMAKE_TESTDRIVER_AFTER_TESTMAIN can be set to have code that will be placed directly after the call to the test main function.

define_property

Define and document custom properties.

```
define_property(<GLOBAL | DIRECTORY | TARGET | SOURCE |
                 TEST | VARIABLE | CACHED_VARIABLE>
                 PROPERTY <name> [INHERITED]
                 BRIEF_DOCS <brief-doc> [docs...]
                 FULL_DOCS <full-doc> [docs...])
```

Define one property in a scope for use with the set_property and get_property commands. This is primarily useful to associate documentation with property names that may be retrieved with the get_property command. The first argument determines the kind of scope in which the property should be used. It must be one of the following:

```
GLOBAL     = associated with the global namespace
DIRECTORY  = associated with one directory
TARGET     = associated with one target
SOURCE     = associated with one source file
TEST       = associated with a test named with add_test
VARIABLE   = documents a CMake language variable
CACHED_VARIABLE = documents a CMake cache variable
```

Note that unlike set_property and get_property no actual scope needs to be given; only the kind of scope is important.

The required PROPERTY option is immediately followed by the name of the property being defined.

If the INHERITED option then the get_property command will chain up to the next higher scope when the requested property is not set in the scope given to the command. DIRECTORY scope chains to GLOBAL.

TARGET, SOURCE, and TEST chain to DIRECTORY.

The BRIEF_DOCS and FULL_DOCS options are followed by strings to be associated with the property as its brief and full documentation. Corresponding options to the get_property command will retrieve the documentation.

elseif

Starts the elseif portion of an if block.

```
elseif(expression)
```

See the if command.

else

Starts the else portion of an if block.

```
else(expression)
```

See the if command.

enable_language

Enable a language (CXX/C/Fortran/etc)

```
enable_language(<lang> [OPTIONAL] )
```

This command enables support for the named language in CMake. This is the same as the project command but does not create any of the extra variables that are created by the project command. Example languages are CXX, C, Fortran.

This command must be called in file scope, not in a function call. Furthermore, it must be called in the highest directory common to all targets using the named language directly for compiling sources or indirectly through link dependencies. It is simplest to enable all needed languages in the top-level directory of a project.

The OPTIONAL keyword is a placeholder for future implementation and does not currently work.

enable_testing

Enable testing for current directory and below.

```
enable_testing()
```

Enables testing for this directory and below. See also the add_test command. Note that ctest expects to find a test file in the build directory root. Therefore, this command should be in the source directory root.

endforeach

Ends a list of commands in a FOREACH block.

```
endforeach(expression)
```

See the FOREACH command.

endfunction

Ends a list of commands in a function block.

```
endfunction(expression)
```

See the function command.

endif

Ends a list of commands in an if block.

```
endif(expression)
```

See the if command.

endmacro

Ends a list of commands in a macro block.

```
endmacro(expression)
```

See the macro command.

endwhile

Ends a list of commands in a while block.

```
endwhile(expression)
```

See the while command.

execute_process

Execute one or more child processes.

```
execute_process(COMMAND <cmd1> [args1...]]
                [COMMAND <cmd2> [args2...] [...]]
                [WORKING_DIRECTORY <directory>]
                [TIMEOUT <seconds>]
                [RESULT_VARIABLE <variable>]
                [OUTPUT_VARIABLE <variable>]
                [ERROR_VARIABLE <variable>]
                [INPUT_FILE <file>]
                [OUTPUT_FILE <file>]
                [ERROR_FILE <file>]
                [OUTPUT_QUIET]
                [ERROR_QUIET]
                [OUTPUT_STRIP_TRAILING_WHITESPACE]
                [ERROR_STRIP_TRAILING_WHITESPACE])
```

Runs the given sequence of one or more commands with the standard output of each process piped to the standard input of the next. A single standard error pipe is used for all processes.

Options:

COMMAND A child process command line.

> CMake executes the child process using operating system APIs directly. All arguments are passed VERBATIM to the child process. No intermediate shell is used, so shell operators such as > are treated as normal arguments. (Use the INPUT_*, OUTPUT_*, and ERROR_* options to redirect stdin, stdout, and stderr.)

WORKING_DIRECTORY The named directory will be set as the current working directory of the child processes.

TIMEOUT The child processes will be terminated if they do not finish in the specified number of seconds (fractions are allowed).

RESULT_VARIABLE The variable will be set to contain the result of running the processes. This will be an integer return code from the last child or a string describing an error condition.

OUTPUT_VARIABLE, ERROR_VARIABLE The variable named will be set with the contents of the standard output and standard error pipes, respectively. If the same variable is named for both pipes their output will be merged in the order produced.

INPUT_FILE, OUTPUT_FILE, ERROR_FILE The file named will be attached to the standard input of the first process, standard output of the last process, or standard error of all processes, respectively.

OUTPUT_QUIET, ERROR_QUIET The standard output or standard error results will be quietly ignored.

If more than one OUTPUT_* or ERROR_* option is given for the same pipe the precedence is not specified. If no OUTPUT_* or ERROR_* options are given the output will be shared with the corresponding pipes of the CMake process itself.

The execute_process() (page 285) command is a newer more powerful version of exec_program() (page 346), but the old command has been kept for compatibility. Both commands run while CMake is processing the project prior to build system generation. Use `add_custom_target()` (page 272) and `add_custom_command()` (page 269) to create custom commands that run at build time.

export

Export targets from the build tree for use by outside projects.

```
export(EXPORT <export-name> [NAMESPACE <namespace>] [FILE <filename>])
```

Create a file <filename> that may be included by outside projects to import targets from the current project's build tree. This is useful during cross-compiling to build utility executables that can run on the host platform in one project and then import them into another project being compiled for the target platform. If the NAMESPACE option is given the <namespace> string will be prepended to all target names written to the file.

Target installations are associated with the export <export-name> using the EXPORT option of the `install(TARGETS)` (page 317) command.

The file created by this command is specific to the build tree and should never be installed. See the install(EXPORT) command to export targets from an installation tree.

The properties set on the generated IMPORTED targets will have the same values as the final values of the input TARGETS.

```
export(TARGETS [target1 [target2 [...]]] [NAMESPACE <namespace>]
       [APPEND] FILE <filename> [EXPORT_LINK_INTERFACE_LIBRARIES])
```

This signature is similar to the `EXPORT` signature, but targets are listed explicitly rather than specified as an export-name. If the APPEND option is given the generated code will be appended to the file instead of over-writing it. The EXPORT_LINK_INTERFACE_LIBRARIES keyword, if present, causes the contents of the properties matching `(IMPORTED_)?LINK_INTERFACE_LIBRARIES(_<CONFIG>)?` to be exported, when policy CMP0022 is NEW. If a library target is included in the export but a target to which it links is not included the behavior is unspecified.

```
export(PACKAGE <name>)
```

Store the current build directory in the CMake user package registry for package <name>. The find_package command may consider the directory while searching for package <name>. This helps dependent projects find and use a package from the current project's build tree without help from the user. Note that the entry in the package registry that this command creates works only in conjunction with a package configuration file (<name>Config.cmake) that works with the build tree. In some cases, for example for packaging and for system wide installations, it is not desirable to write the user package registry. If the `CMAKE_EXPORT_NO_PACKAGE_REGISTRY` (page 641) variable is enabled, the `export(PACKAGE)` command will do nothing.

file

File manipulation command.

```
file(WRITE <filename> <content>...)
file(APPEND <filename> <content>...)
```

Write <content> into a file called <filename>. If the file does not exist, it will be created. If the file already exists, WRITE mode will overwrite it and APPEND mode will append to the end. (If the file is a build input, use the configure_file() (page 282) command to update the file only when its content changes.)

```
file(READ <filename> <variable>
     [OFFSET <offset>] [LIMIT <max-in>] [HEX])
```

Read content from a file called <filename> and store it in a <variable>. Optionally start from the given <offset> and read at most <max-in> bytes. The HEX option causes data to be converted to a hexadecimal representation (useful for binary data).

```
file(STRINGS <filename> <variable> [<options>...])
```

Parse a list of ASCII strings from <filename> and store it in <variable>. Binary data in the file are ignored. Carriage return ($\r$, CR) characters are ignored. The options are:

LENGTH_MAXIMUM <max-len> Consider only strings of at most a given length.

LENGTH_MINIMUM <min-len> Consider only strings of at least a given length.

LIMIT_COUNT <max-num> Limit the number of distinct strings to be extracted.

LIMIT_INPUT <max-in> Limit the number of input bytes to read from the file.

LIMIT_OUTPUT <max-out> Limit the number of total bytes to store in the <variable>.

NEWLINE_CONSUME Treat newline characters ($\n$, LF) as part of string content instead of terminating at them.

NO_HEX_CONVERSION Intel Hex and Motorola S-record files are automatically converted to binary while reading unless this option is given.

REGEX <regex> Consider only strings that match the given regular expression.

ENCODING <encoding-type> Consider strings of a given encoding. "UTF-8" is currently supported.

For example, the code

```
file(STRINGS myfile.txt myfile)
```

stores a list in the variable myfile in which each item is a line from the input file.

```
file(<MD5|SHA1|SHA224|SHA256|SHA384|SHA512> <filename> <variable>)
```

Compute a cryptographic hash of the content of <filename> and store it in a <variable>.

```
file(GLOB <variable> [RELATIVE <path>] [<globbing-expressions>...])
file(GLOB_RECURSE <variable> [RELATIVE <path>]
     [FOLLOW_SYMLINKS] [<globbing-expressions>...])
```

Generate a list of files that match the <globbing-expressions> and store it into the <variable>. Globbing expressions are similar to regular expressions, but much simpler. If RELATIVE flag is specified, the results will be returned as relative paths to the given path.

Note: We do not recommend using GLOB to collect a list of source files from your source tree. If no CMakeLists.txt file changes when a source is added or removed then the generated build system cannot know when to ask CMake to regenerate.

Examples of globbing expressions include:

```
*.cxx      - match all files with extension cxx
*.vt?      - match all files with extension vta,...,vtz
f[3-5].txt - match files f3.txt, f4.txt, f5.txt
```

The GLOB_RECURSE mode will traverse all the subdirectories of the matched directory and match the files. Subdirectories that are symlinks are only traversed if FOLLOW_SYMLINKS is given or policy CMP0009 (page 542) is not set to NEW.

Examples of recursive globbing include:

```
/dir/*.py  - match all python files in /dir and subdirectories
```

```
file(RENAME <oldname> <newname>)
```

Move a file or directory within a filesystem from <oldname> to <newname>, replacing the destination atomically.

```
file(REMOVE [<files>...])
file(REMOVE_RECURSE [<files>...])
```

Remove the given files. The REMOVE_RECURSE mode will remove the given files and directories, also non-empty directories

```
file(MAKE_DIRECTORY [<directories>...])
```

Create the given directories and their parents as needed.

```
file(RELATIVE_PATH <variable> <directory> <file>)
```

Compute the relative path from a <directory> to a <file> and store it in the <variable>.

```
file(TO_CMAKE_PATH "<path>" <variable>)
file(TO_NATIVE_PATH "<path>" <variable>)
```

The TO_CMAKE_PATH mode converts a native <path> into a cmake-style path with forward-slashes (/). The input can be a single path or a system search path like $ENV{PATH}. A search path will be converted to a cmake-style list separated by ; characters.

The TO_NATIVE_PATH mode converts a cmake-style <path> into a native path with platform-specific slashes (\ on Windows and / elsewhere).

Always use double quotes around the <path> to be sure it is treated as a single argument to this command.

```
file(DOWNLOAD <url> <file> [<options>...])
file(UPLOAD   <file> <url> [<options>...])
```

The DOWNLOAD mode downloads the given <url> to a local <file>. The UPLOAD mode uploads a local <file> to a given <url>.

Options to both DOWNLOAD and UPLOAD are:

INACTIVITY_TIMEOUT <seconds> Terminate the operation after a period of inactivity.

LOG <variable> Store a human-readable log of the operation in a variable.

SHOW_PROGRESS Print progress information as status messages until the operation is complete.

STATUS <variable> Store the resulting status of the operation in a variable. The status is a ; separated list of length 2. The first element is the numeric return value for the operation, and the second element is a string value for the error. A 0 numeric error means no error in the operation.

TIMEOUT <seconds> Terminate the operation after a given total time has elapsed.

Additional options to DOWNLOAD are:

EXPECTED_HASH ALGO=<value>

Verify that the downloaded content hash matches the expected value, where ALGO is one of MD5, SHA1, SHA224, SHA256, SHA384, or SHA512. If it does not match, the operation fails with an error.

EXPECTED_MD5 <value> Historical short-hand for EXPECTED_HASH MD5=<value>.

TLS_VERIFY <ON|OFF> Specify whether to verify the server certificate for `https://` URLs. The default is to *not* verify.

TLS_CAINFO <file> Specify a custom Certificate Authority file for `https://` URLs.

For `https://` URLs CMake must be built with OpenSSL support. `TLS/SSL` certificates are not checked by default. Set `TLS_VERIFY` to `ON` to check certificates and/or use `EXPECTED_HASH` to verify downloaded content. If neither TLS option is given CMake will check variables `CMAKE_TLS_VERIFY` and `CMAKE_TLS_CAINFO`, respectively.

```
file(TIMESTAMP <filename> <variable> [<format>] [UTC])
```

Compute a string representation of the modification time of `<filename>` and store it in `<variable>`. Should the command be unable to obtain a timestamp variable will be set to the empty string ("").

See the `string(TIMESTAMP)` (page 335) command for documentation of the `<format>` and UTC options.

```
file(GENERATE OUTPUT output-file
     <INPUT input-file|CONTENT content>
     [CONDITION expression])
```

Generate an output file for each build configuration supported by the current `CMake Generator` (page 360). Evaluate `generator expressions` (page 356) from the input content to produce the output content. The options are:

CONDITION <condition> Generate the output file for a particular configuration only if the condition is true. The condition must be either `0` or `1` after evaluating generator expressions.

CONTENT <content> Use the content given explicitly as input.

INPUT <input-file> Use the content from a given file as input.

OUTPUT <output-file> Specify the output file name to generate. Use generator expressions such as `$<CONFIG>` to specify a configuration-specific output file name. Multiple configurations may generate the same output file only if the generated content is identical. Otherwise, the `<output-file>` must evaluate to an unique name for each configuration.

Exactly one `CONTENT` or `INPUT` option must be given. A specific `OUTPUT` file may be named by at most one invocation of `file(GENERATE)`. Generated files are modified on subsequent cmake runs only if their content is changed.

```
file(<COPY|INSTALL> <files>... DESTINATION <dir>
     [FILE_PERMISSIONS <permissions>...]
     [DIRECTORY_PERMISSIONS <permissions>...]
     [NO_SOURCE_PERMISSIONS] [USE_SOURCE_PERMISSIONS]
     [FILES_MATCHING]
```

```
    [[PATTERN <pattern> | REGEX <regex>]
     [EXCLUDE] [PERMISSIONS <permissions>...]] [...])
```

The COPY signature copies files, directories, and symlinks to a destination folder. Relative input paths are evaluated with respect to the current source directory, and a relative destination is evaluated with respect to the current build directory. Copying preserves input file timestamps, and optimizes out a file if it exists at the destination with the same timestamp. Copying preserves input permissions unless explicit permissions or NO_SOURCE_PERMISSIONS are given (default is USE_SOURCE_PERMISSIONS). See the install(DIRECTORY) (page 317) command for documentation of permissions, PATTERN, REGEX, and EXCLUDE options.

The INSTALL signature differs slightly from COPY: it prints status messages (subject to the CMAKE_INSTALL_MESSAGE (page 645) variable), and NO_SOURCE_PERMISSIONS is default. Installation scripts generated by the install() (page 317) command use this signature (with some undocumented options for internal use).

find_file

A short-hand signature is:

```
find_file (<VAR> name1 [path1 path2 ...])
```

The general signature is:

```
find_file (
        <VAR>
        name | NAMES name1 [name2 ...]
        [HINTS path1 [path2 ... ENV var]]
        [PATHS path1 [path2 ... ENV var]]
        [PATH_SUFFIXES suffix1 [suffix2 ...]]
        [DOC "cache documentation string"]
        [NO_DEFAULT_PATH]
        [NO_CMAKE_ENVIRONMENT_PATH]
        [NO_CMAKE_PATH]
        [NO_SYSTEM_ENVIRONMENT_PATH]
        [NO_CMAKE_SYSTEM_PATH]
        [CMAKE_FIND_ROOT_PATH_BOTH |
         ONLY_CMAKE_FIND_ROOT_PATH |
         NO_CMAKE_FIND_ROOT_PATH]
        )
```

This command is used to find a full path to named file. A cache entry named by <VAR> is created to store the result of this command. If the full path to a file is found the result is stored in the variable and the search will not be repeated unless the variable is cleared. If nothing is found, the result will be <VAR>-NOTFOUND, and the search will be attempted again the next time find_file is invoked with the same variable. The name of the full path to a file that is searched for is specified by the names listed after the NAMES argument. Additional search locations can be specified after the PATHS argument. If ENV var is found in the HINTS or PATHS section the environment variable var will be read and converted from a system environment variable to a cmake style list of paths. For example ENV PATH would be a way to list the system path variable. The argument after DOC will be used for the documentation string in the cache. PATH_SUFFIXES specifies additional subdirectories to check below each search path.

If NO_DEFAULT_PATH is specified, then no additional paths are added to the search. If NO_DEFAULT_PATH is not specified, the search process is as follows:

1. Search paths specified in cmake-specific cache variables. These are intended to be used on the command line with a -DVAR=value. This can be skipped if NO_CMAKE_PATH is passed.

   - <prefix>/include/<arch> if CMAKE_LIBRARY_ARCHITECTURE is set, and <prefix>/include for each <prefix> in CMAKE_PREFIX_PATH

   - CMAKE_INCLUDE_PATH

   - CMAKE_FRAMEWORK_PATH

2. Search paths specified in cmake-specific environment variables. These are intended to be set in the user's shell configuration. This can be skipped if NO_CMAKE_ENVIRONMENT_PATH is passed.

   - <prefix>/include/<arch> if CMAKE_LIBRARY_ARCHITECTURE is set, and <prefix>/include for each <prefix> in CMAKE_PREFIX_PATH

   - CMAKE_INCLUDE_PATH

   - CMAKE_FRAMEWORK_PATH

3. Search the paths specified by the HINTS option. These should be paths computed by system introspection, such as a hint provided by the location of another item already found. Hard-coded guesses should be specified with the PATHS option.

4. Search the standard system environment variables. This can be skipped if NO_SYSTEM_ENVIRONMENT_PATH is an argument.

   - PATH and INCLUDE

5. Search cmake variables defined in the Platform files for the current system. This can be skipped if NO_CMAKE_SYSTEM_PATH is passed.

   - <prefix>/include/<arch> if CMAKE_LIBRARY_ARCHITECTURE is set, and <prefix>/include for each <prefix> in CMAKE_SYSTEM_PREFIX_PATH

   - CMAKE_SYSTEM_INCLUDE_PATH

   - CMAKE_SYSTEM_FRAMEWORK_PATH

6. Search the paths specified by the PATHS option or in the short-hand version of the command. These are typically hard-coded guesses.

On Darwin or systems supporting OS X Frameworks, the cmake variable CMAKE_FIND_FRAMEWORK can be set to empty or one of the following:

- FIRST: Try to find frameworks before standard libraries or headers. This is the default on Darwin.

- LAST: Try to find frameworks after standard libraries or headers.

- ONLY: Only try to find frameworks.

- NEVER: Never try to find frameworks.

On Darwin or systems supporting OS X Application Bundles, the cmake variable CMAKE_FIND_APPBUNDLE can be set to empty or one of the following:

- FIRST: Try to find application bundles before standard programs. This is the default on Darwin.

- LAST: Try to find application bundles after standard programs.

- ONLY: Only try to find application bundles.

- NEVER: Never try to find application bundles.

The CMake variable CMAKE_FIND_ROOT_PATH (page 643) specifies one or more directories to be prepended to all other search directories. This effectively "re-roots" the entire search under given locations. Paths which are descendants of the CMAKE_STAGING_PREFIX (page 648) are excluded from this re-rooting, because that variable is always a path on the host system. By default the CMAKE_FIND_ROOT_PATH (page 643) is empty.

The CMAKE_SYSROOT (page 641) variable can also be used to specify exactly one directory to use as a prefix. Setting CMAKE_SYSROOT (page 641) also has other effects. See the documentation for that variable for more.

These variables are especially useful when cross-compiling to point to the root directory of the target environment and CMake will search there too. By default at first the directories listed in CMAKE_FIND_ROOT_PATH (page 643) are searched, then the CMAKE_SYSROOT (page 641) directory is searched, and then the non-rooted directories will be searched. The default behavior can be adjusted by setting CMAKE_FIND_ROOT_PATH_MODE_INCLUDE (page 643). This behavior can be manually overridden on a per-call basis. By using CMAKE_FIND_ROOT_PATH_BOTH the search order will be as described above. If NO_CMAKE_FIND_ROOT_PATH is used then CMAKE_FIND_ROOT_PATH (page 643) will not be used. If ONLY_CMAKE_FIND_ROOT_PATH is used then only the re-rooted directories and directories below CMAKE_STAGING_PREFIX (page 648) will be searched.

The default search order is designed to be most-specific to least-specific for common use cases. Projects may override the order by simply calling the command multiple times and using the NO_* options:

```
find_file (<VAR> NAMES name PATHS paths... NO_DEFAULT_PATH)
find_file (<VAR> NAMES name)
```

Once one of the calls succeeds the result variable will be set and stored in the cache so that no call will search again.

find_library

A short-hand signature is:

```
find_library (<VAR> name1 [path1 path2 ...])
```

The general signature is:

```
find_library (
        <VAR>
        name | NAMES name1 [name2 ...] [NAMES_PER_DIR]
        [HINTS path1 [path2 ... ENV var]]
        [PATHS path1 [path2 ... ENV var]]
        [PATH_SUFFIXES suffix1 [suffix2 ...]]
        [DOC "cache documentation string"]
        [NO_DEFAULT_PATH]
        [NO_CMAKE_ENVIRONMENT_PATH]
        [NO_CMAKE_PATH]
        [NO_SYSTEM_ENVIRONMENT_PATH]
        [NO_CMAKE_SYSTEM_PATH]
        [CMAKE_FIND_ROOT_PATH_BOTH |
         ONLY_CMAKE_FIND_ROOT_PATH |
         NO_CMAKE_FIND_ROOT_PATH]
    )
```

This command is used to find a library. A cache entry named by <VAR> is created to store the result of this command. If the library is found the result is stored in the variable and the search will not be repeated unless the variable is cleared. If nothing is found, the result will be <VAR>-NOTFOUND, and the search will be attempted again the next time find_library is invoked with the same variable. The name of the library that is searched for is specified by the names listed after the NAMES argument. Additional search locations can be specified after the PATHS argument. If ENV var is found in the HINTS or PATHS section the environment variable var will be read and converted from a system environment variable to a cmake style list of paths. For example ENV PATH would be a way to list the system path variable. The argument after DOC will be used for the documentation string in the cache. PATH_SUFFIXES specifies additional subdirectories to check below each search path.

If NO_DEFAULT_PATH is specified, then no additional paths are added to the search. If NO_DEFAULT_PATH is not specified, the search process is as follows:

1. Search paths specified in cmake-specific cache variables. These are intended to be used on the command line with a -DVAR=value. This can be skipped if NO_CMAKE_PATH is passed.

   - <prefix>/lib/<arch> if CMAKE_LIBRARY_ARCHITECTURE is set, and <prefix>/lib for each <prefix> in CMAKE_PREFIX_PATH

   - CMAKE_LIBRARY_PATH

   - CMAKE_FRAMEWORK_PATH

2. Search paths specified in cmake-specific environment variables. These are intended to be set in the user's shell configuration. This can be skipped if NO_CMAKE_ENVIRONMENT_PATH is passed.

   - <prefix>/lib/<arch> if CMAKE_LIBRARY_ARCHITECTURE is set, and <prefix>/lib for each <prefix> in CMAKE_PREFIX_PATH

   - CMAKE_LIBRARY_PATH

   - CMAKE_FRAMEWORK_PATH

3. Search the paths specified by the HINTS option. These should be paths computed by system introspection, such as a hint provided by the location of another item already found. Hard-coded guesses should be specified with the PATHS option.

4. Search the standard system environment variables. This can be skipped if NO_SYSTEM_ENVIRONMENT_PATH is an argument.

   • PATH and LIB

5. Search cmake variables defined in the Platform files for the current system. This can be skipped if NO_CMAKE_SYSTEM_PATH is passed.

   • <prefix>/lib/<arch> if CMAKE_LIBRARY_ARCHITECTURE is set, and <prefix>/lib for each <prefix> in CMAKE_SYSTEM_PREFIX_PATH

   • CMAKE_SYSTEM_LIBRARY_PATH

   • CMAKE_SYSTEM_FRAMEWORK_PATH

6. Search the paths specified by the PATHS option or in the short-hand version of the command. These are typically hard-coded guesses.

On Darwin or systems supporting OS X Frameworks, the cmake variable CMAKE_FIND_FRAMEWORK can be set to empty or one of the following:

• FIRST: Try to find frameworks before standard libraries or headers. This is the default on Darwin.

• LAST: Try to find frameworks after standard libraries or headers.

• ONLY: Only try to find frameworks.

• NEVER: Never try to find frameworks.

On Darwin or systems supporting OS X Application Bundles, the cmake variable CMAKE_FIND_APPBUNDLE can be set to empty or one of the following:

• FIRST: Try to find application bundles before standard programs. This is the default on Darwin.

• LAST: Try to find application bundles after standard programs.

• ONLY: Only try to find application bundles.

• NEVER: Never try to find application bundles.

The CMake variable `CMAKE_FIND_ROOT_PATH` (page 643) specifies one or more directories to be prepended to all other search directories. This effectively "re-roots" the entire search under given locations. Paths which are descendants of the `CMAKE_STAGING_PREFIX` (page 648) are excluded from this re-rooting, because that variable is always a path on the host system. By default the `CMAKE_FIND_ROOT_PATH` (page 643) is empty.

The `CMAKE_SYSROOT` (page 641) variable can also be used to specify exactly one directory to use as a prefix. Setting `CMAKE_SYSROOT` (page 641) also has other effects. See the documentation for that variable for more.

These variables are especially useful when cross-compiling to point to the root directory of the target environment and CMake will search there too. By default at first the directories listed in

CMAKE_FIND_ROOT_PATH (page 643) are searched, then the CMAKE_SYSROOT (page 641) directory is searched, and then the non-rooted directories will be searched. The default behavior can be adjusted by setting CMAKE_FIND_ROOT_PATH_MODE_LIBRARY (page 643). This behavior can be manually overridden on a per-call basis. By using CMAKE_FIND_ROOT_PATH_BOTH the search order will be as described above. If NO_CMAKE_FIND_ROOT_PATH is used then CMAKE_FIND_ROOT_PATH (page 643) will not be used. If ONLY_CMAKE_FIND_ROOT_PATH is used then only the re-rooted directories and directories below CMAKE_STAGING_PREFIX (page 648) will be searched.

The default search order is designed to be most-specific to least-specific for common use cases. Projects may override the order by simply calling the command multiple times and using the NO_* options:

```
find_library (<VAR> NAMES name PATHS paths... NO_DEFAULT_PATH)
find_library (<VAR> NAMES name)
```

Once one of the calls succeeds the result variable will be set and stored in the cache so that no call will search again.

When more than one value is given to the NAMES option this command by default will consider one name at a time and search every directory for it. The NAMES_PER_DIR option tells this command to consider one directory at a time and search for all names in it.

If the library found is a framework, then VAR will be set to the full path to the framework <fullPath>/A.framework. When a full path to a framework is used as a library, CMake will use a -framework A, and a -F<fullPath> to link the framework to the target.

If the global property FIND_LIBRARY_USE_LIB64_PATHS is set all search paths will be tested as normal, with "64/" appended, and with all matches of "lib/" replaced with "lib64/". This property is automatically set for the platforms that are known to need it if at least one of the languages supported by the PROJECT command is enabled.

find_package

Load settings for an external project.

```
find_package(<package> [version] [EXACT] [QUIET] [MODULE]
             [REQUIRED] [[COMPONENTS] [components...]]
             [OPTIONAL_COMPONENTS components...]
             [NO_POLICY_SCOPE])
```

Finds and loads settings from an external project. <package>_FOUND will be set to indicate whether the package was found. When the package is found package-specific information is provided through variables and *Imported Targets* documented by the package itself. The QUIET option disables messages if the package cannot be found. The MODULE option disables the second signature documented below. The REQUIRED option stops processing with an error message if the package cannot be found.

A package-specific list of required components may be listed after the COMPONENTS option (or after the REQUIRED option if present). Additional optional components may be listed after OPTIONAL_COMPONENTS. Available components and their influence on whether a package is considered to be found are defined by the target package.

The [version] argument requests a version with which the package found should be compatible (format is major[.minor[.patch[.tweak]]]). The EXACT option requests that the version be matched exactly. If no [version] and/or component list is given to a recursive invocation inside a find-module, the corresponding arguments are forwarded automatically from the outer call (including the EXACT flag for [version]). Version support is currently provided only on a package-by-package basis (details below).

User code should generally look for packages using the above simple signature. The remainder of this command documentation specifies the full command signature and details of the search process. Project maintainers wishing to provide a package to be found by this command are encouraged to read on.

The command has two modes by which it searches for packages: "Module" mode and "Config" mode. Module mode is available when the command is invoked with the above reduced signature. CMake searches for a file called Find<package>.cmake in the CMAKE_MODULE_PATH (page 646) followed by the CMake installation. If the file is found, it is read and processed by CMake. It is responsible for finding the package, checking the version, and producing any needed messages. Many find-modules provide limited or no support for versioning; check the module documentation. If no module is found and the MODULE option is not given the command proceeds to Config mode.

The complete Config mode command signature is:

```
find_package(<package> [version] [EXACT] [QUIET]
             [REQUIRED] [[COMPONENTS] [components...]]
             [CONFIG|NO_MODULE]
             [NO_POLICY_SCOPE]
             [NAMES name1 [name2 ...]]
             [CONFIGS config1 [config2 ...]]
             [HINTS path1 [path2 ... ]]
             [PATHS path1 [path2 ... ]]
             [PATH_SUFFIXES suffix1 [suffix2 ...]]
             [NO_DEFAULT_PATH]
             [NO_CMAKE_ENVIRONMENT_PATH]
             [NO_CMAKE_PATH]
             [NO_SYSTEM_ENVIRONMENT_PATH]
             [NO_CMAKE_PACKAGE_REGISTRY]
             [NO_CMAKE_BUILDS_PATH]
             [NO_CMAKE_SYSTEM_PATH]
             [NO_CMAKE_SYSTEM_PACKAGE_REGISTRY]
             [CMAKE_FIND_ROOT_PATH_BOTH |
              ONLY_CMAKE_FIND_ROOT_PATH |
              NO_CMAKE_FIND_ROOT_PATH])
```

The CONFIG option may be used to skip Module mode explicitly and switch to Config mode. It is synonymous to using NO_MODULE. Config mode is also implied by use of options not specified in the reduced signature.

Config mode attempts to locate a configuration file provided by the package to be found. A cache entry called <package>_DIR is created to hold the directory containing the file. By default the command searches for a package with the name <package>. If the NAMES option is given the names following it are used instead of <package>. The command searches for a file called <name>Config.cmake or <lower-case-name>-config.cmake for each name specified. A replacement set of possible configuration file names may be given using the CONFIGS option. The search procedure is specified below. Once found, the configuration file is read and processed by CMake. Since the file is provided by the package it already knows the location of package contents. The full path to the configuration file is stored in the cmake variable <package>_CONFIG.

All configuration files which have been considered by CMake while searching for an installation of the package with an appropriate version are stored in the cmake variable <package>_CONSIDERED_CONFIGS, the associated versions in <package>_CONSIDERED_VERSIONS.

If the package configuration file cannot be found CMake will generate an error describing the problem unless the QUIET argument is specified. If REQUIRED is specified and the package is not found a fatal error is generated and the configure step stops executing. If <package>_DIR has been set to a directory not containing a configuration file CMake will ignore it and search from scratch.

When the [version] argument is given Config mode will only find a version of the package that claims compatibility with the requested version (format is major[.minor[.patch[.tweak]]]). If the EXACT option is given only a version of the package claiming an exact match of the requested version may be found. CMake does not establish any convention for the meaning of version numbers. Package version numbers are checked by "version" files provided by the packages themselves. For a candidate package configuration file <config-file>.cmake the corresponding version file is located next to it and named either <config-file>-version.cmake or <config-file>Version.cmake. If no such version file is available then the configuration file is assumed to not be compatible with any requested version. A basic version file containing generic version matching code can be created using the CMakePackageConfigHelpers (page 383) module. When a version file is found it is loaded to check the requested version number. The version file is loaded in a nested scope in which the following variables have been defined:

PACKAGE_FIND_NAME the <package> name

PACKAGE_FIND_VERSION full requested version string

PACKAGE_FIND_VERSION_MAJOR major version if requested, else 0

PACKAGE_FIND_VERSION_MINOR minor version if requested, else 0

PACKAGE_FIND_VERSION_PATCH patch version if requested, else 0

PACKAGE_FIND_VERSION_TWEAK tweak version if requested, else 0

PACKAGE_FIND_VERSION_COUNT number of version components, 0 to 4

The version file checks whether it satisfies the requested version and sets these variables:

PACKAGE_VERSION full provided version string

PACKAGE_VERSION_EXACT true if version is exact match

PACKAGE_VERSION_COMPATIBLE true if version is compatible

PACKAGE_VERSION_UNSUITABLE true if unsuitable as any version

These variables are checked by the find_package command to determine whether the configuration file provides an acceptable version. They are not available after the find_package call returns. If the version is acceptable the following variables are set:

<package>_VERSION full provided version string

<package>_VERSION_MAJOR major version if provided, else 0

<package>_VERSION_MINOR minor version if provided, else 0

<package>_VERSION_PATCH patch version if provided, else 0

<package>_VERSION_TWEAK tweak version if provided, else 0

<package>_VERSION_COUNT number of version components, 0 to 4

and the corresponding package configuration file is loaded. When multiple package configuration files are available whose version files claim compatibility with the version requested it is unspecified which one is chosen. No attempt is made to choose a highest or closest version number.

Config mode provides an elaborate interface and search procedure. Much of the interface is provided for completeness and for use internally by find-modules loaded by Module mode. Most user code should simply call:

```
find_package(<package> [major[.minor]] [EXACT] [REQUIRED|QUIET])
```

in order to find a package. Package maintainers providing CMake package configuration files are encouraged to name and install them such that the procedure outlined below will find them without requiring use of additional options.

CMake constructs a set of possible installation prefixes for the package. Under each prefix several directories are searched for a configuration file. The tables below show the directories searched. Each entry is meant for installation trees following Windows (W), UNIX (U), or Apple (A) conventions:

```
<prefix>/                                              (W)
<prefix>/(cmake|CMake)/                                (W)
<prefix>/<name>*/                                      (W)
<prefix>/<name>*/(cmake|CMake)/                        (W)
<prefix>/(lib/<arch>|lib|share)/cmake/<name>*/         (U)
<prefix>/(lib/<arch>|lib|share)/<name>*/               (U)
<prefix>/(lib/<arch>|lib|share)/<name>*/(cmake|CMake)/ (U)
```

On systems supporting OS X Frameworks and Application Bundles the following directories are searched for frameworks or bundles containing a configuration file:

```
<prefix>/<name>.framework/Resources/                   (A)
<prefix>/<name>.framework/Resources/CMake/             (A)
<prefix>/<name>.framework/Versions/*/Resources/        (A)
<prefix>/<name>.framework/Versions/*/Resources/CMake/  (A)
<prefix>/<name>.app/Contents/Resources/                (A)
<prefix>/<name>.app/Contents/Resources/CMake/          (A)
```

In all cases the <name> is treated as case-insensitive and corresponds to any of the names specified (<package> or names given by NAMES). Paths with lib/<arch> are enabled if the CMAKE_LIBRARY_ARCHITECTURE (page 652) variable is set. If PATH_SUFFIXES is specified the suffixes are appended to each (W) or (U) directory entry one-by-one.

This set of directories is intended to work in cooperation with projects that provide configuration files in their installation trees. Directories above marked with (W) are intended for installations on Windows where the prefix may point at the top of an application's installation directory. Those marked with (U) are intended for installations on UNIX platforms where the prefix is shared by multiple packages. This is merely a convention, so all (W) and (U) directories are still searched on all platforms. Directories marked with (A) are intended for installations on Apple platforms. The cmake variables CMAKE_FIND_FRAMEWORK and CMAKE_FIND_APPBUNDLE determine the order of preference as specified below.

The set of installation prefixes is constructed using the following steps. If NO_DEFAULT_PATH is specified all NO_* options are enabled.

1. Search paths specified in cmake-specific cache variables. These are intended to be used on the command line with a -DVAR=value. This can be skipped if NO_CMAKE_PATH is passed:

```
CMAKE_PREFIX_PATH
CMAKE_FRAMEWORK_PATH
CMAKE_APPBUNDLE_PATH
```

2. Search paths specified in cmake-specific environment variables. These are intended to be set in the user's shell configuration. This can be skipped if NO_CMAKE_ENVIRONMENT_PATH is passed:

```
<package>_DIR
CMAKE_PREFIX_PATH
CMAKE_FRAMEWORK_PATH
CMAKE_APPBUNDLE_PATH
```

3. Search paths specified by the HINTS option. These should be paths computed by system introspection, such as a hint provided by the location of another item already found. Hard-coded guesses should be specified with the PATHS option.

4. Search the standard system environment variables. This can be skipped if NO_SYSTEM_ENVIRONMENT_PATH is passed. Path entries ending in /bin or /sbin are automatically converted to their parent directories:

```
PATH
```

5. Search project build trees recently configured in a cmake-gui(1) (page 261). This can be skipped if NO_CMAKE_BUILDS_PATH is passed. It is intended for the case when a user is building multiple dependent projects one after another. (This step is implemented only on Windows.)

6. Search paths stored in the CMake *User Package Registry*. This can be skipped if NO_CMAKE_PACKAGE_REGISTRY is passed or by setting the CMAKE_FIND_PACKAGE_NO_PACKAGE_REGISTRY (page 642) to TRUE. See the cmake-packages(7) manual for details on the user package registry.

7. Search cmake variables defined in the Platform files for the current system. This can be skipped if NO_CMAKE_SYSTEM_PATH is passed:

```
CMAKE_SYSTEM_PREFIX_PATH
CMAKE_SYSTEM_FRAMEWORK_PATH
CMAKE_SYSTEM_APPBUNDLE_PATH
```

8. Search paths stored in the CMake *System Package Registry.* This can be skipped if `NO_CMAKE_SYSTEM_PACKAGE_REGISTRY` is passed or by setting the `CMAKE_FIND_PACKAGE_NO_SYSTEM_PACKAGE_REGISTRY` (page 642) to `TRUE`. See the `cmake-packages(7)` manual for details on the system package registry.

9. Search paths specified by the `PATHS` option. These are typically hard-coded guesses.

On Darwin or systems supporting OS X Frameworks, the cmake variable CMAKE_FIND_FRAMEWORK can be set to empty or one of the following:

- FIRST: Try to find frameworks before standard libraries or headers. This is the default on Darwin.

- LAST: Try to find frameworks after standard libraries or headers.

- ONLY: Only try to find frameworks.

- NEVER: Never try to find frameworks.

On Darwin or systems supporting OS X Application Bundles, the cmake variable CMAKE_FIND_APPBUNDLE can be set to empty or one of the following:

- FIRST: Try to find application bundles before standard programs. This is the default on Darwin.

- LAST: Try to find application bundles after standard programs.

- ONLY: Only try to find application bundles.

- NEVER: Never try to find application bundles.

The CMake variable `CMAKE_FIND_ROOT_PATH` (page 643) specifies one or more directories to be prepended to all other search directories. This effectively "re-roots" the entire search under given locations. Paths which are descendants of the `CMAKE_STAGING_PREFIX` (page 648) are excluded from this re-rooting, because that variable is always a path on the host system. By default the `CMAKE_FIND_ROOT_PATH` (page 643) is empty.

The `CMAKE_SYSROOT` (page 641) variable can also be used to specify exactly one directory to use as a prefix. Setting `CMAKE_SYSROOT` (page 641) also has other effects. See the documentation for that variable for more.

These variables are especially useful when cross-compiling to point to the root directory of the target environment and CMake will search there too. By default at first the directories listed in `CMAKE_FIND_ROOT_PATH` (page 643) are searched, then the `CMAKE_SYSROOT` (page 641) directory is searched, and then the non-rooted directories will be searched. The default behavior can be adjusted by setting `CMAKE_FIND_ROOT_PATH_MODE_PACKAGE` (page 643). This behavior can be manually overridden on a per-call basis. By using CMAKE_FIND_ROOT_PATH_BOTH the search order will be as described above. If NO_CMAKE_FIND_ROOT_PATH is used then `CMAKE_FIND_ROOT_PATH` (page 643) will not be used. If ONLY_CMAKE_FIND_ROOT_PATH is used then only the re-rooted directories and directories below `CMAKE_STAGING_PREFIX` (page 648) will be searched.

The default search order is designed to be most-specific to least-specific for common use cases. Projects may override the order by simply calling the command multiple times and using the `NO_*` options:

```
find_package (<package> PATHS paths... NO_DEFAULT_PATH)
find_package (<package>)
```

Once one of the calls succeeds the result variable will be set and stored in the cache so that no call will search again.

Every non-REQUIRED `find_package` call can be disabled by setting the CMAKE_DISABLE_FIND_PACKAGE_<PackageName> (page 640) variable to TRUE.

When loading a find module or package configuration file `find_package` defines variables to provide information about the call arguments (and restores their original state before returning):

CMAKE_FIND_PACKAGE_NAME the <package> name which is searched for

<package>_FIND_REQUIRED true if REQUIRED option was given

<package>_FIND_QUIETLY true if QUIET option was given

<package>_FIND_VERSION full requested version string

<package>_FIND_VERSION_MAJOR major version if requested, else 0

<package>_FIND_VERSION_MINOR minor version if requested, else 0

<package>_FIND_VERSION_PATCH patch version if requested, else 0

<package>_FIND_VERSION_TWEAK tweak version if requested, else 0

<package>_FIND_VERSION_COUNT number of version components, 0 to 4

<package>_FIND_VERSION_EXACT true if EXACT option was given

<package>_FIND_COMPONENTS list of requested components

<package>_FIND_REQUIRED_<c> true if component <c> is required, false if component <c> is optional

In Module mode the loaded find module is responsible to honor the request detailed by these variables; see the find module for details. In Config mode `find_package` handles REQUIRED, QUIET, and [version] options automatically but leaves it to the package configuration file to handle components in a way that makes sense for the package. The package configuration file may set <package>_FOUND to false to tell `find_package` that component requirements are not satisfied.

See the `cmake_policy()` (page 280) command documentation for discussion of the NO_POLICY_SCOPE option.

find_path

A short-hand signature is:

```
find_path (<VAR> name1 [path1 path2 ...])
```

The general signature is:

```
find_path (
        <VAR>
        name | NAMES name1 [name2 ...]
        [HINTS path1 [path2 ... ENV var]]
        [PATHS path1 [path2 ... ENV var]]
        [PATH_SUFFIXES suffix1 [suffix2 ...]]
        [DOC "cache documentation string"]
        [NO_DEFAULT_PATH]
        [NO_CMAKE_ENVIRONMENT_PATH]
        [NO_CMAKE_PATH]
        [NO_SYSTEM_ENVIRONMENT_PATH]
        [NO_CMAKE_SYSTEM_PATH]
        [CMAKE_FIND_ROOT_PATH_BOTH |
         ONLY_CMAKE_FIND_ROOT_PATH |
         NO_CMAKE_FIND_ROOT_PATH]
        )
```

This command is used to find a directory containing the named file. A cache entry named by <VAR> is created to store the result of this command. If the file in a directory is found the result is stored in the variable and the search will not be repeated unless the variable is cleared. If nothing is found, the result will be <VAR>-NOTFOUND, and the search will be attempted again the next time find_path is invoked with the same variable. The name of the file in a directory that is searched for is specified by the names listed after the NAMES argument. Additional search locations can be specified after the PATHS argument. If ENV var is found in the HINTS or PATHS section the environment variable var will be read and converted from a system environment variable to a cmake style list of paths. For example ENV PATH would be a way to list the system path variable. The argument after DOC will be used for the documentation string in the cache. PATH_SUFFIXES specifies additional subdirectories to check below each search path.

If NO_DEFAULT_PATH is specified, then no additional paths are added to the search. If NO_DEFAULT_PATH is not specified, the search process is as follows:

1. Search paths specified in cmake-specific cache variables. These are intended to be used on the command line with a -DVAR=value. This can be skipped if NO_CMAKE_PATH is passed.

   - <prefix>/include/<arch> if CMAKE_LIBRARY_ARCHITECTURE is set, and <prefix>/include for each <prefix> in CMAKE_PREFIX_PATH

   - CMAKE_INCLUDE_PATH

   - CMAKE_FRAMEWORK_PATH

2. Search paths specified in cmake-specific environment variables. These are intended to be set in the user's shell configuration. This can be skipped if NO_CMAKE_ENVIRONMENT_PATH is passed.

   - <prefix>/include/<arch> if CMAKE_LIBRARY_ARCHITECTURE is set, and <prefix>/include for each <prefix> in CMAKE_PREFIX_PATH

   - CMAKE_INCLUDE_PATH

   - CMAKE_FRAMEWORK_PATH

3. Search the paths specified by the HINTS option. These should be paths computed by system introspection, such as a hint provided by the location of another item already found. Hard-coded guesses should be specified with the PATHS option.

4. Search the standard system environment variables. This can be skipped if NO_SYSTEM_ENVIRONMENT_PATH is an argument.

   - PATH and INCLUDE

5. Search cmake variables defined in the Platform files for the current system. This can be skipped if NO_CMAKE_SYSTEM_PATH is passed.

   - <prefix>/include/<arch> if CMAKE_LIBRARY_ARCHITECTURE is set, and <prefix>/include for each <prefix> in CMAKE_SYSTEM_PREFIX_PATH

   - CMAKE_SYSTEM_INCLUDE_PATH

   - CMAKE_SYSTEM_FRAMEWORK_PATH

6. Search the paths specified by the PATHS option or in the short-hand version of the command. These are typically hard-coded guesses.

On Darwin or systems supporting OS X Frameworks, the cmake variable CMAKE_FIND_FRAMEWORK can be set to empty or one of the following:

- FIRST: Try to find frameworks before standard libraries or headers. This is the default on Darwin.

- LAST: Try to find frameworks after standard libraries or headers.

- ONLY: Only try to find frameworks.

- NEVER: Never try to find frameworks.

On Darwin or systems supporting OS X Application Bundles, the cmake variable CMAKE_FIND_APPBUNDLE can be set to empty or one of the following:

- FIRST: Try to find application bundles before standard programs. This is the default on Darwin.

- LAST: Try to find application bundles after standard programs.

- ONLY: Only try to find application bundles.

- NEVER: Never try to find application bundles.

The CMake variable `CMAKE_FIND_ROOT_PATH` (page 643) specifies one or more directories to be prepended to all other search directories. This effectively "re-roots" the entire search under given locations. Paths which are descendants of the `CMAKE_STAGING_PREFIX` (page 648) are excluded from this re-rooting, because that variable is always a path on the host system. By default the `CMAKE_FIND_ROOT_PATH` (page 643) is empty.

The `CMAKE_SYSROOT` (page 641) variable can also be used to specify exactly one directory to use as a prefix. Setting `CMAKE_SYSROOT` (page 641) also has other effects. See the documentation for that variable for more.

These variables are especially useful when cross-compiling to point to the root directory of the target environment and CMake will search there too. By default at first the directories listed in

CMAKE_FIND_ROOT_PATH (page 643) are searched, then the CMAKE_SYSROOT (page 641) directory is searched, and then the non-rooted directories will be searched. The default behavior can be adjusted by setting CMAKE_FIND_ROOT_PATH_MODE_INCLUDE (page 643). This behavior can be manually overridden on a per-call basis. By using CMAKE_FIND_ROOT_PATH_BOTH the search order will be as described above. If NO_CMAKE_FIND_ROOT_PATH is used then CMAKE_FIND_ROOT_PATH (page 643) will not be used. If ONLY_CMAKE_FIND_ROOT_PATH is used then only the re-rooted directories and directories below CMAKE_STAGING_PREFIX (page 648) will be searched.

The default search order is designed to be most-specific to least-specific for common use cases. Projects may override the order by simply calling the command multiple times and using the NO_* options:

```
find_path (<VAR> NAMES name PATHS paths... NO_DEFAULT_PATH)
find_path (<VAR> NAMES name)
```

Once one of the calls succeeds the result variable will be set and stored in the cache so that no call will search again.

When searching for frameworks, if the file is specified as A/b.h, then the framework search will look for A.framework/Headers/b.h. If that is found the path will be set to the path to the framework. CMake will convert this to the correct -F option to include the file.

find_program

A short-hand signature is:

```
find_program (<VAR> name1 [path1 path2 ...])
```

The general signature is:

```
find_program (
        <VAR>
        name | NAMES name1 [name2 ...]
        [HINTS path1 [path2 ... ENV var]]
        [PATHS path1 [path2 ... ENV var]]
        [PATH_SUFFIXES suffix1 [suffix2 ...]]
        [DOC "cache documentation string"]
        [NO_DEFAULT_PATH]
        [NO_CMAKE_ENVIRONMENT_PATH]
        [NO_CMAKE_PATH]
        [NO_SYSTEM_ENVIRONMENT_PATH]
        [NO_CMAKE_SYSTEM_PATH]
        [CMAKE_FIND_ROOT_PATH_BOTH |
         ONLY_CMAKE_FIND_ROOT_PATH |
         NO_CMAKE_FIND_ROOT_PATH]
        )
```

This command is used to find a program. A cache entry named by <VAR> is created to store the result of this command. If the program is found the result is stored in the variable and the search will not be repeated unless the variable is cleared. If nothing is found, the result will be <VAR>-NOTFOUND, and the search will be attempted again the next time find_program is invoked with the same variable. The name of the program that is searched for is specified by the names listed after the NAMES argument. Additional search locations can be specified after the PATHS argument. If ENV var is found in the HINTS or PATHS section the environment variable var will be read and converted from a system environment variable to a cmake style list of paths. For example ENV PATH would be a way to list the system path variable. The argument after DOC will be used for the documentation string in the cache. PATH_SUFFIXES specifies additional subdirectories to check below each search path.

If NO_DEFAULT_PATH is specified, then no additional paths are added to the search. If NO_DEFAULT_PATH is not specified, the search process is as follows:

1. Search paths specified in cmake-specific cache variables. These are intended to be used on the command line with a -DVAR=value. This can be skipped if NO_CMAKE_PATH is passed.

    - <prefix>/[s]bin for each <prefix> in CMAKE_PREFIX_PATH

    - CMAKE_PROGRAM_PATH

    - CMAKE_APPBUNDLE_PATH

2. Search paths specified in cmake-specific environment variables. These are intended to be set in the user's shell configuration. This can be skipped if NO_CMAKE_ENVIRONMENT_PATH is passed.

    - <prefix>/[s]bin for each <prefix> in CMAKE_PREFIX_PATH

    - CMAKE_PROGRAM_PATH

    - CMAKE_APPBUNDLE_PATH

3. Search the paths specified by the HINTS option. These should be paths computed by system introspection, such as a hint provided by the location of another item already found. Hard-coded guesses should be specified with the PATHS option.

4. Search the standard system environment variables. This can be skipped if NO_SYSTEM_ENVIRONMENT_PATH is an argument.

    - PATH

5. Search cmake variables defined in the Platform files for the current system. This can be skipped if NO_CMAKE_SYSTEM_PATH is passed.

    - <prefix>/[s]bin for each <prefix> in CMAKE_SYSTEM_PREFIX_PATH

    - CMAKE_SYSTEM_PROGRAM_PATH

    - CMAKE_SYSTEM_APPBUNDLE_PATH

6. Search the paths specified by the PATHS option or in the short-hand version of the command. These are typically hard-coded guesses.

On Darwin or systems supporting OS X Frameworks, the cmake variable CMAKE_FIND_FRAMEWORK can be set to empty or one of the following:

- FIRST: Try to find frameworks before standard libraries or headers. This is the default on Darwin.

- LAST: Try to find frameworks after standard libraries or headers.

- ONLY: Only try to find frameworks.

- NEVER: Never try to find frameworks.

On Darwin or systems supporting OS X Application Bundles, the cmake variable CMAKE_FIND_APPBUNDLE can be set to empty or one of the following:

- FIRST: Try to find application bundles before standard programs. This is the default on Darwin.

- LAST: Try to find application bundles after standard programs.

- ONLY: Only try to find application bundles.

- NEVER: Never try to find application bundles.

The CMake variable CMAKE_FIND_ROOT_PATH (page 643) specifies one or more directories to be prepended to all other search directories. This effectively "re-roots" the entire search under given locations. Paths which are descendants of the CMAKE_STAGING_PREFIX (page 648) are excluded from this re-rooting, because that variable is always a path on the host system. By default the CMAKE_FIND_ROOT_PATH (page 643) is empty.

The CMAKE_SYSROOT (page 641) variable can also be used to specify exactly one directory to use as a prefix. Setting CMAKE_SYSROOT (page 641) also has other effects. See the documentation for that variable for more.

These variables are especially useful when cross-compiling to point to the root directory of the target environment and CMake will search there too. By default at first the directories listed in CMAKE_FIND_ROOT_PATH (page 643) are searched, then the CMAKE_SYSROOT (page 641) directory is searched, and then the non-rooted directories will be searched. The default behavior can be adjusted by setting CMAKE_FIND_ROOT_PATH_MODE_PROGRAM (page 644). This behavior can be manually overridden on a per-call basis. By using CMAKE_FIND_ROOT_PATH_BOTH the search order will be as described above. If NO_CMAKE_FIND_ROOT_PATH is used then CMAKE_FIND_ROOT_PATH (page 643) will not be used. If ONLY_CMAKE_FIND_ROOT_PATH is used then only the re-rooted directories and directories below CMAKE_STAGING_PREFIX (page 648) will be searched.

The default search order is designed to be most-specific to least-specific for common use cases. Projects may override the order by simply calling the command multiple times and using the NO_* options:

```
find_program (<VAR> NAMES name PATHS paths... NO_DEFAULT_PATH)
find_program (<VAR> NAMES name)
```

Once one of the calls succeeds the result variable will be set and stored in the cache so that no call will search again.

fltk_wrap_ui

Create FLTK user interfaces Wrappers.

```
fltk_wrap_ui(resultingLibraryName source1
             source2 ... sourceN )
```

Produce .h and .cxx files for all the .fl and .fld files listed. The resulting .h and .cxx files will be added to a variable named resultingLibraryName_FLTK_UI_SRCS which should be added to your library.

foreach

Evaluate a group of commands for each value in a list.

```
foreach(loop_var arg1 arg2 ...)
  COMMAND1(ARGS ...)
  COMMAND2(ARGS ...)
  ...
endforeach(loop_var)
```

All commands between foreach and the matching endforeach are recorded without being invoked. Once the endforeach is evaluated, the recorded list of commands is invoked once for each argument listed in the original foreach command. Before each iteration of the loop "${loop_var}" will be set as a variable with the current value in the list.

```
foreach(loop_var RANGE total)
foreach(loop_var RANGE start stop [step])
```

Foreach can also iterate over a generated range of numbers. There are three types of this iteration:

- When specifying single number, the range will have elements 0 to "total".

- When specifying two numbers, the range will have elements from the first number to the second number.

- The third optional number is the increment used to iterate from the first number to the second number.

```
foreach(loop_var IN [LISTS [list1 [...]]]
                    [ITEMS [item1 [...]]])
```

Iterates over a precise list of items. The LISTS option names list-valued variables to be traversed, including empty elements (an empty string is a zero-length list). (Note macro arguments are not variables.) The ITEMS option ends argument parsing and includes all arguments following it in the iteration.

function

Start recording a function for later invocation as a command.

```
function(<name> [arg1 [arg2 [arg3 ...]]])
  COMMAND1(ARGS ...)
  COMMAND2(ARGS ...)
  ...
endfunction(<name>)
```

Define a function named <name> that takes arguments named arg1 arg2 arg3 (...). Commands listed after function, but before the matching endfunction, are not invoked until the function is invoked. When it is invoked, the commands recorded in the function are first modified by replacing formal parameters (${arg1}) with the arguments passed, and then invoked as normal commands. In addition to referencing the formal parameters you can reference the variable ARGC which will be set to the number of arguments passed into the function as well as ARGV0 ARGV1 ARGV2 ... which will have the actual values of the arguments passed in. This facilitates creating functions with optional arguments. Additionally ARGV holds the list of all arguments given to the function and ARGN holds the list of arguments past the last expected argument.

A function opens a new scope: see set(var PARENT_SCOPE) for details.

See the cmake_policy() command documentation for the behavior of policies inside functions.

get_cmake_property

Get a property of the CMake instance.

```
get_cmake_property(VAR property)
```

Get a property from the CMake instance. The value of the property is stored in the variable VAR. If the property is not found, VAR will be set to "NOTFOUND". Some supported properties include: VARIABLES, CACHE_VARIABLES, COMMANDS, MACROS, and COMPONENTS.

See also the more general get_property() command.

get_directory_property

Get a property of DIRECTORY scope.

```
get_directory_property(<variable> [DIRECTORY <dir>] <prop-name>)
```

Store a property of directory scope in the named variable. If the property is not defined the empty-string is returned. The DIRECTORY argument specifies another directory from which to retrieve the property value. The specified directory must have already been traversed by CMake.

```
get_directory_property(<variable> [DIRECTORY <dir>]
                       DEFINITION <var-name>)
```

Get a variable definition from a directory. This form is useful to get a variable definition from another directory.

See also the more general get_property() command.

get_filename_component

Get a specific component of a full filename.

```
get_filename_component(<VAR> <FileName> <COMP> [CACHE])
```

Set <VAR> to a component of <FileName>, where <COMP> is one of:

```
DIRECTORY = Directory without file name
NAME      = File name without directory
EXT       = File name longest extension (.b.c from d/a.b.c)
NAME_WE   = File name without directory or longest extension
ABSOLUTE  = Full path to file
REALPATH  = Full path to existing file with symlinks resolved
PATH      = Legacy alias for DIRECTORY (use for CMake <= 2.8.11)
```

Paths are returned with forward slashes and have no trailing slahes. The longest file extension is always considered. If the optional CACHE argument is specified, the result variable is added to the cache.

```
get_filename_component(<VAR> FileName
                       PROGRAM [PROGRAM_ARGS <ARG_VAR>]
                       [CACHE])
```

The program in FileName will be found in the system search path or left as a full path. If PROGRAM_ARGS is present with PROGRAM, then any command-line arguments present in the FileName string are split from the program name and stored in <ARG_VAR>. This is used to separate a program name from its arguments in a command line string.

get_property

Get a property.

```
get_property(<variable>
             <GLOBAL                |
              DIRECTORY [dir]       |
              TARGET    <target>  |
              SOURCE    <source>  |
              INSTALL   <file>    |
              TEST      <test>    |
              CACHE     <entry>   |
              VARIABLE>
             PROPERTY <name>
             [SET | DEFINED | BRIEF_DOCS | FULL_DOCS])
```

Get one property from one object in a scope. The first argument specifies the variable in which to store the result. The second argument determines the scope from which to get the property. It must be one of the following:

GLOBAL Scope is unique and does not accept a name.

DIRECTORY Scope defaults to the current directory but another directory (already processed by CMake) may be named by full or relative path.

TARGET Scope must name one existing target.

SOURCE Scope must name one source file.

INSTALL Scope must name one installed file path.

TEST Scope must name one existing test.

CACHE Scope must name one cache entry.

VARIABLE Scope is unique and does not accept a name.

The required PROPERTY option is immediately followed by the name of the property to get. If the property is not set an empty value is returned. If the SET option is given the variable is set to a boolean value indicating whether the property has been set. If the DEFINED option is given the variable is set to a boolean value indicating whether the property has been defined such as with the define_property() (page 283) command. If BRIEF_DOCS or FULL_DOCS is given then the variable is set to a string containing documentation for the requested property. If documentation is requested for a property that has not been defined NOTFOUND is returned.

get_source_file_property

Get a property for a source file.

```
get_source_file_property(VAR file property)
```

Get a property from a source file. The value of the property is stored in the variable VAR. If the property is not found, VAR will be set to "NOTFOUND". Use set_source_files_properties to set property values. Source file properties usually control how the file is built. One property that is always there is LOCATION

See also the more general get_property() command.

get_target_property

Get a property from a target.

```
get_target_property(VAR target property)
```

Get a property from a target. The value of the property is stored in the variable VAR. If the property is not found, VAR will be set to "NOTFOUND". Use set_target_properties to set property values. Properties are usually used to control how a target is built, but some query the target instead. This command can get properties for any target so far created. The targets do not need to be in the current CMakeLists.txt file.

See also the more general get_property() command.

get_test_property

Get a property of the test.

```
get_test_property(test property VAR)
```

Get a property from the test. The value of the property is stored in the variable VAR. If the test or property is not found, VAR will be set to "NOTFOUND". For a list of standard properties you can type cmake –help-property-list.

See also the more general get_property() command.

if

Conditionally execute a group of commands.

```
if(expression)
  # then section.
  COMMAND1(ARGS ...)
  COMMAND2(ARGS ...)
  ...
elseif(expression2)
  # elseif section.
  COMMAND1(ARGS ...)
  COMMAND2(ARGS ...)
  ...
else(expression)
  # else section.
  COMMAND1(ARGS ...)
  COMMAND2(ARGS ...)
  ...
endif(expression)
```

Evaluates the given expression. If the result is true, the commands in the THEN section are invoked. Otherwise, the commands in the else section are invoked. The elseif and else sections are optional. You may have multiple elseif clauses. Note that the expression in the else and endif clause is optional. Long expressions can be used and there is a traditional order of precedence. Parenthetical expressions are evaluated first followed by unary tests such as EXISTS, COMMAND, and DEFINED. Then any binary tests such as EQUAL, LESS, GREATER, STRLESS, STRGREATER, STREQUAL, and MATCHES will be evaluated. Then boolean NOT operators and finally boolean AND and then OR operators will be evaluated.

Possible expressions are:

if(<constant>) True if the constant is 1, ON, YES, TRUE, Y, or a non-zero number. False if the constant is 0, OFF, NO, FALSE, N, IGNORE, NOTFOUND, the empty string, or ends in the suffix -NOTFOUND. Named boolean constants are case-insensitive. If the argument is not one of these specific constants, it is treated as a variable or string and the following signature is used.

if(<variable|string>) True if given a variable that is defined to a value that is not a false constant. False otherwise. (Note macro arguments are not variables.)

if(NOT <expression>) True if the expression is not true.

if(<expr1> AND <expr2>) True if both expressions would be considered true individually.

if(<expr1> OR <expr2>) True if either expression would be considered true individually.

if(COMMAND command-name) True if the given name is a command, macro or function that can be invoked.

if(POLICY policy-id) True if the given name is an existing policy (of the form CMP<NNNN>).

if(TARGET target-name) True if the given name is an existing logical target name such as those created by the `add_executable()` (page 273), `add_library()` (page 274), or `add_custom_target()` (page 272) commands.

if(EXISTS path-to-file-or-directory) True if the named file or directory exists. Behavior is well-defined only for full paths.

if(file1 IS_NEWER_THAN file2) True if file1 is newer than file2 or if one of the two files doesn't exist. Behavior is well-defined only for full paths. If the file time stamps are exactly the same, an `IS_NEWER_THAN` comparison returns true, so that any dependent build operations will occur in the event of a tie. This includes the case of passing the same file name for both file1 and file2.

if(IS_DIRECTORY path-to-directory) True if the given name is a directory. Behavior is well-defined only for full paths.

if(IS_SYMLINK file-name) True if the given name is a symbolic link. Behavior is well-defined only for full paths.

if(IS_ABSOLUTE path) True if the given path is an absolute path.

if(<variable|string> MATCHES regex) True if the given string or variable's value matches the given regular expression.

if(<variable|string> LESS <variable|string>) True if the given string or variable's value is a valid number and less than that on the right.

if(<variable|string> GREATER <variable|string>) True if the given string or variable's value is a valid number and greater than that on the right.

if(<variable|string> EQUAL <variable|string>) True if the given string or variable's value is a valid number and equal to that on the right.

if(<variable|string> STRLESS <variable|string>) True if the given string or variable's value is lexicographically less than the string or variable on the right.

if(<variable|string> STRGREATER <variable|string>) True if the given string or variable's value is lexicographically greater than the string or variable on the right.

if(<variable|string> STREQUAL <variable|string>) True if the given string or variable's value is lexicographically equal to the string or variable on the right.

if(<variable|string> VERSION_LESS <variable|string>) Component-wise integer version number comparison (version format is `major[.minor[.patch[.tweak]]]`).

if(<variable|string> VERSION_EQUAL <variable|string>) Component-wise integer version number comparison (version format is `major[.minor[.patch[.tweak]]]`).

if(<variable|string> VERSION_GREATER <variable|string>) Component-wise integer version number comparison (version format is `major[.minor[.patch[.tweak]]]`).

if(DEFINED <variable>) True if the given variable is defined. It does not matter if the variable is true or false just if it has been set. (Note macro arguments are not variables.)

if((expression) AND (expression OR (expression))) The expressions inside the parenthesis are evaluated first and then the remaining expression is evaluated as in the previous examples. Where there are nested parenthesis the innermost are evaluated as part of evaluating the expression that contains them.

The if command was written very early in CMake's history, predating the `${}` variable evaluation syntax, and for convenience evaluates variables named by its arguments as shown in the above signatures. Note that normal variable evaluation with `${}` applies before the if command even receives the arguments. Therefore code like:

```
set(var1 OFF)
set(var2 "var1")
if(${var2})
```

appears to the if command as:

```
if(var1)
```

and is evaluated according to the `if(<variable>)` case documented above. The result is `OFF` which is false. However, if we remove the `${}` from the example then the command sees:

```
if(var2)
```

which is true because `var2` is defined to "var1" which is not a false constant.

Automatic evaluation applies in the other cases whenever the above-documented signature accepts `<variable|string>`:

- The left hand argument to `MATCHES` is first checked to see if it is a defined variable, if so the variable's value is used, otherwise the original value is used.

- If the left hand argument to `MATCHES` is missing it returns false without error

- Both left and right hand arguments to `LESS`, `GREATER`, and `EQUAL` are independently tested to see if they are defined variables, if so their defined values are used otherwise the original value is used.

- Both left and right hand arguments to `STRLESS`, `STREQUAL`, and `STRGREATER` are independently tested to see if they are defined variables, if so their defined values are used otherwise the original value is used.

- Both left and right hand arguments to `VERSION_LESS`, `VERSION_EQUAL`, and `VERSION_GREATER` are independently tested to see if they are defined variables, if so their defined values are used otherwise the original value is used.

- The right hand argument to `NOT` is tested to see if it is a boolean constant, if so the value is used, otherwise it is assumed to be a variable and it is dereferenced.

- The left and right hand arguments to `AND` and `OR` are independently tested to see if they are boolean constants, if so they are used as such, otherwise they are assumed to be variables and are dereferenced.

To prevent ambiguity, potential variable or keyword names can be specified in a *Quoted Argument* or a *Bracket Argument*. A quoted or bracketed variable or keyword will be interpreted as a string and not dereferenced or interpreted. See policy `CMP0054` (page 558).

include_directories

Add include directories to the build.

```
include_directories([AFTER|BEFORE] [SYSTEM] dir1 [dir2 ...])
```

Add the given directories to those the compiler uses to search for include files. Relative paths are interpreted as relative to the current source directory.

The include directories are added to the INCLUDE_DIRECTORIES (page 570) directory property for the current CMakeLists file. They are also added to the INCLUDE_DIRECTORIES (page 591) target property for each target in the current CMakeLists file. The target property values are the ones used by the generators.

By default the directories specified are appended onto the current list of directories. This default behavior can be changed by setting CMAKE_INCLUDE_DIRECTORIES_BEFORE (page 644) to ON. By using AFTER or BEFORE explicitly, you can select between appending and prepending, independent of the default.

If the SYSTEM option is given, the compiler will be told the directories are meant as system include directories on some platforms. Signalling this setting might achieve effects such as the compiler skipping warnings, or these fixed-install system files not being considered in dependency calculations - see compiler docs.

Arguments to include_directories may use "generator expressions" with the syntax "$<...>". See the cmake-generator-expressions(7) (page 356) manual for available expressions. See the cmake-buildsystem(7) manual for more on defining buildsystem properties.

include_external_msproject

Include an external Microsoft project file in a workspace.

```
include_external_msproject(projectname location
                           [TYPE projectTypeGUID]
                           [GUID projectGUID]
                           [PLATFORM platformName]
                           dep1 dep2 ...)
```

Includes an external Microsoft project in the generated workspace file. Currently does nothing on UNIX. This will create a target named [projectname]. This can be used in the add_dependencies command to make things depend on the external project.

TYPE, GUID and PLATFORM are optional parameters that allow one to specify the type of project, id (GUID) of the project and the name of the target platform. This is useful for projects requiring values other than the default (e.g. WIX projects). These options are not supported by the Visual Studio 6 generator.

include_regular_expression

Set the regular expression used for dependency checking.

```
include_regular_expression(regex_match [regex_complain])
```

Set the regular expressions used in dependency checking. Only files matching regex_match will be traced as dependencies. Only files matching regex_complain will generate warnings if they cannot be found (standard header paths are not searched). The defaults are:

```
regex_match    = "^.*$" (match everything)
regex_complain = "^$" (match empty string only)
```

include

Load and run CMake code from a file or module.

```
include(<file|module> [OPTIONAL] [RESULT_VARIABLE <VAR>]
                      [NO_POLICY_SCOPE])
```

Load and run CMake code from the file given. Variable reads and writes access the scope of the caller (dynamic scoping). If OPTIONAL is present, then no error is raised if the file does not exist. If RE-SULT_VARIABLE is given the variable will be set to the full filename which has been included or NOT-FOUND if it failed.

If a module is specified instead of a file, the file with name <modulename>.cmake is searched first in CMAKE_MODULE_PATH, then in the CMake module directory. There is one exception to this: if the file which calls include() is located itself in the CMake module directory, then first the CMake module directory is searched and CMAKE_MODULE_PATH afterwards. See also policy CMP0017.

See the cmake_policy() command documentation for discussion of the NO_POLICY_SCOPE option.

install

Specify rules to run at install time.

Introduction

This command generates installation rules for a project. Rules specified by calls to this command within a source directory are executed in order during installation. The order across directories is not defined.

There are multiple signatures for this command. Some of them define installation options for files and targets. Options common to multiple signatures are covered here but they are valid only for signatures that specify them. The common options are:

DESTINATION Specify the directory on disk to which a file will be installed. If a full path (with a leading slash or drive letter) is given it is used directly. If a relative path is given it is interpreted relative to the value of the CMAKE_INSTALL_PREFIX (page 645) variable. The prefix can be relocated at install time using the DESTDIR mechanism explained in the CMAKE_INSTALL_PREFIX (page 645) variable documentation.

PERMISSIONS Specify permissions for installed files. Valid permissions are OWNER_READ, OWNER_WRITE, OWNER_EXECUTE, GROUP_READ, GROUP_WRITE, GROUP_EXECUTE, WORLD_READ, WORLD_WRITE, WORLD_EXECUTE, SETUID, and SETGID. Permissions that do not make sense on certain platforms are ignored on those platforms.

CONFIGURATIONS Specify a list of build configurations for which the install rule applies (Debug, Release, etc.).

COMPONENT Specify an installation component name with which the install rule is associated, such as "runtime" or "development". During component-specific installation only install rules associated with the given component name will be executed. During a full installation all components are installed. If COMPONENT is not provided a default component "Unspecified" is created. The default component name may be controlled with the CMAKE_INSTALL_DEFAULT_COMPONENT_NAME (page 645) variable.

RENAME Specify a name for an installed file that may be different from the original file. Renaming is allowed only when a single file is installed by the command.

OPTIONAL Specify that it is not an error if the file to be installed does not exist.

Command signatures that install files may print messages during installation. Use the CMAKE_INSTALL_MESSAGE (page 645) variable to control which messages are printed.

Installing Targets

```
install(TARGETS targets... [EXPORT <export-name>]
        [[ARCHIVE|LIBRARY|RUNTIME|FRAMEWORK|BUNDLE|
          PRIVATE_HEADER|PUBLIC_HEADER|RESOURCE]
         [DESTINATION <dir>]
         [INCLUDES DESTINATION [<dir> ...]]
         [PERMISSIONS permissions...]
         [CONFIGURATIONS [Debug|Release|...]]
         [COMPONENT <component>]
         [OPTIONAL] [NAMELINK_ONLY|NAMELINK_SKIP]
        ] [...])
```

The TARGETS form specifies rules for installing targets from a project. There are five kinds of target files that may be installed: ARCHIVE, LIBRARY, RUNTIME, FRAMEWORK, and BUNDLE. Executables are treated as RUNTIME targets, except that those marked with the MACOSX_BUNDLE property are treated as BUNDLE targets on OS X. Static libraries are always treated as ARCHIVE targets. Module libraries are always treated as LIBRARY targets. For non-DLL platforms shared libraries are treated as LIBRARY targets, except that those marked with the FRAMEWORK property are treated as FRAMEWORK targets on OS X. For DLL platforms the DLL part of a shared library is treated as a RUNTIME target and the corresponding import library is treated as an ARCHIVE target. All Windows-based systems including Cygwin are DLL platforms. The ARCHIVE, LIBRARY, RUNTIME, and FRAMEWORK arguments change the type of target to which the subsequent properties apply. If none is given the installation properties apply to all target types. If only one is given then only targets of that type will be installed (which can be used to install just a DLL or just an import library). The INCLUDES DESTINATION specifies a list of directories which will be added to the

INTERFACE_INCLUDE_DIRECTORIES (page 593) target property of the <targets> when exported by the install(EXPORT) (page 317) command. If a relative path is specified, it is treated as relative to the $<INSTALL_PREFIX>.

The PRIVATE_HEADER, PUBLIC_HEADER, and RESOURCE arguments cause subsequent properties to be applied to installing a FRAMEWORK shared library target's associated files on non-Apple platforms. Rules defined by these arguments are ignored on Apple platforms because the associated files are installed into the appropriate locations inside the framework folder. See documentation of the PRIVATE_HEADER (page 606), PUBLIC_HEADER (page 606), and RESOURCE (page 606) target properties for details.

Either NAMELINK_ONLY or NAMELINK_SKIP may be specified as a LIBRARY option. On some platforms a versioned shared library has a symbolic link such as:

```
lib<name>.so -> lib<name>.so.1
```

where lib<name>.so.1 is the soname of the library and lib<name>.so is a "namelink" allowing linkers to find the library when given -l<name>. The NAMELINK_ONLY option causes installation of only the namelink when a library target is installed. The NAMELINK_SKIP option causes installation of library files other than the namelink when a library target is installed. When neither option is given both portions are installed. On platforms where versioned shared libraries do not have namelinks or when a library is not versioned the NAMELINK_SKIP option installs the library and the NAMELINK_ONLY option installs nothing. See the VERSION (page 609) and SOVERSION (page 608) target properties for details on creating versioned shared libraries.

One or more groups of properties may be specified in a single call to the TARGETS form of this command. A target may be installed more than once to different locations. Consider hypothetical targets myExe, mySharedLib, and myStaticLib. The code:

```
install(TARGETS myExe mySharedLib myStaticLib
        RUNTIME DESTINATION bin
        LIBRARY DESTINATION lib
        ARCHIVE DESTINATION lib/static)
install(TARGETS mySharedLib DESTINATION /some/full/path)
```

will install myExe to <prefix>/bin and myStaticLib to <prefix>/lib/static. On non-DLL platforms mySharedLib will be installed to <prefix>/lib and /some/full/path. On DLL platforms the mySharedLib DLL will be installed to <prefix>/bin and /some/full/path and its import library will be installed to <prefix>/lib/static and /some/full/path.

The EXPORT option associates the installed target files with an export called <export-name>. It must appear before any RUNTIME, LIBRARY, or ARCHIVE options. To actually install the export file itself, call install(EXPORT), documented below.

Installing a target with the EXCLUDE_FROM_ALL (page 585) target property set to TRUE has undefined behavior.

Installing Files

```
install(<FILES|PROGRAMS> files... DESTINATION <dir>
        [PERMISSIONS permissions...]
        [CONFIGURATIONS [Debug|Release|...]]
        [COMPONENT <component>]
        [RENAME <name>] [OPTIONAL])
```

The FILES form specifies rules for installing files for a project. File names given as relative paths are interpreted with respect to the current source directory. Files installed by this form are by default given permissions OWNER_WRITE, OWNER_READ, GROUP_READ, and WORLD_READ if no PERMISSIONS argument is given.

The PROGRAMS form is identical to the FILES form except that the default permissions for the installed file also include OWNER_EXECUTE, GROUP_EXECUTE, and WORLD_EXECUTE. This form is intended to install programs that are not targets, such as shell scripts. Use the TARGETS form to install targets built within the project.

The list of files... given to FILES or PROGRAMS may use "generator expressions" with the syntax $<...>. See the cmake-generator-expressions(7) (page 356) manual for available expressions. However, if any item begins in a generator expression it must evaluate to a full path.

Installing Directories

```
install(DIRECTORY dirs... DESTINATION <dir>
        [FILE_PERMISSIONS permissions...]
        [DIRECTORY_PERMISSIONS permissions...]
        [USE_SOURCE_PERMISSIONS] [OPTIONAL] [MESSAGE_NEVER]
        [CONFIGURATIONS [Debug|Release|...]]
        [COMPONENT <component>] [FILES_MATCHING]
        [[PATTERN <pattern> | REGEX <regex>]
         [EXCLUDE] [PERMISSIONS permissions...]] [...])
```

The DIRECTORY form installs contents of one or more directories to a given destination. The directory structure is copied verbatim to the destination. The last component of each directory name is appended to the destination directory but a trailing slash may be used to avoid this because it leaves the last component empty. Directory names given as relative paths are interpreted with respect to the current source directory. If no input directory names are given the destination directory will be created but nothing will be installed into it. The FILE_PERMISSIONS and DIRECTORY_PERMISSIONS options specify permissions given to files and directories in the destination. If USE_SOURCE_PERMISSIONS is specified and FILE_PERMISSIONS is not, file permissions will be copied from the source directory structure. If no permissions are specified files will be given the default permissions specified in the FILES form of the command, and the directories will be given the default permissions specified in the PROGRAMS form of the command.

The MESSAGE_NEVER option disables file installation status output.

Installation of directories may be controlled with fine granularity using the PATTERN or REGEX options. These "match" options specify a globbing pattern or regular expression to match directories or files encountered within input directories. They may be used to apply certain options (see below) to a subset of the files and directories encountered. The full path to each input file or directory (with forward slashes) is matched against the expression. A PATTERN will match only complete file names: the portion of the full path matching the pattern must occur at the end of the file name and be preceded by a slash. A REGEX will match any portion of the full path but it may use / and $ to simulate the PATTERN behavior. By default all files and directories are installed whether or not they are matched. The FILES_MATCHING option may be given before the first match option to disable installation of files (but not directories) not matched by any expression. For example, the code

```
install(DIRECTORY src/ DESTINATION include/myproj
        FILES_MATCHING PATTERN "*.h")
```

will extract and install header files from a source tree.

Some options may follow a PATTERN or REGEX expression and are applied only to files or directories matching them. The EXCLUDE option will skip the matched file or directory. The PERMISSIONS option overrides the permissions setting for the matched file or directory. For example the code

```
install(DIRECTORY icons scripts/ DESTINATION share/myproj
        PATTERN "CVS" EXCLUDE
        PATTERN "scripts/*"
        PERMISSIONS OWNER_EXECUTE OWNER_WRITE OWNER_READ
                    GROUP_EXECUTE GROUP_READ)
```

will install the icons directory to share/myproj/icons and the scripts directory to share/myproj. The icons will get default file permissions, the scripts will be given specific permissions, and any CVS directories will be excluded.

Custom Installation Logic

```
install([[SCRIPT <file>] [CODE <code>]]
        [COMPONENT <component>] [...])
```

The SCRIPT form will invoke the given CMake script files during installation. If the script file name is a relative path it will be interpreted with respect to the current source directory. The CODE form will invoke the given CMake code during installation. Code is specified as a single argument inside a double-quoted string. For example, the code

```
install(CODE "MESSAGE(\"Sample install message.\")")
```

will print a message during installation.

Installing Exports

```
install(EXPORT <export-name> DESTINATION <dir>
        [NAMESPACE <namespace>] [FILE <name>.cmake]
        [PERMISSIONS permissions...]
```

```
          [CONFIGURATIONS [Debug|Release|...]]
          [EXPORT_LINK_INTERFACE_LIBRARIES]
          [COMPONENT <component>])
```

The EXPORT form generates and installs a CMake file containing code to import targets from the installation tree into another project. Target installations are associated with the export <export-name> using the EXPORT option of the install(TARGETS) signature documented above. The NAMESPACE option will prepend <namespace> to the target names as they are written to the import file. By default the generated file will be called <export-name>.cmake but the FILE option may be used to specify a different name. The value given to the FILE option must be a file name with the .cmake extension. If a CONFIGURATIONS option is given then the file will only be installed when one of the named configurations is installed. Additionally, the generated import file will reference only the matching target configurations. The EXPORT_LINK_INTERFACE_LIBRARIES keyword, if present, causes the contents of the properties matching (IMPORTED_)?LINK_INTERFACE_LIBRARIES(_<CONFIG>)? to be exported, when policy CMP0022 (page 546) is NEW. If a COMPONENT option is specified that does not match that given to the targets associated with <export-name> the behavior is undefined. If a library target is included in the export but a target to which it links is not included the behavior is unspecified.

The EXPORT form is useful to help outside projects use targets built and installed by the current project. For example, the code

```
install(TARGETS myexe EXPORT myproj DESTINATION bin)
install(EXPORT myproj NAMESPACE mp_ DESTINATION lib/myproj)
```

will install the executable myexe to <prefix>/bin and code to import it in the file <prefix>/lib/myproj/myproj.cmake. An outside project may load this file with the include command and reference the myexe executable from the installation tree using the imported target name mp_myexe as if the target were built in its own tree.

Note: This command supercedes the install_targets() (page 348) command and the PRE_INSTALL_SCRIPT (page 623) and POST_INSTALL_SCRIPT (page 623) target properties. It also replaces the FILES forms of the install_files() (page 347) and install_programs() (page 348) commands. The processing order of these install rules relative to those generated by install_targets() (page 348), install_files() (page 347), and install_programs() (page 348) commands is not defined.

---

link_directories

Specify directories in which the linker will look for libraries.

```
link_directories(directory1 directory2 ...)
```

Specify the paths in which the linker should search for libraries. The command will apply only to targets created after it is called. Relative paths given to this command are interpreted as relative to the current source directory, see CMP0015.

Note that this command is rarely necessary. Library locations returned by find_package() and find_library() are absolute paths. Pass these absolute library file paths directly to the target_link_libraries() command. CMake will ensure the linker finds them.

list

List operations.

```
list(LENGTH <list> <output variable>)
list(GET <list> <element index> [<element index> ...]
     <output variable>)
list(APPEND <list> [<element> ...])
list(FIND <list> <value> <output variable>)
list(INSERT <list> <element_index> <element> [<element> ...])
list(REMOVE_ITEM <list> <value> [<value> ...])
list(REMOVE_AT <list> <index> [<index> ...])
list(REMOVE_DUPLICATES <list>)
list(REVERSE <list>)
list(SORT <list>)
```

LENGTH will return a given list's length.

GET will return list of elements specified by indices from the list.

APPEND will append elements to the list.

FIND will return the index of the element specified in the list or -1 if it wasn't found.

INSERT will insert elements to the list to the specified location.

REMOVE_AT and REMOVE_ITEM will remove items from the list. The difference is that REMOVE_ITEM will remove the given items, while REMOVE_AT will remove the items at the given indices.

REMOVE_DUPLICATES will remove duplicated items in the list.

REVERSE reverses the contents of the list in-place.

SORT sorts the list in-place alphabetically.

The list subcommands APPEND, INSERT, REMOVE_AT, REMOVE_ITEM, REMOVE_DUPLICATES, REVERSE and SORT may create new values for the list within the current CMake variable scope. Similar to the SET command, the LIST command creates new variable values in the current scope, even if the list itself is actually defined in a parent scope. To propagate the results of these operations upwards, use SET with PARENT_SCOPE, SET with CACHE INTERNAL, or some other means of value propagation.

NOTES: A list in cmake is a ; separated group of strings. To create a list the set command can be used. For example, set(var a b c d e) creates a list with a;b;c;d;e, and set(var "a b c d e") creates a string or a list with one item in it. (Note macro arguments are not variables, and therefore cannot be used in LIST commands.)

When specifying index values, if <element index> is 0 or greater, it is indexed from the beginning of the list, with 0 representing the first list element. If <element index> is -1 or lesser, it is indexed from the end of the list, with -1 representing the last list element. Be careful when counting with negative indices: they do not start from 0. -0 is equivalent to 0, the first list element.

load_cache

Load in the values from another project's CMake cache.

```
load_cache(pathToCacheFile READ_WITH_PREFIX
           prefix entry1...)
```

Read the cache and store the requested entries in variables with their name prefixed with the given prefix. This only reads the values, and does not create entries in the local project's cache.

```
load_cache(pathToCacheFile [EXCLUDE entry1...]
           [INCLUDE_INTERNALS entry1...])
```

Load in the values from another cache and store them in the local project's cache as internal entries. This is useful for a project that depends on another project built in a different tree. EXCLUDE option can be used to provide a list of entries to be excluded. INCLUDE_INTERNALS can be used to provide a list of internal entries to be included. Normally, no internal entries are brought in. Use of this form of the command is strongly discouraged, but it is provided for backward compatibility.

load_command

Disallowed. See CMake Policy CMP0031 (page 550).

Load a command into a running CMake.

```
load_command(COMMAND_NAME <loc1> [loc2 ...])
```

The given locations are searched for a library whose name is cmCOMMAND_NAME. If found, it is loaded as a module and the command is added to the set of available CMake commands. Usually, TRY_COMPILE is used before this command to compile the module. If the command is successfully loaded a variable named

```
CMAKE_LOADED_COMMAND_<COMMAND_NAME>
```

will be set to the full path of the module that was loaded. Otherwise the variable will not be set.

macro

Start recording a macro for later invocation as a command.

```
macro(<name> [arg1 [arg2 [arg3 ...]]])
  COMMAND1(ARGS ...)
  COMMAND2(ARGS ...)
  ...
endmacro(<name>)
```

Define a macro named <name> that takes arguments named arg1 arg2 arg3 (...). Commands listed after macro, but before the matching endmacro, are not invoked until the macro is invoked. When it is invoked, the commands recorded in the macro are first modified by replacing formal parameters (${arg1}) with the arguments passed, and then invoked as normal commands. In addition to referencing the formal parameters you can reference the values ${ARGC} which will be set to the number of arguments passed into the function as well as ${ARGV0} ${ARGV1} ${ARGV2} ... which will have the actual values of the arguments passed in. This facilitates creating macros with optional arguments. Additionally ${ARGV} holds the list of all arguments given to the macro and ${ARGN} holds the list of arguments past the last expected argument.

See the cmake_policy() command documentation for the behavior of policies inside macros.

Macro Argument Caveats

Note that the parameters to a macro and values such as ARGN are not variables in the usual CMake sense. They are string replacements much like the C preprocessor would do with a macro. Therefore you will NOT be able to use commands like:

```
if(ARGV1) # ARGV1 is not a variable
foreach(loop_var IN LISTS ARGN) # ARGN is not a variable
```

In the first case you can use if(${ARGV1}), in the second case, you can use foreach(loop_var ${ARGN}) but this will skip empty arguments. If you need to include them, you can use:

```
set(list_var "${ARGN}")
foreach(loop_var IN LISTS list_var)
```

Note that if you have a variable with the same name in the scope from which the macro is called, using unreferenced names will use the existing variable instead of the arguments. For example:

```
macro(_BAR)
  foreach(arg IN LISTS ARGN)
    [...]
  endforeach()
endmacro()

function(_FOO)
  _bar(x y z)
endfunction()

_foo(a b c)
```

Will loop over a;b;c and not over x;y;z as one might be expecting. If you want true CMake variables and/or better CMake scope control you should look at the function command.

mark_as_advanced

Mark cmake cached variables as advanced.

```
mark_as_advanced([CLEAR|FORCE] VAR [VAR2 ...])
```

Mark the named cached variables as advanced. An advanced variable will not be displayed in any of the cmake GUIs unless the show advanced option is on. If CLEAR is the first argument advanced variables are changed back to unadvanced. If FORCE is the first argument, then the variable is made advanced. If neither FORCE nor CLEAR is specified, new values will be marked as advanced, but if the variable already has an advanced/non-advanced state, it will not be changed.

It does nothing in script mode.

math

Mathematical expressions.

```
math(EXPR <output variable> <math expression>)
```

EXPR evaluates mathematical expression and returns result in the output variable. Example mathematical expression is '5 * (10 + 13)'. Supported operators are + - * / % | & ^ ~ << >> * / %. They have the same meaning as they do in C code.

message

Display a message to the user.

```
message([<mode>] "message to display" ...)
```

The optional <mode> keyword determines the type of message:

```
(none)         = Important information
STATUS         = Incidental information
WARNING        = CMake Warning, continue processing
AUTHOR_WARNING = CMake Warning (dev), continue processing
SEND_ERROR     = CMake Error, continue processing,
                         but skip generation
FATAL_ERROR    = CMake Error, stop processing and generation
DEPRECATION    = CMake Deprecation Error or Warning if variable
                 CMAKE_ERROR_DEPRECATED or CMAKE_WARN_DEPRECATED
                 is enabled, respectively, else no message.
```

The CMake command-line tool displays STATUS messages on stdout and all other message types on stderr. The CMake GUI displays all messages in its log area. The interactive dialogs (ccmake and CMakeSetup) show STATUS messages one at a time on a status line and other messages in interactive pop-up boxes.

CMake Warning and Error message text displays using a simple markup language. Non-indented text is formatted in line-wrapped paragraphs delimited by newlines. Indented text is considered pre-formatted.

option

Provides an option that the user can optionally select.

```
option(<option_variable> "help string describing option"
       [initial value])
```

Provide an option for the user to select as ON or OFF. If no initial value is provided, OFF is used.

If you have options that depend on the values of other options, see the module help for CMakeDependentOption.

project

Set a name, version, and enable languages for the entire project.

```
project(<PROJECT-NAME> [LANGUAGES] [<language-name>...])
project(<PROJECT-NAME>
        [VERSION <major>[.<minor>[.<patch>[.<tweak>]]]]
        [LANGUAGES <language-name>...])
```

Sets the name of the project and stores the name in the PROJECT_NAME (page 637) variable. Additionally this sets variables

- PROJECT_SOURCE_DIR (page 638), <PROJECT-NAME>_SOURCE_DIR (page 637)
- PROJECT_BINARY_DIR (page 636), <PROJECT-NAME>_BINARY_DIR (page 636)

If VERSION is specified, given components must be non-negative integers. If VERSION is not specified, the default version is the empty string. The VERSION option may not be used unless policy CMP0048 (page 556) is set to NEW.

The project() (page 327) command stores the version number and its components in variables

- PROJECT_VERSION (page 638), <PROJECT-NAME>_VERSION (page 637)
- PROJECT_VERSION_MAJOR (page 638), <PROJECT-NAME>_VERSION_MAJOR (page 637)
- PROJECT_VERSION_MINOR (page 638), <PROJECT-NAME>_VERSION_MINOR (page 637)
- PROJECT_VERSION_PATCH (page 638), <PROJECT-NAME>_VERSION_PATCH (page 637)
- PROJECT_VERSION_TWEAK (page 638), <PROJECT-NAME>_VERSION_TWEAK (page 637)

Variables corresponding to unspecified versions are set to the empty string (if policy CMP0048 (page 556) is set to NEW).

Optionally you can specify which languages your project supports. Example languages are C, CXX (i.e. C++), Fortran, etc. By default C and CXX are enabled if no language options are given. Specify language NONE, or use the LANGUAGES keyword and list no languages, to skip enabling any languages.

If a variable exists called CMAKE_PROJECT_<PROJECT-NAME>_INCLUDE (page 648), the file pointed to by that variable will be included as the last step of the project command.

The top-level CMakeLists.txt file for a project must contain a literal, direct call to the project() (page 327) command; loading one through the include() (page 317) command is not sufficient. If no such call exists CMake will implicitly add one to the top that enables the default languages (C and CXX).

qt_wrap_cpp

Create Qt Wrappers.

```
qt_wrap_cpp(resultingLibraryName DestName
            SourceLists ...)
```

Produce moc files for all the .h files listed in the SourceLists. The moc files will be added to the library using the DestName source list.

qt_wrap_ui

Create Qt user interfaces Wrappers.

```
qt_wrap_ui(resultingLibraryName HeadersDestName
           SourcesDestName SourceLists ...)
```

Produce .h and .cxx files for all the .ui files listed in the SourceLists. The .h files will be added to the library using the HeadersDestNamesource list. The .cxx files will be added to the library using the SourcesDestNamesource list.

remove_definitions

Removes -D define flags added by add_definitions.

```
remove_definitions(-DFOO -DBAR ...)
```

Removes flags (added by add_definitions) from the compiler command line for sources in the current directory and below.

return

Return from a file, directory or function.

```
return()
```

Returns from a file, directory or function. When this command is encountered in an included file (via include() or find_package()), it causes processing of the current file to stop and control is returned to the including file. If it is encountered in a file which is not included by another file, e.g. a CMakeLists.txt, control is returned to the parent directory if there is one. If return is called in a function, control is returned to the caller of the function. Note that a macro is not a function and does not handle return like a function does.

separate_arguments

Parse space-separated arguments into a semicolon-separated list.

```
separate_arguments(<var> <UNIX|WINDOWS>_COMMAND "<args>")
```

Parses a unix- or windows-style command-line string "<args>" and stores a semicolon-separated list of the arguments in <var>. The entire command line must be given in one "<args>" argument.

The UNIX_COMMAND mode separates arguments by unquoted whitespace. It recognizes both single-quote and double-quote pairs. A backslash escapes the next literal character (" is "); there are no special escapes (n is just n).

The WINDOWS_COMMAND mode parses a windows command-line using the same syntax the runtime library uses to construct argv at startup. It separates arguments by whitespace that is not double-quoted. Backslashes are literal unless they precede double-quotes. See the MSDN article "Parsing C Command-Line Arguments" for details.

```
separate_arguments(VARIABLE)
```

Convert the value of VARIABLE to a semi-colon separated list. All spaces are replaced with ';'. This helps with generating command lines.

set_directory_properties

Set a property of the directory.

```
set_directory_properties(PROPERTIES prop1 value1 prop2 value2)
```

Set a property for the current directory and subdirectories. If the property is not found, CMake will report an error. The properties include: INCLUDE_DIRECTORIES, LINK_DIRECTORIES, INCLUDE_REGULAR_EXPRESSION, and ADDITIONAL_MAKE_CLEAN_FILES. ADDITIONAL_MAKE_CLEAN_FILES is a list of files that will be cleaned as a part of "make clean" stage.

set_property

Set a named property in a given scope.

```
set_property(<GLOBAL                            |
              DIRECTORY [dir]                    |
              TARGET    [target1 [target2 ...]] |
              SOURCE    [src1 [src2 ...]]        |
              INSTALL   [file1 [file2 ...]]      |
              TEST      [test1 [test2 ...]]      |
              CACHE     [entry1 [entry2 ...]]> |
             [APPEND] [APPEND_STRING]
             PROPERTY <name> [value1 [value2 ...]])
```

Set one property on zero or more objects of a scope. The first argument determines the scope in which the property is set. It must be one of the following:

GLOBAL Scope is unique and does not accept a name.

DIRECTORY Scope defaults to the current directory but another directory (already processed by CMake) may be named by full or relative path.

TARGET Scope may name zero or more existing targets.

SOURCE Scope may name zero or more source files. Note that source file properties are visible only to targets added in the same directory (CMakeLists.txt).

INSTALL Scope may name zero or more installed file paths. These are made available to CPack to influence deployment.

> Both the property key and value may use generator expressions. Specific properties may apply to installed files and/or directories.

> Path components have to be separated by forward slashes, must be normalized and are case sensitive.

> To reference the installation prefix itself with a relative path use ".".

> Currently installed file properties are only defined for the WIX generator where the given paths are relative to the installation prefix.

TEST Scope may name zero or more existing tests.

CACHE Scope must name zero or more cache existing entries.

The required PROPERTY option is immediately followed by the name of the property to set. Remaining arguments are used to compose the property value in the form of a semicolon-separated list. If the APPEND option is given the list is appended to any existing property value. If the APPEND_STRING option is given the string is append to any existing property value as string, i.e. it results in a longer string and not a list of strings.

set

Set a CMake, cache or environment variable to a given value.

```
set(<variable> <value>
    [[CACHE <type> <docstring> [FORCE]] | PARENT_SCOPE])
```

Within CMake sets <variable> to the value <value>. <value> is expanded before <variable> is set to it. Normally, set will set a regular CMake variable. If CACHE is present, then the <variable> is put in the cache instead, unless it is already in the cache. See section 'Variable types in CMake' below for details of regular and cache variables and their interactions. If CACHE is used, <type> and <docstring> are required. <type> is used by the CMake GUI to choose a widget with which the user sets a value. The value for <type> may be one of

```
FILEPATH = File chooser dialog.
PATH     = Directory chooser dialog.
STRING   = Arbitrary string.
BOOL     = Boolean ON/OFF checkbox.
INTERNAL = No GUI entry (used for persistent variables).
```

If <type> is INTERNAL, the cache variable is marked as internal, and will not be shown to the user in tools like cmake-gui. This is intended for values that should be persisted in the cache, but which users should not normally change. INTERNAL implies FORCE.

Normally, set(...CACHE...) creates cache variables, but does not modify them. If FORCE is specified, the value of the cache variable is set, even if the variable is already in the cache. This should normally be avoided, as it will remove any changes to the cache variable's value by the user.

If PARENT_SCOPE is present, the variable will be set in the scope above the current scope. Each new directory or function creates a new scope. This command will set the value of a variable into the parent directory or calling function (whichever is applicable to the case at hand). PARENT_SCOPE cannot be combined with CACHE.

If <value> is not specified then the variable is removed instead of set. See also: the unset() command.

```
set(<variable> <value1> ... <valueN>)
```

In this case <variable> is set to a semicolon separated list of values.

<variable> can be an environment variable such as:

```
set( ENV{PATH} /home/martink )
```

in which case the environment variable will be set.

* Variable types in CMake *

In CMake there are two types of variables: normal variables and cache variables. Normal variables are meant for the internal use of the script (just like variables in most programming languages); they are not persisted across CMake runs. Cache variables (unless set with INTERNAL) are mostly intended for configuration settings where the first CMake run determines a suitable default value, which the user can then override, by editing the cache with tools such as ccmake or cmake-gui. Cache variables are stored in the CMake cache file, and are persisted across CMake runs.

Both types can exist at the same time with the same name but different values. When ${FOO} is evaluated, CMake first looks for a normal variable 'FOO' in scope and uses it if set. If and only if no normal variable exists then it falls back to the cache variable 'FOO'.

Some examples:

The code 'set(FOO "x")' sets the normal variable 'FOO'. It does not touch the cache, but it will hide any existing cache value 'FOO'.

The code 'set(FOO "x" CACHE ...)' checks for 'FOO' in the cache, ignoring any normal variable of the same name. If 'FOO' is in the cache then nothing happens to either the normal variable or the cache variable. If 'FOO' is not in the cache, then it is added to the cache.

Finally, whenever a cache variable is added or modified by a command, CMake also *removes* the normal variable of the same name from the current scope so that an immediately following evaluation of it will expose the newly cached value.

Normally projects should avoid using normal and cache variables of the same name, as this interaction can be hard to follow. However, in some situations it can be useful. One example (used by some projects):

A project has a subproject in its source tree. The child project has its own CMakeLists.txt, which is included from the parent CMakeLists.txt using add_subdirectory(). Now, if the parent and the child project provide the same option (for example a compiler option), the parent gets the first chance to add a user-editable option to the cache. Normally, the child would then use the same value that the parent uses. However, it may be necessary to hard-code the value for the child project's option while still allowing the user to edit the value used by the parent project. The parent project can achieve this simply by setting a normal variable with the same name as the option in a scope sufficient to hide the option's cache variable from the child completely. The parent has already set the cache variable, so the child's set(...CACHE...) will do nothing, and evaluating the option variable will use the value from the normal variable, which hides the cache variable.

set_source_files_properties

Source files can have properties that affect how they are built.

```
set_source_files_properties([file1 [file2 [...]]]
                            PROPERTIES prop1 value1
                            [prop2 value2 [...]])
```

Set properties associated with source files using a key/value paired list. See properties documentation for those known to CMake. Unrecognized properties are ignored. Source file properties are visible only to targets added in the same directory (CMakeLists.txt).

set_target_properties

Targets can have properties that affect how they are built.

```
set_target_properties(target1 target2 ...
                      PROPERTIES prop1 value1
                      prop2 value2 ...)
```

Set properties on a target. The syntax for the command is to list all the files you want to change, and then provide the values you want to set next. You can use any prop value pair you want and extract it later with the GET_TARGET_PROPERTY command.

Properties that affect the name of a target's output file are as follows. The PREFIX and SUFFIX properties override the default target name prefix (such as "lib") and suffix (such as ".so"). IMPORT_PREFIX and IM-PORT_SUFFIX are the equivalent properties for the import library corresponding to a DLL (for SHARED library targets). OUTPUT_NAME sets the real name of a target when it is built and can be used to help create two targets of the same name even though CMake requires unique logical target names. There is also a <CON-FIG>_OUTPUT_NAME that can set the output name on a per-configuration basis. <CONFIG>_POSTFIX sets a postfix for the real name of the target when it is built under the configuration named by <CONFIG> (in upper-case, such as "DEBUG_POSTFIX"). The value of this property is initialized when the target is created to the value of the variable CMAKE_<CONFIG>_POSTFIX (except for executable targets because earlier CMake versions which did not use this variable for executables).

The LINK_FLAGS property can be used to add extra flags to the link step of a target. LINK_FLAGS_<CONFIG> will add to the configuration <CONFIG>, for example, DEBUG, RELEASE, MINSIZEREL, RELWITHDEBINFO. DEFINE_SYMBOL sets the name of the preprocessor symbol defined when compiling sources in a shared library. If not set here then it is set to target_EXPORTS by default (with some substitutions if the target is not a valid C identifier). This is useful for headers to know whether they are being included from inside their library or outside to properly setup dllexport/dllimport decorations. The COMPILE_FLAGS property sets additional compiler flags used to build sources within the target. It may also be used to pass additional preprocessor definitions.

The LINKER_LANGUAGE property is used to change the tool used to link an executable or shared library. The default is set the language to match the files in the library. CXX and C are common values for this property.

For shared libraries VERSION and SOVERSION can be used to specify the build version and API version respectively. When building or installing appropriate symlinks are created if the platform supports symlinks and the linker supports so-names. If only one of both is specified the missing is assumed to have the same version number. For executables VERSION can be used to specify the build version. When building or installing appropriate symlinks are created if the platform supports symlinks. For shared libraries and executables on Windows the VERSION attribute is parsed to extract a "major.minor" version number. These numbers are used as the image version of the binary.

There are a few properties used to specify RPATH rules. INSTALL_RPATH is a semicolon-separated list specifying the rpath to use in installed targets (for platforms that support it). IN-STALL_RPATH_USE_LINK_PATH is a boolean that if set to true will append directories in the linker search path and outside the project to the INSTALL_RPATH. SKIP_BUILD_RPATH is a boolean specifying whether to skip automatic generation of an rpath allowing the target to run from the build tree. BUILD_WITH_INSTALL_RPATH is a boolean specifying whether to link the target in the build tree with the INSTALL_RPATH. This takes precedence over SKIP_BUILD_RPATH and avoids the need for relinking before installation. INSTALL_NAME_DIR is a string specifying the directory portion of the "install_name" field of shared libraries on Mac OSX to use in the installed targets. When the target is created the values of the variables CMAKE_INSTALL_RPATH, CMAKE_INSTALL_RPATH_USE_LINK_PATH, CMAKE_SKIP_BUILD_RPATH, CMAKE_BUILD_WITH_INSTALL_RPATH, and CMAKE_INSTALL_NAME_DIR are used to initialize these properties.

PROJECT_LABEL can be used to change the name of the target in an IDE like visual studio. VS_KEYWORD can be set to change the visual studio keyword, for example Qt integration works better if this is set to Qt4VSv1.0.

VS_SCC_PROJECTNAME, VS_SCC_LOCALPATH, VS_SCC_PROVIDER and VS_SCC_AUXPATH can be set to add support for source control bindings in a Visual Studio project file.

VS_GLOBAL_<variable> can be set to add a Visual Studio project-specific global variable. Qt integration works better if VS_GLOBAL_QtVersion is set to the Qt version FindQt4.cmake found. For example, "4.7.3"

The PRE_INSTALL_SCRIPT and POST_INSTALL_SCRIPT properties are the old way to specify CMake scripts to run before and after installing a target. They are used only when the old INSTALL_TARGETS command is used to install the target. Use the INSTALL command instead.

The EXCLUDE_FROM_DEFAULT_BUILD property is used by the visual studio generators. If it is set to 1 the target will not be part of the default build when you select "Build Solution". This can also be set on a per-configuration basis using EXCLUDE_FROM_DEFAULT_BUILD_<CONFIG>.

set_tests_properties

Set a property of the tests.

```
set_tests_properties(test1 [test2...] PROPERTIES prop1 value1 prop2 value2)
```

Set a property for the tests. If the test is not found, CMake will report an error. Generator expressions will be expanded the same as supported by the test's add_test call. The properties include:

WILL_FAIL: If set to true, this will invert the pass/fail flag of the test.

PASS_REGULAR_EXPRESSION: If set, the test output will be checked against the specified regular expressions and at least one of the regular expressions has to match, otherwise the test will fail.

```
Example: PASS_REGULAR_EXPRESSION "TestPassed;All ok"
```

FAIL_REGULAR_EXPRESSION: If set, if the output will match to one of specified regular expressions, the test will fail.

```
Example: FAIL_REGULAR_EXPRESSION "[^a-z]Error;ERROR;Failed"
```

Both PASS_REGULAR_EXPRESSION and FAIL_REGULAR_EXPRESSION expect a list of regular expressions.

TIMEOUT: Setting this will limit the test runtime to the number of seconds specified.

site_name

Set the given variable to the name of the computer.

```
site_name(variable)
```

source_group

Define a grouping for source files in IDE project generation.

```
source_group(<name> [FILES <src>...] [REGULAR_EXPRESSION <regex>])
```

Defines a group into which sources will be placed in project files. This is intended to set up file tabs in Visual Studio. The options are:

FILES Any source file specified explicitly will be placed in group `<name>`. Relative paths are interpreted with respect to the current source directory.

REGULAR_EXPRESSION Any source file whose name matches the regular expression will be placed in group `<name>`.

If a source file matches multiple groups, the *last* group that explicitly lists the file with `FILES` will be favored, if any. If no group explicitly lists the file, the *last* group whose regular expression matches the file will be favored.

The `<name>` of the group may contain backslashes to specify subgroups:

```
source_group(outer\\inner ...)
```

For backwards compatibility, the short-hand signature

```
source_group(<name> <regex>)
```

is equivalent to

```
source_group(<name> REGULAR_EXPRESSION <regex>)
```

string

String operations.

```
string(REGEX MATCH <regular_expression>
       <output variable> <input> [<input>...])
string(REGEX MATCHALL <regular_expression>
       <output variable> <input> [<input>...])
string(REGEX REPLACE <regular_expression>
       <replace_expression> <output variable>
       <input> [<input>...])
string(REPLACE <match_string>
       <replace_string> <output variable>
       <input> [<input>...])
string(CONCAT <output variable> [<input>...])
string(<MD5|SHA1|SHA224|SHA256|SHA384|SHA512>
       <output variable> <input>)
string(COMPARE EQUAL <string1> <string2> <output variable>)
string(COMPARE NOTEQUAL <string1> <string2> <output variable>)
string(COMPARE LESS <string1> <string2> <output variable>)
string(COMPARE GREATER <string1> <string2> <output variable>)
string(ASCII <number> [<number> ...] <output variable>)
string(CONFIGURE <string1> <output variable>
       [@ONLY] [ESCAPE_QUOTES])
string(TOUPPER <string1> <output variable>)
string(TOLOWER <string1> <output variable>)
string(LENGTH <string> <output variable>)
string(SUBSTRING <string> <begin> <length> <output variable>)
```

```
string(STRIP <string> <output variable>)
string(RANDOM [LENGTH <length>] [ALPHABET <alphabet>]
       [RANDOM_SEED <seed>] <output variable>)
string(FIND <string> <substring> <output variable> [REVERSE])
string(TIMESTAMP <output variable> [<format string>] [UTC])
string(MAKE_C_IDENTIFIER <input string> <output variable>)
string(GENEX_STRIP <input string> <output variable>)
string(UUID <output variable> NAMESPACE <namespace> NAME <name>
       TYPE <MD5|SHA1> [UPPER])
```

REGEX MATCH will match the regular expression once and store the match in the output variable.

REGEX MATCHALL will match the regular expression as many times as possible and store the matches in the output variable as a list.

REGEX REPLACE will match the regular expression as many times as possible and substitute the replacement expression for the match in the output. The replace expression may refer to paren-delimited subexpressions of the match using 1, 2, ..., 9. Note that two backslashes (\1) are required in CMake code to get a backslash through argument parsing.

REPLACE will replace all occurrences of match_string in the input with replace_string and store the result in the output.

CONCAT will concatenate all the input arguments together and store the result in the named output variable.

MD5, SHA1, SHA224, SHA256, SHA384, and SHA512 will compute a cryptographic hash of the input string.

COMPARE EQUAL/NOTEQUAL/LESS/GREATER will compare the strings and store true or false in the output variable.

ASCII will convert all numbers into corresponding ASCII characters.

CONFIGURE will transform a string like CONFIGURE_FILE transforms a file.

TOUPPER/TOLOWER will convert string to upper/lower characters.

LENGTH will return a given string's length.

SUBSTRING will return a substring of a given string. If length is -1 the remainder of the string starting at begin will be returned.

STRIP will return a substring of a given string with leading and trailing spaces removed.

RANDOM will return a random string of given length consisting of characters from the given alphabet. Default length is 5 characters and default alphabet is all numbers and upper and lower case letters. If an integer RANDOM_SEED is given, its value will be used to seed the random number generator.

FIND will return the position where the given substring was found in the supplied string. If the REVERSE flag was used, the command will search for the position of the last occurrence of the specified substring.

The following characters have special meaning in regular expressions:

```
^            Matches at beginning of input
$            Matches at end of input
.            Matches any single character
[ ]          Matches any character(s) inside the brackets
[^ ]         Matches any character(s) not inside the brackets
 -           Inside brackets, specifies an inclusive range between
             characters on either side e.g. [a-f] is [abcdef]
             To match a literal - using brackets, make it the first
             or the last character e.g. [+*/-] matches basic
             mathematical operators.
*            Matches preceding pattern zero or more times
+            Matches preceding pattern one or more times
?            Matches preceding pattern zero or once only
|            Matches a pattern on either side of the |
()           Saves a matched subexpression, which can be referenced
             in the REGEX REPLACE operation. Additionally it is saved
             by all regular expression-related commands, including
             e.g. if( MATCHES ), in the variables CMAKE_MATCH_(0..9).
```

$*$, $+$ and $?$ have higher precedence than concatenation. | has lower precedence than concatenation. This means that the regular expression "^ab+d$" matches "abbd" but not "ababd", and the regular expression "^(ab|cd)$" matches "ab" but not "abd".

TIMESTAMP will write a string representation of the current date and/or time to the output variable.

Should the command be unable to obtain a timestamp the output variable will be set to the empty string "".

The optional UTC flag requests the current date/time representation to be in Coordinated Universal Time (UTC) rather than local time.

The optional <format string> may contain the following format specifiers:

```
%d           The day of the current month (01-31).
%H           The hour on a 24-hour clock (00-23).
%I           The hour on a 12-hour clock (01-12).
%j           The day of the current year (001-366).
%m           The month of the current year (01-12).
%M           The minute of the current hour (00-59).
%S           The second of the current minute.
             60 represents a leap second. (00-60)
%U           The week number of the current year (00-53).
%w           The day of the current week. 0 is Sunday. (0-6)
%y           The last two digits of the current year (00-99)
%Y           The current year.
```

Unknown format specifiers will be ignored and copied to the output as-is.

If no explicit <format string> is given it will default to:

```
%Y-%m-%dT%H:%M:%S     for local time.
%Y-%m-%dT%H:%M:%SZ    for UTC.
```

C.1. cmake-commands(7)

MAKE_C_IDENTIFIER will write a string which can be used as an identifier in C.

GENEX_STRIP will strip any `generator expressions` (page 356) from the `input string` and store the result in the `output variable`.

UUID creates a univerally unique identifier (aka GUID) as per RFC4122 based on the hash of the combined values of <namespace> (which itself has to be a valid UUID) and <name>. The hash algorithm can be either MD5 (Version 3 UUID) or SHA1 (Version 5 UUID). A UUID has the format xxxxxxxx-xxxx-xxxx-xxxx-xxxxxxxxxxxx where each *x* represents a lower case hexadecimal character. Where required an uppercase representation can be requested with the optional UPPER flag.

target_compile_definitions

Add compile definitions to a target.

```
target_compile_definitions(<target>
  <INTERFACE|PUBLIC|PRIVATE> [items1...]
  [<INTERFACE|PUBLIC|PRIVATE> [items2...] ...])
```

Specify compile definitions to use when compiling a given <target. The named <target> must have been created by a command such as add_executable() (page 273) or add_library() (page 274) and must not be an *Imported Target*.

The INTERFACE, PUBLIC and PRIVATE keywords are required to specify the scope of the following arguments. PRIVATE and PUBLIC items will populate the COMPILE_DEFINITIONS (page 580) property of <target>. PUBLIC and INTERFACE items will populate the INTERFACE_COMPILE_DEFINITIONS (page 592) property of <target>. The following arguments specify compile definitions. Repeated calls for the same <target> append items in the order called.

Arguments to target_compile_definitions may use "generator expressions" with the syntax $<...>. See the cmake-generator-expressions(7) (page 356) manual for available expressions. See the cmake-buildsystem(7) manual for more on defining buildsystem properties.

target_compile_features

Add expected compiler features to a target.

```
target_compile_features(<target> <PRIVATE|PUBLIC|INTERFACE> <feature> [...])
```

Specify compiler features required when compiling a given target. If the feature is not listed in the CMAKE_C_COMPILE_FEATURES (page 667) variable or CMAKE_CXX_COMPILE_FEATURES (page 668) variable, then an error will be reported by CMake. If the use of the feature requires an additional compiler flag, such as -std=gnu++11, the flag will be added automatically.

The INTERFACE, PUBLIC and PRIVATE keywords are required to specify the scope of the features. PRIVATE and PUBLIC items will populate the COMPILE_FEATURES (page 581) property of <target>. PUBLIC and INTERFACE items will populate the INTERFACE_COMPILE_FEATURES (page 593) property of <target>. Repeated calls for the same <target> append items.

The named <target> must have been created by a command such as add_executable() (page 273) or add_library() (page 274) and must not be an IMPORTED target.

Arguments to target_compile_features may use "generator expressions" with the syntax $<...>. See the cmake-generator-expressions(7) (page 356) manual for available expressions. See the cmake-compile-features(7) manual for information on compile features.

target_compile_options

Add compile options to a target.

```
target_compile_options(<target> [BEFORE]
  <INTERFACE|PUBLIC|PRIVATE> [items1...]
  [<INTERFACE|PUBLIC|PRIVATE> [items2...] ...])
```

Specify compile options to use when compiling a given target. The named <target> must have been created by a command such as add_executable() (page 273) or add_library() (page 274) and must not be an *IMPORTED Target*. If BEFORE is specified, the content will be prepended to the property instead of being appended.

This command can be used to add any options, but alternative commands exist to add preprocessor definitions (target_compile_definitions() (page 338) and add_definitions() (page 273)) or include directories (target_include_directories() (page 339) and include_directories() (page 316)). See documentation of the directory (page 581) and :prop_tgt:' target <COMPILE_OPTIONS>' COMPILE_OPTIONS properties.

The INTERFACE, PUBLIC and PRIVATE keywords are required to specify the scope of the following arguments. PRIVATE and PUBLIC items will populate the COMPILE_OPTIONS (page 581) property of <target>. PUBLIC and INTERFACE items will populate the INTERFACE_COMPILE_OPTIONS (page 593) property of <target>. The following arguments specify compile options. Repeated calls for the same <target> append items in the order called.

Arguments to target_compile_options may use "generator expressions" with the syntax $<...>. See the cmake-generator-expressions(7) (page 356) manual for available expressions. See the cmake-buildsystem(7) manual for more on defining buildsystem properties.

target_include_directories

Add include directories to a target.

```
target_include_directories(<target> [SYSTEM] [BEFORE]
  <INTERFACE|PUBLIC|PRIVATE> [items1...]
  [<INTERFACE|PUBLIC|PRIVATE> [items2...] ...])
```

Specify include directories to use when compiling a given target. The named <target> must have been created by a command such as add_executable() (page 273) or add_library() (page 274) and must not be an IMPORTED (page 590) target.

If BEFORE is specified, the content will be prepended to the property instead of being appended.

The INTERFACE, PUBLIC and PRIVATE keywords are required to specify the scope of the following arguments. PRIVATE and PUBLIC items will populate the INCLUDE_DIRECTORIES (page 591) property of <target>. PUBLIC and INTERFACE items will populate the INTERFACE_INCLUDE_DIRECTORIES (page 593) property of <target>. The following arguments specify include directories.

Specified include directories may be absolute paths or relative paths. Repeated calls for the same <target> append items in the order called. If SYSTEM is specified, the compiler will be told the directories are meant as system include directories on some platforms (signalling this setting might achieve effects such as the compiler skipping warnings, or these fixed-install system files not being considered in dependency calculations - see compiler docs). If SYSTEM is used together with PUBLIC or INTERFACE, the INTERFACE_SYSTEM_INCLUDE_DIRECTORIES (page 595) target property will be populated with the specified directories.

Arguments to target_include_directories may use "generator expressions" with the syntax $<...>. See the cmake-generator-expressions(7) (page 356) manual for available expressions. See the cmake-buildsystem(7) manual for more on defining buildsystem properties.

Include directories usage requirements commonly differ between the build-tree and the install-tree. The BUILD_INTERFACE and INSTALL_INTERFACE generator expressions can be used to describe separate usage requirements based on the usage location. Relative paths are allowed within the INSTALL_INTERFACE expression and are interpreted relative to the installation prefix. For example:

```
target_include_directories(mylib PUBLIC
  $<BUILD_INTERFACE:${CMAKE_CURRENT_SOURCE_DIR}/include/mylib>
  $<INSTALL_INTERFACE:include/mylib>  # <prefix>/include/mylib
)
```

target_link_libraries

Link a target to given libraries.

```
target_link_libraries(<target> [item1 [item2 [...]]]
                    [[debug|optimized|general] <item>] ...)
```

Specify libraries or flags to use when linking a given target. The named <target> must have been created in the current directory by a command such as add_executable() (page 273) or add_library() (page 274). The remaining arguments specify library names or flags. Repeated calls for the same <target> append items in the order called.

If a library name matches that of another target in the project a dependency will automatically be added in the build system to make sure the library being linked is up-to-date before the target links. Item names starting with -, but not -l or -framework, are treated as linker flags. Note that such flags will be treated like any other library link item for purposes of transitive dependencies, so they are generally safe to specify only as private link items that will not propagate to dependents of <target>.

A debug, optimized, or general keyword indicates that the library immediately following it is to be used only for the corresponding build configuration. The debug keyword corresponds to the Debug configuration (or to configurations named in the DEBUG_CONFIGURATIONS (page 563) global property if it is set). The optimized keyword corresponds to all other configurations. The general keyword corresponds to all configurations, and is purely optional (assumed if omitted). Higher granularity may be achieved for per-configuration rules by creating and linking to *IMPORTED library targets*.

Library dependencies are transitive by default with this signature. When this target is linked into another target then the libraries linked to this target will appear on the link line for the other target too. This transitive "link interface" is stored in the INTERFACE_LINK_LIBRARIES (page 594) target property and may be overridden by setting the property directly. When CMP0022 (page 546) is not set to NEW, transitive linking is built in but may be overridden by the LINK_INTERFACE_LIBRARIES (page 598) property. Calls to other signatures of this command may set the property making any libraries linked exclusively by this signature private.

CMake will also propagate *usage requirements* from linked library targets. Usage requirements of dependencies affect compilation of sources in the <target>.

If an <item> is a library in a Mac OX framework, the Headers directory of the framework will also be processed as a *usage requirement*. This has the same effect as passing the framework directory as an include directory.

```
target_link_libraries(<target>
                <PRIVATE|PUBLIC|INTERFACE> <lib> ...
                [<PRIVATE|PUBLIC|INTERFACE> <lib> ... ] ...])
```

The PUBLIC, PRIVATE and INTERFACE keywords can be used to specify both the link dependencies and the link interface in one command. Libraries and targets following PUBLIC are linked to, and are made part of the link interface. Libraries and targets following PRIVATE are linked to, but are not made part of the link interface. Libraries following INTERFACE are appended to the link interface and are not used for linking <target>.

```
target_link_libraries(<target> LINK_INTERFACE_LIBRARIES
                [[debug|optimized|general] <lib>] ...)
```

The LINK_INTERFACE_LIBRARIES mode appends the libraries to the INTERFACE_LINK_LIBRARIES (page 594) target property instead of using them for linking. If policy CMP0022 (page 546) is not NEW, then this mode also appends libraries to the LINK_INTERFACE_LIBRARIES (page 598) and its per-configuration equivalent.

This signature is for compatibility only. Prefer the INTERFACE mode instead.

Libraries specified as debug are wrapped in a generator expression to correspond to debug builds. If policy CMP0022 (page 546) is not NEW, the libraries are also appended to the LINK_INTERFACE_LIBRARIES_DEBUG (page 598) property (or to the properties corresponding to configurations listed in the DEBUG_CONFIGURATIONS (page 563) global property if it is set). Libraries specified as optimized are appended to the INTERFACE_LINK_LIBRARIES (page 594) property. If policy CMP0022 (page 546) is not NEW, they are also appended to the LINK_INTERFACE_LIBRARIES (page 598) property. Libraries specified as `general` (or without any keyword) are treated as if specified for both `debug` and `optimized`.

```
target_link_libraries(<target>
                <LINK_PRIVATE|LINK_PUBLIC>
                  [[debug|optimized|general] <lib>] ...
                [<LINK_PRIVATE|LINK_PUBLIC>
                  [[debug|optimized|general] <lib>] ...])
```

The `LINK_PUBLIC` and `LINK_PRIVATE` modes can be used to specify both the link dependencies and the link interface in one command.

This signature is for compatibility only. Prefer the `PUBLIC` or `PRIVATE` keywords instead.

Libraries and targets following `LINK_PUBLIC` are linked to, and are made part of the `INTERFACE_LINK_LIBRARIES` (page 594). If policy `CMP0022` (page 546) is not `NEW`, they are also made part of the `LINK_INTERFACE_LIBRARIES` (page 598). Libraries and targets following `LINK_PRIVATE` are linked to, but are not made part of the `INTERFACE_LINK_LIBRARIES` (page 594) (or `LINK_INTERFACE_LIBRARIES` (page 598)).

The library dependency graph is normally acyclic (a DAG), but in the case of mutually-dependent `STATIC` libraries CMake allows the graph to contain cycles (strongly connected components). When another target links to one of the libraries, CMake repeats the entire connected component. For example, the code

```
add_library(A STATIC a.c)
add_library(B STATIC b.c)
target_link_libraries(A B)
target_link_libraries(B A)
add_executable(main main.c)
target_link_libraries(main A)
```

links `main` to `A B A B`. While one repetition is usually sufficient, pathological object file and symbol arrangements can require more. One may handle such cases by manually repeating the component in the last `target_link_libraries` call. However, if two archives are really so interdependent they should probably be combined into a single archive.

Arguments to target_link_libraries may use "generator expressions" with the syntax `$<...>`. Note however, that generator expressions will not be used in OLD handling of `CMP0003` (page 539) or `CMP0004` (page 540). See the `cmake-generator-expressions(7)` (page 356) manual for available expressions. See the `cmake-buildsystem(7)` manual for more on defining buildsystem properties.

target_sources

Add sources to a target.

```
target_sources(<target>
  <INTERFACE|PUBLIC|PRIVATE> [items1...]
  [<INTERFACE|PUBLIC|PRIVATE> [items2...] ...])
```

Specify sources to use when compiling a given target. The named `<target>` must have been created by a command such as `add_executable()` (page 273) or `add_library()` (page 274) and must not be an *IMPORTED Target.*

The `INTERFACE`, `PUBLIC` and `PRIVATE` keywords are required to specify the scope of the following arguments. `PRIVATE` and `PUBLIC` items will populate the `SOURCES` (page 608) property of `<target>`. `PUBLIC` and `INTERFACE` items will populate the `INTERFACE_SOURCES` (page 594) property of `<target>`. The following arguments specify sources. Repeated calls for the same `<target>` append items in the order called.

Targets with `INTERFACE_SOURCES` (page 594) may not be exported with the `export()` (page 287) or `install(EXPORT)` (page 317) commands. This limitation may be lifted in a future version of CMake.

Arguments to `target_sources` may use "generator expressions" with the syntax `$<...>`. See the `cmake-generator-expressions(7)` (page 356) manual for available expressions. See the `cmake-buildsystem(7)` manual for more on defining buildsystem properties.

try_compile

Try building some code.

```
try_compile(RESULT_VAR <bindir> <srcdir>
            <projectName> [targetName] [CMAKE_FLAGS flags...]
            [OUTPUT_VARIABLE <var>])
```

Try building a project. In this form, srcdir should contain a complete CMake project with a CMakeLists.txt file and all sources. The bindir and srcdir will not be deleted after this command is run. Specify targetName to build a specific target instead of the 'all' or 'ALL_BUILD' target.

```
try_compile(RESULT_VAR <bindir> <srcfile|SOURCES srcfile...>
            [CMAKE_FLAGS flags...]
            [COMPILE_DEFINITIONS flags...]
            [LINK_LIBRARIES libs...]
            [OUTPUT_VARIABLE <var>]
            [COPY_FILE <fileName> [COPY_FILE_ERROR <var>]])
```

Try building an executable from one or more source files. In this form the user need only supply one or more source files that include a definition for 'main'. CMake will create a CMakeLists.txt file to build the source(s) as an executable. Specify COPY_FILE to get a copy of the linked executable at the given fileName and optionally COPY_FILE_ERROR to capture any error.

In this version all files in bindir/CMakeFiles/CMakeTmp will be cleaned automatically. For debugging, –debug-trycompile can be passed to cmake to avoid this clean. However, multiple sequential try_compile operations reuse this single output directory. If you use –debug-trycompile, you can only debug one try_compile call at a time. The recommended procedure is to protect all try_compile calls in your project by `if(NOT DEFINED RESULT_VAR)` logic, configure with cmake all the way through once, then delete the cache entry associated with the try_compile call of interest, and then re-run cmake again with –debug-trycompile.

Some extra flags that can be included are, INCLUDE_DIRECTORIES, LINK_DIRECTORIES, and LINK_LIBRARIES. COMPILE_DEFINITIONS are -Ddefinition that will be passed to the compile line.

The srcfile signature also accepts a LINK_LIBRARIES argument which may contain a list of libraries or IMPORTED targets which will be linked to in the generated project. If LINK_LIBRARIES is specified as a parameter to try_compile, then any LINK_LIBRARIES passed as CMAKE_FLAGS will be ignored.

try_compile creates a CMakeList.txt file on the fly that looks like this:

```
add_definitions( <expanded COMPILE_DEFINITIONS from calling cmake>)
include_directories(${INCLUDE_DIRECTORIES})
link_directories(${LINK_DIRECTORIES})
add_executable(cmTryCompileExec sources)
target_link_libraries(cmTryCompileExec ${LINK_LIBRARIES})
```

In both versions of the command, if OUTPUT_VARIABLE is specified, then the output from the build process is stored in the given variable. The success or failure of the try_compile, i.e. TRUE or FALSE respectively, is returned in RESULT_VAR. CMAKE_FLAGS can be used to pass -DVAR:TYPE=VALUE flags to the cmake that is run during the build. Set variable CMAKE_TRY_COMPILE_CONFIGURATION to choose a build configuration.

try_run

Try compiling and then running some code.

```
try_run(RUN_RESULT_VAR COMPILE_RESULT_VAR
        bindir srcfile [CMAKE_FLAGS <Flags>]
        [COMPILE_DEFINITIONS <flags>]
        [COMPILE_OUTPUT_VARIABLE comp]
        [RUN_OUTPUT_VARIABLE run]
        [OUTPUT_VARIABLE var]
        [ARGS <arg1> <arg2>...])
```

Try compiling a srcfile. Return TRUE or FALSE for success or failure in COMPILE_RESULT_VAR. Then if the compile succeeded, run the executable and return its exit code in RUN_RESULT_VAR. If the executable was built, but failed to run, then RUN_RESULT_VAR will be set to FAILED_TO_RUN. COMPILE_OUTPUT_VARIABLE specifies the variable where the output from the compile step goes. RUN_OUTPUT_VARIABLE specifies the variable where the output from the running executable goes.

For compatibility reasons OUTPUT_VARIABLE is still supported, which gives you the output from the compile and run step combined.

Cross compiling issues

When cross compiling, the executable compiled in the first step usually cannot be run on the build host. try_run() checks the CMAKE_CROSSCOMPILING variable to detect whether CMake is in crosscompiling mode. If that's the case, it will still try to compile the executable, but it will not try to run the executable. Instead it will create cache variables which must be filled by the user or by presetting them in some CMake script file to the values the executable would have produced if it had been run on its actual target platform. These variables are RUN_RESULT_VAR (explanation see above) and if RUN_OUTPUT_VARIABLE (or OUTPUT_VARIABLE) was used, an additional cache variable RUN_RESULT_VAR__COMPILE_RESULT_VAR__TRYRUN_OUTPUT.This is intended to hold stdout and stderr from the executable.

In order to make cross compiling your project easier, use try_run only if really required. If you use try_run, use RUN_OUTPUT_VARIABLE (or OUTPUT_VARIABLE) only if really required. Using them will require that when crosscompiling, the cache variables will have to be set manually to the output of the executable. You can also "guard" the calls to try_run with if(CMAKE_CROSSCOMPILING) and provide an easy-to-preset alternative for this case.

Set variable CMAKE_TRY_COMPILE_CONFIGURATION to choose a build configuration.

unset

Unset a variable, cache variable, or environment variable.

```
unset(<variable> [CACHE | PARENT_SCOPE])
```

Removes the specified variable causing it to become undefined. If CACHE is present then the variable is removed from the cache instead of the current scope.

If PARENT_SCOPE is present then the variable is removed from the scope above the current scope. See the same option in the set() command for further details.

<variable> can be an environment variable such as:

```
unset(ENV{LD_LIBRARY_PATH})
```

in which case the variable will be removed from the current environment.

variable_watch

Watch the CMake variable for change.

```
variable_watch(<variable name> [<command to execute>])
```

If the specified variable changes, the message will be printed about the variable being changed. If the command is specified, the command will be executed. The command will receive the following arguments: COMMAND(<variable> <access> <value> <current list file> <stack>)

while

Evaluate a group of commands while a condition is true

```
while(condition)
  COMMAND1(ARGS ...)
  COMMAND2(ARGS ...)
  ...
endwhile(condition)
```

All commands between while and the matching endwhile are recorded without being invoked. Once the endwhile is evaluated, the recorded list of commands is invoked as long as the condition is true. The condition is evaluated using the same logic as the if command.

C.1.2 Deprecated Commands

These commands are available only for compatibility with older versions of CMake. Do not use them in new code.

build_name

Disallowed. See CMake Policy CMP0036 (page 551).

Use ${CMAKE_SYSTEM} and ${CMAKE_CXX_COMPILER} instead.

```
build_name(variable)
```

Sets the specified variable to a string representing the platform and compiler settings. These values are now available through the CMAKE_SYSTEM and CMAKE_CXX_COMPILER variables.

exec_program

Deprecated. Use the execute_process() command instead.

Run an executable program during the processing of the CMakeList.txt file.

```
exec_program(Executable [directory in which to run]
             [ARGS <arguments to executable>]
             [OUTPUT_VARIABLE <var>]
             [RETURN_VALUE <var>])
```

The executable is run in the optionally specified directory. The executable can include arguments if it is double quoted, but it is better to use the optional ARGS argument to specify arguments to the program. This is because cmake will then be able to escape spaces in the executable path. An optional argument OUTPUT_VARIABLE specifies a variable in which to store the output. To capture the return value of the execution, provide a RETURN_VALUE. If OUTPUT_VARIABLE is specified, then no output will go to the stdout/stderr of the console running cmake.

export_library_dependencies

Disallowed. See CMake Policy CMP0033 (page 551).

Use install(EXPORT) (page 317) or export() (page 287) command.

This command generates an old-style library dependencies file. Projects requiring CMake 2.6 or later should not use the command. Use instead the install(EXPORT) command to help export targets from an installation tree and the export() command to export targets from a build tree.

The old-style library dependencies file does not take into account per-configuration names of libraries or the LINK_INTERFACE_LIBRARIES target property.

```
export_library_dependencies(<file> [APPEND])
```

Create a file named <file> that can be included into a CMake listfile with the INCLUDE command. The file will contain a number of SET commands that will set all the variables needed for library dependency information. This should be the last command in the top level CMakeLists.txt file of the project. If the APPEND option is specified, the SET commands will be appended to the given file instead of replacing it.

install_files

Deprecated. Use the install(FILES) command instead.

This command has been superceded by the install command. It is provided for compatibility with older CMake code. The FILES form is directly replaced by the FILES form of the install command. The regexp form can be expressed more clearly using the GLOB form of the file command.

```
install_files(<dir> extension file file ...)
```

Create rules to install the listed files with the given extension into the given directory. Only files existing in the current source tree or its corresponding location in the binary tree may be listed. If a file specified already has an extension, that extension will be removed first. This is useful for providing lists of source files such as foo.cxx when you want the corresponding foo.h to be installed. A typical extension is '.h'.

```
install_files(<dir> regexp)
```

Any files in the current source directory that match the regular expression will be installed.

```
install_files(<dir> FILES file file ...)
```

Any files listed after the FILES keyword will be installed explicitly from the names given. Full paths are allowed in this form.

The directory <dir> is relative to the installation prefix, which is stored in the variable CMAKE_INSTALL_PREFIX.

install_programs

Deprecated. Use the install(PROGRAMS) command instead.

This command has been superceded by the install command. It is provided for compatibility with older CMake code. The FILES form is directly replaced by the PROGRAMS form of the INSTALL command. The regexp form can be expressed more clearly using the GLOB form of the FILE command.

```
install_programs(<dir> file1 file2 [file3 ...])
install_programs(<dir> FILES file1 [file2 ...])
```

Create rules to install the listed programs into the given directory. Use the FILES argument to guarantee that the file list version of the command will be used even when there is only one argument.

```
install_programs(<dir> regexp)
```

In the second form any program in the current source directory that matches the regular expression will be installed.

This command is intended to install programs that are not built by cmake, such as shell scripts. See the TARGETS form of the INSTALL command to create installation rules for targets built by cmake.

The directory <dir> is relative to the installation prefix, which is stored in the variable CMAKE_INSTALL_PREFIX.

install_targets

Deprecated. Use the install(TARGETS) command instead.

This command has been superceded by the install command. It is provided for compatibility with older CMake code.

```
install_targets(<dir> [RUNTIME_DIRECTORY dir] target target)
```

Create rules to install the listed targets into the given directory. The directory <dir> is relative to the installation prefix, which is stored in the variable CMAKE_INSTALL_PREFIX. If RUNTIME_DIRECTORY is specified, then on systems with special runtime files (Windows DLL), the files will be copied to that directory.

link_libraries

Deprecated. Use the target_link_libraries() command instead.

Link libraries to all targets added later.

```
link_libraries(library1 <debug | optimized> library2 ...)
```

Specify a list of libraries to be linked into any following targets (typically added with the add_executable or add_library calls). This command is passed down to all subdirectories. The debug and optimized strings may be used to indicate that the next library listed is to be used only for that specific type of build.

make_directory

Deprecated. Use the file(MAKE_DIRECTORY) command instead.

```
make_directory(directory)
```

Creates the specified directory. Full paths should be given. Any parent directories that do not exist will also be created. Use with care.

output_required_files

Disallowed. See CMake Policy CMP0032 (page 550).

Approximate C preprocessor dependency scanning.

This command exists only because ancient CMake versions provided it. CMake handles preprocessor dependency scanning automatically using a more advanced scanner.

```
output_required_files(srcfile outputfile)
```

Outputs a list of all the source files that are required by the specified srcfile. This list is written into outputfile. This is similar to writing out the dependencies for srcfile except that it jumps from .h files into .cxx, .c and .cpp files if possible.

remove

Deprecated. Use the list(REMOVE_ITEM) command instead.

```
remove(VAR VALUE VALUE ...)
```

Removes VALUE from the variable VAR. This is typically used to remove entries from a vector (e.g. semicolon separated list). VALUE is expanded.

subdir_depends

Disallowed. See CMake Policy CMP0029 (page 549).

Does nothing.

```
subdir_depends(subdir dep1 dep2 ...)
```

Does not do anything. This command used to help projects order parallel builds correctly. This functionality is now automatic.

subdirs

Deprecated. Use the add_subdirectory() command instead.

Add a list of subdirectories to the build.

```
subdirs(dir1 dir2 ...[EXCLUDE_FROM_ALL exclude_dir1 exclude_dir2 ...]
        [PREORDER] )
```

Add a list of subdirectories to the build. The add_subdirectory command should be used instead of subdirs although subdirs will still work. This will cause any CMakeLists.txt files in the sub directories to be processed by CMake. Any directories after the PREORDER flag are traversed first by makefile builds, the PREORDER flag has no effect on IDE projects. Any directories after the EXCLUDE_FROM_ALL marker will not be included in the top level makefile or project file. This is useful for having CMake create makefiles or projects for a set of examples in a project. You would want CMake to generate makefiles or project files for all the examples at the same time, but you would not want them to show up in the top level project or be built each time make is run from the top.

use_mangled_mesa

Disallowed. See CMake Policy CMP0030 (page 550).

Copy mesa headers for use in combination with system GL.

```
use_mangled_mesa(PATH_TO_MESA OUTPUT_DIRECTORY)
```

The path to mesa includes, should contain gl_mangle.h. The mesa headers are copied to the specified output directory. This allows mangled mesa headers to override other GL headers by being added to the include directory path earlier.

utility_source

Disallowed. See CMake Policy CMP0034 (page 551).

Specify the source tree of a third-party utility.

```
utility_source(cache_entry executable_name
               path_to_source [file1 file2 ...])
```

When a third-party utility's source is included in the distribution, this command specifies its location and name. The cache entry will not be set unless the path_to_source and all listed files exist. It is assumed that the source tree of the utility will have been built before it is needed.

When cross compiling CMake will print a warning if a utility_source() command is executed, because in many cases it is used to build an executable which is executed later on. This doesn't work when cross compiling, since the executable can run only on their target platform. So in this case the cache entry has to be adjusted manually so it points to an executable which is runnable on the build host.

variable_requires

Disallowed. See CMake Policy CMP0035 (page 551).

Use the if() command instead.

Assert satisfaction of an option's required variables.

```
variable_requires(TEST_VARIABLE RESULT_VARIABLE
                  REQUIRED_VARIABLE1
                  REQUIRED_VARIABLE2 ...)
```

The first argument (TEST_VARIABLE) is the name of the variable to be tested, if that variable is false nothing else is done. If TEST_VARIABLE is true, then the next argument (RESULT_VARIABLE) is a variable that is set to true if all the required variables are set. The rest of the arguments are variables that must be true or not set to NOTFOUND to avoid an error. If any are not true, an error is reported.

write_file

Deprecated. Use the file(WRITE) command instead.

```
write_file(filename "message to write"... [APPEND])
```

The first argument is the file name, the rest of the arguments are messages to write. If the argument APPEND is specified, then the message will be appended.

NOTE 1: file(WRITE ... and file(APPEND ... do exactly the same as this one but add some more functionality.

NOTE 2: When using write_file the produced file cannot be used as an input to CMake (CONFIGURE_FILE, source file ...) because it will lead to an infinite loop. Use configure_file if you want to generate input files to CMake.

C.1.3 CTest Commands

These commands are available only in ctest scripts.

ctest_build

Build the project.

```
ctest_build([BUILD build_dir] [TARGET target] [RETURN_VALUE res]
            [APPEND][NUMBER_ERRORS val] [NUMBER_WARNINGS val])
```

Builds the given build directory and stores results in Build.xml. If no BUILD is given, the CTEST_BINARY_DIRECTORY variable is used.

The TARGET variable can be used to specify a build target. If none is specified, the "all" target will be built.

The RETURN_VALUE option specifies a variable in which to store the return value of the native build tool. The NUMBER_ERRORS and NUMBER_WARNINGS options specify variables in which to store the number of build errors and warnings detected.

The APPEND option marks results for append to those previously submitted to a dashboard server since the last ctest_start. Append semantics are defined by the dashboard server in use.

If set, the contents of the variable CTEST_BUILD_FLAGS are passed as additional arguments to the underlying build command. This can e.g. be used to trigger a parallel build using the -j option of make. See ProcessorCount (page 525) for an example.

ctest_configure

Configure the project build tree.

```
ctest_configure([BUILD build_dir] [SOURCE source_dir] [APPEND]
                [OPTIONS options] [RETURN_VALUE res])
```

Configures the given build directory and stores results in Configure.xml. If no BUILD is given, the CTEST_BINARY_DIRECTORY variable is used. If no SOURCE is given, the CTEST_SOURCE_DIRECTORY variable is used. The OPTIONS argument specifies command line arguments to pass to the configuration tool. The RETURN_VALUE option specifies a variable in which to store the return value of the native build tool.

The APPEND option marks results for append to those previously submitted to a dashboard server since the last ctest_start. Append semantics are defined by the dashboard server in use.

ctest_coverage

Collect coverage tool results.

```
ctest_coverage([BUILD build_dir] [RETURN_VALUE res] [APPEND]
               [LABELS label1 [label2 [...]]])
```

Perform the coverage of the given build directory and stores results in Coverage.xml. The second argument is a variable that will hold value.

The LABELS option filters the coverage report to include only source files labeled with at least one of the labels specified.

The APPEND option marks results for append to those previously submitted to a dashboard server since the last ctest_start. Append semantics are defined by the dashboard server in use.

ctest_empty_binary_directory

empties the binary directory

```
ctest_empty_binary_directory( directory )
```

Removes a binary directory. This command will perform some checks prior to deleting the directory in an attempt to avoid malicious or accidental directory deletion.

ctest_memcheck

Run tests with a dynamic analysis tool.

```
ctest_memcheck([BUILD build_dir] [RETURN_VALUE res] [APPEND]
          [START start number] [END end number]
          [STRIDE stride number] [EXCLUDE exclude regex ]
          [INCLUDE include regex]
          [EXCLUDE_LABEL exclude regex]
          [INCLUDE_LABEL label regex]
          [PARALLEL_LEVEL level] )
```

Tests the given build directory and stores results in MemCheck.xml. The second argument is a variable that will hold value. Optionally, you can specify the starting test number START, the ending test number END, the number of tests to skip between each test STRIDE, a regular expression for tests to run INCLUDE, or a regular expression for tests not to run EXCLUDE. EXCLUDE_LABEL and INCLUDE_LABEL are regular expressions for tests to be included or excluded by the test property LABEL. PARALLEL_LEVEL should be set to a positive number representing the number of tests to be run in parallel.

The APPEND option marks results for append to those previously submitted to a dashboard server since the last ctest_start. Append semantics are defined by the dashboard server in use.

ctest_read_custom_files

read CTestCustom files.

```
ctest_read_custom_files( directory ... )
```

Read all the CTestCustom.ctest or CTestCustom.cmake files from the given directory.

ctest_run_script

runs a ctest -S script

```
ctest_run_script([NEW_PROCESS] script_file_name script_file_name1
          script_file_name2 ... [RETURN_VALUE var])
```

Runs a script or scripts much like if it was run from ctest -S. If no argument is provided then the current script is run using the current settings of the variables. If NEW_PROCESS is specified then each script will be run in a separate process.If RETURN_VALUE is specified the return value of the last script run will be put into var.

ctest_sleep

sleeps for some amount of time

```
ctest_sleep(<seconds>)
```

Sleep for given number of seconds.

```
ctest_sleep(<time1> <duration> <time2>)
```

Sleep for t=(time1 + duration - time2) seconds if t > 0.

ctest_start

Starts the testing for a given model

```
ctest_start(Model [TRACK <track>] [APPEND] [source [binary]])
```

Starts the testing for a given model. The command should be called after the binary directory is initialized. If the 'source' and 'binary' directory are not specified, it reads the CTEST_SOURCE_DIRECTORY (page 680) and CTEST_BINARY_DIRECTORY (page 675). If the track is specified, the submissions will go to the specified track. If APPEND is used, the existing TAG is used rather than creating a new one based on the current time stamp.

If the CTEST_CHECKOUT_COMMAND (page 676) variable (or the CTEST_CVS_CHECKOUT (page 677) variable) is set, its content is treated as command-line. The command is invoked with the current working directory set to the parent of the source directory, even if the source directory already exists. This can be used to create the source tree from a version control repository.

ctest_submit

Submit results to a dashboard server.

```
ctest_submit([PARTS ...] [FILES ...]
             [RETRY_COUNT count]
             [RETRY_DELAY delay]
             [RETURN_VALUE res]
             )
```

By default all available parts are submitted if no PARTS or FILES are specified. The PARTS option lists a subset of parts to be submitted. Valid part names are:

```
Start      = nothing
Update     = ctest_update results, in Update.xml
Configure  = ctest_configure results, in Configure.xml
Build      = ctest_build results, in Build.xml
Test       = ctest_test results, in Test.xml
Coverage   = ctest_coverage results, in Coverage.xml
```

```
MemCheck    = ctest_memcheck results, in DynamicAnalysis.xml
Notes       = Files listed by CTEST_NOTES_FILES, in Notes.xml
ExtraFiles  = Files listed by CTEST_EXTRA_SUBMIT_FILES
Upload      = Files prepared for upload by ctest_upload(), in Upload.xml
Submit      = nothing
```

The FILES option explicitly lists specific files to be submitted. Each individual file must exist at the time of the call.

The RETRY_DELAY option specifies how long in seconds to wait after a timed-out submission before attempting to re-submit.

The RETRY_COUNT option specifies how many times to retry a timed-out submission.

ctest_test

Run tests in the project build tree.

```
ctest_test([BUILD build_dir] [APPEND]
           [START start number] [END end number]
           [STRIDE stride number] [EXCLUDE exclude regex ]
           [INCLUDE include regex] [RETURN_VALUE res]
           [EXCLUDE_LABEL exclude regex]
           [INCLUDE_LABEL label regex]
           [PARALLEL_LEVEL level]
           [SCHEDULE_RANDOM on]
           [STOP_TIME time of day])
```

Tests the given build directory and stores results in Test.xml. The second argument is a variable that will hold value. Optionally, you can specify the starting test number START, the ending test number END, the number of tests to skip between each test STRIDE, a regular expression for tests to run INCLUDE, or a regular expression for tests to not run EXCLUDE. EXCLUDE_LABEL and INCLUDE_LABEL are regular expression for test to be included or excluded by the test property LABEL. PARALLEL_LEVEL should be set to a positive number representing the number of tests to be run in parallel. SCHEDULE_RANDOM will launch tests in a random order, and is typically used to detect implicit test dependencies. STOP_TIME is the time of day at which the tests should all stop running.

The APPEND option marks results for append to those previously submitted to a dashboard server since the last ctest_start. Append semantics are defined by the dashboard server in use.

ctest_update

Update the work tree from version control.

```
ctest_update([SOURCE source] [RETURN_VALUE res])
```

Updates the given source directory and stores results in Update.xml. If no SOURCE is given, the CTEST_SOURCE_DIRECTORY variable is used. The RETURN_VALUE option specifies a variable in which to store the result, which is the number of files updated or -1 on error.

ctest_upload

Upload files to a dashboard server.

```
ctest_upload(FILES ...)
```

Pass a list of files to be sent along with the build results to the dashboard server.

C.2 cmake-generator-expressions(7)

C.2.1 Introduction

Generator expressions are evaluated during build system generation to produce information specific to each build configuration.

Generator expressions are allowed in the context of many target properties, such as LINK_LIBRARIES (page 599), INCLUDE_DIRECTORIES (page 591), COMPILE_DEFINITIONS (page 580) and others. They may also be used when using commands to populate those properties, such as target_link_libraries() (page 340), target_include_directories() (page 339), target_compile_definitions() (page 338) and others.

This means that they enable conditional linking, conditional definitions used when compiling, and conditional include directories and more. The conditions may be based on the build configuration, target properties, platform information or any other queryable information.

C.2.2 Logical Expressions

Logical expressions are used to create conditional output. The basic expressions are the 0 and 1 expressions. Because other logical expressions evaluate to either 0 or 1, they can be composed to create conditional output:

```
$<$<CONFIG:Debug>:DEBUG_MODE>
```

expands to DEBUG_MODE when the Debug configuration is used, and otherwise expands to nothing.

Available logical expressions are:

$<0:...> Empty string (ignores ...)

$<1:...> Content of ...

$<BOOL:...> 1 if the ... is true, else 0

`$<AND:?[,?]...>` 1 if all ? are 1, else 0

> The ? must always be either 0 or 1 in boolean expressions.

`$<OR:?[,?]...>` 0 if all ? are 0, else 1

`$<NOT:?>` 0 if ? is 1, else 1

`$<STREQUAL:a,b>` 1 if a is STREQUAL b, else 0

`$<EQUAL:a,b>` 1 if a is EQUAL b in a numeric comparison, else 0

`$<CONFIG:cfg>` 1 if config is `cfg`, else 0. This is a case-insensitive comparison. The mapping in `MAP_IMPORTED_CONFIG_<CONFIG>` (page 602) is also considered by this expression when it is evaluated on a property on an `IMPORTED` (page 590) target.

`$<PLATFORM_ID:comp>` 1 if the CMake-id of the platform matches `comp`, otherwise 0.

`$<C_COMPILER_ID:comp>` 1 if the CMake-id of the C compiler matches `comp`, otherwise 0.

`$<CXX_COMPILER_ID:comp>` 1 if the CMake-id of the CXX compiler matches `comp`, otherwise 0.

`$<VERSION_GREATER:v1,v2>` 1 if v1 is a version greater than v2, else 0.

`$<VERSION_LESS:v1,v2>` 1 if v1 is a version less than v2, else 0.

`$<VERSION_EQUAL:v1,v2>` 1 if v1 is the same version as v2, else 0.

`$<C_COMPILER_VERSION:ver>` 1 if the version of the C compiler matches `ver`, otherwise 0.

`$<CXX_COMPILER_VERSION:ver>` 1 if the version of the CXX compiler matches `ver`, otherwise 0.

`$<TARGET_POLICY:pol>` 1 if the policy `pol` was NEW when the 'head' target was created, else 0. If the policy was not set, the warning message for the policy will be emitted. This generator expression only works for a subset of policies.

`$<COMPILE_FEATURES:feature[,feature]...>` 1 if all of the `feature` features are available for the 'head' target, and 0 otherwise. If this expression is used while evaluating the link implementation of a target and if any dependency transitively increases the required `C_STANDARD` (page 578) or `CXX_STANDARD` (page 583) for the 'head' target, an error is reported. See the `cmake-compile-features(7)` manual for information on compile features.

C.2.3 Informational Expressions

These expressions expand to some information. The information may be used directly, eg:

```
include_directories(/usr/include/$<CXX_COMPILER_ID>/)
```

expands to `/usr/include/GNU/` or `/usr/include/Clang/` etc, depending on the Id of the compiler.

These expressions may also may be combined with logical expressions:

```
$<$<VERSION_LESS:$<CXX_COMPILER_VERSION>,4.2.0>:OLD_COMPILER>
```

expands to `OLD_COMPILER` if the `CMAKE_CXX_COMPILER_VERSION` (page 671) is less than 4.2.0.

Available informational expressions are:

$<CONFIGURATION> Configuration name. Deprecated. Use `CONFIG` instead.

$<CONFIG> Configuration name

$<PLATFORM_ID> The CMake-id of the platform. See also the `CMAKE_SYSTEM_NAME` (page 653) variable.

$<C_COMPILER_ID> The CMake-id of the C compiler used. See also the `CMAKE_<LANG>_COMPILER_ID` (page 670) variable.

$<CXX_COMPILER_ID> The CMake-id of the CXX compiler used. See also the `CMAKE_<LANG>_COMPILER_ID` (page 670) variable.

$<C_COMPILER_VERSION> The version of the C compiler used. See also the `CMAKE_<LANG>_COMPILER_VERSION` (page 671) variable.

$<CXX_COMPILER_VERSION> The version of the CXX compiler used. See also the `CMAKE_<LANG>_COMPILER_VERSION` (page 671) variable.

$<TARGET_FILE:tgt> Full path to main file (.exe, .so.1.2, .a) where `tgt` is the name of a target.

$<TARGET_FILE_NAME:tgt> Name of main file (.exe, .so.1.2, .a).

$<TARGET_FILE_DIR:tgt> Directory of main file (.exe, .so.1.2, .a).

$<TARGET_LINKER_FILE:tgt> File used to link (.a, .lib, .so) where `tgt` is the name of a target.

$<TARGET_LINKER_FILE_NAME:tgt> Name of file used to link (.a, .lib, .so).

$<TARGET_LINKER_FILE_DIR:tgt> Directory of file used to link (.a, .lib, .so).

$<TARGET_SONAME_FILE:tgt> File with soname (.so.3) where `tgt` is the name of a target.

$<TARGET_SONAME_FILE_NAME:tgt> Name of file with soname (.so.3).

$<TARGET_SONAME_FILE_DIR:tgt> Directory of with soname (.so.3).

$<TARGET_PDB_FILE:tgt> Full path to the linker generated program database file (.pdb) where `tgt` is the name of a target.

See also the `PDB_NAME` (page 604) and `PDB_OUTPUT_DIRECTORY` (page 605) target properties and their configuration specific variants `PDB_NAME_<CONFIG>` (page 604) and `PDB_OUTPUT_DIRECTORY_<CONFIG>` (page 604).

$<TARGET_PDB_FILE_NAME:tgt> Name of the linker generated program database file (.pdb).

$<TARGET_PDB_FILE_DIR:tgt> Directory of the linker generated program database file (.pdb).

$<TARGET_PROPERTY:tgt,prop> Value of the property `prop` on the target `tgt`.

Note that `tgt` is not added as a dependency of the target this expression is evaluated on.

$<TARGET_PROPERTY:prop> Value of the property `prop` on the target on which the generator expression is evaluated.

$<INSTALL_PREFIX> Content of the install prefix when the target is exported via install(EXPORT) (page 317) and empty otherwise.

C.2.4 Output Expressions

These expressions generate output, in some cases depending on an input. These expressions may be combined with other expressions for information or logical comparison:

```
-I$<JOIN:$<TARGET_PROPERTY:INCLUDE_DIRECTORIES>, -I>
```

generates a string of the entries in the INCLUDE_DIRECTORIES (page 591) target property with each entry preceeded by -I. Note that a more-complete use in this situation would require first checking if the INCLUDE_DIRECTORIES property is non-empty:

```
$<$<BOOL:${prop}>:-I$<JOIN:${prop}, -I>>
```

where ${prop} refers to a helper variable:

```
set(prop "$<TARGET_PROPERTY:INCLUDE_DIRECTORIES>")
```

Available output expressions are:

$<JOIN:list,...> Joins the list with the content of ...

$<ANGLE-R> A literal >. Used to compare strings which contain a > for example.

$<COMMA> A literal ,. Used to compare strings which contain a , for example.

$<SEMICOLON> A literal ;. Used to prevent list expansion on an argument with ;.

$<TARGET_NAME:...> Marks ... as being the name of a target. This is required if exporting targets to multiple dependent export sets. The ... must be a literal name of a target- it may not contain generator expressions.

$<LINK_ONLY:...> Content of ... except when evaluated in a link interface while propagating *Target Usage Requirements*, in which case it is the empty string. Intended for use only in an INTERFACE_LINK_LIBRARIES (page 594) target property, perhaps via the target_link_libraries() (page 340) command, to specify private link dependencies without other usage requirements.

$<INSTALL_INTERFACE:...> Content of ... when the property is exported using install(EXPORT) (page 317), and empty otherwise.

$<BUILD_INTERFACE:...> Content of ... when the property is exported using export() (page 287), or when the target is used by another target in the same buildsystem. Expands to the empty string otherwise.

$<LOWER_CASE:...> Content of ... converted to lower case.

$<UPPER_CASE:...> Content of ... converted to upper case.

$<MAKE_C_IDENTIFIER:...> Content of ... converted to a C identifier.

$<TARGET_OBJECTS:objLib> List of objects resulting from build of `objLib`. `objLib` must be an object of type `OBJECT_LIBRARY`. This expression may only be used in the sources of `add_library()` (page 274) and `add_executable()` (page 273) commands.

C.3 cmake-generators(7)

C.3.1 Introduction

A *CMake Generator* is responsible for writing the input files for a native build system. Exactly one of the CMake Generators (page 360) must be selected for a build tree to determine what native build system is to be used. Optionally one of the Extra Generators (page 364) may be selected as a variant of some of the Command-Line Build Tool Generators (page 360) to produce project files for an auxiliary IDE.

CMake Generators are platform-specific so each may be available only on certain platforms. The `cmake(1)` (page 235) command-line tool `--help` output lists available generators on the current platform. Use its `-G` option to specify the generator for a new build tree. The `cmake-gui(1)` (page 261) offers interactive selection of a generator when creating a new build tree.

C.3.2 CMake Generators

Command-Line Build Tool Generators

These generators support command-line build tools. In order to use them, one must launch CMake from a command-line prompt whose environment is already configured for the chosen compiler and build tool.

Borland Makefiles

Generates Borland makefiles.

MSYS Makefiles

Generates makefiles for use with MSYS `make` under the MSYS shell.

Use this generator in a MSYS shell prompt and using `make` as the build tool. The generated makefiles use `/bin/sh` as the shell to launch build rules. They are not compatible with a Windows command prompt.

To build under a Windows command prompt, use the `MinGW Makefiles` (page 360) generator.

MinGW Makefiles

Generates makefiles for use with `mingw32-make` under a Windows command prompt.

Use this generator under a Windows command prompt with MinGW in the PATH and using mingw32-make as the build tool. The generated makefiles use cmd.exe as the shell to launch build rules. They are not compatible with MSYS or a unix shell.

To build under the MSYS shell, use the MSYS Makefiles (page 360) generator.

NMake Makefiles

Generates NMake makefiles.

NMake Makefiles JOM

Generates JOM makefiles.

Ninja

Generates build.ninja files (experimental).

A build.ninja file is generated into the build tree. Recent versions of the ninja program can build the project through the "all" target. An "install" target is also provided.

Unix Makefiles

Generates standard UNIX makefiles.

A hierarchy of UNIX makefiles is generated into the build tree. Any standard UNIX-style make program can build the project through the default make target. A "make install" target is also provided.

Watcom WMake

Generates Watcom WMake makefiles.

IDE Build Tool Generators

These generators support Integrated Development Environment (IDE) project files. Since the IDEs configure their own environment one may launch CMake from any environment.

Visual Studio 6

Generates Visual Studio 6 project files.

Visual Studio 7

Generates Visual Studio .NET 2002 project files.

Visual Studio 7 .NET 2003

Generates Visual Studio .NET 2003 project files.

Visual Studio 8 2005

Generates Visual Studio 8 2005 project files.

The CMAKE_GENERATOR_PLATFORM (page 628) variable may be set to specify a target platform name.

For compatibility with CMake versions prior to 3.1, one may specify a target platform name optionally at the end of this generator name:

Visual Studio 8 2005 Win64 Specify target platform x64.

Visual Studio 8 2005 <WinCE-SDK> Specify target platform matching a Windows CE SDK name.

Visual Studio 9 2008

Generates Visual Studio 9 2008 project files.

The CMAKE_GENERATOR_PLATFORM (page 628) variable may be set to specify a target platform name.

For compatibility with CMake versions prior to 3.1, one may specify a target platform name optionally at the end of this generator name:

Visual Studio 9 2008 Win64 Specify target platform x64.

Visual Studio 9 2008 IA64 Specify target platform Itanium.

Visual Studio 9 2008 <WinCE-SDK> Specify target platform matching a Windows CE SDK name.

Visual Studio 10 2010

Generates Visual Studio 10 (VS 2010) project files.

The CMAKE_GENERATOR_PLATFORM (page 628) variable may be set to specify a target platform name.

For compatibility with CMake versions prior to 3.1, one may specify a target platform name optionally at the end of this generator name:

Visual Studio 10 2010 Win64 Specify target platform x64.

Visual Studio 10 2010 IA64 Specify target platform `Itanium`.

For compatibility with CMake versions prior to 3.0, one may specify this generator using the name `Visual Studio 10` without the year component.

Visual Studio 11 2012

Generates Visual Studio 11 (VS 2012) project files.

The `CMAKE_GENERATOR_PLATFORM` (page 628) variable may be set to specify a target platform name.

For compatibility with CMake versions prior to 3.1, one may specify a target platform name optionally at the end of this generator name:

Visual Studio 11 2012 Win64 Specify target platform `x64`.

Visual Studio 11 2012 ARM Specify target platform `ARM`.

Visual Studio 11 2012 <WinCE-SDK> Specify target platform matching a Windows CE SDK name.

For compatibility with CMake versions prior to 3.0, one may specify this generator using the name "Visual Studio 11" without the year component.

Visual Studio 12 2013

Generates Visual Studio 12 (VS 2013) project files.

The `CMAKE_GENERATOR_PLATFORM` (page 628) variable may be set to specify a target platform name.

For compatibility with CMake versions prior to 3.1, one may specify a target platform name optionally at the end of this generator name:

Visual Studio 12 2013 Win64 Specify target platform `x64`.

Visual Studio 12 2013 ARM Specify target platform `ARM`.

For compatibility with CMake versions prior to 3.0, one may specify this generator using the name "Visual Studio 12" without the year component.

Visual Studio 14 2015

Generates Visual Studio 14 (VS 2015) project files.

The `CMAKE_GENERATOR_PLATFORM` (page 628) variable may be set to specify a target platform name.

For compatibility with CMake versions prior to 3.1, one may specify a target platform name optionally at the end of this generator name:

Visual Studio 14 2015 Win64 Specify target platform `x64`.

Visual Studio 14 2015 ARM Specify target platform ARM.

Xcode

Generate Xcode project files.

C.3.3 Extra Generators

Some of the CMake Generators (page 360) listed in the cmake(1) (page 235) command-line tool --help output may have variants that specify an extra generator for an auxiliary IDE tool. Such generator names have the form <extra-generator> - <main-generator>. The following extra generators are known to CMake.

CodeBlocks

Generates CodeBlocks project files.

Project files for CodeBlocks will be created in the top directory and in every subdirectory which features a CMakeLists.txt file containing a PROJECT() call. Additionally a hierarchy of makefiles is generated into the build tree. The appropriate make program can build the project through the default make target. A "make install" target is also provided.

This "extra" generator may be specified as:

CodeBlocks - MinGW Makefiles Generate with MinGW Makefiles (page 360).

CodeBlocks - NMake Makefiles Generate with NMake Makefiles (page 361).

CodeBlocks - Ninja Generate with Ninja (page 361).

CodeBlocks - Unix Makefiles Generate with Unix Makefiles (page 361).

CodeLite

Generates CodeLite project files.

Project files for CodeLite will be created in the top directory and in every subdirectory which features a CMakeLists.txt file containing a PROJECT() call. The appropriate make program can build the project through the default make target. A "make install" target is also provided.

This "extra" generator may be specified as:

CodeLite - MinGW Makefiles Generate with MinGW Makefiles (page 360).

CodeLite - NMake Makefiles Generate with NMake Makefiles (page 361).

CodeLite - Ninja Generate with Ninja (page 361).

CodeLite - Unix Makefiles Generate with Unix Makefiles (page 361).

Eclipse CDT4

Generates Eclipse CDT 4.0 project files.

Project files for Eclipse will be created in the top directory. In out of source builds, a linked resource to the top level source directory will be created. Additionally a hierarchy of makefiles is generated into the build tree. The appropriate make program can build the project through the default make target. A "make install" target is also provided.

This "extra" generator may be specified as:

Eclipse CDT4 - MinGW Makefiles Generate with MinGW Makefiles (page 360).

Eclipse CDT4 - NMake Makefiles Generate with NMake Makefiles (page 361).

Eclipse CDT4 - Ninja Generate with Ninja (page 361).

Eclipse CDT4 - Unix Makefiles Generate with Unix Makefiles (page 361).

KDevelop3

Generates KDevelop 3 project files.

Project files for KDevelop 3 will be created in the top directory and in every subdirectory which features a CMakeLists.txt file containing a PROJECT() call. If you change the settings using KDevelop cmake will try its best to keep your changes when regenerating the project files. Additionally a hierarchy of UNIX makefiles is generated into the build tree. Any standard UNIX-style make program can build the project through the default make target. A "make install" target is also provided.

This "extra" generator may be specified as:

KDevelop3 - Unix Makefiles Generate with Unix Makefiles (page 361).

KDevelop3 Generate with Unix Makefiles (page 361).

> For historical reasons this extra generator may be specified directly as the main generator and it will be used as the extra generator with Unix Makefiles (page 361) automatically.

Kate

Generates Kate project files.

A project file for Kate will be created in the top directory in the top level build directory. To use it in kate, the Project plugin must be enabled. The project file is loaded in kate simply by opening the Project-Name.kateproject file in the editor. If the kate Build-plugin is enabled, all targets generated by CMake are available for building.

This "extra" generator may be specified as:

Kate — MinGW Makefiles Generate with MinGW Makefiles (page 360).

Kate — NMake Makefiles Generate with NMake Makefiles (page 361).

Kate — Ninja Generate with Ninja (page 361).

Kate — Unix Makefiles Generate with Unix Makefiles (page 361).

Sublime Text 2

Generates Sublime Text 2 project files.

Project files for Sublime Text 2 will be created in the top directory and in every subdirectory which features a CMakeLists.txt file containing a PROJECT() call. Additionally Makefiles (or build.ninja files) are generated into the build tree. The appropriate make program can build the project through the default make target. A "make install" target is also provided.

This "extra" generator may be specified as:

Sublime Text 2 — MinGW Makefiles Generate with MinGW Makefiles (page 360).

Sublime Text 2 — NMake Makefiles Generate with NMake Makefiles (page 361).

Sublime Text 2 — Ninja Generate with Ninja (page 361).

Sublime Text 2 — Unix Makefiles Generate with Unix Makefiles (page 361).

C.4 cmake-modules(7)

C.4.1 All Modules

AddFileDependencies

ADD_FILE_DEPENDENCIES(source_file depend_files...)

Adds the given files as dependencies to source_file

BundleUtilities

Functions to help assemble a standalone bundle application.

A collection of CMake utility functions useful for dealing with .app bundles on the Mac and bundle-like directories on any OS.

The following functions are provided by this module:

```
fixup_bundle
copy_and_fixup_bundle
verify_app
get_bundle_main_executable
get_dotapp_dir
get_bundle_and_executable
get_bundle_all_executables
get_item_key
get_item_rpaths
clear_bundle_keys
set_bundle_key_values
get_bundle_keys
copy_resolved_item_into_bundle
copy_resolved_framework_into_bundle
fixup_bundle_item
verify_bundle_prerequisites
verify_bundle_symlinks
```

Requires CMake 2.6 or greater because it uses function, break and PARENT_SCOPE. Also depends on GetPrerequisites.cmake.

```
FIXUP_BUNDLE(<app> <libs> <dirs>)
```

Fix up a bundle in-place and make it standalone, such that it can be drag-n-drop copied to another machine and run on that machine as long as all of the system libraries are compatible.

If you pass plugins to fixup_bundle as the libs parameter, you should install them or copy them into the bundle before calling fixup_bundle. The "libs" parameter is a list of libraries that must be fixed up, but that cannot be determined by otool output analysis. (i.e., plugins)

Gather all the keys for all the executables and libraries in a bundle, and then, for each key, copy each prerequisite into the bundle. Then fix each one up according to its own list of prerequisites.

Then clear all the keys and call verify_app on the final bundle to ensure that it is truly standalone.

```
COPY_AND_FIXUP_BUNDLE(<src> <dst> <libs> <dirs>)
```

Makes a copy of the bundle <src> at location <dst> and then fixes up the new copied bundle in-place at <dst>...

```
VERIFY_APP(<app>)
```

Verifies that an application <app> appears valid based on running analysis tools on it. Calls "message(FATAL_ERROR" if the application is not verified.

```
GET_BUNDLE_MAIN_EXECUTABLE(<bundle> <result_var>)
```

The result will be the full path name of the bundle's main executable file or an "error:" prefixed string if it could not be determined.

```
GET_DOTAPP_DIR(<exe> <dotapp_dir_var>)
```

Returns the nearest parent dir whose name ends with ".app" given the full path to an executable. If there is no such parent dir, then simply return the dir containing the executable.

The returned directory may or may not exist.

```
GET_BUNDLE_AND_EXECUTABLE(<app> <bundle_var> <executable_var> <valid_var>)
```

Takes either a ".app" directory name or the name of an executable nested inside a ".app" directory and returns the path to the ".app" directory in <bundle_var> and the path to its main executable in <executable_var>

```
GET_BUNDLE_ALL_EXECUTABLES(<bundle> <exes_var>)
```

Scans the given bundle recursively for all executable files and accumulates them into a variable.

```
GET_ITEM_KEY(<item> <key_var>)
```

Given a file (item) name, generate a key that should be unique considering the set of libraries that need copying or fixing up to make a bundle standalone. This is essentially the file name including extension with "." replaced by "_"

This key is used as a prefix for CMake variables so that we can associate a set of variables with a given item based on its key.

```
CLEAR_BUNDLE_KEYS(<keys_var>)
```

Loop over the list of keys, clearing all the variables associated with each key. After the loop, clear the list of keys itself.

Caller of get_bundle_keys should call clear_bundle_keys when done with list of keys.

```
SET_BUNDLE_KEY_VALUES(<keys_var> <context> <item> <exepath> <dirs>
                      <copyflag> [<rpaths>])
```

Add a key to the list (if necessary) for the given item. If added, also set all the variables associated with that key.

```
GET_BUNDLE_KEYS(<app> <libs> <dirs> <keys_var>)
```

Loop over all the executable and library files within the bundle (and given as extra <libs>) and accumulate a list of keys representing them. Set values associated with each key such that we can loop over all of them and copy prerequisite libs into the bundle and then do appropriate install_name_tool fixups.

```
COPY_RESOLVED_ITEM_INTO_BUNDLE(<resolved_item> <resolved_embedded_item>)
```

Copy a resolved item into the bundle if necessary. Copy is not necessary if the resolved_item is "the same as" the resolved_embedded_item.

```
COPY_RESOLVED_FRAMEWORK_INTO_BUNDLE(<resolved_item> <resolved_embedded_item>)
```

Copy a resolved framework into the bundle if necessary. Copy is not necessary if the resolved_item is "the same as" the resolved_embedded_item.

By default, BU_COPY_FULL_FRAMEWORK_CONTENTS is not set. If you want full frameworks embedded in your bundles, set BU_COPY_FULL_FRAMEWORK_CONTENTS to ON before calling fixup_bundle. By default, COPY_RESOLVED_FRAMEWORK_INTO_BUNDLE copies the framework dylib itself plus the framework Resources directory.

```
FIXUP_BUNDLE_ITEM(<resolved_embedded_item> <exepath> <dirs>)
```

Get the direct/non-system prerequisites of the resolved embedded item. For each prerequisite, change the way it is referenced to the value of the _EMBEDDED_ITEM keyed variable for that prerequisite. (Most likely changing to an "@executable_path" style reference.)

This function requires that the resolved_embedded_item be "inside" the bundle already. In other words, if you pass plugins to fixup_bundle as the libs parameter, you should install them or copy them into the bundle before calling fixup_bundle. The "libs" parameter is a list of libraries that must be fixed up, but that cannot be determined by otool output analysis. (i.e., plugins)

Also, change the id of the item being fixed up to its own _EMBEDDED_ITEM value.

Accumulate changes in a local variable and make *one* call to install_name_tool at the end of the function with all the changes at once.

If the BU_CHMOD_BUNDLE_ITEMS variable is set then bundle items will be marked writable before install_name_tool tries to change them.

```
VERIFY_BUNDLE_PREREQUISITES(<bundle> <result_var> <info_var>)
```

Verifies that the sum of all prerequisites of all files inside the bundle are contained within the bundle or are "system" libraries, presumed to exist everywhere.

```
VERIFY_BUNDLE_SYMLINKS(<bundle> <result_var> <info_var>)
```

Verifies that any symlinks found in the bundle point to other files that are already also in the bundle... Anything that points to an external file causes this function to fail the verification.

CheckCCompilerFlag

Check whether the C compiler supports a given flag.

CHECK_C_COMPILER_FLAG(<flag> <var>)

```
<flag> - the compiler flag
<var>  - variable to store the result
         Will be created as an internal cache variable.
```

This internally calls the check_c_source_compiles macro and sets CMAKE_REQUIRED_DEFINITIONS to <flag>. See help for CheckCSourceCompiles for a listing of variables that can otherwise modify the build. The result only tells that the compiler does not give an error message when it encounters the flag. If the flag has any effect or even a specific one is beyond the scope of this module.

CheckCSourceCompiles

Check if given C source compiles and links into an executable

CHECK_C_SOURCE_COMPILES(<code> <var> [FAIL_REGEX <fail-regex>])

```
<code>       - source code to try to compile, must define 'main'
<var>        - variable to store whether the source code compiled
               Will be created as an internal cache variable.
<fail-regex> - fail if test output matches this regex
```

The following variables may be set before calling this macro to modify the way the check is run:

```
CMAKE_REQUIRED_FLAGS = string of compile command line flags
CMAKE_REQUIRED_DEFINITIONS = list of macros to define (-DFOO=bar)
CMAKE_REQUIRED_INCLUDES = list of include directories
CMAKE_REQUIRED_LIBRARIES = list of libraries to link
CMAKE_REQUIRED_QUIET = execute quietly without messages
```

CheckCSourceRuns

Check if the given C source code compiles and runs.

CHECK_C_SOURCE_RUNS(<code> <var>)

```
<code>    - source code to try to compile
<var>     - variable to store the result
            (1 for success, empty for failure)
            Will be created as an internal cache variable.
```

The following variables may be set before calling this macro to modify the way the check is run:

```
CMAKE_REQUIRED_FLAGS = string of compile command line flags
CMAKE_REQUIRED_DEFINITIONS = list of macros to define (-DFOO=bar)
CMAKE_REQUIRED_INCLUDES = list of include directories
CMAKE_REQUIRED_LIBRARIES = list of libraries to link
CMAKE_REQUIRED_QUIET = execute quietly without messages
```

CheckCXXCompilerFlag

Check whether the CXX compiler supports a given flag.

CHECK_CXX_COMPILER_FLAG(<flag> <var>)

```
<flag> - the compiler flag
<var>  - variable to store the result
```

This internally calls the check_cxx_source_compiles macro and sets CMAKE_REQUIRED_DEFINITIONS to <flag>. See help for CheckCXXSourceCompiles for a listing of variables that can otherwise modify the build. The result only tells that the compiler does not give an error message when it encounters the flag. If the flag has any effect or even a specific one is beyond the scope of this module.

CheckCXXSourceCompiles

Check if given C++ source compiles and links into an executable

CHECK_CXX_SOURCE_COMPILES(<code> <var> [FAIL_REGEX <fail-regex>])

```
<code>       - source code to try to compile, must define 'main'
<var>        - variable to store whether the source code compiled
               Will be created as an internal cache variable.
<fail-regex> - fail if test output matches this regex
```

The following variables may be set before calling this macro to modify the way the check is run:

```
CMAKE_REQUIRED_FLAGS = string of compile command line flags
CMAKE_REQUIRED_DEFINITIONS = list of macros to define (-DFOO=bar)
CMAKE_REQUIRED_INCLUDES = list of include directories
CMAKE_REQUIRED_LIBRARIES = list of libraries to link
CMAKE_REQUIRED_QUIET = execute quietly without messages
```

CheckCXXSourceRuns

Check if the given C++ source code compiles and runs.

CHECK_CXX_SOURCE_RUNS(<code> <var>)

```
<code>  - source code to try to compile
<var>   - variable to store the result
          (1 for success, empty for failure)
          Will be created as an internal cache variable.
```

The following variables may be set before calling this macro to modify the way the check is run:

```
CMAKE_REQUIRED_FLAGS = string of compile command line flags
CMAKE_REQUIRED_DEFINITIONS = list of macros to define (-DFOO=bar)
CMAKE_REQUIRED_INCLUDES = list of include directories
CMAKE_REQUIRED_LIBRARIES = list of libraries to link
CMAKE_REQUIRED_QUIET = execute quietly without messages
```

CheckCXXSymbolExists

Check if a symbol exists as a function, variable, or macro in C++

CHECK_CXX_SYMBOL_EXISTS(<symbol> <files> <variable>)

Check that the <symbol> is available after including given header <files> and store the result in a <variable>. Specify the list of files in one argument as a semicolon-separated list. CHECK_CXX_SYMBOL_EXISTS() can be used to check in C++ files, as opposed to CHECK_SYMBOL_EXISTS(), which works only for C.

If the header files define the symbol as a macro it is considered available and assumed to work. If the header files declare the symbol as a function or variable then the symbol must also be available for linking. If the symbol is a type or enum value it will not be recognized (consider using CheckTypeSize or CheckCSource-Compiles).

The following variables may be set before calling this macro to modify the way the check is run:

```
CMAKE_REQUIRED_FLAGS = string of compile command line flags
CMAKE_REQUIRED_DEFINITIONS = list of macros to define (-DFOO=bar)
CMAKE_REQUIRED_INCLUDES = list of include directories
CMAKE_REQUIRED_LIBRARIES = list of libraries to link
CMAKE_REQUIRED_QUIET = execute quietly without messages
```

CheckFortranFunctionExists

macro which checks if the Fortran function exists

CHECK_FORTRAN_FUNCTION_EXISTS(FUNCTION VARIABLE)

```
FUNCTION - the name of the Fortran function
VARIABLE - variable to store the result
           Will be created as an internal cache variable.
```

The following variables may be set before calling this macro to modify the way the check is run:

```
CMAKE_REQUIRED_LIBRARIES = list of libraries to link
```

CheckFortranSourceCompiles

Check if given Fortran source compiles and links into an executable:

```
CHECK_Fortran_SOURCE_COMPILES(<code> <var> [FAIL_REGEX <fail-regex>])
```

The arguments are:

<code> Source code to try to compile. It must define a PROGRAM entry point.

<var> Variable to store whether the source code compiled. Will be created as an internal cache variable.

<fail-regex> Fail if test output matches this regex.

The following variables may be set before calling this macro to modify the way the check is run:

```
CMAKE_REQUIRED_FLAGS = string of compile command line flags
CMAKE_REQUIRED_DEFINITIONS = list of macros to define (-DFOO=bar)
CMAKE_REQUIRED_INCLUDES = list of include directories
```

```
CMAKE_REQUIRED_LIBRARIES = list of libraries to link
CMAKE_REQUIRED_QUIET = execute quietly without messages
```

CheckFunctionExists

Check if a C function can be linked

CHECK_FUNCTION_EXISTS(<function> <variable>)

Check that the <function> is provided by libraries on the system and store the result in a <variable>. This does not verify that any system header file declares the function, only that it can be found at link time (consider using CheckSymbolExists). <variable> will be created as an internal cache variable.

The following variables may be set before calling this macro to modify the way the check is run:

```
CMAKE_REQUIRED_FLAGS = string of compile command line flags
CMAKE_REQUIRED_DEFINITIONS = list of macros to define (-DFOO=bar)
CMAKE_REQUIRED_INCLUDES = list of include directories
CMAKE_REQUIRED_LIBRARIES = list of libraries to link
CMAKE_REQUIRED_QUIET = execute quietly without messages
```

CheckIncludeFileCXX

Check if the include file exists.

```
CHECK_INCLUDE_FILE_CXX(INCLUDE VARIABLE)
```

```
INCLUDE   - name of include file
VARIABLE - variable to return result
           Will be created as an internal cache variable.
```

An optional third argument is the CFlags to add to the compile line or you can use CMAKE_REQUIRED_FLAGS.

The following variables may be set before calling this macro to modify the way the check is run:

```
CMAKE_REQUIRED_FLAGS = string of compile command line flags
CMAKE_REQUIRED_DEFINITIONS = list of macros to define (-DFOO=bar)
CMAKE_REQUIRED_INCLUDES = list of include directories
CMAKE_REQUIRED_QUIET = execute quietly without messages
```

CheckIncludeFile

macro which checks the include file exists.

CHECK_INCLUDE_FILE(INCLUDE VARIABLE)

```
INCLUDE  - name of include file
VARIABLE - variable to return result
           Will be created as an internal cache variable.
```

an optional third argument is the CFlags to add to the compile line or you can use CMAKE_REQUIRED_FLAGS

The following variables may be set before calling this macro to modify the way the check is run:

```
CMAKE_REQUIRED_FLAGS = string of compile command line flags
CMAKE_REQUIRED_DEFINITIONS = list of macros to define (-DFOO=bar)
CMAKE_REQUIRED_INCLUDES = list of include directories
CMAKE_REQUIRED_QUIET = execute quietly without messages
```

CheckIncludeFiles

Check if the files can be included

CHECK_INCLUDE_FILES(INCLUDE VARIABLE)

```
INCLUDE  - list of files to include
VARIABLE - variable to return result
           Will be created as an internal cache variable.
```

The following variables may be set before calling this macro to modify the way the check is run:

```
CMAKE_REQUIRED_FLAGS = string of compile command line flags
CMAKE_REQUIRED_DEFINITIONS = list of macros to define (-DFOO=bar)
CMAKE_REQUIRED_INCLUDES = list of include directories
CMAKE_REQUIRED_QUIET = execute quietly without messages
```

CheckLanguage

Check if a language can be enabled

Usage:

```
check_language(<lang>)
```

where <lang> is a language that may be passed to enable_language() such as "Fortran". If CMAKE_<lang>_COMPILER is already defined the check does nothing. Otherwise it tries enabling the language in a test project. The result is cached in CMAKE_<lang>_COMPILER as the compiler that was found, or NOTFOUND if the language cannot be enabled.

Example:

```
check_language(Fortran)
if(CMAKE_Fortran_COMPILER)
  enable_language(Fortran)
```

```
else()
  message(STATUS "No Fortran support")
endif()
```

CheckLibraryExists

Check if the function exists.

CHECK_LIBRARY_EXISTS (LIBRARY FUNCTION LOCATION VARIABLE)

```
LIBRARY  - the name of the library you are looking for
FUNCTION - the name of the function
LOCATION - location where the library should be found
VARIABLE - variable to store the result
           Will be created as an internal cache variable.
```

The following variables may be set before calling this macro to modify the way the check is run:

```
CMAKE_REQUIRED_FLAGS = string of compile command line flags
CMAKE_REQUIRED_DEFINITIONS = list of macros to define (-DFOO=bar)
CMAKE_REQUIRED_LIBRARIES = list of libraries to link
CMAKE_REQUIRED_QUIET = execute quietly without messages
```

CheckPrototypeDefinition

Check if the protoype we expect is correct.

check_prototype_definition(FUNCTION PROTOTYPE RETURN HEADER VARIABLE)

```
FUNCTION - The name of the function (used to check if prototype exists)
PROTOTYPE- The prototype to check.
RETURN - The return value of the function.
HEADER - The header files required.
VARIABLE - The variable to store the result.
           Will be created as an internal cache variable.
```

Example:

```
check_prototype_definition(getpwent_r
 "struct passwd *getpwent_r(struct passwd *src, char *buf, int buflen)"
 "NULL"
 "unistd.h;pwd.h"
 SOLARIS_GETPWENT_R)
```

The following variables may be set before calling this macro to modify the way the check is run:

```
CMAKE_REQUIRED_FLAGS = string of compile command line flags
CMAKE_REQUIRED_DEFINITIONS = list of macros to define (-DFOO=bar)
CMAKE_REQUIRED_INCLUDES = list of include directories
```

```
CMAKE_REQUIRED_LIBRARIES = list of libraries to link
CMAKE_REQUIRED_QUIET = execute quietly without messages
```

CheckStructHasMember

Check if the given struct or class has the specified member variable

```
CHECK_STRUCT_HAS_MEMBER(<struct> <member> <header> <variable>
                        [LANGUAGE <language>])
```

```
<struct> - the name of the struct or class you are interested in
<member> - the member which existence you want to check
<header> - the header(s) where the prototype should be declared
<variable> - variable to store the result
<language> - the compiler to use (C or CXX)
```

The following variables may be set before calling this macro to modify the way the check is run:

```
CMAKE_REQUIRED_FLAGS = string of compile command line flags
CMAKE_REQUIRED_DEFINITIONS = list of macros to define (-DFOO=bar)
CMAKE_REQUIRED_INCLUDES = list of include directories
CMAKE_REQUIRED_LIBRARIES = list of libraries to link
CMAKE_REQUIRED_QUIET = execute quietly without messages
```

Example: CHECK_STRUCT_HAS_MEMBER("struct   timeval"   tv_sec   sys/select.h
HAVE_TIMEVAL_TV_SEC LANGUAGE C)

CheckSymbolExists

Check if a symbol exists as a function, variable, or macro

CHECK_SYMBOL_EXISTS(<symbol> <files> <variable>)

Check that the <symbol> is available after including given header <files> and store the result in a <variable>. Specify the list of files in one argument as a semicolon-separated list. <variable> will be created as an internal cache variable.

If the header files define the symbol as a macro it is considered available and assumed to work. If the header files declare the symbol as a function or variable then the symbol must also be available for linking. If the symbol is a type or enum value it will not be recognized (consider using CheckTypeSize or CheckCSource-Compiles). If the check needs to be done in C++, consider using CHECK_CXX_SYMBOL_EXISTS(), which does the same as CHECK_SYMBOL_EXISTS(), but in C++.

The following variables may be set before calling this macro to modify the way the check is run:

```
CMAKE_REQUIRED_FLAGS = string of compile command line flags
CMAKE_REQUIRED_DEFINITIONS = list of macros to define (-DFOO=bar)
CMAKE_REQUIRED_INCLUDES = list of include directories
```

```
CMAKE_REQUIRED_LIBRARIES = list of libraries to link
CMAKE_REQUIRED_QUIET = execute quietly without messages
```

CheckTypeSize

Check sizeof a type

```
CHECK_TYPE_SIZE(TYPE VARIABLE [BUILTIN_TYPES_ONLY]
                          [LANGUAGE <language>])
```

Check if the type exists and determine its size. On return, "HAVE_${VARIABLE}" holds the existence of the type, and "${VARIABLE}" holds one of the following:

```
<size> = type has non-zero size <size>
"0"    = type has arch-dependent size (see below)
""     = type does not exist
```

Both `HAVE_${VARIABLE}` and `${VARIABLE}` will be created as internal cache variables.

Furthermore, the variable "${VARIABLE}_CODE" holds C preprocessor code to define the macro "${VARIABLE}" to the size of the type, or leave the macro undefined if the type does not exist.

The variable "${VARIABLE}" may be "0" when CMAKE_OSX_ARCHITECTURES has multiple architectures for building OS X universal binaries. This indicates that the type size varies across architectures. In this case "${VARIABLE}_CODE" contains C preprocessor tests mapping from each architecture macro to the corresponding type size. The list of architecture macros is stored in "${VARIABLE}_KEYS", and the value for each key is stored in "${VARIABLE}-${KEY}".

If the BUILTIN_TYPES_ONLY option is not given, the macro checks for headers <sys/types.h>, <stdint.h>, and <stddef.h>, and saves results in HAVE_SYS_TYPES_H, HAVE_STDINT_H, and HAVE_STDDEF_H. The type size check automatically includes the available headers, thus supporting checks of types defined in the headers.

If LANGUAGE is set, the specified compiler will be used to perform the check. Acceptable values are C and CXX

Despite the name of the macro you may use it to check the size of more complex expressions, too. To check e.g. for the size of a struct member you can do something like this:

```
check_type_size("((struct something*)0)->member" SIZEOF_MEMBER)
```

The following variables may be set before calling this macro to modify the way the check is run:

```
CMAKE_REQUIRED_FLAGS = string of compile command line flags
CMAKE_REQUIRED_DEFINITIONS = list of macros to define (-DFOO=bar)
CMAKE_REQUIRED_INCLUDES = list of include directories
CMAKE_REQUIRED_LIBRARIES = list of libraries to link
CMAKE_REQUIRED_QUIET = execute quietly without messages
CMAKE_EXTRA_INCLUDE_FILES = list of extra headers to include
```

CheckVariableExists

Check if the variable exists.

```
CHECK_VARIABLE_EXISTS(VAR VARIABLE)
```

```
VAR       - the name of the variable
VARIABLE - variable to store the result
            Will be created as an internal cache variable.
```

This macro is only for C variables.

The following variables may be set before calling this macro to modify the way the check is run:

```
CMAKE_REQUIRED_FLAGS = string of compile command line flags
CMAKE_REQUIRED_DEFINITIONS = list of macros to define (-DFOO=bar)
CMAKE_REQUIRED_LIBRARIES = list of libraries to link
CMAKE_REQUIRED_QUIET = execute quietly without messages
```

CMakeAddFortranSubdirectory

Use MinGW gfortran from VS if a fortran compiler is not found.

The 'add_fortran_subdirectory' function adds a subdirectory to a project that contains a fortran only sub-project. The module will check the current compiler and see if it can support fortran. If no fortran compiler is found and the compiler is MSVC, then this module will find the MinGW gfortran. It will then use an external project to build with the MinGW tools. It will also create imported targets for the libraries created. This will only work if the fortran code is built into a dll, so BUILD_SHARED_LIBS is turned on in the project. In addition the CMAKE_GNUtoMS option is set to on, so that the MS .lib files are created. Usage is as follows:

```
cmake_add_fortran_subdirectory(
  <subdir>                   # name of subdirectory
  PROJECT <project_name>     # project name in subdir top CMakeLists.txt
  ARCHIVE_DIR <dir>          # dir where project places .lib files
  RUNTIME_DIR <dir>          # dir where project places .dll files
  LIBRARIES <lib>...         # names of library targets to import
  LINK_LIBRARIES             # link interface libraries for LIBRARIES
    [LINK_LIBS <lib> <dep>...]...
  CMAKE_COMMAND_LINE ...     # extra command line flags to pass to cmake
  NO_EXTERNAL_INSTALL        # skip installation of external project
  )
```

Relative paths in ARCHIVE_DIR and RUNTIME_DIR are interpreted with respect to the build directory corresponding to the source directory in which the function is invoked.

Limitations:

NO_EXTERNAL_INSTALL is required for forward compatibility with a future version that supports installation of the external project binaries during "make install".

CMakeBackwardCompatibilityCXX

define a bunch of backwards compatibility variables

```
CMAKE_ANSI_CXXFLAGS - flag for ansi c++
CMAKE_HAS_ANSI_STRING_STREAM - has <strstream>
include(TestForANSIStreamHeaders)
include(CheckIncludeFileCXX)
include(TestForSTDNamespace)
include(TestForANSIForScope)
```

CMakeDependentOption

Macro to provide an option dependent on other options.

This macro presents an option to the user only if a set of other conditions are true. When the option is not presented a default value is used, but any value set by the user is preserved for when the option is presented again. Example invocation:

```
CMAKE_DEPENDENT_OPTION(USE_FOO "Use Foo" ON
                       "USE_BAR;NOT USE_ZOT" OFF)
```

If USE_BAR is true and USE_ZOT is false, this provides an option called USE_FOO that defaults to ON. Otherwise, it sets USE_FOO to OFF. If the status of USE_BAR or USE_ZOT ever changes, any value for the USE_FOO option is saved so that when the option is re-enabled it retains its old value.

CMakeDetermineVSServicePack

Deprecated. Do not use.

The functionality of this module has been superseded by the CMAKE_<LANG>_COMPILER_VERSION (page 671) variable that contains the compiler version number.

Determine the Visual Studio service pack of the 'cl' in use.

Usage:

```
if(MSVC)
  include(CMakeDetermineVSServicePack)
  DetermineVSServicePack( my_service_pack )
  if( my_service_pack )
    message(STATUS "Detected: ${my_service_pack}")
  endif()
endif()
```

Function DetermineVSServicePack sets the given variable to one of the following values or an empty string if unknown:

```
vc80, vc80sp1
vc90, vc90sp1
vc100, vc100sp1
vc110, vc110sp1, vc110sp2, vc110sp3, vc110sp4
```

CMakeExpandImportedTargets

```
CMAKE_EXPAND_IMPORTED_TARGETS(<var> LIBRARIES lib1 lib2...libN
                              [CONFIGURATION <config>])
```

CMAKE_EXPAND_IMPORTED_TARGETS() takes a list of libraries and replaces all imported targets contained in this list with their actual file paths of the referenced libraries on disk, including the libraries from their link interfaces. If a CONFIGURATION is given, it uses the respective configuration of the imported targets if it exists. If no CONFIGURATION is given, it uses the first configuration from ${CMAKE_CONFIGURATION_TYPES} if set, otherwise ${CMAKE_BUILD_TYPE}. This macro is used by all Check*.cmake files which use try_compile() or try_run() and support CMAKE_REQUIRED_LIBRARIES , so that these checks support imported targets in CMAKE_REQUIRED_LIBRARIES:

```
cmake_expand_imported_targets(expandedLibs
  LIBRARIES ${CMAKE_REQUIRED_LIBRARIES}
  CONFIGURATION "${CMAKE_TRY_COMPILE_CONFIGURATION}" )
```

CMakeFindDependencyMacro

```
find_dependency(<dep> [<version> [EXACT]])
```

find_dependency() wraps a find_package() (page 297) call for a package dependency. It is designed to be used in a <package>Config.cmake file, and it forwards the correct parameters for EXACT, QUIET and REQUIRED which were passed to the original find_package() (page 297) call. It also sets an informative diagnostic message if the dependency could not be found.

CMakeFindFrameworks

helper module to find OSX frameworks

CMakeFindPackageMode

This file is executed by cmake when invoked with –find-package. It expects that the following variables are set using -D:

NAME name of the package

COMPILER_ID the CMake compiler ID for which the result is, i.e. GNU/Intel/Clang/MSVC, etc.

LANGUAGE language for which the result will be used, i.e. C/CXX/Fortan/ASM

MODE

> **EXIST** only check for existence of the given package

> **COMPILE** print the flags needed for compiling an object file which uses the given package

> **LINK** print the flags needed for linking when using the given package

QUIET if TRUE, don't print anything

CMakeForceCompiler

This module defines macros intended for use by cross-compiling toolchain files when CMake is not able to automatically detect the compiler identification.

Macro CMAKE_FORCE_C_COMPILER has the following signature:

```
CMAKE_FORCE_C_COMPILER(<compiler> <compiler-id>)
```

It sets CMAKE_C_COMPILER to the given compiler and the cmake internal variable CMAKE_C_COMPILER_ID to the given compiler-id. It also bypasses the check for working compiler and basic compiler information tests.

Macro CMAKE_FORCE_CXX_COMPILER has the following signature:

```
CMAKE_FORCE_CXX_COMPILER(<compiler> <compiler-id>)
```

It sets CMAKE_CXX_COMPILER to the given compiler and the cmake internal variable CMAKE_CXX_COMPILER_ID to the given compiler-id. It also bypasses the check for working compiler and basic compiler information tests.

Macro CMAKE_FORCE_Fortran_COMPILER has the following signature:

```
CMAKE_FORCE_Fortran_COMPILER(<compiler> <compiler-id>)
```

It sets CMAKE_Fortran_COMPILER to the given compiler and the cmake internal variable CMAKE_Fortran_COMPILER_ID to the given compiler-id. It also bypasses the check for working compiler and basic compiler information tests.

So a simple toolchain file could look like this:

```
include (CMakeForceCompiler)
set(CMAKE_SYSTEM_NAME Generic)
CMAKE_FORCE_C_COMPILER   (chc12 MetrowerksHicross)
CMAKE_FORCE_CXX_COMPILER (chc12 MetrowerksHicross)
```

CMakeGraphVizOptions

The builtin graphviz support of CMake.

Variables specific to the graphviz support

CMake can generate graphviz files, showing the dependencies between the targets in a project and also external libraries which are linked against. When CMake is run with the –graphiz=foo option, it will produce

- a foo.dot file showing all dependencies in the project

- a foo.dot.<target> file for each target, file showing on which other targets the respective target depends

- a foo.dot.<target>.dependers file, showing which other targets depend on the respective target

This can result in huge graphs. Using the file CMakeGraphVizOptions.cmake the look and content of the generated graphs can be influenced. This file is searched first in ${CMAKE_BINARY_DIR} and then in ${CMAKE_SOURCE_DIR}. If found, it is read and the variables set in it are used to adjust options for the generated graphviz files.

GRAPHVIZ_GRAPH_TYPE
>The graph type

>>•Mandatory : NO

>>•Default : "digraph"

GRAPHVIZ_GRAPH_NAME
>The graph name.

>>•Mandatory : NO

>>•Default : "GG"

GRAPHVIZ_GRAPH_HEADER
>The header written at the top of the graphviz file.

>>•Mandatory : NO

>>•Default : "node [n fontsize = "12"];"

GRAPHVIZ_NODE_PREFIX
>The prefix for each node in the graphviz file.

>>•Mandatory : NO

>>•Default : "node"

GRAPHVIZ_EXECUTABLES
>Set this to FALSE to exclude executables from the generated graphs.

>>•Mandatory : NO

>>•Default : TRUE

GRAPHVIZ_STATIC_LIBS
>Set this to FALSE to exclude static libraries from the generated graphs.

>>•Mandatory : NO

•Default : TRUE

GRAPHVIZ_SHARED_LIBS

Set this to FALSE to exclude shared libraries from the generated graphs.

•Mandatory : NO

•Default : TRUE

GRAPHVIZ_MODULE_LIBS

Set this to FALSE to exclude module libraries from the generated graphs.

•Mandatory : NO

•Default : TRUE

GRAPHVIZ_EXTERNAL_LIBS

Set this to FALSE to exclude external libraries from the generated graphs.

•Mandatory : NO

•Default : TRUE

GRAPHVIZ_IGNORE_TARGETS

A list of regular expressions for ignoring targets.

•Mandatory : NO

•Default : empty

GRAPHVIZ_GENERATE_PER_TARGET

Set this to FALSE to exclude per target graphs `foo.dot.<target>`.

•Mandatory : NO

•Default : TRUE

GRAPHVIZ_GENERATE_DEPENDERS

Set this to FALSE to exclude depender graphs `foo.dot.<target>.dependers`.

•Mandatory : NO

•Default : TRUE

CMakePackageConfigHelpers

Helpers functions for creating config files that can be included by other projects to find and use a package.

Adds the `configure_package_config_file()` (page 384) and `write_basic_package_version_file()` (page 385) commands.

Generating a Package Configuration File

`configure_package_config_file`
Create a config file for a project:

```
configure_package_config_file(<input> <output>
    INSTALL_DESTINATION <path>
    [PATH_VARS <var1> <var2> ... <varN>]
    [NO_SET_AND_CHECK_MACRO]
    [NO_CHECK_REQUIRED_COMPONENTS_MACRO]
    [INSTALL_PREFIX <path>]
    )
```

`configure_package_config_file()` should be used instead of the plain `configure_file()` (page 282) command when creating the `<Name>Config.cmake` or `<Name>-config.cmake` file for installing a project or library. It helps making the resulting package relocatable by avoiding hardcoded paths in the installed `Config.cmake` file.

In a `FooConfig.cmake` file there may be code like this to make the install destinations know to the using project:

```
set(FOO_INCLUDE_DIR    "@CMAKE_INSTALL_FULL_INCLUDEDIR@" )
set(FOO_DATA_DIR    "@CMAKE_INSTALL_PREFIX@/@RELATIVE_DATA_INSTALL_DIR@" )
set(FOO_ICONS_DIR    "@CMAKE_INSTALL_PREFIX@/share/icons" )
...logic to determine installedPrefix from the own location...
set(FOO_CONFIG_DIR    "${installedPrefix}/@CONFIG_INSTALL_DIR@" )
```

All 4 options shown above are not sufficient, since the first 3 hardcode the absolute directory locations, and the 4th case works only if the logic to determine the `installedPrefix` is correct, and if `CONFIG_INSTALL_DIR` contains a relative path, which in general cannot be guaranteed. This has the effect that the resulting `FooConfig.cmake` file would work poorly under Windows and OSX, where users are used to choose the install location of a binary package at install time, independent from how `CMAKE_INSTALL_PREFIX` (page 645) was set at build/cmake time.

Using `configure_package_config_file` helps. If used correctly, it makes the resulting `FooConfig.cmake` file relocatable. Usage:

1. write a `FooConfig.cmake.in` file as you are used to

2. insert a line containing only the string `@PACKAGE_INIT@`

3. instead of `set(FOO_DIR "@SOME_INSTALL_DIR@")`, use `set(FOO_DIR "@PACKAGE_SOME_INSTALL_DIR@")` (this must be after the `@PACKAGE_INIT@` line)

4. instead of using the normal `configure_file()` (page 282), use `configure_package_config_file()`

The `<input>` and `<output>` arguments are the input and output file, the same way as in `configure_file()` (page 282).

The `<path>` given to `INSTALL_DESTINATION` must be the destination where the `FooConfig.cmake` file will be installed to. This path can either be absolute, or relative to the `INSTALL_PREFIX` path.

The variables `<var1>` to `<varN>` given as `PATH_VARS` are the variables which contain install destinations. For each of them the macro will create a helper variable `PACKAGE_<var...>`. These helper variables must be used in the `FooConfig.cmake.in` file for setting the installed location. They are calculated by `configure_package_config_file` so that they are always relative to the installed location of the package. This works both for relative and also for absolute locations. For absolute locations it works only if the absolute location is a subdirectory of `INSTALL_PREFIX`.

If the `INSTALL_PREFIX` argument is passed, this is used as base path to calculate all the relative paths. The `<path>` argument must be an absolute path. If this argument is not passed, the `CMAKE_INSTALL_PREFIX` (page 645) variable will be used instead. The default value is good when generating a FooConfig.cmake file to use your package from the install tree. When generating a FooConfig.cmake file to use your package from the build tree this option should be used.

By default `configure_package_config_file` also generates two helper macros, `set_and_check()` and `check_required_components()` into the `FooConfig.cmake` file.

`set_and_check()` should be used instead of the normal `set()` command for setting directories and file locations. Additionally to setting the variable it also checks that the referenced file or directory actually exists and fails with a `FATAL_ERROR` otherwise. This makes sure that the created `FooConfig.cmake` file does not contain wrong references. When using the `NO_SET_AND_CHECK_MACRO`, this macro is not generated into the `FooConfig.cmake` file.

`check_required_components(<package_name>)` should be called at the end of the `FooConfig.cmake` file if the package supports components. This macro checks whether all requested, non-optional components have been found, and if this is not the case, sets the `Foo_FOUND` variable to `FALSE`, so that the package is considered to be not found. It does that by testing the `Foo_<Component>_FOUND` variables for all requested required components. When using the `NO_CHECK_REQUIRED_COMPONENTS_MACRO` option, this macro is not generated into the `FooConfig.cmake` file.

For an example see below the documentation for `write_basic_package_version_file()` (page 385).

Generating a Package Version File

write_basic_package_version_file
Create a version file for a project:

```
write_basic_package_version_file(<filename>
  [VERSION <major.minor.patch>]
  COMPATIBILITY <AnyNewerVersion|SameMajorVersion|ExactVersion> )
```

Writes a file for use as `<package>ConfigVersion.cmake` file to `<filename>`. See the documentation of `find_package()` (page 297) for details on this.

`<filename>` is the output filename, it should be in the build tree. `<major.minor.patch>` is the version number of the project to be installed.

If no `VERSION` is given, the `PROJECT_VERSION` (page 638) variable is used. If this hasn't been set, it errors out.

The `COMPATIBILITY` mode `AnyNewerVersion` means that the installed package version will be considered compatible if it is newer or exactly the same as the requested version. This mode should be used for packages which are fully backward compatible, also across major versions. If `SameMajorVersion` is used instead, then the behaviour differs from `AnyNewerVersion` in that the major version number must be the same as requested, e.g. version 2.0 will not be considered compatible if 1.0 is requested. This mode should be used for packages which guarantee backward compatibility within the same major version. If `ExactVersion` is used, then the package is only considered compatible if the requested version matches exactly its own version number (not considering the tweak version). For example, version 1.2.3 of a package is only considered compatible to requested version 1.2.3. This mode is for packages without compatibility guarantees. If your project has more elaborated version matching rules, you will need to write your own custom `ConfigVersion.cmake` file instead of using this macro.

Internally, this macro executes `configure_file()` (page 282) to create the resulting version file. Depending on the `COMPATIBLITY`, either the file `BasicConfigVersion-SameMajorVersion.cmake.in` or `BasicConfigVersion-AnyNewerVersion.cmake.in` is used. Please note that these two files are internal to CMake and you should not call `configure_file()` (page 282) on them yourself, but they can be used as starting point to create more sophisticted custom `ConfigVersion.cmake` files.

Example Generating Package Files

Example using both `configure_package_config_file()` (page 384) and `write_basic_package_version_file()`:

`CMakeLists.txt`:

```
set(INCLUDE_INSTALL_DIR include/ ... CACHE )
set(LIB_INSTALL_DIR lib/ ... CACHE )
set(SYSCONFIG_INSTALL_DIR etc/foo/ ... CACHE )
...
include(CMakePackageConfigHelpers)
configure_package_config_file(FooConfig.cmake.in
  ${CMAKE_CURRENT_BINARY_DIR}/FooConfig.cmake
  INSTALL_DESTINATION ${LIB_INSTALL_DIR}/Foo/cmake
  PATH_VARS INCLUDE_INSTALL_DIR SYSCONFIG_INSTALL_DIR)
write_basic_package_version_file(
  ${CMAKE_CURRENT_BINARY_DIR}/FooConfigVersion.cmake
  VERSION 1.2.3
  COMPATIBILITY SameMajorVersion )
install(FILES ${CMAKE_CURRENT_BINARY_DIR}/FooConfig.cmake
            ${CMAKE_CURRENT_BINARY_DIR}/FooConfigVersion.cmake
      DESTINATION ${LIB_INSTALL_DIR}/Foo/cmake )
```

FooConfig.cmake.in:

```
set(FOO_VERSION x.y.z)
...
@PACKAGE_INIT@
...
set_and_check(FOO_INCLUDE_DIR "@PACKAGE_INCLUDE_INSTALL_DIR@")
set_and_check(FOO_SYSCONFIG_DIR "@PACKAGE_SYSCONFIG_INSTALL_DIR@")

check_required_components(Foo)
```

CMakeParseArguments

CMAKE_PARSE_ARGUMENTS(<prefix> <options> <one_value_keywords> <multi_value_keywords> args...)

CMAKE_PARSE_ARGUMENTS() is intended to be used in macros or functions for parsing the arguments given to that macro or function. It processes the arguments and defines a set of variables which hold the values of the respective options.

The <options> argument contains all options for the respective macro, i.e. keywords which can be used when calling the macro without any value following, like e.g. the OPTIONAL keyword of the install() command.

The <one_value_keywords> argument contains all keywords for this macro which are followed by one value, like e.g. DESTINATION keyword of the install() command.

The <multi_value_keywords> argument contains all keywords for this macro which can be followed by more than one value, like e.g. the TARGETS or FILES keywords of the install() command.

When done, CMAKE_PARSE_ARGUMENTS() will have defined for each of the keywords listed in <options>, <one_value_keywords> and <multi_value_keywords> a variable composed of the given <prefix> followed by "_" and the name of the respective keyword. These variables will then hold the respective value from the argument list. For the <options> keywords this will be TRUE or FALSE.

All remaining arguments are collected in a variable <prefix>_UNPARSED_ARGUMENTS, this can be checked afterwards to see whether your macro was called with unrecognized parameters.

As an example here a my_install() macro, which takes similar arguments as the real install() command:

```
function(MY_INSTALL)
  set(options OPTIONAL FAST)
  set(oneValueArgs DESTINATION RENAME)
  set(multiValueArgs TARGETS CONFIGURATIONS)
  cmake_parse_arguments(MY_INSTALL "${options}" "${oneValueArgs}"
                        "${multiValueArgs}" ${ARGN} )
  ...
```

Assume my_install() has been called like this:

```
my_install(TARGETS foo bar DESTINATION bin OPTIONAL blub)
```

After the cmake_parse_arguments() call the macro will have set the following variables:

```
MY_INSTALL_OPTIONAL = TRUE
MY_INSTALL_FAST = FALSE (this option was not used when calling my_install()
MY_INSTALL_DESTINATION = "bin"
MY_INSTALL_RENAME = "" (was not used)
MY_INSTALL_TARGETS = "foo;bar"
MY_INSTALL_CONFIGURATIONS = "" (was not used)
MY_INSTALL_UNPARSED_ARGUMENTS = "blub" (no value expected after "OPTIONAL"
```

You can then continue and process these variables.

Keywords terminate lists of values, e.g. if directly after a one_value_keyword another recognized keyword follows, this is interpreted as the beginning of the new option. E.g. my_install(TARGETS foo DESTINATION OPTIONAL) would result in MY_INSTALL_DESTINATION set to "OPTIONAL", but MY_INSTALL_DESTINATION would be empty and MY_INSTALL_OPTIONAL would be set to TRUE therefor.

CMakePrintHelpers

Convenience macros for printing properties and variables, useful e.g. for debugging.

```
CMAKE_PRINT_PROPERTIES([TARGETS target1 .. targetN]
                       [SOURCES source1 .. sourceN]
                       [DIRECTORIES dir1 .. dirN]
                       [TESTS test1 .. testN]
                       [CACHE_ENTRIES entry1 .. entryN]
                       PROPERTIES prop1 .. propN )
```

This macro prints the values of the properties of the given targets, source files, directories, tests or cache entries. Exactly one of the scope keywords must be used. Example:

```
cmake_print_properties(TARGETS foo bar PROPERTIES
                       LOCATION INTERFACE_INCLUDE_DIRS)
```

This will print the LOCATION and INTERFACE_INCLUDE_DIRS properties for both targets foo and bar.

CMAKE_PRINT_VARIABLES(var1 var2 .. varN)

This macro will print the name of each variable followed by its value. Example:

```
cmake_print_variables(CMAKE_C_COMPILER CMAKE_MAJOR_VERSION DOES_NOT_EXIST)
```

Gives:

```
-- CMAKE_C_COMPILER="/usr/bin/gcc" ; CMAKE_MAJOR_VERSION="2" ; DOES_NOT_EXIST=""
```

CMakePrintSystemInformation

print system information

This file can be used for diagnostic purposes just include it in a project to see various internal CMake variables.

CMakePushCheckState

This module defines three macros: CMAKE_PUSH_CHECK_STATE() CMAKE_POP_CHECK_STATE() and CMAKE_RESET_CHECK_STATE() These macros can be used to save, restore and reset (i.e., clear contents) the state of the variables CMAKE_REQUIRED_FLAGS, CMAKE_REQUIRED_DEFINITIONS, CMAKE_REQUIRED_LIBRARIES and CMAKE_REQUIRED_INCLUDES used by the various Check-files coming with CMake, like e.g. check_function_exists() etc. The variable contents are pushed on a stack, pushing multiple times is supported. This is useful e.g. when executing such tests in a Find-module, where they have to be set, but after the Find-module has been executed they should have the same value as they had before.

CMAKE_PUSH_CHECK_STATE() macro receives optional argument RESET. Whether it's specified, CMAKE_PUSH_CHECK_STATE() will set all CMAKE_REQUIRED_* variables to empty values, same as CMAKE_RESET_CHECK_STATE() call will do.

Usage:

```
cmake_push_check_state(RESET)
set(CMAKE_REQUIRED_DEFINITIONS -DSOME_MORE_DEF)
check_function_exists(...)
cmake_reset_check_state()
set(CMAKE_REQUIRED_DEFINITIONS -DANOTHER_DEF)
check_function_exists(...)
cmake_pop_check_state()
```

CMakeVerifyManifest

CMakeVerifyManifest.cmake

This script is used to verify that embedded manifests and side by side manifests for a project match. To run this script, cd to a directory and run the script with cmake -P. On the command line you can pass in versions that are OK even if not found in the .manifest files. For example, cmake -Dallow_versions=8.0.50608.0 -PCmakeVerifyManifest.cmake could be used to allow an embedded manifest of 8.0.50608.0 to be used in a project even if that version was not found in the .manifest file.

CPackBundle

CPack Bundle generator (Mac OS X) specific options

Variables specific to CPack Bundle generator

Installers built on Mac OS X using the Bundle generator use the aforementioned DragNDrop (CPACK_DMG_xxx) variables, plus the following Bundle-specific parameters (CPACK_BUNDLE_xxx).

CPACK_BUNDLE_NAME

The name of the generated bundle. This appears in the OSX finder as the bundle name. Required.

CPACK_BUNDLE_PLIST

Path to an OSX plist file that will be used for the generated bundle. This assumes that the caller has generated or specified their own Info.plist file. Required.

CPACK_BUNDLE_ICON

Path to an OSX icon file that will be used as the icon for the generated bundle. This is the icon that appears in the OSX finder for the bundle, and in the OSX dock when the bundle is opened. Required.

CPACK_BUNDLE_STARTUP_COMMAND

Path to a startup script. This is a path to an executable or script that will be run whenever an end-user double-clicks the generated bundle in the OSX Finder. Optional.

CPackComponent

Build binary and source package installers

Variables concerning CPack Components

The CPackComponent module is the module which handles the component part of CPack. See CPack module for general information about CPack.

For certain kinds of binary installers (including the graphical installers on Mac OS X and Windows), CPack generates installers that allow users to select individual application components to install. The contents of each of the components are identified by the COMPONENT argument of CMake's INSTALL command. These components can be annotated with user-friendly names and descriptions, inter-component dependencies, etc., and grouped in various ways to customize the resulting installer. See the cpack_add_* commands, described below, for more information about component-specific installations.

Component-specific installation allows users to select specific sets of components to install during the install process. Installation components are identified by the COMPONENT argument of CMake's INSTALL commands, and should be further described by the following CPack commands:

CPACK_COMPONENTS_ALL

The list of component to install.

The default value of this variable is computed by CPack and contains all components defined by the project. The user may set it to only include the specified components.

CPACK_<GENNAME>_COMPONENT_INSTALL

Enable/Disable component install for CPack generator <GENNAME>.

Each CPack Generator (RPM, DEB, ARCHIVE, NSIS, DMG, etc...) has a legacy default behavior. e.g. RPM builds monolithic whereas NSIS builds component. One can change the default behavior by setting this variable to 0/1 or OFF/ON.

CPACK_COMPONENTS_GROUPING

Specify how components are grouped for multi-package component-aware CPack generators.

Some generators like RPM or ARCHIVE family (TGZ, ZIP, ...) generates several packages files when asked for component packaging. They group the component differently depending on the value of this variable:

- •ONE_PER_GROUP (default): creates one package file per component group

- •ALL_COMPONENTS_IN_ONE : creates a single package with all (requested) component

- •IGNORE : creates one package per component, i.e. IGNORE component group

One can specify different grouping for different CPack generator by using a CPACK_PROJECT_CONFIG_FILE.

CPACK_COMPONENT_<compName>_DISPLAY_NAME

The name to be displayed for a component.

CPACK_COMPONENT_<compName>_DESCRIPTION

The description of a component.

CPACK_COMPONENT_<compName>_GROUP

The group of a component.

CPACK_COMPONENT_<compName>_DEPENDS

The dependencies (list of components) on which this component depends.

CPACK_COMPONENT_<compName>_REQUIRED

True is this component is required.

cpack_add_component

Describes a CPack installation component named by the COMPONENT argument to a CMake INSTALL command.

```
cpack_add_component(compname
              [DISPLAY_NAME name]
              [DESCRIPTION description]
              [HIDDEN | REQUIRED | DISABLED ]
              [GROUP group]
              [DEPENDS comp1 comp2 ... ]
              [INSTALL_TYPES type1 type2 ... ]
              [DOWNLOADED]
              [ARCHIVE_FILE filename])
```

The cmake_add_component command describes an installation component, which the user can opt to install or remove as part of the graphical installation process. compname is the name of the component, as provided to the COMPONENT argument of one or more CMake INSTALL commands.

DISPLAY_NAME is the displayed name of the component, used in graphical installers to display the component name. This value can be any string.

DESCRIPTION is an extended description of the component, used in graphical installers to give the user additional information about the component. Descriptions can span multiple lines using \n as the line separator. Typically, these descriptions should be no more than a few lines long.

HIDDEN indicates that this component will be hidden in the graphical installer, so that the user cannot directly change whether it is installed or not.

REQUIRED indicates that this component is required, and therefore will always be installed. It will be visible in the graphical installer, but it cannot be unselected. (Typically, required components are shown greyed out).

DISABLED indicates that this component should be disabled (unselected) by default. The user is free to select this component for installation, unless it is also HIDDEN.

DEPENDS lists the components on which this component depends. If this component is selected, then each of the components listed must also be selected. The dependency information is encoded within the installer itself, so that users cannot install inconsistent sets of components.

GROUP names the component group of which this component is a part. If not provided, the component will be a standalone component, not part of any component group. Component groups are described with the cpack_add_component_group command, detailed below.

INSTALL_TYPES lists the installation types of which this component is a part. When one of these installations types is selected, this component will automatically be selected. Installation types are described with the cpack_add_install_type command, detailed below.

DOWNLOADED indicates that this component should be downloaded on-the-fly by the installer, rather than packaged in with the installer itself. For more information, see the cpack_configure_downloads command.

ARCHIVE_FILE provides a name for the archive file created by CPack to be used for downloaded components. If not supplied, CPack will create a file with some name based on CPACK_PACKAGE_FILE_NAME and the name of the component. See cpack_configure_downloads for more information.

cpack_add_component_group

Describes a group of related CPack installation components.

```
cpack_add_component_group(groupname
                  [DISPLAY_NAME name]
                  [DESCRIPTION description]
                  [PARENT_GROUP parent]
                  [EXPANDED]
                  [BOLD_TITLE])
```

The cpack_add_component_group describes a group of installation components, which will be placed together within the listing of options. Typically, component groups allow the user to select/deselect all of the components within a single group via a single group-level option. Use component groups to reduce the complexity of installers with many options. groupname is an arbitrary name used to identify the group in the GROUP argument of the cpack_add_component command, which is used to place a component in a group. The name of the group must not conflict with the name of any component.

DISPLAY_NAME is the displayed name of the component group, used in graphical installers to display the component group name. This value can be any string.

DESCRIPTION is an extended description of the component group, used in graphical installers to give the user additional information about the components within that group. Descriptions can span multiple lines using \n as the line separator. Typically, these descriptions should be no more than a few lines long.

PARENT_GROUP, if supplied, names the parent group of this group. Parent groups are used to establish a hierarchy of groups, providing an arbitrary hierarchy of groups.

EXPANDED indicates that, by default, the group should show up as "expanded", so that the user immediately sees all of the components within the group. Otherwise, the group will initially show up as a single entry.

BOLD_TITLE indicates that the group title should appear in bold, to call the user's attention to the group.

cpack_add_install_type

Add a new installation type containing a set of predefined component selections to the graphical installer.

```
cpack_add_install_type(typename
                       [DISPLAY_NAME name])
```

The cpack_add_install_type command identifies a set of preselected components that represents a common use case for an application. For example, a "Developer" install type might include an application along with its header and library files, while an "End user" install type might just include the application's executable. Each component identifies itself with one or more install types via the INSTALL_TYPES argument to cpack_add_component.

DISPLAY_NAME is the displayed name of the install type, which will typically show up in a drop-down box within a graphical installer. This value can be any string.

cpack_configure_downloads

Configure CPack to download selected components on-the-fly as part of the installation process.

```
cpack_configure_downloads(site
                          [UPLOAD_DIRECTORY dirname]
                          [ALL]
                          [ADD_REMOVE|NO_ADD_REMOVE])
```

The cpack_configure_downloads command configures installation-time downloads of selected components. For each downloadable component, CPack will create an archive containing the contents of that component, which should be uploaded to the given site. When the user selects that component for installation, the installer will download and extract the component in place. This feature is useful for creating small installers that only download the requested components, saving bandwidth. Additionally, the installers are small enough that they will be installed as part of the normal installation process, and the "Change" button in Windows Add/Remove

---

Programs control panel will allow one to add or remove parts of the application after the original installation. On Windows, the downloaded-components functionality requires the ZipDLL plug-in for NSIS, available at:

```
http://nsis.sourceforge.net/ZipDLL_plug-in
```

On Mac OS X, installers that download components on-the-fly can only be built and installed on system using Mac OS X 10.5 or later.

The site argument is a URL where the archives for downloadable components will reside, e.g., http://www.cmake.org/files/2.6.1/installer/ All of the archives produced by CPack should be uploaded to that location.

UPLOAD_DIRECTORY is the local directory where CPack will create the various archives for each of the components. The contents of this directory should be uploaded to a location accessible by the URL given in the site argument. If omitted, CPack will use the directory CPackUploads inside the CMake binary directory to store the generated archives.

The ALL flag indicates that all components be downloaded. Otherwise, only those components explicitly marked as DOWNLOADED or that have a specified ARCHIVE_FILE will be downloaded. Additionally, the ALL option implies ADD_REMOVE (unless NO_ADD_REMOVE is specified).

ADD_REMOVE indicates that CPack should install a copy of the installer that can be called from Windows' Add/Remove Programs dialog (via the "Modify" button) to change the set of installed components. NO_ADD_REMOVE turns off this behavior. This option is ignored on Mac OS X.

CPackCygwin

Cygwin CPack generator (Cygwin).

Variables specific to CPack Cygwin generator

The following variable is specific to installers build on and/or for Cygwin:

CPACK_CYGWIN_PATCH_NUMBER
> The Cygwin patch number. FIXME: This documentation is incomplete.

CPACK_CYGWIN_PATCH_FILE
> The Cygwin patch file. FIXME: This documentation is incomplete.

CPACK_CYGWIN_BUILD_SCRIPT
> The Cygwin build script. FIXME: This documentation is incomplete.

CPackDeb

The builtin (binary) CPack Deb generator (Unix only)

Variables specific to CPack Debian (DEB) generator

CPackDeb may be used to create Deb package using CPack. CPackDeb is a CPack generator thus it uses the CPACK_XXX variables used by CPack : http://www.cmake.org/Wiki/CMake:CPackConfiguration. CPackDeb generator should work on any linux host but it will produce better deb package when Debian specific tools 'dpkg-xxx' are usable on the build system.

CPackDeb has specific features which are controlled by the specifics CPACK_DEBIAN_XXX variables.You'll find a detailed usage on the wiki: http://www.cmake.org/Wiki/CMake:CPackPackageGenerators#DEB_.28UNIX_only.29

However as a handy reminder here comes the list of specific variables:

CPACK_DEBIAN_PACKAGE_NAME

> •Mandatory : YES

> •Default : CPACK_PACKAGE_NAME (lower case)

The debian package summary

CPACK_DEBIAN_PACKAGE_VERSION

> •Mandatory : YES

> •Default : CPACK_PACKAGE_VERSION

The debian package version

CPACK_DEBIAN_PACKAGE_ARCHITECTURE

> •Mandatory : YES

> •Default : Output of dpkg –print-architecture (or i386 if dpkg is not found)

The debian package architecture

CPACK_DEBIAN_PACKAGE_DEPENDS

> •Mandatory : NO

> •Default : -

May be used to set deb dependencies.

CPACK_DEBIAN_PACKAGE_MAINTAINER

> •Mandatory : YES

> •Default : CPACK_PACKAGE_CONTACT

The debian package maintainer

CPACK_DEBIAN_PACKAGE_DESCRIPTION

> •Mandatory : YES

> •Default : CPACK_PACKAGE_DESCRIPTION_SUMMARY

The debian package description

CPACK_DEBIAN_PACKAGE_SECTION

- Mandatory : YES

- Default : 'devel'

CPACK_DEBIAN_COMPRESSION_TYPE

- Mandatory : YES

- Default : 'gzip'

Possible values are: lzma, xz, bzip2 and gzip.

CPACK_DEBIAN_PACKAGE_PRIORITY

- Mandatory : YES

- Default : 'optional'

The debian package priority

CPACK_DEBIAN_PACKAGE_HOMEPAGE

- Mandatory : NO

- Default : -

The URL of the web site for this package, preferably (when applicable) the site from which the original source can be obtained and any additional upstream documentation or information may be found. The content of this field is a simple URL without any surrounding characters such as <>.

CPACK_DEBIAN_PACKAGE_SHLIBDEPS

- Mandatory : NO

- Default : OFF

May be set to ON in order to use dpkg-shlibdeps to generate better package dependency list. You may need set CMAKE_INSTALL_RPATH toi appropriate value if you use this feature, because if you don't dpkg-shlibdeps may fail to find your own shared libs. See http://www.cmake.org/Wiki/CMake_RPATH_handling.

CPACK_DEBIAN_PACKAGE_DEBUG

- Mandatory : NO

- Default : -

May be set when invoking cpack in order to trace debug information during CPackDeb run.

CPACK_DEBIAN_PACKAGE_PREDEPENDS

- Mandatory : NO

- Default : -

see http://www.debian.org/doc/debian-policy/ch-relationships.html#s-binarydeps This field is like Depends, except that it also forces dpkg to complete installation of the packages named before even starting the installation of the package which declares the pre-dependency.

CPACK_DEBIAN_PACKAGE_ENHANCES

- Mandatory : NO

- Default : -

see http://www.debian.org/doc/debian-policy/ch-relationships.html#s-binarydeps This field is similar to Suggests but works in the opposite direction. It is used to declare that a package can enhance the functionality of another package.

CPACK_DEBIAN_PACKAGE_BREAKS

- Mandatory : NO

- Default : -

see http://www.debian.org/doc/debian-policy/ch-relationships.html#s-binarydeps When one binary package declares that it breaks another, dpkg will refuse to allow the package which declares Breaks be installed unless the broken package is deconfigured first, and it will refuse to allow the broken package to be reconfigured.

CPACK_DEBIAN_PACKAGE_CONFLICTS

- Mandatory : NO

- Default : -

see http://www.debian.org/doc/debian-policy/ch-relationships.html#s-binarydeps When one binary package declares a conflict with another using a Conflicts field, dpkg will refuse to allow them to be installed on the system at the same time.

CPACK_DEBIAN_PACKAGE_PROVIDES

- Mandatory : NO

- Default : -

see http://www.debian.org/doc/debian-policy/ch-relationships.html#s-binarydeps A virtual package is one which appears in the Provides control field of another package.

CPACK_DEBIAN_PACKAGE_REPLACES

- Mandatory : NO

- Default : -

see http://www.debian.org/doc/debian-policy/ch-relationships.html#s-binarydeps Packages can declare in their control file that they should overwrite files in certain other packages, or completely replace other packages.

CPACK_DEBIAN_PACKAGE_RECOMMENDS

- Mandatory : NO

•Default : -

see http://www.debian.org/doc/debian-policy/ch-relationships.html#s-binarydeps Allows packages to declare a strong, but not absolute, dependency on other packages.

CPACK_DEBIAN_PACKAGE_SUGGESTS

•Mandatory : NO

•Default : -

see http://www.debian.org/doc/debian-policy/ch-relationships.html#s-binarydeps Allows packages to declare a suggested package install grouping.

CPACK_DEBIAN_PACKAGE_CONTROL_EXTRA

•Mandatory : NO

•Default : -

This variable allow advanced user to add custom script to the control.tar.gz Typical usage is for conf-files, postinst, postrm, prerm. Usage:

```
set(CPACK_DEBIAN_PACKAGE_CONTROL_EXTRA
    "${CMAKE_CURRENT_SOURCE_DIR/prerm;${CMAKE_CURRENT_SOURCE_DIR}/postrm")
```

CPackDMG

DragNDrop CPack generator (Mac OS X).

Variables specific to CPack DragNDrop generator

The following variables are specific to the DragNDrop installers built on Mac OS X:

CPACK_DMG_VOLUME_NAME
The volume name of the generated disk image. Defaults to CPACK_PACKAGE_FILE_NAME.

CPACK_DMG_FORMAT
The disk image format. Common values are UDRO (UDIF read-only), UDZO (UDIF zlib-compressed) or UDBZ (UDIF bzip2-compressed). Refer to hdiutil(1) for more information on other available formats.

CPACK_DMG_DS_STORE
Path to a custom DS_Store file. This .DS_Store file e.g. can be used to specify the Finder window position/geometry and layout (such as hidden toolbars, placement of the icons etc.). This file has to be generated by the Finder (either manually or through OSA-script) using a normal folder from which the .DS_Store file can then be extracted.

CPACK_DMG_BACKGROUND_IMAGE
Path to a background image file. This file will be used as the background for the Finder Window when

the disk image is opened. By default no background image is set. The background image is applied after applying the custom .DS_Store file.

CPACK_COMMAND_HDIUTIL

Path to the hdiutil(1) command used to operate on disk image files on Mac OS X. This variable can be used to override the automatically detected command (or specify its location if the auto-detection fails to find it.)

CPACK_COMMAND_SETFILE

Path to the SetFile(1) command used to set extended attributes on files and directories on Mac OS X. This variable can be used to override the automatically detected command (or specify its location if the auto-detection fails to find it.)

CPACK_COMMAND_REZ

Path to the Rez(1) command used to compile resources on Mac OS X. This variable can be used to override the automatically detected command (or specify its location if the auto-detection fails to find it.)

CPackIFW

This module looks for the location of the command line utilities supplied with the Qt Installer Framework (QtIFW[1]).

The module also defines several commands to control the behavior of the CPack `IFW` generator.

Overview

CPack `IFW` generator helps you to create online and offline binary cross-platform installers with a graphical user interface.

CPack IFW generator prepares project installation and generates configuration and meta information for QtIFW[2] tools.

The QtIFW[3] provides a set of tools and utilities to create installers for the supported desktop Qt platforms: Linux, Microsoft Windows, and Mac OS X.

You should also install QtIFW[4] to use CPack `IFW` generator. If you don't use a default path for the installation, please set the used path in the variable `QTIFWDIR`.

Variables

You can use the following variables to change behavior of CPack `IFW` generator.

---

[1] http://qt-project.org/doc/qtinstallerframework/index.html
[2] http://qt-project.org/doc/qtinstallerframework/index.html
[3] http://qt-project.org/doc/qtinstallerframework/index.html
[4] http://qt-project.org/doc/qtinstallerframework/index.html

Package
CPACK_IFW_PACKAGE_TITLE
> Name of the installer as displayed on the title bar. By default used CPACK_PACKAGE_DESCRIPTION_SUMMARY (page 413)

CPACK_IFW_PACKAGE_PUBLISHER
> Publisher of the software (as shown in the Windows Control Panel). By default used CPACK_PACKAGE_VENDOR (page 412)

CPACK_IFW_PRODUCT_URL
> URL to a page that contains product information on your web site.

CPACK_IFW_PACKAGE_ICON
> Filename for a custom installer icon. The actual file is '.icns' (Mac OS X), '.ico' (Windows). No functionality on Unix.

CPACK_IFW_PACKAGE_WINDOW_ICON
> Filename for a custom window icon in PNG format for the Installer application.

CPACK_IFW_PACKAGE_LOGO
> Filename for a logo is used as QWizard::LogoPixmap.

CPACK_IFW_TARGET_DIRECTORY
> Default target directory for installation. By default used "@ApplicationsDir@/CPACK_PACKAGE_INSTALL_DIRECTORY (page 413)"
>
> You can use predefined variables.

CPACK_IFW_ADMIN_TARGET_DIRECTORY
> Default target directory for installation with administrator rights.
>
> You can use predefined variables.

CPACK_IFW_PACKAGE_GROUP
> The group, which will be used to configure the root package

CPACK_IFW_PACKAGE_NAME
> The root package name, which will be used if configuration group is not specified

CPACK_IFW_REPOSITORIES_ALL
> The list of remote repositories.
>
> The default value of this variable is computed by CPack and contains all repositories added with command cpack_ifw_add_repository() (page 402)

CPACK_IFW_DOWNLOAD_ALL
> If this is ON all components will be downloaded. By default is OFF or used value from CPACK_DOWNLOAD_ALL if set

Components
CPACK_IFW_RESOLVE_DUPLICATE_NAMES
> Resolve duplicate names when installing components with groups.

CPACK_IFW_PACKAGES_DIRECTORIES
    Additional prepared packages dirs that will be used to resolve dependent components.

Tools

CPACK_IFW_BINARYCREATOR_EXECUTABLE
    The path to "binarycreator" command line client.

    This variable is cached and can be configured user if need.

CPACK_IFW_REPOGEN_EXECUTABLE
    The path to "repogen" command line client.

    This variable is cached and can be configured user if need.

Commands

The module defines the following commands:

cpack_ifw_configure_component

Sets the arguments specific to the CPack IFW generator.

```
cpack_ifw_configure_component(<compname> [COMMON]
                    [NAME <name>]
                    [VERSION <version>]
                    [SCRIPT <script>]
                    [PRIORITY <priority>]
                    [DEPENDS <com_id> ...]
                    [LICENSES <display_name> <file_path> ...])
```

This command should be called after cpack_add_component command.

COMMON if set, then the component will be packaged and installed as part of a group to which it belongs.

VERSION is version of component. By default used CPACK_PACKAGE_VERSION (page 415).

SCRIPT is a relative or absolute path to operations script for this component.

NAME is used to create domain-like identification for this component. By default used origin component name.

PRIORITY is priority of the component in the tree.

DEPENDS list of dependency component identifiers in QtIFW[5] style.

LICENSES pair of <display_name> and <file_path> of license text for this component. You can specify more then one license.

---

[5] http://qt-project.org/doc/qtinstallerframework/index.html

cpack_ifw_configure_component_group

Sets the arguments specific to the CPack IFW generator.

```
cpack_ifw_configure_component_group(<grpname>
                    [VERSION <version>]
                    [NAME <name>]
                    [SCRIPT <script>]
                    [PRIORITY <priority>]
                    [LICENSES <display_name> <file_path> ...])
```

This command should be called after cpack_add_component_group command.

VERSION is version of component group. By default used CPACK_PACKAGE_VERSION (page 415).

NAME is used to create domain-like identification for this component group. By default used origin component group name.

SCRIPT is a relative or absolute path to operations script for this component group.

PRIORITY is priority of the component group in the tree.

LICENSES pair of <display_name> and <file_path> of license text for this component group. You can specify more then one license.

---

cpack_ifw_add_repository

Add QtIFW[6] specific remote repository.

```
cpack_ifw_add_repository(<reponame> [DISABLED]
                    URL <url>
                    [USERNAME <username>]
                    [PASSWORD <password>]
                    [DISPLAY_NAME <display_name>])
```

This macro will also add the <reponame> repository to a variable CPACK_IFW_REPOSITORIES_ALL (page 400)

DISABLED if set, then the repository will be disabled by default.

URL is points to a list of available components.

USERNAME is used as user on a protected repository.

PASSWORD is password to use on a protected repository.

DISPLAY_NAME is string to display instead of the URL.

---

[6]http://qt-project.org/doc/qtinstallerframework/index.html

Example usage

```
set(CPACK_PACKAGE_NAME "MyPackage")
set(CPACK_PACKAGE_DESCRIPTION_SUMMARY "MyPackage Installation Example")
set(CPACK_PACKAGE_VERSION "1.0.0") # Version of installer

include(CPack)
include(CPackIFW)

cpack_add_component(myapp
    DISPLAY_NAME "MyApp"
    DESCRIPTION "My Application")
cpack_ifw_configure_component(myapp
    VERSION "1.2.3" # Version of component
    SCRIPT "operations.qs")
cpack_add_component(mybigplugin
    DISPLAY_NAME "MyBigPlugin"
    DESCRIPTION "My Big Downloadable Plugin"
    DOWNLOADED)
cpack_ifw_add_repository(myrepo
    URL "http://example.com/ifw/repo/myapp"
    DISPLAY_NAME "My Application Repository")
```

Online installer

By default CPack IFW generator makes offline installer. This means that all components will be packaged into a binary file.

To make a component downloaded, you must set the DOWNLOADED option in cpack_add_component() (page 391).

Then you would use the command cpack_configure_downloads() (page 393). If you set ALL option all components will be downloaded.

You also can use command cpack_ifw_add_repository() (page 402) and variable CPACK_IFW_DOWNLOAD_ALL (page 400) for more specific configuration.

CPack IFW generator creates "repository" dir in current binary dir. You would copy content of this dir to specified site(url).

See Also

Qt Installer Framework Manual:

> **Index page** http://qt-project.org/doc/qtinstallerframework/index.html
>
> **Component Scripting** http://qt-project.org/doc/qtinstallerframework/scripting.html

Predefined Variables http://qt-project.org/doc/qtinstallerframework/scripting.html#predefined-variables

Download Qt Installer Framework for you platform from Qt Project site: http://download.qt-project.org/official_releases/qt-installer-framework/

CPackNSIS

CPack NSIS generator specific options

Variables specific to CPack NSIS generator

The following variables are specific to the graphical installers built on Windows using the Nullsoft Installation System.

CPACK_NSIS_INSTALL_ROOT
> The default installation directory presented to the end user by the NSIS installer is under this root dir. The full directory presented to the end user is: ${CPACK_NSIS_INSTALL_ROOT}/${CPACK_PACKAGE_INSTALL_DIRECTORY}

CPACK_NSIS_MUI_ICON
> An icon filename. The name of a *.ico file used as the main icon for the generated install program.

CPACK_NSIS_MUI_UNIICON
> An icon filename. The name of a *.ico file used as the main icon for the generated uninstall program.

CPACK_NSIS_INSTALLER_MUI_ICON_CODE
> undocumented.

CPACK_NSIS_EXTRA_PREINSTALL_COMMANDS
> Extra NSIS commands that will be added to the beginning of the install Section, before your install tree is available on the target system.

CPACK_NSIS_EXTRA_INSTALL_COMMANDS
> Extra NSIS commands that will be added to the end of the install Section, after your install tree is available on the target system.

CPACK_NSIS_EXTRA_UNINSTALL_COMMANDS
> Extra NSIS commands that will be added to the uninstall Section, before your install tree is removed from the target system.

CPACK_NSIS_COMPRESSOR
> The arguments that will be passed to the NSIS SetCompressor command.

CPACK_NSIS_ENABLE_UNINSTALL_BEFORE_INSTALL
> Ask about uninstalling previous versions first. If this is set to "ON", then an installer will look for previous installed versions and if one is found, ask the user whether to uninstall it before proceeding with the install.

CPACK_NSIS_MODIFY_PATH

Modify PATH toggle. If this is set to "ON", then an extra page will appear in the installer that will allow the user to choose whether the program directory should be added to the system PATH variable.

CPACK_NSIS_DISPLAY_NAME

The display name string that appears in the Windows Add/Remove Program control panel

CPACK_NSIS_PACKAGE_NAME

The title displayed at the top of the installer.

CPACK_NSIS_INSTALLED_ICON_NAME

A path to the executable that contains the installer icon.

CPACK_NSIS_HELP_LINK

URL to a web site providing assistance in installing your application.

CPACK_NSIS_URL_INFO_ABOUT

URL to a web site providing more information about your application.

CPACK_NSIS_CONTACT

Contact information for questions and comments about the installation process.

CPACK_NSIS_CREATE_ICONS_EXTRA

Additional NSIS commands for creating start menu shortcuts.

CPACK_NSIS_DELETE_ICONS_EXTRA

Additional NSIS commands to uninstall start menu shortcuts.

CPACK_NSIS_EXECUTABLES_DIRECTORY

Creating NSIS start menu links assumes that they are in 'bin' unless this variable is set. For example, you would set this to 'exec' if your executables are in an exec directory.

CPACK_NSIS_MUI_FINISHPAGE_RUN

Specify an executable to add an option to run on the finish page of the NSIS installer.

CPACK_NSIS_MENU_LINKS

Specify links in [application] menu. This should contain a list of pair "link" "link name". The link may be an URL or a path relative to installation prefix. Like:

```
set(CPACK_NSIS_MENU_LINKS
    "doc/cmake-@CMake_VERSION_MAJOR@.@CMake_VERSION_MINOR@/cmake.html"
    "CMake Help" "http://www.cmake.org" "CMake Web Site")
```

CPackPackageMaker

PackageMaker CPack generator (Mac OS X).

Variables specific to CPack PackageMaker generator

The following variable is specific to installers built on Mac OS X using PackageMaker:

CPACK_OSX_PACKAGE_VERSION

The version of Mac OS X that the resulting PackageMaker archive should be compatible with. Different versions of Mac OS X support different features. For example, CPack can only build component-based installers for Mac OS X 10.4 or newer, and can only build installers that download component son-the-fly for Mac OS X 10.5 or newer. If left blank, this value will be set to the minimum version of Mac OS X that supports the requested features. Set this variable to some value (e.g., 10.4) only if you want to guarantee that your installer will work on that version of Mac OS X, and don't mind missing extra features available in the installer shipping with later versions of Mac OS X.

CPackRPM

The builtin (binary) CPack RPM generator (Unix only)

Variables specific to CPack RPM generator

CPackRPM may be used to create RPM package using CPack. CPackRPM is a CPack generator thus it uses the CPACK_XXX variables used by CPack : http://www.cmake.org/Wiki/CMake:CPackConfiguration

However CPackRPM has specific features which are controlled by the specifics CPACK_RPM_XXX variables. CPackRPM is a component aware generator so when CPACK_RPM_COMPONENT_INSTALL is ON some more CPACK_RPM_<ComponentName>_XXXX variables may be used in order to have component specific values. Note however that <componentName> refers to the **grouping name**. This may be either a component name or a component GROUP name. Usually those vars correspond to RPM spec file entities, one may find information about spec files here http://www.rpm.org/wiki/Docs. You'll find a detailed usage of CPackRPM on the wiki:

```
http://www.cmake.org/Wiki/CMake:CPackPackageGenerators#RPM_.28Unix_Only.29
```

However as a handy reminder here comes the list of specific variables:

CPACK_RPM_PACKAGE_SUMMARY
The RPM package summary.

> •Mandatory : YES

> •Default : CPACK_PACKAGE_DESCRIPTION_SUMMARY

CPACK_RPM_PACKAGE_NAME
The RPM package name.

> •Mandatory : YES

> •Default : CPACK_PACKAGE_NAME

CPACK_RPM_PACKAGE_VERSION
The RPM package version.

> •Mandatory : YES

> •Default : CPACK_PACKAGE_VERSION

CPACK_RPM_PACKAGE_ARCHITECTURE

The RPM package architecture.

- •Mandatory : NO

- •Default : -

This may be set to "noarch" if you know you are building a noarch package.

CPACK_RPM_PACKAGE_RELEASE

The RPM package release.

- •Mandatory : YES

- •Default : 1

This is the numbering of the RPM package itself, i.e. the version of the packaging and not the version of the content (see CPACK_RPM_PACKAGE_VERSION). One may change the default value if the previous packaging was buggy and/or you want to put here a fancy Linux distro specific numbering.

CPACK_RPM_PACKAGE_LICENSE

The RPM package license policy.

- •Mandatory : YES

- •Default : "unknown"

CPACK_RPM_PACKAGE_GROUP

The RPM package group.

- •Mandatory : YES

- •Default : "unknown"

CPACK_RPM_PACKAGE_VENDOR

The RPM package vendor.

- •Mandatory : YES

- •Default : CPACK_PACKAGE_VENDOR if set or "unknown"

CPACK_RPM_PACKAGE_URL

The projects URL.

- •Mandatory : NO

- •Default : -

CPACK_RPM_PACKAGE_DESCRIPTION

RPM package description.

- •Mandatory : YES

- •Default : CPACK_PACKAGE_DESCRIPTION_FILE if set or "no package description available"

CPACK_RPM_COMPRESSION_TYPE

RPM compression type.

•Mandatory : NO

•Default : -

May be used to override RPM compression type to be used to build the RPM. For example some Linux distribution now default to lzma or xz compression whereas older cannot use such RPM. Using this one can enforce compression type to be used. Possible value are: lzma, xz, bzip2 and gzip.

CPACK_RPM_PACKAGE_REQUIRES

RPM spec requires field.

•Mandatory : NO

•Default : -

May be used to set RPM dependencies (requires). Note that you must enclose the complete requires string between quotes, for example:

```
set(CPACK_RPM_PACKAGE_REQUIRES "python >= 2.5.0, cmake >= 2.8")
```

The required package list of an RPM file could be printed with:

```
rpm -qp --requires file.rpm
```

CPACK_RPM_PACKAGE_SUGGESTS

RPM spec suggest field.

•Mandatory : NO

•Default : -

May be used to set weak RPM dependencies (suggests). Note that you must enclose the complete requires string between quotes.

CPACK_RPM_PACKAGE_PROVIDES

RPM spec provides field.

•Mandatory : NO

•Default : -

May be used to set RPM dependencies (provides). The provided package list of an RPM file could be printed with:

```
rpm -qp --provides file.rpm
```

CPACK_RPM_PACKAGE_OBSOLETES

RPM spec obsoletes field.

•Mandatory : NO

•Default : -

May be used to set RPM packages that are obsoleted by this one.

CPACK_RPM_PACKAGE_RELOCATABLE
>
> build a relocatable RPM.
>
> > •Mandatory : NO
> >
> > •Default : CPACK_PACKAGE_RELOCATABLE
>
> If this variable is set to TRUE or ON CPackRPM will try to build a relocatable RPM package. A relocatable RPM may be installed using:

```
rpm --prefix or --relocate
```

> in order to install it at an alternate place see rpm(8). Note that currently this may fail if CPACK_SET_DESTDIR is set to ON. If CPACK_SET_DESTDIR is set then you will get a warning message but if there is file installed with absolute path you'll get unexpected behavior.

CPACK_RPM_SPEC_INSTALL_POST
>
> > •Mandatory : NO
> >
> > •Default : -
> >
> > •Deprecated: YES
>
> This way of specifying post-install script is deprecated, use CPACK_RPM_POST_INSTALL_SCRIPT_FILE. May be used to set an RPM post-install command inside the spec file. For example setting it to "/bin/true" may be used to prevent rpmbuild to strip binaries.

CPACK_RPM_SPEC_MORE_DEFINE
>
> RPM extended spec definitions lines.
>
> > •Mandatory : NO
> >
> > •Default : -
>
> May be used to add any %define lines to the generated spec file.

CPACK_RPM_PACKAGE_DEBUG
>
> Toggle CPackRPM debug output.
>
> > •Mandatory : NO
> >
> > •Default : -
>
> May be set when invoking cpack in order to trace debug information during CPack RPM run. For example you may launch CPack like this:

```
cpack -D CPACK_RPM_PACKAGE_DEBUG=1 -G RPM
```

CPACK_RPM_USER_BINARY_SPECFILE
>
> A user provided spec file.
>
> > •Mandatory : NO
> >
> > •Default : -

May be set by the user in order to specify a USER binary spec file to be used by CPackRPM instead of generating the file. The specified file will be processed by configure_file(@ONLY). One can provide a component specific file by setting CPACK_RPM_<componentName>_USER_BINARY_SPECFILE.

CPACK_RPM_GENERATE_USER_BINARY_SPECFILE_TEMPLATE

Spec file template.

> • Mandatory : NO

> • Default : -

If set CPack will generate a template for USER specified binary spec file and stop with an error. For example launch CPack like this:

```
cpack -D CPACK_RPM_GENERATE_USER_BINARY_SPECFILE_TEMPLATE=1 -G RPM
```

The user may then use this file in order to hand-craft is own binary spec file which may be used with CPACK_RPM_USER_BINARY_SPECFILE.

CPACK_RPM_PRE_INSTALL_SCRIPT_FILE
CPACK_RPM_PRE_UNINSTALL_SCRIPT_FILE

> • Mandatory : NO

> • Default : -

May be used to embed a pre (un)installation script in the spec file. The refered script file(s) will be read and directly put after the %pre or %preun section If CPACK_RPM_COMPONENT_INSTALL is set to ON the (un)install script for each component can be overridden with CPACK_RPM_<COMPONENT>_PRE_INSTALL_SCRIPT_FILE and CPACK_RPM_<COMPONENT>_PRE_UNINSTALL_SCRIPT_FILE. One may verify which scriptlet has been included with:

```
rpm -qp --scripts  package.rpm
```

CPACK_RPM_POST_INSTALL_SCRIPT_FILE
CPACK_RPM_POST_UNINSTALL_SCRIPT_FILE

> • Mandatory : NO

> • Default : -

May be used to embed a post (un)installation script in the spec file. The refered script file(s) will be read and directly put after the %post or %postun section. If CPACK_RPM_COMPONENT_INSTALL is set to ON the (un)install script for each component can be overridden with CPACK_RPM_<COMPONENT>_POST_INSTALL_SCRIPT_FILE and CPACK_RPM_<COMPONENT>_POST_UNINSTALL_SCRIPT_FILE. One may verify which scriptlet has been included with:

```
rpm -qp --scripts  package.rpm
```

CPACK_RPM_USER_FILELIST
CPACK_RPM_<COMPONENT>_USER_FILELIST

•Mandatory : NO

•Default : -

May be used to explicitly specify %(<directive>) file line in the spec file. Like %config(noreplace) or any other directive that be found in the %files section. Since CPackRPM is generating the list of files (and directories) the user specified files of the CPACK_RPM_<COMPONENT>_USER_FILELIST list will be removed from the generated list.

CPACK_RPM_CHANGELOG_FILE
RPM changelog file.

•Mandatory : NO

•Default : -

May be used to embed a changelog in the spec file. The refered file will be read and directly put after the %changelog section.

CPACK_RPM_EXCLUDE_FROM_AUTO_FILELIST
list of path to be excluded.

•Mandatory : NO

•Default : /etc /etc/init.d /usr /usr/share /usr/share/doc /usr/bin /usr/lib /usr/lib64 /usr/include

May be used to exclude path (directories or files) from the auto-generated list of paths discovered by CPack RPM. The defaut value contains a reasonable set of values if the variable is not defined by the user. If the variable is defined by the user then CPackRPM will NOT any of the default path. If you want to add some path to the default list then you can use CPACK_RPM_EXCLUDE_FROM_AUTO_FILELIST_ADDITION variable.

CPACK_RPM_EXCLUDE_FROM_AUTO_FILELIST_ADDITION
additional list of path to be excluded.

•Mandatory : NO

•Default : -

May be used to add more exclude path (directories or files) from the initial default list of excluded paths. See CPACK_RPM_EXCLUDE_FROM_AUTO_FILELIST.

CPack

Build binary and source package installers.

Variables common to all CPack generators

The CPack module generates binary and source installers in a variety of formats using the cpack program. Inclusion of the CPack module adds two new targets to the resulting makefiles, package and package_source, which build the binary and source installers, respectively. The generated binary installers contain everything installed via CMake's INSTALL command (and the deprecated INSTALL_FILES, INSTALL_PROGRAMS, and INSTALL_TARGETS commands).

For certain kinds of binary installers (including the graphical installers on Mac OS X and Windows), CPack generates installers that allow users to select individual application components to install. See CPackComponent module for that.

The CPACK_GENERATOR variable has different meanings in different contexts. In your CMakeLists.txt file, CPACK_GENERATOR is a *list of generators*: when run with no other arguments, CPack will iterate over that list and produce one package for each generator. In a CPACK_PROJECT_CONFIG_FILE, though, CPACK_GENERATOR is a *string naming a single generator*. If you need per-cpack- generator logic to control *other* cpack settings, then you need a CPACK_PROJECT_CONFIG_FILE.

The CMake source tree itself contains a CPACK_PROJECT_CONFIG_FILE. See the top level file CMakeC-PackOptions.cmake.in for an example.

If set, the CPACK_PROJECT_CONFIG_FILE is included automatically on a per-generator basis. It only need contain overrides.

Here's how it works:

- cpack runs

- it includes CPackConfig.cmake

- it iterates over the generators listed in that file's CPACK_GENERATOR list variable (unless told to use just a specific one via -G on the command line...)

- foreach generator, it then

  - sets CPACK_GENERATOR to the one currently being iterated

  - includes the CPACK_PROJECT_CONFIG_FILE

  - produces the package for that generator

This is the key: For each generator listed in CPACK_GENERATOR in CPackConfig.cmake, cpack will *reset* CPACK_GENERATOR internally to *the one currently being used* and then include the CPACK_PROJECT_CONFIG_FILE.

Before including this CPack module in your CMakeLists.txt file, there are a variety of variables that can be set to customize the resulting installers. The most commonly-used variables are:

CPACK_PACKAGE_NAME
> The name of the package (or application). If not specified, defaults to the project name.

CPACK_PACKAGE_VENDOR
> The name of the package vendor. (e.g., "Kitware").

CPACK_PACKAGE_DIRECTORY
> The directory in which CPack is doing its packaging. If it is not set then this will default (internally) to the build dir. This variable may be defined in CPack config file or from the cpack command line option "-B". If set the command line option override the value found in the config file.

CPACK_PACKAGE_VERSION_MAJOR

Package major Version

CPACK_PACKAGE_VERSION_MINOR

Package minor Version

CPACK_PACKAGE_VERSION_PATCH

Package patch Version

CPACK_PACKAGE_DESCRIPTION_FILE

A text file used to describe the project. Used, for example, the introduction screen of a CPack-generated Windows installer to describe the project.

CPACK_PACKAGE_DESCRIPTION_SUMMARY

Short description of the project (only a few words).

CPACK_PACKAGE_FILE_NAME

The name of the package file to generate, not including the extension. For example, cmake-2.6.1-Linux-i686. The default value is:

```
${CPACK_PACKAGE_NAME}-${CPACK_PACKAGE_VERSION}-${CPACK_SYSTEM_NAME}.
```

CPACK_PACKAGE_INSTALL_DIRECTORY

Installation directory on the target system. This may be used by some CPack generators like NSIS to create an installation directory e.g., "CMake 2.5" below the installation prefix. All installed element will be put inside this directory.

CPACK_PACKAGE_ICON

A branding image that will be displayed inside the installer (used by GUI installers).

CPACK_PROJECT_CONFIG_FILE

CPack-time project CPack configuration file. This file included at cpack time, once per generator after CPack has set CPACK_GENERATOR to the actual generator being used. It allows per-generator setting of CPACK_* variables at cpack time.

CPACK_RESOURCE_FILE_LICENSE

License to be embedded in the installer. It will typically be displayed to the user by the produced installer (often with an explicit "Accept" button, for graphical installers) prior to installation. This license file is NOT added to installed file but is used by some CPack generators like NSIS. If you want to install a license file (may be the same as this one) along with your project you must add an appropriate CMake INSTALL command in your CMakeLists.txt.

CPACK_RESOURCE_FILE_README

ReadMe file to be embedded in the installer. It typically describes in some detail the purpose of the project during the installation. Not all CPack generators uses this file.

CPACK_RESOURCE_FILE_WELCOME

Welcome file to be embedded in the installer. It welcomes users to this installer. Typically used in the graphical installers on Windows and Mac OS X.

CPACK_MONOLITHIC_INSTALL

Disables the component-based installation mechanism. When set the component specification is ignored and all installed items are put in a single "MONOLITHIC" package. Some CPack generators do monolithic packaging by default and may be asked to do component packaging by setting CPACK_<GENNAME>_COMPONENT_INSTALL to 1/TRUE.

CPACK_GENERATOR

List of CPack generators to use. If not specified, CPack will create a set of options CPACK_BINARY_<GENNAME> (e.g., CPACK_BINARY_NSIS) allowing the user to enable/disable individual generators. This variable may be used on the command line as well as in:

```
cpack -D CPACK_GENERATOR="ZIP;TGZ" /path/to/build/tree
```

CPACK_OUTPUT_CONFIG_FILE

The name of the CPack binary configuration file. This file is the CPack configuration generated by the CPack module for binary installers. Defaults to CPackConfig.cmake.

CPACK_PACKAGE_EXECUTABLES

Lists each of the executables and associated text label to be used to create Start Menu shortcuts. For example, setting this to the list ccmake;CMake will create a shortcut named "CMake" that will execute the installed executable ccmake. Not all CPack generators use it (at least NSIS, WIX and OSXX11 do).

CPACK_STRIP_FILES

List of files to be stripped. Starting with CMake 2.6.0 CPACK_STRIP_FILES will be a boolean variable which enables stripping of all files (a list of files evaluates to TRUE in CMake, so this change is compatible).

The following CPack variables are specific to source packages, and will not affect binary packages:

CPACK_SOURCE_PACKAGE_FILE_NAME

The name of the source package. For example cmake-2.6.1.

CPACK_SOURCE_STRIP_FILES

List of files in the source tree that will be stripped. Starting with CMake 2.6.0 CPACK_SOURCE_STRIP_FILES will be a boolean variable which enables stripping of all files (a list of files evaluates to TRUE in CMake, so this change is compatible).

CPACK_SOURCE_GENERATOR

List of generators used for the source packages. As with CPACK_GENERATOR, if this is not specified then CPack will create a set of options (e.g., CPACK_SOURCE_ZIP) allowing users to select which packages will be generated.

CPACK_SOURCE_OUTPUT_CONFIG_FILE

The name of the CPack source configuration file. This file is the CPack configuration generated by the CPack module for source installers. Defaults to CPackSourceConfig.cmake.

CPACK_SOURCE_IGNORE_FILES

Pattern of files in the source tree that won't be packaged when building a source package. This is a list of regular expression patterns (that must be properly escaped), e.g., /CVS/;/\.svn/;\.swp$;\.#;/#;.*~;cscope.*

The following variables are for advanced uses of CPack:

CPACK_CMAKE_GENERATOR

What CMake generator should be used if the project is CMake project. Defaults to the value of CMAKE_GENERATOR few users will want to change this setting.

CPACK_INSTALL_CMAKE_PROJECTS

List of four values that specify what project to install. The four values are: Build directory, Project Name, Project Component, Directory. If omitted, CPack will build an installer that installers everything.

CPACK_SYSTEM_NAME

System name, defaults to the value of ${CMAKE_SYSTEM_NAME}.

CPACK_PACKAGE_VERSION

Package full version, used internally. By default, this is built from CPACK_PACKAGE_VERSION_MAJOR, CPACK_PACKAGE_VERSION_MINOR, and CPACK_PACKAGE_VERSION_PATCH.

CPACK_TOPLEVEL_TAG

Directory for the installed files.

CPACK_INSTALL_COMMANDS

Extra commands to install components.

CPACK_INSTALLED_DIRECTORIES

Extra directories to install.

CPACK_PACKAGE_INSTALL_REGISTRY_KEY

Registry key used when installing this project. This is only used by installer for Windows. The default value is based on the installation directory.

CPACK_CREATE_DESKTOP_LINKS

List of desktop links to create. Each desktop link requires a corresponding start menu shortcut as created by CPACK_PACKAGE_EXECUTABLES (page 414).

CPACK_BINARY_<GENNAME>

CPack generated options for binary generators. The CPack.cmake module generates (when CPACK_GENERATOR is not set) a set of CMake options (see CMake option command) which may then be used to select the CPack generator(s) to be used when launching the package target.

Provide options to choose generators we might check here if the required tools for the generates exist and set the defaults according to the results

CPackWIX

CPack WiX generator specific options

Variables specific to CPack WiX generator

The following variables are specific to the installers built on Windows using WiX.

CPACK_WIX_UPGRADE_GUID

Upgrade GUID (`Product/@UpgradeCode`)

Will be automatically generated unless explicitly provided.

It should be explicitly set to a constant generated globally unique identifier (GUID) to allow your installers to replace existing installations that use the same GUID.

You may for example explicitly set this variable in your CMakeLists.txt to the value that has been generated per default. You should not use GUIDs that you did not generate yourself or which may belong to other projects.

A GUID shall have the following fixed length syntax:

```
XXXXXXXX-XXXX-XXXX-XXXX-XXXXXXXXXXXX
```

(each X represents an uppercase hexadecimal digit)

CPACK_WIX_PRODUCT_GUID

Product GUID (`Product/@Id`)

Will be automatically generated unless explicitly provided.

If explicitly provided this will set the Product Id of your installer.

The installer will abort if it detects a pre-existing installation that uses the same GUID.

The GUID shall use the syntax described for CPACK_WIX_UPGRADE_GUID.

CPACK_WIX_LICENSE_RTF

RTF License File

If CPACK_RESOURCE_FILE_LICENSE has an .rtf extension it is used as-is.

If CPACK_RESOURCE_FILE_LICENSE has an .txt extension it is implicitly converted to RTF by the WiX Generator. The expected encoding of the .txt file is UTF-8.

With CPACK_WIX_LICENSE_RTF you can override the license file used by the WiX Generator in case CPACK_RESOURCE_FILE_LICENSE is in an unsupported format or the .txt -> .rtf conversion does not work as expected.

CPACK_WIX_PRODUCT_ICON

The Icon shown next to the program name in Add/Remove programs.

If set, this icon is used in place of the default icon.

CPACK_WIX_UI_REF

This variable allows you to override the Id of the `<UIRef>` element in the WiX template.

The default is `WixUI_InstallDir` in case no CPack components have been defined and `WixUI_FeatureTree` otherwise.

CPACK_WIX_UI_BANNER

The bitmap will appear at the top of all installer pages other than the welcome and completion dialogs.

If set, this image will replace the default banner image.

This image must be 493 by 58 pixels.

CPACK_WIX_UI_DIALOG

Background bitmap used on the welcome and completion dialogs.

If this variable is set, the installer will replace the default dialog image.

This image must be 493 by 312 pixels.

CPACK_WIX_PROGRAM_MENU_FOLDER

Start menu folder name for launcher.

If this variable is not set, it will be initialized with CPACK_PACKAGE_NAME

CPACK_WIX_CULTURES

Language(s) of the installer

Languages are compiled into the WixUI extension library. To use them, simply provide the name of the culture. If you specify more than one culture identifier in a comma or semicolon delimited list, the first one that is found will be used. You can find a list of supported languages at: http://wix.sourceforge.net/manual-wix3/WixUI_localization.htm

CPACK_WIX_TEMPLATE

Template file for WiX generation

If this variable is set, the specified template will be used to generate the WiX wxs file. This should be used if further customization of the output is required.

If this variable is not set, the default MSI template included with CMake will be used.

CPACK_WIX_PATCH_FILE

Optional XML file with fragments to be inserted into generated WiX sources

This optional variable can be used to specify an XML file that the WiX generator will use to inject fragments into its generated source files.

Patch files understood by the CPack WiX generator roughly follow this RELAX NG compact schema:

```
start = CPackWiXPatch

CPackWiXPatch = element CPackWiXPatch { CPackWiXFragment* }

CPackWiXFragment = element CPackWiXFragment
{
    attribute Id { string },
    fragmentContent*
}

fragmentContent = element * - CPackWiXFragment
{
    (attribute * { text } | text | fragmentContent)*
}
```

Currently fragments can be injected into most Component, File and Directory elements.

The following example illustrates how this works.

Given that the WiX generator creates the following XML element:

```
<Component Id="CM_CP_applications.bin.my_libapp.exe" Guid="*"/>
```

The following XML patch file may be used to inject an Environment element into it:

```
<CPackWiXPatch>
  <CPackWiXFragment Id="CM_CP_applications.bin.my_libapp.exe">
    <Environment Id="MyEnvironment" Action="set"
     Name="MyVariableName" Value="MyVariableValue"/>
  </CPackWiXFragment>
</CPackWiXPatch>
```

CPACK_WIX_EXTRA_SOURCES

Extra WiX source files

This variable provides an optional list of extra WiX source files (.wxs) that should be compiled and linked. The full path to source files is required.

CPACK_WIX_EXTRA_OBJECTS

Extra WiX object files or libraries

This variable provides an optional list of extra WiX object (.wixobj) and/or WiX library (.wixlib) files. The full path to objects and libraries is required.

CPACK_WIX_EXTENSIONS

This variable provides a list of additional extensions for the WiX tools light and candle.

CPACK_WIX_<TOOL>_EXTENSIONS

This is the tool specific version of CPACK_WIX_EXTENSIONS. <TOOL> can be either LIGHT or CANDLE.

CPACK_WIX_<TOOL>_EXTRA_FLAGS

This list variable allows you to pass additional flags to the WiX tool <TOOL>.

Use it at your own risk. Future versions of CPack may generate flags which may be in conflict with your own flags.

<TOOL> can be either LIGHT or CANDLE.

CPACK_WIX_CMAKE_PACKAGE_REGISTRY

If this variable is set the generated installer will create an entry in the windows registry key HKEY_LOCAL_MACHINE\Software\Kitware\CMake\Packages\<package> The value for <package> is provided by this variable.

Assuming you also install a CMake configuration file this will allow other CMake projects to find your package with the find_package() (page 297) command.

CPACK_WIX_PROPERTY_<PROPERTY>

This variable can be used to provide a value for the Windows Installer property <PROPERTY>

The follwing list contains some example properties that can be used to customize information under "Programs and Features" (also known as "Add or Remove Programs")

- ARPCOMMENTS - Comments
- ARPHELPLINK - Help and support information URL
- ARPURLINFOABOUT - General information URL
- URLUPDATEINFO - Update information URL
- ARPHELPTELEPHONE - Help and support telephone number
- ARPSIZE - Size (in kilobytes) of the application

CTest

Configure a project for testing with CTest/CDash

Include this module in the top CMakeLists.txt file of a project to enable testing with CTest and dashboard submissions to CDash:

```
project(MyProject)
...
include(CTest)
```

The module automatically creates a BUILD_TESTING option that selects whether to enable testing support (ON by default). After including the module, use code like

```
if(BUILD_TESTING)
  # ... CMake code to create tests ...
endif()
```

to creating tests when testing is enabled.

To enable submissions to a CDash server, create a CTestConfig.cmake file at the top of the project with content such as

```
set(CTEST_PROJECT_NAME "MyProject")
set(CTEST_NIGHTLY_START_TIME "01:00:00 UTC")
set(CTEST_DROP_METHOD "http")
set(CTEST_DROP_SITE "my.cdash.org")
set(CTEST_DROP_LOCATION "/submit.php?project=MyProject")
set(CTEST_DROP_SITE_CDASH TRUE)
```

(the CDash server can provide the file to a project administrator who configures 'MyProject'). Settings in the config file are shared by both this CTest module and the CTest command-line tool's dashboard script mode (ctest -S).

While building a project for submission to CDash, CTest scans the build output for errors and warnings and reports them with surrounding context from the build log. This generic approach works for all build tools, but does not give details about the command invocation that produced a given problem. One may get more detailed reports by adding

```
set(CTEST_USE_LAUNCHERS 1)
```

to the CTestConfig.cmake file. When this option is enabled, the CTest module tells CMake's Makefile generators to invoke every command in the generated build system through a CTest launcher program. (Currently the CTEST_USE_LAUNCHERS option is ignored on non-Makefile generators.) During a manual build each launcher transparently runs the command it wraps. During a CTest-driven build for submission to CDash each launcher reports detailed information when its command fails or warns. (Setting CTEST_USE_LAUNCHERS in CTestConfig.cmake is convenient, but also adds the launcher overhead even for manual builds. One may instead set it in a CTest dashboard script and add it to the CMake cache for the build tree.)

CTestScriptMode

This file is read by ctest in script mode (-S)

CTestUseLaunchers

Set the RULE_LAUNCH_* global properties when CTEST_USE_LAUNCHERS is on.

CTestUseLaunchers is automatically included when you include(CTest). However, it is split out into its own module file so projects can use the CTEST_USE_LAUNCHERS functionality independently.

To use launchers, set CTEST_USE_LAUNCHERS to ON in a ctest -S dashboard script, and then also set it in the cache of the configured project. Both cmake and ctest need to know the value of it for the launchers to work properly. CMake needs to know in order to generate proper build rules, and ctest, in order to produce the proper error and warning analysis.

For convenience, you may set the ENV variable CTEST_USE_LAUNCHERS_DEFAULT in your ctest -S script, too. Then, as long as your CMakeLists uses include(CTest) or include(CTestUseLaunchers), it will use the value of the ENV variable to initialize a CTEST_USE_LAUNCHERS cache variable. This cache variable initialization only occurs if CTEST_USE_LAUNCHERS is not already defined.

Dart

Configure a project for testing with CTest or old Dart Tcl Client

This file is the backwards-compatibility version of the CTest module. It supports using the old Dart 1 Tcl client for driving dashboard submissions as well as testing with CTest. This module should be included in the CMakeLists.txt file at the top of a project. Typical usage:

```
include(Dart)
if(BUILD_TESTING)
  # ... testing related CMake code ...
endif()
```

The BUILD_TESTING option is created by the Dart module to determine whether testing support should be enabled. The default is ON.

DeployQt4

Functions to help assemble a standalone Qt4 executable.

A collection of CMake utility functions useful for deploying Qt4 executables.

The following functions are provided by this module:

```
write_qt4_conf
resolve_qt4_paths
fixup_qt4_executable
install_qt4_plugin_path
install_qt4_plugin
install_qt4_executable
```

Requires CMake 2.6 or greater because it uses function and PARENT_SCOPE. Also depends on BundleUtilities.cmake.

```
WRITE_QT4_CONF(<qt_conf_dir> <qt_conf_contents>)
```

Writes a qt.conf file with the <qt_conf_contents> into <qt_conf_dir>.

```
RESOLVE_QT4_PATHS(<paths_var> [<executable_path>])
```

Loop through <paths_var> list and if any don't exist resolve them relative to the <executable_path> (if supplied) or the CMAKE_INSTALL_PREFIX.

```
FIXUP_QT4_EXECUTABLE(<executable>
  [<qtplugins> <libs> <dirs> <plugins_dir> <request_qt_conf>])
```

Copies Qt plugins, writes a Qt configuration file (if needed) and fixes up a Qt4 executable using BundleUtilities so it is standalone and can be drag-and-drop copied to another machine as long as all of the system libraries are compatible.

<executable> should point to the executable to be fixed-up.

<qtplugins> should contain a list of the names or paths of any Qt plugins to be installed.

<libs> will be passed to BundleUtilities and should be a list of any already installed plugins, libraries or executables to also be fixed-up.

<dirs> will be passed to BundleUtilities and should contain and directories to be searched to find library dependencies.

<plugins_dir> allows an custom plugins directory to be used.

<request_qt_conf> will force a qt.conf file to be written even if not needed.

```
INSTALL_QT4_PLUGIN_PATH(plugin executable copy installed_plugin_path_var
                        <plugins_dir> <component> <configurations>)
```

Install (or copy) a resolved <plugin> to the default plugins directory (or <plugins_dir>) relative to <executable> and store the result in <installed_plugin_path_var>.

If <copy> is set to TRUE then the plugins will be copied rather than installed. This is to allow this module to be used at CMake time rather than install time.

If <component> is set then anything installed will use this COMPONENT.

```
INSTALL_QT4_PLUGIN(plugin executable copy installed_plugin_path_var
                   <plugins_dir> <component>)
```

Install (or copy) an unresolved <plugin> to the default plugins directory (or <plugins_dir>) relative to <executable> and store the result in <installed_plugin_path_var>. See documentation of INSTALL_QT4_PLUGIN_PATH.

```
INSTALL_QT4_EXECUTABLE(<executable>
  [<qtplugins> <libs> <dirs> <plugins_dir> <request_qt_conf> <component>])
```

Installs Qt plugins, writes a Qt configuration file (if needed) and fixes up a Qt4 executable using BundleUtilities so it is standalone and can be drag-and-drop copied to another machine as long as all of the system libraries are compatible. The executable will be fixed-up at install time. <component> is the COMPONENT used for bundle fixup and plugin installation. See documentation of FIXUP_QT4_BUNDLE.

Documentation

DocumentationVTK.cmake

This file provides support for the VTK documentation framework. It relies on several tools (Doxygen, Perl, etc).

ExternalData

Manage data files stored outside source tree

Use this module to unambiguously reference data files stored outside the source tree and fetch them at build time from arbitrary local and remote content-addressed locations. Functions provided by this module recognize arguments with the syntax DATA{<name>} as references to external data, replace them with full paths to local copies of those data, and create build rules to fetch and update the local copies.

The DATA{} syntax is literal and the <name> is a full or relative path within the source tree. The source tree must contain either a real data file at <name> or a "content link" at <name><ext> containing a hash of the real file using a hash algorithm corresponding to <ext>. For example, the argument DATA{img.png} may be satisfied by either a real img.png file in the current source directory or a img.png.md5 file containing its MD5 sum.

The ExternalData_Expand_Arguments function evaluates DATA{} references in its arguments and constructs a new list of arguments:

```
ExternalData_Expand_Arguments(
  <target>    # Name of data management target
  <outVar>    # Output variable
  [args...]   # Input arguments, DATA{} allowed
  )
```

It replaces each DATA{} reference in an argument with the full path of a real data file on disk that will exist after the <target> builds.

The ExternalData_Add_Test function wraps around the CMake add_test() (page 277) command but supports DATA{} references in its arguments:

```
ExternalData_Add_Test(
  <target>    # Name of data management target
  ...         # Arguments of add_test(), DATA{} allowed
  )
```

It passes its arguments through ExternalData_Expand_Arguments and then invokes the add_test() (page 277) command using the results.

The ExternalData_Add_Target function creates a custom target to manage local instances of data files stored externally:

```
ExternalData_Add_Target(
  <target>    # Name of data management target
  )
```

It creates custom commands in the target as necessary to make data files available for each DATA{} reference previously evaluated by other functions provided by this module. A list of URL templates may be provided in the variable ExternalData_URL_TEMPLATES using the placeholders %(algo) and %(hash) in each template. Data fetch rules try each URL template in order by substituting the hash algorithm name for %(algo) and the hash value for %(hash).

The following hash algorithms are supported:

%(algo)	<ext>	Description
MD5	.md5	Message-Digest Algorithm 5, RFC 1321
SHA1	.sha1	US Secure Hash Algorithm 1, RFC 3174
SHA224	.sha224	US Secure Hash Algorithms, RFC 4634
SHA256	.sha256	US Secure Hash Algorithms, RFC 4634
SHA384	.sha384	US Secure Hash Algorithms, RFC 4634
SHA512	.sha512	US Secure Hash Algorithms, RFC 4634

Note that the hashes are used only for unique data identification and download verification.

Example usage:

```
include(ExternalData)
set(ExternalData_URL_TEMPLATES "file:///local/%(algo)/%(hash)"
                               "file:////host/share/%(algo)/%(hash)"
                               "http://data.org/%(algo)/%(hash)")
ExternalData_Add_Test(MyData
  NAME MyTest
  COMMAND MyExe DATA{MyInput.png}
  )
ExternalData_Add_Target(MyData)
```

When test `MyTest` runs the `DATA{MyInput.png}` argument will be replaced by the full path to a real instance of the data file `MyInput.png` on disk. If the source tree contains a content link such as `MyInput.png.md5` then the `MyData` target creates a real `MyInput.png` in the build tree.

The `DATA{}` syntax can be told to fetch a file series using the form `DATA{<name>,:}`, where the `:` is literal. If the source tree contains a group of files or content links named like a series then a reference to one member adds rules to fetch all of them. Although all members of a series are fetched, only the file originally named by the `DATA{}` argument is substituted for it. The default configuration recognizes file series names ending with `#.ext`, `_#.ext`, `.#.ext`, or `-#.ext` where `#` is a sequence of decimal digits and `.ext` is any single extension. Configure it with a regex that parses `<number>` and `<suffix>` parts from the end of `<name>`:

```
ExternalData_SERIES_PARSE = regex of the form (<number>)(<suffix>)$
```

For more complicated cases set:

```
ExternalData_SERIES_PARSE = regex with at least two () groups
ExternalData_SERIES_PARSE_PREFIX = <prefix> regex group number, if any
ExternalData_SERIES_PARSE_NUMBER = <number> regex group number
ExternalData_SERIES_PARSE_SUFFIX = <suffix> regex group number
```

Configure series number matching with a regex that matches the `<number>` part of series members named `<prefix><number><suffix>`:

```
ExternalData_SERIES_MATCH = regex matching <number> in all series members
```

Note that the `<suffix>` of a series does not include a hash-algorithm extension.

The `DATA{}` syntax can alternatively match files associated with the named file and contained in the same directory. Associated files may be specified by options using the syntax `DATA{<name>,<opt1>,<opt2>,...}`. Each option may specify one file by name or specify a regular expression to match file names using the syntax `REGEX:<regex>`. For example, the arguments:

```
DATA{MyData/MyInput.mhd,MyInput.img}                    # File pair
DATA{MyData/MyFrames00.png,REGEX:MyFrames[0-9]+\.png}   # Series
```

will pass `MyInput.mha` and `MyFrames00.png` on the command line but ensure that the associated files are present next to them.

The `DATA{}` syntax may reference a directory using a trailing slash and a list of associated files. The form `DATA{<name>/,<opt1>,<opt2>,...}` adds rules to fetch any files in the directory that match one of the associated file options. For example, the argument DATA{MyDataDir/,REGEX:.*} will pass the full path to a MyDataDir directory on the command line and ensure that the directory contains files corresponding to every file or content link in the MyDataDir source directory.

The variable ExternalData_LINK_CONTENT may be set to the name of a supported hash algorithm to enable automatic conversion of real data files referenced by the DATA{} syntax into content links. For each such <file> a content link named <file><ext> is created. The original file is renamed to the form .ExternalData_<algo>_<hash> to stage it for future transmission to one of the locations in the list of URL templates (by means outside the scope of this module). The data fetch rule created for the content link will use the staged object if it cannot be found using any URL template.

The variable ExternalData_OBJECT_STORES may be set to a list of local directories that store objects using the layout <dir>/%(algo)/%(hash). These directories will be searched first for a needed object. If the object is not available in any store then it will be fetched remotely using the URL templates and added to the first local store listed. If no stores are specified the default is a location inside the build tree.

The variable ExternalData_SOURCE_ROOT may be set to the highest source directory containing any path named by a DATA{} reference. The default is CMAKE_SOURCE_DIR. ExternalData_SOURCE_ROOT and CMAKE_SOURCE_DIR must refer to directories within a single source distribution (e.g. they come together in one tarball).

The variable ExternalData_BINARY_ROOT may be set to the directory to hold the real data files named by expanded DATA{} references. The default is CMAKE_BINARY_DIR. The directory layout will mirror that of content links under ExternalData_SOURCE_ROOT.

Variables ExternalData_TIMEOUT_INACTIVITY and ExternalData_TIMEOUT_ABSOLUTE set the download inactivity and absolute timeouts, in seconds. The defaults are 60 seconds and 300 seconds, respectively. Set either timeout to 0 seconds to disable enforcement.

ExternalProject

Create custom targets to build projects in external trees

The ExternalProject_Add function creates a custom target to drive download, update/patch, configure, build, install and test steps of an external project:

```
ExternalProject_Add(<name>        # Name for custom target
  [DEPENDS projects...]           # Targets on which the project depends
  [PREFIX dir]                    # Root dir for entire project
  [LIST_SEPARATOR sep]            # Sep to be replaced by ; in cmd lines
  [TMP_DIR dir]                   # Directory to store temporary files
  [STAMP_DIR dir]                 # Directory to store step timestamps
  [EXCLUDE_FROM_ALL 1]            # The "all" target does not depend on this
#--Download step--------------
  [DOWNLOAD_NAME fname]           # File name to store (if not end of URL)
  [DOWNLOAD_DIR dir]              # Directory to store downloaded files
  [DOWNLOAD_COMMAND cmd...]       # Command to download source tree
  [DOWNLOAD_NO_PROGRESS 1]        # Disable download progress reports
  [CVS_REPOSITORY cvsroot]        # CVSROOT of CVS repository
```

```
  [CVS_MODULE mod]              # Module to checkout from CVS repo
  [CVS_TAG tag]                 # Tag to checkout from CVS repo
  [SVN_REPOSITORY url]          # URL of Subversion repo
  [SVN_REVISION -r<rev>]        # Revision to checkout from Subversion repo
  [SVN_USERNAME john ]          # Username for Subversion checkout and update
  [SVN_PASSWORD doe ]           # Password for Subversion checkout and update
  [SVN_TRUST_CERT 1 ]           # Trust the Subversion server site certificate
  [GIT_REPOSITORY url]          # URL of git repo
  [GIT_TAG tag]                 # Git branch name, commit id or tag
  [GIT_SUBMODULES modules...]   # Git submodules that shall be updated, all if empty
  [HG_REPOSITORY url]           # URL of mercurial repo
  [HG_TAG tag]                  # Mercurial branch name, commit id or tag
  [URL /.../src.tgz]            # Full path or URL of source
  [URL_HASH ALGO=value]         # Hash of file at URL
  [URL_MD5 md5]                 # Equivalent to URL_HASH MD5=md5
  [TLS_VERIFY bool]             # Should certificate for https be checked
  [TLS_CAINFO file]             # Path to a certificate authority file
  [TIMEOUT seconds]             # Time allowed for file download operations
#--Update/Patch step----------
  [UPDATE_COMMAND cmd...]       # Source work-tree update command
  [PATCH_COMMAND cmd...]        # Command to patch downloaded source
#--Configure step-------------
  [SOURCE_DIR dir]              # Source dir to be used for build
  [CONFIGURE_COMMAND cmd...]    # Build tree configuration command
  [CMAKE_COMMAND /.../cmake]    # Specify alternative cmake executable
  [CMAKE_GENERATOR gen]         # Specify generator for native build
  [CMAKE_GENERATOR_PLATFORM p]  # Generator-specific platform name
  [CMAKE_GENERATOR_TOOLSET t]   # Generator-specific toolset name
  [CMAKE_ARGS args...]          # Arguments to CMake command line
  [CMAKE_CACHE_ARGS args...]    # Initial cache args with form -Dvar:string=on
#--Build step-----------------
  [BINARY_DIR dir]              # Specify build dir location
  [BUILD_COMMAND cmd...]        # Command to drive the native build
  [BUILD_IN_SOURCE 1]           # Use source dir for build dir
  [BUILD_ALWAYS 1]              # No stamp file, build step always runs
#--Install step--------------
  [INSTALL_DIR dir]             # Installation prefix
  [INSTALL_COMMAND cmd...]      # Command to drive install after build
#--Test step-----------------
  [TEST_BEFORE_INSTALL 1]       # Add test step executed before install step
  [TEST_AFTER_INSTALL 1]        # Add test step executed after install step
  [TEST_COMMAND cmd...]         # Command to drive test
#--Output logging------------
  [LOG_DOWNLOAD 1]              # Wrap download in script to log output
  [LOG_UPDATE 1]                # Wrap update in script to log output
  [LOG_CONFIGURE 1]             # Wrap configure in script to log output
  [LOG_BUILD 1]                 # Wrap build in script to log output
  [LOG_TEST 1]                  # Wrap test in script to log output
  [LOG_INSTALL 1]               # Wrap install in script to log output
```

```
#--Custom targets-------------
  [STEP_TARGETS st1 st2 ...]  # Generate custom targets for these steps
  )
```

The *_DIR options specify directories for the project, with default directories computed as follows. If the PREFIX option is given to ExternalProject_Add() or the EP_PREFIX directory property is set, then an external project is built and installed under the specified prefix:

```
TMP_DIR      = <prefix>/tmp
STAMP_DIR    = <prefix>/src/<name>-stamp
DOWNLOAD_DIR = <prefix>/src
SOURCE_DIR   = <prefix>/src/<name>
BINARY_DIR   = <prefix>/src/<name>-build
INSTALL_DIR  = <prefix>
```

Otherwise, if the EP_BASE directory property is set then components of an external project are stored under the specified base:

```
TMP_DIR      = <base>/tmp/<name>
STAMP_DIR    = <base>/Stamp/<name>
DOWNLOAD_DIR = <base>/Download/<name>
SOURCE_DIR   = <base>/Source/<name>
BINARY_DIR   = <base>/Build/<name>
INSTALL_DIR  = <base>/Install/<name>
```

If no PREFIX, EP_PREFIX, or EP_BASE is specified then the default is to set PREFIX to <name>-prefix. Relative paths are interpreted with respect to the build directory corresponding to the source directory in which ExternalProject_Add is invoked.

If SOURCE_DIR is explicitly set to an existing directory the project will be built from it. Otherwise a download step must be specified using one of the DOWNLOAD_COMMAND, CVS_*, SVN_*, or URL options. The URL option may refer locally to a directory or source tarball, or refer to a remote tarball (e.g. http://.../src.tgz).

The ExternalProject_Add_Step function adds a custom step to an external project:

```
ExternalProject_Add_Step(<name> <step> # Names of project and custom step
  [COMMAND cmd...]              # Command line invoked by this step
  [COMMENT "text..."]           # Text printed when step executes
  [DEPENDEES steps...]          # Steps on which this step depends
  [DEPENDERS steps...]          # Steps that depend on this step
  [DEPENDS files...]            # Files on which this step depends
  [ALWAYS 1]                    # No stamp file, step always runs
  [EXCLUDE_FROM_MAIN 1]         # Main target does not depend on this step
  [WORKING_DIRECTORY dir]       # Working directory for command
  [LOG 1]                       # Wrap step in script to log output
  )
```

The command line, comment, and working directory of every standard and custom step is processed to replace tokens <SOURCE_DIR>, <BINARY_DIR>, <INSTALL_DIR>, and <TMP_DIR> with corresponding property values.

Any builtin step that specifies a `<step>_COMMAND cmd...` or custom step that specifies a `COMMAND cmd...` may specify additional command lines using the form `COMMAND cmd...`. At build time the commands will be executed in order and aborted if any one fails. For example:

```
... BUILD_COMMAND make COMMAND echo done ...
```

specifies to run `make` and then `echo done` during the build step. Whether the current working directory is preserved between commands is not defined. Behavior of shell operators like `&&` is not defined.

The `ExternalProject_Get_Property` function retrieves external project target properties:

```
ExternalProject_Get_Property(<name> [prop1 [prop2 [...]]])
```

It stores property values in variables of the same name. Property names correspond to the keyword argument names of `ExternalProject_Add`.

The `ExternalProject_Add_StepTargets` function generates custom targets for the steps listed:

```
ExternalProject_Add_StepTargets(<name> [step1 [step2 [...]]])
```

If `STEP_TARGETS` is set then `ExternalProject_Add_StepTargets` is automatically called at the end of matching calls to `ExternalProject_Add_Step`. Pass `STEP_TARGETS` explicitly to individual `ExternalProject_Add` calls, or implicitly to all `ExternalProject_Add` calls by setting the directory property `EP_STEP_TARGETS`.

If `STEP_TARGETS` is not set, clients may still manually call `ExternalProject_Add_StepTargets` after calling `ExternalProject_Add` or `ExternalProject_Add_Step`.

This functionality is provided to make it easy to drive the steps independently of each other by specifying targets on build command lines. For example, you may be submitting to a sub-project based dashboard, where you want to drive the configure portion of the build, then submit to the dashboard, followed by the build portion, followed by tests. If you invoke a custom target that depends on a step halfway through the step dependency chain, then all the previous steps will also run to ensure everything is up to date.

For example, to drive configure, build and test steps independently for each `ExternalProject_Add` call in your project, write the following line prior to any `ExternalProject_Add` calls in your `CMakeLists.txt` file:

```
set_property(DIRECTORY PROPERTY EP_STEP_TARGETS configure build test)
```

FeatureSummary

Macros for generating a summary of enabled/disabled features

This module provides the macros feature_summary(), set_package_properties() and add_feature_info(). For compatibility it also still provides set_package_info(), set_feature_info(), print_enabled_features() and print_disabled_features().

These macros can be used to generate a summary of enabled and disabled packages and/or feature for a build tree:

```
-- The following OPTIONAL packages have been found:
LibXml2 (required version >= 2.4), XML processing lib, <http://xmlsoft.org>
   * Enables HTML-import in MyWordProcessor
   * Enables odt-export in MyWordProcessor
PNG , A PNG image library. , <http://www.libpng.org/pub/png/>
   * Enables saving screenshots
-- The following OPTIONAL packages have not been found:
Lua51 , The Lua scripting language. , <http://www.lua.org>
   * Enables macros in MyWordProcessor
Foo , Foo provides cool stuff.
```

```
FEATURE_SUMMARY( [FILENAME <file>]
                 [APPEND]
                 [VAR <variable_name>]
                 [INCLUDE_QUIET_PACKAGES]
                 [FATAL_ON_MISSING_REQUIRED_PACKAGES]
                 [DESCRIPTION "Found packages:"]
                 WHAT (ALL | PACKAGES_FOUND | PACKAGES_NOT_FOUND
                       | ENABLED_FEATURES | DISABLED_FEATURES]
                 )
```

The FEATURE_SUMMARY() macro can be used to print information about enabled or disabled packages or features of a project. By default, only the names of the features/packages will be printed and their required version when one was specified. Use SET_PACKAGE_PROPERTIES() to add more useful information, like e.g. a download URL for the respective package or their purpose in the project.

The WHAT option is the only mandatory option. Here you specify what information will be printed:

ALL print everything

ENABLED_FEATURES the list of all features which are enabled

DISABLED_FEATURES the list of all features which are disabled

PACKAGES_FOUND the list of all packages which have been found

PACKAGES_NOT_FOUND the list of all packages which have not been found

OPTIONAL_PACKAGES_FOUND only those packages which have been found which have the type OPTIONAL

OPTIONAL_PACKAGES_NOT_FOUND only those packages which have not been found which have the type OPTIONAL

RECOMMENDED_PACKAGES_FOUND only those packages which have been found which have the type RECOMMENDED

RECOMMENDED_PACKAGES_NOT_FOUND only those packages which have not been found which have the type RECOMMENDED

REQUIRED_PACKAGES_FOUND only those packages which have been found which have the type RE-QUIRED

REQUIRED_PACKAGES_NOT_FOUND only those packages which have not been found which have the type REQUIRED

RUNTIME_PACKAGES_FOUND only those packages which have been found which have the type RUN-TIME

RUNTIME_PACKAGES_NOT_FOUND only those packages which have not been found which have the type RUNTIME

With the exception of the ALL value, these values can be combined in order to customize the output. For example:

```
feature_summary(WHAT ENABLED_FEATURES DISABLED_FEATURES)
```

If a FILENAME is given, the information is printed into this file. If APPEND is used, it is appended to this file, otherwise the file is overwritten if it already existed. If the VAR option is used, the information is "printed" into the specified variable. If FILENAME is not used, the information is printed to the terminal. Using the DESCRIPTION option a description or headline can be set which will be printed above the actual content. If INCLUDE_QUIET_PACKAGES is given, packages which have been searched with find_package(... QUIET) will also be listed. By default they are skipped. If FATAL_ON_MISSING_REQUIRED_PACKAGES is given, CMake will abort if a package which is marked as REQUIRED has not been found.

Example 1, append everything to a file:

```
feature_summary(WHAT ALL
                FILENAME ${CMAKE_BINARY_DIR}/all.log APPEND)
```

Example 2, print the enabled features into the variable enabledFeaturesText, including QUIET packages:

```
feature_summary(WHAT ENABLED_FEATURES
                INCLUDE_QUIET_PACKAGES
                DESCRIPTION "Enabled Features:"
                VAR enabledFeaturesText)
message(STATUS "${enabledFeaturesText}")
```

```
SET_PACKAGE_PROPERTIES(<name> PROPERTIES
                    [ URL <url> ]
                    [ DESCRIPTION <description> ]
                    [ TYPE (RUNTIME|OPTIONAL|RECOMMENDED|REQUIRED) ]
                    [ PURPOSE <purpose> ]
                    )
```

Use this macro to set up information about the named package, which can then be displayed via FEATURE_SUMMARY(). This can be done either directly in the Find-module or in the project which uses the module after the find_package() call. The features for which information can be set are added automatically by the find_package() command.

URL: this should be the homepage of the package, or something similar. Ideally this is set already directly in the Find-module.

DESCRIPTION: A short description what that package is, at most one sentence. Ideally this is set already directly in the Find-module.

TYPE: What type of dependency has the using project on that package. Default is OPTIONAL. In this case it is a package which can be used by the project when available at buildtime, but it also work without. RECOMMENDED is similar to OPTIONAL, i.e. the project will build if the package is not present, but the functionality of the resulting binaries will be severly limited. If a REQUIRED package is not available at buildtime, the project may not even build. This can be combined with the FA-TAL_ON_MISSING_REQUIRED_PACKAGES argument for feature_summary(). Last, a RUNTIME package is a package which is actually not used at all during the build, but which is required for actually running the resulting binaries. So if such a package is missing, the project can still be built, but it may not work later on. If set_package_properties() is called multiple times for the same package with different TYPEs, the TYPE is only changed to higher TYPEs (RUNTIME < OPTIONAL < RECOMMENDED < REQUIRED), lower TYPEs are ignored. The TYPE property is project-specific, so it cannot be set by the Find-module, but must be set in the project.

PURPOSE: This describes which features this package enables in the project, i.e. it tells the user what functionality he gets in the resulting binaries. If set_package_properties() is called multiple times for a package, all PURPOSE properties are appended to a list of purposes of the package in the project. As the TYPE property, also the PURPOSE property is project-specific, so it cannot be set by the Find-module, but must be set in the project.

Example for setting the info for a package:

```
find_package(LibXml2)
set_package_properties(LibXml2 PROPERTIES
                       DESCRIPTION "A XML processing library."
                       URL "http://xmlsoft.org/")
```

```
set_package_properties(LibXml2 PROPERTIES
                       TYPE RECOMMENDED
                       PURPOSE "Enables HTML-import in MyWordProcessor")
...
set_package_properties(LibXml2 PROPERTIES
                       TYPE OPTIONAL
                       PURPOSE "Enables odt-export in MyWordProcessor")
```

```
find_package(DBUS)
set_package_properties(DBUS PROPERTIES
  TYPE RUNTIME
  PURPOSE "Necessary to disable the screensaver during a presentation" )
```

```
ADD_FEATURE_INFO(<name> <enabled> <description>)
```

Use this macro to add information about a feature with the given <name>. <enabled> contains whether this feature is enabled or not, <description> is a text describing the feature. The information can be displayed using feature_summary() for ENABLED_FEATURES and DISABLED_FEATURES respectively.

Example for setting the info for a feature:

```
option(WITH_FOO "Help for foo" ON)
add_feature_info(Foo WITH_FOO "The Foo feature provides very cool stuff.")
```

The following macros are provided for compatibility with previous CMake versions:

```
SET_PACKAGE_INFO(<name> <description> [<url> [<purpose>] ] )
```

Use this macro to set up information about the named package, which can then be displayed via FEA-TURE_SUMMARY(). This can be done either directly in the Find-module or in the project which uses the module after the find_package() call. The features for which information can be set are added automatically by the find_package() command.

```
PRINT_ENABLED_FEATURES()
```

Does the same as FEATURE_SUMMARY(WHAT ENABLED_FEATURES DESCRIPTION "Enabled features:")

```
PRINT_DISABLED_FEATURES()
```

Does the same as FEATURE_SUMMARY(WHAT DISABLED_FEATURES DESCRIPTION "Disabled features:")

```
SET_FEATURE_INFO(<name> <description> [<url>] )
```

Does the same as SET_PACKAGE_INFO(<name> <description> <url>)

FindALSA

Find alsa

Find the alsa libraries (asound)

```
This module defines the following variables:
   ALSA_FOUND       - True if ALSA_INCLUDE_DIR & ALSA_LIBRARY are found
   ALSA_LIBRARIES   - Set when ALSA_LIBRARY is found
   ALSA_INCLUDE_DIRS - Set when ALSA_INCLUDE_DIR is found
```

```
ALSA_INCLUDE_DIR - where to find asoundlib.h, etc.
ALSA_LIBRARY     - the asound library
ALSA_VERSION_STRING - the version of alsa found (since CMake 2.8.8)
```

FindArmadillo

Find Armadillo

Find the Armadillo C++ library

Using Armadillo:

```
find_package(Armadillo REQUIRED)
include_directories(${ARMADILLO_INCLUDE_DIRS})
add_executable(foo foo.cc)
target_link_libraries(foo ${ARMADILLO_LIBRARIES})
```

This module sets the following variables:

```
ARMADILLO_FOUND - set to true if the library is found
ARMADILLO_INCLUDE_DIRS - list of required include directories
ARMADILLO_LIBRARIES - list of libraries to be linked
ARMADILLO_VERSION_MAJOR - major version number
ARMADILLO_VERSION_MINOR - minor version number
ARMADILLO_VERSION_PATCH - patch version number
ARMADILLO_VERSION_STRING - version number as a string (ex: "1.0.4")
ARMADILLO_VERSION_NAME - name of the version (ex: "Antipodean Antileech")
```

FindASPELL

Try to find ASPELL

Once done this will define

```
ASPELL_FOUND - system has ASPELL
ASPELL_EXECUTABLE - the ASPELL executable
ASPELL_INCLUDE_DIR - the ASPELL include directory
ASPELL_LIBRARIES - The libraries needed to use ASPELL
ASPELL_DEFINITIONS - Compiler switches required for using ASPELL
```

FindAVIFile

Locate AVIFILE library and include paths

AVIFILE (http://avifile.sourceforge.net/)is a set of libraries for i386 machines to use various AVI codecs. Support is limited beyond Linux. Windows provides native AVI support, and so doesn't need this library. This module defines

```
AVIFILE_INCLUDE_DIR, where to find avifile.h , etc.
AVIFILE_LIBRARIES, the libraries to link against
AVIFILE_DEFINITIONS, definitions to use when compiling
AVIFILE_FOUND, If false, don't try to use AVIFILE
```

FindBISON

Find bison executable and provides macros to generate custom build rules

The module defines the following variables:

```
BISON_EXECUTABLE - path to the bison program
BISON_VERSION - version of bison
BISON_FOUND - true if the program was found
```

The minimum required version of bison can be specified using the standard CMake syntax, e.g. find_package(BISON 2.1.3)

If bison is found, the module defines the macros:

```
BISON_TARGET(<Name> <YaccInput> <CodeOutput> [VERBOSE <file>]
            [COMPILE_FLAGS <string>])
```

which will create a custom rule to generate a parser. <YaccInput> is the path to a yacc file. <CodeOutput> is the name of the source file generated by bison. A header file is also be generated, and contains the token list. If COMPILE_FLAGS option is specified, the next parameter is added in the bison command line. if VERBOSE option is specified, <file> is created and contains verbose descriptions of the grammar and parser. The macro defines a set of variables:

```
BISON_${Name}_DEFINED - true is the macro ran successfully
BISON_${Name}_INPUT - The input source file, an alias for <YaccInput>
BISON_${Name}_OUTPUT_SOURCE - The source file generated by bison
BISON_${Name}_OUTPUT_HEADER - The header file generated by bison
BISON_${Name}_OUTPUTS - The sources files generated by bison
BISON_${Name}_COMPILE_FLAGS - Options used in the bison command line
```

```
===================================================================
Example:
```

```
find_package(BISON)
BISON_TARGET(MyParser parser.y ${CMAKE_CURRENT_BINARY_DIR}/parser.cpp)
add_executable(Foo main.cpp ${BISON_MyParser_OUTPUTS})
===================================================================
```

FindBLAS

Find BLAS library

This module finds an installed fortran library that implements the BLAS linear-algebra interface (see http://www.netlib.org/blas/). The list of libraries searched for is taken from the autoconf macro file, acx_blas.m4 (distributed at http://ac-archive.sourceforge.net/ac-archive/acx_blas.html).

This module sets the following variables:

```
BLAS_FOUND - set to true if a library implementing the BLAS interface
  is found
BLAS_LINKER_FLAGS - uncached list of required linker flags (excluding -l
  and -L).
BLAS_LIBRARIES - uncached list of libraries (using full path name) to
  link against to use BLAS
```

```
BLAS95_LIBRARIES - uncached list of libraries (using full path name)
  to link against to use BLAS95 interface
BLAS95_FOUND - set to true if a library implementing the BLAS f95 interface
  is found
BLA_STATIC  if set on this determines what kind of linkage we do (static)
BLA_VENDOR  if set checks only the specified vendor, if not set checks
  all the possibilities
BLA_F95     if set on tries to find the f95 interfaces for BLAS/LAPACK
```

######### ## List of vendors (BLA_VENDOR) valid in this module # Goto,ATLAS PhiPACK,CXML,DXML,SunPerf,SCSL,SGIMATH,IBMESSL,Intel10_32 (intel mkl v10 32 bit),Intel10_64lp (intel mkl v10 64 bit,lp thread model, lp64 model), # Intel10_64lp_seq (intel mkl v10 64 bit,sequential code, lp64 model), # Intel(older versions of mkl 32 and 64 bit), ACML,ACML_MP,ACML_GPU,Apple, NAS, Generic C/CXX should be enabled to use Intel mkl

FindBacktrace

Find provider for backtrace(3).

Checks if OS supports backtrace(3) via either libc or custom library. This module defines the following variables:

Backtrace_HEADER The header file needed for backtrace(3). Cached. Could be forcibly set by user.

Backtrace_INCLUDE_DIRS The include directories needed to use backtrace(3) header.

Backtrace_LIBRARIES The libraries (linker flags) needed to use backtrace(3), if any.

Backtrace_FOUND Is set if and only if backtrace(3) support detected.

The following cache variables are also available to set or use:

Backtrace_LIBRARY The external library providing backtrace, if any.

Backtrace_INCLUDE_DIR The directory holding the backtrace(3) header.

Typical usage is to generate of header file using configure_file() with the contents like the following:

```
#cmakedefine01 Backtrace_FOUND
#if Backtrace_FOUND
# include <${Backtrace_HEADER}>
#endif
```

And then reference that generated header file in actual source.

FindBoost

Find Boost include dirs and libraries

Use this module by invoking find_package with the form:

```
find_package(Boost
  [version] [EXACT]        # Minimum or EXACT version e.g. 1.36.0
  [REQUIRED]               # Fail with error if Boost is not found
  [COMPONENTS <libs>...]   # Boost libraries by their canonical name
  )                        # e.g. "date_time" for "libboost_date_time"
```

This module finds headers and requested component libraries OR a CMake package configuration file provided by a "Boost CMake" build. For the latter case skip to the "Boost CMake" section below. For the former case results are reported in variables:

```
Boost_FOUND                    - True if headers and requested libraries were found
Boost_INCLUDE_DIRS             - Boost include directories
Boost_LIBRARY_DIRS             - Link directories for Boost libraries
Boost_LIBRARIES                - Boost component libraries to be linked
Boost_<C>_FOUND                - True if component <C> was found (<C> is upper-case)
Boost_<C>_LIBRARY              - Libraries to link for component <C> (may include
                                 target_link_libraries debug/optimized keywords)
Boost_VERSION                  - BOOST_VERSION value from boost/version.hpp
Boost_LIB_VERSION              - Version string appended to library filenames
Boost_MAJOR_VERSION            - Boost major version number (X in X.y.z)
Boost_MINOR_VERSION            - Boost minor version number (Y in x.Y.z)
Boost_SUBMINOR_VERSION         - Boost subminor version number (Z in x.y.Z)
Boost_LIB_DIAGNOSTIC_DEFINITIONS (Windows)
                               - Pass to add_definitions() to have diagnostic
                                 information about Boost's automatic linking
                                 displayed during compilation
```

This module reads hints about search locations from variables:

```
BOOST_ROOT                - Preferred installation prefix
 (or BOOSTROOT)
BOOST_INCLUDEDIR          - Preferred include directory e.g. <prefix>/include
BOOST_LIBRARYDIR          - Preferred library directory e.g. <prefix>/lib
Boost_NO_SYSTEM_PATHS     - Set to ON to disable searching in locations not
                            specified by these hint variables. Default is OFF.
Boost_ADDITIONAL_VERSIONS
                          - List of Boost versions not known to this module
                            (Boost install locations may contain the version)
```

and saves search results persistently in CMake cache entries:

```
Boost_INCLUDE_DIR          - Directory containing Boost headers
Boost_LIBRARY_DIR          - Directory containing Boost libraries
Boost_<C>_LIBRARY_DEBUG    - Component <C> library debug variant
Boost_<C>_LIBRARY_RELEASE  - Component <C> library release variant
```

Users may set these hints or results as cache entries. Projects should not read these entries directly but instead use the above result variables. Note that some hint names start in upper-case "BOOST". One may specify these as environment variables if they are not specified as CMake variables or cache entries.

This module first searches for the Boost header files using the above hint variables (excluding BOOST_LIBRARYDIR) and saves the result in Boost_INCLUDE_DIR. Then it searches for requested component libraries using the above hints (excluding BOOST_INCLUDEDIR and Boost_ADDITIONAL_VERSIONS), "lib" directories near Boost_INCLUDE_DIR, and the library name configuration settings below. It saves the library directory in Boost_LIBRARY_DIR and individual library locations in Boost_<C>_LIBRARY_DEBUG and Boost_<C>_LIBRARY_RELEASE. When one changes settings used by previous searches in the same build tree (excluding environment variables) this module discards previous search results affected by the changes and searches again.

Boost libraries come in many variants encoded in their file name. Users or projects may tell this module which variant to find by setting variables:

```
Boost_USE_MULTITHREADED      - Set to OFF to use the non-multithreaded
                               libraries ('mt' tag).  Default is ON.
Boost_USE_STATIC_LIBS        - Set to ON to force the use of the static
                               libraries.  Default is OFF.
Boost_USE_STATIC_RUNTIME     - Set to ON or OFF to specify whether to use
                               libraries linked statically to the C++ runtime
                               ('s' tag).  Default is platform dependent.
Boost_USE_DEBUG_RUNTIME      - Set to ON or OFF to specify whether to use
                               libraries linked to the MS debug C++ runtime
                               ('g' tag).  Default is ON.
Boost_USE_DEBUG_PYTHON       - Set to ON to use libraries compiled with a
                               debug Python build ('y' tag). Default is OFF.
Boost_USE_STLPORT            - Set to ON to use libraries compiled with
                               STLPort ('p' tag).  Default is OFF.
Boost_USE_STLPORT_DEPRECATED_NATIVE_IOSTREAMS
                             - Set to ON to use libraries compiled with
                               STLPort deprecated "native iostreams"
                               ('n' tag).  Default is OFF.
Boost_COMPILER               - Set to the compiler-specific library suffix
                               (e.g. "-gcc43").  Default is auto-computed
                               for the C++ compiler in use.
Boost_THREADAPI              - Suffix for "thread" component library name,
                               such as "pthread" or "win32".  Names with
                               and without this suffix will both be tried.
Boost_NAMESPACE              - Alternate namespace used to build boost with
                               e.g. if set to "myboost", will search for
                               myboost_thread instead of boost_thread.
```

Other variables one may set to control this module are:

```
Boost_DEBUG                  - Set to ON to enable debug output from FindBoost.
                               Please enable this before filing any bug report.
Boost_DETAILED_FAILURE_MSG
                             - Set to ON to add detailed information to the
                               failure message even when the REQUIRED option
                               is not given to the find_package call.
Boost_REALPATH               - Set to ON to resolve symlinks for discovered
                               libraries to assist with packaging.  For example,
```

```
                                       the "system" component library may be resolved to
                                       "/usr/lib/libboost_system.so.1.42.0" instead of
                                       "/usr/lib/libboost_system.so".  This does not
                                       affect linking and should not be enabled unless
                                       the user needs this information.
```

On Visual Studio and Borland compilers Boost headers request automatic linking to corresponding libraries. This requires matching libraries to be linked explicitly or available in the link library search path. In this case setting Boost_USE_STATIC_LIBS to OFF may not achieve dynamic linking. Boost automatic linking typically requests static libraries with a few exceptions (such as Boost.Python). Use:

```
add_definitions(${Boost_LIB_DIAGNOSTIC_DEFINITIONS})
```

to ask Boost to report information about automatic linking requests.

Example to find Boost headers only:

```
find_package(Boost 1.36.0)
if(Boost_FOUND)
  include_directories(${Boost_INCLUDE_DIRS})
  add_executable(foo foo.cc)
endif()
```

Example to find Boost headers and some *static* libraries:

```
set(Boost_USE_STATIC_LIBS        ON) # only find static libs
set(Boost_USE_MULTITHREADED      ON)
set(Boost_USE_STATIC_RUNTIME    OFF)
find_package(Boost 1.36.0 COMPONENTS date_time filesystem system ...)
if(Boost_FOUND)
  include_directories(${Boost_INCLUDE_DIRS})
  add_executable(foo foo.cc)
  target_link_libraries(foo ${Boost_LIBRARIES})
endif()
```

Boost CMake

If Boost was built using the boost-cmake project it provides a package configuration file for use with find_package's Config mode. This module looks for the package configuration file called BoostConfig.cmake or boost-config.cmake and stores the result in cache entry "Boost_DIR". If found, the package configuration file is loaded and this module returns with no further action. See documentation of the Boost CMake package configuration for details on what it provides.

Set Boost_NO_BOOST_CMAKE to ON to disable the search for boost-cmake.

FindBullet

Try to find the Bullet physics engine

This module defines the following variables

```
BULLET_FOUND - Was bullet found
BULLET_INCLUDE_DIRS - the Bullet include directories
BULLET_LIBRARIES - Link to this, by default it includes
                   all bullet components (Dynamics,
                   Collision, LinearMath, & SoftBody)
```

This module accepts the following variables

```
BULLET_ROOT - Can be set to bullet install path or Windows build path
```

FindBZip2

Try to find BZip2

Once done this will define

```
BZIP2_FOUND - system has BZip2
BZIP2_INCLUDE_DIR - the BZip2 include directory
BZIP2_LIBRARIES - Link these to use BZip2
BZIP2_NEED_PREFIX - this is set if the functions are prefixed with BZ2_
BZIP2_VERSION_STRING - the version of BZip2 found (since CMake 2.8.8)
```

FindCABLE

Find CABLE

This module finds if CABLE is installed and determines where the include files and libraries are. This code sets the following variables:

```
CABLE              the path to the cable executable
CABLE_TCL_LIBRARY  the path to the Tcl wrapper library
CABLE_INCLUDE_DIR  the path to the include directory
```

To build Tcl wrappers, you should add shared library and link it to ${CABLE_TCL_LIBRARY}. You should also add ${CABLE_INCLUDE_DIR} as an include directory.

FindCoin3D

Find Coin3D (Open Inventor)

Coin3D is an implementation of the Open Inventor API. It provides data structures and algorithms for 3D visualization http://www.coin3d.org/

This module defines the following variables

```
COIN3D_FOUND              - system has Coin3D - Open Inventor
COIN3D_INCLUDE_DIRS       - where the Inventor include directory can be found
COIN3D_LIBRARIES          - Link to this to use Coin3D
```

FindCUDA

Tools for building CUDA C files: libraries and build dependencies.

This script locates the NVIDIA CUDA C tools. It should work on linux, windows, and mac and should be reasonably up to date with CUDA C releases.

This script makes use of the standard find_package arguments of <VERSION>, REQUIRED and QUIET. CUDA_FOUND will report if an acceptable version of CUDA was found.

The script will prompt the user to specify CUDA_TOOLKIT_ROOT_DIR if the prefix cannot be determined by the location of nvcc in the system path and REQUIRED is specified to find_package(). To use a different installed version of the toolkit set the environment variable CUDA_BIN_PATH before running cmake (e.g. CUDA_BIN_PATH=/usr/local/cuda1.0 instead of the default /usr/local/cuda) or set CUDA_TOOLKIT_ROOT_DIR after configuring. If you change the value of CUDA_TOOLKIT_ROOT_DIR, various components that depend on the path will be relocated.

It might be necessary to set CUDA_TOOLKIT_ROOT_DIR manually on certain platforms, or to use a cuda runtime not installed in the default location. In newer versions of the toolkit the cuda library is included with the graphics driver- be sure that the driver version matches what is needed by the cuda runtime version.

The following variables affect the behavior of the macros in the script (in alphebetical order). Note that any of these flags can be changed multiple times in the same directory before calling CUDA_ADD_EXECUTABLE, CUDA_ADD_LIBRARY, CUDA_COMPILE, CUDA_COMPILE_PTX, CUDA_COMPILE_FATBIN, CUDA_COMPILE_CUBIN or CUDA_WRAP_SRCS:

```
CUDA_64_BIT_DEVICE_CODE (Default matches host bit size)
-- Set to ON to compile for 64 bit device code, OFF for 32 bit device code.
   Note that making this different from the host code when generating object
   or C files from CUDA code just won't work, because size_t gets defined by
   nvcc in the generated source.  If you compile to PTX and then load the
   file yourself, you can mix bit sizes between device and host.

CUDA_ATTACH_VS_BUILD_RULE_TO_CUDA_FILE (Default ON)
-- Set to ON if you want the custom build rule to be attached to the source
   file in Visual Studio.  Turn OFF if you add the same cuda file to multiple
   targets.

   This allows the user to build the target from the CUDA file; however, bad
   things can happen if the CUDA source file is added to multiple targets.
   When performing parallel builds it is possible for the custom build
   command to be run more than once and in parallel causing cryptic build
   errors.  VS runs the rules for every source file in the target, and a
   source can have only one rule no matter how many projects it is added to.
   When the rule is run from multiple targets race conditions can occur on
```

the generated file. Eventually everything will get built, but if the user is unaware of this behavior, there may be confusion. It would be nice if this script could detect the reuse of source files across multiple targets and turn the option off for the user, but no good solution could be found.

CUDA_BUILD_CUBIN (Default OFF)
-- Set to ON to enable and extra compilation pass with the -cubin option in Device mode. The output is parsed and register, shared memory usage is printed during build.

CUDA_BUILD_EMULATION (Default OFF for device mode)
-- Set to ON for Emulation mode. -D_DEVICEEMU is defined for CUDA C files when CUDA_BUILD_EMULATION is TRUE.

CUDA_GENERATED_OUTPUT_DIR (Default CMAKE_CURRENT_BINARY_DIR)
-- Set to the path you wish to have the generated files placed. If it is blank output files will be placed in CMAKE_CURRENT_BINARY_DIR. Intermediate files will always be placed in CMAKE_CURRENT_BINARY_DIR/CMakeFiles.

CUDA_HOST_COMPILATION_CPP (Default ON)
-- Set to OFF for C compilation of host code.

CUDA_HOST_COMPILER (Default CMAKE_C_COMPILER, $(VCInstallDir)/bin for VS)
-- Set the host compiler to be used by nvcc. Ignored if -ccbin or --compiler-bindir is already present in the CUDA_NVCC_FLAGS or CUDA_NVCC_FLAGS_<CONFIG> variables. For Visual Studio targets $(VCInstallDir)/bin is a special value that expands out to the path when the command is run from withing VS.

CUDA_NVCC_FLAGS
CUDA_NVCC_FLAGS_<CONFIG>
-- Additional NVCC command line arguments. NOTE: multiple arguments must be semi-colon delimited (e.g. --compiler-options;-Wall)

CUDA_PROPAGATE_HOST_FLAGS (Default ON)
-- Set to ON to propagate CMAKE_{C,CXX}_FLAGS and their configuration dependent counterparts (e.g. CMAKE_C_FLAGS_DEBUG) automatically to the host compiler through nvcc's -Xcompiler flag. This helps make the generated host code match the rest of the system better. Sometimes certain flags give nvcc problems, and this will help you turn the flag propagation off. This does not affect the flags supplied directly to nvcc via CUDA_NVCC_FLAGS or through the OPTION flags specified through CUDA_ADD_LIBRARY, CUDA_ADD_EXECUTABLE, or CUDA_WRAP_SRCS. Flags used for shared library compilation are not affected by this flag.

CUDA_SEPARABLE_COMPILATION (Default OFF)
-- If set this will enable separable compilation for all CUDA runtime object files. If used outside of CUDA_ADD_EXECUTABLE and CUDA_ADD_LIBRARY

```
    (e.g. calling CUDA_WRAP_SRCS directly),
    CUDA_COMPUTE_SEPARABLE_COMPILATION_OBJECT_FILE_NAME and
    CUDA_LINK_SEPARABLE_COMPILATION_OBJECTS should be called.

CUDA_VERBOSE_BUILD (Default OFF)
-- Set to ON to see all the commands used when building the CUDA file.  When
   using a Makefile generator the value defaults to VERBOSE (run make
   VERBOSE=1 to see output), although setting CUDA_VERBOSE_BUILD to ON will
   always print the output.
```

The script creates the following macros (in alphebetical order):

```
CUDA_ADD_CUFFT_TO_TARGET( cuda_target )
-- Adds the cufft library to the target (can be any target).  Handles whether
   you are in emulation mode or not.

CUDA_ADD_CUBLAS_TO_TARGET( cuda_target )
-- Adds the cublas library to the target (can be any target).  Handles
   whether you are in emulation mode or not.

CUDA_ADD_EXECUTABLE( cuda_target file0 file1 ...
                     [WIN32] [MACOSX_BUNDLE] [EXCLUDE_FROM_ALL] [OPTIONS ...] )
-- Creates an executable "cuda_target" which is made up of the files
   specified.  All of the non CUDA C files are compiled using the standard
   build rules specified by CMAKE and the cuda files are compiled to object
   files using nvcc and the host compiler.  In addition CUDA_INCLUDE_DIRS is
   added automatically to include_directories().  Some standard CMake target
   calls can be used on the target after calling this macro
   (e.g. set_target_properties and target_link_libraries), but setting
   properties that adjust compilation flags will not affect code compiled by
   nvcc.  Such flags should be modified before calling CUDA_ADD_EXECUTABLE,
   CUDA_ADD_LIBRARY or CUDA_WRAP_SRCS.

CUDA_ADD_LIBRARY( cuda_target file0 file1 ...
                  [STATIC | SHARED | MODULE] [EXCLUDE_FROM_ALL] [OPTIONS ...] )
-- Same as CUDA_ADD_EXECUTABLE except that a library is created.

CUDA_BUILD_CLEAN_TARGET()
-- Creates a convience target that deletes all the dependency files
   generated.  You should make clean after running this target to ensure the
   dependency files get regenerated.

CUDA_COMPILE( generated_files file0 file1 ... [STATIC | SHARED | MODULE]
              [OPTIONS ...] )
-- Returns a list of generated files from the input source files to be used
   with ADD_LIBRARY or ADD_EXECUTABLE.

CUDA_COMPILE_PTX( generated_files file0 file1 ... [OPTIONS ...] )
-- Returns a list of PTX files generated from the input source files.
```

```
CUDA_COMPILE_FATBIN( generated_files file0 file1 ... [OPTIONS ...] )
-- Returns a list of FATBIN files generated from the input source files.

CUDA_COMPILE_CUBIN( generated_files file0 file1 ... [OPTIONS ...] )
-- Returns a list of CUBIN files generated from the input source files.

CUDA_COMPUTE_SEPARABLE_COMPILATION_OBJECT_FILE_NAME( output_file_var
                                                    cuda_target
                                                    object_files )
-- Compute the name of the intermediate link file used for separable
   compilation. This file name is typically passed into
   CUDA_LINK_SEPARABLE_COMPILATION_OBJECTS. output_file_var is produced
   based on cuda_target the list of objects files that need separable
   compilation as specified by object_files. If the object_files list is
   empty, then output_file_var will be empty. This function is called
   automatically for CUDA_ADD_LIBRARY and CUDA_ADD_EXECUTABLE. Note that
   this is a function and not a macro.

CUDA_INCLUDE_DIRECTORIES( path0 path1 ... )
-- Sets the directories that should be passed to nvcc
   (e.g. nvcc -Ipath0 -Ipath1 ... ). These paths usually contain other .cu
   files.



CUDA_LINK_SEPARABLE_COMPILATION_OBJECTS( output_file_var cuda_target
                                         nvcc_flags object_files)

-- Generates the link object required by separable compilation from the given
   object files. This is called automatically for CUDA_ADD_EXECUTABLE and
   CUDA_ADD_LIBRARY, but can be called manually when using CUDA_WRAP_SRCS
   directly. When called from CUDA_ADD_LIBRARY or CUDA_ADD_EXECUTABLE the
   nvcc_flags passed in are the same as the flags passed in via the OPTIONS
   argument. The only nvcc flag added automatically is the bitness flag as
   specified by CUDA_64_BIT_DEVICE_CODE. Note that this is a function
   instead of a macro.

CUDA_WRAP_SRCS ( cuda_target format generated_files file0 file1 ...
                 [STATIC | SHARED | MODULE] [OPTIONS ...] )
-- This is where all the magic happens. CUDA_ADD_EXECUTABLE,
   CUDA_ADD_LIBRARY, CUDA_COMPILE, and CUDA_COMPILE_PTX all call this
   function under the hood.

   Given the list of files (file0 file1 ... fileN) this macro generates
   custom commands that generate either PTX or linkable objects (use "PTX" or
   "OBJ" for the format argument to switch). Files that don't end with .cu
   or have the HEADER_FILE_ONLY property are ignored.

   The arguments passed in after OPTIONS are extra command line options to
```

give to nvcc. You can also specify per configuration options by specifying the name of the configuration followed by the options. General options must preceed configuration specific options. Not all configurations need to be specified, only the ones provided will be used.

```
OPTIONS -DFLAG=2 "-DFLAG_OTHER=space in flag"
DEBUG -g
RELEASE --use_fast_math
RELWITHDEBINFO --use_fast_math;-g
MINSIZEREL --use_fast_math
```

For certain configurations (namely VS generating object files with CUDA_ATTACH_VS_BUILD_RULE_TO_CUDA_FILE set to ON), no generated file will be produced for the given cuda file. This is because when you add the cuda file to Visual Studio it knows that this file produces an object file and will link in the resulting object file automatically.

This script will also generate a separate cmake script that is used at build time to invoke nvcc. This is for several reasons.

1. nvcc can return negative numbers as return values which confuses Visual Studio into thinking that the command succeeded. The script now checks the error codes and produces errors when there was a problem.

2. nvcc has been known to not delete incomplete results when it encounters problems. This confuses build systems into thinking the target was generated when in fact an unusable file exists. The script now deletes the output files if there was an error.

3. By putting all the options that affect the build into a file and then make the build rule dependent on the file, the output files will be regenerated when the options change.

This script also looks at optional arguments STATIC, SHARED, or MODULE to determine when to target the object compilation for a shared library. BUILD_SHARED_LIBS is ignored in CUDA_WRAP_SRCS, but it is respected in CUDA_ADD_LIBRARY. On some systems special flags are added for building objects intended for shared libraries. A preprocessor macro, <target_name>_EXPORTS is defined when a shared library compilation is detected.

Flags passed into add_definitions with -D or /D are passed along to nvcc.

The script defines the following variables:

```
CUDA_VERSION_MAJOR    -- The major version of cuda as reported by nvcc.
CUDA_VERSION_MINOR    -- The minor version.
CUDA_VERSION
CUDA_VERSION_STRING   -- CUDA_VERSION_MAJOR.CUDA_VERSION_MINOR
```

```
CUDA_TOOLKIT_ROOT_DIR -- Path to the CUDA Toolkit (defined if not set).
CUDA_SDK_ROOT_DIR     -- Path to the CUDA SDK.  Use this to find files in the
                         SDK.  This script will not directly support finding
                         specific libraries or headers, as that isn't
                         supported by NVIDIA.  If you want to change
                         libraries when the path changes see the
                         FindCUDA.cmake script for an example of how to clear
                         these variables.  There are also examples of how to
                         use the CUDA_SDK_ROOT_DIR to locate headers or
                         libraries, if you so choose (at your own risk).
CUDA_INCLUDE_DIRS     -- Include directory for cuda headers. Added automatically
                         for CUDA_ADD_EXECUTABLE and CUDA_ADD_LIBRARY.
CUDA_LIBRARIES        -- Cuda RT library.
CUDA_CUFFT_LIBRARIES  -- Device or emulation library for the Cuda FFT
                         implementation (alternative to:
                         CUDA_ADD_CUFFT_TO_TARGET macro)
CUDA_CUBLAS_LIBRARIES -- Device or emulation library for the Cuda BLAS
                         implementation (alterative to:
                         CUDA_ADD_CUBLAS_TO_TARGET macro).
CUDA_cupti_LIBRARY    -- CUDA Profiling Tools Interface library.
                         Only available for CUDA version 4.0+.
CUDA_curand_LIBRARY   -- CUDA Random Number Generation library.
                         Only available for CUDA version 3.2+.
CUDA_cusparse_LIBRARY -- CUDA Sparse Matrix library.
                         Only available for CUDA version 3.2+.
CUDA_npp_LIBRARY      -- NVIDIA Performance Primitives lib.
                         Only available for CUDA version 4.0+.
CUDA_nppc_LIBRARY     -- NVIDIA Performance Primitives lib (core).
                         Only available for CUDA version 5.5+.
CUDA_nppi_LIBRARY     -- NVIDIA Performance Primitives lib (image processing).
                         Only available for CUDA version 5.5+.
CUDA_npps_LIBRARY     -- NVIDIA Performance Primitives lib (signal processing).
                         Only available for CUDA version 5.5+.
CUDA_nvcuvenc_LIBRARY -- CUDA Video Encoder library.
                         Only available for CUDA version 3.2+.
                         Windows only.
CUDA_nvcuvid_LIBRARY  -- CUDA Video Decoder library.
                         Only available for CUDA version 3.2+.
                         Windows only.
```

FindCups

Try to find the Cups printing system

Once done this will define

```
CUPS_FOUND - system has Cups
CUPS_INCLUDE_DIR - the Cups include directory
```

```
CUPS_LIBRARIES - Libraries needed to use Cups
CUPS_VERSION_STRING - version of Cups found (since CMake 2.8.8)
Set CUPS_REQUIRE_IPP_DELETE_ATTRIBUTE to TRUE if you need a version which
features this function (i.e. at least 1.1.19)
```

FindCURL

Find curl

Find the native CURL headers and libraries.

```
CURL_INCLUDE_DIRS   - where to find curl/curl.h, etc.
CURL_LIBRARIES      - List of libraries when using curl.
CURL_FOUND          - True if curl found.
CURL_VERSION_STRING - the version of curl found (since CMake 2.8.8)
```

FindCurses

Find the curses or ncurses include file and library.

Result Variables

This module defines the following variables:

CURSES_FOUND True if Curses is found.

CURSES_INCLUDE_DIRS The include directories needed to use Curses.

CURSES_LIBRARIES The libraries needed to use Curses.

CURSES_HAVE_CURSES_H True if curses.h is available.

CURSES_HAVE_NCURSES_H True if ncurses.h is available.

CURSES_HAVE_NCURSES_NCURSES_H True if ncurses/ncurses.h is available.

CURSES_HAVE_NCURSES_CURSES_H True if ncurses/curses.h is available.

Set CURSES_NEED_NCURSES to TRUE before the find_package(Curses) call if NCurses functionality is required.

Backward Compatibility

The following variable are provided for backward compatibility:

CURSES_INCLUDE_DIR Path to Curses include. Use CURSES_INCLUDE_DIRS instead.

CURSES_LIBRARY Path to Curses library. Use CURSES_LIBRARIES instead.

FindCVS

The module defines the following variables:

```
CVS_EXECUTABLE - path to cvs command line client
CVS_FOUND - true if the command line client was found
```

Example usage:

```
find_package(CVS)
if(CVS_FOUND)
  message("CVS found: ${CVS_EXECUTABLE}")
endif()
```

FindCxxTest

Find CxxTest

Find the CxxTest suite and declare a helper macro for creating unit tests and integrating them with CTest. For more details on CxxTest see http://cxxtest.tigris.org

INPUT Variables

```
CXXTEST_USE_PYTHON [deprecated since 1.3]
    Only used in the case both Python & Perl
    are detected on the system to control
    which CxxTest code generator is used.
    Valid only for CxxTest version 3.
```

```
NOTE: In older versions of this Find Module,
this variable controlled if the Python test
generator was used instead of the Perl one,
regardless of which scripting language the
user had installed.
```

```
CXXTEST_TESTGEN_ARGS (since CMake 2.8.3)
    Specify a list of options to pass to the CxxTest code
    generator.  If not defined, --error-printer is
    passed.
```

OUTPUT Variables

```
CXXTEST_FOUND
    True if the CxxTest framework was found
CXXTEST_INCLUDE_DIRS
    Where to find the CxxTest include directory
CXXTEST_PERL_TESTGEN_EXECUTABLE
    The perl-based test generator
CXXTEST_PYTHON_TESTGEN_EXECUTABLE
    The python-based test generator
```

```
CXXTEST_TESTGEN_EXECUTABLE (since CMake 2.8.3)
    The test generator that is actually used (chosen using user preferences
    and interpreters found in the system)
CXXTEST_TESTGEN_INTERPRETER (since CMake 2.8.3)
    The full path to the Perl or Python executable on the system
```

MACROS for optional use by CMake users:

```
CXXTEST_ADD_TEST(<test_name> <gen_source_file> <input_files_to_testgen...>)
    Creates a CxxTest runner and adds it to the CTest testing suite
    Parameters:
        test_name               The name of the test
        gen_source_file         The generated source filename to be
                                generated by CxxTest
        input_files_to_testgen  The list of header files containing the
                                CxxTest::TestSuite's to be included in
                                this runner
```

```
#===============
Example Usage:
```

```
find_package(CxxTest)
if(CXXTEST_FOUND)
    include_directories(${CXXTEST_INCLUDE_DIR})
    enable_testing()
```

```
    CXXTEST_ADD_TEST(unittest_foo foo_test.cc
                     ${CMAKE_CURRENT_SOURCE_DIR}/foo_test.h)
    target_link_libraries(unittest_foo foo) # as needed
endif()
```

```
This will (if CxxTest is found):
1. Invoke the testgen executable to autogenerate foo_test.cc in the
   binary tree from "foo_test.h" in the current source directory.
2. Create an executable and test called unittest_foo.
```

```
#=============
Example foo_test.h:
```

```
#include <cxxtest/TestSuite.h>
```

```
class MyTestSuite : public CxxTest::TestSuite
{
public:
   void testAddition( void )
   {
      TS_ASSERT( 1 + 1 > 1 );
      TS_ASSERT_EQUALS( 1 + 1, 2 );
   }
};
```

FindCygwin

this module looks for Cygwin

FindDart

Find DART

This module looks for the dart testing software and sets DART_ROOT to point to where it found it.

FindDCMTK

find DCMTK libraries and applications

FindDevIL

This module locates the developer's image library. http://openil.sourceforge.net/

This module sets:

```
IL_LIBRARIES -    the name of the IL library. These include the full path to
                  the core DevIL library. This one has to be linked into the
                  application.
ILU_LIBRARIES -   the name of the ILU library. Again, the full path. This
                  library is for filters and effects, not actual loading. It
                  doesn't have to be linked if the functionality it provides
                  is not used.
ILUT_LIBRARIES -  the name of the ILUT library. Full path. This part of the
                  library interfaces with OpenGL. It is not strictly needed
                  in applications.
IL_INCLUDE_DIR -  where to find the il.h, ilu.h and ilut.h files.
IL_FOUND -        this is set to TRUE if all the above variables were set.
                  This will be set to false if ILU or ILUT are not found,
                  even if they are not needed. In most systems, if one
                  library is found all the others are as well. That's the
                  way the DevIL developers release it.
```

FindDoxygen

This module looks for Doxygen and the path to Graphviz's dot

Doxygen is a documentation generation tool. Please see http://www.doxygen.org

This module accepts the following optional variables:

```
DOXYGEN_SKIP_DOT          = If true this module will skip trying to find Dot
                            (an optional component often used by Doxygen)
```

This modules defines the following variables:

```
DOXYGEN_EXECUTABLE        = The path to the doxygen command.
DOXYGEN_FOUND             = Was Doxygen found or not?
DOXYGEN_VERSION           = The version reported by doxygen --version
```

```
DOXYGEN_DOT_EXECUTABLE = The path to the dot program used by doxygen.
DOXYGEN_DOT_FOUND      = Was Dot found or not?
```

For compatibility with older versions of CMake, the now-deprecated variable DOXYGEN_DOT_PATH is set to the path to the directory containing dot as reported in DOXYGEN_DOT_EXECUTABLE. The path may have forward slashes even on Windows and is not suitable for direct substitution into a Doxyfile.in template. If you need this value, use get_filename_component() (page 310) to compute it from DOXYGEN_DOT_EXECUTABLE directly, and perhaps the file(TO_NATIVE_PATH) (page 287) command to prepare the path for a Doxygen configuration file.

FindEXPAT

Find expat

Find the native EXPAT headers and libraries.

```
EXPAT_INCLUDE_DIRS - where to find expat.h, etc.
EXPAT_LIBRARIES    - List of libraries when using expat.
EXPAT_FOUND        - True if expat found.
```

FindFLEX

Find flex executable and provides a macro to generate custom build rules

The module defines the following variables:

```
FLEX_FOUND - true is flex executable is found
FLEX_EXECUTABLE - the path to the flex executable
FLEX_VERSION - the version of flex
FLEX_LIBRARIES - The flex libraries
FLEX_INCLUDE_DIRS - The path to the flex headers
```

The minimum required version of flex can be specified using the standard syntax, e.g. find_package(FLEX 2.5.13)

If flex is found on the system, the module provides the macro:

```
FLEX_TARGET(Name FlexInput FlexOutput [COMPILE_FLAGS <string>])
```

which creates a custom command to generate the <FlexOutput> file from the <FlexInput> file. If COM-PILE_FLAGS option is specified, the next parameter is added to the flex command line. Name is an alias used to get details of this custom command. Indeed the macro defines the following variables:

```
FLEX_${Name}_DEFINED - true is the macro ran successfully
FLEX_${Name}_OUTPUTS - the source file generated by the custom rule, an
alias for FlexOutput
FLEX_${Name}_INPUT - the flex source file, an alias for ${FlexInput}
```

Flex scanners oftenly use tokens defined by Bison: the code generated by Flex depends of the header generated by Bison. This module also defines a macro:

```
ADD_FLEX_BISON_DEPENDENCY(FlexTarget BisonTarget)
```

which adds the required dependency between a scanner and a parser where <FlexTarget> and <BisonTarget> are the first parameters of respectively FLEX_TARGET and BISON_TARGET macros.

```
===============================================================================
Example:
```

```
find_package(BISON)
find_package(FLEX)
```

```
BISON_TARGET(MyParser parser.y ${CMAKE_CURRENT_BINARY_DIR}/parser.cpp)
FLEX_TARGET(MyScanner lexer.l  ${CMAKE_CURRENT_BINARY_DIR}/lexer.cpp)
ADD_FLEX_BISON_DEPENDENCY(MyScanner MyParser)
```

```
 include_directories(${CMAKE_CURRENT_BINARY_DIR})
 add_executable(Foo
    Foo.cc
    ${BISON_MyParser_OUTPUTS}
    ${FLEX_MyScanner_OUTPUTS}
 )
===============================================================================
```

FindFLTK2

Find the native FLTK2 includes and library

The following settings are defined

```
FLTK2_FLUID_EXECUTABLE, where to find the Fluid tool
FLTK2_WRAP_UI, This enables the FLTK2_WRAP_UI command
FLTK2_INCLUDE_DIR, where to find include files
FLTK2_LIBRARIES, list of fltk2 libraries
FLTK2_FOUND, Don't use FLTK2 if false.
```

The following settings should not be used in general.

```
FLTK2_BASE_LIBRARY    = the full path to fltk2.lib
FLTK2_GL_LIBRARY      = the full path to fltk2_gl.lib
FLTK2_IMAGES_LIBRARY = the full path to fltk2_images.lib
```

FindFLTK

Find the native FLTK includes and library

By default FindFLTK.cmake will search for all of the FLTK components and add them to the FLTK_LIBRARIES variable.

```
You can limit the components which get placed in FLTK_LIBRARIES by
defining one or more of the following three options:
```

```
FLTK_SKIP_OPENGL, set to true to disable searching for opengl and
                  the FLTK GL library
FLTK_SKIP_FORMS, set to true to disable searching for fltk_forms
FLTK_SKIP_IMAGES, set to true to disable searching for fltk_images
```

```
FLTK_SKIP_FLUID, set to true if the fluid binary need not be present
                 at build time
```

The following variables will be defined:

```
FLTK_FOUND, True if all components not skipped were found
FLTK_INCLUDE_DIR, where to find include files
FLTK_LIBRARIES, list of fltk libraries you should link against
FLTK_FLUID_EXECUTABLE, where to find the Fluid tool
FLTK_WRAP_UI, This enables the FLTK_WRAP_UI command
```

The following cache variables are assigned but should not be used. See the FLTK_LIBRARIES variable instead.

```
FLTK_BASE_LIBRARY    = the full path to fltk.lib
FLTK_GL_LIBRARY      = the full path to fltk_gl.lib
FLTK_FORMS_LIBRARY   = the full path to fltk_forms.lib
FLTK_IMAGES_LIBRARY = the full path to fltk_images.lib
```

FindFreetype

Locate FreeType library

This module defines

```
FREETYPE_LIBRARIES, the library to link against
FREETYPE_FOUND, if false, do not try to link to FREETYPE
FREETYPE_INCLUDE_DIRS, where to find headers.
```

```
FREETYPE_VERSION_STRING, the version of freetype found (since CMake 2.8.8)
This is the concatenation of the paths:
FREETYPE_INCLUDE_DIR_ft2build
FREETYPE_INCLUDE_DIR_freetype2
```

$FREETYPE_DIR is an environment variable that would correspond to the ./configure – prefix=$FREETYPE_DIR used in building FREETYPE.

FindGCCXML

Find the GCC-XML front-end executable.

This module will define the following variables:

```
GCCXML - the GCC-XML front-end executable.
```

FindGDAL

Locate gdal

This module accepts the following environment variables:

```
GDAL_DIR or GDAL_ROOT - Specify the location of GDAL
```

This module defines the following CMake variables:

```
GDAL_FOUND - True if libgdal is found
GDAL_LIBRARY - A variable pointing to the GDAL library
GDAL_INCLUDE_DIR - Where to find the headers
```

FindGettext

Find GNU gettext tools

This module looks for the GNU gettext tools. This module defines the following values:

```
GETTEXT_MSGMERGE_EXECUTABLE: the full path to the msgmerge tool.
GETTEXT_MSGFMT_EXECUTABLE: the full path to the msgfmt tool.
GETTEXT_FOUND: True if gettext has been found.
GETTEXT_VERSION_STRING: the version of gettext found (since CMake 2.8.8)
```

Additionally it provides the following macros:

GETTEXT_CREATE_TRANSLATIONS (outputFile [ALL] file1 ... fileN)

```
This will create a target "translations" which will convert the
given input po files into the binary output mo file. If the
ALL option is used, the translations will also be created when
building the default target.
```

GETTEXT_PROCESS_POT_FILE(<potfile> [ALL] [INSTALL_DESTINATION <destdir>] LAN-GUAGES <lang1> <lang2> ...)

```
Process the given pot file to mo files.
If INSTALL_DESTINATION is given then automatically install rules will
be created, the language subdirectory will be taken into account
(by default use share/locale/).
If ALL is specified, the pot file is processed when building the all traget.
It creates a custom target "potfile".
```

GETTEXT_PROCESS_PO_FILES(<lang> [ALL] [INSTALL_DESTINATION <dir>] PO_FILES <po1> <po2> ...)

```
Process the given po files to mo files for the given language.
If INSTALL_DESTINATION is given then automatically install rules will
be created, the language subdirectory will be taken into account
(by default use share/locale/).
If ALL is specified, the po files are processed when building the all traget.
It creates a custom target "pofiles".
```

FindGIF

This module searches giflib and defines GIF_LIBRARIES - libraries to link to in order to use GIF GIF_FOUND, if false, do not try to link GIF_INCLUDE_DIR, where to find the headers GIF_VERSION, reports either version 4 or 3 (for everything before version 4)

The minimum required version of giflib can be specified using the standard syntax, e.g. find_package(GIF 4)

$GIF_DIR is an environment variable that would correspond to the ./configure –prefix=$GIF_DIR

FindGit

The module defines the following variables:

```
GIT_EXECUTABLE - path to git command line client
GIT_FOUND - true if the command line client was found
GIT_VERSION_STRING - the version of git found (since CMake 2.8.8)
```

Example usage:

```
find_package(Git)
if(GIT_FOUND)
```

```
  message("git found: ${GIT_EXECUTABLE}")
endif()
```

FindGLEW

Find the OpenGL Extension Wrangler Library (GLEW)

IMPORTED Targets

This module defines the IMPORTED (page 590) target GLEW::GLEW, if GLEW has been found.

Result Variables

This module defines the following variables:

```
GLEW_INCLUDE_DIRS - include directories for GLEW
GLEW_LIBRARIES - libraries to link against GLEW
GLEW_FOUND - true if GLEW has been found and can be used
```

FindGLUT

try to find glut library and include files.

IMPORTED Targets

This module defines the IMPORTED (page 590) targets:

GLUT::GLUT Defined if the system has GLUT.

Result Variables

This module sets the following variables:

```
GLUT_INCLUDE_DIR, where to find GL/glut.h, etc.
GLUT_LIBRARIES, the libraries to link against
GLUT_FOUND, If false, do not try to use GLUT.
```

Also defined, but not for general use are:

```
GLUT_glut_LIBRARY = the full path to the glut library.
GLUT_Xmu_LIBRARY  = the full path to the Xmu library.
GLUT_Xi_LIBRARY   = the full path to the Xi Library.
```

FindGnuplot

this module looks for gnuplot

Once done this will define

```
GNUPLOT_FOUND - system has Gnuplot
GNUPLOT_EXECUTABLE - the Gnuplot executable
GNUPLOT_VERSION_STRING - the version of Gnuplot found (since CMake 2.8.8)
```

GNUPLOT_VERSION_STRING will not work for old versions like 3.7.1.

FindGnuTLS

Try to find the GNU Transport Layer Security library (gnutls)

Once done this will define

```
GNUTLS_FOUND - System has gnutls
GNUTLS_INCLUDE_DIR - The gnutls include directory
GNUTLS_LIBRARIES - The libraries needed to use gnutls
GNUTLS_DEFINITIONS - Compiler switches required for using gnutls
```

FindGTest

Locate the Google C++ Testing Framework.

Defines the following variables:

```
GTEST_FOUND - Found the Google Testing framework
GTEST_INCLUDE_DIRS - Include directories
```

Also defines the library variables below as normal variables. These contain debug/optimized keywords when a debugging library is found.

```
GTEST_BOTH_LIBRARIES - Both libgtest & libgtest-main
GTEST_LIBRARIES - libgtest
GTEST_MAIN_LIBRARIES - libgtest-main
```

Accepts the following variables as input:

```
GTEST_ROOT - (as a CMake or environment variable)
             The root directory of the gtest install prefix
```

```
GTEST_MSVC_SEARCH - If compiling with MSVC, this variable can be set to
                    "MD" or "MT" to enable searching a GTest build tree
                    (defaults: "MD")
```

Example Usage:

```
enable_testing()
find_package(GTest REQUIRED)
include_directories(${GTEST_INCLUDE_DIRS})
```

```
add_executable(foo foo.cc)
target_link_libraries(foo ${GTEST_BOTH_LIBRARIES})
```

```
add_test(AllTestsInFoo foo)
```

If you would like each Google test to show up in CTest as a test you may use the following macro. NOTE: It will slow down your tests by running an executable for each test and test fixture. You will also have to rerun CMake after adding or removing tests or test fixtures.

GTEST_ADD_TESTS(executable extra_args ARGN)

```
executable = The path to the test executable
extra_args = Pass a list of extra arguments to be passed to
             executable enclosed in quotes (or "" for none)
ARGN =       A list of source files to search for tests & test
             fixtures. Or AUTO to find them from executable target.
```

```
Example:
   set(FooTestArgs --foo 1 --bar 2)
   add_executable(FooTest FooUnitTest.cc)
   GTEST_ADD_TESTS(FooTest "${FooTestArgs}" AUTO)
```

FindGTK2

FindGTK2.cmake

This module can find the GTK2 widget libraries and several of its other optional components like gtkmm, glade, and glademm.

NOTE: If you intend to use version checking, CMake 2.6.2 or later is

```
required.
```

Specify one or more of the following components as you call this find module. See example below.

```
gtk
gtkmm
glade
glademm
```

The following variables will be defined for your use

```
GTK2_FOUND - Were all of your specified components found?
GTK2_INCLUDE_DIRS - All include directories
GTK2_LIBRARIES - All libraries
GTK2_DEFINITIONS - Additional compiler flags
```

```
GTK2_VERSION - The version of GTK2 found (x.y.z)
GTK2_MAJOR_VERSION - The major version of GTK2
GTK2_MINOR_VERSION - The minor version of GTK2
GTK2_PATCH_VERSION - The patch version of GTK2
```

Optional variables you can define prior to calling this module:

```
GTK2_DEBUG - Enables verbose debugging of the module
GTK2_ADDITIONAL_SUFFIXES - Allows defining additional directories to
                           search for include files
```

================= Example Usage:

```
Call find_package() once, here are some examples to pick from:
```

```
Require GTK 2.6 or later
    find_package(GTK2 2.6 REQUIRED gtk)
```

```
Require GTK 2.10 or later and Glade
    find_package(GTK2 2.10 REQUIRED gtk glade)
```

```
Search for GTK/GTKMM 2.8 or later
    find_package(GTK2 2.8 COMPONENTS gtk gtkmm)
```

```
if(GTK2_FOUND)
    include_directories(${GTK2_INCLUDE_DIRS})
    add_executable(mygui mygui.cc)
    target_link_libraries(mygui ${GTK2_LIBRARIES})
endif()
```

FindGTK

try to find GTK (and glib) and GTKGLArea

```
GTK_INCLUDE_DIR    - Directories to include to use GTK
GTK_LIBRARIES      - Files to link against to use GTK
GTK_FOUND          - GTK was found
GTK_GL_FOUND       - GTK's GL features were found
```

FindHDF5

Find HDF5, a library for reading and writing self describing array data.

This module invokes the HDF5 wrapper compiler that should be installed alongside HDF5. Depending upon the HDF5 Configuration, the wrapper compiler is called either h5cc or h5pcc. If this succeeds, the module will then call the compiler with the -show argument to see what flags are used when compiling an HDF5 client application.

The module will optionally accept the COMPONENTS argument. If no COMPONENTS are specified, then the find module will default to finding only the HDF5 C library. If one or more COMPONENTS are specified, the module will attempt to find the language bindings for the specified components. The only valid components are C, CXX, Fortran, HL, and Fortran_HL. If the COMPONENTS argument is not given, the module will attempt to find only the C bindings.

On UNIX systems, this module will read the variable HDF5_USE_STATIC_LIBRARIES to determine whether or not to prefer a static link to a dynamic link for HDF5 and all of it's dependencies. To use this feature, make sure that the HDF5_USE_STATIC_LIBRARIES variable is set before the call to find_package.

To provide the module with a hint about where to find your HDF5 installation, you can set the environment variable HDF5_ROOT. The Find module will then look in this path when searching for HDF5 executables, paths, and libraries.

In addition to finding the includes and libraries required to compile an HDF5 client application, this module also makes an effort to find tools that come with the HDF5 distribution that may be useful for regression testing.

This module will define the following variables:

```
HDF5_INCLUDE_DIRS - Location of the hdf5 includes
HDF5_INCLUDE_DIR - Location of the hdf5 includes (deprecated)
HDF5_DEFINITIONS - Required compiler definitions for HDF5
HDF5_C_LIBRARIES - Required libraries for the HDF5 C bindings.
HDF5_CXX_LIBRARIES - Required libraries for the HDF5 C++ bindings
HDF5_Fortran_LIBRARIES - Required libraries for the HDF5 Fortran bindings
HDF5_HL_LIBRARIES - Required libraries for the HDF5 high level API
HDF5_Fortran_HL_LIBRARIES - Required libraries for the high level Fortran
                            bindings.
HDF5_LIBRARIES - Required libraries for all requested bindings
HDF5_FOUND - true if HDF5 was found on the system
HDF5_LIBRARY_DIRS - the full set of library directories
HDF5_IS_PARALLEL - Whether or not HDF5 was found with parallel IO support
HDF5_C_COMPILER_EXECUTABLE - the path to the HDF5 C wrapper compiler
HDF5_CXX_COMPILER_EXECUTABLE - the path to the HDF5 C++ wrapper compiler
HDF5_Fortran_COMPILER_EXECUTABLE - the path to the HDF5 Fortran wrapper compiler
HDF5_DIFF_EXECUTABLE - the path to the HDF5 dataset comparison tool
```

FindHg

Extract information from a mercurial working copy.

The module defines the following variables:

```
HG_EXECUTABLE - path to mercurial command line client (hg)
HG_FOUND - true if the command line client was found
HG_VERSION_STRING - the version of mercurial found
```

If the command line client executable is found the following macro is defined:

```
HG_WC_INFO(<dir> <var-prefix>)
```

Hg_WC_INFO extracts information of a mercurial working copy at a given location. This macro defines the following variables:

```
<var-prefix>_WC_CHANGESET - current changeset
<var-prefix>_WC_REVISION - current revision
```

Example usage:

```
find_package(Hg)
if(HG_FOUND)
  message("hg found: ${HG_EXECUTABLE}")
  HG_WC_INFO(${PROJECT_SOURCE_DIR} Project)
  message("Current revision is ${Project_WC_REVISION}")
  message("Current changeset is ${Project_WC_CHANGESET}")
endif()
```

FindHSPELL

Try to find Hspell

Once done this will define

```
HSPELL_FOUND - system has Hspell
HSPELL_INCLUDE_DIR - the Hspell include directory
HSPELL_LIBRARIES - The libraries needed to use Hspell
HSPELL_DEFINITIONS - Compiler switches required for using Hspell
```

```
HSPELL_VERSION_STRING - The version of Hspell found (x.y)
HSPELL_MAJOR_VERSION  - the major version of Hspell
HSPELL_MINOR_VERSION  - The minor version of Hspell
```

FindHTMLHelp

This module looks for Microsoft HTML Help Compiler

It defines:

```
HTML_HELP_COMPILER     : full path to the Compiler (hhc.exe)
HTML_HELP_INCLUDE_PATH : include path to the API (htmlhelp.h)
HTML_HELP_LIBRARY      : full path to the library (htmlhelp.lib)
```

FindIce

Find the ZeroC Internet Communication Engine (ICE) programs, libraries and datafiles.

This module supports multiple components. Components can include any of: `Freeze`, `Glacier2`, `Ice`, `IceBox`, `IceDB`, `IceGrid`, `IcePatch`, `IceSSL`, `IceStorm`, `IceUtil`, `IceXML`, or `Slice`.

This module reports information about the Ice installation in several variables. General variables:

```
Ice_VERSION - Ice release version
Ice_FOUND - true if the main programs and libraries were found
Ice_LIBRARIES - component libraries to be linked
Ice_INCLUDE_DIRS - the directories containing the Ice headers
Ice_SLICE_DIRS - the directories containing the Ice slice interface
                 definitions
```

Ice programs are reported in:

```
Ice_SLICE2CPP_EXECUTABLE - path to slice2cpp executable
Ice_SLICE2CS_EXECUTABLE - path to slice2cs executable
Ice_SLICE2FREEZEJ_EXECUTABLE - path to slice2freezej executable
Ice_SLICE2FREEZE_EXECUTABLE - path to slice2freeze executable
Ice_SLICE2HTML_EXECUTABLE - path to slice2html executable
Ice_SLICE2JAVA_EXECUTABLE - path to slice2java executable
Ice_SLICE2PHP_EXECUTABLE - path to slice2php executable
Ice_SLICE2PY_EXECUTABLE - path to slice2py executable
Ice_SLICE2RB_EXECUTABLE - path to slice2rb executable
```

Ice component libraries are reported in:

```
Ice_<C>_FOUND - ON if component was found
Ice_<C>_LIBRARIES - libraries for component
```

Note that $<C>$ is the uppercased name of the component.

This module reads hints about search results from:

```
Ice_HOME - the root of the Ice installation
```

The environment variable `ICE_HOME` may also be used; the Ice_HOME variable takes precedence.

The following cache variables may also be set:

```
Ice_<P>_EXECUTABLE - the path to executable <P>
Ice_INCLUDE_DIR - the directory containing the Ice headers
Ice_SLICE_DIR - the directory containing the Ice slice interface
                definitions
Ice_<C>_LIBRARY - the library for component <C>
```

Note: In most cases none of the above variables will require setting, unless multiple Ice versions are available and a specific version is required. On Windows, the most recent version of Ice will be found through the registry. On Unix, the programs, headers and libraries will usually be in standard locations, but Ice_SLICE_DIRS might not be automatically detected (commonly known locations are searched). All the other variables are defaulted using Ice_HOME, if set. It's possible to set Ice_HOME and selectively specify alternative locations for the other components; this might be required for e.g. newer versions of Visual Studio if the heuristics are not sufficient to identify the correct programs and libraries for the specific Visual Studio version.

Other variables one may set to control this module are:

```
Ice_DEBUG - Set to ON to enable debug output from FindIce.
```

FindIcotool

Find icotool

This module looks for icotool. This module defines the following values:

```
ICOTOOL_EXECUTABLE: the full path to the icotool tool.
ICOTOOL_FOUND: True if icotool has been found.
ICOTOOL_VERSION_STRING: the version of icotool found.
```

FindImageMagick

Find the ImageMagick binary suite.

This module will search for a set of ImageMagick tools specified as components in the FIND_PACKAGE call. Typical components include, but are not limited to (future versions of ImageMagick might have additional components not listed here):

```
animate
compare
composite
conjure
convert
display
identify
import
mogrify
montage
stream
```

If no component is specified in the FIND_PACKAGE call, then it only searches for the ImageMagick executable directory. This code defines the following variables:

```
ImageMagick_FOUND                     - TRUE if all components are found.
ImageMagick_EXECUTABLE_DIR            - Full path to executables directory.
ImageMagick_<component>_FOUND         - TRUE if <component> is found.
ImageMagick_<component>_EXECUTABLE    - Full path to <component> executable.
ImageMagick_VERSION_STRING            - the version of ImageMagick found
                                        (since CMake 2.8.8)
```

ImageMagick_VERSION_STRING will not work for old versions like 5.2.3.

There are also components for the following ImageMagick APIs:

```
Magick++
MagickWand
MagickCore
```

For these components the following variables are set:

```
ImageMagick_FOUND                       - TRUE if all components are found.
ImageMagick_INCLUDE_DIRS                - Full paths to all include dirs.
ImageMagick_LIBRARIES                   - Full paths to all libraries.
ImageMagick_<component>_FOUND           - TRUE if <component> is found.
ImageMagick_<component>_INCLUDE_DIRS    - Full path to <component> include dirs.
ImageMagick_<component>_LIBRARIES       - Full path to <component> libraries.
```

Example Usages:

```
find_package(ImageMagick)
find_package(ImageMagick COMPONENTS convert)
find_package(ImageMagick COMPONENTS convert mogrify display)
find_package(ImageMagick COMPONENTS Magick++)
find_package(ImageMagick COMPONENTS Magick++ convert)
```

Note that the standard FIND_PACKAGE features are supported (i.e., QUIET, REQUIRED, etc.).

FindITK

This module no longer exists.

This module existed in versions of CMake prior to 3.1, but became only a thin wrapper around `find_package(ITK NO_MODULE)` to provide compatibility for projects using long-outdated conventions. Now `find_package(ITK)` will search for `ITKConfig.cmake` directly.

FindJasper

Try to find the Jasper JPEG2000 library

Once done this will define

```
JASPER_FOUND - system has Jasper
JASPER_INCLUDE_DIR - the Jasper include directory
JASPER_LIBRARIES - the libraries needed to use Jasper
JASPER_VERSION_STRING - the version of Jasper found (since CMake 2.8.8)
```

FindJava

Find Java

This module finds if Java is installed and determines where the include files and libraries are. The caller may set variable JAVA_HOME to specify a Java installation prefix explicitly.

This module sets the following result variables:

```
Java_JAVA_EXECUTABLE     = the full path to the Java runtime
Java_JAVAC_EXECUTABLE    = the full path to the Java compiler
Java_JAVAH_EXECUTABLE    = the full path to the Java header generator
Java_JAVADOC_EXECUTABLE  = the full path to the Java documention generator
Java_JAR_EXECUTABLE      = the full path to the Java archiver
Java_VERSION_STRING      = Version of java found, eg. 1.6.0_12
Java_VERSION_MAJOR       = The major version of the package found.
Java_VERSION_MINOR       = The minor version of the package found.
Java_VERSION_PATCH       = The patch version of the package found.
Java_VERSION_TWEAK       = The tweak version of the package found (after '_')
Java_VERSION             = This is set to: $major.$minor.$patch(.$tweak)
```

The minimum required version of Java can be specified using the standard CMake syntax, e.g. find_package(Java 1.5)

NOTE: ${Java_VERSION} and ${Java_VERSION_STRING} are not guaranteed to be identical. For example some java version may return: Java_VERSION_STRING = 1.5.0_17 and Java_VERSION = 1.5.0.17

another example is the Java OEM, with: Java_VERSION_STRING = 1.6.0-oem and Java_VERSION = 1.6.0

For these components the following variables are set:

```
Java_FOUND                  - TRUE if all components are found.
Java_INCLUDE_DIRS           - Full paths to all include dirs.
Java_LIBRARIES              - Full paths to all libraries.
Java_<component>_FOUND      - TRUE if <component> is found.
```

Example Usages:

```
find_package(Java)
find_package(Java COMPONENTS Runtime)
find_package(Java COMPONENTS Development)
```

FindJNI

Find JNI java libraries.

This module finds if Java is installed and determines where the include files and libraries are. It also determines what the name of the library is. The caller may set variable JAVA_HOME to specify a Java installation prefix explicitly.

This module sets the following result variables:

```
JNI_INCLUDE_DIRS      = the include dirs to use
JNI_LIBRARIES         = the libraries to use
JNI_FOUND             = TRUE if JNI headers and libraries were found.
JAVA_AWT_LIBRARY      = the path to the jawt library
JAVA_JVM_LIBRARY      = the path to the jvm library
JAVA_INCLUDE_PATH     = the include path to jni.h
JAVA_INCLUDE_PATH2    = the include path to jni_md.h
JAVA_AWT_INCLUDE_PATH = the include path to jawt.h
```

FindJPEG

Find JPEG

Find the native JPEG includes and library This module defines

```
JPEG_INCLUDE_DIR, where to find jpeglib.h, etc.
JPEG_LIBRARIES, the libraries needed to use JPEG.
JPEG_FOUND, If false, do not try to use JPEG.
```

also defined, but not for general use are

```
JPEG_LIBRARY, where to find the JPEG library.
```

FindKDE3

Find the KDE3 include and library dirs, KDE preprocessors and define a some macros

This module defines the following variables:

KDE3_DEFINITIONS compiler definitions required for compiling KDE software

KDE3_INCLUDE_DIR the KDE include directory

KDE3_INCLUDE_DIRS the KDE and the Qt include directory, for use with include_directories()

KDE3_LIB_DIR the directory where the KDE libraries are installed, for use with link_directories()

QT_AND_KDECORE_LIBS this contains both the Qt and the kdecore library

KDE3_DCOPIDL_EXECUTABLE the dcopidl executable

KDE3_DCOPIDL2CPP_EXECUTABLE the dcopidl2cpp executable

KDE3_KCFGC_EXECUTABLE the kconfig_compiler executable

KDE3_FOUND set to TRUE if all of the above has been found

The following user adjustable options are provided:

KDE3_BUILD_TESTS enable this to build KDE testcases

It also adds the following macros (from KDE3Macros.cmake) SRCS_VAR is always the variable which contains the list of source files for your application or library.

KDE3_AUTOMOC(file1 ... fileN)

```
Call this if you want to have automatic moc file handling.
This means if you include "foo.moc" in the source file foo.cpp
a moc file for the header foo.h will be created automatically.
You can set the property SKIP_AUTOMAKE using set_source_files_properties()
to exclude some files in the list from being processed.
```

KDE3_ADD_MOC_FILES(SRCS_VAR file1 ... fileN)

```
If you don't use the KDE3_AUTOMOC() macro, for the files
listed here moc files will be created (named "foo.moc.cpp")
```

KDE3_ADD_DCOP_SKELS(SRCS_VAR header1.h ... headerN.h)

```
Use this to generate DCOP skeletions from the listed headers.
```

KDE3_ADD_DCOP_STUBS(SRCS_VAR header1.h ... headerN.h)

```
Use this to generate DCOP stubs from the listed headers.
```

KDE3_ADD_UI_FILES(SRCS_VAR file1.ui ... fileN.ui)

```
Use this to add the Qt designer ui files to your application/library.
```

KDE3_ADD_KCFG_FILES(SRCS_VAR file1.kcfgc ... fileN.kcfgc)

```
Use this to add KDE kconfig compiler files to your application/library.
```

KDE3_INSTALL_LIBTOOL_FILE(target)

```
This will create and install a simple libtool file for the given target.
```

KDE3_ADD_EXECUTABLE(name file1 ... fileN)

```
Currently identical to add_executable(), may provide some advanced
features in the future.
```

KDE3_ADD_KPART(name [WITH_PREFIX] file1 ... fileN)

```
Create a KDE plugin (KPart, kioslave, etc.) from the given source files.
If WITH_PREFIX is given, the resulting plugin will have the prefix "lib",
otherwise it won't.
It creates and installs an appropriate libtool la-file.
```

KDE3_ADD_KDEINIT_EXECUTABLE(name file1 ... fileN)

```
Create a KDE application in the form of a module loadable via kdeinit.
A library named kdeinit_<name> will be created and a small executable
which links to it.
```

The option KDE3_ENABLE_FINAL to enable all-in-one compilation is no longer supported.

Author: Alexander Neundorf <neundorf@kde.org[7]>

FindKDE4

Find KDE4 and provide all necessary variables and macros to compile software for it. It looks for KDE 4 in the following directories in the given order:

```
CMAKE_INSTALL_PREFIX
KDEDIRS
/opt/kde4
```

Please look in FindKDE4Internal.cmake and KDE4Macros.cmake for more information. They are installed with the KDE 4 libraries in $KDEDIRS/share/apps/cmake/modules/.

Author: Alexander Neundorf <neundorf@kde.org[8]>

FindLAPACK

Find LAPACK library

This module finds an installed fortran library that implements the LAPACK linear-algebra interface (see http://www.netlib.org/lapack/).

The approach follows that taken for the autoconf macro file, acx_lapack.m4 (distributed at http://ac-archive.sourceforge.net/ac-archive/acx_lapack.html).

This module sets the following variables:

```
LAPACK_FOUND - set to true if a library implementing the LAPACK interface
  is found
LAPACK_LINKER_FLAGS - uncached list of required linker flags (excluding -l
  and -L).
LAPACK_LIBRARIES - uncached list of libraries (using full path name) to
  link against to use LAPACK
LAPACK95_LIBRARIES - uncached list of libraries (using full path name) to
  link against to use LAPACK95
LAPACK95_FOUND - set to true if a library implementing the LAPACK f95
  interface is found
BLA_STATIC  if set on this determines what kind of linkage we do (static)
BLA_VENDOR  if set checks only the specified vendor, if not set checks
  all the possibilities
BLA_F95     if set on tries to find the f95 interfaces for BLAS/LAPACK
```

List of vendors (BLA_VENDOR) valid in this module # Intel(mkl), ACML,Apple, NAS, Generic

---

[7]neundorf@kde.org
[8]neundorf@kde.org

FindLATEX

Find Latex

This module finds if Latex is installed and determines where the executables are. This code sets the following variables:

```
LATEX_COMPILER:         path to the LaTeX compiler
PDFLATEX_COMPILER:      path to the PdfLaTeX compiler
BIBTEX_COMPILER:        path to the BibTeX compiler
MAKEINDEX_COMPILER:     path to the MakeIndex compiler
DVIPS_CONVERTER:        path to the DVIPS converter
PS2PDF_CONVERTER:       path to the PS2PDF converter
LATEX2HTML_CONVERTER:   path to the LaTeX2Html converter
```

FindLibArchive

Find libarchive library and headers

The module defines the following variables:

```
LibArchive_FOUND          - true if libarchive was found
LibArchive_INCLUDE_DIRS - include search path
LibArchive_LIBRARIES      - libraries to link
LibArchive_VERSION        - libarchive 3-component version number
```

FindLibLZMA

Find LibLZMA

Find LibLZMA headers and library

```
LIBLZMA_FOUND             - True if liblzma is found.
LIBLZMA_INCLUDE_DIRS      - Directory where liblzma headers are located.
LIBLZMA_LIBRARIES         - Lzma libraries to link against.
LIBLZMA_HAS_AUTO_DECODER  - True if lzma_auto_decoder() is found (required).
LIBLZMA_HAS_EASY_ENCODER  - True if lzma_easy_encoder() is found (required).
LIBLZMA_HAS_LZMA_PRESET   - True if lzma_lzma_preset() is found (required).
LIBLZMA_VERSION_MAJOR     - The major version of lzma
LIBLZMA_VERSION_MINOR     - The minor version of lzma
LIBLZMA_VERSION_PATCH     - The patch version of lzma
LIBLZMA_VERSION_STRING    - version number as a string (ex: "5.0.3")
```

FindLibXml2

Try to find the LibXml2 xml processing library

Once done this will define

```
LIBXML2_FOUND - System has LibXml2
LIBXML2_INCLUDE_DIR - The LibXml2 include directory
LIBXML2_LIBRARIES - The libraries needed to use LibXml2
LIBXML2_DEFINITIONS - Compiler switches required for using LibXml2
LIBXML2_XMLLINT_EXECUTABLE - The XML checking tool xmllint coming with LibXml2
LIBXML2_VERSION_STRING - the version of LibXml2 found (since CMake 2.8.8)
```

FindLibXslt

Try to find the LibXslt library

Once done this will define

```
LIBXSLT_FOUND - system has LibXslt
LIBXSLT_INCLUDE_DIR - the LibXslt include directory
LIBXSLT_LIBRARIES - Link these to LibXslt
LIBXSLT_DEFINITIONS - Compiler switches required for using LibXslt
LIBXSLT_VERSION_STRING - version of LibXslt found (since CMake 2.8.8)
```

Additionally, the following two variables are set (but not required for using xslt):

LIBXSLT_EXSLT_LIBRARIES Link to these if you need to link against the exslt library.

LIBXSLT_XSLTPROC_EXECUTABLE Contains the full path to the xsltproc executable if found.

FindLua50

Locate Lua library This module defines

```
LUA50_FOUND, if false, do not try to link to Lua
LUA_LIBRARIES, both lua and lualib
LUA_INCLUDE_DIR, where to find lua.h and lualib.h (and probably lauxlib.h)
```

Note that the expected include convention is

```
#include "lua.h"
```

and not

```
#include <lua/lua.h>
```

This is because, the lua location is not standardized and may exist in locations other than lua/

FindLua51

Locate Lua library This module defines

```
LUA51_FOUND, if false, do not try to link to Lua
LUA_LIBRARIES
LUA_INCLUDE_DIR, where to find lua.h
LUA_VERSION_STRING, the version of Lua found (since CMake 2.8.8)
```

Note that the expected include convention is

```
#include "lua.h"
```

and not

```
#include <lua/lua.h>
```

This is because, the lua location is not standardized and may exist in locations other than lua/

FindLua

Locate Lua library This module defines

```
LUA_FOUND           - if false, do not try to link to Lua
LUA_LIBRARIES       - both lua and lualib
LUA_INCLUDE_DIR     - where to find lua.h
LUA_VERSION_STRING  - the version of Lua found
LUA_VERSION_MAJOR   - the major version of Lua
LUA_VERSION_MINOR   - the minor version of Lua
LUA_VERSION_PATCH   - the patch version of Lua
```

Note that the expected include convention is

```
#include "lua.h"
```

and not

```
#include <lua/lua.h>
```

This is because, the lua location is not standardized and may exist in locations other than lua/

FindMatlab

this module looks for Matlab

Defines:

```
MATLAB_INCLUDE_DIR: include path for mex.h, engine.h
MATLAB_LIBRARIES:   required libraries: libmex, etc
MATLAB_MEX_LIBRARY: path to libmex.lib
MATLAB_MX_LIBRARY:  path to libmx.lib
MATLAB_ENG_LIBRARY: path to libeng.lib
```

FindMFC

Find MFC on Windows

Find the native MFC - i.e. decide if an application can link to the MFC libraries.

```
MFC_FOUND - Was MFC support found
```

You don't need to include anything or link anything to use it.

FindMotif

Try to find Motif (or lesstif)

Once done this will define:

```
MOTIF_FOUND          - system has MOTIF
MOTIF_INCLUDE_DIR    - include paths to use Motif
MOTIF_LIBRARIES      - Link these to use Motif
```

FindMPEG2

Find the native MPEG2 includes and library

This module defines

```
MPEG2_INCLUDE_DIR, path to mpeg2dec/mpeg2.h, etc.
MPEG2_LIBRARIES, the libraries required to use MPEG2.
MPEG2_FOUND, If false, do not try to use MPEG2.
```

also defined, but not for general use are

```
MPEG2_mpeg2_LIBRARY, where to find the MPEG2 library.
MPEG2_vo_LIBRARY, where to find the vo library.
```

FindMPEG

Find the native MPEG includes and library

This module defines

```
MPEG_INCLUDE_DIR, where to find MPEG.h, etc.
MPEG_LIBRARIES, the libraries required to use MPEG.
MPEG_FOUND, If false, do not try to use MPEG.
```

also defined, but not for general use are

```
MPEG_mpeg2_LIBRARY, where to find the MPEG library.
MPEG_vo_LIBRARY, where to find the vo library.
```

FindMPI

Find a Message Passing Interface (MPI) implementation

The Message Passing Interface (MPI) is a library used to write high-performance distributed-memory parallel applications, and is typically deployed on a cluster. MPI is a standard interface (defined by the MPI forum) for which many implementations are available. All of them have somewhat different include paths, libraries to link against, etc., and this module tries to smooth out those differences.

=== Variables ===

This module will set the following variables per language in your project, where <lang> is one of C, CXX, or Fortran:

```
MPI_<lang>_FOUND            TRUE if FindMPI found MPI flags for <lang>
MPI_<lang>_COMPILER         MPI Compiler wrapper for <lang>
MPI_<lang>_COMPILE_FLAGS    Compilation flags for MPI programs
MPI_<lang>_INCLUDE_PATH     Include path(s) for MPI header
MPI_<lang>_LINK_FLAGS       Linking flags for MPI programs
MPI_<lang>_LIBRARIES        All libraries to link MPI programs against
```

Additionally, FindMPI sets the following variables for running MPI programs from the command line:

```
MPIEXEC                     Executable for running MPI programs
MPIEXEC_NUMPROC_FLAG        Flag to pass to MPIEXEC before giving
                            it the number of processors to run on
MPIEXEC_PREFLAGS            Flags to pass to MPIEXEC directly
                            before the executable to run.
MPIEXEC_POSTFLAGS           Flags to pass to MPIEXEC after other flags
```

=== Usage ===

To use this module, simply call FindMPI from a CMakeLists.txt file, or run find_package(MPI), then run CMake. If you are happy with the auto- detected configuration for your language, then you're done. If not, you have two options:

```
1. Set MPI_<lang>_COMPILER to the MPI wrapper (mpicc, etc.) of your
   choice and reconfigure.  FindMPI will attempt to determine all the
   necessary variables using THAT compiler's compile and link flags.
2. If this fails, or if your MPI implementation does not come with
   a compiler wrapper, then set both MPI_<lang>_LIBRARIES and
   MPI_<lang>_INCLUDE_PATH.  You may also set any other variables
   listed above, but these two are required.  This will circumvent
   autodetection entirely.
```

When configuration is successful, MPI_<lang>_COMPILER will be set to the compiler wrapper for <lang>, if it was found. MPI_<lang>_FOUND and other variables above will be set if any MPI implementation was found for <lang>, regardless of whether a compiler was found.

When using MPIEXEC to execute MPI applications, you should typically use all of the MPIEXEC flags as follows:

```
${MPIEXEC} ${MPIEXEC_NUMPROC_FLAG} PROCS
  ${MPIEXEC_PREFLAGS} EXECUTABLE ${MPIEXEC_POSTFLAGS} ARGS
```

where PROCS is the number of processors on which to execute the program, EXECUTABLE is the MPI program, and ARGS are the arguments to pass to the MPI program.

=== Backward Compatibility ===

For backward compatibility with older versions of FindMPI, these variables are set, but deprecated:

```
MPI_FOUND           MPI_COMPILER        MPI_LIBRARY
MPI_COMPILE_FLAGS   MPI_INCLUDE_PATH    MPI_EXTRA_LIBRARY
MPI_LINK_FLAGS      MPI_LIBRARIES
```

In new projects, please use the MPI_<lang>_XXX equivalents.

FindOpenAL

Locate OpenAL This module defines OPENAL_LIBRARY OPENAL_FOUND, if false, do not try to link to OpenAL OPENAL_INCLUDE_DIR, where to find the headers

$OPENALDIR is an environment variable that would correspond to the ./configure –prefix=$OPENALDIR used in building OpenAL.

Created by Eric Wing. This was influenced by the FindSDL.cmake module.

FindOpenCL

Try to find OpenCL

Once done this will define:

```
OpenCL_FOUND           - True if OpenCL was found
OpenCL_INCLUDE_DIRS    - include directories for OpenCL
OpenCL_LIBRARIES       - link against this library to use OpenCL
OpenCL_VERSION_STRING  - Highest supported OpenCL version (eg. 1.2)
OpenCL_VERSION_MAJOR   - The major version of the OpenCL implementation
OpenCL_VERSION_MINOR   - The minor version of the OpenCL implementation
```

The module will also define two cache variables:

```
OpenCL_INCLUDE_DIR     - the OpenCL include directory
OpenCL_LIBRARY         - the path to the OpenCL library
```

FindOpenGL

FindModule for OpenGL and GLU.

Result Variables

This module sets the following variables:

OPENGL_FOUND True, if the system has OpenGL.

OPENGL_XMESA_FOUND True, if the system has XMESA.

OPENGL_GLU_FOUND True, if the system has GLU.

OPENGL_INCLUDE_DIR Path to the OpenGL include directory.

OPENGL_LIBRARIES Paths to the OpenGL and GLU libraries.

If you want to use just GL you can use these values:

OPENGL_gl_LIBRARY Path to the OpenGL library.

OPENGL_glu_LIBRARY Path to the GLU library.

OSX Specific

On OSX default to using the framework version of OpenGL. People will have to change the cache values of OPENGL_glu_LIBRARY and OPENGL_gl_LIBRARY to use OpenGL with X11 on OSX.

FindOpenMP

Finds OpenMP support

This module can be used to detect OpenMP support in a compiler. If the compiler supports OpenMP, the flags required to compile with OpenMP support are returned in variables for the different languages. The variables may be empty if the compiler does not need a special flag to support OpenMP.

The following variables are set:

```
OpenMP_C_FLAGS - flags to add to the C compiler for OpenMP support
OpenMP_CXX_FLAGS - flags to add to the CXX compiler for OpenMP support
OpenMP_Fortran_FLAGS - flags to add to the Fortran compiler for OpenMP support
OPENMP_FOUND - true if openmp is detected
```

Supported compilers can be found at http://openmp.org/wp/openmp-compilers/

FindOpenSceneGraph

Find OpenSceneGraph

This module searches for the OpenSceneGraph core "osg" library as well as OpenThreads, and whatever additional COMPONENTS (nodekits) that you specify.

```
See http://www.openscenegraph.org
```

NOTE: To use this module effectively you must either require CMake >= 2.6.3 with cmake_minimum_required(VERSION 2.6.3) or download and place FindOpenThreads.cmake, Find-osg_functions.cmake, Findosg.cmake, and Find<etc>.cmake files into your CMAKE_MODULE_PATH.

This module accepts the following variables (note mixed case)

```
OpenSceneGraph_DEBUG - Enable debugging output
```

```
OpenSceneGraph_MARK_AS_ADVANCED - Mark cache variables as advanced
                                  automatically
```

The following environment variables are also respected for finding the OSG and it's various components. CMAKE_PREFIX_PATH can also be used for this (see find_library() CMake documentation).

<MODULE>_DIR (where MODULE is of the form "OSGVOLUME" and there is a FindosgVolume.cmake file)

OSG_DIR

OSGDIR

OSG_ROOT

[CMake 2.8.10]: The CMake variable OSG_DIR can now be used as well to influence detection, instead of needing to specify an environment variable.

This module defines the following output variables:

```
OPENSCENEGRAPH_FOUND - Was the OSG and all of the specified components found?
```

```
OPENSCENEGRAPH_VERSION - The version of the OSG which was found
```

```
OPENSCENEGRAPH_INCLUDE_DIRS - Where to find the headers
```

```
OPENSCENEGRAPH_LIBRARIES - The OSG libraries
```

```
================================ Example Usage:
```

```
find_package(OpenSceneGraph 2.0.0 REQUIRED osgDB osgUtil)
    # libOpenThreads & libosg automatically searched
include_directories(${OPENSCENEGRAPH_INCLUDE_DIRS})
```

```
add_executable(foo foo.cc)
target_link_libraries(foo ${OPENSCENEGRAPH_LIBRARIES})
```

FindOpenSSL

Try to find the OpenSSL encryption library

Once done this will define

```
OPENSSL_ROOT_DIR - Set this variable to the root installation of OpenSSL
```

Read-Only variables:

```
OPENSSL_FOUND - system has the OpenSSL library
OPENSSL_INCLUDE_DIR - the OpenSSL include directory
OPENSSL_LIBRARIES - The libraries needed to use OpenSSL
OPENSSL_VERSION - This is set to $major.$minor.$revision$path (eg. 0.9.8s)
```

FindOpenThreads

OpenThreads is a C++ based threading library. Its largest userbase seems to OpenSceneGraph so you might notice I accept OSGDIR as an environment path. I consider this part of the Findosg* suite used to find OpenSceneGraph components. Each component is separate and you must opt in to each module.

Locate OpenThreads This module defines OPENTHREADS_LIBRARY OPENTHREADS_FOUND, if false, do not try to link to OpenThreads OPENTHREADS_INCLUDE_DIR, where to find the headers

$OPENTHREADS_DIR is an environment variable that would correspond to the ./configure – prefix=$OPENTHREADS_DIR used in building osg.

[CMake 2.8.10]: The CMake variables OPENTHREADS_DIR or OSG_DIR can now be used as well to influence detection, instead of needing to specify an environment variable.

Created by Eric Wing.

FindosgAnimation

This is part of the Findosg* suite used to find OpenSceneGraph components. Each component is separate and you must opt in to each module. You must also opt into OpenGL and OpenThreads (and Producer if needed) as these modules won't do it for you. This is to allow you control over your own system piece by piece in case you need to opt out of certain components or change the Find behavior for a particular module (perhaps because the default FindOpenGL.cmake module doesn't work with your system as an example). If you want to use a more convenient module that includes everything, use the FindOpenSceneGraph.cmake instead of the Findosg*.cmake modules.

Locate osgAnimation This module defines

OSGANIMATION_FOUND - Was osgAnimation found? OSGANIMATION_INCLUDE_DIR - Where to find the headers OSGANIMATION_LIBRARIES - The libraries to link against for the OSG (use this)

OSGANIMATION_LIBRARY - The OSG library OSGANIMATION_LIBRARY_DEBUG - The OSG debug library

$OSGDIR is an environment variable that would correspond to the ./configure –prefix=$OSGDIR used in building osg.

Created by Eric Wing.

FindosgDB

This is part of the Findosg* suite used to find OpenSceneGraph components. Each component is separate and you must opt in to each module. You must also opt into OpenGL and OpenThreads (and Producer if needed) as these modules won't do it for you. This is to allow you control over your own system piece by piece in case you need to opt out of certain components or change the Find behavior for a particular module (perhaps because the default FindOpenGL.cmake module doesn't work with your system as an example). If you want to use a more convenient module that includes everything, use the FindOpenSceneGraph.cmake instead of the Findosg*.cmake modules.

Locate osgDB This module defines

OSGDB_FOUND - Was osgDB found? OSGDB_INCLUDE_DIR - Where to find the headers OS-GDB_LIBRARIES - The libraries to link against for the osgDB (use this)

OSGDB_LIBRARY - The osgDB library OSGDB_LIBRARY_DEBUG - The osgDB debug library

$OSGDIR is an environment variable that would correspond to the ./configure –prefix=$OSGDIR used in building osg.

Created by Eric Wing.

Findosg_functions

This CMake file contains two macros to assist with searching for OSG libraries and nodekits. Please see FindOpenSceneGraph.cmake for full documentation.

FindosgFX

This is part of the Findosg* suite used to find OpenSceneGraph components. Each component is separate and you must opt in to each module. You must also opt into OpenGL and OpenThreads (and Producer if needed) as these modules won't do it for you. This is to allow you control over your own system piece by piece in case you need to opt out of certain components or change the Find behavior for a particular module (perhaps because the default FindOpenGL.cmake module doesn't work with your system as an example). If you want to use a more convenient module that includes everything, use the FindOpenSceneGraph.cmake instead of the Findosg*.cmake modules.

Locate osgFX This module defines

OSGFX_FOUND - Was osgFX found?   OSGFX_INCLUDE_DIR - Where to find the headers OS-GFX_LIBRARIES - The libraries to link against for the osgFX (use this)

OSGFX_LIBRARY - The osgFX library OSGFX_LIBRARY_DEBUG - The osgFX debug library

$OSGDIR is an environment variable that would correspond to the ./configure –prefix=$OSGDIR used in building osg.

Created by Eric Wing.

FindosgGA

This is part of the Findosg* suite used to find OpenSceneGraph components. Each component is separate and you must opt in to each module. You must also opt into OpenGL and OpenThreads (and Producer if needed) as these modules won't do it for you. This is to allow you control over your own system piece by piece in case you need to opt out of certain components or change the Find behavior for a particular module (perhaps because the default FindOpenGL.cmake module doesn't work with your system as an example). If you want to use a more convenient module that includes everything, use the FindOpenSceneGraph.cmake instead of the Findosg*.cmake modules.

Locate osgGA This module defines

OSGGA_FOUND - Was osgGA found?   OSGGA_INCLUDE_DIR - Where to find the headers OSGGA_LIBRARIES - The libraries to link against for the osgGA (use this)

OSGGA_LIBRARY - The osgGA library OSGGA_LIBRARY_DEBUG - The osgGA debug library

$OSGDIR is an environment variable that would correspond to the ./configure –prefix=$OSGDIR used in building osg.

Created by Eric Wing.

FindosgIntrospection

This is part of the Findosg* suite used to find OpenSceneGraph components. Each component is separate and you must opt in to each module. You must also opt into OpenGL and OpenThreads (and Producer if needed) as these modules won't do it for you. This is to allow you control over your own system piece by piece in case you need to opt out of certain components or change the Find behavior for a particular module (perhaps because the default FindOpenGL.cmake module doesn't work with your system as an example). If you want to use a more convenient module that includes everything, use the FindOpenSceneGraph.cmake instead of the Findosg*.cmake modules.

Locate osgINTROSPECTION This module defines

OSGINTROSPECTION_FOUND - Was osgIntrospection found? OSGINTROSPECTION_INCLUDE_DIR - Where to find the headers OSGINTROSPECTION_LIBRARIES - The libraries to link for osgIntrospection (use this)

OSGINTROSPECTION_LIBRARY - The osgIntrospection library OSGINTROSPEC-TION_LIBRARY_DEBUG - The osgIntrospection debug library

$OSGDIR is an environment variable that would correspond to the ./configure –prefix=$OSGDIR used in building osg.

Created by Eric Wing.

FindosgManipulator

This is part of the Findosg* suite used to find OpenSceneGraph components. Each component is separate and you must opt in to each module. You must also opt into OpenGL and OpenThreads (and Producer if needed) as these modules won't do it for you. This is to allow you control over your own system piece by piece in case you need to opt out of certain components or change the Find behavior for a particular module (perhaps because the default FindOpenGL.cmake module doesn't work with your system as an example). If you want to use a more convenient module that includes everything, use the FindOpenSceneGraph.cmake instead of the Findosg*.cmake modules.

Locate osgManipulator This module defines

OSGMANIPULATOR_FOUND - Was osgManipulator found? OSGMANIPULATOR_INCLUDE_DIR - Where to find the headers OSGMANIPULATOR_LIBRARIES - The libraries to link for osgManipulator (use this)

OSGMANIPULATOR_LIBRARY - The osgManipulator library OSGMANIPULA-TOR_LIBRARY_DEBUG - The osgManipulator debug library

$OSGDIR is an environment variable that would correspond to the ./configure –prefix=$OSGDIR used in building osg.

Created by Eric Wing.

FindosgParticle

This is part of the Findosg* suite used to find OpenSceneGraph components. Each component is separate and you must opt in to each module. You must also opt into OpenGL and OpenThreads (and Producer if needed) as these modules won't do it for you. This is to allow you control over your own system piece by piece in case you need to opt out of certain components or change the Find behavior for a particular module (perhaps because the default FindOpenGL.cmake module doesn't work with your system as an example). If you want to use a more convenient module that includes everything, use the FindOpenSceneGraph.cmake instead of the Findosg*.cmake modules.

Locate osgParticle This module defines

OSGPARTICLE_FOUND - Was osgParticle found? OSGPARTICLE_INCLUDE_DIR - Where to find the headers OSGPARTICLE_LIBRARIES - The libraries to link for osgParticle (use this)

OSGPARTICLE_LIBRARY - The osgParticle library OSGPARTICLE_LIBRARY_DEBUG - The osgParticle debug library

$OSGDIR is an environment variable that would correspond to the ./configure –prefix=$OSGDIR used in building osg.

Created by Eric Wing.

FindosgPresentation

This is part of the Findosg* suite used to find OpenSceneGraph components. Each component is separate and you must opt in to each module. You must also opt into OpenGL and OpenThreads (and Producer if needed) as these modules won't do it for you. This is to allow you control over your own system piece by piece in case you need to opt out of certain components or change the Find behavior for a particular module (perhaps because the default FindOpenGL.cmake module doesn't work with your system as an example). If you want to use a more convenient module that includes everything, use the FindOpenSceneGraph.cmake instead of the Findosg*.cmake modules.

Locate osgPresentation This module defines

OSGPRESENTATION_FOUND - Was osgPresentation found? OSGPRESENTATION_INCLUDE_DIR - Where to find the headers OSGPRESENTATION_LIBRARIES - The libraries to link for osgPresentation (use this)

OSGPRESENTATION_LIBRARY - The osgPresentation library OSGPRESENTA-TION_LIBRARY_DEBUG - The osgPresentation debug library

$OSGDIR is an environment variable that would correspond to the ./configure –prefix=$OSGDIR used in building osg.

Created by Eric Wing. Modified to work with osgPresentation by Robert Osfield, January 2012.

FindosgProducer

This is part of the Findosg* suite used to find OpenSceneGraph components. Each component is separate and you must opt in to each module. You must also opt into OpenGL and OpenThreads (and Producer if needed) as these modules won't do it for you. This is to allow you control over your own system piece by piece in case you need to opt out of certain components or change the Find behavior for a particular module (perhaps because the default FindOpenGL.cmake module doesn't work with your system as an example). If you want to use a more convenient module that includes everything, use the FindOpenSceneGraph.cmake instead of the Findosg*.cmake modules.

Locate osgProducer This module defines

OSGPRODUCER_FOUND - Was osgProducer found? OSGPRODUCER_INCLUDE_DIR - Where to find the headers OSGPRODUCER_LIBRARIES - The libraries to link for osgProducer (use this)

OSGPRODUCER_LIBRARY - The osgProducer library OSGPRODUCER_LIBRARY_DEBUG - The osg-Producer debug library

$OSGDIR is an environment variable that would correspond to the ./configure –prefix=$OSGDIR used in building osg.

Created by Eric Wing.

FindosgQt

This is part of the Findosg* suite used to find OpenSceneGraph components. Each component is separate and you must opt in to each module. You must also opt into OpenGL and OpenThreads (and Producer if needed) as these modules won't do it for you. This is to allow you control over your own system piece by piece in case you need to opt out of certain components or change the Find behavior for a particular module (perhaps because the default FindOpenGL.cmake module doesn't work with your system as an example). If you want to use a more convenient module that includes everything, use the FindOpenSceneGraph.cmake instead of the Findosg*.cmake modules.

Locate osgQt This module defines

OSGQT_FOUND - Was osgQt found? OSGQT_INCLUDE_DIR - Where to find the headers OS-GQT_LIBRARIES - The libraries to link for osgQt (use this)

OSGQT_LIBRARY - The osgQt library OSGQT_LIBRARY_DEBUG - The osgQt debug library

$OSGDIR is an environment variable that would correspond to the ./configure –prefix=$OSGDIR used in building osg.

Created by Eric Wing. Modified to work with osgQt by Robert Osfield, January 2012.

Findosg

NOTE: It is highly recommended that you use the new FindOpenSceneGraph.cmake introduced in CMake 2.6.3 and not use this Find module directly.

This is part of the Findosg* suite used to find OpenSceneGraph components. Each component is separate and you must opt in to each module. You must also opt into OpenGL and OpenThreads (and Producer if needed) as these modules won't do it for you. This is to allow you control over your own system piece by piece in case you need to opt out of certain components or change the Find behavior for a particular module (perhaps because the default FindOpenGL.cmake module doesn't work with your system as an example). If you want to use a more convenient module that includes everything, use the FindOpenSceneGraph.cmake instead of the Findosg*.cmake modules.

Locate osg This module defines

OSG_FOUND - Was the Osg found? OSG_INCLUDE_DIR - Where to find the headers OSG_LIBRARIES - The libraries to link against for the OSG (use this)

OSG_LIBRARY - The OSG library OSG_LIBRARY_DEBUG - The OSG debug library

$OSGDIR is an environment variable that would correspond to the ./configure –prefix=$OSGDIR used in building osg.

Created by Eric Wing.

FindosgShadow

This is part of the Findosg* suite used to find OpenSceneGraph components. Each component is separate and you must opt in to each module. You must also opt into OpenGL and OpenThreads (and Producer if needed) as these modules won't do it for you. This is to allow you control over your own system piece by piece in case you need to opt out of certain components or change the Find behavior for a particular module (perhaps because the default FindOpenGL.cmake module doesn't work with your system as an example). If you want to use a more convenient module that includes everything, use the FindOpenSceneGraph.cmake instead of the Findosg*.cmake modules.

Locate osgShadow This module defines

OSGSHADOW_FOUND - Was osgShadow found? OSGSHADOW_INCLUDE_DIR - Where to find the headers OSGSHADOW_LIBRARIES - The libraries to link for osgShadow (use this)

OSGSHADOW_LIBRARY - The osgShadow library OSGSHADOW_LIBRARY_DEBUG - The osgShadow debug library

$OSGDIR is an environment variable that would correspond to the ./configure –prefix=$OSGDIR used in building osg.

Created by Eric Wing.

FindosgSim

This is part of the Findosg* suite used to find OpenSceneGraph components. Each component is separate and you must opt in to each module. You must also opt into OpenGL and OpenThreads (and Producer if needed) as these modules won't do it for you. This is to allow you control over your own system piece by piece in case you need to opt out of certain components or change the Find behavior for a particular module (perhaps because the default FindOpenGL.cmake module doesn't work with your system as an example). If you want to use a more convenient module that includes everything, use the FindOpenSceneGraph.cmake instead of the Findosg*.cmake modules.

Locate osgSim This module defines

OSGSIM_FOUND - Was osgSim found? OSGSIM_INCLUDE_DIR - Where to find the headers OSGSIM_LIBRARIES - The libraries to link for osgSim (use this)

OSGSIM_LIBRARY - The osgSim library OSGSIM_LIBRARY_DEBUG - The osgSim debug library

$OSGDIR is an environment variable that would correspond to the ./configure –prefix=$OSGDIR used in building osg.

Created by Eric Wing.

FindosgTerrain

This is part of the Findosg* suite used to find OpenSceneGraph components. Each component is separate and you must opt in to each module. You must also opt into OpenGL and OpenThreads (and Producer if needed)

as these modules won't do it for you. This is to allow you control over your own system piece by piece in case you need to opt out of certain components or change the Find behavior for a particular module (perhaps because the default FindOpenGL.cmake module doesn't work with your system as an example). If you want to use a more convenient module that includes everything, use the FindOpenSceneGraph.cmake instead of the Findosg*.cmake modules.

Locate osgTerrain This module defines

OSGTERRAIN_FOUND - Was osgTerrain found? OSGTERRAIN_INCLUDE_DIR - Where to find the headers OSGTERRAIN_LIBRARIES - The libraries to link for osgTerrain (use this)

OSGTERRAIN_LIBRARY - The osgTerrain library OSGTERRAIN_LIBRARY_DEBUG - The osgTerrain debug library

$OSGDIR is an environment variable that would correspond to the ./configure –prefix=$OSGDIR used in building osg.

Created by Eric Wing.

FindosgText

This is part of the Findosg* suite used to find OpenSceneGraph components. Each component is separate and you must opt in to each module. You must also opt into OpenGL and OpenThreads (and Producer if needed) as these modules won't do it for you. This is to allow you control over your own system piece by piece in case you need to opt out of certain components or change the Find behavior for a particular module (perhaps because the default FindOpenGL.cmake module doesn't work with your system as an example). If you want to use a more convenient module that includes everything, use the FindOpenSceneGraph.cmake instead of the Findosg*.cmake modules.

Locate osgText This module defines

OSGTEXT_FOUND - Was osgText found? OSGTEXT_INCLUDE_DIR - Where to find the headers OSG-TEXT_LIBRARIES - The libraries to link for osgText (use this)

OSGTEXT_LIBRARY - The osgText library OSGTEXT_LIBRARY_DEBUG - The osgText debug library

$OSGDIR is an environment variable that would correspond to the ./configure –prefix=$OSGDIR used in building osg.

Created by Eric Wing.

FindosgUtil

This is part of the Findosg* suite used to find OpenSceneGraph components. Each component is separate and you must opt in to each module. You must also opt into OpenGL and OpenThreads (and Producer if needed) as these modules won't do it for you. This is to allow you control over your own system piece by piece in case you need to opt out of certain components or change the Find behavior for a particular module (perhaps because the default FindOpenGL.cmake module doesn't work with your system as an example). If you want to use a more convenient module that includes everything, use the FindOpenSceneGraph.cmake instead of the Findosg*.cmake modules.

Locate osgUtil This module defines

OSGUTIL_FOUND - Was osgUtil found? OSGUTIL_INCLUDE_DIR - Where to find the headers OSGUTIL_LIBRARIES - The libraries to link for osgUtil (use this)

OSGUTIL_LIBRARY - The osgUtil library OSGUTIL_LIBRARY_DEBUG - The osgUtil debug library

$OSGDIR is an environment variable that would correspond to the ./configure –prefix=$OSGDIR used in building osg.

Created by Eric Wing.

FindosgViewer

This is part of the Findosg* suite used to find OpenSceneGraph components. Each component is separate and you must opt in to each module. You must also opt into OpenGL and OpenThreads (and Producer if needed) as these modules won't do it for you. This is to allow you control over your own system piece by piece in case you need to opt out of certain components or change the Find behavior for a particular module (perhaps because the default FindOpenGL.cmake module doesn't work with your system as an example). If you want to use a more convenient module that includes everything, use the FindOpenSceneGraph.cmake instead of the Findosg*.cmake modules.

Locate osgViewer This module defines

OSGVIEWER_FOUND - Was osgViewer found? OSGVIEWER_INCLUDE_DIR - Where to find the headers OSGVIEWER_LIBRARIES - The libraries to link for osgViewer (use this)

OSGVIEWER_LIBRARY - The osgViewer library OSGVIEWER_LIBRARY_DEBUG - The osgViewer debug library

$OSGDIR is an environment variable that would correspond to the ./configure –prefix=$OSGDIR used in building osg.

Created by Eric Wing.

FindosgVolume

This is part of the Findosg* suite used to find OpenSceneGraph components. Each component is separate and you must opt in to each module. You must also opt into OpenGL and OpenThreads (and Producer if needed) as these modules won't do it for you. This is to allow you control over your own system piece by piece in case you need to opt out of certain components or change the Find behavior for a particular module (perhaps because the default FindOpenGL.cmake module doesn't work with your system as an example). If you want to use a more convenient module that includes everything, use the FindOpenSceneGraph.cmake instead of the Findosg*.cmake modules.

Locate osgVolume This module defines

OSGVOLUME_FOUND - Was osgVolume found? OSGVOLUME_INCLUDE_DIR - Where to find the headers OSGVOLUME_LIBRARIES - The libraries to link for osgVolume (use this)

OSGVOLUME_LIBRARY - The osgVolume library OSGVOLUME_LIBRARY_DEBUG - The osgVolume debug library

$OSGDIR is an environment variable that would correspond to the ./configure –prefix=$OSGDIR used in building osg.

Created by Eric Wing.

FindosgWidget

This is part of the Findosg* suite used to find OpenSceneGraph components. Each component is separate and you must opt in to each module. You must also opt into OpenGL and OpenThreads (and Producer if needed) as these modules won't do it for you. This is to allow you control over your own system piece by piece in case you need to opt out of certain components or change the Find behavior for a particular module (perhaps because the default FindOpenGL.cmake module doesn't work with your system as an example). If you want to use a more convenient module that includes everything, use the FindOpenSceneGraph.cmake instead of the Findosg*.cmake modules.

Locate osgWidget This module defines

OSGWIDGET_FOUND - Was osgWidget found? OSGWIDGET_INCLUDE_DIR - Where to find the headers OSGWIDGET_LIBRARIES - The libraries to link for osgWidget (use this)

OSGWIDGET_LIBRARY - The osgWidget library OSGWIDGET_LIBRARY_DEBUG - The osgWidget debug library

$OSGDIR is an environment variable that would correspond to the ./configure –prefix=$OSGDIR used in building osg.

FindosgWidget.cmake tweaked from Findosg* suite as created by Eric Wing.

FindPackageHandleStandardArgs

FIND_PACKAGE_HANDLE_STANDARD_ARGS(<name> ...)

This function is intended to be used in FindXXX.cmake modules files. It handles the REQUIRED, QUIET and version-related arguments to find_package(). It also sets the <packagename>_FOUND variable. The package is considered found if all variables <var1>... listed contain valid results, e.g. valid filepaths.

There are two modes of this function. The first argument in both modes is the name of the Find-module where it is called (in original casing).

The first simple mode looks like this:

```
FIND_PACKAGE_HANDLE_STANDARD_ARGS(<name>
  (DEFAULT_MSG|"Custom failure message") <var1>...<varN> )
```

If the variables <var1> to <varN> are all valid, then <UPPERCASED_NAME>_FOUND will be set to TRUE. If DEFAULT_MSG is given as second argument, then the function will generate itself useful success and error messages. You can also supply a custom error message for the failure case. This is not recommended.

The second mode is more powerful and also supports version checking:

```
FIND_PACKAGE_HANDLE_STANDARD_ARGS(NAME
  [FOUND_VAR <resultVar>]
  [REQUIRED_VARS <var1>...<varN>]
  [VERSION_VAR   <versionvar>]
  [HANDLE_COMPONENTS]
  [CONFIG_MODE]
  [FAIL_MESSAGE "Custom failure message"] )
```

In this mode, the name of the result-variable can be set either to either <UPPERCASED_NAME>_FOUND or <OriginalCase_Name>_FOUND using the FOUND_VAR option. Other names for the result-variable are not allowed. So for a Find-module named FindFooBar.cmake, the two possible names are FooBar_FOUND and FOOBAR_FOUND. It is recommended to use the original case version. If the FOUND_VAR option is not used, the default is <UPPERCASED_NAME>_FOUND.

As in the simple mode, if <var1> through <varN> are all valid, <packagename>_FOUND will be set to TRUE. After REQUIRED_VARS the variables which are required for this package are listed. Following VERSION_VAR the name of the variable can be specified which holds the version of the package which has been found. If this is done, this version will be checked against the (potentially) specified required version used in the find_package() call. The EXACT keyword is also handled. The default messages include information about the required version and the version which has been actually found, both if the version is ok or not. If the package supports components, use the HANDLE_COMPONENTS option to enable handling them. In this case, find_package_handle_standard_args() will report which components have been found and which are missing, and the <packagename>_FOUND variable will be set to FALSE if any of the required components (i.e. not the ones listed after OPTIONAL_COMPONENTS) are missing. Use the option CONFIG_MODE if your FindXXX.cmake module is a wrapper for a find_package(... NO_MODULE) call. In this case VERSION_VAR will be set to <NAME>_VERSION and the macro will automatically check whether the Config module was found. Via FAIL_MESSAGE a custom failure message can be specified, if this is not used, the default message will be displayed.

Example for mode 1:

```
find_package_handle_standard_args(LibXml2   DEFAULT_MSG
  LIBXML2_LIBRARY LIBXML2_INCLUDE_DIR)
```

LibXml2 is considered to be found, if both LIBXML2_LIBRARY and LIBXML2_INCLUDE_DIR are valid. Then also LIBXML2_FOUND is set to TRUE. If it is not found and REQUIRED was used, it fails with FATAL_ERROR, independent whether QUIET was used or not. If it is found, success will be reported, including the content of <var1>. On repeated Cmake runs, the same message won't be printed again.

Example for mode 2:

```
find_package_handle_standard_args(LibXslt
  FOUND_VAR LibXslt_FOUND
```

```
REQUIRED_VARS LibXslt_LIBRARIES LibXslt_INCLUDE_DIRS
VERSION_VAR LibXslt_VERSION_STRING)
```

In this case, LibXslt is considered to be found if the variable(s) listed after REQUIRED_VAR are all valid, i.e. LibXslt_LIBRARIES and LibXslt_INCLUDE_DIRS in this case. The result will then be stored in LibXslt_FOUND . Also the version of LibXslt will be checked by using the version contained in LibXslt_VERSION_STRING. Since no FAIL_MESSAGE is given, the default messages will be printed.

Another example for mode 2:

```
find_package(Automoc4 QUIET NO_MODULE HINTS /opt/automoc4)
find_package_handle_standard_args(Automoc4  CONFIG_MODE)
```

In this case, FindAutmoc4.cmake wraps a call to find_package(Automoc4 NO_MODULE) and adds an additional search directory for automoc4. Here the result will be stored in AUTOMOC4_FOUND. The following FIND_PACKAGE_HANDLE_STANDARD_ARGS() call produces a proper success/error message.

FindPackageMessage

FIND_PACKAGE_MESSAGE(<name> "message for user" "find result details")

This macro is intended to be used in FindXXX.cmake modules files. It will print a message once for each unique find result. This is useful for telling the user where a package was found. The first argument specifies the name (XXX) of the package. The second argument specifies the message to display. The third argument lists details about the find result so that if they change the message will be displayed again. The macro also obeys the QUIET argument to the find_package command.

Example:

```
if(X11_FOUND)
  FIND_PACKAGE_MESSAGE(X11 "Found X11: ${X11_X11_LIB}"
    "[${X11_X11_LIB}][${X11_INCLUDE_DIR}]")
else()
  ...
endif()
```

FindPerlLibs

Find Perl libraries

This module finds if PERL is installed and determines where the include files and libraries are. It also determines what the name of the library is. This code sets the following variables:

```
PERLLIBS_FOUND      = True if perl.h & libperl were found
PERL_INCLUDE_PATH  = path to where perl.h is found
PERL_LIBRARY        = path to libperl
PERL_EXECUTABLE    = full path to the perl binary
```

The minimum required version of Perl can be specified using the standard syntax, e.g. find_package(PerlLibs 6.0)

```
The following variables are also available if needed
(introduced after CMake 2.6.4)
```

```
PERL_SITESEARCH     = path to the sitesearch install dir
PERL_SITELIB        = path to the sitelib install directory
PERL_VENDORARCH     = path to the vendor arch install directory
PERL_VENDORLIB      = path to the vendor lib install directory
PERL_ARCHLIB        = path to the arch lib install directory
PERL_PRIVLIB        = path to the priv lib install directory
PERL_EXTRA_C_FLAGS  = Compilation flags used to build perl
```

FindPerl

Find perl

this module looks for Perl

```
PERL_EXECUTABLE       - the full path to perl
PERL_FOUND            - If false, don't attempt to use perl.
PERL_VERSION_STRING   - version of perl found (since CMake 2.8.8)
```

FindPHP4

Find PHP4

This module finds if PHP4 is installed and determines where the include files and libraries are. It also determines what the name of the library is. This code sets the following variables:

```
PHP4_INCLUDE_PATH     = path to where php.h can be found
PHP4_EXECUTABLE       = full path to the php4 binary
```

FindPhysFS

Locate PhysFS library This module defines PHYSFS_LIBRARY, the name of the library to link against PHYSFS_FOUND, if false, do not try to link to PHYSFS PHYSFS_INCLUDE_DIR, where to find physfs.h

$PHYSFSDIR is an environment variable that would correspond to the ./configure –prefix=$PHYSFSDIR used in building PHYSFS.

Created by Eric Wing.

FindPike

Find Pike

This module finds if PIKE is installed and determines where the include files and libraries are. It also determines what the name of the library is. This code sets the following variables:

```
PIKE_INCLUDE_PATH       = path to where program.h is found
PIKE_EXECUTABLE         = full path to the pike binary
```

FindPkgConfig

A *pkg-config* module for CMake.

Finds the `pkg-config` executable and add the `pkg_check_modules()` (page 489) and `pkg_search_module()` (page 490) commands.

In order to find the `pkg-config` executable, it uses the `PKG_CONFIG_EXECUTABLE` (page 491) variable or the `PKG_CONFIG` environment variable first.

pkg_check_modules

Checks for all the given modules.

```
pkg_check_modules(<PREFIX> [REQUIRED] [QUIET]
                  [NO_CMAKE_PATH] [NO_CMAKE_ENVIRONMENT_PATH]
                  <MODULE> [<MODULE>]*)
```

When the `REQUIRED` argument was set, macros will fail with an error when module(s) could not be found.

When the `QUIET` argument is set, no status messages will be printed.

By default, if `CMAKE_MINIMUM_REQUIRED_VERSION` (page 630) is 3.1 or later, or if `PKG_CONFIG_USE_CMAKE_PREFIX_PATH` (page 491) is set, the `CMAKE_PREFIX_PATH` (page 647), `CMAKE_FRAMEWORK_PATH` (page 644), and `CMAKE_APPBUNDLE_PATH` (page 639) cache and environment variables will be added to `pkg-config` search path. The `NO_CMAKE_PATH` and `NO_CMAKE_ENVIRONMENT_PATH` arguments disable this behavior for the cache variables and the environment variables, respectively.

It sets the following variables:

```
PKG_CONFIG_FOUND          ... if pkg-config executable was found
PKG_CONFIG_EXECUTABLE     ... pathname of the pkg-config program
PKG_CONFIG_VERSION_STRING ... the version of the pkg-config program found
                              (since CMake 2.8.8)
```

For the following variables two sets of values exist; first one is the common one and has the given PREFIX. The second set contains flags which are given out when `pkg-config` was called with the `--static` option.

```
<XPREFIX>_FOUND          ... set to 1 if module(s) exist
<XPREFIX>_LIBRARIES      ... only the libraries (w/o the '-l')
<XPREFIX>_LIBRARY_DIRS   ... the paths of the libraries (w/o the '-L')
<XPREFIX>_LDFLAGS        ... all required linker flags
<XPREFIX>_LDFLAGS_OTHER  ... all other linker flags
<XPREFIX>_INCLUDE_DIRS   ... the '-I' preprocessor flags (w/o the '-I')
<XPREFIX>_CFLAGS         ... all required cflags
<XPREFIX>_CFLAGS_OTHER   ... the other compiler flags
```

```
<XPREFIX> = <PREFIX>        for common case
<XPREFIX> = <PREFIX>_STATIC for static linking
```

There are some special variables whose prefix depends on the count of given modules. When there is only one module, <PREFIX> stays unchanged. When there are multiple modules, the prefix will be changed to <PREFIX>_<MODNAME>:

```
<XPREFIX>_VERSION    ... version of the module
<XPREFIX>_PREFIX     ... prefix-directory of the module
<XPREFIX>_INCLUDEDIR ... include-dir of the module
<XPREFIX>_LIBDIR     ... lib-dir of the module
```

```
<XPREFIX> = <PREFIX>  when |MODULES| == 1, else
<XPREFIX> = <PREFIX>_<MODNAME>
```

A <MODULE> parameter can have the following formats:

```
{MODNAME}              ... matches any version
{MODNAME}>={VERSION} ... at least version <VERSION> is required
{MODNAME}={VERSION}  ... exactly version <VERSION> is required
{MODNAME}<={VERSION} ... modules must not be newer than <VERSION>
```

Examples

```
pkg_check_modules (GLIB2   glib-2.0)
```

```
pkg_check_modules (GLIB2   glib-2.0>=2.10)
```

Requires at least version 2.10 of glib2 and defines e.g. GLIB2_VERSION=2.10.3

```
pkg_check_modules (FOO     glib-2.0>=2.10 gtk+-2.0)
```

Requires both glib2 and gtk2, and defines e.g. FOO_glib-2.0_VERSION=2.10.3 and FOO_gtk+-2.0_VERSION=2.8.20

```
pkg_check_modules (XRENDER REQUIRED xrender)
```

Defines for example:

```
XRENDER_LIBRARIES=Xrender;X11``
XRENDER_STATIC_LIBRARIES=Xrender;X11;pthread;Xau;Xdmcp
```

`pkg_search_module`

Same as `pkg_check_modules()` (page 489), but instead it checks for given modules and uses the first working one.

```
pkg_search_module(<PREFIX> [REQUIRED] [QUIET]
                   [NO_CMAKE_PATH] [NO_CMAKE_ENVIRONMENT_PATH]
                   <MODULE> [<MODULE>]*)
```

Examples

```
pkg_search_module (BAR      libxml-2.0 libxml2 libxml>=2)
```

`PKG_CONFIG_EXECUTABLE`

Path to the pkg-config executable.

`PKG_CONFIG_USE_CMAKE_PREFIX_PATH`

Whether `pkg_check_modules()` (page 489) and `pkg_search_module()` (page 490) should add the paths in `CMAKE_PREFIX_PATH` (page 647), `CMAKE_FRAMEWORK_PATH` (page 644), and `CMAKE_APPBUNDLE_PATH` (page 639) cache and environment variables to `pkg-config` search path.

If this variable is not set, this behavior is enabled by default if `CMAKE_MINIMUM_REQUIRED_VERSION` (page 630) is 3.1 or later, disabled otherwise.

FindPNG

Find the native PNG includes and library

This module searches libpng, the library for working with PNG images.

It defines the following variables

PNG_INCLUDE_DIRS where to find png.h, etc.

PNG_LIBRARIES the libraries to link against to use PNG.

PNG_DEFINITIONS You should add_definitons(${PNG_DEFINITIONS}) before compiling code that includes png library files.

PNG_FOUND If false, do not try to use PNG.

PNG_VERSION_STRING the version of the PNG library found (since CMake 2.8.8)

Also defined, but not for general use are

PNG_LIBRARY where to find the PNG library.

For backward compatiblity the variable PNG_INCLUDE_DIR is also set. It has the same value as PNG_INCLUDE_DIRS.

Since PNG depends on the ZLib compression library, none of the above will be defined unless ZLib can be found.

FindPostgreSQL

Find the PostgreSQL installation.

In Windows, we make the assumption that, if the PostgreSQL files are installed, the default directory will be C:Program FilesPostgreSQL.

This module defines

```
PostgreSQL_LIBRARIES - the PostgreSQL libraries needed for linking
PostgreSQL_INCLUDE_DIRS - the directories of the PostgreSQL headers
PostgreSQL_VERSION_STRING - the version of PostgreSQL found (since CMake 2.8.8)
```

FindProducer

Though Producer isn't directly part of OpenSceneGraph, its primary user is OSG so I consider this part of the Findosg* suite used to find OpenSceneGraph components. You'll notice that I accept OSGDIR as an environment path.

Each component is separate and you must opt in to each module. You must also opt into OpenGL (and OpenThreads?) as these modules won't do it for you. This is to allow you control over your own system piece by piece in case you need to opt out of certain components or change the Find behavior for a particular module (perhaps because the default FindOpenGL.cmake module doesn't work with your system as an example). If you want to use a more convenient module that includes everything, use the FindOpenSceneGraph.cmake instead of the Findosg*.cmake modules.

Locate Producer This module defines PRODUCER_LIBRARY PRODUCER_FOUND, if false, do not try to link to Producer PRODUCER_INCLUDE_DIR, where to find the headers

$PRODUCER_DIR is an environment variable that would correspond to the ./configure – prefix=$PRODUCER_DIR used in building osg.

Created by Eric Wing.

FindProtobuf

Locate and configure the Google Protocol Buffers library.

The following variables can be set and are optional:

PROTOBUF_SRC_ROOT_FOLDER When compiling with MSVC, if this cache variable is set the protobuf-default VS project build locations (vsprojects/Debug & vsprojects/Release) will be searched for libraries and binaries.

PROTOBUF_IMPORT_DIRS List of additional directories to be searched for imported .proto files.

Defines the following variables:

PROTOBUF_FOUND Found the Google Protocol Buffers library (libprotobuf & header files)

PROTOBUF_INCLUDE_DIRS Include directories for Google Protocol Buffers

PROTOBUF_LIBRARIES The protobuf libraries

PROTOBUF_PROTOC_LIBRARIES The protoc libraries

PROTOBUF_LITE_LIBRARIES The protobuf-lite libraries

The following cache variables are also available to set or use:

PROTOBUF_LIBRARY The protobuf library

PROTOBUF_PROTOC_LIBRARY The protoc library

PROTOBUF_INCLUDE_DIR The include directory for protocol buffers

PROTOBUF_PROTOC_EXECUTABLE The protoc compiler

PROTOBUF_LIBRARY_DEBUG The protobuf library (debug)

PROTOBUF_PROTOC_LIBRARY_DEBUG The protoc library (debug)

PROTOBUF_LITE_LIBRARY The protobuf lite library

PROTOBUF_LITE_LIBRARY_DEBUG The protobuf lite library (debug)

Example:

```
find_package(Protobuf REQUIRED)
include_directories(${PROTOBUF_INCLUDE_DIRS})
include_directories(${CMAKE_CURRENT_BINARY_DIR})
protobuf_generate_cpp(PROTO_SRCS PROTO_HDRS foo.proto)
add_executable(bar bar.cc ${PROTO_SRCS} ${PROTO_HDRS})
target_link_libraries(bar ${PROTOBUF_LIBRARIES})
```

Note: The PROTOBUF_GENERATE_CPP macro and add_executable() or add_library() calls only work properly within the same directory.

protobuf_generate_cpp

Add custom commands to process .proto files:

```
protobuf_generate_cpp (<SRCS> <HDRS> [<ARGN>...])
```

SRCS Variable to define with autogenerated source files

HDRS Variable to define with autogenerated header files

ARGN .proto files

FindPythonInterp

Find python interpreter

This module finds if Python interpreter is installed and determines where the executables are. This code sets the following variables:

```
PYTHONINTERP_FOUND          - Was the Python executable found
PYTHON_EXECUTABLE           - path to the Python interpreter
```

```
PYTHON_VERSION_STRING       - Python version found e.g. 2.5.2
PYTHON_VERSION_MAJOR        - Python major version found e.g. 2
PYTHON_VERSION_MINOR        - Python minor version found e.g. 5
PYTHON_VERSION_PATCH        - Python patch version found e.g. 2
```

The Python_ADDITIONAL_VERSIONS variable can be used to specify a list of version numbers that should be taken into account when searching for Python. You need to set this variable before calling find_package(PythonInterp).

If also calling find_package(PythonLibs), call find_package(PythonInterp) first to get the currently active Python version by default with a consistent version of PYTHON_LIBRARIES.

FindPythonLibs

Find python libraries

This module finds if Python is installed and determines where the include files and libraries are. It also determines what the name of the library is. This code sets the following variables:

```
PYTHONLIBS_FOUND            - have the Python libs been found
PYTHON_LIBRARIES            - path to the python library
PYTHON_INCLUDE_PATH         - path to where Python.h is found (deprecated)
PYTHON_INCLUDE_DIRS         - path to where Python.h is found
PYTHON_DEBUG_LIBRARIES      - path to the debug library (deprecated)
PYTHONLIBS_VERSION_STRING   - version of the Python libs found (since CMake 2.8.8)
```

The Python_ADDITIONAL_VERSIONS variable can be used to specify a list of version numbers that should be taken into account when searching for Python. You need to set this variable before calling find_package(PythonLibs).

If you'd like to specify the installation of Python to use, you should modify the following cache variables:

```
PYTHON_LIBRARY              - path to the python library
PYTHON_INCLUDE_DIR          - path to where Python.h is found
```

If also calling find_package(PythonInterp), call find_package(PythonInterp) first to get the currently active Python version by default with a consistent version of PYTHON_LIBRARIES.

FindQt3

Locate Qt include paths and libraries

This module defines:

```
QT_INCLUDE_DIR       - where to find qt.h, etc.
QT_LIBRARIES         - the libraries to link against to use Qt.
QT_DEFINITIONS       - definitions to use when
                       compiling code that uses Qt.
QT_FOUND             - If false, don't try to use Qt.
QT_VERSION_STRING    - the version of Qt found
```

If you need the multithreaded version of Qt, set QT_MT_REQUIRED to TRUE

Also defined, but not for general use are:

```
QT_MOC_EXECUTABLE, where to find the moc tool.
QT_UIC_EXECUTABLE, where to find the uic tool.
QT_QT_LIBRARY, where to find the Qt library.
QT_QTMAIN_LIBRARY, where to find the qtmain
 library. This is only required by Qt3 on Windows.
```

FindQt4

Finding and Using Qt4

This module can be used to find Qt4. The most important issue is that the Qt4 qmake is available via the system path. This qmake is then used to detect basically everything else. This module defines a number of IMPORTED (page 590) targets, macros and variables.

Typical usage could be something like:

```
set (CMAKE_AUTOMOC ON)
set (CMAKE_INCLUDE_CURRENT_DIR ON)
find_package(Qt4 4.4.3 REQUIRED QtGui QtXml)
add_executable(myexe main.cpp)
target_link_libraries(myexe Qt4::QtGui Qt4::QtXml)
```

Note: When using IMPORTED (page 590) targets, the qtmain.lib static library is automatically linked on Windows for WIN32 (page 612) executables. To disable that globally, set the QT4_NO_LINK_QTMAIN variable before finding Qt4. To disable that for a particular executable, set the QT4_NO_LINK_QTMAIN target property to TRUE on the executable.

Qt Build Tools

Qt relies on some bundled tools for code generation, such as moc for meta-object code generation,``uic`` for widget layout and population, and rcc for virtual filesystem content generation. These tools may be automatically invoked by cmake(1) (page 235) if the appropriate conditions are met. See cmake-qt(7) for more.

Qt Macros

In some cases it can be necessary or useful to invoke the Qt build tools in a more-manual way. Several macros are available to add targets for such uses.

```
macro QT4_WRAP_CPP(outfiles inputfile ... [TARGET tgt] OPTIONS ...)
       create moc code from a list of files containing Qt class with
       the Q_OBJECT declaration.  Per-directory preprocessor definitions
       are also added.  If the <tgt> is specified, the
       INTERFACE_INCLUDE_DIRECTORIES and INTERFACE_COMPILE_DEFINITIONS from
       the <tgt> are passed to moc.  Options may be given to moc, such as
       those found when executing "moc -help".
```

```
macro QT4_WRAP_UI(outfiles inputfile ... OPTIONS ...)
       create code from a list of Qt designer ui files.
       Options may be given to uic, such as those found
       when executing "uic -help"
```

```
macro QT4_ADD_RESOURCES(outfiles inputfile ... OPTIONS ...)
       create code from a list of Qt resource files.
       Options may be given to rcc, such as those found
       when executing "rcc -help"
```

```
macro QT4_GENERATE_MOC(inputfile outputfile [TARGET tgt])
       creates a rule to run moc on infile and create outfile.
       Use this if for some reason QT4_WRAP_CPP() isn't appropriate, e.g.
       because you need a custom filename for the moc file or something
       similar.  If the <tgt> is specified, the
       INTERFACE_INCLUDE_DIRECTORIES and INTERFACE_COMPILE_DEFINITIONS from
       the <tgt> are passed to moc.
```

```
macro QT4_ADD_DBUS_INTERFACE(outfiles interface basename)
       Create the interface header and implementation files with the
       given basename from the given interface xml file and add it to
       the list of sources.

       You can pass additional parameters to the qdbusxml2cpp call by setting
       properties on the input file:

       INCLUDE the given file will be included in the generate interface header

       CLASSNAME the generated class is named accordingly

       NO_NAMESPACE the generated class is not wrapped in a namespace
```

```
macro QT4_ADD_DBUS_INTERFACES(outfiles inputfile ... )
       Create the interface header and implementation files
       for all listed interface xml files.
       The basename will be automatically determined from the name
```

of the xml file.

The source file properties described for
QT4_ADD_DBUS_INTERFACE also apply here.

macro QT4_ADD_DBUS_ADAPTOR(outfiles xmlfile parentheader parentclassname
                    [basename] [classname])
create a dbus adaptor (header and implementation file) from the xml file
describing the interface, and add it to the list of sources. The adaptor
forwards the calls to a parent class, defined in parentheader and named
parentclassname. The name of the generated files will be
<basename>adaptor.{cpp,h} where basename defaults to the basename of the
xml file.
If <classname> is provided, then it will be used as the classname of the
adaptor itself.

macro QT4_GENERATE_DBUS_INTERFACE(header [interfacename] OPTIONS ...)
generate the xml interface file from the given header.
If the optional argument interfacename is omitted, the name of the
interface file is constructed from the basename of the header with
the suffix .xml appended.
Options may be given to qdbuscpp2xml, such as those found when
executing "qdbuscpp2xml --help"

macro QT4_CREATE_TRANSLATION(qm_files directories ... sources ...
                    ts_files ... OPTIONS ...)
out: qm_files
in: directories sources ts_files
options: flags to pass to lupdate, such as -extensions to specify
extensions for a directory scan.
generates commands to create .ts (vie lupdate) and .qm
(via lrelease) - files from directories and/or sources. The ts files are
created and/or updated in the source tree (unless given with full paths).
The qm files are generated in the build tree.
Updating the translations can be done by adding the qm_files
to the source list of your library/executable, so they are
always updated, or by adding a custom target to control when
they get updated/generated.

macro QT4_ADD_TRANSLATION(qm_files ts_files ...)
out: qm_files
in: ts_files
generates commands to create .qm from .ts - files. The generated
filenames can be found in qm_files. The ts_files
must exist and are not updated in any way.

macro QT4_AUTOMOC(sourcefile1 sourcefile2 ... [TARGET tgt])
The qt4_automoc macro is obsolete. Use the CMAKE_AUTOMOC feature instead.
This macro is still experimental.

```
It can be used to have moc automatically handled.
So if you have the files foo.h and foo.cpp, and in foo.h a
a class uses the Q_OBJECT macro, moc has to run on it. If you don't
want to use QT4_WRAP_CPP() (which is reliable and mature), you can insert
#include "foo.moc"
in foo.cpp and then give foo.cpp as argument to QT4_AUTOMOC(). This will
scan all listed files at cmake-time for such included moc files and if it
finds them cause a rule to be generated to run moc at build time on the
accompanying header file foo.h.
If a source file has the SKIP_AUTOMOC property set it will be ignored by
this macro.
If the <tgt> is specified, the INTERFACE_INCLUDE_DIRECTORIES and
INTERFACE_COMPILE_DEFINITIONS from the <tgt> are passed to moc.
```

```
function QT4_USE_MODULES( target [link_type] modules...)
     This function is obsolete. Use target_link_libraries with IMPORTED targets
     instead.
     Make <target> use the <modules> from Qt. Using a Qt module means
     to link to the library, add the relevant include directories for the
     module, and add the relevant compiler defines for using the module.
     Modules are roughly equivalent to components of Qt4, so usage would be
     something like:
        qt4_use_modules(myexe Core Gui Declarative)
     to use QtCore, QtGui and QtDeclarative. The optional <link_type> argument
     can be specified as either LINK_PUBLIC or LINK_PRIVATE to specify the
     same argument to the target_link_libraries call.
```

IMPORTED Targets

A particular Qt library may be used by using the corresponding IMPORTED (page 590) target with the target_link_libraries() (page 340) command:

```
target_link_libraries(myexe Qt4::QtGui Qt4::QtXml)
```

Using a target in this way causes :cmake(1)' to use the appropriate include directories and compile definitions for the target when compiling myexe.

Targets are aware of their dependencies, so for example it is not necessary to list Qt4::QtCore if another Qt library is listed, and it is not necessary to list Qt4::QtGui if Qt4::QtDeclarative is listed. Targets may be tested for existence in the usual way with the if(TARGET) (page 313) command.

The Qt toolkit may contain both debug and release libraries. cmake(1) (page 235) will choose the appropriate version based on the build configuration.

Qt4::QtCore The QtCore target

Qt4::QtGui The QtGui target

Qt4::Qt3Support The Qt3Support target

`Qt4::QtAssistant` The QtAssistant target

`Qt4::QtAssistantClient` The QtAssistantClient target

`Qt4::QAxContainer` The QAxContainer target (Windows only)

`Qt4::QAxServer` The QAxServer target (Windows only)

`Qt4::QtDBus` The QtDBus target

`Qt4::QtDesigner` The QtDesigner target

`Qt4::QtDesignerComponents` The QtDesignerComponents target

`Qt4::QtHelp` The QtHelp target

`Qt4::QtMotif` The QtMotif target

`Qt4::QtMultimedia` The QtMultimedia target

`Qt4::QtNetwork` The QtNetwork target

`Qt4::QtNsPLugin` The QtNsPLugin target

`Qt4::QtOpenGL` The QtOpenGL target

`Qt4::QtScript` The QtScript target

`Qt4::QtScriptTools` The QtScriptTools target

`Qt4::QtSql` The QtSql target

`Qt4::QtSvg` The QtSvg target

`Qt4::QtTest` The QtTest target

`Qt4::QtUiTools` The QtUiTools target

`Qt4::QtWebKit` The QtWebKit target

`Qt4::QtXml` The QtXml target

`Qt4::QtXmlPatterns` The QtXmlPatterns target

`Qt4::phonon` The phonon target

Result Variables

Below is a detailed list of variables that FindQt4.cmake sets.

`Qt4_FOUND` If false, don't try to use Qt 4.

`QT_FOUND` If false, don't try to use Qt. This variable is for compatibility only.

`QT4_FOUND` If false, don't try to use Qt 4. This variable is for compatibility only.

`QT_VERSION_MAJOR` The major version of Qt found.

QT_VERSION_MINOR The minor version of Qt found.

QT_VERSION_PATCH The patch version of Qt found.

FindQt

Searches for all installed versions of Qt.

This should only be used if your project can work with multiple versions of Qt. If not, you should just directly use FindQt4 or FindQt3. If multiple versions of Qt are found on the machine, then The user must set the option DESIRED_QT_VERSION to the version they want to use. If only one version of qt is found on the machine, then the DESIRED_QT_VERSION is set to that version and the matching FindQt3 or FindQt4 module is included. Once the user sets DESIRED_QT_VERSION, then the FindQt3 or FindQt4 module is included.

```
QT_REQUIRED if this is set to TRUE then if CMake can
            not find Qt4 or Qt3 an error is raised
            and a message is sent to the user.
```

```
DESIRED_QT_VERSION OPTION is created
QT4_INSTALLED is set to TRUE if qt4 is found.
QT3_INSTALLED is set to TRUE if qt3 is found.
```

FindQuickTime

Locate QuickTime This module defines QUICKTIME_LIBRARY QUICKTIME_FOUND, if false, do not try to link to gdal QUICKTIME_INCLUDE_DIR, where to find the headers

$QUICKTIME_DIR is an environment variable that would correspond to the ./configure – prefix=$QUICKTIME_DIR

Created by Eric Wing.

FindRTI

Try to find M&S HLA RTI libraries

This module finds if any HLA RTI is installed and locates the standard RTI include files and libraries.

RTI is a simulation infrastructure standardized by IEEE and SISO. It has a well defined C++ API that assures that simulation applications are independent on a particular RTI implementation.

```
http://en.wikipedia.org/wiki/Run-Time_Infrastructure_(simulation)
```

This code sets the following variables:

```
RTI_INCLUDE_DIR = the directory where RTI includes file are found
RTI_LIBRARIES = The libraries to link against to use RTI
RTI_DEFINITIONS = -DRTI_USES_STD_FSTREAM
RTI_FOUND = Set to FALSE if any HLA RTI was not found
```

Report problems to <certi-devel@nongnu.org[9]>

FindRuby

Find Ruby

This module finds if Ruby is installed and determines where the include files and libraries are. Ruby 1.8, 1.9, 2.0 and 2.1 are supported.

The minimum required version of Ruby can be specified using the standard syntax, e.g. find_package(Ruby 1.8)

It also determines what the name of the library is. This code sets the following variables:

RUBY_EXECUTABLE full path to the ruby binary

RUBY_INCLUDE_DIRS include dirs to be used when using the ruby library

RUBY_LIBRARY full path to the ruby library

RUBY_VERSION the version of ruby which was found, e.g. "1.8.7"

RUBY_FOUND set to true if ruby ws found successfully

Also:

RUBY_INCLUDE_PATH same as RUBY_INCLUDE_DIRS, only provided for compatibility reasons, don't use it

FindSDL_image

Locate SDL_image library

This module defines:

```
SDL_IMAGE_LIBRARIES, the name of the library to link against
SDL_IMAGE_INCLUDE_DIRS, where to find the headers
SDL_IMAGE_FOUND, if false, do not try to link against
SDL_IMAGE_VERSION_STRING - human-readable string containing the
                           version of SDL_image
```

For backward compatiblity the following variables are also set:

---

[9]certi-devel@nongnu.org

```
SDLIMAGE_LIBRARY (same value as SDL_IMAGE_LIBRARIES)
SDLIMAGE_INCLUDE_DIR (same value as SDL_IMAGE_INCLUDE_DIRS)
SDLIMAGE_FOUND (same value as SDL_IMAGE_FOUND)
```

$SDLDIR is an environment variable that would correspond to the ./configure –prefix=$SDLDIR used in building SDL.

Created by Eric Wing. This was influenced by the FindSDL.cmake module, but with modifications to recognize OS X frameworks and additional Unix paths (FreeBSD, etc).

FindSDL_mixer

Locate SDL_mixer library

This module defines:

```
SDL_MIXER_LIBRARIES, the name of the library to link against
SDL_MIXER_INCLUDE_DIRS, where to find the headers
SDL_MIXER_FOUND, if false, do not try to link against
SDL_MIXER_VERSION_STRING - human-readable string containing the
                        version of SDL_mixer
```

For backward compatiblity the following variables are also set:

```
SDLMIXER_LIBRARY (same value as SDL_MIXER_LIBRARIES)
SDLMIXER_INCLUDE_DIR (same value as SDL_MIXER_INCLUDE_DIRS)
SDLMIXER_FOUND (same value as SDL_MIXER_FOUND)
```

$SDLDIR is an environment variable that would correspond to the ./configure –prefix=$SDLDIR used in building SDL.

Created by Eric Wing. This was influenced by the FindSDL.cmake module, but with modifications to recognize OS X frameworks and additional Unix paths (FreeBSD, etc).

FindSDL_net

Locate SDL_net library

This module defines:

```
SDL_NET_LIBRARIES, the name of the library to link against
SDL_NET_INCLUDE_DIRS, where to find the headers
SDL_NET_FOUND, if false, do not try to link against
SDL_NET_VERSION_STRING - human-readable string containing the version of SDL_net
```

For backward compatiblity the following variables are also set:

```
SDLNET_LIBRARY (same value as SDL_NET_LIBRARIES)
SDLNET_INCLUDE_DIR (same value as SDL_NET_INCLUDE_DIRS)
SDLNET_FOUND (same value as SDL_NET_FOUND)
```

$SDLDIR is an environment variable that would correspond to the ./configure –prefix=$SDLDIR used in building SDL.

Created by Eric Wing. This was influenced by the FindSDL.cmake module, but with modifications to recognize OS X frameworks and additional Unix paths (FreeBSD, etc).

FindSDL

Locate SDL library

This module defines

```
SDL_LIBRARY, the name of the library to link against
SDL_FOUND, if false, do not try to link to SDL
SDL_INCLUDE_DIR, where to find SDL.h
SDL_VERSION_STRING, human-readable string containing the version of SDL
```

This module responds to the flag:

```
SDL_BUILDING_LIBRARY
    If this is defined, then no SDL_main will be linked in because
    only applications need main().
    Otherwise, it is assumed you are building an application and this
    module will attempt to locate and set the proper link flags
    as part of the returned SDL_LIBRARY variable.
```

Don't forget to include SDLmain.h and SDLmain.m your project for the OS X framework based version. (Other versions link to -lSDLmain which this module will try to find on your behalf.) Also for OS X, this module will automatically add the -framework Cocoa on your behalf.

Additional Note: If you see an empty SDL_LIBRARY_TEMP in your configuration and no SDL_LIBRARY, it means CMake did not find your SDL library (SDL.dll, libsdl.so, SDL.framework, etc). Set SDL_LIBRARY_TEMP to point to your SDL library, and configure again. Similarly, if you see an empty SDLMAIN_LIBRARY, you should set this value as appropriate. These values are used to generate the final SDL_LIBRARY variable, but when these values are unset, SDL_LIBRARY does not get created.

$SDLDIR is an environment variable that would correspond to the ./configure –prefix=$SDLDIR used in building SDL. l.e.galup 9-20-02

Modified by Eric Wing. Added code to assist with automated building by using environmental variables and providing a more controlled/consistent search behavior. Added new modifications to recognize OS X frameworks and additional Unix paths (FreeBSD, etc). Also corrected the header search path to follow "proper" SDL guidelines. Added a search for SDLmain which is needed by some platforms. Added a search for threads which is needed by some platforms. Added needed compile switches for MinGW.

On OSX, this will prefer the Framework version (if found) over others. People will have to manually change the cache values of SDL_LIBRARY to override this selection or set the CMake environment CMAKE_INCLUDE_PATH to modify the search paths.

Note that the header path has changed from SDL/SDL.h to just SDL.h This needed to change because "proper" SDL convention is #include "SDL.h", not <SDL/SDL.h>. This is done for portability reasons because not all systems place things in SDL/ (see FreeBSD).

FindSDL_sound

Locates the SDL_sound library

This module depends on SDL being found and must be called AFTER FindSDL.cmake is called.

This module defines

```
SDL_SOUND_INCLUDE_DIR, where to find SDL_sound.h
SDL_SOUND_FOUND, if false, do not try to link to SDL_sound
SDL_SOUND_LIBRARIES, this contains the list of libraries that you need
  to link against. This is a read-only variable and is marked INTERNAL.
SDL_SOUND_EXTRAS, this is an optional variable for you to add your own
  flags to SDL_SOUND_LIBRARIES. This is prepended to SDL_SOUND_LIBRARIES.
  This is available mostly for cases this module failed to anticipate for
  and you must add additional flags. This is marked as ADVANCED.
SDL_SOUND_VERSION_STRING, human-readable string containing the
  version of SDL_sound
```

This module also defines (but you shouldn't need to use directly)

```
SDL_SOUND_LIBRARY, the name of just the SDL_sound library you would link
against. Use SDL_SOUND_LIBRARIES for you link instructions and not this one.
```

And might define the following as needed

```
MIKMOD_LIBRARY
MODPLUG_LIBRARY
OGG_LIBRARY
VORBIS_LIBRARY
SMPEG_LIBRARY
FLAC_LIBRARY
SPEEX_LIBRARY
```

Typically, you should not use these variables directly, and you should use SDL_SOUND_LIBRARIES which contains SDL_SOUND_LIBRARY and the other audio libraries (if needed) to successfully compile on your system.

Created by Eric Wing. This module is a bit more complicated than the other FindSDL* family modules. The reason is that SDL_sound can be compiled in a large variety of different ways which are independent of platform. SDL_sound may dynamically link against other 3rd party libraries to get additional codec support, such as Ogg Vorbis, SMPEG, ModPlug, MikMod, FLAC, Speex, and potentially others. Under some circumstances which I don't fully understand, there seems to be a requirement that dependent libraries of libraries you use must also be explicitly linked against in order to successfully compile. SDL_sound does not currently have any system in place to know how it was compiled. So this CMake module does the hard work in trying to discover which 3rd party libraries are required for building (if any). This module uses a brute force approach to create a test program that uses SDL_sound, and then tries to build it. If the build fails, it parses the error output for known symbol names to figure out which libraries are needed.

Responds to the $SDLDIR and $SDLSOUNDDIR environmental variable that would correspond to the ./configure –prefix=$SDLDIR used in building SDL.

On OSX, this will prefer the Framework version (if found) over others. People will have to manually change the cache values of SDL_LIBRARY to override this selectionor set the CMake environment CMAKE_INCLUDE_PATH to modify the search paths.

FindSDL_ttf

Locate SDL_ttf library

This module defines:

```
SDL_TTF_LIBRARIES, the name of the library to link against
SDL_TTF_INCLUDE_DIRS, where to find the headers
SDL_TTF_FOUND, if false, do not try to link against
SDL_TTF_VERSION_STRING - human-readable string containing the version of SDL_ttf
```

For backward compatiblity the following variables are also set:

```
SDLTTF_LIBRARY (same value as SDL_TTF_LIBRARIES)
SDLTTF_INCLUDE_DIR (same value as SDL_TTF_INCLUDE_DIRS)
SDLTTF_FOUND (same value as SDL_TTF_FOUND)
```

$SDLDIR is an environment variable that would correspond to the ./configure –prefix=$SDLDIR used in building SDL.

Created by Eric Wing. This was influenced by the FindSDL.cmake module, but with modifications to recognize OS X frameworks and additional Unix paths (FreeBSD, etc).

FindSelfPackers

Find upx

This module looks for some executable packers (i.e. software that compress executables or shared libs into on-the-fly self-extracting executables or shared libs. Examples:

```
UPX: http://wildsau.idv.uni-linz.ac.at/mfx/upx.html
```

FindSquish

– Typical Use

This module can be used to find Squish. Currently Squish versions 3 and 4 are supported.

```
SQUISH_FOUND                  If false, don't try to use Squish
SQUISH_VERSION                The full version of Squish found
SQUISH_VERSION_MAJOR          The major version of Squish found
SQUISH_VERSION_MINOR          The minor version of Squish found
SQUISH_VERSION_PATCH          The patch version of Squish found
```

```
SQUISH_INSTALL_DIR            The Squish installation directory
                              (containing bin, lib, etc)
SQUISH_SERVER_EXECUTABLE      The squishserver executable
SQUISH_CLIENT_EXECUTABLE      The squishrunner executable
```

```
SQUISH_INSTALL_DIR_FOUND          Was the install directory found?
SQUISH_SERVER_EXECUTABLE_FOUND    Was the server executable found?
SQUISH_CLIENT_EXECUTABLE_FOUND    Was the client executable found?
```

It provides the function squish_v4_add_test() for adding a squish test to cmake using Squish 4.x:

```
squish_v4_add_test(cmakeTestName
  AUT targetName SUITE suiteName TEST squishTestName
  [SETTINGSGROUP group] [PRE_COMMAND command] [POST_COMMAND command] )
```

The arguments have the following meaning:

cmakeTestName this will be used as the first argument for add_test()

AUT targetName the name of the cmake target which will be used as AUT, i.e. the executable which will be tested.

SUITE suiteName this is either the full path to the squish suite, or just the last directory of the suite, i.e. the suite name. In this case the CMakeLists.txt which calls squish_add_test() must be located in the parent directory of the suite directory.

TEST squishTestName the name of the squish test, i.e. the name of the subdirectory of the test inside the suite directory.

SETTINGSGROUP group if specified, the given settings group will be used for executing the test. If not specified, the groupname will be "CTest_<username>"

PRE_COMMAND command if specified, the given command will be executed before starting the squish test.

POST_COMMAND command same as PRE_COMMAND, but after the squish test has been executed.

```
enable_testing()
find_package(Squish 4.0)
if (SQUISH_FOUND)
   squish_v4_add_test(myTestName
```

```
     AUT myApp
     SUITE ${CMAKE_SOURCE_DIR}/tests/mySuite
     TEST someSquishTest
     SETTINGSGROUP myGroup
     )
endif ()
```

For users of Squish version 3.x the macro squish_v3_add_test() is provided:

```
squish_v3_add_test(testName applicationUnderTest testCase envVars testWrapper)
Use this macro to add a test using Squish 3.x.
```

```
enable_testing()
find_package(Squish)
if (SQUISH_FOUND)
  squish_v3_add_test(myTestName myApplication testCase envVars testWrapper)
endif ()
```

macro SQUISH_ADD_TEST(testName applicationUnderTest testCase envVars testWrapper)

```
This is deprecated. Use SQUISH_V3_ADD_TEST() if you are using Squish 3.x instead.
```

FindSubversion

Extract information from a subversion working copy

The module defines the following variables:

```
Subversion_SVN_EXECUTABLE - path to svn command line client
Subversion_VERSION_SVN - version of svn command line client
Subversion_FOUND - true if the command line client was found
SUBVERSION_FOUND - same as Subversion_FOUND, set for compatiblity reasons
```

The minimum required version of Subversion can be specified using the standard syntax, e.g. find_package(Subversion 1.4)

If the command line client executable is found two macros are defined:

```
Subversion_WC_INFO(<dir> <var-prefix>)
Subversion_WC_LOG(<dir> <var-prefix>)
```

Subversion_WC_INFO extracts information of a subversion working copy at a given location. This macro defines the following variables:

```
<var-prefix>_WC_URL - url of the repository (at <dir>)
<var-prefix>_WC_ROOT - root url of the repository
<var-prefix>_WC_REVISION - current revision
<var-prefix>_WC_LAST_CHANGED_AUTHOR - author of last commit
<var-prefix>_WC_LAST_CHANGED_DATE - date of last commit
```

```
<var-prefix>_WC_LAST_CHANGED_REV - revision of last commit
<var-prefix>_WC_INFO - output of command 'svn info <dir>'
```

Subversion_WC_LOG retrieves the log message of the base revision of a subversion working copy at a given location. This macro defines the variable:

```
<var-prefix>_LAST_CHANGED_LOG - last log of base revision
```

Example usage:

```
find_package(Subversion)
if(SUBVERSION_FOUND)
  Subversion_WC_INFO(${PROJECT_SOURCE_DIR} Project)
  message("Current revision is ${Project_WC_REVISION}")
  Subversion_WC_LOG(${PROJECT_SOURCE_DIR} Project)
  message("Last changed log is ${Project_LAST_CHANGED_LOG}")
endif()
```

FindSWIG

Find SWIG

This module finds an installed SWIG. It sets the following variables:

```
SWIG_FOUND - set to true if SWIG is found
SWIG_DIR - the directory where swig is installed
SWIG_EXECUTABLE - the path to the swig executable
SWIG_VERSION   - the version number of the swig executable
```

The minimum required version of SWIG can be specified using the standard syntax, e.g. find_package(SWIG 1.1)

All information is collected from the SWIG_EXECUTABLE so the version to be found can be changed from the command line by means of setting SWIG_EXECUTABLE

FindTCL

TK_INTERNAL_PATH was removed.

This module finds if Tcl is installed and determines where the include files and libraries are. It also determines what the name of the library is. This code sets the following variables:

```
TCL_FOUND           = Tcl was found
TK_FOUND            = Tk was found
TCLTK_FOUND         = Tcl and Tk were found
TCL_LIBRARY         = path to Tcl library (tcl tcl80)
TCL_INCLUDE_PATH    = path to where tcl.h can be found
TCL_TCLSH           = path to tclsh binary (tcl tcl80)
```

```
TK_LIBRARY              = path to Tk library (tk tk80 etc)
TK_INCLUDE_PATH         = path to where tk.h can be found
TK_WISH                 = full path to the wish executable
```

In an effort to remove some clutter and clear up some issues for people who are not necessarily Tcl/Tk gurus/developpers, some variables were moved or removed. Changes compared to CMake 2.4 are:

```
=> they were only useful for people writing Tcl/Tk extensions.
=> these libs are not packaged by default with Tcl/Tk distributions.
   Even when Tcl/Tk is built from source, several flavors of debug libs
   are created and there is no real reason to pick a single one
   specifically (say, amongst tcl84g, tcl84gs, or tcl84sgx).
   Let's leave that choice to the user by allowing him to assign
   TCL_LIBRARY to any Tcl library, debug or not.
=> this ended up being only a Win32 variable, and there is a lot of
   confusion regarding the location of this file in an installed Tcl/Tk
   tree anyway (see 8.5 for example). If you need the internal path at
   this point it is safer you ask directly where the *source* tree is
   and dig from there.
```

FindTclsh

Find tclsh

This module finds if TCL is installed and determines where the include files and libraries are. It also determines what the name of the library is. This code sets the following variables:

```
TCLSH_FOUND = TRUE if tclsh has been found
TCL_TCLSH = the path to the tclsh executable
```

In cygwin, look for the cygwin version first. Don't look for it later to avoid finding the cygwin version on a Win32 build.

FindTclStub

TCL_STUB_LIBRARY_DEBUG and TK_STUB_LIBRARY_DEBUG were removed.

This module finds Tcl stub libraries. It first finds Tcl include files and libraries by calling FindTCL.cmake. How to Use the Tcl Stubs Library:

```
http://tcl.activestate.com/doc/howto/stubs.html
```

Using Stub Libraries:

```
http://safari.oreilly.com/0130385603/ch48lev1sec3
```

This code sets the following variables:

```
TCL_STUB_LIBRARY          = path to Tcl stub library
TK_STUB_LIBRARY           = path to Tk stub library
TTK_STUB_LIBRARY          = path to ttk stub library
```

In an effort to remove some clutter and clear up some issues for people who are not necessarily Tcl/Tk gurus/developpers, some variables were moved or removed. Changes compared to CMake 2.4 are:

```
=> these libs are not packaged by default with Tcl/Tk distributions.
   Even when Tcl/Tk is built from source, several flavors of debug libs
   are created and there is no real reason to pick a single one
   specifically (say, amongst tclstub84g, tclstub84gs, or tclstub84sgx).
   Let's leave that choice to the user by allowing him to assign
   TCL_STUB_LIBRARY to any Tcl library, debug or not.
```

FindThreads

This module determines the thread library of the system.

The following variables are set

```
CMAKE_THREAD_LIBS_INIT        - the thread library
CMAKE_USE_SPROC_INIT          - are we using sproc?
CMAKE_USE_WIN32_THREADS_INIT  - using WIN32 threads?
CMAKE_USE_PTHREADS_INIT       - are we using pthreads
CMAKE_HP_PTHREADS_INIT        - are we using hp pthreads
```

The following import target is created

```
Threads::Threads
```

For systems with multiple thread libraries, caller can set

```
CMAKE_THREAD_PREFER_PTHREAD
```

If the use of the -pthread compiler and linker flag is prefered then the caller can set

```
THREADS_PREFER_PTHREAD_FLAG
```

Please note that the compiler flag can only be used with the imported target. Use of both the imported target as well as this switch is highly recommended for new code.

FindTIFF

Find TIFF library

Find the native TIFF includes and library This module defines

```
TIFF_INCLUDE_DIR, where to find tiff.h, etc.
TIFF_LIBRARIES, libraries to link against to use TIFF.
TIFF_FOUND, If false, do not try to use TIFF.
```

also defined, but not for general use are

```
TIFF_LIBRARY, where to find the TIFF library.
```

FindUnixCommands

Find unix commands from cygwin

This module looks for some usual Unix commands.

FindVTK

This module no longer exists.

This module existed in versions of CMake prior to 3.1, but became only a thin wrapper around `find_package(VTK NO_MODULE)` to provide compatibility for projects using long-outdated conventions. Now `find_package(VTK)` will search for `VTKConfig.cmake` directly.

FindWget

Find wget

This module looks for wget. This module defines the following values:

```
WGET_EXECUTABLE: the full path to the wget tool.
WGET_FOUND: True if wget has been found.
```

FindWish

Find wish installation

This module finds if TCL is installed and determines where the include files and libraries are. It also determines what the name of the library is. This code sets the following variables:

```
TK_WISH = the path to the wish executable
```

if UNIX is defined, then it will look for the cygwin version first

FindwxWidgets

Find a wxWidgets (a.k.a., wxWindows) installation.

This module finds if wxWidgets is installed and selects a default configuration to use. wxWidgets is a modular library. To specify the modules that you will use, you need to name them as components to the package:

find_package(wxWidgets COMPONENTS core base ...)

There are two search branches: a windows style and a unix style. For windows, the following variables are searched for and set to defaults in case of multiple choices. Change them if the defaults are not desired (i.e., these are the only variables you should change to select a configuration):

```
wxWidgets_ROOT_DIR            - Base wxWidgets directory
                                (e.g., C:/wxWidgets-2.6.3).
wxWidgets_LIB_DIR             - Path to wxWidgets libraries
                                (e.g., C:/wxWidgets-2.6.3/lib/vc_lib).
wxWidgets_CONFIGURATION       - Configuration to use
                                (e.g., msw, mswd, mswu, mswunivud, etc.)
wxWidgets_EXCLUDE_COMMON_LIBRARIES
                              - Set to TRUE to exclude linking of
                                commonly required libs (e.g., png tiff
                                jpeg zlib regex expat).
```

For unix style it uses the wx-config utility. You can select between debug/release, unicode/ansi, universal/non-universal, and static/shared in the QtDialog or ccmake interfaces by turning ON/OFF the following variables:

```
wxWidgets_USE_DEBUG
wxWidgets_USE_UNICODE
wxWidgets_USE_UNIVERSAL
wxWidgets_USE_STATIC
```

There is also a wxWidgets_CONFIG_OPTIONS variable for all other options that need to be passed to the wx-config utility. For example, to use the base toolkit found in the /usr/local path, set the variable (before calling the FIND_PACKAGE command) as such:

```
set(wxWidgets_CONFIG_OPTIONS --toolkit=base --prefix=/usr)
```

The following are set after the configuration is done for both windows and unix style:

```
wxWidgets_FOUND              - Set to TRUE if wxWidgets was found.
wxWidgets_INCLUDE_DIRS       - Include directories for WIN32
                                i.e., where to find "wx/wx.h" and
                                "wx/setup.h"; possibly empty for unices.
wxWidgets_LIBRARIES          - Path to the wxWidgets libraries.
wxWidgets_LIBRARY_DIRS       - compile time link dirs, useful for
                                rpath on UNIX. Typically an empty string
                                in WIN32 environment.
wxWidgets_DEFINITIONS        - Contains defines required to compile/link
                                against WX, e.g. WXUSINGDLL
wxWidgets_DEFINITIONS_DEBUG- Contains defines required to compile/link
```

```
wxWidgets_CXX_FLAGS         against WX debug builds, e.g. __WXDEBUG__
                          - Include dirs and compiler flags for
                            unices, empty on WIN32. Essentially
                            "`wx-config --cxxflags`".
wxWidgets_USE_FILE        - Convenience include file.
```

Sample usage:

```
# Note that for MinGW users the order of libs is important!
find_package(wxWidgets COMPONENTS net gl core base)
if(wxWidgets_FOUND)
  include(${wxWidgets_USE_FILE})
  # and for each of your dependent executable/library targets:
  target_link_libraries(<YourTarget> ${wxWidgets_LIBRARIES})
endif()
```

If wxWidgets is required (i.e., not an optional part):

```
find_package(wxWidgets REQUIRED net gl core base)
include(${wxWidgets_USE_FILE})
# and for each of your dependent executable/library targets:
target_link_libraries(<YourTarget> ${wxWidgets_LIBRARIES})
```

FindwxWindows

Find wxWindows (wxWidgets) installation

This module finds if wxWindows/wxWidgets is installed and determines where the include files and libraries are. It also determines what the name of the library is. Please note this file is DEPRECATED and replaced by FindwxWidgets.cmake. This code sets the following variables:

```
WXWINDOWS_FOUND       = system has WxWindows
WXWINDOWS_LIBRARIES   = path to the wxWindows libraries
                        on Unix/Linux with additional
                        linker flags from
                        "wx-config --libs"
CMAKE_WXWINDOWS_CXX_FLAGS  = Compiler flags for wxWindows,
                             essentially "`wx-config --cxxflags`"
                             on Linux
WXWINDOWS_INCLUDE_DIR      = where to find "wx/wx.h" and "wx/setup.h"
WXWINDOWS_LINK_DIRECTORIES = link directories, useful for rpath on
                             Unix
WXWINDOWS_DEFINITIONS      = extra defines
```

OPTIONS If you need OpenGL support please

```
set(WXWINDOWS_USE_GL 1)
```

in your CMakeLists.txt *before* you include this file.

```
HAVE_ISYSTEM        - true required to replace -I by -isystem on g++
```

For convenience include Use_wxWindows.cmake in your project's CMakeLists.txt using include(${CMAKE_CURRENT_LIST_DIR}/Use_wxWindows.cmake).

USAGE

```
set(WXWINDOWS_USE_GL 1)
find_package(wxWindows)
```

NOTES wxWidgets 2.6.x is supported for monolithic builds e.g. compiled in wx/build/msw dir as:

```
nmake -f makefile.vc BUILD=debug SHARED=0 USE_OPENGL=1 MONOLITHIC=1
```

DEPRECATED

```
CMAKE_WX_CAN_COMPILE
WXWINDOWS_LIBRARY
CMAKE_WX_CXX_FLAGS
WXWINDOWS_INCLUDE_PATH
```

AUTHOR Jan Woetzel <http://www.mip.informatik.uni-kiel.de/~jw> (07/2003-01/2006)

FindXercesC

Find the Apache Xerces-C++ validating XML parser headers and libraries.

This module reports information about the Xerces installation in several variables. General variables:

```
XercesC_FOUND - true if the Xerces headers and libraries were found
XercesC_VERSION - Xerces release version
XercesC_INCLUDE_DIRS - the directory containing the Xerces headers
XercesC_LIBRARIES - Xerces libraries to be linked
```

The following cache variables may also be set:

```
XercesC_INCLUDE_DIR - the directory containing the Xerces headers
XercesC_LIBRARY - the Xerces library
```

FindX11

Find X11 installation

Try to find X11 on UNIX systems. The following values are defined

```
X11_FOUND        - True if X11 is available
X11_INCLUDE_DIR  - include directories to use X11
X11_LIBRARIES    - link against these to use X11
```

and also the following more fine grained variables:

```
X11_ICE_INCLUDE_PATH,           X11_ICE_LIB,          X11_ICE_FOUND
X11_SM_INCLUDE_PATH,            X11_SM_LIB,           X11_SM_FOUND
X11_X11_INCLUDE_PATH,           X11_X11_LIB
X11_Xaccessrules_INCLUDE_PATH,                        X11_Xaccess_FOUND
X11_Xaccessstr_INCLUDE_PATH,                          X11_Xaccess_FOUND
X11_Xau_INCLUDE_PATH,           X11_Xau_LIB,          X11_Xau_FOUND
X11_Xcomposite_INCLUDE_PATH,    X11_Xcomposite_LIB,   X11_Xcomposite_FOUND
X11_Xcursor_INCLUDE_PATH,       X11_Xcursor_LIB,      X11_Xcursor_FOUND
X11_Xdamage_INCLUDE_PATH,       X11_Xdamage_LIB,      X11_Xdamage_FOUND
X11_Xdmcp_INCLUDE_PATH,         X11_Xdmcp_LIB,        X11_Xdmcp_FOUND
X11_Xext_LIB,        X11_Xext_FOUND
X11_dpms_INCLUDE_PATH,          (in X11_Xext_LIB),    X11_dpms_FOUND
X11_XShm_INCLUDE_PATH,          (in X11_Xext_LIB),    X11_XShm_FOUND
X11_Xshape_INCLUDE_PATH,        (in X11_Xext_LIB),    X11_Xshape_FOUND
X11_xf86misc_INCLUDE_PATH,      X11_Xxf86misc_LIB,    X11_xf86misc_FOUND
X11_xf86vmode_INCLUDE_PATH,     X11_Xxf86vm_LIB       X11_xf86vmode_FOUND
X11_Xfixes_INCLUDE_PATH,        X11_Xfixes_LIB,       X11_Xfixes_FOUND
X11_Xft_INCLUDE_PATH,           X11_Xft_LIB,          X11_Xft_FOUND
X11_Xi_INCLUDE_PATH,            X11_Xi_LIB,           X11_Xi_FOUND
X11_Xinerama_INCLUDE_PATH,      X11_Xinerama_LIB,     X11_Xinerama_FOUND
X11_Xinput_INCLUDE_PATH,        X11_Xinput_LIB,       X11_Xinput_FOUND
X11_Xkb_INCLUDE_PATH,                                 X11_Xkb_FOUND
X11_Xkblib_INCLUDE_PATH,                              X11_Xkb_FOUND
X11_Xkbfile_INCLUDE_PATH,       X11_Xkbfile_LIB,      X11_Xkbfile_FOUND
X11_Xmu_INCLUDE_PATH,           X11_Xmu_LIB,          X11_Xmu_FOUND
X11_Xpm_INCLUDE_PATH,           X11_Xpm_LIB,          X11_Xpm_FOUND
X11_XTest_INCLUDE_PATH,         X11_XTest_LIB,        X11_XTest_FOUND
X11_Xrandr_INCLUDE_PATH,        X11_Xrandr_LIB,       X11_Xrandr_FOUND
X11_Xrender_INCLUDE_PATH,       X11_Xrender_LIB,      X11_Xrender_FOUND
X11_Xscreensaver_INCLUDE_PATH,  X11_Xscreensaver_LIB, X11_Xscreensaver_FOUND
X11_Xt_INCLUDE_PATH,            X11_Xt_LIB,           X11_Xt_FOUND
X11_Xutil_INCLUDE_PATH,                               X11_Xutil_FOUND
X11_Xv_INCLUDE_PATH,            X11_Xv_LIB,           X11_Xv_FOUND
X11_XSync_INCLUDE_PATH,         (in X11_Xext_LIB),    X11_XSync_FOUND
```

FindXMLRPC

Find xmlrpc

Find the native XMLRPC headers and libraries.

```
XMLRPC_INCLUDE_DIRS     - where to find xmlrpc.h, etc.
XMLRPC_LIBRARIES        - List of libraries when using xmlrpc.
XMLRPC_FOUND            - True if xmlrpc found.
```

XMLRPC modules may be specified as components for this find module. Modules may be listed by running "xmlrpc-c-config". Modules include:

```
c++              C++ wrapper code
libwww-client    libwww-based client
cgi-server       CGI-based server
abyss-server     ABYSS-based server
```

Typical usage:

```
find_package(XMLRPC REQUIRED libwww-client)
```

FindZLIB

Find the native ZLIB includes and library.

IMPORTED Targets

This module defines IMPORTED (page 590) target ZLIB::ZLIB, if ZLIB has been found.

Result Variables

This module defines the following variables:

```
ZLIB_INCLUDE_DIRS   - where to find zlib.h, etc.
ZLIB_LIBRARIES      - List of libraries when using zlib.
ZLIB_FOUND          - True if zlib found.
```

```
ZLIB_VERSION_STRING - The version of zlib found (x.y.z)
ZLIB_VERSION_MAJOR  - The major version of zlib
ZLIB_VERSION_MINOR  - The minor version of zlib
ZLIB_VERSION_PATCH  - The patch version of zlib
ZLIB_VERSION_TWEAK  - The tweak version of zlib
```

Backward Compatibility

The following variable are provided for backward compatibility

```
ZLIB_MAJOR_VERSION  - The major version of zlib
ZLIB_MINOR_VERSION  - The minor version of zlib
ZLIB_PATCH_VERSION  - The patch version of zlib
```

Hints

A user may set ZLIB_ROOT to a zlib installation root to tell this module where to look.

FortranCInterface

Fortran/C Interface Detection

This module automatically detects the API by which C and Fortran languages interact. Variables indicate if the mangling is found:

```
FortranCInterface_GLOBAL_FOUND = Global subroutines and functions
FortranCInterface_MODULE_FOUND = Module subroutines and functions
                                 (declared by "MODULE PROCEDURE")
```

A function is provided to generate a C header file containing macros to mangle symbol names:

```
FortranCInterface_HEADER(<file>
                        [MACRO_NAMESPACE <macro-ns>]
                        [SYMBOL_NAMESPACE <ns>]
                        [SYMBOLS [<module>:]<function> ...])
```

It generates in <file> definitions of the following macros:

```
#define FortranCInterface_GLOBAL (name,NAME) ...
#define FortranCInterface_GLOBAL_(name,NAME) ...
#define FortranCInterface_MODULE (mod,name, MOD,NAME) ...
#define FortranCInterface_MODULE_(mod,name, MOD,NAME) ...
```

These macros mangle four categories of Fortran symbols, respectively:

```
- Global symbols without '_': call mysub()
- Global symbols with '_'    : call my_sub()
- Module symbols without '_': use mymod; call mysub()
- Module symbols with '_'    : use mymod; call my_sub()
```

If mangling for a category is not known, its macro is left undefined. All macros require raw names in both lower case and upper case. The MACRO_NAMESPACE option replaces the default "FortranCInterface (page 517)" prefix with a given namespace "<macro-ns>".

The SYMBOLS option lists symbols to mangle automatically with C preprocessor definitions:

```
<function>          ==> #define <ns><function> ...
<module>:<function> ==> #define <ns><module>_<function> ...
```

If the mangling for some symbol is not known then no preprocessor definition is created, and a warning is displayed. The SYMBOL_NAMESPACE option prefixes all preprocessor definitions generated by the SYMBOLS option with a given namespace "<ns>".

Example usage:

```
include(FortranCInterface)
FortranCInterface_HEADER(FC.h MACRO_NAMESPACE "FC_")
```

This creates a "FC.h" header that defines mangling macros FC_GLOBAL(), FC_GLOBAL_(), FC_MODULE(), and FC_MODULE_().

Example usage:

```
include(FortranCInterface)
FortranCInterface_HEADER(FCMangle.h
                         MACRO_NAMESPACE "FC_"
                         SYMBOL_NAMESPACE "FC_"
                         SYMBOLS mysub mymod:my_sub)
```

This creates a "FCMangle.h" header that defines the same FC_*() mangling macros as the previous example plus preprocessor symbols FC_mysub and FC_mymod_my_sub.

Another function is provided to verify that the Fortran and C/C++ compilers work together:

```
FortranCInterface_VERIFY([CXX] [QUIET])
```

It tests whether a simple test executable using Fortran and C (and C++ when the CXX option is given) compiles and links successfully. The result is stored in the cache entry FortranCInterface_VERIFIED_C (or FortranCInterface_VERIFIED_CXX if CXX is given) as a boolean. If the check fails and QUIET is not given the function terminates with a FATAL_ERROR message describing the problem. The purpose of this check is to stop a build early for incompatible compiler combinations. The test is built in the Release configuration.

FortranCInterface is aware of possible GLOBAL and MODULE manglings for many Fortran compilers, but it also provides an interface to specify new possible manglings. Set the variables

```
FortranCInterface_GLOBAL_SYMBOLS
FortranCInterface_MODULE_SYMBOLS
```

before including FortranCInterface to specify manglings of the symbols "MySub", "My_Sub", "MyModule:MySub", and "My_Module:My_Sub". For example, the code:

```
set(FortranCInterface_GLOBAL_SYMBOLS mysub_ my_sub__ MYSUB_)
  #                                   ^^^^^  ^^^^^^   ^^^^^
set(FortranCInterface_MODULE_SYMBOLS
    __mymodule_MOD_mysub __my_module_MOD_my_sub)
  # ^^^^^^^^^         ^^^^^   ^^^^^^^^^      ^^^^^^
include(FortranCInterface)
```

tells FortranCInterface to try given GLOBAL and MODULE manglings. (The carets point at raw symbol names for clarity in this example but are not needed.)

GenerateExportHeader

Function for generation of export macros for libraries

This module provides the function GENERATE_EXPORT_HEADER().

The GENERATE_EXPORT_HEADER function can be used to generate a file suitable for preprocessor inclusion which contains EXPORT macros to be used in library classes:

```
GENERATE_EXPORT_HEADER( LIBRARY_TARGET
        [BASE_NAME <base_name>]
        [EXPORT_MACRO_NAME <export_macro_name>]
        [EXPORT_FILE_NAME <export_file_name>]
        [DEPRECATED_MACRO_NAME <deprecated_macro_name>]
        [NO_EXPORT_MACRO_NAME <no_export_macro_name>]
        [STATIC_DEFINE <static_define>]
        [NO_DEPRECATED_MACRO_NAME <no_deprecated_macro_name>]
        [DEFINE_NO_DEPRECATED]
        [PREFIX_NAME <prefix_name>]
)
```

The target properties CXX_VISIBILITY_PRESET (page 596) and VISIBILITY_INLINES_HIDDEN (page 609) can be used to add the appropriate compile flags for targets. See the documentation of those target properties, and the convenience variables CMAKE_CXX_VISIBILITY_PRESET (page 660) and CMAKE_VISIBILITY_INLINES_HIDDEN (page 666).

By default GENERATE_EXPORT_HEADER() generates macro names in a file name determined by the name of the library. This means that in the simplest case, users of GenerateExportHeader will be equivalent to:

```
set(CMAKE_CXX_VISIBILITY_PRESET hidden)
set(CMAKE_VISIBILITY_INLINES_HIDDEN 1)
add_library(somelib someclass.cpp)
generate_export_header(somelib)
install(TARGETS somelib DESTINATION ${LIBRARY_INSTALL_DIR})
install(FILES
 someclass.h
 ${PROJECT_BINARY_DIR}/somelib_export.h DESTINATION ${INCLUDE_INSTALL_DIR}
)
```

And in the ABI header files:

```
#include "somelib_export.h"
class SOMELIB_EXPORT SomeClass {
  ...
};
```

The CMake fragment will generate a file in the ${CMAKE_CURRENT_BINARY_DIR} called somelib_export.h containing the macros SOMELIB_EXPORT, SOMELIB_NO_EXPORT, SOMELIB_DEPRECATED, SOMELIB_DEPRECATED_EXPORT and SOMELIB_DEPRECATED_NO_EXPORT. The resulting file should be installed with other headers in the library.

The BASE_NAME argument can be used to override the file name and the names used for the macros:

```
add_library(somelib someclass.cpp)
generate_export_header(somelib
  BASE_NAME other_name
)
```

Generates a file called `other_name_export.h` containing the macros `OTHER_NAME_EXPORT`, `OTHER_NAME_NO_EXPORT` and `OTHER_NAME_DEPRECATED` etc.

The `BASE_NAME` may be overridden by specifiying other options in the function. For example:

```
add_library(somelib someclass.cpp)
generate_export_header(somelib
  EXPORT_MACRO_NAME OTHER_NAME_EXPORT
)
```

creates the macro `OTHER_NAME_EXPORT` instead of `SOMELIB_EXPORT`, but other macros and the generated file name is as default:

```
add_library(somelib someclass.cpp)
generate_export_header(somelib
  DEPRECATED_MACRO_NAME KDE_DEPRECATED
)
```

creates the macro `KDE_DEPRECATED` instead of `SOMELIB_DEPRECATED`.

If `LIBRARY_TARGET` is a static library, macros are defined without values.

If the same sources are used to create both a shared and a static library, the uppercased symbol `${BASE_NAME}_STATIC_DEFINE` should be used when building the static library:

```
add_library(shared_variant SHARED ${lib_SRCS})
add_library(static_variant ${lib_SRCS})
generate_export_header(shared_variant BASE_NAME libshared_and_static)
set_target_properties(static_variant PROPERTIES
  COMPILE_FLAGS -DLIBSHARED_AND_STATIC_STATIC_DEFINE)
```

This will cause the export macros to expand to nothing when building the static library.

If `DEFINE_NO_DEPRECATED` is specified, then a macro `${BASE_NAME}_NO_DEPRECATED` will be defined This macro can be used to remove deprecated code from preprocessor output:

```
option(EXCLUDE_DEPRECATED "Exclude deprecated parts of the library" FALSE)
if (EXCLUDE_DEPRECATED)
  set(NO_BUILD_DEPRECATED DEFINE_NO_DEPRECATED)
endif()
generate_export_header(somelib ${NO_BUILD_DEPRECATED})
```

And then in somelib:

```
class SOMELIB_EXPORT SomeClass
{
public:
#ifndef SOMELIB_NO_DEPRECATED
  SOMELIB_DEPRECATED void oldMethod();
#endif
};
```

```
#ifndef SOMELIB_NO_DEPRECATED
void SomeClass::oldMethod() {   }
#endif
```

If `PREFIX_NAME` is specified, the argument will be used as a prefix to all generated macros.

For example:

```
generate_export_header(somelib PREFIX_NAME VTK_)
```

Generates the macros `VTK_SOMELIB_EXPORT` etc.

```
ADD_COMPILER_EXPORT_FLAGS( [<output_variable>] )
```

The `ADD_COMPILER_EXPORT_FLAGS` function adds `-fvisibility=hidden` to `CMAKE_CXX_FLAGS` (page 672) if supported, and is a no-op on Windows which does not need extra compiler flags for exporting support. You may optionally pass a single argument to `ADD_COMPILER_EXPORT_FLAGS` that will be populated with the `CXX_FLAGS` required to enable visibility support for the compiler/architecture in use.

This function is deprecated. Set the target properties `CXX_VISIBILITY_PRESET` (page 596) and `VISIBILITY_INLINES_HIDDEN` (page 609) instead.

GetPrerequisites

Functions to analyze and list executable file prerequisites.

This module provides functions to list the .dll, .dylib or .so files that an executable or shared library file depends on. (Its prerequisites.)

It uses various tools to obtain the list of required shared library files:

```
dumpbin (Windows)
objdump (MinGW on Windows)
ldd (Linux/Unix)
otool (Mac OSX)
```

The following functions are provided by this module:

```
get_prerequisites
list_prerequisites
list_prerequisites_by_glob
gp_append_unique
is_file_executable
gp_item_default_embedded_path
   (projects can override with gp_item_default_embedded_path_override)
gp_resolve_item
   (projects can override with gp_resolve_item_override)
gp_resolved_file_type
```

```
 (projects can override with gp_resolved_file_type_override)
gp_file_type
```

Requires CMake 2.6 or greater because it uses function, break, return and PARENT_SCOPE.

```
GET_PREREQUISITES(<target> <prerequisites_var> <exclude_system> <recurse>
                   <exepath> <dirs> [<rpaths>])
```

Get the list of shared library files required by <target>. The list in the variable named <prerequisites_var> should be empty on first entry to this function. On exit, <prerequisites_var> will contain the list of required shared library files.

<target> is the full path to an executable file. <prerequisites_var> is the name of a CMake variable to contain the results. <exclude_system> must be 0 or 1 indicating whether to include or exclude "system" prerequisites. If <recurse> is set to 1 all prerequisites will be found recursively, if set to 0 only direct prerequisites are listed. <exepath> is the path to the top level executable used for @executable_path replacment on the Mac. <dirs> is a list of paths where libraries might be found: these paths are searched first when a target without any path info is given. Then standard system locations are also searched: PATH, Framework locations, /usr/lib...

```
LIST_PREREQUISITES(<target> [<recurse> [<exclude_system> [<verbose>]]])
```

Print a message listing the prerequisites of <target>.

<target> is the name of a shared library or executable target or the full path to a shared library or executable file. If <recurse> is set to 1 all prerequisites will be found recursively, if set to 0 only direct prerequisites are listed. <exclude_system> must be 0 or 1 indicating whether to include or exclude "system" prerequisites. With <verbose> set to 0 only the full path names of the prerequisites are printed, set to 1 extra informatin will be displayed.

```
LIST_PREREQUISITES_BY_GLOB(<glob_arg> <glob_exp>)
```

Print the prerequisites of shared library and executable files matching a globbing pattern. <glob_arg> is GLOB or GLOB_RECURSE and <glob_exp> is a globbing expression used with "file(GLOB" or "file(GLOB_RECURSE" to retrieve a list of matching files. If a matching file is executable, its prerequisites are listed.

Any additional (optional) arguments provided are passed along as the optional arguments to the list_prerequisites calls.

```
GP_APPEND_UNIQUE(<list_var> <value>)
```

Append <value> to the list variable <list_var> only if the value is not already in the list.

```
IS_FILE_EXECUTABLE(<file> <result_var>)
```

Return 1 in <result_var> if <file> is a binary executable, 0 otherwise.

```
GP_ITEM_DEFAULT_EMBEDDED_PATH(<item> <default_embedded_path_var>)
```

Return the path that others should refer to the item by when the item is embedded inside a bundle.

Override on a per-project basis by providing a project-specific gp_item_default_embedded_path_override function.

```
GP_RESOLVE_ITEM(<context> <item> <exepath> <dirs> <resolved_item_var>
                [<rpaths>])
```

Resolve an item into an existing full path file.

Override on a per-project basis by providing a project-specific gp_resolve_item_override function.

```
GP_RESOLVED_FILE_TYPE(<original_file> <file> <exepath> <dirs> <type_var>
                      [<rpaths>])
```

Return the type of <file> with respect to <original_file>. String describing type of prerequisite is returned in variable named <type_var>.

Use <exepath> and <dirs> if necessary to resolve non-absolute <file> values – but only for non-embedded items.

Possible types are:

```
system
local
embedded
other
```

Override on a per-project basis by providing a project-specific gp_resolved_file_type_override function.

```
GP_FILE_TYPE(<original_file> <file> <type_var>)
```

Return the type of <file> with respect to <original_file>. String describing type of prerequisite is returned in variable named <type_var>.

Possible types are:

```
system
local
embedded
other
```

GNUInstallDirs

Define GNU standard installation directories

Provides install directory variables as defined for GNU software:

http://www.gnu.org/prep/standards/html_node/Directory-Variables.html

Inclusion of this module defines the following variables:

CMAKE_INSTALL_<dir> destination for files of a given type

CMAKE_INSTALL_FULL_<dir> corresponding absolute path

where <dir> is one of:

BINDIR user executables (bin)

SBINDIR system admin executables (sbin)

LIBEXECDIR program executables (libexec)

SYSCONFDIR read-only single-machine data (etc)

SHAREDSTATEDIR modifiable architecture-independent data (com)

LOCALSTATEDIR modifiable single-machine data (var)

LIBDIR object code libraries (lib or lib64 or lib/<multiarch-tuple> on Debian)

INCLUDEDIR C header files (include)

OLDINCLUDEDIR C header files for non-gcc (/usr/include)

DATAROOTDIR read-only architecture-independent data root (share)

DATADIR read-only architecture-independent data (DATAROOTDIR)

INFODIR info documentation (DATAROOTDIR/info)

LOCALEDIR locale-dependent data (DATAROOTDIR/locale)

MANDIR man documentation (DATAROOTDIR/man)

DOCDIR documentation root (DATAROOTDIR/doc/PROJECT_NAME)

Each CMAKE_INSTALL_<dir> value may be passed to the DESTINATION options of install() commands for the corresponding file type. If the includer does not define a value the above-shown default will be used and the value will appear in the cache for editing by the user. Each CMAKE_INSTALL_FULL_<dir> value contains an absolute path constructed from the corresponding destination by prepending (if necessary) the value of CMAKE_INSTALL_PREFIX.

InstallRequiredSystemLibraries

By including this file, all library files listed in the variable CMAKE_INSTALL_SYSTEM_RUNTIME_LIBS will be installed with install(PROGRAMS ...) into bin for WIN32 and lib for non-WIN32. If CMAKE_INSTALL_SYSTEM_RUNTIME_LIBS_SKIP is set to TRUE before including this file, then the INSTALL command is not called. The user can use the variable CMAKE_INSTALL_SYSTEM_RUNTIME_LIBS to use a custom install command and install them however they want. If it is the MSVC compiler, then the microsoft run time libraries will be found and automatically added to the CMAKE_INSTALL_SYSTEM_RUNTIME_LIBS, and installed. If CMAKE_INSTALL_DEBUG_LIBRARIES is set and it is the MSVC compiler, then the debug libraries are installed when available. If CMAKE_INSTALL_DEBUG_LIBRARIES_ONLY is set then only the debug libraries are installed when both debug and release are available. If CMAKE_INSTALL_MFC_LIBRARIES is set then the MFC run time libraries are installed as well as the CRT run time libraries. If CMAKE_INSTALL_OPENMP_LIBRARIES is set then the OpenMP run time libraries are installed as well. If CMAKE_INSTALL_SYSTEM_RUNTIME_DESTINATION is set then the libraries are installed to that directory rather than the default. If CMAKE_INSTALL_SYSTEM_RUNTIME_LIBS_NO_WARNINGS is NOT set, then this file warns about required files that do not exist. You can set this variable to ON before including this file to avoid the warning. For example, the Visual Studio Express editions do not include the redistributable files, so if you include this file on a machine with only VS Express installed, you'll get the warning.

MacroAddFileDependencies

MACRO_ADD_FILE_DEPENDENCIES(<_file> depend_files...)

Using the macro MACRO_ADD_FILE_DEPENDENCIES() is discouraged. There are usually better ways to specify the correct dependencies.

MACRO_ADD_FILE_DEPENDENCIES(<_file> depend_files...) is just a convenience wrapper around the OBJECT_DEPENDS source file property. You can just use set_property(SOURCE <file> APPEND PROPERTY OBJECT_DEPENDS depend_files) instead.

ProcessorCount

ProcessorCount(var)

Determine the number of processors/cores and save value in ${var}

Sets the variable named ${var} to the number of physical cores available on the machine if the information can be determined. Otherwise it is set to 0. Currently this functionality is implemented for AIX, cygwin, FreeBSD, HPUX, IRIX, Linux, Mac OS X, QNX, Sun and Windows.

This function is guaranteed to return a positive integer (>=1) if it succeeds. It returns 0 if there's a problem determining the processor count.

Example use, in a ctest -S dashboard script:

```
include(ProcessorCount)
ProcessorCount(N)
if(NOT N EQUAL 0)
  set(CTEST_BUILD_FLAGS -j${N})
  set(ctest_test_args ${ctest_test_args} PARALLEL_LEVEL ${N})
endif()
```

This function is intended to offer an approximation of the value of the number of compute cores available on the current machine, such that you may use that value for parallel building and parallel testing. It is meant to help utilize as much of the machine as seems reasonable. Of course, knowledge of what else might be running on the machine simultaneously should be used when deciding whether to request a machine's full capacity all for yourself.

SelectLibraryConfigurations

select_library_configurations(basename)

This macro takes a library base name as an argument, and will choose good values for basename_LIBRARY, basename_LIBRARIES, basename_LIBRARY_DEBUG, and basename_LIBRARY_RELEASE depending on what has been found and set. If only basename_LIBRARY_RELEASE is defined, basename_LIBRARY will be set to the release value, and basename_LIBRARY_DEBUG will be set to basename_LIBRARY_DEBUG-NOTFOUND. If only basename_LIBRARY_DEBUG is defined, then basename_LIBRARY will take the debug value, and basename_LIBRARY_RELEASE will be set to basename_LIBRARY_RELEASE-NOTFOUND.

If the generator supports configuration types, then basename_LIBRARY and basename_LIBRARIES will be set with debug and optimized flags specifying the library to be used for the given configuration. If no build type has been set or the generator in use does not support configuration types, then basename_LIBRARY and basename_LIBRARIES will take only the release value, or the debug value if the release one is not set.

SquishTestScript

This script launches a GUI test using Squish. You should not call the script directly; instead, you should access it via the SQUISH_ADD_TEST macro that is defined in FindSquish.cmake.

This script starts the Squish server, launches the test on the client, and finally stops the squish server. If any of these steps fail (including if the tests do not pass) then a fatal error is raised.

TestBigEndian

Define macro to determine endian type

Check if the system is big endian or little endian

```
TEST_BIG_ENDIAN(VARIABLE)
VARIABLE - variable to store the result to
```

TestCXXAcceptsFlag

Deprecated. See `CheckCXXCompilerFlag` (page 370).

Check if the CXX compiler accepts a flag.

```
CHECK_CXX_ACCEPTS_FLAG(<flags> <variable>)
```

<flags> the flags to try

<variable> variable to store the result

TestForANSIForScope

Check for ANSI for scope support

Check if the compiler restricts the scope of variables declared in a for-init-statement to the loop body.

```
CMAKE_NO_ANSI_FOR_SCOPE - holds result
```

TestForANSIStreamHeaders

Test for compiler support of ANSI stream headers iostream, etc.

check if the compiler supports the standard ANSI iostream header (without the .h)

```
CMAKE_NO_ANSI_STREAM_HEADERS - defined by the results
```

TestForSSTREAM

Test for compiler support of ANSI sstream header

check if the compiler supports the standard ANSI sstream header

```
CMAKE_NO_ANSI_STRING_STREAM - defined by the results
```

TestForSTDNamespace

Test for std:: namespace support

check if the compiler supports std:: on stl classes

```
CMAKE_NO_STD_NAMESPACE - defined by the results
```

UseEcos

This module defines variables and macros required to build eCos application.

This file contains the following macros: ECOS_ADD_INCLUDE_DIRECTORIES() - add the eCos include dirs ECOS_ADD_EXECUTABLE(name source1 ... sourceN) - create an eCos executable ECOS_ADJUST_DIRECTORY(VAR source1 ... sourceN) - adjusts the path of the source files and puts the result into VAR

Macros for selecting the toolchain: ECOS_USE_ARM_ELF_TOOLS() - enable the ARM ELF toolchain for the directory where it is called ECOS_USE_I386_ELF_TOOLS() - enable the i386 ELF toolchain for the directory where it is called ECOS_USE_PPC_EABI_TOOLS() - enable the PowerPC toolchain for the directory where it is called

It contains the following variables: ECOS_DEFINITIONS ECOSCONFIG_EXECUTABLE ECOS_CONFIG_FILE - defaults to ecos.ecc, if your eCos configuration file has a different name, adjust this variable for internal use only:

```
ECOS_ADD_TARGET_LIB
```

UseJavaClassFilelist

This script create a list of compiled Java class files to be added to a jar file. This avoids including cmake files which get created in the binary directory.

UseJava

Use Module for Java

This file provides functions for Java. It is assumed that FindJava.cmake has already been loaded. See FindJava.cmake for information on how to load Java into your CMake project.

```
add_jar(target_name
        [SOURCES] source1 [source2 ...] [resource1 ...]
        [INCLUDE_JARS jar1 [jar2 ...]]
        [ENTRY_POINT entry]
        [VERSION version]
        [OUTPUT_NAME name]
        [OUTPUT_DIR dir]
        )
```

This command creates a <target_name>.jar. It compiles the given source files (source) and adds the given resource files (resource) to the jar file. If only resource files are given then just a jar file is created. The list of include jars are added to the classpath when compiling the java sources and also to the dependencies of the target. INCLUDE_JARS also accepts other target names created by add_jar. For backwards compatibility, jar files listed as sources are ignored (as they have been since the first version of this module).

The default OUTPUT_DIR can also be changed by setting the variable CMAKE_JAVA_TARGET_OUTPUT_DIR.

Additional instructions:

```
To add compile flags to the target you can set these flags with
the following variable:
```

```
set(CMAKE_JAVA_COMPILE_FLAGS -nowarn)
```

```
To add a path or a jar file to the class path you can do this
with the CMAKE_JAVA_INCLUDE_PATH variable.
```

```
set(CMAKE_JAVA_INCLUDE_PATH /usr/share/java/shibboleet.jar)
```

```
To use a different output name for the target you can set it with:
```

```
add_jar(foobar foobar.java OUTPUT_NAME shibboleet.jar)
```

```
To use a different output directory than CMAKE_CURRENT_BINARY_DIR
you can set it with:
```

```
add_jar(foobar foobar.java OUTPUT_DIR ${PROJECT_BINARY_DIR}/bin)
```

To define an entry point in your jar you can set it with the ENTRY_POINT
named argument:

```
add_jar(example ENTRY_POINT com/examples/MyProject/Main)
```

To define a custom manifest for the jar, you can set it with the manifest
named argument:

```
add_jar(example MANIFEST /path/to/manifest)
```

To add a VERSION to the target output name you can set it using
the VERSION named argument to add_jar. This will create a jar file with the
name shibboleet-1.0.0.jar and will create a symlink shibboleet.jar
pointing to the jar with the version information.

```
add_jar(shibboleet shibbotleet.java VERSION 1.2.0)
```

If the target is a JNI library, utilize the following commands to
create a JNI symbolic link:

```
set(CMAKE_JNI_TARGET TRUE)
add_jar(shibboleet shibbotleet.java VERSION 1.2.0)
install_jar(shibboleet ${LIB_INSTALL_DIR}/shibboleet)
install_jni_symlink(shibboleet ${JAVA_LIB_INSTALL_DIR})
```

If a single target needs to produce more than one jar from its
java source code, to prevent the accumulation of duplicate class
files in subsequent jars, set/reset CMAKE_JAR_CLASSES_PREFIX prior
to calling the add_jar() function:

```
set(CMAKE_JAR_CLASSES_PREFIX com/redhat/foo)
add_jar(foo foo.java)
```

```
set(CMAKE_JAR_CLASSES_PREFIX com/redhat/bar)
add_jar(bar bar.java)
```

Target Properties:

```
The add_jar() functions sets some target properties. You can get these
properties with the
   get_property(TARGET <target_name> PROPERTY <propery_name>)
command.
```

INSTALL_FILES	The files which should be installed. This is used by install_jar().
JNI_SYMLINK	The JNI symlink which should be installed. This is used by install_jni_symlink().

```
JAR_FILE              The location of the jar file so that you can include
                      it.
CLASS_DIR             The directory where the class files can be found. For
                      example to use them with javah.
```

```
find_jar(<VAR>
         name | NAMES name1 [name2 ...]
         [PATHS path1 [path2 ... ENV var]]
         [VERSIONS version1 [version2]]
         [DOC "cache documentation string"]
         )
```

This command is used to find a full path to the named jar. A cache entry named by <VAR> is created to stor
the result of this command. If the full path to a jar is found the result is stored in the variable and the search
will not repeated unless the variable is cleared. If nothing is found, the result will be <VAR>-NOTFOUND,
and the search will be attempted again next time find_jar is invoked with the same variable. The name of
the full path to a file that is searched for is specified by the names listed after NAMES argument. Additional
search locations can be specified after the PATHS argument. If you require special a version of a jar file you
can specify it with the VERSIONS argument. The argument after DOC will be used for the documentation
string in the cache.

```
install_jar(TARGET_NAME DESTINATION)
```

This command installs the TARGET_NAME files to the given DESTINATION. It should be called in the
same scope as add_jar() or it will fail.

```
install_jni_symlink(TARGET_NAME DESTINATION)
```

This command installs the TARGET_NAME JNI symlinks to the given DESTINATION. It should be called
in the same scope as add_jar() or it will fail.

```
create_javadoc(<VAR>
               PACKAGES pkg1 [pkg2 ...]
               [SOURCEPATH <sourcepath>]
               [CLASSPATH <classpath>]
               [INSTALLPATH <install path>]
               [DOCTITLE "the documentation title"]
               [WINDOWTITLE "the title of the document"]
               [AUTHOR TRUE|FALSE]
               [USE TRUE|FALSE]
               [VERSION TRUE|FALSE]
               )
```

Create java documentation based on files or packages. For more details please read the javadoc manpage.

There are two main signatures for create_javadoc. The first signature works with package names on a path
with source files:

```
Example:
create_javadoc(my_example_doc
```

```
    PACKAGES com.exmaple.foo com.example.bar
    SOURCEPATH "${CMAKE_CURRENT_SOURCE_DIR}"
    CLASSPATH ${CMAKE_JAVA_INCLUDE_PATH}
    WINDOWTITLE "My example"
    DOCTITLE "<h1>My example</h1>"
    AUTHOR TRUE
    USE TRUE
    VERSION TRUE
)
```

The second signature for create_javadoc works on a given list of files.

```
create_javadoc(<VAR>
                FILES file1 [file2 ...]
                [CLASSPATH <classpath>]
                [INSTALLPATH <install path>]
                [DOCTITLE "the documentation title"]
                [WINDOWTITLE "the title of the document"]
                [AUTHOR TRUE|FALSE]
                [USE TRUE|FALSE]
                [VERSION TRUE|FALSE]
                )
```

Example:

```
create_javadoc(my_example_doc
  FILES ${example_SRCS}
  CLASSPATH ${CMAKE_JAVA_INCLUDE_PATH}
  WINDOWTITLE "My example"
  DOCTITLE "<h1>My example</h1>"
  AUTHOR TRUE
  USE TRUE
  VERSION TRUE
)
```

Both signatures share most of the options. These options are the same as what you can find in the javadoc manpage. Please look at the manpage for CLASSPATH, DOCTITLE, WINDOWTITLE, AUTHOR, USE and VERSION.

The documentation will be by default installed to

```
${CMAKE_INSTALL_PREFIX}/share/javadoc/<VAR>
```

if you don't set the INSTALLPATH.

UseJavaSymlinks

Helper script for UseJava.cmake

UsePkgConfig

Obsolete pkg-config module for CMake, use FindPkgConfig instead.

This module defines the following macro:

PKGCONFIG(package includedir libdir linkflags cflags)

Calling PKGCONFIG will fill the desired information into the 4 given arguments, e.g. PKGCONFIG(libart-2.0 LIBART_INCLUDE_DIR LIBART_LINK_DIR LIBART_LINK_FLAGS LIBART_CFLAGS) if pkg-config was NOT found or the specified software package doesn't exist, the variable will be empty when the function returns, otherwise they will contain the respective information

UseSWIG

Defines the following macros for use with SWIG:

```
SWIG_ADD_MODULE(name language [ files ])
 - Define swig module with given name and specified language
SWIG_LINK_LIBRARIES(name [ libraries ])
 - Link libraries to swig module
```

Source files properties on module files can be set before the invocation of the SWIG_ADD_MODULE macro to specify special behavior of SWIG.

The source file property CPLUSPLUS calls SWIG in c++ mode, e.g.:

```
set_property(SOURCE mymod.i PROPERTY CPLUSPLUS ON)
swig_add_module(mymod python mymod.i)
```

The source file property SWIG_FLAGS adds custom flags to the SWIG executable.

The source-file property SWIG_MODULE_NAME have to be provided to specify the actual import name of the module in the target language if it cannot be scanned automatically from source or different from the module file basename.:

```
set_property(SOURCE mymod.i PROPERTY SWIG_MODULE_NAME mymod_realname)
```

To get the name of the swig module target library, use: ${SWIG_MODULE_${name}_REAL_NAME}.

Also some variables can be set to specify special behavior of SWIG.

CMAKE_SWIG_FLAGS can be used to add special flags to all swig calls.

Another special variable is CMAKE_SWIG_OUTDIR, it allows one to specify where to write all the swig generated module (swig -outdir option)

The name-specific variable SWIG_MODULE_<name>_EXTRA_DEPS may be used to specify extra dependencies for the generated modules.

If the source file generated by swig need some special flag you can use:

```
set_source_files_properties( ${swig_generated_file_fullname}
                             PROPERTIES COMPILE_FLAGS "-bla")
```

UsewxWidgets

Convenience include for using wxWidgets library.

Determines if wxWidgets was FOUND and sets the appropriate libs, incdirs, flags, etc. IN-CLUDE_DIRECTORIES and LINK_DIRECTORIES are called.

USAGE

```
# Note that for MinGW users the order of libs is important!
find_package(wxWidgets REQUIRED net gl core base)
include(${wxWidgets_USE_FILE})
# and for each of your dependent executable/library targets:
target_link_libraries(<YourTarget> ${wxWidgets_LIBRARIES})
```

DEPRECATED

```
LINK_LIBRARIES is not called in favor of adding dependencies per target.
```

AUTHOR

```
Jan Woetzel <jw -at- mip.informatik.uni-kiel.de>
```

Use_wxWindows

This convenience include finds if wxWindows is installed and set the appropriate libs, incdirs, flags etc. author Jan Woetzel <jw -at- mip.informatik.uni-kiel.de> (07/2003)

USAGE:

```
just include Use_wxWindows.cmake
in your projects CMakeLists.txt
```

include(${CMAKE_MODULE_PATH}/Use_wxWindows.cmake)

```
if you are sure you need GL then
```

set(WXWINDOWS_USE_GL 1)

```
*before* you include this file.
```

WriteBasicConfigVersionFile

```
WRITE_BASIC_CONFIG_VERSION_FILE( filename
  [VERSION major.minor.patch]
  COMPATIBILITY (AnyNewerVersion|SameMajorVersion)
  )
```

Deprecated, see WRITE_BASIC_PACKAGE_VERSION_FILE(), it is identical.

WriteCompilerDetectionHeader

This module provides the function write_compiler_detection_header().

The WRITE_COMPILER_DETECTION_HEADER function can be used to generate a file suitable for pre-processor inclusion which contains macros to be used in source code:

```
write_compiler_detection_header(
        FILE <file>
        PREFIX <prefix>
        COMPILERS <compiler> [...]
        FEATURES <feature> [...]
        [VERSION <version>]
        [PROLOG <prolog>]
        [EPILOG <epilog>]
)
```

The write_compiler_detection_header function generates the file <file> with macros which all have the prefix <prefix>.

VERSION may be used to specify the API version to be generated. Future versions of CMake may introduce alternative APIs. A given API is selected by any <version> value greater than or equal to the version of CMake that introduced the given API and less than the version of CMake that introduced its succeeding API. The value of the CMAKE_MINIMUM_REQUIRED_VERSION (page 630) variable is used if no explicit version is specified. (As of CMake version 3.1.0 there is only one API version.)

PROLOG may be specified as text content to write at the start of the header. EPILOG may be specified as text content to write at the end of the header

At least one <compiler> and one <feature> must be listed. Compilers which are known to CMake, but not specified are detected and a preprocessor #error is generated for them. A preprocessor macro matching <PREFIX>_COMPILER_IS_<compiler> is generated for each compiler known to CMake to contain the value 0 or 1.

Possible compiler identifiers are documented with the CMAKE_<LANG>_COMPILER_ID (page 670) variable. Available features in this version of CMake are listed in the CMAKE_C_KNOWN_FEATURES (page 560) and CMAKE_CXX_KNOWN_FEATURES (page 560) global properties.

See the cmake-compile-features(7) manual for information on compile features.

Feature Test Macros

For each compiler, a preprocessor macro is generated matching <PREFIX>_COMPILER_IS_<compiler> which has the content either 0 or 1, depending on the compiler in use. Preprocessor macros for compiler version components are generated matching <PREFIX>_COMPILER_VERSION_MAJOR <PREFIX>_COMPILER_VERSION_MINOR and <PREFIX>_COMPILER_VERSION_PATCH containing decimal values for the corresponding compiler version components, if defined.

A preprocessor test is generated based on the compiler version denoting whether each feature is enabled. A preprocessor macro matching <PREFIX>_COMPILER_<FEATURE>, where <FEATURE> is the uppercase <feature> name, is generated to contain the value 0 or 1 depending on whether the compiler in use supports the feature:

```
write_compiler_detection_header(
  FILE climbingstats_compiler_detection.h
  PREFIX ClimbingStats
  COMPILERS GNU Clang
  FEATURES cxx_variadic_templates
)
```

```
#if ClimbingStats_COMPILER_CXX_VARIADIC_TEMPLATES
template<typename... T>
void someInterface(T t...) { /* ... */ }
#else
// Compatibility versions
template<typename T1>
void someInterface(T1 t1) { /* ... */ }
template<typename T1, typename T2>
void someInterface(T1 t1, T2 t2) { /* ... */ }
template<typename T1, typename T2, typename T3>
void someInterface(T1 t1, T2 t2, T3 t3) { /* ... */ }
#endif
```

Symbol Macros

Some additional symbol-defines are created for particular features for use as symbols which may be conditionally defined empty:

```
class MyClass ClimbingStats_FINAL
{
    ClimbingStats_CONSTEXPR int someInterface() { return 42; }
};
```

The ClimbingStats_FINAL macro will expand to final if the compiler (and its flags) support the cxx_final feature, and the ClimbingStats_CONSTEXPR macro will expand to constexpr if cxx_constexpr is supported.

The following features generate corresponding symbol defines:

Feature	Define	Symbol
c_restrict	<PREFIX>_RESTRICT	restrict
cxx_constexpr	<PREFIX>_CONSTEXPR	constexpr
cxx_deleted_functions	<PREFIX>_DELETED_FUNCTION	= delete
cxx_extern_templates	<PREFIX>_EXTERN_TEMPLATE	extern
cxx_final	<PREFIX>_FINAL	final
cxx_noexcept	<PREFIX>_NOEXCEPT	noexcept
cxx_noexcept	<PREFIX>_NOEXCEPT_EXPR(X)	noexcept(X)
cxx_override	<PREFIX>_OVERRIDE	override

Compatibility Implementation Macros

Some features are suitable for wrapping in a macro with a backward compatibility implementation if the compiler does not support the feature.

When the cxx_static_assert feature is not provided by the compiler, a compatibility implementation is available via the <PREFIX>_STATIC_ASSERT(COND) and <PREFIX>_STATIC_ASSERT_MSG(COND, MSG) function-like macros. The macros expand to static_assert where that compiler feature is available, and to a compatibility implementation otherwise. In the first form, the condition is stringified in the message field of static_assert. In the second form, the message MSG is passed to the message field of static_assert, or ignored if using the backward compatibility implementation.

The cxx_attribute_deprecated feature provides a macro definition <PREFIX>_DEPRECATED, which expands to either the standard [[deprecated]] attribute or a compiler-specific decorator such as __attribute__((__deprecated__)) used by GNU compilers.

The cxx_alignas feature provides a macro definition <PREFIX>_ALIGNAS which expands to either the standard alignas decorator or a compiler-specific decorator such as __attribute__ ((__aligned__)) used by GNU compilers.

The cxx_alignof feature provides a macro definition <PREFIX>_ALIGNOF which expands to either the standard alignof decorator or a compiler-specific decorator such as __alignof__ used by GNU compilers.

Feature	Define	Symbol
cxx_alignas	<PREFIX>_ALIGNAS	alignas
cxx_alignof	<PREFIX>_ALIGNOF	alignof
cxx_nullptr	<PREFIX>_NULLPTR	nullptr
cxx_static_assert	<PREFIX>_STATIC_ASSERT	static_assert
cxx_static_assert	<PREFIX>_STATIC_ASSERT_MSG	static_assert
cxx_attribute_deprecated	<PREFIX>_DEPRECATED	[[deprecated]]
cxx_attribute_deprecated	<PREFIX>_DEPRECATED_MSG	[[deprecated]]

A use-case which arises with such deprecation macros is the deprecation of an entire library. In that case, all public API in the library may be decorated with the <PREFIX>_DEPRECATED macro. This results in very noisy build output when building the library itself, so the macro may be may be defined to empty in that case when building the deprecated library:

```
add_library(compat_support ${srcs})
target_compile_definitions(compat_support
  PRIVATE
    CompatSupport_DEPRECATED=
)
```

C.5 cmake-policies(7)

C.5.1 Introduction

Policies in CMake are used to preserve backward compatible behavior across multiple releases. When a new policy is introduced, newer CMake versions will begin to warn about the backward compatible behavior. It is possible to disable the warning by explicitly requesting the OLD, or backward compatible behavior using the cmake_policy() (page 280) command. It is also possible to request NEW, or non-backward compatible behavior for a policy, also avoiding the warning. Each policy can also be set to either NEW or OLD behavior explicitly on the command line with the CMAKE_POLICY_DEFAULT_CMP<NNNN> (page 647) variable.

The cmake_minimum_required() (page 280) command does more than report an error if a too-old version of CMake is used to build a project. It also sets all policies introduced in that CMake version or earlier to NEW behavior. To manage policies without increasing the minimum required CMake version, the if(POLICY) (page 313) command may be used:

```
if(POLICY CMP0990)
  cmake_policy(SET CMP0990 NEW)
endif()
```

This has the effect of using the NEW behavior with newer CMake releases which users may be using and not issuing a compatibility warning.

The setting of a policy is confined in some cases to not propagate to the parent scope. For example, if the files read by the include() (page 317) command or the find_package() (page 297) command contain a use of cmake_policy() (page 280), that policy setting will not affect the caller by default. Both commands accept an optional NO_POLICY_SCOPE keyword to control this behavior.

The CMAKE_MINIMUM_REQUIRED_VERSION (page 630) variable may also be used to determine whether to report an error on use of deprecated macros or functions.

C.5.2 All Policies

CMP0000

A minimum required CMake version must be specified.

CMake requires that projects specify the version of CMake to which they have been written. This policy has been put in place so users trying to build the project may be told when they need to update their CMake. Specifying a version also helps the project build with CMake versions newer than that specified. Use the cmake_minimum_required command at the top of your main CMakeLists.txt file:

```
cmake_minimum_required(VERSION <major>.<minor>)
```

where "<major>.<minor>" is the version of CMake you want to support (such as "2.6"). The command will ensure that at least the given version of CMake is running and help newer versions be compatible with the project. See documentation of cmake_minimum_required for details.

Note that the command invocation must appear in the CMakeLists.txt file itself; a call in an included file is not sufficient. However, the cmake_policy command may be called to set policy CMP0000 to OLD or NEW behavior explicitly. The OLD behavior is to silently ignore the missing invocation. The NEW behavior is to issue an error instead of a warning. An included file may set CMP0000 explicitly to affect how this policy is enforced for the main CMakeLists.txt file.

This policy was introduced in CMake version 2.6.0.

CMP0001

CMAKE_BACKWARDS_COMPATIBILITY should no longer be used.

The OLD behavior is to check CMAKE_BACKWARDS_COMPATIBILITY and present it to the user. The NEW behavior is to ignore CMAKE_BACKWARDS_COMPATIBILITY completely.

In CMake 2.4 and below the variable CMAKE_BACKWARDS_COMPATIBILITY was used to request compatibility with earlier versions of CMake. In CMake 2.6 and above all compatibility issues are handled by policies and the cmake_policy command. However, CMake must still check CMAKE_BACKWARDS_COMPATIBILITY for projects written for CMake 2.4 and below.

This policy was introduced in CMake version 2.6.0. CMake version 3.1.0 warns when the policy is not set and uses OLD behavior. Use the cmake_policy command to set it to OLD or NEW explicitly.

CMP0002

Logical target names must be globally unique.

Targets names created with add_executable, add_library, or add_custom_target are logical build target names. Logical target names must be globally unique because:

```
- Unique names may be referenced unambiguously both in CMake
  code and on make tool command lines.
- Logical names are used by Xcode and VS IDE generators
  to produce meaningful project names for the targets.
```

The logical name of executable and library targets does not have to correspond to the physical file names built. Consider using the OUTPUT_NAME target property to create two targets with the same physical name while keeping logical names distinct. Custom targets must simply have globally unique names (unless one uses the global property ALLOW_DUPLICATE_CUSTOM_TARGETS with a Makefiles generator).

This policy was introduced in CMake version 2.6.0. CMake version 3.1.0 warns when the policy is not set and uses OLD behavior. Use the cmake_policy command to set it to OLD or NEW explicitly.

CMP0003

Libraries linked via full path no longer produce linker search paths.

This policy affects how libraries whose full paths are NOT known are found at link time, but was created due to a change in how CMake deals with libraries whose full paths are known. Consider the code

```
target_link_libraries(myexe /path/to/libA.so)
```

CMake 2.4 and below implemented linking to libraries whose full paths are known by splitting them on the link line into separate components consisting of the linker search path and the library name. The example code might have produced something like

```
... -L/path/to -lA ...
```

in order to link to library A. An analysis was performed to order multiple link directories such that the linker would find library A in the desired location, but there are cases in which this does not work. CMake versions 2.6 and above use the more reliable approach of passing the full path to libraries directly to the linker in most cases. The example code now produces something like

```
... /path/to/libA.so ....
```

Unfortunately this change can break code like

```
target_link_libraries(myexe /path/to/libA.so B)
```

where "B" is meant to find "/path/to/libB.so". This code is wrong because the user is asking the linker to find library B but has not provided a linker search path (which may be added with the link_directories command). However, with the old linking implementation the code would work accidentally because the linker search path added for library A allowed library B to be found.

In order to support projects depending on linker search paths added by linking to libraries with known full paths, the OLD behavior for this policy will add the linker search paths even though they are not needed for their own libraries. When this policy is set to OLD, CMake will produce a link line such as

```
... -L/path/to /path/to/libA.so -lB ...
```

which will allow library B to be found as it was previously. When this policy is set to NEW, CMake will produce a link line such as

```
... /path/to/libA.so -lB ...
```

which more accurately matches what the project specified.

The setting for this policy used when generating the link line is that in effect when the target is created by an add_executable or add_library command. For the example described above, the code

```
cmake_policy(SET CMP0003 OLD) # or cmake_policy(VERSION 2.4)
add_executable(myexe myexe.c)
target_link_libraries(myexe /path/to/libA.so B)
```

will work and suppress the warning for this policy. It may also be updated to work with the corrected linking approach:

```
cmake_policy(SET CMP0003 NEW) # or cmake_policy(VERSION 2.6)
link_directories(/path/to) # needed to find library B
add_executable(myexe myexe.c)
target_link_libraries(myexe /path/to/libA.so B)
```

Even better, library B may be specified with a full path:

```
add_executable(myexe myexe.c)
target_link_libraries(myexe /path/to/libA.so /path/to/libB.so)
```

When all items on the link line have known paths CMake does not check this policy so it has no effect.

Note that the warning for this policy will be issued for at most one target. This avoids flooding users with messages for every target when setting the policy once will probably fix all targets.

This policy was introduced in CMake version 2.6.0. CMake version 3.1.0 warns when the policy is not set and uses OLD behavior. Use the cmake_policy command to set it to OLD or NEW explicitly.

CMP0004

Libraries linked may not have leading or trailing whitespace.

CMake versions 2.4 and below silently removed leading and trailing whitespace from libraries linked with code like

```
target_link_libraries(myexe " A ")
```

This could lead to subtle errors in user projects.

The OLD behavior for this policy is to silently remove leading and trailing whitespace. The NEW behavior for this policy is to diagnose the existence of such whitespace as an error. The setting for this policy used when checking the library names is that in effect when the target is created by an add_executable or add_library command.

This policy was introduced in CMake version 2.6.0. CMake version 3.1.0 warns when the policy is not set and uses OLD behavior. Use the cmake_policy command to set it to OLD or NEW explicitly.

CMP0005

Preprocessor definition values are now escaped automatically.

This policy determines whether or not CMake should generate escaped preprocessor definition values added via add_definitions. CMake versions 2.4 and below assumed that only trivial values would be given for macros in add_definitions calls. It did not attempt to escape non-trivial values such as string literals in generated build rules. CMake versions 2.6 and above support escaping of most values, but cannot assume the user has not added escapes already in an attempt to work around limitations in earlier versions.

The OLD behavior for this policy is to place definition values given to add_definitions directly in the generated build rules without attempting to escape anything. The NEW behavior for this policy is to generate correct escapes for all native build tools automatically. See documentation of the COMPILE_DEFINITIONS target property for limitations of the escaping implementation.

This policy was introduced in CMake version 2.6.0. CMake version 3.1.0 warns when the policy is not set and uses OLD behavior. Use the cmake_policy command to set it to OLD or NEW explicitly.

CMP0006

Installing MACOSX_BUNDLE targets requires a BUNDLE DESTINATION.

This policy determines whether the install(TARGETS) command must be given a BUNDLE DESTINATION when asked to install a target with the MACOSX_BUNDLE property set. CMake 2.4 and below did not distinguish application bundles from normal executables when installing targets. CMake 2.6 provides a BUNDLE option to the install(TARGETS) command that specifies rules specific to application bundles on the Mac. Projects should use this option when installing a target with the MACOSX_BUNDLE property set.

The OLD behavior for this policy is to fall back to the RUNTIME DESTINATION if a BUNDLE DESTINATION is not given. The NEW behavior for this policy is to produce an error if a bundle target is installed without a BUNDLE DESTINATION.

This policy was introduced in CMake version 2.6.0. CMake version 3.1.0 warns when the policy is not set and uses OLD behavior. Use the cmake_policy command to set it to OLD or NEW explicitly.

CMP0007

list command no longer ignores empty elements.

This policy determines whether the list command will ignore empty elements in the list. CMake 2.4 and below list commands ignored all empty elements in the list. For example, a;b;;c would have length 3 and not 4. The OLD behavior for this policy is to ignore empty list elements. The NEW behavior for this policy is to correctly count empty elements in a list.

This policy was introduced in CMake version 2.6.0. CMake version 3.1.0 warns when the policy is not set and uses OLD behavior. Use the cmake_policy command to set it to OLD or NEW explicitly.

CMP0008

Libraries linked by full-path must have a valid library file name.

In CMake 2.4 and below it is possible to write code like

```
target_link_libraries(myexe /full/path/to/somelib)
```

where "somelib" is supposed to be a valid library file name such as "libsomelib.a" or "somelib.lib". For Makefile generators this produces an error at build time because the dependency on the full path cannot be found. For VS IDE and Xcode generators this used to work by accident because CMake would always split off the library directory and ask the linker to search for the library by name (-lsomelib or somelib.lib). Despite the failure with Makefiles, some projects have code like this and build only with VS and/or Xcode. This version of CMake prefers to pass the full path directly to the native build tool, which will fail in this case because it does not name a valid library file.

This policy determines what to do with full paths that do not appear to name a valid library file. The OLD behavior for this policy is to split the library name from the path and ask the linker to search for it. The NEW behavior for this policy is to trust the given path and pass it directly to the native build tool unchanged.

This policy was introduced in CMake version 2.6.1. CMake version 3.1.0 warns when the policy is not set and uses OLD behavior. Use the cmake_policy command to set it to OLD or NEW explicitly.

CMP0009

FILE GLOB_RECURSE calls should not follow symlinks by default.

In CMake 2.6.1 and below, FILE GLOB_RECURSE calls would follow through symlinks, sometimes coming up with unexpectedly large result sets because of symlinks to top level directories that contain hundreds of thousands of files.

This policy determines whether or not to follow symlinks encountered during a FILE GLOB_RECURSE call. The OLD behavior for this policy is to follow the symlinks. The NEW behavior for this policy is not to follow the symlinks by default, but only if FOLLOW_SYMLINKS is given as an additional argument to the FILE command.

This policy was introduced in CMake version 2.6.2. CMake version 3.1.0 warns when the policy is not set and uses OLD behavior. Use the cmake_policy command to set it to OLD or NEW explicitly.

CMP0010

Bad variable reference syntax is an error.

In CMake 2.6.2 and below, incorrect variable reference syntax such as a missing close-brace ("${FOO") was reported but did not stop processing of CMake code. This policy determines whether a bad variable reference is an error. The OLD behavior for this policy is to warn about the error, leave the string untouched, and continue. The NEW behavior for this policy is to report an error.

If CMP0053 (page 558) is set to NEW, this policy has no effect and is treated as always being NEW.

This policy was introduced in CMake version 2.6.3. CMake version 3.1.0 warns when the policy is not set and uses OLD behavior. Use the cmake_policy command to set it to OLD or NEW explicitly.

CMP0011

Included scripts do automatic cmake_policy PUSH and POP.

In CMake 2.6.2 and below, CMake Policy settings in scripts loaded by the include() and find_package() commands would affect the includer. Explicit invocations of cmake_policy(PUSH) and cmake_policy(POP) were required to isolate policy changes and protect the includer. While some scripts intend to affect the policies of their includer, most do not. In CMake 2.6.3 and above, include() and find_package() by default PUSH and POP an entry on the policy stack around an included script, but provide a NO_POLICY_SCOPE option to disable it. This policy determines whether or not to imply NO_POLICY_SCOPE for compatibility. The OLD behavior for this policy is to imply NO_POLICY_SCOPE for include() and find_package() commands. The NEW behavior for this policy is to allow the commands to do their default cmake_policy PUSH and POP.

This policy was introduced in CMake version 2.6.3. CMake version 3.1.0 warns when the policy is not set and uses OLD behavior. Use the cmake_policy command to set it to OLD or NEW explicitly.

CMP0012

if() recognizes numbers and boolean constants.

In CMake versions 2.6.4 and lower the if() command implicitly dereferenced arguments corresponding to variables, even those named like numbers or boolean constants, except for 0 and 1. Numbers and boolean constants such as true, false, yes, no, on, off, y, n, notfound, ignore (all case insensitive) were recognized in some cases but not all. For example, the code "if(TRUE)" might have evaluated as false. Numbers such as 2 were recognized only in boolean expressions like "if(NOT 2)" (leading to false) but not as a single-argument like "if(2)" (also leading to false). Later versions of CMake prefer to treat numbers and boolean constants literally, so they should not be used as variable names.

The OLD behavior for this policy is to implicitly dereference variables named like numbers and boolean constants. The NEW behavior for this policy is to recognize numbers and boolean constants without dereferencing variables with such names.

This policy was introduced in CMake version 2.8.0. CMake version 3.1.0 warns when the policy is not set and uses OLD behavior. Use the cmake_policy command to set it to OLD or NEW explicitly.

CMP0013

Duplicate binary directories are not allowed.

CMake 2.6.3 and below silently permitted add_subdirectory() calls to create the same binary directory multiple times. During build system generation files would be written and then overwritten in the build tree and could lead to strange behavior. CMake 2.6.4 and above explicitly detect duplicate binary directories. CMake 2.6.4 always considers this case an error. In CMake 2.8.0 and above this policy determines whether or not the case is an error. The OLD behavior for this policy is to allow duplicate binary directories. The NEW behavior for this policy is to disallow duplicate binary directories with an error.

This policy was introduced in CMake version 2.8.0. CMake version 3.1.0 warns when the policy is not set and uses OLD behavior. Use the cmake_policy command to set it to OLD or NEW explicitly.

CMP0014

Input directories must have CMakeLists.txt.

CMake versions before 2.8 silently ignored missing CMakeLists.txt files in directories referenced by add_subdirectory() or subdirs(), treating them as if present but empty. In CMake 2.8.0 and above this policy determines whether or not the case is an error. The OLD behavior for this policy is to silently ignore the problem. The NEW behavior for this policy is to report an error.

This policy was introduced in CMake version 2.8.0. CMake version 3.1.0 warns when the policy is not set and uses OLD behavior. Use the cmake_policy command to set it to OLD or NEW explicitly.

CMP0015

link_directories() treats paths relative to the source dir.

In CMake 2.8.0 and lower the link_directories() command passed relative paths unchanged to the linker. In CMake 2.8.1 and above the link_directories() command prefers to interpret relative paths with respect to CMAKE_CURRENT_SOURCE_DIR, which is consistent with include_directories() and other commands. The OLD behavior for this policy is to use relative paths verbatim in the linker command. The NEW behavior for this policy is to convert relative paths to absolute paths by appending the relative path to CMAKE_CURRENT_SOURCE_DIR.

This policy was introduced in CMake version 2.8.1. CMake version 3.1.0 warns when the policy is not set and uses OLD behavior. Use the cmake_policy command to set it to OLD or NEW explicitly.

CMP0016

target_link_libraries() reports error if its only argument is not a target.

In CMake 2.8.2 and lower the target_link_libraries() command silently ignored if it was called with only one argument, and this argument wasn't a valid target. In CMake 2.8.3 and above it reports an error in this case.

This policy was introduced in CMake version 2.8.3. CMake version 3.1.0 warns when the policy is not set and uses OLD behavior. Use the cmake_policy command to set it to OLD or NEW explicitly.

CMP0017

Prefer files from the CMake module directory when including from there.

Starting with CMake 2.8.4, if a cmake-module shipped with CMake (i.e. located in the CMake module directory) calls include() or find_package(), the files located in the CMake module directory are preferred over the files in CMAKE_MODULE_PATH. This makes sure that the modules belonging to CMake always get those files included which they expect, and against which they were developed and tested. In all other cases, the files found in CMAKE_MODULE_PATH still take precedence over the ones in the CMake module directory. The OLD behavior is to always prefer files from CMAKE_MODULE_PATH over files from the CMake modules directory.

This policy was introduced in CMake version 2.8.4. CMake version 3.1.0 warns when the policy is not set and uses OLD behavior. Use the cmake_policy command to set it to OLD or NEW explicitly.

CMP0018

Ignore CMAKE_SHARED_LIBRARY_<Lang>_FLAGS variable.

CMake 2.8.8 and lower compiled sources in SHARED and MODULE libraries using the value of the undocumented CMAKE_SHARED_LIBRARY_<Lang>_FLAGS platform variable. The variable contained platform-specific flags needed to compile objects for shared libraries. Typically it included a flag such as -fPIC for position independent code but also included other flags needed on certain platforms. CMake 2.8.9 and higher prefer instead to use the POSITION_INDEPENDENT_CODE target property to determine what targets should be position independent, and new undocumented platform variables to select flags while ignoring CMAKE_SHARED_LIBRARY_<Lang>_FLAGS completely.

The default for either approach produces identical compilation flags, but if a project modifies CMAKE_SHARED_LIBRARY_<Lang>_FLAGS from its original value this policy determines which approach to use.

The OLD behavior for this policy is to ignore the POSITION_INDEPENDENT_CODE property for all targets and use the modified value of CMAKE_SHARED_LIBRARY_<Lang>_FLAGS for SHARED and MODULE libraries.

The NEW behavior for this policy is to ignore CMAKE_SHARED_LIBRARY_<Lang>_FLAGS whether it is modified or not and honor the POSITION_INDEPENDENT_CODE target property.

This policy was introduced in CMake version 2.8.9. CMake version 3.1.0 warns when the policy is not set and uses OLD behavior. Use the cmake_policy command to set it to OLD or NEW explicitly.

CMP0019

Do not re-expand variables in include and link information.

CMake 2.8.10 and lower re-evaluated values given to the include_directories, link_directories, and link_libraries commands to expand any leftover variable references at the end of the configuration step. This was for strict compatibility with VERY early CMake versions because all variable references are now normally evaluated during CMake language processing. CMake 2.8.11 and higher prefer to skip the extra evaluation.

The OLD behavior for this policy is to re-evaluate the values for strict compatibility. The NEW behavior for this policy is to leave the values untouched.

This policy was introduced in CMake version 2.8.11. CMake version 3.1.0 warns when the policy is not set and uses OLD behavior. Use the cmake_policy command to set it to OLD or NEW explicitly.

CMP0020

Automatically link Qt executables to qtmain target on Windows.

CMake 2.8.10 and lower required users of Qt to always specify a link dependency to the qtmain.lib static library manually on Windows. CMake 2.8.11 gained the ability to evaluate generator expressions while determining the link dependencies from IMPORTED targets. This allows CMake itself to automatically link executables which link to Qt to the qtmain.lib library when using IMPORTED Qt targets. For applications already linking to qtmain.lib, this should have little impact. For applications which supply their own alternative WinMain implementation and for applications which use the QAxServer library, this automatic linking will need to be disabled as per the documentation.

The OLD behavior for this policy is not to link executables to qtmain.lib automatically when they link to the QtCore IMPORTED target. The NEW behavior for this policy is to link executables to qtmain.lib automatically when they link to QtCore IMPORTED target.

This policy was introduced in CMake version 2.8.11. CMake version 3.1.0 warns when the policy is not set and uses OLD behavior. Use the cmake_policy command to set it to OLD or NEW explicitly.

CMP0021

Fatal error on relative paths in INCLUDE_DIRECTORIES target property.

CMake 2.8.10.2 and lower allowed the INCLUDE_DIRECTORIES target property to contain relative paths. The base path for such relative entries is not well defined. CMake 2.8.12 issues a FATAL_ERROR if the INCLUDE_DIRECTORIES property contains a relative path.

The OLD behavior for this policy is not to warn about relative paths in the INCLUDE_DIRECTORIES target property. The NEW behavior for this policy is to issue a FATAL_ERROR if INCLUDE_DIRECTORIES contains a relative path.

This policy was introduced in CMake version 2.8.12. CMake version 3.1.0 warns when the policy is not set and uses OLD behavior. Use the cmake_policy command to set it to OLD or NEW explicitly.

CMP0022

INTERFACE_LINK_LIBRARIES defines the link interface.

CMake 2.8.11 constructed the 'link interface' of a target from properties matching `(IMPORTED_)?LINK_INTERFACE_LIBRARIES(_<CONFIG>)?`. The modern way to specify config-sensitive content is to use generator expressions and the `IMPORTED_` prefix makes uniform processing of the link interface with generator expressions impossible. The INTERFACE_LINK_LIBRARIES target property was introduced as a replacement in CMake 2.8.12. This new property is named consistently with the INTERFACE_COMPILE_DEFINITIONS, INTERFACE_INCLUDE_DIRECTORIES and INTERFACE_COMPILE_OPTIONS properties. For in-build targets, CMake will use the INTERFACE_LINK_LIBRARIES property as the source of the link interface only if policy CMP0022 is NEW. When exporting a target which has this policy set to NEW, only the INTERFACE_LINK_LIBRARIES property will be processed and generated for the IMPORTED target by default. A new option to the install(EXPORT) and export commands allows export of the old-style properties for compatibility with downstream users of CMake versions older than 2.8.12. The target_link_libraries command will no longer populate the properties matching LINK_INTERFACE_LIBRARIES(_<CONFIG>)? if this policy is NEW.

Warning-free future-compatible code which works with CMake 2.8.7 onwards can be written by using the `LINK_PRIVATE` and `LINK_PUBLIC` keywords of `target_link_libraries()` (page 340).

The OLD behavior for this policy is to ignore the INTERFACE_LINK_LIBRARIES property for in-build targets. The NEW behavior for this policy is to use the INTERFACE_LINK_LIBRARIES property for in-build targets, and ignore the old properties matching `(IMPORTED_)?LINK_INTERFACE_LIBRARIES(_<CONFIG>)?`.

This policy was introduced in CMake version 2.8.12. CMake version 3.1.0 warns when the policy is not set and uses OLD behavior. Use the cmake_policy command to set it to OLD or NEW explicitly.

CMP0023

Plain and keyword target_link_libraries signatures cannot be mixed.

CMake 2.8.12 introduced the target_link_libraries signature using the PUBLIC, PRIVATE, and INTERFACE keywords to generalize the LINK_PUBLIC and LINK_PRIVATE keywords introduced in CMake 2.8.7. Use of signatures with any of these keywords sets the link interface of a target explicitly, even if empty. This produces confusing behavior when used in combination with the historical behavior of the plain target_link_libraries signature. For example, consider the code:

```
target_link_libraries(mylib A)
target_link_libraries(mylib PRIVATE B)
```

After the first line the link interface has not been set explicitly so CMake would use the link implementation, A, as the link interface. However, the second line sets the link interface to empty. In order to avoid this subtle behavior CMake now prefers to disallow mixing the plain and keyword signatures of target_link_libraries for a single target.

The OLD behavior for this policy is to allow keyword and plain target_link_libraries signatures to be mixed. The NEW behavior for this policy is to not to allow mixing of the keyword and plain signatures.

This policy was introduced in CMake version 2.8.12. CMake version 3.1.0 warns when the policy is not set and uses OLD behavior. Use the cmake_policy command to set it to OLD or NEW explicitly.

CMP0024

Disallow include export result.

CMake 2.8.12 and lower allowed use of the include() command with the result of the export() command. This relies on the assumption that the export() command has an immediate effect at configure-time during a cmake run. Certain properties of targets are not fully determined until later at generate-time, such as the link language and complete list of link libraries. Future refactoring will change the effect of the export() command to be executed at generate-time. Use ALIAS targets instead in cases where the goal is to refer to targets by another name.

The OLD behavior for this policy is to allow including the result of an export() command. The NEW behavior for this policy is not to allow including the result of an export() command.

This policy was introduced in CMake version 3.0. CMake version 3.1.0 warns when the policy is not set and uses OLD behavior. Use the cmake_policy command to set it to OLD or NEW explicitly.

CMP0025

Compiler id for Apple Clang is now `AppleClang`.

CMake 3.0 and above recognize that Apple Clang is a different compiler than upstream Clang and that they have different version numbers. CMake now prefers to present this to projects by setting the `CMAKE_<LANG>_COMPILER_ID` (page 670) variable to `AppleClang` instead of `Clang`. However, existing projects may assume the compiler id for Apple Clang is just `Clang` as it was in CMake versions prior to 3.0. Therefore this policy determines for Apple Clang which compiler id to report in the `CMAKE_<LANG>_COMPILER_ID` (page 670) variable after language <LANG> is enabled by the `project()` (page 327) or `enable_language()` (page 284) command. The policy must be set prior to the invocation of either command.

The OLD behavior for this policy is to use compiler id `Clang`. The NEW behavior for this policy is to use compiler id `AppleClang`.

This policy was introduced in CMake version 3.0. Use the `cmake_policy()` (page 280) command to set this policy to OLD or NEW explicitly. Unlike most policies, CMake version 3.1.0 does *not* warn by default when this policy is not set and simply uses OLD behavior. See documentation of the `CMAKE_POLICY_WARNING_CMP0025` (page 647) variable to control the warning.

CMP0026

Disallow use of the LOCATION target property.

CMake 2.8.12 and lower allowed reading the LOCATION target property (and configuration-specific variants) to determine the eventual location of build targets. This relies on the assumption that all necessary information is available at configure-time to determine the final location and filename of the target. However, this property is not fully determined until later at generate-time. At generate time, the $<TARGET_FILE> generator expression can be used to determine the eventual LOCATION of a target output.

Code which reads the LOCATION target property can be ported to use the $<TARGET_FILE> generator expression together with the file(GENERATE) subcommand to generate a file containing the target location.

The OLD behavior for this policy is to allow reading the LOCATION properties from build-targets. The NEW behavior for this policy is to not to allow reading the LOCATION properties from build-targets.

This policy was introduced in CMake version 3.0. CMake version 3.1.0 warns when the policy is not set and uses OLD behavior. Use the cmake_policy command to set it to OLD or NEW explicitly.

CMP0027

Conditionally linked imported targets with missing include directories.

CMake 2.8.11 introduced introduced the concept of INTERFACE_INCLUDE_DIRECTORIES, and a check at cmake time that the entries in the INTERFACE_INCLUDE_DIRECTORIES of an IMPORTED target actually exist. CMake 2.8.11 also introduced generator expression support in the target_link_libraries command. However, if an imported target is linked as a result of a generator expression evaluation, the entries in the INTERFACE_INCLUDE_DIRECTORIES of that target were not checked for existence as they should be.

The OLD behavior of this policy is to report a warning if an entry in the INTER-FACE_INCLUDE_DIRECTORIES of a generator-expression conditionally linked IMPORTED target does not exist.

The NEW behavior of this policy is to report an error if an entry in the INTER-FACE_INCLUDE_DIRECTORIES of a generator-expression conditionally linked IMPORTED target does not exist.

This policy was introduced in CMake version 3.0. CMake version 3.1.0 warns when the policy is not set and uses OLD behavior. Use the cmake_policy command to set it to OLD or NEW explicitly.

CMP0028

Double colon in target name means ALIAS or IMPORTED target.

CMake 2.8.12 and lower allowed the use of targets and files with double colons in target_link_libraries, with some buildsystem generators.

The use of double-colons is a common pattern used to namespace IMPORTED targets and ALIAS targets. When computing the link dependencies of a target, the name of each dependency could either be a target, or a file on disk. Previously, if a target was not found with a matching name, the name was considered to refer to a file on disk. This can lead to confusing error messages if there is a typo in what should be a target name.

The OLD behavior for this policy is to search for targets, then files on disk, even if the search term contains double-colons. The NEW behavior for this policy is to issue a FATAL_ERROR if a link dependency contains double-colons but is not an IMPORTED target or an ALIAS target.

This policy was introduced in CMake version 3.0. CMake version 3.1.0 warns when the policy is not set and uses OLD behavior. Use the cmake_policy command to set it to OLD or NEW explicitly.

CMP0029

The subdir_depends() (page 349) command should not be called.

The implementation of this command has been empty since December 2001 but was kept in CMake for compatibility for a long time.

CMake >= 3.0 prefer that this command never be called. The OLD behavior for this policy is to allow the command to be called. The NEW behavior for this policy is to issue a FATAL_ERROR when the command is called.

This policy was introduced in CMake version 3.0. CMake version 3.1.0 warns when the policy is not set and uses OLD behavior. Use the cmake_policy command to set it to OLD or NEW explicitly.

CMP0030

The use_mangled_mesa() (page 350) command should not be called.

This command was created in September 2001 to support VTK before modern CMake language and custom command capabilities. VTK has not used it in years.

CMake >= 3.0 prefer that this command never be called. The OLD behavior for this policy is to allow the command to be called. The NEW behavior for this policy is to issue a FATAL_ERROR when the command is called.

This policy was introduced in CMake version 3.0. CMake version 3.1.0 warns when the policy is not set and uses OLD behavior. Use the cmake_policy command to set it to OLD or NEW explicitly.

CMP0031

The load_command() (page 324) command should not be called.

This command was added in August 2002 to allow projects to add arbitrary commands implemented in C or C++. However, it does not work when the toolchain in use does not match the ABI of the CMake process. It has been mostly superseded by the macro() (page 324) and function() (page 309) commands.

CMake >= 3.0 prefer that this command never be called. The OLD behavior for this policy is to allow the command to be called. The NEW behavior for this policy is to issue a FATAL_ERROR when the command is called.

This policy was introduced in CMake version 3.0. CMake version 3.1.0 warns when the policy is not set and uses OLD behavior. Use the cmake_policy command to set it to OLD or NEW explicitly.

CMP0032

The output_required_files() (page 349) command should not be called.

This command was added in June 2001 to expose the then-current CMake implicit dependency scanner. CMake's real implicit dependency scanner has evolved since then but is not exposed through this command. The scanning capabilities of this command are very limited and this functionality is better achieved through dedicated outside tools.

CMake >= 3.0 prefer that this command never be called. The OLD behavior for this policy is to allow the command to be called. The NEW behavior for this policy is to issue a FATAL_ERROR when the command is called.

This policy was introduced in CMake version 3.0. CMake version 3.1.0 warns when the policy is not set and uses OLD behavior. Use the cmake_policy command to set it to OLD or NEW explicitly.

CMP0033

The `export_library_dependencies()` (page 347) command should not be called.

This command was added in January 2003 to export `<tgt>_LIB_DEPENDS` internal CMake cache entries to a file for installation with a project. This was used at the time to allow transitive link dependencies to work for applications outside of the original build tree of a project. The functionality has been superseded by the `export()` (page 287) and `install(EXPORT)` (page 317) commands.

CMake >= 3.0 prefer that this command never be called. The OLD behavior for this policy is to allow the command to be called. The NEW behavior for this policy is to issue a FATAL_ERROR when the command is called.

This policy was introduced in CMake version 3.0. CMake version 3.1.0 warns when the policy is not set and uses OLD behavior. Use the cmake_policy command to set it to OLD or NEW explicitly.

CMP0034

The `utility_source()` (page 350) command should not be called.

This command was introduced in March 2001 to help build executables used to generate other files. This approach has long been replaced by `add_executable()` (page 273) combined with `add_custom_command()` (page 269).

CMake >= 3.0 prefer that this command never be called. The OLD behavior for this policy is to allow the command to be called. The NEW behavior for this policy is to issue a FATAL_ERROR when the command is called.

This policy was introduced in CMake version 3.0. CMake version 3.1.0 warns when the policy is not set and uses OLD behavior. Use the cmake_policy command to set it to OLD or NEW explicitly.

CMP0035

The `variable_requires()` (page 351) command should not be called.

This command was introduced in November 2001 to perform some conditional logic. It has long been replaced by the `if()` (page 313) command.

CMake >= 3.0 prefer that this command never be called. The OLD behavior for this policy is to allow the command to be called. The NEW behavior for this policy is to issue a FATAL_ERROR when the command is called.

This policy was introduced in CMake version 3.0. CMake version 3.1.0 warns when the policy is not set and uses OLD behavior. Use the cmake_policy command to set it to OLD or NEW explicitly.

CMP0036

The `build_name()` (page 346) command should not be called.

This command was added in May 2001 to compute a name for the current operating system and compiler combination. The command has long been documented as discouraged and replaced by the CMAKE_SYSTEM (page 653) and CMAKE_<LANG>_COMPILER (page 671) variables.

CMake >= 3.0 prefer that this command never be called. The OLD behavior for this policy is to allow the command to be called. The NEW behavior for this policy is to issue a FATAL_ERROR when the command is called.

This policy was introduced in CMake version 3.0. CMake version 3.1.0 warns when the policy is not set and uses OLD behavior. Use the cmake_policy command to set it to OLD or NEW explicitly.

CMP0037

Target names should not be reserved and should match a validity pattern.

CMake 2.8.12 and lower allowed creating targets using add_library() (page 274), add_executable() (page 273) and add_custom_target() (page 272) with unrestricted choice for the target name. Newer cmake features such as cmake-generator-expressions(7) (page 356) and some diagnostics expect target names to match a restricted pattern.

Target names may contain upper and lower case letters, numbers, the underscore character (_), dot(.), plus(+) and minus(-). As a special case, ALIAS targets and IMPORTED targets may contain two consequtive colons.

Target names reserved by one or more CMake generators are not allowed. Among others these include "all", "help" and "test".

The OLD behavior for this policy is to allow creating targets with reserved names or which do not match the validity pattern. The NEW behavior for this policy is to report an error if an add_* command is used with an invalid target name.

This policy was introduced in CMake version 3.0. CMake version 3.1.0 warns when the policy is not set and uses OLD behavior. Use the cmake_policy command to set it to OLD or NEW explicitly.

CMP0038

Targets may not link directly to themselves.

CMake 2.8.12 and lower allowed a build target to link to itself directly with a target_link_libraries() (page 340) call. This is an indicator of a bug in user code.

The OLD behavior for this policy is to ignore targets which list themselves in their own link implementation. The NEW behavior for this policy is to report an error if a target attempts to link to itself.

This policy was introduced in CMake version 3.0. CMake version 3.1.0 warns when the policy is not set and uses OLD behavior. Use the cmake_policy command to set it to OLD or NEW explicitly.

CMP0039

Utility targets may not have link dependencies.

CMake 2.8.12 and lower allowed using utility targets in the left hand side position of the `target_link_libraries()` (page 340) command. This is an indicator of a bug in user code.

The OLD behavior for this policy is to ignore attempts to set the link libraries of utility targets. The NEW behavior for this policy is to report an error if an attempt is made to set the link libraries of a utility target.

This policy was introduced in CMake version 3.0. CMake version 3.1.0 warns when the policy is not set and uses OLD behavior. Use the cmake_policy command to set it to OLD or NEW explicitly.

CMP0040

The target in the TARGET signature of add_custom_command() must exist.

CMake 2.8.12 and lower silently ignored a custom command created with the TARGET signature of `add_custom_command()` (page 269) if the target is unknown.

The OLD behavior for this policy is to ignore custom commands for unknown targets. The NEW behavior for this policy is to report an error if the target referenced in `add_custom_command()` (page 269) is unknown.

This policy was introduced in CMake version 3.0. CMake version 3.1.0 warns when the policy is not set and uses OLD behavior. Use the cmake_policy command to set it to OLD or NEW explicitly.

CMP0041

Error on relative include with generator expression.

Diagnostics in CMake 2.8.12 and lower silently ignored an entry in the `INTERFACE_INCLUDE_DIRECTORIES` (page 593) of a target if it contained a generator expression at any position.

The path entries in that target property should not be relative. High-level API should ensure that by adding either a source directory or a install directory prefix, as appropriate.

As an additional diagnostic, the `INTERFACE_INCLUDE_DIRECTORIES` (page 593) generated on an `IMPORTED` (page 590) target for the install location should not contain paths in the source directory or the build directory.

The OLD behavior for this policy is to ignore relative path entries if they contain a generator expression. The NEW behavior for this policy is to report an error if a generator expression appears in another location and the path is relative.

This policy was introduced in CMake version 3.0. CMake version 3.1.0 warns when the policy is not set and uses OLD behavior. Use the cmake_policy command to set it to OLD or NEW explicitly.

CMP0042

`MACOSX_RPATH` (page 602) is enabled by default.

CMake 2.8.12 and newer has support for using @rpath in a target's install name. This was enabled by setting the target property MACOSX_RPATH (page 602). The @rpath in an install name is a more flexible and powerful mechanism than @executable_path or @loader_path for locating shared libraries.

CMake 3.0 and later prefer this property to be ON by default. Projects wanting @rpath in a target's install name may remove any setting of the INSTALL_NAME_DIR (page 592) and CMAKE_INSTALL_NAME_DIR (page 660) variables.

This policy was introduced in CMake version 3.0. CMake version 3.1.0 warns when the policy is not set and uses OLD behavior. Use the cmake_policy command to set it to OLD or NEW explicitly.

CMP0043

Ignore COMPILE_DEFINITIONS_<Config> properties

CMake 2.8.12 and lower allowed setting the COMPILE_DEFINITIONS_<CONFIG> (page 622) target property and COMPILE_DEFINITIONS_<CONFIG> (page 622) directory property to apply configuration-specific compile definitions.

Since CMake 2.8.10, the COMPILE_DEFINITIONS (page 580) property has supported generator expressions (page 356) for setting configuration-dependent content. The continued existence of the suffixed variables is redundant, and causes a maintenance burden. Population of the COMPILE_DEFINITIONS_DEBUG (page 622) property may be replaced with a population of COMPILE_DEFINITIONS (page 580) directly or via target_compile_definitions() (page 338):

```
# Old Interfaces:
set_property(TARGET tgt APPEND PROPERTY
  COMPILE_DEFINITIONS_DEBUG DEBUG_MODE
)
set_property(DIRECTORY APPEND PROPERTY
  COMPILE_DEFINITIONS_DEBUG DIR_DEBUG_MODE
)

# New Interfaces:
set_property(TARGET tgt APPEND PROPERTY
  COMPILE_DEFINITIONS $<$<CONFIG:Debug>:DEBUG_MODE>
)
target_compile_definitions(tgt PRIVATE $<$<CONFIG:Debug>:DEBUG_MODE>)
set_property(DIRECTORY APPEND PROPERTY
  COMPILE_DEFINITIONS $<$<CONFIG:Debug>:DIR_DEBUG_MODE>
)
```

The OLD behavior for this policy is to consume the content of the suffixed COMPILE_DEFINITIONS_<CONFIG> (page 622) target property when generating the compilation command. The NEW behavior for this policy is to ignore the content of the COMPILE_DEFINITIONS_<CONFIG> (page 622) target property .

This policy was introduced in CMake version 3.0. CMake version 3.1.0 warns when the policy is not set and uses OLD behavior. Use the cmake_policy command to set it to OLD or NEW explicitly.

CMP0044

Case sensitive `<LANG>_COMPILER_ID` generator expressions

CMake 2.8.12 introduced the `<LANG>_COMPILER_ID generator expressions` (page 356) to allow comparison of the `CMAKE_<LANG>_COMPILER_ID` (page 670) with a test value. The possible valid values are lowercase, but the comparison with the test value was performed case-insensitively.

The OLD behavior for this policy is to perform a case-insensitive comparison with the value in the `<LANG>_COMPILER_ID` expression. The NEW behavior for this policy is to perform a case-sensitive comparison with the value in the `<LANG>_COMPILER_ID` expression.

This policy was introduced in CMake version 3.0. CMake version 3.1.0 warns when the policy is not set and uses OLD behavior. Use the cmake_policy command to set it to OLD or NEW explicitly.

CMP0045

Error on non-existent target in get_target_property.

In CMake 2.8.12 and lower, the `get_target_property()` (page 312) command accepted a non-existent target argument without issuing any error or warning. The result variable is set to a `-NOTFOUND` value.

The OLD behavior for this policy is to issue no warning and set the result variable to a `-NOTFOUND` value. The NEW behavior for this policy is to issue a `FATAL_ERROR` if the command is called with a non-existent target.

This policy was introduced in CMake version 3.0. CMake version 3.1.0 warns when the policy is not set and uses OLD behavior. Use the cmake_policy command to set it to OLD or NEW explicitly.

CMP0046

Error on non-existent dependency in add_dependencies.

CMake 2.8.12 and lower silently ignored non-existent dependencies listed in the `add_dependencies()` (page 273) command.

The OLD behavior for this policy is to silently ignore non-existent dependencies. The NEW behavior for this policy is to report an error if non-existent dependencies are listed in the `add_dependencies()` (page 273) command.

This policy was introduced in CMake version 3.0. CMake version 3.1.0 warns when the policy is not set and uses OLD behavior. Use the cmake_policy command to set it to OLD or NEW explicitly.

CMP0047

Use `QCC` compiler id for the qcc drivers on QNX.

CMake 3.0 and above recognize that the QNX qcc compiler driver is different from the GNU compiler. CMake now prefers to present this to projects by setting the `CMAKE_<LANG>_COMPILER_ID` (page 670) variable to QCC instead of GNU. However, existing projects may assume the compiler id for QNX qcc is just GNU as it was in CMake versions prior to 3.0. Therefore this policy determines for QNX qcc which compiler id to report in the CMAKE_<LANG>_COMPILER_ID (page 670) variable after language <LANG> is enabled by the project() (page 327) or enable_language() (page 284) command. The policy must be set prior to the invocation of either command.

The OLD behavior for this policy is to use the GNU compiler id for the qcc and QCC compiler drivers. The NEW behavior for this policy is to use the QCC compiler id for those drivers.

This policy was introduced in CMake version 3.0. Use the cmake_policy() (page 280) command to set this policy to OLD or NEW explicitly. Unlike most policies, CMake version 3.1.0 does *not* warn by default when this policy is not set and simply uses OLD behavior. See documentation of the CMAKE_POLICY_WARNING_CMP0047 (page 647) variable to control the warning.

CMP0048

The project() (page 327) command manages VERSION variables.

CMake version 3.0 introduced the VERSION option of the project() (page 327) command to specify a project version as well as the name. In order to keep PROJECT_VERSION (page 638) and related variables consistent with variable PROJECT_NAME (page 637) it is necessary to set the VERSION variables to the empty string when no VERSION is given to project() (page 327). However, this can change behavior for existing projects that set VERSION variables themselves since project() (page 327) may now clear them. This policy controls the behavior for compatibility with such projects.

The OLD behavior for this policy is to leave VERSION variables untouched. The NEW behavior for this policy is to set VERSION as documented by the project() (page 327) command.

This policy was introduced in CMake version 3.0. CMake version 3.1.0 warns when the policy is not set and uses OLD behavior. Use the cmake_policy command to set it to OLD or NEW explicitly.

CMP0049

Do not expand variables in target source entries.

CMake 2.8.12 and lower performed and extra layer of variable expansion when evaluating source file names:

```
set(a_source foo.c)
add_executable(foo \${a_source})
```

This was undocumented behavior.

The OLD behavior for this policy is to expand such variables when processing the target sources. The NEW behavior for this policy is to issue an error if such variables need to be expanded.

This policy was introduced in CMake version 3.0. CMake version 3.1.0 warns when the policy is not set and uses OLD behavior. Use the cmake_policy command to set it to OLD or NEW explicitly.

CMP0050

Disallow add_custom_command SOURCE signatures.

CMake 2.8.12 and lower allowed a signature for `add_custom_command()` (page 269) which specified an input to a command. This was undocumented behavior. Modern use of CMake associates custom commands with their output, rather than their input.

The OLD behavior for this policy is to allow the use of `add_custom_command()` (page 269) SOURCE signatures. The NEW behavior for this policy is to issue an error if such a signature is used.

This policy was introduced in CMake version 3.0. CMake version 3.1.0 warns when the policy is not set and uses OLD behavior. Use the cmake_policy command to set it to OLD or NEW explicitly.

CMP0051

List TARGET_OBJECTS in SOURCES target property.

CMake 3.0 and lower did not include the `TARGET_OBJECTS generator expression` (page 356) when returning the `SOURCES` (page 608) target property.

Configure-time CMake code is not able to handle generator expressions. If using the `SOURCES` (page 608) target property at configure time, it may be necessary to first remove generator expressions using the `string(GENEX_STRIP)` (page 335) command. Generate-time CMake code such as `file(GENERATE)` (page 287) can handle the content without stripping.

The `OLD` behavior for this policy is to omit `TARGET_OBJECTS` expressions from the `SOURCES` (page 608) target property. The `NEW` behavior for this policy is to include `TARGET_OBJECTS` expressions in the output.

This policy was introduced in CMake version 3.1. CMake version 3.1.0 warns when the policy is not set and uses `OLD` behavior. Use the `cmake_policy()` (page 280) command to set it to `OLD` or `NEW` explicitly.

CMP0052

Reject source and build dirs in installed INTERFACE_INCLUDE_DIRECTORIES.

CMake 3.0 and lower allowed subdirectories of the source directory or build directory to be in the `INTERFACE_INCLUDE_DIRECTORIES` (page 593) of installed and exported targets, if the directory was also a subdirectory of the installation prefix. This makes the installation depend on the existence of the source dir or binary dir, and the installation will be broken if either are removed after installation.

See *Include Directories and Usage Requirements* for more on specifying include directories for targets.

The OLD behavior for this policy is to export the content of the `INTERFACE_INCLUDE_DIRECTORIES` (page 593) with the source or binary directory. The NEW behavior for this policy is to issue an error if such a directory is used.

This policy was introduced in CMake version 3.1. CMake version 3.1.0 warns when the policy is not set and uses `OLD` behavior. Use the `cmake_policy()` (page 280) command to set it to `OLD` or `NEW` explicitly.

CMP0053

Simplify variable reference and escape sequence evaluation.

CMake 3.1 introduced a much faster implementation of evaluation of the *Variable References* and *Escape Sequences* documented in the `cmake-language(7)` manual. While the behavior is identical to the legacy implementation in most cases, some corner cases were cleaned up to simplify the behavior. Specifically:

- Expansion of `@VAR@` reference syntax defined by the `configure_file()` (page 282) and `string(CONFIGURE)` (page 335) commands is no longer performed in other contexts.

- Literal `${VAR}` reference syntax may contain only alphanumeric characters (A-Z, a-z, 0-9) and the characters `_`, `.`, `/`, `-`, and `+`. Variables with other characters in their name may still be referenced indirectly, e.g.

```
set(varname "otherwise & disallowed $ characters")
message("${${varname}}")
```

- The setting of policy `CMP0010` (page 542) is not considered, so improper variable reference syntax is always an error.

- More characters are allowed to be escaped in variable names. Previously, only `()#" \@^` were valid characters to escape. Now any non-alphanumeric, non-semicolon, non-NUL character may be escaped following the `escape_identity` production in the *Escape Sequences* section of the `cmake-language(7)` manual.

The `OLD` behavior for this policy is to honor the legacy behavior for variable references and escape sequences. The `NEW` behavior is to use the simpler variable expansion and escape sequence evaluation rules.

This policy was introduced in CMake version 3.1. CMake version 3.1.0 warns when the policy is not set and uses `OLD` behavior. Use the `cmake_policy()` (page 280) command to set it to `OLD` or `NEW` explicitly.

CMP0054

Only interpret `if()` (page 313) arguments as variables or keywords when unquoted.

CMake 3.1 and above no longer implicitly dereference variables or interpret keywords in an `if()` (page 313) command argument when it is a *Quoted Argument* or a *Bracket Argument*.

The `OLD` behavior for this policy is to dereference variables and interpret keywords even if they are quoted or bracketed. The `NEW` behavior is to not dereference variables or interpret keywords that have been quoted or bracketed.

Given the following partial example:

```
set(MONKEY 1)
set(ANIMAL MONKEY)

if("${ANIMAL}" STREQUAL "MONKEY")
```

After explicit expansion of variables this gives:

```
if("MONKEY" STREQUAL "MONKEY")
```

With the policy set to OLD implicit expansion reduces this semantically to:

```
if("1" STREQUAL "1")
```

With the policy set to NEW the quoted arguments will not be further dereferenced:

```
if("MONKEY" STREQUAL "MONKEY")
```

This policy was introduced in CMake version 3.1. CMake version 3.1.0 warns when the policy is not set and uses OLD behavior. Use the cmake_policy() (page 280) command to set it to OLD or NEW explicitly.

C.6 cmake-properties(7)

C.6.1 Properties of Global Scope

ALLOW_DUPLICATE_CUSTOM_TARGETS

Allow duplicate custom targets to be created.

Normally CMake requires that all targets built in a project have globally unique logical names (see policy CMP0002). This is necessary to generate meaningful project file names in Xcode and VS IDE generators. It also allows the target names to be referenced unambiguously.

Makefile generators are capable of supporting duplicate custom target names. For projects that care only about Makefile generators and do not wish to support Xcode or VS IDE generators, one may set this property to true to allow duplicate custom targets. The property allows multiple add_custom_target command calls in different directories to specify the same target name. However, setting this property will cause non-Makefile generators to produce an error and refuse to generate the project.

AUTOGEN_TARGETS_FOLDER

Name of FOLDER (page 585) for *_automoc targets that are added automatically by CMake for targets for which AUTOMOC (page 575) is enabled.

If not set, CMake uses the FOLDER (page 585) property of the parent target as a default value for this property. See also the documentation for the FOLDER (page 585) target property and the AUTOMOC (page 575) target property.

AUTOMOC_TARGETS_FOLDER

Name of FOLDER (page 585) for *_automoc targets that are added automatically by CMake for targets for which AUTOMOC (page 575) is enabled.

This property is obsolete. Use AUTOGEN_TARGETS_FOLDER (page 559) instead.

If not set, CMake uses the FOLDER (page 585) property of the parent target as a default value for this property. See also the documentation for the FOLDER (page 585) target property and the AUTOMOC (page 575) target property.

CMAKE_C_KNOWN_FEATURES

List of C features known to this version of CMake.

The features listed in this global property may be known to be available to the C compiler. If the feature is available with the C compiler, it will be listed in the CMAKE_C_COMPILE_FEATURES (page 667) variable.

The features listed here may be used with the target_compile_features() (page 338) command. See the cmake-compile-features(7) manual for information on compile features.

The features known to this version of CMake are:

c_function_prototypes Function prototypes, as defined in ISO/IEC 9899:1990.

c_restrict restrict keyword, as defined in ISO/IEC 9899:1999.

c_static_assert Static assert, as defined in ISO/IEC 9899:2011.

c_variadic_macros Variadic macros, as defined in ISO/IEC 9899:1999.

CMAKE_CXX_KNOWN_FEATURES

List of C++ features known to this version of CMake.

The features listed in this global property may be known to be available to the C++ compiler. If the feature is available with the C++ compiler, it will be listed in the CMAKE_CXX_COMPILE_FEATURES (page 668) variable.

The features listed here may be used with the target_compile_features() (page 338) command. See the cmake-compile-features(7) manual for information on compile features.

The features known to this version of CMake are:

cxx_aggregate_default_initializers Aggregate default initializers, as defined in N3605[10].

cxx_alias_templates Template aliases, as defined in N2258[11].

cxx_alignas Alignment control alignas, as defined in N2341[12].

cxx_alignof Alignment control alignof, as defined in N2341[13].

cxx_attributes Generic attributes, as defined in N2761[14].

---

[10]http://www.open-std.org/jtc1/sc22/wg21/docs/papers/2013/n3605.html
[11]http://www.open-std.org/jtc1/sc22/wg21/docs/papers/2007/n2258.pdf
[12]http://www.open-std.org/jtc1/sc22/wg21/docs/papers/2007/n2341.pdf
[13]http://www.open-std.org/jtc1/sc22/wg21/docs/papers/2007/n2341.pdf
[14]http://www.open-std.org/jtc1/sc22/wg21/docs/papers/2008/n2761.pdf

cxx_attribute_deprecated [[deprecated]] attribute, as defined in N3760[15].

cxx_auto_type Automatic type deduction, as defined in N1984[16].

cxx_binary_literals Binary literals, as defined in N3472[17].

cxx_constexpr Constant expressions, as defined in N2235[18].

cxx_contextual_conversions Contextual conversions, as defined in N3323[19].

cxx_decltype_incomplete_return_types Decltype on incomplete return types, as defined in N3276[20].

cxx_decltype Decltype, as defined in N2343[21].

cxx_decltype_auto decltype(auto) semantics, as defined in N3638[22].

cxx_default_function_template_args Default template arguments for function templates, as defined in DR226[23]

cxx_defaulted_functions Defaulted functions, as defined in N2346[24].

cxx_defaulted_move_initializers Defaulted move initializers, as defined in N3053[25].

cxx_delegating_constructors Delegating constructors, as defined in N1986[26].

cxx_deleted_functions Deleted functions, as defined in N2346[27].

cxx_digit_separators Digit separators, as defined in N3781[28].

cxx_enum_forward_declarations Enum forward declarations, as defined in N2764[29].

cxx_explicit_conversions Explicit conversion operators, as defined in N2437[30].

cxx_extended_friend_declarations Extended friend declarations, as defined in N1791[31].

cxx_extern_templates Extern templates, as defined in N1987[32].

cxx_final Override control final keyword, as defined in N2928[33].

---

[15] http://www.open-std.org/jtc1/sc22/wg21/docs/papers/2013/n3760.html
[16] http://www.open-std.org/jtc1/sc22/wg21/docs/papers/2006/n1984.pdf
[17] http://www.open-std.org/jtc1/sc22/wg21/docs/papers/2012/n3472.pdf
[18] http://www.open-std.org/jtc1/sc22/wg21/docs/papers/2007/n2235.pdf
[19] http://www.open-std.org/jtc1/sc22/wg21/docs/papers/2012/n3323.pdf
[20] http://www.open-std.org/jtc1/sc22/wg21/docs/papers/2011/n3276.pdf
[21] http://www.open-std.org/jtc1/sc22/wg21/docs/papers/2007/n2343.pdf
[22] http://www.open-std.org/jtc1/sc22/wg21/docs/papers/2013/n3638.html
[23] http://www.open-std.org/jtc1/sc22/wg21/docs/cwg_defects.html#226
[24] http://www.open-std.org/jtc1/sc22/wg21/docs/papers/2007/n2346.htm
[25] http://www.open-std.org/jtc1/sc22/wg21/docs/papers/2010/n3053.html
[26] http://www.open-std.org/jtc1/sc22/wg21/docs/papers/2006/n1986.pdf
[27] http://www.open-std.org/jtc1/sc22/wg21/docs/papers/2007/n2346.htm
[28] http://www.open-std.org/jtc1/sc22/wg21/docs/papers/2013/n3781.pdf
[29] http://www.open-std.org/jtc1/sc22/wg21/docs/papers/2008/n2764.pdf
[30] http://www.open-std.org/jtc1/sc22/wg21/docs/papers/2007/n2437.pdf
[31] http://www.open-std.org/jtc1/sc22/wg21/docs/papers/2005/n1791.pdf
[32] http://www.open-std.org/jtc1/sc22/wg21/docs/papers/2006/n1987.htm
[33] http://www.open-std.org/JTC1/SC22/WG21/docs/papers/2009/n2928.htm

cxx_func_identifier Predefined __`func`__ identifier, as defined in N2340[34].

cxx_generalized_initializers Initializer lists, as defined in N2672[35].

cxx_generic_lambdas Generic lambdas, as defined in N3649[36].

cxx_inheriting_constructors Inheriting constructors, as defined in N2540[37].

cxx_inline_namespaces Inline namespaces, as defined in N2535[38].

cxx_lambdas Lambda functions, as defined in N2927[39].

cxx_lambda_init_captures Initialized lambda captures, as defined in N3648[40].

cxx_local_type_template_args Local and unnamed types as template arguments, as defined in N2657[41].

cxx_long_long_type `long long` type, as defined in N1811[42].

cxx_noexcept Exception specifications, as defined in N3050[43].

cxx_nonstatic_member_init Non-static data member initialization, as defined in N2756[44].

cxx_nullptr Null pointer, as defined in N2431[45].

cxx_override Override control `override` keyword, as defined in N2928[46].

cxx_range_for Range-based for, as defined in N2930[47].

cxx_raw_string_literals Raw string literals, as defined in N2442[48].

cxx_reference_qualified_functions Reference qualified functions, as defined in N2439[49].

cxx_relaxed_constexpr Relaxed constexpr, as defined in N3652[50].

cxx_return_type_deduction Return type deduction on normal functions, as defined in N3386[51].

cxx_right_angle_brackets Right angle bracket parsing, as defined in N1757[52].

---

[34] http://www.open-std.org/jtc1/sc22/wg21/docs/papers/2007/n2340.htm
[35] http://www.open-std.org/jtc1/sc22/wg21/docs/papers/2008/n2672.htm
[36] http://www.open-std.org/jtc1/sc22/wg21/docs/papers/2013/n3649.html
[37] http://www.open-std.org/jtc1/sc22/wg21/docs/papers/2008/n2540.htm
[38] http://www.open-std.org/jtc1/sc22/wg21/docs/papers/2008/n2535.htm
[39] http://www.open-std.org/jtc1/sc22/wg21/docs/papers/2009/n2927.pdf
[40] http://www.open-std.org/jtc1/sc22/wg21/docs/papers/2013/n3648.html
[41] http://www.open-std.org/jtc1/sc22/wg21/docs/papers/2008/n2657.htm
[42] http://www.open-std.org/jtc1/sc22/wg21/docs/papers/2005/n1811.pdf
[43] http://www.open-std.org/jtc1/sc22/wg21/docs/papers/2010/n3050.html
[44] http://www.open-std.org/jtc1/sc22/wg21/docs/papers/2008/n2756.htm
[45] http://www.open-std.org/jtc1/sc22/wg21/docs/papers/2007/n2431.pdf
[46] http://www.open-std.org/JTC1/SC22/WG21/docs/papers/2009/n2928.htm
[47] http://www.open-std.org/jtc1/sc22/wg21/docs/papers/2009/n2930.html
[48] http://www.open-std.org/jtc1/sc22/wg21/docs/papers/2007/n2442.htm
[49] http://www.open-std.org/jtc1/sc22/wg21/docs/papers/2007/n2439.htm
[50] http://www.open-std.org/jtc1/sc22/wg21/docs/papers/2013/n3652.html
[51] http://www.open-std.org/jtc1/sc22/wg21/docs/papers/2012/n3386.html
[52] http://www.open-std.org/jtc1/sc22/wg21/docs/papers/2005/n1757.html

cxx_rvalue_references R-value references, as defined in N2118[53].

cxx_sizeof_member Size of non-static data members, as defined in N2253[54].

cxx_static_assert Static assert, as defined in N1720[55].

cxx_strong_enums Strongly typed enums, as defined in N2347[56].

cxx_thread_local Thread-local variables, as defined in N2659[57].

cxx_trailing_return_types Automatic function return type, as defined in N2541[58].

cxx_unicode_literals Unicode string literals, as defined in N2442[59].

cxx_uniform_initialization Uniform intialization, as defined in N2640[60].

cxx_unrestricted_unions Unrestricted unions, as defined in N2544[61].

cxx_user_literals User-defined literals, as defined in N2765[62].

cxx_variable_templates Variable templates, as defined in N3651[63].

cxx_variadic_macros Variadic macros, as defined in N1653[64].

cxx_variadic_templates Variadic templates, as defined in N2242[65].

cxx_template_template_parameters Template template parameters, as defined in `ISO/IEC 14882:1998`.

DEBUG_CONFIGURATIONS

Specify which configurations are for debugging.

The value must be a semi-colon separated list of configuration names. Currently this property is used only by the target_link_libraries command (see its documentation for details). Additional uses may be defined in the future.

This property must be set at the top level of the project and before the first target_link_libraries command invocation. If any entry in the list does not match a valid configuration for the project the behavior is undefined.

---

[53] http://www.open-std.org/jtc1/sc22/wg21/docs/papers/2006/n2118.html
[54] http://www.open-std.org/jtc1/sc22/wg21/docs/papers/2007/n2253.html
[55] http://www.open-std.org/jtc1/sc22/wg21/docs/papers/2004/n1720.html
[56] http://www.open-std.org/jtc1/sc22/wg21/docs/papers/2007/n2347.pdf
[57] http://www.open-std.org/jtc1/sc22/wg21/docs/papers/2008/n2659.htm
[58] http://www.open-std.org/jtc1/sc22/wg21/docs/papers/2008/n2541.htm
[59] http://www.open-std.org/jtc1/sc22/wg21/docs/papers/2007/n2442.htm
[60] http://www.open-std.org/jtc1/sc22/wg21/docs/papers/2008/n2640.pdf
[61] http://www.open-std.org/jtc1/sc22/wg21/docs/papers/2008/n2544.pdf
[62] http://www.open-std.org/jtc1/sc22/wg21/docs/papers/2008/n2765.pdf
[63] http://www.open-std.org/jtc1/sc22/wg21/docs/papers/2013/n3651.pdf
[64] http://www.open-std.org/jtc1/sc22/wg21/docs/papers/2004/n1653.htm
[65] http://www.open-std.org/jtc1/sc22/wg21/docs/papers/2007/n2242.pdf

DISABLED_FEATURES

List of features which are disabled during the CMake run.

List of features which are disabled during the CMake run. By default it contains the names of all packages which were not found. This is determined using the <NAME>_FOUND variables. Packages which are searched QUIET are not listed. A project can add its own features to this list. This property is used by the macros in FeatureSummary.cmake.

ENABLED_FEATURES

List of features which are enabled during the CMake run.

List of features which are enabled during the CMake run. By default it contains the names of all packages which were found. This is determined using the <NAME>_FOUND variables. Packages which are searched QUIET are not listed. A project can add its own features to this list. This property is used by the macros in FeatureSummary.cmake.

ENABLED_LANGUAGES

Read-only property that contains the list of currently enabled languages

Set to list of currently enabled languages.

FIND_LIBRARY_USE_LIB64_PATHS

Whether FIND_LIBRARY should automatically search lib64 directories.

FIND_LIBRARY_USE_LIB64_PATHS is a boolean specifying whether the FIND_LIBRARY command should automatically search the lib64 variant of directories called lib in the search path when building 64-bit binaries.

FIND_LIBRARY_USE_OPENBSD_VERSIONING

Whether FIND_LIBRARY should find OpenBSD-style shared libraries.

This property is a boolean specifying whether the FIND_LIBRARY command should find shared libraries with OpenBSD-style versioned extension: ".so.<major>.<minor>". The property is set to true on OpenBSD and false on other platforms.

GLOBAL_DEPENDS_DEBUG_MODE

Enable global target dependency graph debug mode.

CMake automatically analyzes the global inter-target dependency graph at the beginning of native build system generation. This property causes it to display details of its analysis to stderr.

GLOBAL_DEPENDS_NO_CYCLES

Disallow global target dependency graph cycles.

CMake automatically analyzes the global inter-target dependency graph at the beginning of native build system generation. It reports an error if the dependency graph contains a cycle that does not consist of all STATIC library targets. This property tells CMake to disallow all cycles completely, even among static libraries.

IN_TRY_COMPILE

Read-only property that is true during a try-compile configuration.

True when building a project inside a TRY_COMPILE or TRY_RUN command.

PACKAGES_FOUND

List of packages which were found during the CMake run.

List of packages which were found during the CMake run. Whether a package has been found is determined using the <NAME>_FOUND variables.

PACKAGES_NOT_FOUND

List of packages which were not found during the CMake run.

List of packages which were not found during the CMake run. Whether a package has been found is determined using the <NAME>_FOUND variables.

JOB_POOLS

Ninja only: List of available pools.

A pool is a named integer property and defines the maximum number of concurrent jobs which can be started by a rule assigned to the pool. The JOB_POOLS (page 565) property is a semicolon-separated list of pairs using the syntax NAME=integer (without a space after the equality sign).

For instance:

```
set_property(GLOBAL PROPERTY JOB_POOLS two_jobs=2 ten_jobs=10)
```

Defined pools could be used globally by setting CMAKE_JOB_POOL_COMPILE (page 629) and CMAKE_JOB_POOL_LINK (page 629) or per target by setting the target properties JOB_POOL_COMPILE (page 595) and JOB_POOL_LINK (page 596).

PREDEFINED_TARGETS_FOLDER

Name of FOLDER for targets that are added automatically by CMake.

If not set, CMake uses "CMakePredefinedTargets" as a default value for this property. Targets such as IN-STALL, PACKAGE and RUN_TESTS will be organized into this FOLDER. See also the documentation for the FOLDER target property.

ECLIPSE_EXTRA_NATURES

List of natures to add to the generated Eclipse project file.

Eclipse projects specify language plugins by using natures. This property should be set to the unique identifier for a nature (which looks like a Java package name).

REPORT_UNDEFINED_PROPERTIES

If set, report any undefined properties to this file.

If this property is set to a filename then when CMake runs it will report any properties or variables that were accessed but not defined into the filename specified in this property.

RULE_LAUNCH_COMPILE

Specify a launcher for compile rules.

Makefile generators prefix compiler commands with the given launcher command line. This is intended to allow launchers to intercept build problems with high granularity. Non-Makefile generators currently ignore this property.

RULE_LAUNCH_CUSTOM

Specify a launcher for custom rules.

Makefile generators prefix custom commands with the given launcher command line. This is intended to allow launchers to intercept build problems with high granularity. Non-Makefile generators currently ignore this property.

RULE_LAUNCH_LINK

Specify a launcher for link rules.

Makefile generators prefix link and archive commands with the given launcher command line. This is intended to allow launchers to intercept build problems with high granularity. Non-Makefile generators currently ignore this property.

RULE_MESSAGES

Specify whether to report a message for each make rule.

This property specifies whether Makefile generators should add a progress message describing what each build rule does. If the property is not set the default is ON. Set the property to OFF to disable granular messages and report only as each target completes. This is intended to allow scripted builds to avoid the build time cost of detailed reports. If a CMAKE_RULE_MESSAGES cache entry exists its value initializes the value of this property. Non-Makefile generators currently ignore this property.

TARGET_ARCHIVES_MAY_BE_SHARED_LIBS

Set if shared libraries may be named like archives.

On AIX shared libraries may be named "lib<name>.a". This property is set to true on such platforms.

TARGET_SUPPORTS_SHARED_LIBS

Does the target platform support shared libraries.

TARGET_SUPPORTS_SHARED_LIBS is a boolean specifying whether the target platform supports shared libraries. Basically all current general general purpose OS do so, the exception are usually embedded systems with no or special OSs.

USE_FOLDERS

Use the FOLDER target property to organize targets into folders.

If not set, CMake treats this property as OFF by default. CMake generators that are capable of organizing into a hierarchy of folders use the values of the FOLDER target property to name those folders. See also the documentation for the FOLDER target property.

C.6.2 Properties on Directories

ADDITIONAL_MAKE_CLEAN_FILES

Additional files to clean during the make clean stage.

A list of files that will be cleaned as a part of the "make clean" stage.

CACHE_VARIABLES

List of cache variables available in the current directory.

This read-only property specifies the list of CMake cache variables currently defined. It is intended for debugging purposes.

CLEAN_NO_CUSTOM

Should the output of custom commands be left.

If this is true then the outputs of custom commands for this directory will not be removed during the "make clean" stage.

CMAKE_CONFIGURE_DEPENDS

Tell CMake about additional input files to the configuration process. If any named file is modified the build system will re-run CMake to re-configure the file and generate the build system again.

Specify files as a semicolon-separated list of paths. Relative paths are interpreted as relative to the current source directory.

COMPILE_DEFINITIONS

Preprocessor definitions for compiling a directory's sources.

This property specifies the list of options given so far to the `add_definitions()` (page 273) command.

The `COMPILE_DEFINITIONS` property may be set to a semicolon-separated list of preprocessor definitions using the syntax `VAR` or `VAR=value`. Function-style definitions are not supported. CMake will automatically escape the value correctly for the native build system (note that CMake language syntax may require escapes to specify some values).

This property will be initialized in each directory by its value in the directory's parent.

CMake will automatically drop some definitions that are not supported by the native build tool. The VS6 IDE does not support definition values with spaces (but NMake does).

Disclaimer: Most native build tools have poor support for escaping certain values. CMake has work-arounds for many cases but some values may just not be possible to pass correctly. If a value does not seem to be escaped correctly, do not attempt to work-around the problem by adding escape sequences to the value. Your work-around may break in a future version of CMake that has improved escape support. Instead consider defining the macro in a (configured) header file. Then report the limitation. Known limitations include:

```
#              - broken almost everywhere
;              - broken in VS IDE 7.0 and Borland Makefiles
,              - broken in VS IDE
%              - broken in some cases in NMake
& |            - broken in some cases on MinGW
^ < > \"       - broken in most Make tools on Windows
```

CMake does not reject these values outright because they do work in some cases. Use with caution.

Contents of `COMPILE_DEFINITIONS` may use "generator expressions" with the syntax `$<...>`. See the `cmake-generator-expressions(7)` (page 356) manual for available expressions. See the `cmake-buildsystem(7)` manual for more on defining buildsystem properties.

The corresponding `COMPILE_DEFINITIONS_<CONFIG>` (page 622) property may be set to specify per-configuration definitions. Generator expressions should be preferred instead of setting the alternative property.

COMPILE_OPTIONS

List of options to pass to the compiler.

This property specifies the list of options given so far to the `add_compile_options()` (page 269) command.

This property is used to initialize the `COMPILE_OPTIONS` (page 581) target property when a target is created, which is used by the generators to set the options for the compiler.

Contents of `COMPILE_OPTIONS` may use "generator expressions" with the syntax `$<...>`. See the `cmake-generator-expressions(7)` (page 356) manual for available expressions. See the `cmake-buildsystem(7)` manual for more on defining buildsystem properties.

DEFINITIONS

For CMake 2.4 compatibility only. Use COMPILE_DEFINITIONS instead.

This read-only property specifies the list of flags given so far to the add_definitions command. It is intended for debugging purposes. Use the COMPILE_DEFINITIONS instead.

EXCLUDE_FROM_ALL

Exclude the directory from the all target of its parent.

A property on a directory that indicates if its targets are excluded from the default build target. If it is not, then with a Makefile for example typing make will cause the targets to be built. The same concept applies to the default build of other generators.

IMPLICIT_DEPENDS_INCLUDE_TRANSFORM

Specify #include line transforms for dependencies in a directory.

This property specifies rules to transform macro-like #include lines during implicit dependency scanning of C and C++ source files. The list of rules must be semicolon-separated with each entry of the form "A_MACRO(%)=value-with-%" (the % must be literal). During dependency scanning occurrences of A_MACRO(...) on #include lines will be replaced by the value given with the macro argument substituted for '%'. For example, the entry

```
MYDIR(%)=<mydir/%>
```

will convert lines of the form

```
#include MYDIR(myheader.h)
```

to

```
#include <mydir/myheader.h>
```

allowing the dependency to be followed.

This property applies to sources in all targets within a directory. The property value is initialized in each directory by its value in the directory's parent.

INCLUDE_DIRECTORIES

List of preprocessor include file search directories.

This property specifies the list of directories given so far to the `include_directories()` (page 316) command.

This property is used to populate the INCLUDE_DIRECTORIES (page 591) target property, which is used by the generators to set the include directories for the compiler.

In addition to accepting values from that command, values may be set directly on any directory using the `set_property()` (page 329) command. A directory gets its initial value from its parent directory if it has one. The intial value of the INCLUDE_DIRECTORIES (page 591) target property comes from the value of this property. Both directory and target property values are adjusted by calls to the `include_directories()` (page 316) command.

The target property values are used by the generators to set the include paths for the compiler.

Contents of INCLUDE_DIRECTORIES may use "generator expressions" with the syntax $<...>. See the `cmake-generator-expressions(7)` (page 356) manual for available expressions. See the `cmake-buildsystem(7)` manual for more on defining buildsystem properties.

INCLUDE_REGULAR_EXPRESSION

Include file scanning regular expression.

This read-only property specifies the regular expression used during dependency scanning to match include files that should be followed. See the include_regular_expression command.

INTERPROCEDURAL_OPTIMIZATION_<CONFIG>

Per-configuration interprocedural optimization for a directory.

This is a per-configuration version of INTERPROCEDURAL_OPTIMIZATION. If set, this property overrides the generic property for the named configuration.

INTERPROCEDURAL_OPTIMIZATION

Enable interprocedural optimization for targets in a directory.

If set to true, enables interprocedural optimizations if they are known to be supported by the compiler.

LINK_DIRECTORIES

List of linker search directories.

This read-only property specifies the list of directories given so far to the link_directories command. It is intended for debugging purposes.

LISTFILE_STACK

The current stack of listfiles being processed.

This property is mainly useful when trying to debug errors in your CMake scripts. It returns a list of what list files are currently being processed, in order. So if one listfile does an INCLUDE command then that is effectively pushing the included listfile onto the stack.

MACROS

List of macro commands available in the current directory.

This read-only property specifies the list of CMake macros currently defined. It is intended for debugging purposes. See the macro command.

PARENT_DIRECTORY

Source directory that added current subdirectory.

This read-only property specifies the source directory that added the current source directory as a subdirectory of the build. In the top-level directory the value is the empty-string.

RULE_LAUNCH_COMPILE

Specify a launcher for compile rules.

See the global property of the same name for details. This overrides the global property for a directory.

RULE_LAUNCH_CUSTOM

Specify a launcher for custom rules.

See the global property of the same name for details. This overrides the global property for a directory.

RULE_LAUNCH_LINK

Specify a launcher for link rules.

See the global property of the same name for details. This overrides the global property for a directory.

TEST_INCLUDE_FILE

A cmake file that will be included when ctest is run.

If you specify TEST_INCLUDE_FILE, that file will be included and processed when ctest is run on the directory.

VARIABLES

List of variables defined in the current directory.

This read-only property specifies the list of CMake variables currently defined. It is intended for debugging purposes.

VS_GLOBAL_SECTION_POST_<section>

Specify a postSolution global section in Visual Studio.

Setting a property like this generates an entry of the following form in the solution file:

```
GlobalSection(<section>) = postSolution
  <contents based on property value>
EndGlobalSection
```

The property must be set to a semicolon-separated list of key=value pairs. Each such pair will be transformed into an entry in the solution global section. Whitespace around key and value is ignored. List elements which do not contain an equal sign are skipped.

This property only works for Visual Studio 7 and above; it is ignored on other generators. The property only applies when set on a directory whose CMakeLists.txt contains a project() command.

Note that CMake generates postSolution sections ExtensibilityGlobals and ExtensibilityAddIns by default. If you set the corresponding property, it will override the default section. For example, setting VS_GLOBAL_SECTION_POST_ExtensibilityGlobals will override the default contents of the ExtensibilityGlobals section, while keeping ExtensibilityAddIns on its default.

VS_GLOBAL_SECTION_PRE_<section>

Specify a preSolution global section in Visual Studio.

Setting a property like this generates an entry of the following form in the solution file:

```
GlobalSection(<section>) = preSolution
  <contents based on property value>
EndGlobalSection
```

The property must be set to a semicolon-separated list of key=value pairs. Each such pair will be transformed into an entry in the solution global section. Whitespace around key and value is ignored. List elements which do not contain an equal sign are skipped.

This property only works for Visual Studio 7 and above; it is ignored on other generators. The property only applies when set on a directory whose CMakeLists.txt contains a project() command.

C.6.3 Properties on Targets

ALIASED_TARGET

Name of target aliased by this target.

If this is an *Alias Target*, this property contains the name of the target aliased.

ANDROID_API

Set the Android Target API version (e.g. 15). The version number must be a positive decimal integer. This property is initialized by the value of the CMAKE_ANDROID_API (page 656) variable if it is set when a target is created.

ANDROID_GUI

Build an executable as an application package on Android.

When this property is set to true the executable when built for Android will be created as an application package. This property is initialized by the value of the CMAKE_ANDROID_GUI (page 656) variable if it is set when a target is created.

Add the `AndroidManifest.xml` source file explicitly to the target `add_executable()` (page 273) command invocation to specify the root directory of the application package source.

ARCHIVE_OUTPUT_DIRECTORY_<CONFIG>

Per-configuration output directory for ARCHIVE target files.

This is a per-configuration version of ARCHIVE_OUTPUT_DIRECTORY, but multi-configuration generators (VS, Xcode) do NOT append a per-configuration subdirectory to the specified directory. This property is initialized by the value of the variable CMAKE_ARCHIVE_OUTPUT_DIRECTORY_<CONFIG> if it is set when a target is created.

ARCHIVE_OUTPUT_DIRECTORY

Output directory in which to build ARCHIVE target files.

This property specifies the directory into which archive target files should be built. Multi-configuration generators (VS, Xcode) append a per-configuration subdirectory to the specified directory.

There are three kinds of target files that may be built: archive, library, and runtime. Executables are always treated as runtime targets. Static libraries are always treated as archive targets. Module libraries are always treated as library targets. For non-DLL platforms shared libraries are treated as library targets. For DLL platforms the DLL part of a shared library is treated as a runtime target and the corresponding import library is treated as an archive target. All Windows-based systems including Cygwin are DLL platforms.

This property is initialized by the value of the variable CMAKE_ARCHIVE_OUTPUT_DIRECTORY if it is set when a target is created.

ARCHIVE_OUTPUT_NAME_<CONFIG>

Per-configuration output name for ARCHIVE target files.

This is the configuration-specific version of ARCHIVE_OUTPUT_NAME.

ARCHIVE_OUTPUT_NAME

Output name for ARCHIVE target files.

This property specifies the base name for archive target files. It overrides OUTPUT_NAME and OUTPUT_NAME_<CONFIG> properties.

There are three kinds of target files that may be built: archive, library, and runtime. Executables are always treated as runtime targets. Static libraries are always treated as archive targets. Module libraries are always treated as library targets. For non-DLL platforms shared libraries are treated as library targets. For DLL platforms the DLL part of a shared library is treated as a runtime target and the corresponding import library is treated as an archive target. All Windows-based systems including Cygwin are DLL platforms.

AUTOGEN_TARGET_DEPENDS

Target dependencies of the corresponding _automoc target.

Targets which have their AUTOMOC (page 575) target ON have a corresponding _automoc target which is used to autogenerate generate moc files. As this _automoc target is created at generate-time, it is not possible to define dependencies of it, such as to create inputs for the moc executable.

The AUTOGEN_TARGET_DEPENDS target property can be set instead to a list of dependencies for the _automoc target. The buildsystem will be generated to depend on its contents.

See the cmake-qt(7) manual for more information on using CMake with Qt.

AUTOMOC_MOC_OPTIONS

Additional options for moc when using AUTOMOC (page 575)

This property is only used if the AUTOMOC (page 575) property is ON for this target. In this case, it holds additional command line options which will be used when moc is executed during the build, i.e. it is equivalent to the optional OPTIONS argument of the qt4_wrap_cpp() (page 495) macro.

By default it is empty.

See the cmake-qt(7) manual for more information on using CMake with Qt.

AUTOMOC

Should the target be processed with automoc (for Qt projects).

AUTOMOC is a boolean specifying whether CMake will handle the Qt moc preprocessor automatically, i.e. without having to use the QT4_WRAP_CPP() (page 495) or QT5_WRAP_CPP() macro. Currently Qt4 and Qt5 are supported. When this property is set ON, CMake will scan the source files at build time and invoke moc accordingly. If an #include statement like #include "moc_foo.cpp" is found, the Q_OBJECT class declaration is expected in the header, and moc is run on the header file. If an #include statement like #include "foo.moc" is found, then a Q_OBJECT is expected in the current source file and moc is run on the file itself. Additionally, header files with the same base name (like foo.h) or _p appended to the base name (like foo_p.h) are parsed for Q_OBJECT macros, and if found, moc is also executed on those files. AUTOMOC checks multiple header alternative extensions, such as hpp, hxx etc when searching for headers. The resulting moc files, which are not included as shown above in any of the source files are included in a generated <targetname>_automoc.cpp file, which is compiled as part of the target. This property is initialized by the value of the CMAKE_AUTOMOC (page 657) variable if it is set when a target is created.

Additional command line options for moc can be set via the AUTOMOC_MOC_OPTIONS (page 575) property.

By enabling the CMAKE_AUTOMOC_RELAXED_MODE (page 639) variable the rules for searching the files which will be processed by moc can be relaxed. See the documentation for this variable for more details.

The global property AUTOGEN_TARGETS_FOLDER (page 559) can be used to group the automoc targets together in an IDE, e.g. in MSVS.

See the `cmake-qt(7)` manual for more information on using CMake with Qt.

AUTOUIC

Should the target be processed with autouic (for Qt projects).

`AUTOUIC` is a boolean specifying whether CMake will handle the Qt `uic` code generator automatically, i.e. without having to use the `QT4_WRAP_UI()` (page 495) or `QT5_WRAP_UI()` macro. Currently Qt4 and Qt5 are supported.

When this property is `ON`, CMake will scan the source files at build time and invoke `uic` accordingly. If an `#include` statement like `#include "ui_foo.h"` is found in `foo.cpp`, a `foo.ui` file is expected next to `foo.cpp`, and `uic` is run on the `foo.ui` file. This property is initialized by the value of the `CMAKE_AUTOUIC` (page 657) variable if it is set when a target is created.

Additional command line options for `uic` can be set via the `AUTOUIC_OPTIONS` (page 615) source file property on the `foo.ui` file. The global property `AUTOGEN_TARGETS_FOLDER` (page 559) can be used to group the autouic targets together in an IDE, e.g. in MSVS.

See the `cmake-qt(7)` manual for more information on using CMake with Qt.

AUTOUIC_OPTIONS

Additional options for uic when using `AUTOUIC` (page 576)

This property holds additional command line options which will be used when `uic` is executed during the build via `AUTOUIC` (page 576), i.e. it is equivalent to the optional `OPTIONS` argument of the `qt4_wrap_ui()` (page 495) macro.

By default it is empty.

This property is initialized by the value of the `CMAKE_AUTOUIC_OPTIONS` (page 658) variable if it is set when a target is created.

The options set on the target may be overridden by `AUTOUIC_OPTIONS` (page 615) set on the `.ui` source file.

This property may use "generator expressions" with the syntax `$<...>`. See the `cmake-generator-expressions(7)` (page 356) manual for available expressions.

See the `cmake-qt(7)` manual for more information on using CMake with Qt.

AUTORCC

Should the target be processed with autorcc (for Qt projects).

`AUTORCC` is a boolean specifying whether CMake will handle the Qt `rcc` code generator automatically, i.e. without having to use the `QT4_ADD_RESOURCES()` (page 495) or `QT5_ADD_RESOURCES()` macro. Currently Qt4 and Qt5 are supported.

When this property is ON, CMake will handle .qrc files added as target sources at build time and invoke rcc accordingly. This property is initialized by the value of the CMAKE_AUTORCC (page 657) variable if it is set when a target is created.

Additional command line options for rcc can be set via the AUTORCC_OPTIONS (page 616) source file property on the .qrc file.

The global property AUTOGEN_TARGETS_FOLDER (page 559) can be used to group the autorcc targets together in an IDE, e.g. in MSVS.

See the cmake-qt(7) manual for more information on using CMake with Qt.

AUTORCC_OPTIONS

Additional options for rcc when using AUTORCC (page 576)

This property holds additional command line options which will be used when rcc is executed during the build via AUTORCC (page 576), i.e. it is equivalent to the optional OPTIONS argument of the qt4_add_resources() (page 495) macro.

By default it is empty.

This property is initialized by the value of the CMAKE_AUTORCC_OPTIONS (page 657) variable if it is set when a target is created.

The options set on the target may be overridden by AUTORCC_OPTIONS (page 616) set on the .qrc source file.

See the cmake-qt(7) manual for more information on using CMake with Qt.

BUILD_WITH_INSTALL_RPATH

Should build tree targets have install tree rpaths.

BUILD_WITH_INSTALL_RPATH is a boolean specifying whether to link the target in the build tree with the INSTALL_RPATH. This takes precedence over SKIP_BUILD_RPATH and avoids the need for relinking before installation. This property is initialized by the value of the variable CMAKE_BUILD_WITH_INSTALL_RPATH if it is set when a target is created.

BUNDLE_EXTENSION

The file extension used to name a BUNDLE target on the Mac.

The default value is "bundle" - you can also use "plugin" or whatever file extension is required by the host app for your bundle.

BUNDLE

This target is a CFBundle on the Mac.

If a module library target has this property set to true it will be built as a CFBundle when built on the mac. It will have the directory structure required for a CFBundle and will be suitable to be used for creating Browser Plugins or other application resources.

C_EXTENSIONS

Boolean specifying whether compiler specific extensions are requested.

This property specifies whether compiler specific extensions should be used. For some compilers, this results in adding a flag such as -std=gnu11 instead of -std=c11 to the compile line. This property is ON by default.

See the cmake-compile-features(7) manual for information on compile features.

This property is initialized by the value of the CMAKE_C_EXTENSIONS (page 667) variable if it is set when a target is created.

C_STANDARD

The C standard whose features are requested to build this target.

This property specifies the C standard whose features are requested to build this target. For some compilers, this results in adding a flag such as -std=gnu11 to the compile line.

Supported values are 90, 99 and 11.

If the value requested does not result in a compile flag being added for the compiler in use, a previous standard flag will be added instead. This means that using:

```
set_property(TARGET tgt PROPERTY C_STANDARD 11)
```

with a compiler which does not support -std=gnu11 or an equivalent flag will not result in an error or warning, but will instead add the -std=gnu99 or -std=gnu90 flag if supported. This "decay" behavior may be controlled with the C_STANDARD_REQUIRED (page 578) target property.

See the cmake-compile-features(7) manual for information on compile features.

This property is initialized by the value of the CMAKE_C_STANDARD (page 667) variable if it is set when a target is created.

C_STANDARD_REQUIRED

Boolean describing whether the value of C_STANDARD (page 578) is a requirement.

If this property is set to ON, then the value of the C_STANDARD (page 578) target property is treated as a requirement. If this property is OFF or unset, the C_STANDARD (page 578) target property is treated as optional and may "decay" to a previous standard if the requested is not available.

See the cmake-compile-features(7) manual for information on compile features.

This property is initialized by the value of the CMAKE_C_STANDARD_REQUIRED (page 667) variable if it is set when a target is created.

COMPATIBLE_INTERFACE_BOOL

Properties which must be compatible with their link interface

The COMPATIBLE_INTERFACE_BOOL property may contain a list of properties for this target which must be consistent when evaluated as a boolean with the INTERFACE variant of the property in all linked dependees. For example, if a property FOO appears in the list, then for each dependee, the INTERFACE_FOO property content in all of its dependencies must be consistent with each other, and with the FOO property in the depender.

Consistency in this sense has the meaning that if the property is set, then it must have the same boolean value as all others, and if the property is not set, then it is ignored.

Note that for each dependee, the set of properties specified in this property must not intersect with the set specified in any of the other *Compatible Interface Properties*.

COMPATIBLE_INTERFACE_NUMBER_MAX

Properties whose maximum value from the link interface will be used.

The COMPATIBLE_INTERFACE_NUMBER_MAX property may contain a list of properties for this target whose maximum value may be read at generate time when evaluated in the INTERFACE variant of the property in all linked dependees. For example, if a property FOO appears in the list, then for each dependee, the INTERFACE_FOO property content in all of its dependencies will be compared with each other and with the FOO property in the depender. When reading the FOO property at generate time, the maximum value will be returned. If the property is not set, then it is ignored.

Note that for each dependee, the set of properties specified in this property must not intersect with the set specified in any of the other *Compatible Interface Properties*.

COMPATIBLE_INTERFACE_NUMBER_MIN

Properties whose maximum value from the link interface will be used.

The COMPATIBLE_INTERFACE_NUMBER_MIN property may contain a list of properties for this target whose minimum value may be read at generate time when evaluated in the INTERFACE variant of the property of all linked dependees. For example, if a property FOO appears in the list, then for each dependee, the INTERFACE_FOO property content in all of its dependencies will be compared with each other and with the FOO property in the depender. When reading the FOO property at generate time, the minimum value will be returned. If the property is not set, then it is ignored.

Note that for each dependee, the set of properties specified in this property must not intersect with the set specified in any of the other *Compatible Interface Properties*.

COMPATIBLE_INTERFACE_STRING

Properties which must be string-compatible with their link interface

The COMPATIBLE_INTERFACE_STRING property may contain a list of properties for this target which must be the same when evaluated as a string in the INTERFACE variant of the property all linked dependees. For example, if a property FOO appears in the list, then for each dependee, the INTERFACE_FOO property content in all of its dependencies must be equal with each other, and with the FOO property in the depender. If the property is not set, then it is ignored.

Note that for each dependee, the set of properties specified in this property must not intersect with the set specified in any of the other *Compatible Interface Properties*.

COMPILE_DEFINITIONS

Preprocessor definitions for compiling a target's sources.

The COMPILE_DEFINITIONS property may be set to a semicolon-separated list of preprocessor definitions using the syntax VAR or VAR=value. Function-style definitions are not supported. CMake will automatically escape the value correctly for the native build system (note that CMake language syntax may require escapes to specify some values).

CMake will automatically drop some definitions that are not supported by the native build tool. The VS6 IDE does not support definition values with spaces (but NMake does).

Disclaimer: Most native build tools have poor support for escaping certain values. CMake has work-arounds for many cases but some values may just not be possible to pass correctly. If a value does not seem to be escaped correctly, do not attempt to work-around the problem by adding escape sequences to the value. Your work-around may break in a future version of CMake that has improved escape support. Instead consider defining the macro in a (configured) header file. Then report the limitation. Known limitations include:

```
#              - broken almost everywhere
;              - broken in VS IDE 7.0 and Borland Makefiles
,              - broken in VS IDE
%              - broken in some cases in NMake
& |            - broken in some cases on MinGW
^ < > \"       - broken in most Make tools on Windows
```

CMake does not reject these values outright because they do work in some cases. Use with caution.

Contents of COMPILE_DEFINITIONS may use "generator expressions" with the syntax $<...>. See the cmake-generator-expressions(7) (page 356) manual for available expressions. See the cmake-buildsystem(7) manual for more on defining buildsystem properties.

The corresponding COMPILE_DEFINITIONS_<CONFIG> (page 622) property may be set to specify per-configuration definitions. Generator expressions should be preferred instead of setting the alternative property.

COMPILE_FEATURES

Compiler features enabled for this target.

The list of features in this property are a subset of the features listed in the CMAKE_CXX_COMPILE_FEATURES (page 668) variable.

Contents of COMPILE_FEATURES may use "generator expressions" with the syntax $<...>. See the cmake-generator-expressions(7) (page 356) manual for available expressions. See the cmake-compile-features(7) manual for information on compile features.

COMPILE_FLAGS

Additional flags to use when compiling this target's sources.

The COMPILE_FLAGS property sets additional compiler flags used to build sources within the target. Use COMPILE_DEFINITIONS to pass additional preprocessor definitions.

This property is deprecated. Use the COMPILE_OPTIONS property or the target_compile_options command instead.

COMPILE_OPTIONS

List of options to pass to the compiler.

This property specifies the list of options specified so far for this property.

This property is intialized by the COMPILE_OPTIONS (page 569) directory property, which is used by the generators to set the options for the compiler.

Contents of COMPILE_OPTIONS may use "generator expressions" with the syntax $<...>. See the cmake-generator-expressions(7) (page 356) manual for available expressions. See the cmake-buildsystem(7) manual for more on defining buildsystem properties.

COMPILE_PDB_NAME

Output name for the MS debug symbol .pdb file generated by the compiler while building source files.

This property specifies the base name for the debug symbols file. If not set, the default is unspecified.

Note: The compiler-generated program database files are specified by the /Fd compiler flag and are not the same as linker-generated program database files specified by the /pdb linker flag. Use the PDB_NAME (page 604) property to specify the latter.

This property is not implemented by the Visual Studio 6 (page 361) generator.

COMPILE_PDB_NAME_<CONFIG>

Per-configuration output name for the MS debug symbol .pdb file generated by the compiler while building source files.

This is the configuration-specific version of COMPILE_PDB_NAME (page 581).

Note: The compiler-generated program database files are specified by the /Fd compiler flag and are not the same as linker-generated program database files specified by the /pdb linker flag. Use the PDB_NAME_<CONFIG> (page 604) property to specify the latter.

This property is not implemented by the Visual Studio 6 (page 361) generator.

COMPILE_PDB_OUTPUT_DIRECTORY

Output directory for the MS debug symbol .pdb file generated by the compiler while building source files.

This property specifies the directory into which the MS debug symbols will be placed by the compiler. This property is initialized by the value of the CMAKE_COMPILE_PDB_OUTPUT_DIRECTORY (page 658) variable if it is set when a target is created.

Note: The compiler-generated program database files are specified by the /Fd compiler flag and are not the same as linker-generated program database files specified by the /pdb linker flag. Use the PDB_OUTPUT_DIRECTORY (page 605) property to specify the latter.

This property is not implemented by the Visual Studio 6 (page 361) generator.

COMPILE_PDB_OUTPUT_DIRECTORY_<CONFIG>

Per-configuration output directory for the MS debug symbol .pdb file generated by the compiler while building source files.

This is a per-configuration version of COMPILE_PDB_OUTPUT_DIRECTORY (page 582), but multi-configuration generators (VS, Xcode) do NOT append a per-configuration subdirectory to the specified directory. This property is initialized by the value of the CMAKE_COMPILE_PDB_OUTPUT_DIRECTORY_<CONFIG> (page 658) variable if it is set when a target is created.

Note: The compiler-generated program database files are specified by the /Fd compiler flag and are not the same as linker-generated program database files specified by the /pdb linker flag. Use the PDB_OUTPUT_DIRECTORY_<CONFIG> (page 604) property to specify the latter.

This property is not implemented by the Visual Studio 6 (page 361) generator.

<CONFIG>_OUTPUT_NAME

Old per-configuration target file base name.

This is a configuration-specific version of OUTPUT_NAME. Use OUTPUT_NAME_<CONFIG> instead.

<CONFIG>_POSTFIX

Postfix to append to the target file name for configuration <CONFIG>.

When building with configuration <CONFIG> the value of this property is appended to the target file name built on disk. For non-executable targets, this property is initialized by the value of the variable CMAKE_<CONFIG>_POSTFIX if it is set when a target is created. This property is ignored on the Mac for Frameworks and App Bundles.

CXX_EXTENSIONS

Boolean specifying whether compiler specific extensions are requested.

This property specifies whether compiler specific extensions should be used. For some compilers, this results in adding a flag such as -std=gnu++11 instead of -std=c++11 to the compile line. This property is ON by default.

See the cmake-compile-features(7) manual for information on compile features.

This property is initialized by the value of the CMAKE_CXX_EXTENSIONS (page 668) variable if it is set when a target is created.

CXX_STANDARD

The C++ standard whose features are requested to build this target.

This property specifies the C++ standard whose features are requested to build this target. For some compilers, this results in adding a flag such as -std=gnu++11 to the compile line.

Supported values are 98, 11 and 14.

If the value requested does not result in a compile flag being added for the compiler in use, a previous standard flag will be added instead. This means that using:

```
set_property(TARGET tgt PROPERTY CXX_STANDARD 11)
```

with a compiler which does not support -std=gnu++11 or an equivalent flag will not result in an error or warning, but will instead add the -std=gnu++98 flag if supported. This "decay" behavior may be controlled with the CXX_STANDARD_REQUIRED (page 584) target property.

See the `cmake-compile-features(7)` manual for information on compile features.

This property is initialized by the value of the `CMAKE_CXX_STANDARD` (page 668) variable if it is set when a target is created.

CXX_STANDARD_REQUIRED

Boolean describing whether the value of `CXX_STANDARD` (page 583) is a requirement.

If this property is set to `ON`, then the value of the `CXX_STANDARD` (page 583) target property is treated as a requirement. If this property is `OFF` or unset, the `CXX_STANDARD` (page 583) target property is treated as optional and may "decay" to a previous standard if the requested is not available.

See the `cmake-compile-features(7)` manual for information on compile features.

This property is initialized by the value of the `CMAKE_CXX_STANDARD_REQUIRED` (page 668) variable if it is set when a target is created.

DEBUG_POSTFIX

See target property <CONFIG>_POSTFIX.

This property is a special case of the more-general <CONFIG>_POSTFIX property for the DEBUG configuration.

DEFINE_SYMBOL

Define a symbol when compiling this target's sources.

DEFINE_SYMBOL sets the name of the preprocessor symbol defined when compiling sources in a shared library. If not set here then it is set to target_EXPORTS by default (with some substitutions if the target is not a valid C identifier). This is useful for headers to know whether they are being included from inside their library or outside to properly setup dllexport/dllimport decorations.

EchoString

A message to be displayed when the target is built.

A message to display on some generators (such as makefiles) when the target is built.

ENABLE_EXPORTS

Specify whether an executable exports symbols for loadable modules.

Normally an executable does not export any symbols because it is the final program. It is possible for an executable to export symbols to be used by loadable modules. When this property is set to true CMake will allow other targets to "link" to the executable with the TARGET_LINK_LIBRARIES command. On all platforms a target-level dependency on the executable is created for targets that link to it. For DLL platforms an import library will be created for the exported symbols and then used for linking. All Windows-based systems including Cygwin are DLL platforms. For non-DLL platforms that require all symbols to be resolved at link time, such as Mac OS X, the module will "link" to the executable using a flag like "-bundle_loader". For other non-DLL platforms the link rule is simply ignored since the dynamic loader will automatically bind symbols when the module is loaded.

EXCLUDE_FROM_ALL

Exclude the target from the all target.

A property on a target that indicates if the target is excluded from the default build target. If it is not, then with a Makefile for example typing make will cause this target to be built. The same concept applies to the default build of other generators. Installing a target with EXCLUDE_FROM_ALL set to true has undefined behavior.

EXCLUDE_FROM_DEFAULT_BUILD_<CONFIG>

Per-configuration version of target exclusion from "Build Solution".

This is the configuration-specific version of EXCLUDE_FROM_DEFAULT_BUILD. If the generic EXCLUDE_FROM_DEFAULT_BUILD is also set on a target, EX-CLUDE_FROM_DEFAULT_BUILD_<CONFIG> takes precedence in configurations for which it has a value.

EXCLUDE_FROM_DEFAULT_BUILD

Exclude target from "Build Solution".

This property is only used by Visual Studio generators 7 and above. When set to TRUE, the target will not be built when you press "Build Solution".

EXPORT_NAME

Exported name for target files.

This sets the name for the IMPORTED target generated when it this target is is exported. If not set, the logical target name is used by default.

FOLDER

Set the folder name. Use to organize targets in an IDE.

Targets with no FOLDER property will appear as top level entities in IDEs like Visual Studio. Targets with the same FOLDER property value will appear next to each other in a folder of that name. To nest folders, use FOLDER values such as 'GUI/Dialogs' with '/' characters separating folder levels.

Fortran_FORMAT

Set to FIXED or FREE to indicate the Fortran source layout.

This property tells CMake whether the Fortran source files in a target use fixed-format or free-format. CMake will pass the corresponding format flag to the compiler. Use the source-specific Fortran_FORMAT property to change the format of a specific source file. If the variable CMAKE_Fortran_FORMAT is set when a target is created its value is used to initialize this property.

Fortran_MODULE_DIRECTORY

Specify output directory for Fortran modules provided by the target.

If the target contains Fortran source files that provide modules and the compiler supports a module output directory this specifies the directory in which the modules will be placed. When this property is not set the modules will be placed in the build directory corresponding to the target's source directory. If the variable CMAKE_Fortran_MODULE_DIRECTORY is set when a target is created its value is used to initialize this property.

Note that some compilers will automatically search the module output directory for modules USEd during compilation but others will not. If your sources USE modules their location must be specified by IN-CLUDE_DIRECTORIES regardless of this property.

FRAMEWORK

This target is a framework on the Mac.

If a shared library target has this property set to true it will be built as a framework when built on the mac. It will have the directory structure required for a framework and will be suitable to be used with the -framework option

GENERATOR_FILE_NAME

Generator's file for this target.

An internal property used by some generators to record the name of the project or dsp file associated with this target. Note that at configure time, this property is only set for targets created by include_external_msproject().

GNUtoMS

Convert GNU import library (.dll.a) to MS format (.lib).

When linking a shared library or executable that exports symbols using GNU tools on Windows (MinGW/MSYS) with Visual Studio installed convert the import library (.dll.a) from GNU to MS format (.lib). Both import libraries will be installed by install(TARGETS) and exported by install(EXPORT) and export() to be linked by applications with either GNU- or MS-compatible tools.

If the variable CMAKE_GNUtoMS is set when a target is created its value is used to initialize this property. The variable must be set prior to the first command that enables a language such as project() or enable_language(). CMake provides the variable as an option to the user automatically when configuring on Windows with GNU tools.

HAS_CXX

Link the target using the C++ linker tool (obsolete).

This is equivalent to setting the LINKER_LANGUAGE property to CXX. See that property's documentation for details.

IMPLICIT_DEPENDS_INCLUDE_TRANSFORM

Specify #include line transforms for dependencies in a target.

This property specifies rules to transform macro-like #include lines during implicit dependency scanning of C and C++ source files. The list of rules must be semicolon-separated with each entry of the form "A_MACRO(%)=value-with-%" (the % must be literal). During dependency scanning occurrences of A_MACRO(...) on #include lines will be replaced by the value given with the macro argument substituted for '%'. For example, the entry

```
MYDIR(%)=<mydir/%>
```

will convert lines of the form

```
#include MYDIR(myheader.h)
```

to

```
#include <mydir/myheader.h>
```

allowing the dependency to be followed.

This property applies to sources in the target on which it is set.

IMPORTED_CONFIGURATIONS

Configurations provided for an IMPORTED target.

Set this to the list of configuration names available for an IMPORTED target. The names correspond to configurations defined in the project from which the target is imported. If the importing project uses a different set of configurations the names may be mapped using the MAP_IMPORTED_CONFIG_<CONFIG> property. Ignored for non-imported targets.

IMPORTED_IMPLIB_<CONFIG>

<CONFIG>-specific version of IMPORTED_IMPLIB property.

Configuration names correspond to those provided by the project from which the target is imported.

IMPORTED_IMPLIB

Full path to the import library for an IMPORTED target.

Set this to the location of the ".lib" part of a windows DLL. Ignored for non-imported targets.

IMPORTED_LINK_DEPENDENT_LIBRARIES_<CONFIG>

<CONFIG>-specific version of IMPORTED_LINK_DEPENDENT_LIBRARIES.

Configuration names correspond to those provided by the project from which the target is imported. If set, this property completely overrides the generic property for the named configuration.

IMPORTED_LINK_DEPENDENT_LIBRARIES

Dependent shared libraries of an imported shared library.

Shared libraries may be linked to other shared libraries as part of their implementation. On some platforms the linker searches for the dependent libraries of shared libraries they are including in the link. Set this property to the list of dependent shared libraries of an imported library. The list should be disjoint from the list of interface libraries in the INTERFACE_LINK_LIBRARIES property. On platforms requiring dependent shared libraries to be found at link time CMake uses this list to add appropriate files or paths to the link command line. Ignored for non-imported targets.

IMPORTED_LINK_INTERFACE_LANGUAGES_<CONFIG>

<CONFIG>-specific version of IMPORTED_LINK_INTERFACE_LANGUAGES.

Configuration names correspond to those provided by the project from which the target is imported. If set, this property completely overrides the generic property for the named configuration.

IMPORTED_LINK_INTERFACE_LANGUAGES

Languages compiled into an IMPORTED static library.

Set this to the list of languages of source files compiled to produce a STATIC IMPORTED library (such as "C" or "CXX"). CMake accounts for these languages when computing how to link a target to the imported library. For example, when a C executable links to an imported C++ static library CMake chooses the C++ linker to satisfy language runtime dependencies of the static library.

This property is ignored for targets that are not STATIC libraries. This property is ignored for non-imported targets.

IMPORTED_LINK_INTERFACE_LIBRARIES_<CONFIG>

<CONFIG>-specific version of IMPORTED_LINK_INTERFACE_LIBRARIES.

Configuration names correspond to those provided by the project from which the target is imported. If set, this property completely overrides the generic property for the named configuration.

This property is ignored if the target also has a non-empty INTERFACE_LINK_LIBRARIES property.

This property is deprecated. Use INTERFACE_LINK_LIBRARIES instead.

IMPORTED_LINK_INTERFACE_LIBRARIES

Transitive link interface of an IMPORTED target.

Set this to the list of libraries whose interface is included when an IMPORTED library target is linked to another target. The libraries will be included on the link line for the target. Unlike the LINK_INTERFACE_LIBRARIES property, this property applies to all imported target types, including STATIC libraries. This property is ignored for non-imported targets.

This property is ignored if the target also has a non-empty INTERFACE_LINK_LIBRARIES property.

This property is deprecated. Use INTERFACE_LINK_LIBRARIES instead.

IMPORTED_LINK_INTERFACE_MULTIPLICITY_<CONFIG>

<CONFIG>-specific version of IMPORTED_LINK_INTERFACE_MULTIPLICITY.

If set, this property completely overrides the generic property for the named configuration.

IMPORTED_LINK_INTERFACE_MULTIPLICITY

Repetition count for cycles of IMPORTED static libraries.

This is LINK_INTERFACE_MULTIPLICITY for IMPORTED targets.

IMPORTED_LOCATION_<CONFIG>

<CONFIG>-specific version of IMPORTED_LOCATION property.

Configuration names correspond to those provided by the project from which the target is imported.

IMPORTED_LOCATION

Full path to the main file on disk for an IMPORTED target.

Set this to the location of an IMPORTED target file on disk. For executables this is the location of the executable file. For bundles on OS X this is the location of the executable file inside Contents/MacOS under the application bundle folder. For static libraries and modules this is the location of the library or module. For shared libraries on non-DLL platforms this is the location of the shared library. For frameworks on OS X this is the location of the library file symlink just inside the framework folder. For DLLs this is the location of the ".dll" part of the library. For UNKNOWN libraries this is the location of the file to be linked. Ignored for non-imported targets.

Projects may skip IMPORTED_LOCATION if the configuration-specific property IM-PORTED_LOCATION_<CONFIG> is set. To get the location of an imported target read one of the LOCATION or LOCATION_<CONFIG> properties.

IMPORTED_NO_SONAME_<CONFIG>

<CONFIG>-specific version of IMPORTED_NO_SONAME property.

Configuration names correspond to those provided by the project from which the target is imported.

IMPORTED_NO_SONAME

Specifies that an IMPORTED shared library target has no "soname".

Set this property to true for an imported shared library file that has no "soname" field. CMake may adjust generated link commands for some platforms to prevent the linker from using the path to the library in place of its missing soname. Ignored for non-imported targets.

IMPORTED

Read-only indication of whether a target is IMPORTED.

The boolean value of this property is `True` for targets created with the IMPORTED option to `add_executable()` (page 273) or `add_library()` (page 274). It is `False` for targets built within the project.

IMPORTED_SONAME_<CONFIG>

<CONFIG>-specific version of IMPORTED_SONAME property.

Configuration names correspond to those provided by the project from which the target is imported.

IMPORTED_SONAME

The "soname" of an IMPORTED target of shared library type.

Set this to the "soname" embedded in an imported shared library. This is meaningful only on platforms supporting the feature. Ignored for non-imported targets.

IMPORT_PREFIX

What comes before the import library name.

Similar to the target property PREFIX, but used for import libraries (typically corresponding to a DLL) instead of regular libraries. A target property that can be set to override the prefix (such as "lib") on an import library name.

IMPORT_SUFFIX

What comes after the import library name.

Similar to the target property SUFFIX, but used for import libraries (typically corresponding to a DLL) instead of regular libraries. A target property that can be set to override the suffix (such as ".lib") on an import library name.

INCLUDE_DIRECTORIES

List of preprocessor include file search directories.

This property specifies the list of directories given so far to the `target_include_directories()` (page 339) command. In addition to accepting values from that command, values may be set directly on any target using the `set_property()` (page 329) command. A target gets its initial value for this property from the value of the INCLUDE_DIRECTORIES (page 570) directory property. Both directory and target property values are adjusted by calls to the `include_directories()` (page 316) command.

The value of this property is used by the generators to set the include paths for the compiler.

Relative paths should not be added to this property directly. Use one of the commands above instead to handle relative paths.

Contents of INCLUDE_DIRECTORIES may use "generator expressions" with the syntax $<...>. See the `cmake-generator-expressions(7)` (page 356) manual for available expressions. See the `cmake-buildsystem(7)` manual for more on defining buildsystem properties.

INSTALL_NAME_DIR

Mac OSX directory name for installed targets.

INSTALL_NAME_DIR is a string specifying the directory portion of the "install_name" field of shared libraries on Mac OSX to use in the installed targets.

INSTALL_RPATH

The rpath to use for installed targets.

A semicolon-separated list specifying the rpath to use in installed targets (for platforms that support it). This property is initialized by the value of the variable CMAKE_INSTALL_RPATH if it is set when a target is created.

INSTALL_RPATH_USE_LINK_PATH

Add paths to linker search and installed rpath.

INSTALL_RPATH_USE_LINK_PATH is a boolean that if set to true will append directories in the linker search path and outside the project to the INSTALL_RPATH. This property is initialized by the value of the variable CMAKE_INSTALL_RPATH_USE_LINK_PATH if it is set when a target is created.

INTERFACE_AUTOUIC_OPTIONS

List of interface options to pass to uic.

Targets may populate this property to publish the options required to use when invoking uic. Consuming targets can add entries to their own AUTOUIC_OPTIONS (page 576) property such as $<TARGET_PROPERTY:foo,INTERFACE_AUTOUIC_OPTIONS> to use the uic options specified in the interface of foo. This is done automatically by the target_link_libraries() (page 340) command.

This property supports generator expressions. See the cmake-generator-expressions(7) (page 356) manual for available expressions.

INTERFACE_COMPILE_DEFINITIONS

List of public compile definitions for a library.

Targets may populate this property to publish the compile definitions required to compile against the headers for the target. Consuming targets can add entries to their own COMPILE_DEFINITIONS (page 580) property such as $<TARGET_PROPERTY:foo,INTERFACE_COMPILE_DEFINITIONS> to use the compile definitions specified in the interface of foo.

Contents of `INTERFACE_COMPILE_DEFINITIONS` may use "generator expressions" with the syntax `$<...>`. See the `cmake-generator-expressions(7)` (page 356) manual for available expressions. See the `cmake-buildsystem(7)` manual for more on defining buildsystem properties.

INTERFACE_COMPILE_FEATURES

List of public compile requirements for a library.

Targets may populate this property to publish the compiler features required to compile against the headers for the target. Consuming targets can add entries to their own `COMPILE_FEATURES` (page 581) property such as `$<TARGET_PROPERTY:foo,INTERFACE_COMPILE_FEATURES>` to require the features specified in the interface of `foo`.

Contents of `INTERFACE_COMPILE_FEATURES` may use "generator expressions" with the syntax `$<...>`. See the `cmake-generator-expressions(7)` (page 356) manual for available expressions. See the `cmake-compile-features(7)` manual for information on compile features.

INTERFACE_COMPILE_OPTIONS

List of interface options to pass to the compiler.

Targets may populate this property to publish the compile options required to compile against the headers for the target. Consuming targets can add entries to their own `COMPILE_OPTIONS` (page 581) property such as `$<TARGET_PROPERTY:foo,INTERFACE_COMPILE_OPTIONS>` to use the compile options specified in the interface of `foo`.

Contents of `INTERFACE_COMPILE_OPTIONS` may use "generator expressions" with the syntax `$<...>`. See the `cmake-generator-expressions(7)` (page 356) manual for available expressions. See the `cmake-buildsystem(7)` manual for more on defining buildsystem properties.

INTERFACE_INCLUDE_DIRECTORIES

List of public include directories for a library.

The `target_include_directories()` (page 339) command populates this property with values given to the `PUBLIC` and `INTERFACE` keywords. Projects may also get and set the property directly.

Targets may populate this property to publish the include directories required to compile against the headers for the target. Consuming targets can add entries to their own `INCLUDE_DIRECTORIES` (page 591) property such as `$<TARGET_PROPERTY:foo,INTERFACE_INCLUDE_DIRECTORIES>` to use the include directories specified in the interface of `foo`.

Contents of `INTERFACE_INCLUDE_DIRECTORIES` may use "generator expressions" with the syntax `$<...>`. See the `cmake-generator-expressions(7)` (page 356) manual for available expressions. See the `cmake-buildsystem(7)` manual for more on defining buildsystem properties.

Include directories usage requirements commonly differ between the build-tree and the install-tree. The `BUILD_INTERFACE` and `INSTALL_INTERFACE` generator expressions can be used to describe separate usage requirements based on the usage location. Relative paths are allowed within the `INSTALL_INTERFACE` expression and are interpreted relative to the installation prefix. For example:

```
set_property(TARGET mylib APPEND PROPERTY INTERFACE_INCLUDE_DIRECTORIES
  $<BUILD_INTERFACE:${CMAKE_CURRENT_SOURCE_DIR}/include/mylib>
  $<INSTALL_INTERFACE:include/mylib>  # <prefix>/include/mylib
  )
```

INTERFACE_LINK_LIBRARIES

List public interface libraries for a library.

This property contains the list of transitive link dependencies. When the target is linked into another target the libraries listed (and recursively their link interface libraries) will be provided to the other target also. This property is overridden by the `LINK_INTERFACE_LIBRARIES` (page 598) or `LINK_INTERFACE_LIBRARIES_<CONFIG>` (page 598) property if policy `CMP0022` (page 546) is `OLD` or unset.

Contents of `INTERFACE_LINK_LIBRARIES` may use "generator expressions" with the syntax `$<...>`. See the `cmake-generator-expressions(7)` (page 356) manual for available expressions. See the `cmake-buildsystem(7)` manual for more on defining buildsystem properties.

INTERFACE_POSITION_INDEPENDENT_CODE

Whether consumers need to create a position-independent target

The `INTERFACE_POSITION_INDEPENDENT_CODE` property informs consumers of this target whether they must set their `POSITION_INDEPENDENT_CODE` (page 605) property to `ON`. If this property is set to `ON`, then the `POSITION_INDEPENDENT_CODE` (page 605) property on all consumers will be set to `ON`. Similarly, if this property is set to `OFF`, then the `POSITION_INDEPENDENT_CODE` (page 605) property on all consumers will be set to `OFF`. If this property is undefined, then consumers will determine their `POSITION_INDEPENDENT_CODE` (page 605) property by other means. Consumers must ensure that the targets that they link to have a consistent requirement for their `INTERFACE_POSITION_INDEPENDENT_CODE` property.

INTERFACE_SOURCES

List of interface sources to pass to the compiler.

Targets may populate this property to publish the sources for consuming targets to compile. Consuming targets can add entries to their own `SOURCES` (page 608) property such as `$<TARGET_PROPERTY:foo,INTERFACE_SOURCES>` to use the sources specified in the interface of foo.

Targets with `INTERFACE_SOURCES` may not be exported with the `export()` (page 287) or `install(EXPORT)` (page 317) commands. This limitation may be lifted in a future version of CMake.

Contents of INTERFACE_SOURCES may use "generator expressions" with the syntax $<...>. See the cmake-generator-expressions(7) (page 356) manual for available expressions. See the cmake-buildsystem(7) manual for more on defining buildsystem properties.

INTERFACE_SYSTEM_INCLUDE_DIRECTORIES

List of public system include directories for a library.

Targets may populate this property to publish the include directories which contain system headers, and therefore should not result in compiler warnings. Consuming targets will then mark the same include directories as system headers.

Contents of INTERFACE_SYSTEM_INCLUDE_DIRECTORIES may use "generator expressions" with the syntax $<...>. See the cmake-generator-expressions(7) (page 356) manual for available expressions. See the cmake-buildsystem(7) manual for more on defining buildsystem properties.

INTERPROCEDURAL_OPTIMIZATION_<CONFIG>

Per-configuration interprocedural optimization for a target.

This is a per-configuration version of INTERPROCEDURAL_OPTIMIZATION. If set, this property overrides the generic property for the named configuration.

INTERPROCEDURAL_OPTIMIZATION

Enable interprocedural optimization for a target.

If set to true, enables interprocedural optimizations if they are known to be supported by the compiler.

JOB_POOL_COMPILE

Ninja only: Pool used for compiling.

The number of parallel compile processes could be limited by defining pools with the global JOB_POOLS (page 565) property and then specifying here the pool name.

For instance:

```
set_property(TARGET myexe PROPERTY JOB_POOL_COMPILE ten_jobs)
```

This property is initialized by the value of CMAKE_JOB_POOL_COMPILE (page 629).

JOB_POOL_LINK

Ninja only: Pool used for linking.

The number of parallel link processes could be limited by defining pools with the global `JOB_POOLS` (page 565) property and then specifing here the pool name.

For instance:

```
set_property(TARGET myexe PROPERTY JOB_POOL_LINK two_jobs)
```

This property is initialized by the value of `CMAKE_JOB_POOL_LINK` (page 629).

LABELS

Specify a list of text labels associated with a target.

Target label semantics are currently unspecified.

<LANG>_VISIBILITY_PRESET

Value for symbol visibility compile flags

The <LANG>_VISIBILITY_PRESET property determines the value passed in a visibility related compile option, such as -fvisibility= for <LANG>. This property only has an affect for libraries and executables with exports. This property is initialized by the value of the variable CMAKE_<LANG>_VISIBILITY_PRESET if it is set when a target is created.

LIBRARY_OUTPUT_DIRECTORY_<CONFIG>

Per-configuration output directory for LIBRARY target files.

This is a per-configuration version of LIBRARY_OUTPUT_DIRECTORY, but multi-configuration generators (VS, Xcode) do NOT append a per-configuration subdirectory to the specified directory. This property is initialized by the value of the variable CMAKE_LIBRARY_OUTPUT_DIRECTORY_<CONFIG> if it is set when a target is created.

LIBRARY_OUTPUT_DIRECTORY

Output directory in which to build LIBRARY target files.

This property specifies the directory into which library target files should be built. Multi-configuration generators (VS, Xcode) append a per-configuration subdirectory to the specified directory.

There are three kinds of target files that may be built: archive, library, and runtime. Executables are always treated as runtime targets. Static libraries are always treated as archive targets. Module libraries are always treated as library targets. For non-DLL platforms shared libraries are treated as library targets. For DLL platforms the DLL part of a shared library is treated as a runtime target and the corresponding import library is treated as an archive target. All Windows-based systems including Cygwin are DLL platforms.

This property is initialized by the value of the variable CMAKE_LIBRARY_OUTPUT_DIRECTORY if it is set when a target is created.

LIBRARY_OUTPUT_NAME_<CONFIG>

Per-configuration output name for LIBRARY target files.

This is the configuration-specific version of LIBRARY_OUTPUT_NAME.

LIBRARY_OUTPUT_NAME

Output name for LIBRARY target files.

This property specifies the base name for library target files. It overrides OUTPUT_NAME and OUT-PUT_NAME_<CONFIG> properties.

There are three kinds of target files that may be built: archive, library, and runtime. Executables are always treated as runtime targets. Static libraries are always treated as archive targets. Module libraries are always treated as library targets. For non-DLL platforms shared libraries are treated as library targets. For DLL platforms the DLL part of a shared library is treated as a runtime target and the corresponding import library is treated as an archive target. All Windows-based systems including Cygwin are DLL platforms.

LINK_DEPENDS_NO_SHARED

Do not depend on linked shared library files.

Set this property to true to tell CMake generators not to add file-level dependencies on the shared library files linked by this target. Modification to the shared libraries will not be sufficient to re-link this target. Logical target-level dependencies will not be affected so the linked shared libraries will still be brought up to date before this target is built.

This property is initialized by the value of the variable CMAKE_LINK_DEPENDS_NO_SHARED if it is set when a target is created.

LINK_DEPENDS

Additional files on which a target binary depends for linking.

Specifies a semicolon-separated list of full-paths to files on which the link rule for this target depends. The target binary will be linked if any of the named files is newer than it.

This property is ignored by non-Makefile generators. It is intended to specify dependencies on "linker scripts" for custom Makefile link rules.

LINKER_LANGUAGE

Specifies language whose compiler will invoke the linker.

For executables, shared libraries, and modules, this sets the language whose compiler is used to link the target (such as "C" or "CXX"). A typical value for an executable is the language of the source file providing the program entry point (main). If not set, the language with the highest linker preference value is the default. See documentation of CMAKE_<LANG>_LINKER_PREFERENCE variables.

If this property is not set by the user, it will be calculated at generate-time by CMake.

LINK_FLAGS_<CONFIG>

Per-configuration linker flags for a target.

This is the configuration-specific version of LINK_FLAGS.

LINK_FLAGS

Additional flags to use when linking this target.

The LINK_FLAGS property can be used to add extra flags to the link step of a target. LINK_FLAGS_<CONFIG> will add to the configuration <CONFIG>, for example, DEBUG, RELEASE, MINSIZEREL, RELWITHDEBINFO.

LINK_INTERFACE_LIBRARIES_<CONFIG>

Per-configuration list of public interface libraries for a target.

This is the configuration-specific version of LINK_INTERFACE_LIBRARIES. If set, this property completely overrides the generic property for the named configuration.

This property is overridden by the INTERFACE_LINK_LIBRARIES property if policy CMP0022 is NEW.

This property is deprecated. Use INTERFACE_LINK_LIBRARIES instead.

LINK_INTERFACE_LIBRARIES

List public interface libraries for a shared library or executable.

By default linking to a shared library target transitively links to targets with which the library itself was linked. For an executable with exports (see the ENABLE_EXPORTS property) no default transitive link dependencies are used. This property replaces the default transitive link dependencies with an explicit list. When the target is linked into another target the libraries listed (and recursively their link interface libraries) will be provided to the other target also. If the list is empty then no transitive link dependencies will be incorporated when this target is linked into another target even if the default set is non-empty. This property is initialized by the value of the variable CMAKE_LINK_INTERFACE_LIBRARIES if it is set when a target is created. This property is ignored for STATIC libraries.

This property is overridden by the INTERFACE_LINK_LIBRARIES property if policy CMP0022 is NEW.

This property is deprecated. Use INTERFACE_LINK_LIBRARIES instead.

LINK_INTERFACE_MULTIPLICITY_<CONFIG>

Per-configuration repetition count for cycles of STATIC libraries.

This is the configuration-specific version of LINK_INTERFACE_MULTIPLICITY. If set, this property completely overrides the generic property for the named configuration.

LINK_INTERFACE_MULTIPLICITY

Repetition count for STATIC libraries with cyclic dependencies.

When linking to a STATIC library target with cyclic dependencies the linker may need to scan more than once through the archives in the strongly connected component of the dependency graph. CMake by default constructs the link line so that the linker will scan through the component at least twice. This property specifies the minimum number of scans if it is larger than the default. CMake uses the largest value specified by any target in a component.

LINK_LIBRARIES

List of direct link dependencies.

This property specifies the list of libraries or targets which will be used for linking. In addition to accepting values from the `target_link_libraries()` (page 340) command, values may be set directly on any target using the `set_property()` (page 329) command.

The value of this property is used by the generators to set the link libraries for the compiler.

Contents of `LINK_LIBRARIES` may use "generator expressions" with the syntax `$<...>`. See the `cmake-generator-expressions(7)` (page 356) manual for available expressions. See the `cmake-buildsystem(7)` manual for more on defining buildsystem properties.

LINK_SEARCH_END_STATIC

End a link line such that static system libraries are used.

Some linkers support switches such as -Bstatic and -Bdynamic to determine whether to use static or shared libraries for -lXXX options. CMake uses these options to set the link type for libraries whose full paths are not known or (in some cases) are in implicit link directories for the platform. By default CMake adds an option at the end of the library list (if necessary) to set the linker search type back to its starting type. This property switches the final linker search type to -Bstatic regardless of how it started. See also LINK_SEARCH_START_STATIC.

LINK_SEARCH_START_STATIC

Assume the linker looks for static libraries by default.

Some linkers support switches such as -Bstatic and -Bdynamic to determine whether to use static or shared libraries for -lXXX options. CMake uses these options to set the link type for libraries whose full paths are not known or (in some cases) are in implicit link directories for the platform. By default the linker search type is assumed to be -Bdynamic at the beginning of the library list. This property switches the assumption to -Bstatic. It is intended for use when linking an executable statically (e.g. with the GNU -static option). See also LINK_SEARCH_END_STATIC.

LOCATION_<CONFIG>

Read-only property providing a target location on disk.

A read-only property that indicates where a target's main file is located on disk for the configuration <CONFIG>. The property is defined only for library and executable targets. An imported target may provide a set of configurations different from that of the importing project. By default CMake looks for an exact-match but otherwise uses an arbitrary available configuration. Use the MAP_IMPORTED_CONFIG_<CONFIG> property to map imported configurations explicitly.

Do not set properties that affect the location of a target after reading this property. These include properties whose names match "(RUNTIME|LIBRARY|ARCHIVE)_OUTPUT_(NAME|DIRECTORY)(_<CONFIG>)?", `(IMPLIB_)?(PREFIX|SUFFIX)`, or "LINKER_LANGUAGE". Failure to follow this rule is not diagnosed and leaves the location of the target undefined.

LOCATION

Read-only location of a target on disk.

For an imported target, this read-only property returns the value of the LOCATION_<CONFIG> property for an unspecified configuration <CONFIG> provided by the target.

For a non-imported target, this property is provided for compatibility with CMake 2.4 and below. It was meant to get the location of an executable target's output file for use in add_custom_command. The path may contain a build-system-specific portion that is replaced at build time with the configuration getting built (such as "$(ConfigurationName)" in VS). In CMake 2.6 and above add_custom_command automatically recognizes a target name in its COMMAND and DEPENDS options and computes the target location. In CMake 2.8.4 and above add_custom_command recognizes generator expressions to refer to target locations anywhere in the command. Therefore this property is not needed for creating custom commands.

Do not set properties that affect the location of a target after reading this property. These include properties whose names match "(RUN-
TIME|LIBRARY|ARCHIVE)_OUTPUT_(NAME|DIRECTORY)(_<CONFIG>)?",
`(IMPLIB_)?(PREFIX|SUFFIX)`, or "LINKER_LANGUAGE". Failure to follow this rule is not
diagnosed and leaves the location of the target undefined.

MACOSX_BUNDLE_INFO_PLIST

Specify a custom Info.plist template for a Mac OS X App Bundle.

An executable target with MACOSX_BUNDLE enabled will be built as an application bundle on Mac OS X.
By default its Info.plist file is created by configuring a template called MacOSXBundleInfo.plist.in located
in the CMAKE_MODULE_PATH. This property specifies an alternative template file name which may be a
full path.

The following target properties may be set to specify content to be configured into the file:

```
MACOSX_BUNDLE_INFO_STRING
MACOSX_BUNDLE_ICON_FILE
MACOSX_BUNDLE_GUI_IDENTIFIER
MACOSX_BUNDLE_LONG_VERSION_STRING
MACOSX_BUNDLE_BUNDLE_NAME
MACOSX_BUNDLE_SHORT_VERSION_STRING
MACOSX_BUNDLE_BUNDLE_VERSION
MACOSX_BUNDLE_COPYRIGHT
```

CMake variables of the same name may be set to affect all targets in a directory that do not have each specific
property set. If a custom Info.plist is specified by this property it may of course hard-code all the settings
instead of using the target properties.

MACOSX_BUNDLE

Build an executable as an application bundle on Mac OS X.

When this property is set to true the executable when built on Mac OS X will be created as an application bundle. This makes it a GUI executable that can be launched from the Finder. See the MA-
COSX_BUNDLE_INFO_PLIST target property for information about creation of the Info.plist file for the
application bundle. This property is initialized by the value of the variable CMAKE_MACOSX_BUNDLE
if it is set when a target is created.

MACOSX_FRAMEWORK_INFO_PLIST

Specify a custom Info.plist template for a Mac OS X Framework.

A library target with FRAMEWORK enabled will be built as a framework on Mac OS X. By default its
Info.plist file is created by configuring a template called MacOSXFrameworkInfo.plist.in located in the

CMAKE_MODULE_PATH. This property specifies an alternative template file name which may be a full path.

The following target properties may be set to specify content to be configured into the file:

```
MACOSX_FRAMEWORK_ICON_FILE
MACOSX_FRAMEWORK_IDENTIFIER
MACOSX_FRAMEWORK_SHORT_VERSION_STRING
MACOSX_FRAMEWORK_BUNDLE_VERSION
```

CMake variables of the same name may be set to affect all targets in a directory that do not have each specific property set. If a custom Info.plist is specified by this property it may of course hard-code all the settings instead of using the target properties.

MACOSX_RPATH

Whether to use rpaths on Mac OS X.

When this property is set to true, the directory portion of the "install_name" field of shared libraries will be @rpath unless overridden by INSTALL_NAME_DIR (page 592). Runtime paths will also be embedded in binaries using this target and can be controlled by the INSTALL_RPATH (page 592) target property. This property is initialized by the value of the variable CMAKE_MACOSX_RPATH (page 662) if it is set when a target is created.

Policy CMP0042 was introduced to change the default value of MACOSX_RPATH to ON. This is because use of @rpath is a more flexible and powerful alternative to @executable_path and @loader_path.

MAP_IMPORTED_CONFIG_<CONFIG>

Map from project configuration to IMPORTED target's configuration.

Set this to the list of configurations of an imported target that may be used for the current project's <CONFIG> configuration. Targets imported from another project may not provide the same set of configuration names available in the current project. Setting this property tells CMake what imported configurations are suitable for use when building the <CONFIG> configuration. The first configuration in the list found to be provided by the imported target is selected. If this property is set and no matching configurations are available, then the imported target is considered to be not found. This property is ignored for non-imported targets.

This property is initialized by the value of the variable CMAKE_MAP_IMPORTED_CONFIG_<CONFIG> if it is set when a target is created.

NAME

Logical name for the target.

Read-only logical name for the target as used by CMake.

NO_SONAME

Whether to set "soname" when linking a shared library or module.

Enable this boolean property if a generated shared library or module should not have "soname" set. Default is to set "soname" on all shared libraries and modules as long as the platform supports it. Generally, use this property only for leaf private libraries or plugins. If you use it on normal shared libraries which other targets link against, on some platforms a linker will insert a full path to the library (as specified at link time) into the dynamic section of the dependent binary. Therefore, once installed, dynamic loader may eventually fail to locate the library for the binary.

NO_SYSTEM_FROM_IMPORTED

Do not treat includes from IMPORTED target interfaces as SYSTEM.

The contents of the INTERFACE_INCLUDE_DIRECTORIES of IMPORTED targets are treated as SYSTEM includes by default. If this property is enabled, the contents of the INTERFACE_INCLUDE_DIRECTORIES of IMPORTED targets are not treated as system includes. This property is initialized by the value of the variable CMAKE_NO_SYSTEM_FROM_IMPORTED if it is set when a target is created.

OSX_ARCHITECTURES_<CONFIG>

Per-configuration OS X binary architectures for a target.

This property is the configuration-specific version of OSX_ARCHITECTURES (page 603).

OSX_ARCHITECTURES

Target specific architectures for OS X.

The OSX_ARCHITECTURES property sets the target binary architecture for targets on OS X (-arch). This property is initialized by the value of the variable CMAKE_OSX_ARCHITECTURES (page 663) if it is set when a target is created. Use OSX_ARCHITECTURES_<CONFIG> (page 603) to set the binary architectures on a per-configuration basis, where <CONFIG> is an upper-case name (e.g. OSX_ARCHITECTURES_DEBUG).

OUTPUT_NAME_<CONFIG>

Per-configuration target file base name.

This is the configuration-specific version of OUTPUT_NAME.

OUTPUT_NAME

Output name for target files.

This sets the base name for output files created for an executable or library target. If not set, the logical target name is used by default.

PDB_NAME_<CONFIG>

Per-configuration output name for the MS debug symbol .pdb file generated by the linker for an executable or shared library target.

This is the configuration-specific version of PDB_NAME (page 604).

Note: This property does not apply to STATIC library targets because no linker is invoked to produce them so they have no linker-generated .pdb file containing debug symbols.

The linker-generated program database files are specified by the /pdb linker flag and are not the same as compiler-generated program database files specified by the /Fd compiler flag. Use the COMPILE_PDB_NAME_<CONFIG> (page 582) property to specify the latter.

This property is not implemented by the Visual Studio 6 (page 361) generator.

PDB_NAME

Output name for the MS debug symbol .pdb file generated by the linker for an executable or shared library target.

This property specifies the base name for the debug symbols file. If not set, the logical target name is used by default.

Note: This property does not apply to STATIC library targets because no linker is invoked to produce them so they have no linker-generated .pdb file containing debug symbols.

The linker-generated program database files are specified by the /pdb linker flag and are not the same as compiler-generated program database files specified by the /Fd compiler flag. Use the COMPILE_PDB_NAME (page 581) property to specify the latter.

This property is not implemented by the Visual Studio 6 (page 361) generator.

PDB_OUTPUT_DIRECTORY_<CONFIG>

Per-configuration output directory for the MS debug symbol .pdb file generated by the linker for an executable or shared library target.

This is a per-configuration version of PDB_OUTPUT_DIRECTORY (page 605), but multi-configuration generators (VS, Xcode) do NOT append a per-configuration subdirectory to the specified directory. This property is initialized by the value of the CMAKE_PDB_OUTPUT_DIRECTORY_<CONFIG> (page 664) variable if it is set when a target is created.

Note: This property does not apply to STATIC library targets because no linker is invoked to produce them so they have no linker-generated .pdb file containing debug symbols.

The linker-generated program database files are specified by the /pdb linker flag and are not the same as compiler-generated program database files specified by the /Fd compiler flag. Use the COMPILE_PDB_OUTPUT_DIRECTORY_<CONFIG> (page 582) property to specify the latter.

This property is not implemented by the Visual Studio 6 (page 361) generator.

PDB_OUTPUT_DIRECTORY

Output directory for the MS debug symbols .pdb file generated by the linker for an executable or shared library target.

This property specifies the directory into which the MS debug symbols will be placed by the linker. This property is initialized by the value of the CMAKE_PDB_OUTPUT_DIRECTORY (page 664) variable if it is set when a target is created.

Note: This property does not apply to STATIC library targets because no linker is invoked to produce them so they have no linker-generated .pdb file containing debug symbols.

The linker-generated program database files are specified by the /pdb linker flag and are not the same as compiler-generated program database files specified by the /Fd compiler flag. Use the COMPILE_PDB_OUTPUT_DIRECTORY (page 582) property to specify the latter.

This property is not implemented by the Visual Studio 6 (page 361) generator.

POSITION_INDEPENDENT_CODE

Whether to create a position-independent target

The POSITION_INDEPENDENT_CODE property determines whether position independent executables or shared libraries will be created. This property is True by default for SHARED and MODULE library targets and False otherwise. This property is initialized by the value of the CMAKE_POSITION_INDEPENDENT_CODE (page 664) variable if it is set when a target is created.

PREFIX

What comes before the library name.

A target property that can be set to override the prefix (such as "lib") on a library name.

PRIVATE_HEADER

Specify private header files in a FRAMEWORK shared library target.

Shared library targets marked with the FRAMEWORK property generate frameworks on OS X and normal shared libraries on other platforms. This property may be set to a list of header files to be placed in the PrivateHeaders directory inside the framework folder. On non-Apple platforms these headers may be installed using the PRIVATE_HEADER option to the install(TARGETS) command.

PROJECT_LABEL

Change the name of a target in an IDE.

Can be used to change the name of the target in an IDE like Visual Studio.

PUBLIC_HEADER

Specify public header files in a FRAMEWORK shared library target.

Shared library targets marked with the FRAMEWORK property generate frameworks on OS X and normal shared libraries on other platforms. This property may be set to a list of header files to be placed in the Headers directory inside the framework folder. On non-Apple platforms these headers may be installed using the PUBLIC_HEADER option to the install(TARGETS) command.

RESOURCE

Specify resource files in a FRAMEWORK shared library target.

Shared library targets marked with the FRAMEWORK property generate frameworks on OS X and normal shared libraries on other platforms. This property may be set to a list of files to be placed in the Resources directory inside the framework folder. On non-Apple platforms these files may be installed using the RE-SOURCE option to the install(TARGETS) command.

RULE_LAUNCH_COMPILE

Specify a launcher for compile rules.

See the global property of the same name for details. This overrides the global and directory property for a target.

RULE_LAUNCH_CUSTOM

Specify a launcher for custom rules.

See the global property of the same name for details. This overrides the global and directory property for a target.

RULE_LAUNCH_LINK

Specify a launcher for link rules.

See the global property of the same name for details. This overrides the global and directory property for a target.

RUNTIME_OUTPUT_DIRECTORY_<CONFIG>

Per-configuration output directory for RUNTIME target files.

This is a per-configuration version of RUNTIME_OUTPUT_DIRECTORY, but multi-configuration generators (VS, Xcode) do NOT append a per-configuration subdirectory to the specified directory. This property is initialized by the value of the variable CMAKE_RUNTIME_OUTPUT_DIRECTORY_<CONFIG> if it is set when a target is created.

RUNTIME_OUTPUT_DIRECTORY

Output directory in which to build RUNTIME target files.

This property specifies the directory into which runtime target files should be built. Multi-configuration generators (VS, Xcode) append a per-configuration subdirectory to the specified directory.

There are three kinds of target files that may be built: archive, library, and runtime. Executables are always treated as runtime targets. Static libraries are always treated as archive targets. Module libraries are always treated as library targets. For non-DLL platforms shared libraries are treated as library targets. For DLL platforms the DLL part of a shared library is treated as a runtime target and the corresponding import library is treated as an archive target. All Windows-based systems including Cygwin are DLL platforms.

This property is initialized by the value of the variable CMAKE_RUNTIME_OUTPUT_DIRECTORY if it is set when a target is created.

RUNTIME_OUTPUT_NAME_<CONFIG>

Per-configuration output name for RUNTIME target files.

This is the configuration-specific version of RUNTIME_OUTPUT_NAME.

RUNTIME_OUTPUT_NAME

Output name for RUNTIME target files.

This property specifies the base name for runtime target files. It overrides OUTPUT_NAME and OUT-PUT_NAME_<CONFIG> properties.

There are three kinds of target files that may be built: archive, library, and runtime. Executables are always treated as runtime targets. Static libraries are always treated as archive targets. Module libraries are always treated as library targets. For non-DLL platforms shared libraries are treated as library targets. For DLL platforms the DLL part of a shared library is treated as a runtime target and the corresponding import library is treated as an archive target. All Windows-based systems including Cygwin are DLL platforms.

SKIP_BUILD_RPATH

Should rpaths be used for the build tree.

SKIP_BUILD_RPATH is a boolean specifying whether to skip automatic generation of an rpath allowing the target to run from the build tree. This property is initialized by the value of the variable CMAKE_SKIP_BUILD_RPATH if it is set when a target is created.

SOURCES

Source names specified for a target.

List of sources specified for a target.

SOVERSION

What version number is this target.

For shared libraries VERSION and SOVERSION can be used to specify the build version and API version respectively. When building or installing appropriate symlinks are created if the platform supports symlinks and the linker supports so-names. If only one of both is specified the missing is assumed to have the same version number. SOVERSION is ignored if NO_SONAME property is set. For shared libraries and executables on Windows the VERSION attribute is parsed to extract a "major.minor" version number. These numbers are used as the image version of the binary.

STATIC_LIBRARY_FLAGS_<CONFIG>

Per-configuration flags for creating a static library.

This is the configuration-specific version of STATIC_LIBRARY_FLAGS.

STATIC_LIBRARY_FLAGS

Extra flags to use when linking static libraries.

Extra flags to use when linking a static library.

SUFFIX

What comes after the target name.

A target property that can be set to override the suffix (such as ".so" or ".exe") on the name of a library, module or executable.

TYPE

The type of the target.

This read-only property can be used to test the type of the given target. It will be one of STATIC_LIBRARY, MODULE_LIBRARY, SHARED_LIBRARY, INTERFACE_LIBRARY, EXECUTABLE or one of the internal target types.

VERSION

What version number is this target.

For shared libraries VERSION and SOVERSION can be used to specify the build version and API version respectively. When building or installing appropriate symlinks are created if the platform supports symlinks and the linker supports so-names. If only one of both is specified the missing is assumed to have the same version number. For executables VERSION can be used to specify the build version. When building or installing appropriate symlinks are created if the platform supports symlinks. For shared libraries and executables on Windows the VERSION attribute is parsed to extract a "major.minor" version number. These numbers are used as the image version of the binary.

VISIBILITY_INLINES_HIDDEN

Whether to add a compile flag to hide symbols of inline functions

The VISIBILITY_INLINES_HIDDEN property determines whether a flag for hiding symbols for inline functions, such as -fvisibility-inlines-hidden, should be used when invoking the compiler. This property only has an affect for libraries and executables with exports. This property is initialized by the value of the CMAKE_VISIBILITY_INLINES_HIDDEN (page 666) if it is set when a target is created.

VS_DOTNET_REFERENCES

Visual Studio managed project .NET references

Adds one or more semicolon-delimited .NET references to a generated Visual Studio project. For example, "System;System.Windows.Forms".

VS_DOTNET_TARGET_FRAMEWORK_VERSION

Specify the .NET target framework version.

Used to specify the .NET target framework version for C++/CLI. For example, "v4.5".

VS_GLOBAL_KEYWORD

Visual Studio project keyword for VS 10 (2010) and newer.

Sets the "keyword" attribute for a generated Visual Studio project. Defaults to "Win32Proj". You may wish to override this value with "ManagedCProj", for example, in a Visual Studio managed C++ unit test project.

Use the VS_KEYWORD (page 610) target property to set the keyword for Visual Studio 9 (2008) and older.

VS_GLOBAL_PROJECT_TYPES

Visual Studio project type(s).

Can be set to one or more UUIDs recognized by Visual Studio to indicate the type of project. This value is copied verbatim into the generated project file. Example for a managed C++ unit testing project:

```
{3AC096D0-A1C2-E12C-1390-A8335801FDAB};{8BC9CEB8-8B4A-11D0-8D11-00A0C91BC942}
```

UUIDs are semicolon-delimited.

VS_GLOBAL_ROOTNAMESPACE

Visual Studio project root namespace.

Sets the "RootNamespace" attribute for a generated Visual Studio project. The attribute will be generated only if this is set.

VS_GLOBAL_<variable>

Visual Studio project-specific global variable.

Tell the Visual Studio generator to set the global variable '<variable>' to a given value in the generated Visual Studio project. Ignored on other generators. Qt integration works better if VS_GLOBAL_QtVersion is set to the version FindQt4.cmake found. For example, "4.7.3"

VS_KEYWORD

Visual Studio project keyword for VS 9 (2008) and older.

Can be set to change the visual studio keyword, for example Qt integration works better if this is set to Qt4VSv1.0.

Use the VS_GLOBAL_KEYWORD (page 610) target property to set the keyword for Visual Studio 10 (2010) and newer.

VS_SCC_AUXPATH

Visual Studio Source Code Control Aux Path.

Can be set to change the visual studio source code control auxpath property.

VS_SCC_LOCALPATH

Visual Studio Source Code Control Local Path.

Can be set to change the visual studio source code control local path property.

VS_SCC_PROJECTNAME

Visual Studio Source Code Control Project.

Can be set to change the visual studio source code control project name property.

VS_SCC_PROVIDER

Visual Studio Source Code Control Provider.

Can be set to change the visual studio source code control provider property.

VS_WINRT_COMPONENT

Mark a target as a Windows Runtime component for the Visual Studio generator. Compile the target with C++/CX language extensions for Windows Runtime. For SHARED and MODULE libraries, this also defines the _WINRT_DLL preprocessor macro.

Note: Currently this is implemented only by Visual Studio generators. Support may be added to other generators in the future.

VS_WINRT_EXTENSIONS

Deprecated. Use VS_WINRT_COMPONENT (page 611) instead. This property was an experimental partial implementation of that one.

VS_WINRT_REFERENCES

Visual Studio project Windows Runtime Metadata references

Adds one or more semicolon-delimited WinRT references to a generated Visual Studio project. For example, "Windows;Windows.UI.Core".

WIN32_EXECUTABLE

Build an executable with a WinMain entry point on windows.

When this property is set to true the executable when linked on Windows will be created with a WinMain() entry point instead of just main(). This makes it a GUI executable instead of a console application. See the CMAKE_MFC_FLAG variable documentation to configure use of MFC for WinMain executables. This property is initialized by the value of the variable CMAKE_WIN32_EXECUTABLE if it is set when a target is created.

XCODE_ATTRIBUTE_<an-attribute>

Set Xcode target attributes directly.

Tell the Xcode generator to set '<an-attribute>' to a given value in the generated Xcode project. Ignored on other generators.

See the `CMAKE_XCODE_ATTRIBUTE_<an-attribute>` (page 666) variable to set attributes on all targets in a directory tree.

C.6.4 Properties on Tests

ATTACHED_FILES_ON_FAIL

Attach a list of files to a dashboard submission if the test fails.

Same as ATTACHED_FILES, but these files will only be included if the test does not pass.

ATTACHED_FILES

Attach a list of files to a dashboard submission.

Set this property to a list of files that will be encoded and submitted to the dashboard as an addition to the test result.

COST

Set this to a floating point value. Tests in a test set will be run in descending order of cost.

This property describes the cost of a test. You can explicitly set this value; tests with higher COST values will run first.

DEPENDS

Specifies that this test should only be run after the specified list of tests.

Set this to a list of tests that must finish before this test is run.

ENVIRONMENT

Specify environment variables that should be defined for running a test.

If set to a list of environment variables and values of the form MYVAR=value those environment variables will be defined while running the test. The environment is restored to its previous state after the test is done.

FAIL_REGULAR_EXPRESSION

If the output matches this regular expression the test will fail.

If set, if the output matches one of specified regular expressions, the test will fail.For example: FAIL_REGULAR_EXPRESSION "[^a-z]Error;ERROR;Failed"

LABELS

Specify a list of text labels associated with a test.

The list is reported in dashboard submissions.

MEASUREMENT

Specify a CDASH measurement and value to be reported for a test.

If set to a name then that name will be reported to CDASH as a named measurement with a value of 1. You may also specify a value by setting MEASUREMENT to "measurement=value".

PASS_REGULAR_EXPRESSION

The output must match this regular expression for the test to pass.

If set, the test output will be checked against the specified regular expressions and at least one of the regular expressions has to match, otherwise the test will fail.

PROCESSORS

How many process slots this test requires

Denotes the number of processors that this test will require. This is typically used for MPI tests, and should be used in conjunction with the ctest_test PARALLEL_LEVEL option.

REQUIRED_FILES

List of files required to run the test.

If set to a list of files, the test will not be run unless all of the files exist.

RESOURCE_LOCK

Specify a list of resources that are locked by this test.

If multiple tests specify the same resource lock, they are guaranteed not to run concurrently.

RUN_SERIAL

Do not run this test in parallel with any other test.

Use this option in conjunction with the ctest_test PARALLEL_LEVEL option to specify that this test should not be run in parallel with any other tests.

SKIP_RETURN_CODE

Return code to mark a test as skipped.

Sometimes only a test itself can determine if all requirements for the test are met. If such a situation should not be considered a hard failure a return code of the process can be specified that will mark the test as "Not Run" if it is encountered.

TIMEOUT

How many seconds to allow for this test.

This property if set will limit a test to not take more than the specified number of seconds to run. If it exceeds that the test process will be killed and ctest will move to the next test. This setting takes precedence over CTEST_TESTING_TIMEOUT.

WILL_FAIL

If set to true, this will invert the pass/fail flag of the test.

This property can be used for tests that are expected to fail and return a non zero return code.

WORKING_DIRECTORY

The directory from which the test executable will be called.

If this is not set it is called from the directory the test executable is located in.

C.6.5 Properties on Source Files

ABSTRACT

Is this source file an abstract class.

A property on a source file that indicates if the source file represents a class that is abstract. This only makes sense for languages that have a notion of an abstract class and it is only used by some tools that wrap classes into other languages.

AUTOUIC_OPTIONS

Additional options for `uic` when using `AUTOUIC` (page 576)

This property holds additional command line options which will be used when `uic` is executed during the build via `AUTOUIC` (page 576), i.e. it is equivalent to the optional `OPTIONS` argument of the `qt4_wrap_ui()` (page 495) macro.

By default it is empty.

The options set on the `.ui` source file may override `AUTOUIC_OPTIONS` (page 576) set on the target.

AUTORCC_OPTIONS

Additional options for `rcc` when using `AUTORCC` (page 576)

This property holds additional command line options which will be used when `rcc` is executed during the build via `AUTORCC` (page 576), i.e. it is equivalent to the optional `OPTIONS` argument of the `qt4_add_resources()` (page 495) macro.

By default it is empty.

The options set on the `.qrc` source file may override `AUTORCC_OPTIONS` (page 577) set on the target.

COMPILE_DEFINITIONS

Preprocessor definitions for compiling a source file.

The COMPILE_DEFINITIONS property may be set to a semicolon-separated list of preprocessor definitions using the syntax VAR or VAR=value. Function-style definitions are not supported. CMake will automatically escape the value correctly for the native build system (note that CMake language syntax may require escapes to specify some values). This property may be set on a per-configuration basis using the name COMPILE_DEFINITIONS_<CONFIG> where <CONFIG> is an upper-case name (ex. "COMPILE_DEFINITIONS_DEBUG").

CMake will automatically drop some definitions that are not supported by the native build tool. The VS6 IDE does not support definition values with spaces (but NMake does). Xcode does not support per-configuration definitions on source files.

Disclaimer: Most native build tools have poor support for escaping certain values. CMake has work-arounds for many cases but some values may just not be possible to pass correctly. If a value does not seem to be escaped correctly, do not attempt to work-around the problem by adding escape sequences to the value. Your work-around may break in a future version of CMake that has improved escape support. Instead consider defining the macro in a (configured) header file. Then report the limitation. Known limitations include:

```
#              - broken almost everywhere
;              - broken in VS IDE 7.0 and Borland Makefiles
,              - broken in VS IDE
%              - broken in some cases in NMake
& |            - broken in some cases on MinGW
^ < > \"       - broken in most Make tools on Windows
```

CMake does not reject these values outright because they do work in some cases. Use with caution.

COMPILE_FLAGS

Additional flags to be added when compiling this source file.

These flags will be added to the list of compile flags when this source file builds. Use COMPILE_DEFINITIONS to pass additional preprocessor definitions.

EXTERNAL_OBJECT

If set to true then this is an object file.

If this property is set to true then the source file is really an object file and should not be compiled. It will still be linked into the target though.

Fortran_FORMAT

Set to FIXED or FREE to indicate the Fortran source layout.

This property tells CMake whether a given Fortran source file uses fixed-format or free-format. CMake will pass the corresponding format flag to the compiler. Consider using the target-wide Fortran_FORMAT property if all source files in a target share the same format.

GENERATED

Is this source file generated as part of the build process.

If a source file is generated by the build process CMake will handle it differently in terms of dependency checking etc. Otherwise having a non-existent source file could create problems.

HEADER_FILE_ONLY

Is this source file only a header file.

A property on a source file that indicates if the source file is a header file with no associated implementation. This is set automatically based on the file extension and is used by CMake to determine if certain dependency information should be computed.

KEEP_EXTENSION

Make the output file have the same extension as the source file.

If this property is set then the file extension of the output file will be the same as that of the source file. Normally the output file extension is computed based on the language of the source file, for example .cxx will go to a .o extension.

LABELS

Specify a list of text labels associated with a source file.

This property has meaning only when the source file is listed in a target whose LABELS property is also set. No other semantics are currently specified.

LANGUAGE

What programming language is the file.

A property that can be set to indicate what programming language the source file is. If it is not set the language is determined based on the file extension. Typical values are CXX C etc. Setting this property for a file means this file will be compiled. Do not set this for headers or files that should not be compiled.

LOCATION

The full path to a source file.

A read only property on a SOURCE FILE that contains the full path to the source file.

MACOSX_PACKAGE_LOCATION

Place a source file inside a Mac OS X bundle, CFBundle, or framework.

Executable targets with the MACOSX_BUNDLE property set are built as Mac OS X application bundles on Apple platforms. Shared library targets with the FRAMEWORK property set are built as Mac OS X frameworks on Apple platforms. Module library targets with the BUNDLE property set are built as Mac OS X CFBundle bundles on Apple platforms. Source files listed in the target with this property set will be copied to a directory inside the bundle or framework content folder specified by the property value. For bundles the content folder is "<name>.app/Contents". For frameworks the content folder is "<name>.framework/Versions/<version>". For cfbundles the content folder is "<name>.bundle/Contents" (unless the extension is changed). See the PUBLIC_HEADER, PRIVATE_HEADER, and RESOURCE target properties for specifying files meant for Headers, PrivateHeaders, or Resources directories.

OBJECT_DEPENDS

Additional files on which a compiled object file depends.

Specifies a semicolon-separated list of full-paths to files on which any object files compiled from this source file depend. An object file will be recompiled if any of the named files is newer than it.

This property need not be used to specify the dependency of a source file on a generated header file that it includes. Although the property was originally introduced for this purpose, it is no longer necessary. If the generated header file is created by a custom command in the same target as the source file, the automatic dependency scanning process will recognize the dependency. If the generated header file is created by another target, an inter-target dependency should be created with the add_dependencies command (if one does not already exist due to linking relationships).

OBJECT_OUTPUTS

Additional outputs for a Makefile rule.

Additional outputs created by compilation of this source file. If any of these outputs is missing the object will be recompiled. This is supported only on Makefile generators and will be ignored on other generators.

SYMBOLIC

Is this just a name for a rule.

If SYMBOLIC (boolean) is set to true the build system will be informed that the source file is not actually created on disk but instead used as a symbolic name for a build rule.

VS_DEPLOYMENT_CONTENT

Mark a source file as content for deployment with a Windows Phone or Windows Store application when built with a Visual Studio generator. The value must evaluate to either 1 or 0 and may use generator expressions (page 356) to make the choice based on the build configuration. The .vcxproj file entry for the source file will be marked either DeploymentContent or ExcludedFromBuild for values 1 and 0, respectively.

VS_DEPLOYMENT_LOCATION

Specifies the deployment location for a content source file with a Windows Phone or Windows Store application when built with a Visual Studio generator. This property is only applicable when using VS_DEPLOYMENT_CONTENT (page 619). The value represent the path relative to the app package and applies to all configurations.

VS_SHADER_ENTRYPOINT

Specifies the name of the entry point for the shader of a .hlsl source file.

VS_SHADER_MODEL

Specifies the shader model of a .hlsl source file. Some shader types can only be used with recent shader models

VS_SHADER_TYPE

Set the VS shader type of a .hlsl source file.

WRAP_EXCLUDE

Exclude this source file from any code wrapping techniques.

Some packages can wrap source files into alternate languages to provide additional functionality. For example, C++ code can be wrapped into Java or Python etc using SWIG etc. If WRAP_EXCLUDE is set to true (1 etc) that indicates that this source file should not be wrapped.

XCODE_EXPLICIT_FILE_TYPE

Set the Xcode `explicitFileType` attribute on its reference to a source file. CMake computes a default based on file extension but can be told explicitly with this property.

See also XCODE_LAST_KNOWN_FILE_TYPE (page 620).

XCODE_LAST_KNOWN_FILE_TYPE

Set the Xcode `lastKnownFileType` attribute on its reference to a source file. CMake computes a default based on file extension but can be told explicitly with this property.

See also XCODE_EXPLICIT_FILE_TYPE (page 620), which is preferred over this property if set.

C.6.6 Properties on Cache Entries

ADVANCED

True if entry should be hidden by default in GUIs.

This is a boolean value indicating whether the entry is considered interesting only for advanced configuration. The mark_as_advanced() command modifies this property.

HELPSTRING

Help associated with entry in GUIs.

This string summarizes the purpose of an entry to help users set it through a CMake GUI.

MODIFIED

Internal management property. Do not set or get.

This is an internal cache entry property managed by CMake to track interactive user modification of entries. Ignore it.

STRINGS

Enumerate possible STRING entry values for GUI selection.

For cache entries with type STRING, this enumerates a set of values. CMake GUIs may use this to provide a selection widget instead of a generic string entry field. This is for convenience only. CMake does not enforce that the value matches one of those listed.

TYPE

Widget type for entry in GUIs.

Cache entry values are always strings, but CMake GUIs present widgets to help users set values. The GUIs use this property as a hint to determine the widget type. Valid TYPE values are:

```
BOOL          = Boolean ON/OFF value.
PATH          = Path to a directory.
FILEPATH      = Path to a file.
STRING        = Generic string value.
INTERNAL      = Do not present in GUI at all.
STATIC        = Value managed by CMake, do not change.
UNINITIALIZED = Type not yet specified.
```

Generally the TYPE of a cache entry should be set by the command which creates it (set, option, find_library, etc.).

VALUE

Value of a cache entry.

This property maps to the actual value of a cache entry. Setting this property always sets the value without checking, so use with care.

C.6.7 Properties on Installed Files

CPACK_NEVER_OVERWRITE

Request that this file not be overwritten on install or reinstall.

The property is currently only supported by the WIX generator.

CPACK_PERMANENT

Request that this file not be removed on uninstall.

The property is currently only supported by the WIX generator.

CPACK_WIX_ACL

Specifies access permissions for files or directories installed by a WiX installer.

The property can contain multiple list entries, each of which has to match the following format.

```
<user>[@<domain>]=<permission>[,<permission>]
```

`<user>` and `<domain>` specify the windows user and domain for which the `<Permission>` element should be generated.

`<permission>` is any of the YesNoType attributes listed here:

```
http://wixtoolset.org/documentation/manual/v3/xsd/wix/permission.html
```

C.6.8 Deprecated Properties on Directories

COMPILE_DEFINITIONS_<CONFIG>

Ignored. See CMake Policy `CMP0043` (page 554).

Per-configuration preprocessor definitions in a directory.

This is the configuration-specific version of `COMPILE_DEFINITIONS` (page 568) where `<CONFIG>` is an upper-case name (ex. `COMPILE_DEFINITIONS_DEBUG`).

This property will be initialized in each directory by its value in the directory's parent.

Contents of `COMPILE_DEFINITIONS_<CONFIG>` may use "generator expressions" with the syntax `$<...>`. See the `cmake-generator-expressions(7)` (page 356) manual for available expressions. See the `cmake-buildsystem(7)` manual for more on defining buildsystem properties.

Generator expressions should be preferred instead of setting this property.

C.6.9 Deprecated Properties on Targets

COMPILE_DEFINITIONS_<CONFIG>

Ignored. See CMake Policy `CMP0043` (page 554).

Per-configuration preprocessor definitions on a target.

This is the configuration-specific version of `COMPILE_DEFINITIONS` (page 580) where `<CONFIG>` is an upper-case name (ex. `COMPILE_DEFINITIONS_DEBUG`).

Contents of `COMPILE_DEFINITIONS_<CONFIG>` may use "generator expressions" with the syntax `$<...>`. See the `cmake-generator-expressions(7)` (page 356) manual for available expressions. See the `cmake-buildsystem(7)` manual for more on defining buildsystem properties.

Generator expressions should be preferred instead of setting this property.

POST_INSTALL_SCRIPT

Deprecated install support.

The PRE_INSTALL_SCRIPT and POST_INSTALL_SCRIPT properties are the old way to specify CMake scripts to run before and after installing a target. They are used only when the old INSTALL_TARGETS command is used to install the target. Use the INSTALL command instead.

PRE_INSTALL_SCRIPT

Deprecated install support.

The PRE_INSTALL_SCRIPT and POST_INSTALL_SCRIPT properties are the old way to specify CMake scripts to run before and after installing a target. They are used only when the old INSTALL_TARGETS command is used to install the target. Use the INSTALL command instead.

C.6.10 Deprecated Properties on Source Files

COMPILE_DEFINITIONS_<CONFIG>

Ignored. See CMake Policy CMP0043 (page 554).

Per-configuration preprocessor definitions on a source file.

This is the configuration-specific version of COMPILE_DEFINITIONS. Note that Xcode does not support per-configuration source file flags so this property will be ignored by the Xcode generator.

C.7 cmake-variables(7)

C.7.1 Variables that Provide Information

CMAKE_ARGC

Number of command line arguments passed to CMake in script mode.

When run in -P script mode, CMake sets this variable to the number of command line arguments. See also CMAKE_ARGV0, 1, 2 ...

CMAKE_ARGV0

Command line argument passed to CMake in script mode.

When run in -P script mode, CMake sets this variable to the first command line argument. It then also sets CMAKE_ARGV1, CMAKE_ARGV2, ... and so on, up to the number of command line arguments given. See also CMAKE_ARGC.

CMAKE_AR

Name of archiving tool for static libraries.

This specifies the name of the program that creates archive or static libraries.

CMAKE_BINARY_DIR

The path to the top level of the build tree.

This is the full path to the top level of the current CMake build tree. For an in-source build, this would be the same as CMAKE_SOURCE_DIR.

CMAKE_BUILD_TOOL

This variable exists only for backwards compatibility. It contains the same value as CMAKE_MAKE_PROGRAM (page 630). Use that variable instead.

CMAKE_CACHEFILE_DIR

The directory with the CMakeCache.txt file.

This is the full path to the directory that has the CMakeCache.txt file in it. This is the same as CMAKE_BINARY_DIR.

CMAKE_CACHE_MAJOR_VERSION

Major version of CMake used to create the CMakeCache.txt file

This stores the major version of CMake used to write a CMake cache file. It is only different when a different version of CMake is run on a previously created cache file.

CMAKE_CACHE_MINOR_VERSION

Minor version of CMake used to create the CMakeCache.txt file

This stores the minor version of CMake used to write a CMake cache file. It is only different when a different version of CMake is run on a previously created cache file.

CMAKE_CACHE_PATCH_VERSION

Patch version of CMake used to create the CMakeCache.txt file

This stores the patch version of CMake used to write a CMake cache file. It is only different when a different version of CMake is run on a previously created cache file.

CMAKE_CFG_INTDIR

Build-time reference to per-configuration output subdirectory.

For native build systems supporting multiple configurations in the build tree (such as Visual Studio and Xcode), the value is a reference to a build-time variable specifying the name of the per-configuration output subdirectory. On Makefile generators this evaluates to "." because there is only one configuration in a build tree. Example values:

```
$(IntDir)         = Visual Studio 6
$(OutDir)         = Visual Studio 7, 8, 9
$(Configuration)  = Visual Studio 10
$(CONFIGURATION)  = Xcode
.                 = Make-based tools
```

Since these values are evaluated by the native build system, this variable is suitable only for use in command lines that will be evaluated at build time. Example of intended usage:

```
add_executable(mytool mytool.c)
add_custom_command(
  OUTPUT out.txt
  COMMAND ${CMAKE_CURRENT_BINARY_DIR}/${CMAKE_CFG_INTDIR}/mytool
          ${CMAKE_CURRENT_SOURCE_DIR}/in.txt out.txt
  DEPENDS mytool in.txt
  )
add_custom_target(drive ALL DEPENDS out.txt)
```

Note that CMAKE_CFG_INTDIR is no longer necessary for this purpose but has been left for compatibility with existing projects. Instead add_custom_command() recognizes executable target names in its COMMAND option, so "${CMAKE_CURRENT_BINARY_DIR}/${CMAKE_CFG_INTDIR}/mytool" can be replaced by just "mytool".

This variable is read-only. Setting it is undefined behavior. In multi-configuration build systems the value of this variable is passed as the value of preprocessor symbol "CMAKE_INTDIR" to the compilation of all source files.

CMAKE_COMMAND

The full path to the cmake executable.

This is the full path to the CMake executable cmake which is useful from custom commands that want to use the cmake -E option for portable system commands. (e.g. /usr/local/bin/cmake

CMAKE_CROSSCOMPILING

Is CMake currently cross compiling.

This variable will be set to true by CMake if CMake is cross compiling. Specifically if the build platform is different from the target platform.

CMAKE_CTEST_COMMAND

Full path to ctest command installed with cmake.

This is the full path to the CTest executable ctest which is useful from custom commands that want to use the cmake -E option for portable system commands.

CMAKE_CURRENT_BINARY_DIR

The path to the binary directory currently being processed.

This the full path to the build directory that is currently being processed by cmake. Each directory added by add_subdirectory will create a binary directory in the build tree, and as it is being processed this variable will be set. For in-source builds this is the current source directory being processed.

CMAKE_CURRENT_LIST_DIR

Full directory of the listfile currently being processed.

As CMake processes the listfiles in your project this variable will always be set to the directory where the listfile which is currently being processed (CMAKE_CURRENT_LIST_FILE) is located. The value has dynamic scope. When CMake starts processing commands in a source file it sets this variable to the directory where this file is located. When CMake finishes processing commands from the file it restores the previous value. Therefore the value of the variable inside a macro or function is the directory of the file invoking the bottom-most entry on the call stack, not the directory of the file containing the macro or function definition.

See also CMAKE_CURRENT_LIST_FILE.

CMAKE_CURRENT_LIST_FILE

Full path to the listfile currently being processed.

As CMake processes the listfiles in your project this variable will always be set to the one currently being processed. The value has dynamic scope. When CMake starts processing commands in a source file it sets this variable to the location of the file. When CMake finishes processing commands from the file it restores the previous value. Therefore the value of the variable inside a macro or function is the file invoking the bottom-most entry on the call stack, not the file containing the macro or function definition.

See also CMAKE_PARENT_LIST_FILE.

CMAKE_CURRENT_LIST_LINE

The line number of the current file being processed.

This is the line number of the file currently being processed by cmake.

CMAKE_CURRENT_SOURCE_DIR

The path to the source directory currently being processed.

This the full path to the source directory that is currently being processed by cmake.

CMAKE_DL_LIBS

Name of library containing dlopen and dlcose.

The name of the library that has dlopen and dlclose in it, usually -ldl on most UNIX machines.

CMAKE_EDIT_COMMAND

Full path to cmake-gui or ccmake. Defined only for Makefile generators when not using an "extra" generator for an IDE.

This is the full path to the CMake executable that can graphically edit the cache. For example, cmake-gui or ccmake.

CMAKE_EXECUTABLE_SUFFIX

The suffix for executables on this platform.

The suffix to use for the end of an executable filename if any, .exe on Windows.

CMAKE_EXECUTABLE_SUFFIX_<LANG> overrides this for language <LANG>.

CMAKE_EXTRA_GENERATOR

The extra generator used to build the project.

When using the Eclipse, CodeBlocks or KDevelop generators, CMake generates Makefiles (CMAKE_GENERATOR) and additionally project files for the respective IDE. This IDE project file generator is stored in CMAKE_EXTRA_GENERATOR (e.g. "Eclipse CDT4").

CMAKE_EXTRA_SHARED_LIBRARY_SUFFIXES

Additional suffixes for shared libraries.

Extensions for shared libraries other than that specified by CMAKE_SHARED_LIBRARY_SUFFIX, if any. CMake uses this to recognize external shared library files during analysis of libraries linked by a target.

CMAKE_FIND_PACKAGE_NAME

Defined by the find_package() (page 297) command while loading a find module to record the caller-specified package name. See command documentation for details.

CMAKE_GENERATOR

The generator used to build the project.

The name of the generator that is being used to generate the build files. (e.g. "Unix Makefiles", "Visual Studio 6", etc.)

CMAKE_GENERATOR_PLATFORM

Generator-specific target platform name specified by user.

Some CMake generators support a target platform name to be given to the native build system to choose a compiler toolchain. If the user specifies a toolset name (e.g. via the cmake -A option) the value will be available in this variable.

The value of this variable should never be modified by project code. A toolchain file specified by the CMAKE_TOOLCHAIN_FILE (page 633) variable may initialize CMAKE_GENERATOR_PLATFORM. Once a given build tree has been initialized with a particular value for this variable, changing the value has undefined behavior.

CMAKE_GENERATOR_TOOLSET

Native build system toolset name specified by user.

Some CMake generators support a toolset name to be given to the native build system to choose a compiler. If the user specifies a toolset name (e.g. via the cmake -T option) the value will be available in this variable.

The value of this variable should never be modified by project code. A toolchain file specified by the CMAKE_TOOLCHAIN_FILE (page 633) variable may initialize CMAKE_GENERATOR_TOOLSET. Once a given build tree has been initialized with a particular value for this variable, changing the value has undefined behavior.

CMAKE_HOME_DIRECTORY

Path to top of source tree.

This is the path to the top level of the source tree.

CMAKE_IMPORT_LIBRARY_PREFIX

The prefix for import libraries that you link to.

The prefix to use for the name of an import library if used on this platform.

CMAKE_IMPORT_LIBRARY_PREFIX_<LANG> overrides this for language <LANG>.

CMAKE_IMPORT_LIBRARY_SUFFIX

The suffix for import libraries that you link to.

The suffix to use for the end of an import library filename if used on this platform.

CMAKE_IMPORT_LIBRARY_SUFFIX_<LANG> overrides this for language <LANG>.

CMAKE_JOB_POOL_COMPILE

This variable is used to initialize the `JOB_POOL_COMPILE` (page 595) property on all the targets. See `JOB_POOL_COMPILE` (page 595) for additional information.

CMAKE_JOB_POOL_LINK

This variable is used to initialize the `JOB_POOL_LINK` (page 596) property on all the targets. See `JOB_POOL_LINK` (page 596) for additional information.

CMAKE_LINK_LIBRARY_SUFFIX

The suffix for libraries that you link to.

The suffix to use for the end of a library filename, .lib on Windows.

CMAKE_MAJOR_VERSION

First version number component of the `CMAKE_VERSION` (page 634) variable.

CMAKE_MAKE_PROGRAM

Tool that can launch the native build system. The value may be the full path to an executable or just the tool name if it is expected to be in the `PATH`.

The tool selected depends on the `CMAKE_GENERATOR` (page 628) used to configure the project:

- The Makefile generators set this to `make`, `gmake`, or a generator-specific tool (e.g. `nmake` for "NMake Makefiles").

  These generators store `CMAKE_MAKE_PROGRAM` in the CMake cache so that it may be edited by the user.

- The Ninja generator sets this to `ninja`.

  This generator stores `CMAKE_MAKE_PROGRAM` in the CMake cache so that it may be edited by the user.

- The Xcode generator sets this to `xcodebuild` (or possibly an otherwise undocumented `cmakexbuild` wrapper implementing some workarounds).

  This generator stores `CMAKE_MAKE_PROGRAM` in the CMake cache so that it may be edited by the user.

- The Visual Studio generators set this to the full path to `MSBuild.exe` (VS >= 10), `devenv.com` (VS 7,8,9), `VCExpress.exe` (VS Express 8,9), or `msdev.exe` (VS 6). (See also variables `CMAKE_VS_MSBUILD_COMMAND` (page 635), `CMAKE_VS_DEVENV_COMMAND` (page 635), and `CMAKE_VS_MSDEV_COMMAND` (page 635).)

  These generators prefer to lookup the build tool at build time rather than to store `CMAKE_MAKE_PROGRAM` in the CMake cache ahead of time. This is because the tools are version-specific and can be located using the Windows Registry. It is also necessary because the proper build tool may depend on the project content (e.g. the Intel Fortran plugin to VS 10 and 11 requires `devenv.com` to build its `.vfproj` project files even though `MSBuild.exe` is normally preferred to support the `CMAKE_GENERATOR_TOOLSET` (page 628)).

  For compatibility with versions of CMake prior to 3.0, if a user or project explicitly adds `CMAKE_MAKE_PROGRAM` to the CMake cache then CMake will use the specified value if possible.

The `CMAKE_MAKE_PROGRAM` variable is set for use by project code. The value is also used by the `cmake(1)` (page 235) `--build` and `ctest(1)` (page 240) `--build-and-test` tools to launch the native build process.

CMAKE_MINIMUM_REQUIRED_VERSION

Version specified to cmake_minimum_required command

Variable containing the VERSION component specified in the cmake_minimum_required command.

CMAKE_MINOR_VERSION

Second version number component of the `CMAKE_VERSION` (page 634) variable.

CMAKE_PARENT_LIST_FILE

Full path to the CMake file that included the current one.

While processing a CMake file loaded by include() or find_package() this variable contains the full path to the file including it. The top of the include stack is always the CMakeLists.txt for the current directory. See also CMAKE_CURRENT_LIST_FILE.

CMAKE_PATCH_VERSION

Third version number component of the `CMAKE_VERSION` (page 634) variable.

CMAKE_PROJECT_NAME

The name of the current project.

This specifies name of the current project from the closest inherited PROJECT command.

CMAKE_RANLIB

Name of randomizing tool for static libraries.

This specifies name of the program that randomizes libraries on UNIX, not used on Windows, but may be present.

CMAKE_ROOT

Install directory for running cmake.

This is the install root for the running CMake and the Modules directory can be found here. This is commonly used in this format: ${CMAKE_ROOT}/Modules

CMAKE_SCRIPT_MODE_FILE

Full path to the -P script file currently being processed.

When run in -P script mode, CMake sets this variable to the full path of the script file. When run to configure a CMakeLists.txt file, this variable is not set.

CMAKE_SHARED_LIBRARY_PREFIX

The prefix for shared libraries that you link to.

The prefix to use for the name of a shared library, lib on UNIX.

CMAKE_SHARED_LIBRARY_PREFIX_<LANG> overrides this for language <LANG>.

CMAKE_SHARED_LIBRARY_SUFFIX

The suffix for shared libraries that you link to.

The suffix to use for the end of a shared library filename, .dll on Windows.

CMAKE_SHARED_LIBRARY_SUFFIX_<LANG> overrides this for language <LANG>.

CMAKE_SHARED_MODULE_PREFIX

The prefix for loadable modules that you link to.

The prefix to use for the name of a loadable module on this platform.

CMAKE_SHARED_MODULE_PREFIX_<LANG> overrides this for language <LANG>.

CMAKE_SHARED_MODULE_SUFFIX

The suffix for shared libraries that you link to.

The suffix to use for the end of a loadable module filename on this platform

CMAKE_SHARED_MODULE_SUFFIX_<LANG> overrides this for language <LANG>.

CMAKE_SIZEOF_VOID_P

Size of a void pointer.

This is set to the size of a pointer on the machine, and is determined by a try compile. If a 64 bit size is found, then the library search path is modified to look for 64 bit libraries first.

CMAKE_SKIP_INSTALL_RULES

Whether to disable generation of installation rules.

If TRUE, cmake will neither generate installaton rules nor will it generate cmake_install.cmake files. This variable is FALSE by default.

CMAKE_SKIP_RPATH

If true, do not add run time path information.

If this is set to TRUE, then the rpath information is not added to compiled executables. The default is to add rpath information if the platform supports it. This allows for easy running from the build tree. To omit RPATH in the install step, but not the build step, use CMAKE_SKIP_INSTALL_RPATH instead.

CMAKE_SOURCE_DIR

The path to the top level of the source tree.

This is the full path to the top level of the current CMake source tree. For an in-source build, this would be the same as CMAKE_BINARY_DIR.

CMAKE_STANDARD_LIBRARIES

Libraries linked into every executable and shared library.

This is the list of libraries that are linked into all executables and libraries.

CMAKE_STATIC_LIBRARY_PREFIX

The prefix for static libraries that you link to.

The prefix to use for the name of a static library, lib on UNIX.

CMAKE_STATIC_LIBRARY_PREFIX_<LANG> overrides this for language <LANG>.

CMAKE_STATIC_LIBRARY_SUFFIX

The suffix for static libraries that you link to.

The suffix to use for the end of a static library filename, .lib on Windows.

CMAKE_STATIC_LIBRARY_SUFFIX_<LANG> overrides this for language <LANG>.

CMAKE_TOOLCHAIN_FILE

Path to toolchain file supplied to cmake(1) (page 235).

This variable is specified on the command line when cross-compiling with CMake. It is the path to a file which is read early in the CMake run and which specifies locations for compilers and toolchain utilities, and other target platform and compiler related information.

CMAKE_TWEAK_VERSION

Defined to 0 for compatibility with code written for older CMake versions that may have defined higher values.

Note: In CMake versions 2.8.2 through 2.8.12, this variable holds the fourth version number component of the CMAKE_VERSION (page 634) variable.

CMAKE_VERBOSE_MAKEFILE

Enable verbose output from Makefile builds.

This variable is a cache entry initialized (to FALSE) by the project() (page 327) command. Users may enable the option in their local build tree to get more verbose output from Makefile builds and show each command line as it is launched.

CMAKE_VERSION

The CMake version string as three non-negative integer components separated by . and possibly followed by − and other information. The first two components represent the feature level and the third component represents either a bug-fix level or development date.

Release versions and release candidate versions of CMake use the format:

```
<major>.<minor>.<patch>[-rc<n>]
```

where the <patch> component is less than 20000000. Development versions of CMake use the format:

```
<major>.<minor>.<date>[-<id>]
```

where the <date> component is of format CCYYMMDD and <id> may contain arbitrary text. This represents development as of a particular date following the <major>.<minor> feature release.

Individual component values are also available in variables:

- CMAKE_MAJOR_VERSION (page 629)
- CMAKE_MINOR_VERSION (page 631)
- CMAKE_PATCH_VERSION (page 631)
- CMAKE_TWEAK_VERSION (page 634)

Use the if() (page 313) command VERSION_LESS, VERSION_EQUAL, or VERSION_GREATER operators to compare version string values against CMAKE_VERSION using a component-wise test. Version component values may be 10 or larger so do not attempt to compare version strings as floating-point numbers.

Note: CMake   versions   2.8.2   through   2.8.12   used   three   components   for   the   fea-

---

ture level. Release versions represented the bug-fix level in a fourth component, i.e. `<major>.<minor>.<patch>[.<tweak>][-rc<n>]`. Development versions represented the development date in the fourth component, i.e. `<major>.<minor>.<patch>.<date>[-<id>]`.

CMake versions prior to 2.8.2 used three components for the feature level and had no bug-fix component. Release versions used an even-valued second component, i.e. `<major>.<even-minor>.<patch>[-rc<n>]`. Development versions used an odd-valued second component with the development date as the third component, i.e. `<major>.<odd-minor>.<date>`.

The CMAKE_VERSION variable is defined by CMake 2.6.3 and higher. Earlier versions defined only the individual component variables.

CMAKE_VS_DEVENV_COMMAND

The generators for `Visual Studio 7` (page 362) and above set this variable to the `devenv.com` command installed with the corresponding Visual Studio version. Note that this variable may be empty on Visual Studio Express editions because they do not provide this tool.

This variable is not defined by other generators even if `devenv.com` is installed on the computer.

The CMAKE_VS_MSBUILD_COMMAND (page 635) is also provided for `Visual Studio 10 2010` (page 362) and above. See also the CMAKE_MAKE_PROGRAM (page 630) variable.

CMAKE_VS_INTEL_Fortran_PROJECT_VERSION

When generating for Visual Studio 7 or greater with the Intel Fortran plugin installed, this specifies the .vfproj project file format version. This is intended for internal use by CMake and should not be used by project code.

CMAKE_VS_MSBUILD_COMMAND

The generators for `Visual Studio 10 2010` (page 362) and above set this variable to the `MSBuild.exe` command installed with the corresponding Visual Studio version.

This variable is not defined by other generators even if `MSBuild.exe` is installed on the computer.

The CMAKE_VS_DEVENV_COMMAND (page 635) is also provided for the non-Express editions of Visual Studio. See also the CMAKE_MAKE_PROGRAM (page 630) variable.

CMAKE_VS_MSDEV_COMMAND

The `Visual Studio 6` (page 361) generator sets this variable to the `msdev.exe` command installed with Visual Studio 6.

This variable is not defined by other generators even if `msdev.exe` is installed on the computer.

See also the CMAKE_MAKE_PROGRAM (page 630) variable.

CMAKE_VS_NsightTegra_VERSION

When using a Visual Studio generator with the CMAKE_SYSTEM_NAME (page 653) variable set to Android, this variable contains the version number of the installed NVIDIA Nsight Tegra Visual Studio Edition.

CMAKE_VS_PLATFORM_NAME

Visual Studio target platform name.

VS 8 and above allow project files to specify a target platform. CMake provides the name of the chosen platform in this variable.

CMAKE_VS_PLATFORM_TOOLSET

Visual Studio Platform Toolset name.

VS 10 and above use MSBuild under the hood and support multiple compiler toolchains. CMake may specify a toolset explicitly, such as "v110" for VS 11 or "Windows7.1SDK" for 64-bit support in VS 10 Express. CMake provides the name of the chosen toolset in this variable.

CMAKE_XCODE_PLATFORM_TOOLSET

Xcode compiler selection.

Xcode supports selection of a compiler from one of the installed toolsets. CMake provides the name of the chosen toolset in this variable, if any is explicitly selected (e.g. via the cmake -T option).

PROJECT_BINARY_DIR

Full path to build directory for project.

This is the binary directory of the most recent project() (page 327) command.

<PROJECT-NAME>_BINARY_DIR

Top level binary directory for the named project.

A variable is created with the name used in the project() (page 327) command, and is the binary directory for the project. This can be useful when add_subdirectory() (page 277) is used to connect several projects.

PROJECT_NAME

Name of the project given to the project command.

This is the name given to the most recent `project()` (page 327) command.

<PROJECT-NAME>_SOURCE_DIR

Top level source directory for the named project.

A variable is created with the name used in the `project()` (page 327) command, and is the source directory for the project. This can be useful when `add_subdirectory()` (page 277) is used to connect several projects.

<PROJECT-NAME>_VERSION

Value given to the VERSION option of the most recent call to the `project()` (page 327) command with project name <PROJECT-NAME>, if any.

See also the component-wise version variables <PROJECT-NAME>_VERSION_MAJOR (page 637), <PROJECT-NAME>_VERSION_MINOR (page 637), <PROJECT-NAME>_VERSION_PATCH (page 637), and <PROJECT-NAME>_VERSION_TWEAK (page 637).

<PROJECT-NAME>_VERSION_MAJOR

First version number component of the <PROJECT-NAME>_VERSION (page 637) variable as set by the `project()` (page 327) command.

<PROJECT-NAME>_VERSION_MINOR

Second version number component of the <PROJECT-NAME>_VERSION (page 637) variable as set by the `project()` (page 327) command.

<PROJECT-NAME>_VERSION_PATCH

Third version number component of the <PROJECT-NAME>_VERSION (page 637) variable as set by the `project()` (page 327) command.

<PROJECT-NAME>_VERSION_TWEAK

Fourth version number component of the <PROJECT-NAME>_VERSION (page 637) variable as set by the `project()` (page 327) command.

PROJECT_SOURCE_DIR

Top level source directory for the current project.

This is the source directory of the most recent `project()` (page 327) command.

PROJECT_VERSION

Value given to the `VERSION` option of the most recent call to the `project()` (page 327) command, if any.

See also the component-wise version variables `PROJECT_VERSION_MAJOR` (page 638), `PROJECT_VERSION_MINOR` (page 638), `PROJECT_VERSION_PATCH` (page 638), and `PROJECT_VERSION_TWEAK` (page 638).

PROJECT_VERSION_MAJOR

First version number component of the `PROJECT_VERSION` (page 638) variable as set by the `project()` (page 327) command.

PROJECT_VERSION_MINOR

Second version number component of the `PROJECT_VERSION` (page 638) variable as set by the `project()` (page 327) command.

PROJECT_VERSION_PATCH

Third version number component of the `PROJECT_VERSION` (page 638) variable as set by the `project()` (page 327) command.

PROJECT_VERSION_TWEAK

Fourth version number component of the `PROJECT_VERSION` (page 638) variable as set by the `project()` (page 327) command.

C.7.2 Variables that Change Behavior

BUILD_SHARED_LIBS

Global flag to cause add_library to create shared libraries if on.

If present and true, this will cause all libraries to be built shared unless the library was explicitly added as a static library. This variable is often added to projects as an OPTION so that each user of a project can decide if they want to build the project using shared or static libraries.

CMAKE_ABSOLUTE_DESTINATION_FILES

List of files which have been installed using an ABSOLUTE DESTINATION path.

This variable is defined by CMake-generated cmake_install.cmake scripts. It can be used (read-only) by programs or scripts that source those install scripts. This is used by some CPack generators (e.g. RPM).

CMAKE_APPBUNDLE_PATH

Search path for OS X application bundles used by the `find_program()` (page 306), and `find_package()` (page 297) commands.

CMAKE_AUTOMOC_RELAXED_MODE

Switch between strict and relaxed automoc mode.

By default, AUTOMOC (page 575) behaves exactly as described in the documentation of the AUTOMOC (page 575) target property. When set to TRUE, it accepts more input and tries to find the correct input file for moc even if it differs from the documented behaviour. In this mode it e.g. also checks whether a header file is intended to be processed by moc when a "foo.moc" file has been included.

Relaxed mode has to be enabled for KDE4 compatibility.

CMAKE_BACKWARDS_COMPATIBILITY

Deprecated. See CMake Policy CMP0001 (page 538) documentation.

CMAKE_BUILD_TYPE

Specifies the build type on single-configuration generators.

This statically specifies what build type (configuration) will be built in this build tree. Possible values are empty, Debug, Release, RelWithDebInfo and MinSizeRel. This variable is only meaningful to single-configuration generators (such as make and Ninja) i.e. those which choose a single configuration when CMake runs to generate a build tree as opposed to multi-configuration generators which offer selection of the build configuration within the generated build environment. There are many per-config properties and variables (usually following clean SOME_VAR_<CONFIG> order conventions), such as CMAKE_C_FLAGS_<CONFIG>, specified as uppercase: CMAKE_C_FLAGS_[DEBUG|RELEASE|RELWITHDEBINFO|MINSIZEREL]. For example, in a build tree configured to build type Debug, CMake will see to having CMAKE_C_FLAGS_DEBUG settings get added to the CMAKE_C_FLAGS settings. See also CMAKE_CONFIGURATION_TYPES.

CMAKE_COLOR_MAKEFILE

Enables color output when using the Makefile generator.

When enabled, the generated Makefiles will produce colored output. Default is ON.

CMAKE_CONFIGURATION_TYPES

Specifies the available build types on multi-config generators.

This specifies what build types (configurations) will be available such as Debug, Release, RelWithDebInfo etc. This has reasonable defaults on most platforms, but can be extended to provide other build types. See also CMAKE_BUILD_TYPE for details of managing configuration data, and CMAKE_CFG_INTDIR.

CMAKE_DEBUG_TARGET_PROPERTIES

Enables tracing output for target properties.

This variable can be populated with a list of properties to generate debug output for when evaluating target properties. Currently it can only be used when evaluating the INCLUDE_DIRECTORIES (page 591), COMPILE_DEFINITIONS (page 580), COMPILE_OPTIONS (page 581), AUTOUIC_OPTIONS (page 576), SOURCES (page 608), COMPILE_FEATURES (page 581), POSITION_INDEPENDENT_CODE (page 605) target properties and any other property listed in COMPATIBLE_INTERFACE_STRING (page 580) and other COMPATIBLE_INTERFACE_ properties. It outputs an origin for each entry in the target property. Default is unset.

CMAKE_DISABLE_FIND_PACKAGE_<PackageName>

Variable for disabling find_package() calls.

Every non-REQUIRED find_package() call in a project can be disabled by setting the variable CMAKE_DISABLE_FIND_PACKAGE_<PackageName> to TRUE. This can be used to build a project without an optional package, although that package is installed.

This switch should be used during the initial CMake run. Otherwise if the package has already been found in a previous CMake run, the variables which have been stored in the cache will still be there. In that case it is recommended to remove the cache variables for this package from the cache using the cache editor or cmake -U

CMAKE_ERROR_DEPRECATED

Whether to issue deprecation errors for macros and functions.

If TRUE, this can be used by macros and functions to issue fatal errors when deprecated macros or functions are used. This variable is FALSE by default.

CMAKE_ERROR_ON_ABSOLUTE_INSTALL_DESTINATION

Ask cmake_install.cmake script to error out as soon as a file with absolute INSTALL DESTINATION is encountered.

The fatal error is emitted before the installation of the offending file takes place. This variable is used by CMake-generated cmake_install.cmake scripts. If one sets this variable to ON while running the script, it may get fatal error messages from the script.

CMAKE_EXPORT_NO_PACKAGE_REGISTRY

Disable the export(PACKAGE) (page 287) command.

In some cases, for example for packaging and for system wide installations, it is not desirable to write the user package registry. If the CMAKE_EXPORT_NO_PACKAGE_REGISTRY (page 641) variable is enabled, the export(PACKAGE) (page 287) command will do nothing.

See also *Disabling the Package Registry*.

CMAKE_SYSROOT

Path to pass to the compiler in the --sysroot flag.

The CMAKE_SYSROOT content is passed to the compiler in the --sysroot flag, if supported. The path is also stripped from the RPATH/RUNPATH if necessary on installation. The CMAKE_SYSROOT is also used to prefix paths searched by the find_* commands.

This variable may only be set in a toolchain file specified by the CMAKE_TOOLCHAIN_FILE (page 633) variable.

CMAKE_FIND_LIBRARY_PREFIXES

Prefixes to prepend when looking for libraries.

This specifies what prefixes to add to library names when the find_library command looks for libraries. On UNIX systems this is typically lib, meaning that when trying to find the foo library it will look for libfoo.

CMAKE_FIND_LIBRARY_SUFFIXES

Suffixes to append when looking for libraries.

This specifies what suffixes to add to library names when the find_library command looks for libraries. On Windows systems this is typically .lib and .dll, meaning that when trying to find the foo library it will look for foo.dll etc.

CMAKE_FIND_NO_INSTALL_PREFIX

Ignore the CMAKE_INSTALL_PREFIX (page 645) when searching for assets.

CMake adds the CMAKE_INSTALL_PREFIX (page 645) and the CMAKE_STAGING_PREFIX (page 648) variable to the CMAKE_SYSTEM_PREFIX_PATH (page 649) by default. This variable may be set on the command line to control that behavior.

Set CMAKE_FIND_NO_INSTALL_PREFIX (page 642) to TRUE to tell find_package not to search in the CMAKE_INSTALL_PREFIX (page 645) or CMAKE_STAGING_PREFIX (page 648) by default. Note that the prefix may still be searched for other reasons, such as being the same prefix as the CMake installation, or for being a built-in system prefix.

CMAKE_FIND_PACKAGE_NO_PACKAGE_REGISTRY

Skip *User Package Registry* in find_package() (page 297) calls.

In some cases, for example to locate only system wide installations, it is not desirable to use the *User Package Registry* when searching for packages. If the CMAKE_FIND_PACKAGE_NO_PACKAGE_REGISTRY (page 642) variable is enabled, all the find_package() (page 297) commands will skip the *User Package Registry* as if they were called with the NO_CMAKE_PACKAGE_REGISTRY argument.

See also *Disabling the Package Registry*.

CMAKE_FIND_PACKAGE_NO_SYSTEM_PACKAGE_REGISTRY

Skip *System Package Registry* in find_package() (page 297) calls.

In some cases, it is not desirable to use the *System Package Registry* when searching for packages. If the CMAKE_FIND_PACKAGE_NO_SYSTEM_PACKAGE_REGISTRY (page 642) variable is enabled, all the find_package() (page 297) commands will skip the *System Package Registry* as if they were called with the NO_CMAKE_SYSTEM_PACKAGE_REGISTRY argument.

See also *Disabling the Package Registry*.

CMAKE_FIND_PACKAGE_WARN_NO_MODULE

Tell find_package to warn if called without an explicit mode.

If find_package is called without an explicit mode option (MODULE, CONFIG or NO_MODULE) and no Find<pkg>.cmake module is in CMAKE_MODULE_PATH then CMake implicitly assumes that the caller intends to search for a package configuration file. If no package configuration file is found then the wording of the failure message must account for both the case that the package is really missing and the case that the project has a bug and failed to provide the intended Find module. If instead the caller specifies an explicit mode option then the failure message can be more specific.

Set CMAKE_FIND_PACKAGE_WARN_NO_MODULE to TRUE to tell find_package to warn when it implicitly assumes Config mode. This helps developers enforce use of an explicit mode in all calls to find_package within a project.

CMAKE_FIND_ROOT_PATH

List of root paths to search on the filesystem.

This variable is most useful when cross-compiling. CMake uses the paths in this list as alternative roots to find filesystem items with `find_package()` (page 297), `find_library()` (page 294) etc.

CMAKE_FIND_ROOT_PATH_MODE_INCLUDE

This variable controls whether the CMAKE_FIND_ROOT_PATH (page 643) and CMAKE_SYSROOT (page 641) are used by `find_file()` (page 292) and `find_path()` (page 303).

If set to ONLY, then only the roots in CMAKE_FIND_ROOT_PATH (page 643) will be searched. If set to NEVER, then the roots in CMAKE_FIND_ROOT_PATH (page 643) will be ignored and only the host system root will be used. If set to BOTH, then the host system paths and the paths in CMAKE_FIND_ROOT_PATH (page 643) will be searched.

CMAKE_FIND_ROOT_PATH_MODE_LIBRARY

This variable controls whether the CMAKE_FIND_ROOT_PATH (page 643) and CMAKE_SYSROOT (page 641) are used by `find_library()` (page 294).

If set to ONLY, then only the roots in CMAKE_FIND_ROOT_PATH (page 643) will be searched. If set to NEVER, then the roots in CMAKE_FIND_ROOT_PATH (page 643) will be ignored and only the host system root will be used. If set to BOTH, then the host system paths and the paths in CMAKE_FIND_ROOT_PATH (page 643) will be searched.

CMAKE_FIND_ROOT_PATH_MODE_PACKAGE

This variable controls whether the CMAKE_FIND_ROOT_PATH (page 643) and CMAKE_SYSROOT (page 641) are used by `find_package()` (page 297).

If set to ONLY, then only the roots in CMAKE_FIND_ROOT_PATH (page 643) will be searched. If set to NEVER, then the roots in CMAKE_FIND_ROOT_PATH (page 643) will be ignored and only the host system root will be used. If set to BOTH, then the host system paths and the paths in CMAKE_FIND_ROOT_PATH (page 643) will be searched.

CMAKE_FIND_ROOT_PATH_MODE_PROGRAM

This variable controls whether the CMAKE_FIND_ROOT_PATH (page 643) and CMAKE_SYSROOT (page 641) are used by find_program() (page 306).

If set to ONLY, then only the roots in CMAKE_FIND_ROOT_PATH (page 643) will be searched. If set to NEVER, then the roots in CMAKE_FIND_ROOT_PATH (page 643) will be ignored and only the host system root will be used. If set to BOTH, then the host system paths and the paths in CMAKE_FIND_ROOT_PATH (page 643) will be searched.

CMAKE_FRAMEWORK_PATH

Search path for OS X frameworks used by the find_library() (page 294), find_package() (page 297), find_path() (page 303), and find_file() (page 292) commands.

CMAKE_IGNORE_PATH

Path to be ignored by FIND_XXX() commands.

Specifies directories to be ignored by searches in FIND_XXX() commands. This is useful in cross-compiled environments where some system directories contain incompatible but possibly linkable libraries. For example, on cross-compiled cluster environments, this allows a user to ignore directories containing libraries meant for the front-end machine that modules like FindX11 (and others) would normally search. By default this is empty; it is intended to be set by the project. Note that CMAKE_IGNORE_PATH takes a list of directory names, NOT a list of prefixes. If you want to ignore paths under prefixes (bin, include, lib, etc.), you'll need to specify them explicitly. See also CMAKE_PREFIX_PATH, CMAKE_LIBRARY_PATH, CMAKE_INCLUDE_PATH, CMAKE_PROGRAM_PATH.

CMAKE_INCLUDE_PATH

Path used for searching by FIND_FILE() and FIND_PATH().

Specifies a path which will be used both by FIND_FILE() and FIND_PATH(). Both commands will check each of the contained directories for the existence of the file which is currently searched. By default it is empty, it is intended to be set by the project. See also CMAKE_SYSTEM_INCLUDE_PATH, CMAKE_PREFIX_PATH.

CMAKE_INCLUDE_DIRECTORIES_BEFORE

Whether to append or prepend directories by default in include_directories() (page 316).

This variable affects the default behavior of the include_directories() (page 316) command. Setting this variable to 'ON' is equivalent to using the BEFORE option in all uses of that command.

CMAKE_INCLUDE_DIRECTORIES_PROJECT_BEFORE

Whether to force prepending of project include directories.

This variable affects the order of include directories generated in compiler command lines. If set to 'ON', it causes the CMAKE_SOURCE_DIR (page 633) and the CMAKE_BINARY_DIR (page 624) to appear first.

CMAKE_INSTALL_DEFAULT_COMPONENT_NAME

Default component used in install() commands.

If an install() command is used without the COMPONENT argument, these files will be grouped into a default component. The name of this default install component will be taken from this variable. It defaults to "Unspecified".

CMAKE_INSTALL_MESSAGE

Specify verbosity of installation script code generated by the install() (page 317) command (using the file(INSTALL) (page 287) command). For paths that are newly installed or updated, installation may print lines like:

```
-- Installing: /some/destination/path
```

For paths that are already up to date, installation may print lines like:

```
-- Up-to-date: /some/destination/path
```

The CMAKE_INSTALL_MESSAGE variable may be set to control which messages are printed:

ALWAYS Print both Installing and Up-to-date messages.

LAZY Print Installing but not Up-to-date messages.

NEVER Print neither Installing nor Up-to-date messages.

Other values have undefined behavior and may not be diagnosed.

If this variable is not set, the default behavior is ALWAYS.

CMAKE_INSTALL_PREFIX

Install directory used by install.

If "make install" is invoked or INSTALL is built, this directory is prepended onto all install directories. This variable defaults to /usr/local on UNIX and c:/Program Files on Windows.

On UNIX one can use the DESTDIR mechanism in order to relocate the whole installation. DESTDIR means DESTination DIRectory. It is commonly used by makefile users in order to install software at non-default location. It is usually invoked like this:

```
make DESTDIR=/home/john install
```

which will install the concerned software using the installation prefix, e.g. "/usr/local" prepended with the DESTDIR value which finally gives "/home/john/usr/local".

WARNING: DESTDIR may not be used on Windows because installation prefix usually contains a drive letter like in "C:/Program Files" which cannot be prepended with some other prefix.

The installation prefix is also added to CMAKE_SYSTEM_PREFIX_PATH so that find_package, find_program, find_library, find_path, and find_file will search the prefix for other software.

Note: Use the GNUInstallDirs (page 523) module to provide GNU-style options for the layout of directories within the installation.

CMAKE_LIBRARY_PATH

Path used for searching by FIND_LIBRARY().

Specifies a path which will be used by FIND_LIBRARY(). FIND_LIBRARY() will check each of the contained directories for the existence of the library which is currently searched. By default it is empty, it is intended to be set by the project. See also CMAKE_SYSTEM_LIBRARY_PATH, CMAKE_PREFIX_PATH.

CMAKE_MFC_FLAG

Tell cmake to use MFC for an executable or dll.

This can be set in a CMakeLists.txt file and will enable MFC in the application. It should be set to 1 for the static MFC library, and 2 for the shared MFC library. This is used in Visual Studio 6 and 7 project files. The CMakeSetup dialog used MFC and the CMakeLists.txt looks like this:

```
add_definitions(-D_AFXDLL)
set(CMAKE_MFC_FLAG 2)
add_executable(CMakeSetup WIN32 ${SRCS})
```

CMAKE_MODULE_PATH

List of directories to search for CMake modules.

Commands like include() and find_package() search for files in directories listed by this variable before checking the default modules that come with CMake.

CMAKE_NOT_USING_CONFIG_FLAGS

Skip _BUILD_TYPE flags if true.

This is an internal flag used by the generators in CMake to tell CMake to skip the _BUILD_TYPE flags.

CMAKE_POLICY_DEFAULT_CMP<NNNN>

Default for CMake Policy CMP<NNNN> when it is otherwise left unset.

Commands cmake_minimum_required(VERSION) and cmake_policy(VERSION) by default leave policies introduced after the given version unset. Set CMAKE_POLICY_DEFAULT_CMP<NNNN> to OLD or NEW to specify the default for policy CMP<NNNN>, where <NNNN> is the policy number.

This variable should not be set by a project in CMake code; use cmake_policy(SET) instead. Users running CMake may set this variable in the cache (e.g. -DCMAKE_POLICY_DEFAULT_CMP<NNNN>=<OLD|NEW>) to set a policy not otherwise set by the project. Set to OLD to quiet a policy warning while using old behavior or to NEW to try building the project with new behavior.

CMAKE_POLICY_WARNING_CMP<NNNN>

Explicitly enable or disable the warning when CMake Policy CMP<NNNN> is not set. This is meaningful only for the few policies that do not warn by default:

- CMAKE_POLICY_WARNING_CMP0025 controls the warning for policy CMP0025 (page 548).
- CMAKE_POLICY_WARNING_CMP0047 controls the warning for policy CMP0047 (page 555).

This variable should not be set by a project in CMake code. Project developers running CMake may set this variable in their cache to enable the warning (e.g. -DCMAKE_POLICY_WARNING_CMP<NNNN>=ON). Alternatively, running cmake(1) (page 235) with the --debug-output or --trace option will also enable the warning.

CMAKE_PREFIX_PATH

Path used for searching by FIND_XXX(), with appropriate suffixes added.

Specifies a path which will be used by the FIND_XXX() commands. It contains the "base" directories, the FIND_XXX() commands append appropriate subdirectories to the base directories. So FIND_PROGRAM() adds /bin to each of the directories in the path, FIND_LIBRARY() appends /lib to each of the directories, and FIND_PATH() and FIND_FILE() append /include . By default it is empty, it is intended to be set by the project. See also CMAKE_SYSTEM_PREFIX_PATH, CMAKE_INCLUDE_PATH, CMAKE_LIBRARY_PATH, CMAKE_PROGRAM_PATH.

CMAKE_PROGRAM_PATH

Path used for searching by FIND_PROGRAM().

Specifies a path which will be used by FIND_PROGRAM(). FIND_PROGRAM() will check each of the contained directories for the existence of the program which is currently searched. By default it is empty, it is intended to be set by the project. See also CMAKE_SYSTEM_PROGRAM_PATH, CMAKE_PREFIX_PATH.

CMAKE_PROJECT_<PROJECT-NAME>_INCLUDE

A CMake language file or module to be included by the `project()` (page 327) command. This is is intended for injecting custom code into project builds without modifying their source.

CMAKE_SKIP_INSTALL_ALL_DEPENDENCY

Don't make the install target depend on the all target.

By default, the "install" target depends on the "all" target. This has the effect, that when "make install" is invoked or INSTALL is built, first the "all" target is built, then the installation starts. If CMAKE_SKIP_INSTALL_ALL_DEPENDENCY is set to TRUE, this dependency is not created, so the installation process will start immediately, independent from whether the project has been completely built or not.

CMAKE_STAGING_PREFIX

This variable may be set to a path to install to when cross-compiling. This can be useful if the path in `CMAKE_SYSROOT` (page 641) is read-only, or otherwise should remain pristine.

The CMAKE_STAGING_PREFIX location is also used as a search prefix by the `find_*` commands. This can be controlled by setting the `CMAKE_FIND_NO_INSTALL_PREFIX` (page 642) variable.

If any RPATH/RUNPATH entries passed to the linker contain the CMAKE_STAGING_PREFIX, the matching path fragments are replaced with the `CMAKE_INSTALL_PREFIX` (page 645).

CMAKE_SYSTEM_IGNORE_PATH

Path to be ignored by FIND_XXX() commands.

Specifies directories to be ignored by searches in FIND_XXX() commands. This is useful in cross-compiled environments where some system directories contain incompatible but possibly linkable libraries. For example, on cross-compiled cluster environments, this allows a user to ignore directories containing libraries meant for the front-end machine that modules like FindX11 (and others) would normally search. By default this contains a list of directories containing incompatible binaries for the host system. See also CMAKE_SYSTEM_PREFIX_PATH, CMAKE_SYSTEM_LIBRARY_PATH, CMAKE_SYSTEM_INCLUDE_PATH, and CMAKE_SYSTEM_PROGRAM_PATH.

CMAKE_SYSTEM_INCLUDE_PATH

Path used for searching by FIND_FILE() and FIND_PATH().

Specifies a path which will be used both by FIND_FILE() and FIND_PATH(). Both commands will check each of the contained directories for the existence of the file which is currently searched. By default it contains the standard directories for the current system. It is NOT intended to be modified by the project, use CMAKE_INCLUDE_PATH for this. See also CMAKE_SYSTEM_PREFIX_PATH.

CMAKE_SYSTEM_LIBRARY_PATH

Path used for searching by FIND_LIBRARY().

Specifies a path which will be used by FIND_LIBRARY(). FIND_LIBRARY() will check each of the contained directories for the existence of the library which is currently searched. By default it contains the standard directories for the current system. It is NOT intended to be modified by the project, use CMAKE_LIBRARY_PATH for this. See also CMAKE_SYSTEM_PREFIX_PATH.

CMAKE_SYSTEM_PREFIX_PATH

Path used for searching by FIND_XXX(), with appropriate suffixes added.

Specifies a path which will be used by the FIND_XXX() commands. It contains the "base" directories, the FIND_XXX() commands append appropriate subdirectories to the base directories. So FIND_PROGRAM() adds /bin to each of the directories in the path, FIND_LIBRARY() appends /lib to each of the directories, and FIND_PATH() and FIND_FILE() append /include . By default this contains the standard directories for the current system, the CMAKE_INSTALL_PREFIX and the CMAKE_STAGING_PREFIX (page 648). It is NOT intended to be modified by the project, use CMAKE_PREFIX_PATH for this. See also CMAKE_SYSTEM_INCLUDE_PATH, CMAKE_SYSTEM_LIBRARY_PATH, CMAKE_SYSTEM_PROGRAM_PATH, and CMAKE_SYSTEM_IGNORE_PATH.

CMAKE_SYSTEM_PROGRAM_PATH

Path used for searching by FIND_PROGRAM().

Specifies a path which will be used by FIND_PROGRAM(). FIND_PROGRAM() will check each of the contained directories for the existence of the program which is currently searched. By default it contains the standard directories for the current system. It is NOT intended to be modified by the project, use CMAKE_PROGRAM_PATH for this. See also CMAKE_SYSTEM_PREFIX_PATH.

CMAKE_USER_MAKE_RULES_OVERRIDE

Specify a CMake file that overrides platform information.

CMake loads the specified file while enabling support for each language from either the project() or enable_language() commands. It is loaded after CMake's builtin compiler and platform information modules have been loaded but before the information is used. The file may set platform information variables to override CMake's defaults.

This feature is intended for use only in overriding information variables that must be set before CMake builds its first test project to check that the compiler for a language works. It should not be used to load a file in cases that a normal include() will work. Use it only as a last resort for behavior that cannot be achieved any other way. For example, one may set CMAKE_C_FLAGS_INIT to change the default value used to initialize CMAKE_C_FLAGS before it is cached. The override file should NOT be used to set anything that could be set after languages are enabled, such as variables like CMAKE_RUNTIME_OUTPUT_DIRECTORY that affect the placement of binaries. Information set in the file will be used for try_compile and try_run builds too.

CMAKE_WARN_DEPRECATED

Whether to issue deprecation warnings for macros and functions.

If TRUE, this can be used by macros and functions to issue deprecation warnings. This variable is FALSE by default.

CMAKE_WARN_ON_ABSOLUTE_INSTALL_DESTINATION

Ask cmake_install.cmake script to warn each time a file with absolute INSTALL DESTINATION is encountered.

This variable is used by CMake-generated cmake_install.cmake scripts. If one sets this variable to ON while running the script, it may get warning messages from the script.

C.7.3 Variables that Describe the System

APPLE

True if running on Mac OS X.

Set to true on Mac OS X.

BORLAND

True if the Borland compiler is being used.

This is set to true if the Borland compiler is being used.

CMAKE_CL_64

Using the 64 bit compiler from Microsoft

Set to true when using the 64 bit cl compiler from Microsoft.

CMAKE_COMPILER_2005

Using the Visual Studio 2005 compiler from Microsoft

Set to true when using the Visual Studio 2005 compiler from Microsoft.

CMAKE_HOST_APPLE

True for Apple OS X operating systems.

Set to true when the host system is Apple OS X.

CMAKE_HOST_SYSTEM_NAME

Name of the OS CMake is running on.

On systems that have the uname command, this variable is set to the output of uname -s. Linux, Windows, and Darwin for Mac OS X are the values found on the big three operating systems.

CMAKE_HOST_SYSTEM_PROCESSOR

The name of the CPU CMake is running on.

On systems that support uname, this variable is set to the output of uname -p, on windows it is set to the value of the environment variable PROCESSOR_ARCHITECTURE.

CMAKE_HOST_SYSTEM

Composit Name of OS CMake is being run on.

This variable is the composite of CMAKE_HOST_SYSTEM_NAME (page 651) and CMAKE_HOST_SYSTEM_VERSION (page 652), e.g. ${CMAKE_HOST_SYSTEM_NAME}-${CMAKE_HOST_SYSTEM_VERSION}. If CMAKE_HOST_SYSTEM_VERSION (page 652) is not set, then this variable is the same as CMAKE_HOST_SYSTEM_NAME (page 651).

CMAKE_HOST_SYSTEM_VERSION

The OS version CMake is running on.

A numeric version string for the system. On systems that support uname, this variable is set to the output of uname -r. On other systems this is set to major-minor version numbers.

CMAKE_HOST_UNIX

True for UNIX and UNIX like operating systems.

Set to true when the host system is UNIX or UNIX like (i.e. APPLE and CYGWIN).

CMAKE_HOST_WIN32

True on windows systems, including win64.

Set to true when the host system is Windows and on Cygwin.

CMAKE_LIBRARY_ARCHITECTURE_REGEX

Regex matching possible target architecture library directory names.

This is used to detect CMAKE_<lang>_LIBRARY_ARCHITECTURE from the implicit linker search path by matching the <arch> name.

CMAKE_LIBRARY_ARCHITECTURE

Target architecture library directory name, if detected.

This is the value of CMAKE_<lang>_LIBRARY_ARCHITECTURE as detected for one of the enabled languages.

CMAKE_OBJECT_PATH_MAX

Maximum object file full-path length allowed by native build tools.

CMake computes for every source file an object file name that is unique to the source file and deterministic with respect to the full path to the source file. This allows multiple source files in a target to share the same name if they lie in different directories without rebuilding when one is added or removed. However, it can produce long full paths in a few cases, so CMake shortens the path using a hashing scheme when the full path to an object file exceeds a limit. CMake has a built-in limit for each platform that is sufficient for common tools, but some native tools may have a lower limit. This variable may be set to specify the limit explicitly. The value must be an integer no less than 128.

CMAKE_SYSTEM_NAME

Name of the OS CMake is building for.

This is the name of the OS on which CMake is targeting. This variable is the same as CMAKE_HOST_SYSTEM_NAME (page 651) if you build for the host system instead of the target system when cross compiling.

CMAKE_SYSTEM_PROCESSOR

The name of the CPU CMake is building for.

This variable is the same as CMAKE_HOST_SYSTEM_PROCESSOR (page 651) if you build for the host system instead of the target system when cross compiling.

CMAKE_SYSTEM

Composit Name of OS CMake is compiling for.

This variable is the composite of CMAKE_SYSTEM_NAME (page 653) and CMAKE_SYSTEM_VERSION (page 653), e.g. ${CMAKE_SYSTEM_NAME}-${CMAKE_SYSTEM_VERSION}. If CMAKE_SYSTEM_VERSION (page 653) is not set, then this variable is the same as CMAKE_SYSTEM_NAME (page 653).

CMAKE_SYSTEM_VERSION

The OS version CMake is building for.

This variable is the same as CMAKE_HOST_SYSTEM_VERSION (page 652) if you build for the host system instead of the target system when cross compiling.

CYGWIN

True for Cygwin.

Set to true when using Cygwin.

ENV

Access environment variables.

Use the syntax $ENV{VAR} to read environment variable VAR. See also the set() command to set ENV{VAR}.

MSVC10

True when using Microsoft Visual C 10.0

Set to true when the compiler is version 10.0 of Microsoft Visual C.

MSVC11

True when using Microsoft Visual C 11.0

Set to true when the compiler is version 11.0 of Microsoft Visual C.

MSVC12

True when using Microsoft Visual C 12.0

Set to true when the compiler is version 12.0 of Microsoft Visual C.

MSVC14

True when using Microsoft Visual C 14.0

Set to true when the compiler is version 14.0 of Microsoft Visual C.

MSVC60

True when using Microsoft Visual C 6.0

Set to true when the compiler is version 6.0 of Microsoft Visual C.

MSVC70

True when using Microsoft Visual C 7.0

Set to true when the compiler is version 7.0 of Microsoft Visual C.

MSVC71

True when using Microsoft Visual C 7.1

Set to true when the compiler is version 7.1 of Microsoft Visual C.

MSVC80

True when using Microsoft Visual C 8.0

Set to true when the compiler is version 8.0 of Microsoft Visual C.

MSVC90

True when using Microsoft Visual C 9.0

Set to true when the compiler is version 9.0 of Microsoft Visual C.

MSVC_IDE

True when using the Microsoft Visual C IDE

Set to true when the target platform is the Microsoft Visual C IDE, as opposed to the command line compiler.

MSVC

True when using Microsoft Visual C

Set to true when the compiler is some version of Microsoft Visual C.

MSVC_VERSION

The version of Microsoft Visual C/C++ being used if any.

Known version numbers are:

```
1200 = VS  6.0
1300 = VS  7.0
1310 = VS  7.1
1400 = VS  8.0
1500 = VS  9.0
1600 = VS 10.0
1700 = VS 11.0
1800 = VS 12.0
1900 = VS 14.0
```

UNIX

True for UNIX and UNIX like operating systems.

Set to true when the target system is UNIX or UNIX like (i.e. APPLE and CYGWIN).

WIN32

True on windows systems, including win64.

Set to true when the target system is Windows.

WINCE

True when the CMAKE_SYSTEM_NAME (page 653) variable is set to WindowsCE.

WINDOWS_PHONE

True when the CMAKE_SYSTEM_NAME (page 653) variable is set to WindowsPhone.

WINDOWS_STORE

True when the CMAKE_SYSTEM_NAME (page 653) variable is set to WindowsStore.

XCODE_VERSION

Version of Xcode (Xcode generator only).

Under the Xcode generator, this is the version of Xcode as specified in "Xcode.app/Contents/version.plist" (such as "3.1.2").

C.7.4 Variables that Control the Build

CMAKE_ANDROID_API

Default value for the ANDROID_API (page 573) target property. See that target property for additional information.

CMAKE_ANDROID_GUI

Default value for the ANDROID_GUI (page 573) target property of executables. See that target property for additional information.

CMAKE_ARCHIVE_OUTPUT_DIRECTORY

Where to put all the ARCHIVE targets when built.

This variable is used to initialize the ARCHIVE_OUTPUT_DIRECTORY property on all the targets. See that target property for additional information.

CMAKE_AUTOMOC_MOC_OPTIONS

Additional options for moc when using CMAKE_AUTOMOC (page 657).

This variable is used to initialize the AUTOMOC_MOC_OPTIONS (page 575) property on all the targets. See that target property for additional information.

CMAKE_AUTOMOC

Whether to handle moc automatically for Qt targets.

This variable is used to initialize the AUTOMOC (page 575) property on all the targets. See that target property for additional information.

CMAKE_AUTORCC

Whether to handle rcc automatically for Qt targets.

This variable is used to initialize the AUTORCC (page 576) property on all the targets. See that target property for additional information.

CMAKE_AUTORCC_OPTIONS

Whether to handle rcc automatically for Qt targets.

This variable is used to initialize the AUTORCC_OPTIONS (page 577) property on all the targets. See that target property for additional information.

CMAKE_AUTOUIC

Whether to handle uic automatically for Qt targets.

This variable is used to initialize the AUTOUIC (page 576) property on all the targets. See that target property for additional information.

CMAKE_AUTOUIC_OPTIONS

Whether to handle `uic` automatically for Qt targets.

This variable is used to initialize the `AUTOUIC_OPTIONS` (page 576) property on all the targets. See that target property for additional information.

CMAKE_BUILD_WITH_INSTALL_RPATH

Use the install path for the RPATH

Normally CMake uses the build tree for the RPATH when building executables etc on systems that use RPATH. When the software is installed the executables etc are relinked by CMake to have the install RPATH. If this variable is set to true then the software is always built with the install path for the RPATH and does not need to be relinked when installed.

CMAKE_COMPILE_PDB_OUTPUT_DIRECTORY

Output directory for MS debug symbol `.pdb` files generated by the compiler while building source files.

This variable is used to initialize the `COMPILE_PDB_OUTPUT_DIRECTORY` (page 582) property on all the targets.

CMAKE_COMPILE_PDB_OUTPUT_DIRECTORY_<CONFIG>

Per-configuration output directory for MS debug symbol `.pdb` files generated by the compiler while building source files.

This is a per-configuration version of `CMAKE_COMPILE_PDB_OUTPUT_DIRECTORY` (page 658). This variable is used to initialize the `COMPILE_PDB_OUTPUT_DIRECTORY_<CONFIG>` (page 582) property on all the targets.

CMAKE_<CONFIG>_POSTFIX

Default filename postfix for libraries under configuration <CONFIG>.

When a non-executable target is created its <CONFIG>_POSTFIX target property is initialized with the value of this variable if it is set.

CMAKE_DEBUG_POSTFIX

See variable CMAKE_<CONFIG>_POSTFIX.

This variable is a special case of the more-general CMAKE_<CONFIG>_POSTFIX variable for the DEBUG configuration.

CMAKE_EXE_LINKER_FLAGS_<CONFIG>

Flags to be used when linking an executable.

Same as CMAKE_C_FLAGS_* but used by the linker when creating executables.

CMAKE_EXE_LINKER_FLAGS

Linker flags to be used to create executables.

These flags will be used by the linker when creating an executable.

CMAKE_Fortran_FORMAT

Set to FIXED or FREE to indicate the Fortran source layout.

This variable is used to initialize the Fortran_FORMAT property on all the targets. See that target property for additional information.

CMAKE_Fortran_MODULE_DIRECTORY

Fortran module output directory.

This variable is used to initialize the Fortran_MODULE_DIRECTORY property on all the targets. See that target property for additional information.

CMAKE_GNUtoMS

Convert GNU import libraries (.dll.a) to MS format (.lib).

This variable is used to initialize the GNUtoMS property on targets when they are created. See that target property for additional information.

CMAKE_INCLUDE_CURRENT_DIR_IN_INTERFACE

Automatically add the current source- and build directories to the INTERFACE_INCLUDE_DIRECTORIES.

If this variable is enabled, CMake automatically adds for each shared library target, static library target, module target and executable target, ${CMAKE_CURRENT_SOURCE_DIR} and ${CMAKE_CURRENT_BINARY_DIR} to the INTERFACE_INCLUDE_DIRECTORIES.By default CMAKE_INCLUDE_CURRENT_DIR_IN_INTERFACE is OFF.

CMAKE_INCLUDE_CURRENT_DIR

Automatically add the current source- and build directories to the include path.

If this variable is enabled, CMake automatically adds in each directory ${CMAKE_CURRENT_SOURCE_DIR} and ${CMAKE_CURRENT_BINARY_DIR} to the include path for this directory. These additional include directories do not propagate down to subdirectories. This is useful mainly for out-of-source builds, where files generated into the build tree are included by files located in the source tree.

By default CMAKE_INCLUDE_CURRENT_DIR is OFF.

CMAKE_INSTALL_NAME_DIR

Mac OS X directory name for installed targets.

CMAKE_INSTALL_NAME_DIR is used to initialize the INSTALL_NAME_DIR property on all targets. See that target property for more information.

CMAKE_INSTALL_RPATH

The rpath to use for installed targets.

A semicolon-separated list specifying the rpath to use in installed targets (for platforms that support it). This is used to initialize the target property INSTALL_RPATH for all targets.

CMAKE_INSTALL_RPATH_USE_LINK_PATH

Add paths to linker search and installed rpath.

CMAKE_INSTALL_RPATH_USE_LINK_PATH is a boolean that if set to true will append directories in the linker search path and outside the project to the INSTALL_RPATH. This is used to initialize the target property INSTALL_RPATH_USE_LINK_PATH for all targets.

CMAKE_<LANG>_VISIBILITY_PRESET

Default value for <LANG>_VISIBILITY_PRESET of targets.

This variable is used to initialize the <LANG>_VISIBILITY_PRESET property on all the targets. See that target property for additional information.

CMAKE_LIBRARY_OUTPUT_DIRECTORY

Where to put all the LIBRARY targets when built.

This variable is used to initialize the LIBRARY_OUTPUT_DIRECTORY property on all the targets. See that target property for additional information.

CMAKE_LIBRARY_PATH_FLAG

The flag to be used to add a library search path to a compiler.

The flag will be used to specify a library directory to the compiler. On most compilers this is "-L".

CMAKE_LINK_DEF_FILE_FLAG

Linker flag to be used to specify a .def file for dll creation.

The flag will be used to add a .def file when creating a dll on Windows; this is only defined on Windows.

CMAKE_LINK_DEPENDS_NO_SHARED

Whether to skip link dependencies on shared library files.

This variable initializes the LINK_DEPENDS_NO_SHARED property on targets when they are created. See that target property for additional information.

CMAKE_LINK_INTERFACE_LIBRARIES

Default value for LINK_INTERFACE_LIBRARIES of targets.

This variable is used to initialize the LINK_INTERFACE_LIBRARIES property on all the targets. See that target property for additional information.

CMAKE_LINK_LIBRARY_FILE_FLAG

Flag to be used to link a library specified by a path to its file.

The flag will be used before a library file path is given to the linker. This is needed only on very few platforms.

CMAKE_LINK_LIBRARY_FLAG

Flag to be used to link a library into an executable.

The flag will be used to specify a library to link to an executable. On most compilers this is "-l".

CMAKE_MACOSX_BUNDLE

Default value for MACOSX_BUNDLE of targets.

This variable is used to initialize the MACOSX_BUNDLE property on all the targets. See that target property for additional information.

CMAKE_MACOSX_RPATH

Whether to use rpaths on Mac OS X.

This variable is used to initialize the MACOSX_RPATH (page 602) property on all targets.

CMAKE_MAP_IMPORTED_CONFIG_<CONFIG>

Default value for MAP_IMPORTED_CONFIG_<CONFIG> of targets.

This variable is used to initialize the MAP_IMPORTED_CONFIG_<CONFIG> property on all the targets. See that target property for additional information.

CMAKE_MODULE_LINKER_FLAGS_<CONFIG>

Flags to be used when linking a module.

Same as CMAKE_C_FLAGS_* but used by the linker when creating modules.

CMAKE_MODULE_LINKER_FLAGS

Linker flags to be used to create modules.

These flags will be used by the linker when creating a module.

CMAKE_NO_BUILTIN_CHRPATH

Do not use the builtin ELF editor to fix RPATHs on installation.

When an ELF binary needs to have a different RPATH after installation than it does in the build tree, CMake uses a builtin editor to change the RPATH in the installed copy. If this variable is set to true then CMake will relink the binary before installation instead of using its builtin editor.

CMAKE_NO_SYSTEM_FROM_IMPORTED

Default value for NO_SYSTEM_FROM_IMPORTED of targets.

This variable is used to initialize the NO_SYSTEM_FROM_IMPORTED property on all the targets. See that target property for additional information.

CMAKE_OSX_ARCHITECTURES

Target specific architectures for OS X.

This variable is used to initialize the OSX_ARCHITECTURES (page 603) property on each target as it is creaed. See that target property for additional information.

The value of this variable should be set prior to the first project() (page 327) or enable_language() (page 284) command invocation because it may influence configuration of the toolchain and flags. It is intended to be set locally by the user creating a build tree.

This variable is ignored on platforms other than OS X.

CMAKE_OSX_DEPLOYMENT_TARGET

Specify the minimum version of OS X on which the target binaries are to be deployed. CMake uses this value for the -mmacosx-version-min flag and to help choose the default SDK (see CMAKE_OSX_SYSROOT (page 663)).

If not set explicitly the value is initialized by the MACOSX_DEPLOYMENT_TARGET environment variable, if set, and otherwise computed based on the host platform.

The value of this variable should be set prior to the first project() (page 327) or enable_language() (page 284) command invocation because it may influence configuration of the toolchain and flags. It is intended to be set locally by the user creating a build tree.

This variable is ignored on platforms other than OS X.

CMAKE_OSX_SYSROOT

Specify the location or name of the OS X platform SDK to be used. CMake uses this value to compute the value of the -isysroot flag or equivalent and to help the find_* commands locate files in the SDK.

If not set explicitly the value is initialized by the SDKROOT environment variable, if set, and otherwise computed based on the CMAKE_OSX_DEPLOYMENT_TARGET (page 663) or the host platform.

The value of this variable should be set prior to the first project() (page 327) or enable_language() (page 284) command invocation because it may influence configuration of the toolchain and flags. It is intended to be set locally by the user creating a build tree.

This variable is ignored on platforms other than OS X.

CMAKE_PDB_OUTPUT_DIRECTORY

Output directory for MS debug symbol `.pdb` files generated by the linker for executable and shared library targets.

This variable is used to initialize the `PDB_OUTPUT_DIRECTORY` (page 605) property on all the targets. See that target property for additional information.

CMAKE_PDB_OUTPUT_DIRECTORY_<CONFIG>

Per-configuration output directory for MS debug symbol `.pdb` files generated by the linker for executable and shared library targets.

This is a per-configuration version of `CMAKE_PDB_OUTPUT_DIRECTORY` (page 664). This variable is used to initialize the `PDB_OUTPUT_DIRECTORY_<CONFIG>` (page 604) property on all the targets. See that target property for additional information.

CMAKE_POSITION_INDEPENDENT_CODE

Default value for POSITION_INDEPENDENT_CODE of targets.

This variable is used to initialize the POSITION_INDEPENDENT_CODE property on all the targets. See that target property for additional information.

CMAKE_RUNTIME_OUTPUT_DIRECTORY

Where to put all the RUNTIME targets when built.

This variable is used to initialize the RUNTIME_OUTPUT_DIRECTORY property on all the targets. See that target property for additional information.

CMAKE_SHARED_LINKER_FLAGS_<CONFIG>

Flags to be used when linking a shared library.

Same as CMAKE_C_FLAGS_* but used by the linker when creating shared libraries.

CMAKE_SHARED_LINKER_FLAGS

Linker flags to be used to create shared libraries.

These flags will be used by the linker when creating a shared library.

CMAKE_SKIP_BUILD_RPATH

Do not include RPATHs in the build tree.

Normally CMake uses the build tree for the RPATH when building executables etc on systems that use RPATH. When the software is installed the executables etc are relinked by CMake to have the install RPATH. If this variable is set to true then the software is always built with no RPATH.

CMAKE_SKIP_INSTALL_RPATH

Do not include RPATHs in the install tree.

Normally CMake uses the build tree for the RPATH when building executables etc on systems that use RPATH. When the software is installed the executables etc are relinked by CMake to have the install RPATH. If this variable is set to true then the software is always installed without RPATH, even if RPATH is enabled when building. This can be useful for example to allow running tests from the build directory with RPATH enabled before the installation step. To omit RPATH in both the build and install steps, use CMAKE_SKIP_RPATH instead.

CMAKE_STATIC_LINKER_FLAGS_<CONFIG>

Flags to be used when linking a static library.

Same as CMAKE_C_FLAGS_* but used by the linker when creating static libraries.

CMAKE_STATIC_LINKER_FLAGS

Linker flags to be used to create static libraries.

These flags will be used by the linker when creating a static library.

CMAKE_TRY_COMPILE_CONFIGURATION

Build configuration used for try_compile and try_run projects.

Projects built by try_compile and try_run are built synchronously during the CMake configuration step. Therefore a specific build configuration must be chosen even if the generated build system supports multiple configurations.

CMAKE_USE_RELATIVE_PATHS

Use relative paths (May not work!).

If this is set to TRUE, then CMake will use relative paths between the source and binary tree. This option does not work for more complicated projects, and relative paths are used when possible. In general, it is not possible to move CMake generated makefiles to a different location regardless of the value of this variable.

CMAKE_VISIBILITY_INLINES_HIDDEN

Default value for VISIBILITY_INLINES_HIDDEN of targets.

This variable is used to initialize the VISIBILITY_INLINES_HIDDEN property on all the targets. See that target property for additional information.

CMAKE_WIN32_EXECUTABLE

Default value for WIN32_EXECUTABLE of targets.

This variable is used to initialize the WIN32_EXECUTABLE property on all the targets. See that target property for additional information.

CMAKE_XCODE_ATTRIBUTE_<an-attribute>

Set Xcode target attributes directly.

Tell the Xcode generator to set '<an-attribute>' to a given value in the generated Xcode project. Ignored on other generators.

See the XCODE_ATTRIBUTE_<an-attribute> (page 612) target property to set attributes on a specific target.

EXECUTABLE_OUTPUT_PATH

Old executable location variable.

The target property RUNTIME_OUTPUT_DIRECTORY supercedes this variable for a target if it is set. Executable targets are otherwise placed in this directory.

LIBRARY_OUTPUT_PATH

Old library location variable.

The target properties ARCHIVE_OUTPUT_DIRECTORY, LIBRARY_OUTPUT_DIRECTORY, and RUNTIME_OUTPUT_DIRECTORY supercede this variable for a target if they are set. Library targets are otherwise placed in this directory.

C.7.5 Variables for Languages

CMAKE_COMPILER_IS_GNU<LANG>

True if the compiler is GNU.

If the selected <LANG> compiler is the GNU compiler then this is TRUE, if not it is FALSE. Unlike the other per-language variables, this uses the GNU syntax for identifying languages instead of the CMake syntax. Recognized values of the <LANG> suffix are:

```
CC = C compiler
CXX = C++ compiler
G77 = Fortran compiler
```

CMAKE_C_COMPILE_FEATURES

List of features known to the C compiler

These features are known to be available for use with the C compiler. This list is a subset of the features listed in the CMAKE_C_KNOWN_FEATURES (page 560) global property.

See the cmake-compile-features(7) manual for information on compile features.

CMAKE_C_EXTENSIONS

Default value for C_EXTENSIONS property of targets.

This variable is used to initialize the C_EXTENSIONS (page 578) property on all targets. See that target property for additional information.

See the cmake-compile-features(7) manual for information on compile features.

CMAKE_C_STANDARD

Default value for C_STANDARD property of targets.

This variable is used to initialize the C_STANDARD (page 578) property on all targets. See that target property for additional information.

See the cmake-compile-features(7) manual for information on compile features.

CMAKE_C_STANDARD_REQUIRED

Default value for C_STANDARD_REQUIRED property of targets.

This variable is used to initialize the C_STANDARD_REQUIRED (page 578) property on all targets. See that target property for additional information.

See the cmake-compile-features(7) manual for information on compile features.

CMAKE_CXX_COMPILE_FEATURES

List of features known to the C++ compiler

These features are known to be available for use with the C++ compiler. This list is a subset of the features listed in the CMAKE_CXX_KNOWN_FEATURES (page 560) global property.

See the cmake-compile-features(7) manual for information on compile features.

CMAKE_CXX_EXTENSIONS

Default value for CXX_EXTENSIONS property of targets.

This variable is used to initialize the CXX_EXTENSIONS (page 583) property on all targets. See that target property for additional information.

See the cmake-compile-features(7) manual for information on compile features.

CMAKE_CXX_STANDARD

Default value for CXX_STANDARD property of targets.

This variable is used to initialize the CXX_STANDARD (page 583) property on all targets. See that target property for additional information.

See the cmake-compile-features(7) manual for information on compile features.

CMAKE_CXX_STANDARD_REQUIRED

Default value for CXX_STANDARD_REQUIRED property of targets.

This variable is used to initialize the CXX_STANDARD_REQUIRED (page 584) property on all targets. See that target property for additional information.

See the cmake-compile-features(7) manual for information on compile features.

CMAKE_Fortran_MODDIR_DEFAULT

Fortran default module output directory.

Most Fortran compilers write .mod files to the current working directory. For those that do not, this is set to "." and used when the Fortran_MODULE_DIRECTORY target property is not set.

CMAKE_Fortran_MODDIR_FLAG

Fortran flag for module output directory.

This stores the flag needed to pass the value of the Fortran_MODULE_DIRECTORY target property to the compiler.

CMAKE_Fortran_MODOUT_FLAG

Fortran flag to enable module output.

Most Fortran compilers write .mod files out by default. For others, this stores the flag needed to enable module output.

CMAKE_INTERNAL_PLATFORM_ABI

An internal variable subject to change.

This is used in determining the compiler ABI and is subject to change.

CMAKE_<LANG>_ARCHIVE_APPEND

Rule variable to append to a static archive.

This is a rule variable that tells CMake how to append to a static archive. It is used in place of CMAKE_<LANG>_CREATE_STATIC_LIBRARY on some platforms in order to support large object counts. See also CMAKE_<LANG>_ARCHIVE_CREATE and CMAKE_<LANG>_ARCHIVE_FINISH.

CMAKE_<LANG>_ARCHIVE_CREATE

Rule variable to create a new static archive.

This is a rule variable that tells CMake how to create a static archive. It is used in place of CMAKE_<LANG>_CREATE_STATIC_LIBRARY on some platforms in order to support large object counts. See also CMAKE_<LANG>_ARCHIVE_APPEND and CMAKE_<LANG>_ARCHIVE_FINISH.

CMAKE_<LANG>_ARCHIVE_FINISH

Rule variable to finish an existing static archive.

This is a rule variable that tells CMake how to finish a static archive. It is used in place of CMAKE_<LANG>_CREATE_STATIC_LIBRARY on some platforms in order to support large object counts. See also CMAKE_<LANG>_ARCHIVE_CREATE and CMAKE_<LANG>_ARCHIVE_APPEND.

CMAKE_<LANG>_COMPILE_OBJECT

Rule variable to compile a single object file.

This is a rule variable that tells CMake how to compile a single object file for the language <LANG>.

CMAKE_<LANG>_COMPILER_ABI

An internal variable subject to change.

This is used in determining the compiler ABI and is subject to change.

CMAKE_<LANG>_COMPILER_ID

Compiler identification string.

A short string unique to the compiler vendor. Possible values include:

```
Absoft = Absoft Fortran (absoft.com)
ADSP = Analog VisualDSP++ (analog.com)
AppleClang = Apple Clang (apple.com)
Clang = LLVM Clang (clang.llvm.org)
Cray = Cray Compiler (cray.com)
Embarcadero, Borland = Embarcadero (embarcadero.com)
G95 = G95 Fortran (g95.org)
GNU = GNU Compiler Collection (gcc.gnu.org)
HP = Hewlett-Packard Compiler (hp.com)
Intel = Intel Compiler (intel.com)
MIPSpro = SGI MIPSpro (sgi.com)
MSVC = Microsoft Visual Studio (microsoft.com)
OpenWatcom = Open Watcom (openwatcom.org)
PGI = The Portland Group (pgroup.com)
PathScale = PathScale (pathscale.com)
SDCC = Small Device C Compiler (sdcc.sourceforge.net)
SunPro = Oracle Solaris Studio (oracle.com)
TI = Texas Instruments (ti.com)
TinyCC = Tiny C Compiler (tinycc.org)
XL, VisualAge, zOS = IBM XL (ibm.com)
```

This variable is not guaranteed to be defined for all compilers or languages.

CMAKE_<LANG>_COMPILER_LOADED

Defined to true if the language is enabled.

When language <LANG> is enabled by project() or enable_language() this variable is defined to 1.

CMAKE_<LANG>_COMPILER

The full path to the compiler for LANG.

This is the command that will be used as the <LANG> compiler. Once set, you can not change this variable.

CMAKE_<LANG>_COMPILER_EXTERNAL_TOOLCHAIN

The external toolchain for cross-compiling, if supported.

Some compiler toolchains do not ship their own auxilliary utilities such as archivers and linkers. The compiler driver may support a command-line argument to specify the location of such tools. CMAKE_<LANG>_COMPILER_EXTERNAL_TOOLCHAIN may be set to a path to a path to the external toolchain and will be passed to the compiler driver if supported.

This variable may only be set in a toolchain file specified by the CMAKE_TOOLCHAIN_FILE (page 633) variable.

CMAKE_<LANG>_COMPILER_TARGET

The target for cross-compiling, if supported.

Some compiler drivers are inherently cross-compilers, such as clang and QNX qcc. These compiler drivers support a command-line argument to specify the target to cross-compile for.

This variable may only be set in a toolchain file specified by the CMAKE_TOOLCHAIN_FILE (page 633) variable.

CMAKE_<LANG>_COMPILER_VERSION

Compiler version string.

Compiler version in major[.minor[.patch[.tweak]]] format. This variable is not guaranteed to be defined for all compilers or languages.

CMAKE_<LANG>_CREATE_SHARED_LIBRARY

Rule variable to create a shared library.

This is a rule variable that tells CMake how to create a shared library for the language <LANG>.

CMAKE_<LANG>_CREATE_SHARED_MODULE

Rule variable to create a shared module.

This is a rule variable that tells CMake how to create a shared library for the language <LANG>.

CMAKE_<LANG>_CREATE_STATIC_LIBRARY

Rule variable to create a static library.

This is a rule variable that tells CMake how to create a static library for the language <LANG>.

CMAKE_<LANG>_FLAGS_DEBUG

Flags for Debug build type or configuration.

<LANG> flags used when CMAKE_BUILD_TYPE is Debug.

CMAKE_<LANG>_FLAGS_MINSIZEREL

Flags for MinSizeRel build type or configuration.

<LANG> flags used when CMAKE_BUILD_TYPE is MinSizeRel.Short for minimum size release.

CMAKE_<LANG>_FLAGS_RELEASE

Flags for Release build type or configuration.

<LANG> flags used when CMAKE_BUILD_TYPE is Release

CMAKE_<LANG>_FLAGS_RELWITHDEBINFO

Flags for RelWithDebInfo type or configuration.

<LANG> flags used when CMAKE_BUILD_TYPE is RelWithDebInfo. Short for Release With Debug Information.

CMAKE_<LANG>_FLAGS

Flags for all build types.

<LANG> flags used regardless of the value of CMAKE_BUILD_TYPE.

CMAKE_<LANG>_IGNORE_EXTENSIONS

File extensions that should be ignored by the build.

This is a list of file extensions that may be part of a project for a given language but are not compiled.

CMAKE_<LANG>_IMPLICIT_INCLUDE_DIRECTORIES

Directories implicitly searched by the compiler for header files.

CMake does not explicitly specify these directories on compiler command lines for language <LANG>. This prevents system include directories from being treated as user include directories on some compilers.

CMAKE_<LANG>_IMPLICIT_LINK_DIRECTORIES

Implicit linker search path detected for language <LANG>.

Compilers typically pass directories containing language runtime libraries and default library search paths when they invoke a linker. These paths are implicit linker search directories for the compiler's language. CMake automatically detects these directories for each language and reports the results in this variable.

When a library in one of these directories is given by full path to target_link_libraries() CMake will generate the -l<name> form on link lines to ensure the linker searches its implicit directories for the library. Note that some toolchains read implicit directories from an environment variable such as LIBRARY_PATH so keep its value consistent when operating in a given build tree.

CMAKE_<LANG>_IMPLICIT_LINK_FRAMEWORK_DIRECTORIES

Implicit linker framework search path detected for language <LANG>.

These paths are implicit linker framework search directories for the compiler's language. CMake automatically detects these directories for each language and reports the results in this variable.

CMAKE_<LANG>_IMPLICIT_LINK_LIBRARIES

Implicit link libraries and flags detected for language <LANG>.

Compilers typically pass language runtime library names and other flags when they invoke a linker. These flags are implicit link options for the compiler's language. CMake automatically detects these libraries and flags for each language and reports the results in this variable.

CMAKE_<LANG>_LIBRARY_ARCHITECTURE

Target architecture library directory name detected for <lang>.

If the <lang> compiler passes to the linker an architecture-specific system library search directory such as <prefix>/lib/<arch> this variable contains the <arch> name if/as detected by CMake.

CMAKE_<LANG>_LINKER_PREFERENCE_PROPAGATES

True if CMAKE_<LANG>_LINKER_PREFERENCE propagates across targets.

This is used when CMake selects a linker language for a target. Languages compiled directly into the target are always considered. A language compiled into static libraries linked by the target is considered if this variable is true.

CMAKE_<LANG>_LINKER_PREFERENCE

Preference value for linker language selection.

The "linker language" for executable, shared library, and module targets is the language whose compiler will invoke the linker. The LINKER_LANGUAGE target property sets the language explicitly. Otherwise, the linker language is that whose linker preference value is highest among languages compiled and linked into the target. See also the CMAKE_<LANG>_LINKER_PREFERENCE_PROPAGATES variable.

CMAKE_<LANG>_LINK_EXECUTABLE

Rule variable to link an executable.

Rule variable to link an executable for the given language.

CMAKE_<LANG>_OUTPUT_EXTENSION

Extension for the output of a compile for a single file.

This is the extension for an object file for the given <LANG>. For example .obj for C on Windows.

CMAKE_<LANG>_PLATFORM_ID

An internal variable subject to change.

This is used in determining the platform and is subject to change.

CMAKE_<LANG>_SIMULATE_ID

Identification string of "simulated" compiler.

Some compilers simulate other compilers to serve as drop-in replacements. When CMake detects such a compiler it sets this variable to what would have been the CMAKE_<LANG>_COMPILER_ID for the simulated compiler.

CMAKE_<LANG>_SIMULATE_VERSION

Version string of "simulated" compiler.

Some compilers simulate other compilers to serve as drop-in replacements. When CMake detects such a compiler it sets this variable to what would have been the CMAKE_<LANG>_COMPILER_VERSION for the simulated compiler.

CMAKE_<LANG>_SIZEOF_DATA_PTR

Size of pointer-to-data types for language <LANG>.

This holds the size (in bytes) of pointer-to-data types in the target platform ABI. It is defined for languages C and CXX (C++).

CMAKE_<LANG>_SOURCE_FILE_EXTENSIONS

Extensions of source files for the given language.

This is the list of extensions for a given language's source files.

CMAKE_USER_MAKE_RULES_OVERRIDE_<LANG>

Specify a CMake file that overrides platform information for <LANG>.

This is a language-specific version of CMAKE_USER_MAKE_RULES_OVERRIDE loaded only when enabling language <LANG>.

C.7.6 Variables for CTest

CTEST_BINARY_DIRECTORY

Specify the CTest `BuildDirectory` setting in a `ctest(1)` (page 240) dashboard client script.

CTEST_BUILD_COMMAND

Specify the CTest `MakeCommand` setting in a `ctest(1)` (page 240) dashboard client script.

CTEST_BUILD_NAME

Specify the CTest `BuildName` setting in a `ctest(1)` (page 240) dashboard client script.

CTEST_BZR_COMMAND

Specify the CTest `BZRCommand` setting in a `ctest(1)` (page 240) dashboard client script.

CTEST_BZR_UPDATE_OPTIONS

Specify the CTest `BZRUpdateOptions` setting in a `ctest(1)` (page 240) dashboard client script.

CTEST_CHECKOUT_COMMAND

Tell the `ctest_start()` (page 354) command how to checkout or initialize the source directory in a `ctest(1)` (page 240) dashboard client script.

CTEST_CONFIGURATION_TYPE

Specify the CTest `DefaultCTestConfigurationType` setting in a `ctest(1)` (page 240) dashboard client script.

CTEST_CONFIGURE_COMMAND

Specify the CTest `ConfigureCommand` setting in a `ctest(1)` (page 240) dashboard client script.

CTEST_COVERAGE_COMMAND

Specify the CTest `CoverageCommand` setting in a `ctest(1)` (page 240) dashboard client script.

Cobertura

Using Cobertura[66] as the coverage generation within your multi-module Java project can generate a series of XML files.

The Cobertura Coverage parser expects to read the coverage data from a single XML file which contains the coverage data for all modules. Cobertura has a program with the ability to merge given cobertura.ser files and then another program to generate a combined XML file from the previous merged file. For command line testing, this can be done by hand prior to CTest looking for the coverage files. For script builds, set the CTEST_COVERAGE_COMMAND variable to point to a file which will perform these same steps, such as a .sh or .bat file.

```
set(CTEST_COVERAGE_COMMAND .../run-coverage-and-consolidate.sh)
```

---

[66] http://cobertura.github.io/cobertura/

---

where the run-coverage-and-consolidate.sh script is perhaps created by the configure_file() (page 282) command and might contain the following code:

```
#!/usr/bin/env bash
CoberturaFiles="$(find "/path/to/source" -name "cobertura.ser")"
SourceDirs="$(find "/path/to/source" -name "java" -type d)"
cobertura-merge --datafile coberturamerge.ser $CoberturaFiles
cobertura-report --datafile coberturamerge.ser --destination . \
                --format xml $SourceDirs
```

The script uses find to capture the paths to all of the cobertura.ser files found below the project's source directory. It keeps the list of files and supplies it as an argument to the cobertura-merge program. The --datafile argument signifies where the result of the merge will be kept.

The combined coberturamerge.ser file is then used to generate the XML report using the cobertura-report program. The call to the cobertura-report program requires some named arguments.

--datafila path to the merged .ser file

--destination path to put the output files(s)

--format file format to write output in: xml or html

The rest of the supplied arguments consist of the full paths to the /src/main/java directories of each module within the souce tree. These directories are needed and should not be forgotten.

CTEST_COVERAGE_EXTRA_FLAGS

Specify the CTest CoverageExtraFlags setting in a ctest(1) (page 240) dashboard client script.

CTEST_CURL_OPTIONS

Specify the CTest CurlOptions setting in a ctest(1) (page 240) dashboard client script.

CTEST_CVS_CHECKOUT

Deprecated. Use CTEST_CHECKOUT_COMMAND (page 676) instead.

CTEST_CVS_COMMAND

Specify the CTest CVSCommand setting in a ctest(1) (page 240) dashboard client script.

CTEST_CVS_UPDATE_OPTIONS

Specify the CTest CVSUpdateOptions setting in a ctest(1) (page 240) dashboard client script.

CTEST_DROP_LOCATION

Specify the CTest DropLocation setting in a ctest (1) (page 240) dashboard client script.

CTEST_DROP_METHOD

Specify the CTest DropMethod setting in a ctest (1) (page 240) dashboard client script.

CTEST_DROP_SITE

Specify the CTest DropSite setting in a ctest (1) (page 240) dashboard client script.

CTEST_DROP_SITE_CDASH

Specify the CTest IsCDash setting in a ctest (1) (page 240) dashboard client script.

CTEST_DROP_SITE_PASSWORD

Specify the CTest DropSitePassword setting in a ctest (1) (page 240) dashboard client script.

CTEST_DROP_SITE_USER

Specify the CTest DropSiteUser setting in a ctest (1) (page 240) dashboard client script.

CTEST_GIT_COMMAND

Specify the CTest GITCommand setting in a ctest (1) (page 240) dashboard client script.

CTEST_GIT_UPDATE_CUSTOM

Specify the CTest GITUpdateCustom setting in a ctest (1) (page 240) dashboard client script.

CTEST_GIT_UPDATE_OPTIONS

Specify the CTest GITUpdateOptions setting in a ctest (1) (page 240) dashboard client script.

CTEST_HG_COMMAND

Specify the CTest HGCommand setting in a ctest (1) (page 240) dashboard client script.

CTEST_HG_UPDATE_OPTIONS

Specify the CTest `HGUpdateOptions` setting in a `ctest(1)` (page 240) dashboard client script.

CTEST_MEMORYCHECK_COMMAND

Specify the CTest `MemoryCheckCommand` setting in a `ctest(1)` (page 240) dashboard client script.

CTEST_MEMORYCHECK_COMMAND_OPTIONS

Specify the CTest `MemoryCheckCommandOptions` setting in a `ctest(1)` (page 240) dashboard client script.

CTEST_MEMORYCHECK_SANITIZER_OPTIONS

Specify the CTest `MemoryCheckSanitizerOptions` setting in a `ctest(1)` (page 240) dashboard client script.

CTEST_MEMORYCHECK_SUPPRESSIONS_FILE

Specify the CTest `MemoryCheckSuppressionFile` setting in a `ctest(1)` (page 240) dashboard client script.

CTEST_MEMORYCHECK_TYPE

Specify the CTest `MemoryCheckType` setting in a `ctest(1)` (page 240) dashboard client script. Valid values are Valgrind, Purify, BoundsChecker, and ThreadSanitizer, AddressSanitizer, MemorySanitizer, and UndefinedBehaviorSanitizer.

CTEST_NIGHTLY_START_TIME

Specify the CTest `NightlyStartTime` setting in a `ctest(1)` (page 240) dashboard client script.

CTEST_P4_CLIENT

Specify the CTest `P4Client` setting in a `ctest(1)` (page 240) dashboard client script.

CTEST_P4_COMMAND

Specify the CTest `P4Command` setting in a `ctest(1)` (page 240) dashboard client script.

CTEST_P4_OPTIONS

Specify the CTest P4Options setting in a ctest(1) (page 240) dashboard client script.

CTEST_P4_UPDATE_OPTIONS

Specify the CTest P4UpdateOptions setting in a ctest(1) (page 240) dashboard client script.

CTEST_SCP_COMMAND

Specify the CTest SCPCommand setting in a ctest(1) (page 240) dashboard client script.

CTEST_SITE

Specify the CTest Site setting in a ctest(1) (page 240) dashboard client script.

CTEST_SOURCE_DIRECTORY

Specify the CTest SourceDirectory setting in a ctest(1) (page 240) dashboard client script.

CTEST_SVN_COMMAND

Specify the CTest SVNCommand setting in a ctest(1) (page 240) dashboard client script.

CTEST_SVN_OPTIONS

Specify the CTest SVNOptions setting in a ctest(1) (page 240) dashboard client script.

CTEST_SVN_UPDATE_OPTIONS

Specify the CTest SVNUpdateOptions setting in a ctest(1) (page 240) dashboard client script.

CTEST_TEST_TIMEOUT

Specify the CTest TimeOut setting in a ctest(1) (page 240) dashboard client script.

CTEST_TRIGGER_SITE

Specify the CTest TriggerSite setting in a ctest(1) (page 240) dashboard client script.

CTEST_UPDATE_COMMAND

Specify the CTest `UpdateCommand` setting in a `ctest(1)` (page 240) dashboard client script.

CTEST_UPDATE_OPTIONS

Specify the CTest `UpdateOptions` setting in a `ctest(1)` (page 240) dashboard client script.

CTEST_UPDATE_VERSION_ONLY

Specify the CTest `UpdateVersionOnly` setting in a `ctest(1)` (page 240) dashboard client script.

CTEST_USE_LAUNCHERS

Specify the CTest `UseLaunchers` setting in a `ctest(1)` (page 240) dashboard client script.

C.7.7 Variables for CPack

CPACK_ABSOLUTE_DESTINATION_FILES

List of files which have been installed using an ABSOLUTE DESTINATION path.

This variable is a Read-Only variable which is set internally by CPack during installation and before packaging using CMAKE_ABSOLUTE_DESTINATION_FILES defined in cmake_install.cmake scripts. The value can be used within CPack project configuration file and/or CPack<GEN>.cmake file of <GEN> generator.

CPACK_COMPONENT_INCLUDE_TOPLEVEL_DIRECTORY

Boolean toggle to include/exclude top level directory (component case).

Similar usage as CPACK_INCLUDE_TOPLEVEL_DIRECTORY but for the component case. See CPACK_INCLUDE_TOPLEVEL_DIRECTORY documentation for the detail.

CPACK_ERROR_ON_ABSOLUTE_INSTALL_DESTINATION

Ask CPack to error out as soon as a file with absolute INSTALL DESTINATION is encountered.

The fatal error is emitted before the installation of the offending file takes place. Some CPack generators, like NSIS,enforce this internally. This variable triggers the definition ofC-MAKE_ERROR_ON_ABSOLUTE_INSTALL_DESTINATION when CPack runsVariables common to all CPack generators

CPACK_INCLUDE_TOPLEVEL_DIRECTORY

Boolean toggle to include/exclude top level directory.

When preparing a package CPack installs the item under the so-called top level directory. The purpose of is to include (set to 1 or ON or TRUE) the top level directory in the package or not (set to 0 or OFF or FALSE).

Each CPack generator has a built-in default value for this variable. E.g. Archive generators (ZIP, TGZ, ...) includes the top level whereas RPM or DEB don't. The user may override the default value by setting this variable.

There is a similar variable CPACK_COMPONENT_INCLUDE_TOPLEVEL_DIRECTORY which may be used to override the behavior for the component packaging case which may have different default value for historical (now backward compatibility) reason.

CPACK_INSTALL_SCRIPT

Extra CMake script provided by the user.

If set this CMake script will be executed by CPack during its local [CPack-private] installation which is done right before packaging the files. The script is not called by e.g.: make install.

CPACK_PACKAGING_INSTALL_PREFIX

The prefix used in the built package.

Each CPack generator has a default value (like /usr). This default value may be overwritten from the CMake-Lists.txt or the cpack command line by setting an alternative value.

e.g. set(CPACK_PACKAGING_INSTALL_PREFIX "/opt")

This is not the same purpose as CMAKE_INSTALL_PREFIX which is used when installing from the build tree without building a package.

CPACK_SET_DESTDIR

Boolean toggle to make CPack use DESTDIR mechanism when packaging.

DESTDIR means DESTination DIRectory. It is commonly used by makefile users in order to install software at non-default location. It is a basic relocation mechanism that should not be used on Windows (see CMAKE_INSTALL_PREFIX documentation). It is usually invoked like this:

```
make DESTDIR=/home/john install
```

which will install the concerned software using the installation prefix, e.g. "/usr/local" prepended with the DESTDIR value which finally gives "/home/john/usr/local". When preparing a package, CPack first installs the items to be packaged in a local (to the build tree) directory by using the same DESTDIR mechanism. Nevertheless, if CPACK_SET_DESTDIR is set then CPack will set DESTDIR before doing the local install. The most noticeable difference is that without CPACK_SET_DESTDIR, CPack uses CPACK_PACKAGING_INSTALL_PREFIX as a prefix whereas with CPACK_SET_DESTDIR set, CPack will use CMAKE_INSTALL_PREFIX as a prefix.

Manually setting CPACK_SET_DESTDIR may help (or simply be necessary) if some install rules uses absolute DESTINATION (see CMake INSTALL command). However, starting with CPack/CMake 2.8.3 RPM and DEB installers tries to handle DESTDIR automatically so that it is seldom necessary for the user to set it.

CPACK_WARN_ON_ABSOLUTE_INSTALL_DESTINATION

Ask CPack to warn each time a file with absolute INSTALL DESTINATION is encountered.

This variable triggers the definition of CMAKE_WARN_ON_ABSOLUTE_INSTALL_DESTINATION when CPack runs cmake_install.cmake scripts.

A

ALL_BUILD
    target, 10, 91
ANT, 3
autoconf, 3
autoconf
    converting to CMake, 99

B

batch commands, 87
binary packages, 123
Borland compiler, 4, 19, 217
build, *see* in-source build, *see* out-of-source build
build
    configurations, 28, 57
build platform, 103
building your project, 16

C

cache
    variables, 19
cache
    Force option, 16
    variable behavior, 27
cache property
    ADVANCED, **620**
    HELPSTRING, **620**
    MODIFIED, **620**
    STRINGS, 26, **620**
    TYPE, **621**
    VALUE, **621**
case sensitivity, 6
ccmake, *see* manual
    running CMake, 10
CDash, 166
CDash
    adding notes, 176
    automatic submission, 177
    backup, 199

client setup, 172
creating a new project, 169
email, 193
expected builds, 193
filtering errors/warnings, 175
logging, 198
mobile support, 198
server setup, 187
sites, 195
specifying the server, 174
submitting results, 169
subprojects, 202
timing, 198
upgrading, 199
cmake, *see* manual
    running CMake, 13
CMake
    benefits, 1
    compiler selection, 13
    extending, 218
    history, 2
    plugins, 218
    porting, 209
    structure, 19
    syntax, 6
    tutorial, 222
    versions, 37
CMake Modules, *see* modules
CMake Policies, *see* policies
cmake-gui, *see* manual
    running CMake, 9
code coverage, 169, 172
command
    add_compile_options, **269**, 273, 569
    add_custom_command, 52, 65, 66, 88, 89, 91, 101, 106, 109, 120, 230, 232, **269**, 274, 287, 551, 553, 557
    add_custom_target, 22, 89, 91, 101, 109, 120, 270, 271, **272**, 272, 287, 314, 552
    add_definitions, 74, 79, 269, **272**, 339, 568
    add_dependencies, 68, **273**, 555
    add_executable, 7, 8, 22, 30, 43, 46, 48, 52, 57, 65, 66,

68, 71, 79, 89, 96, 98, 99, 101, 109, 113, 114, 116, 120, 124, 158, 163, 164, 207, 215, 223, 225, 230, 231, 270, 271, **273**, 276, 278, 314, 338–340, 343, 360, 551, 552, 574, 590

add_library, 22, 30, 38, 40, 49, 50, 52, 57, 65, 67, 79, 99, 101, 113, 207, 215, 219, 225, 230, 232, 271, **274**, 276, 314, 338–340, 343, 360, 552, 590

add_subdirectory, 24, 30, 34, 42, 43, 67, 80, 95, 100, 160, 225, **277**, 636, 637

add_test, 32, 158, 160, 162, 163, 172, 175, 207, 227, 231, **277**, 423

aux_source_directory, **278**

break, 35, **278**

build_command, 252, **279**

build_name, **346**, 551

cmake_host_system_information, **279**

cmake_minimum_required, 8, 37, 42, 44, 45, 183, 223, 231, **280**, 281, 282, 537

cmake_policy, 42–45, **280**, 303, 537, 548, 556–559

configure_file, 64, 100, 113, 145, 224, 229, 231, 270, **282**, 288, 384, 386, 558, 677

configure_package_config_file, 383, **384**, 386

cpack_add_component, **391**, 403

cpack_add_component_group, **392**

cpack_add_install_type, **393**

cpack_configure_downloads, **393**, 403

cpack_ifw_add_repository, 400, **402**, 403

cpack_ifw_configure_component, **401**

cpack_ifw_configure_component_group, **401**

create_test_sourcelist, 163, **282**

ctest_build, 183, 205–207, 252, **351**

ctest_configure, 183, 205, 207, 252, **352**

ctest_coverage, 253, **352**

ctest_empty_binary_directory, 183, **352**

ctest_memcheck, 253, **353**

ctest_read_custom_files, **353**

ctest_run_script, **353**

ctest_sleep, **353**

ctest_start, 183, 205, 207, 249, **354**, 676

ctest_submit, 183, 205, 207, 255, **354**

ctest_test, 183, 205–207, 253, **355**

ctest_update, 205, 207, 249, **355**

ctest_upload, **356**

define_property, **283**, 312

else, 8, 30, **284**

elseif, 31, **284**

enable_language, **284**, 548, 556, 663

enable_testing, 278, **284**

endforeach, 96, **284**

endfunction, **285**

endif, 8, 30, 40, 45, 76, 219, 226, 231, **285**

endmacro, 34, **285**

endwhile, **285**

exec_program, 98, 286, **346**

execute_process, 106, **285**, 286

export, 67, **287**, 343, 347, 359, 551, 594, 641

export_library_dependencies, **346**, 551

ExternalData_Add_Target, 165

ExternalData_Add_Test, 165

file, 74, 98, 121, 270, **287**, 450, 557, 645

find_file, 26, 71, 106, **292**, 643, 644

find_library, 8, 47, 71, 77, 114, 116, **294**, 643, 644

find_package, 38–40, 71, 77, 78, 114, 281, **297**, 380, 385, 418, 537, 628, 639, 642–644

find_path, 71, 106, 114, **303**, 643, 644

find_program, 71, 88, 106, **306**, 639, 644

fltk_wrap_ui, **308**

foreach, 30, 32, 93, 96, 163, 164, **309**

function, 24, 30, 34, 282, **309**, 550

get_cmake_property, 125, **310**

get_directory_property, **310**

get_filename_component, 66, 117, 163, **310**, 450

get_property, 22, 23, **311**

get_source_file_property, **312**

get_target_property, 22, 109, **312**, 555

get_test_property, **312**

if, 8, 24, 30, 34, 35, 37, 40, 45, 76, 114, 219, 226, 231, 274, 276, **313**, 498, 537, 551, 558, 634

include, 25, 38–40, 64, 66, 76, 96, 99, 113, 124, 145, 158, 231, 233, 234, 281, **317**, 328, 537

include_directories, 39, 71, 114, 219, 224, 225, 230, 231, 269, **315**, 339, 570, 591, 644

include_external_msproject, **316**

include_regular_expression, 68, **316**

install, 55, 64, 66, 67, 113, 114, 116, 124, 227, 231, 287, 292, **317**, 319, 343, 347, 359, 551, 594, 645

install_files, 145, 322, **347**

install_programs, 322, **347**

install_targets, 322, **348**

link_directories, 47, **322**

link_libraries, **348**

list, 30, 165, **323**

load_cache, **324**

load_command, **324**, 550

macro, 30, 34, 228, 231, 282, **324**, 550

make_directory, 98, **349**

mark_as_advanced, 16, 26, **325**

math, **326**

message, 32, 34, **326**

option, 26, 79, 100, 226, 231, **326**

output_required_files, 68, **349**, 550

pkg_check_modules, **489**, 489, 491

pkg_search_module, 489, **490**, 491

project, 7, 10, 29, 42, 43, 56, 68, 101, 113, 114, 116, 124, 163, 212, 215, 219, 223, 231, **327**, 327, 328, 548, 556, 634, 636–638, 648, 663

protobuf_generate_cpp, **493**

qt_wrap_cpp, **328**

qt_wrap_ui, **328**

remove, 30, 163, 164, **349**

remove_definitions, **328**

return, 35, **328**

separate_arguments, 30, **328**

set, 7, 8, 15, 24, 25, 34, 39, 40, 52, 64, 68, 76, 93, 96,

113–115, 117, 118, 125, 145, 178, 181, 219, 224, 226, 231, 233, 234, **330**
set_directory_properties, **329**
set_property, 22, 23, 49, 65, 66, 79, 159, 161, 207, 274, 276, **329**, 570, 591, 599
set_source_files_properties, 39, 40, 52, **332**
set_target_properties, 22, 40, 55, 113, 114, 274, 276, **332**
set_tests_properties, 227, 231, **334**
site_name, 256, **334**
source_group, 101, **334**
string, 30, 35, 52, 291, **335**, 557, 558
subdir_depends, **349**, 549
subdirs, 160, **349**
target_compile_definitions, 269, 277, **338**, 339, 356, 554
target_compile_features, **338**, 560
target_compile_options, 276, **339**
target_include_directories, 269, 276, **339**, 339, 356, 591, 593
target_link_libraries, 22, 40, 46–48, 51, 52, 65, 67, 71, 114, 116, 207, 225, 231, 274–277, **340**, 356, 359, 498, 547, 552, 553, 592, 599
target_link_library, 8, 158
target_sources, 277, **342**
try_compile, 71, 73, 100, 107, 121, 219, **343**
try_run, 71, 73, 107, 120, 121, **344**
unset, **345**
use_mangled_mesa, **350**, 550
utility_source, 119, **350**, 551
variable_requires, **350**, 551
variable_watch, **345**
while, 30, 33, **345**
write_basic_package_version_file, 383, **385**, 385
write_file, **351**
command line
    running CMake, 13
comments, 29
comparison, 31
compile flags, 23
compiler specification, 13
compilers, 4, 212
compiling CMake, 5
conditional statements, 30
converting autoconf projects to CMake, 99
converting MakeFiles to CMake, 98
converting Visual Studio projects, 100
copying files, *see* file
CPack, 122
CPack
    components, 136
    DESTDIR, 128
    escape characters, 125
    generators, 126
    variables, 124
cross compiling, 101
cross compiling

hello world, 111
    system introspection, 107
CTest, 160
CTest
    advanced, 183
    building tests, 162
    options, 161
    properties, 159
    regular expressions, 159
    running the tests, 160
    variables, 182
custom commands, 85
custom targets, 91
CVS, 179
cygwin, 123, 144

D

Dart, *see* CDash
Debian, 123, 154
declspec, 51
dependencies, 68
dependency analysis, 14, 23
directory installation, 60
directory property
    ADDITIONAL_MAKE_CLEAN_FILES, **567**
    CACHE_VARIABLES, **568**
    CLEAN_NO_CUSTOM, **568**
    CMAKE_CONFIGURE_DEPENDS, **568**
    COMPILE_DEFINITIONS, 80, 273, **568**, 622
    COMPILE_DEFINITIONS_<CONFIG>, 554, 569, **622**
    COMPILE_OPTIONS, 269, **569**, 581
    DEFINITIONS, **569**
    EXCLUDE_FROM_ALL, 30, **569**
    IMPLICIT_DEPENDS_INCLUDE_TRANSFORM, **569**
    INCLUDE_DIRECTORIES, 49, 316, **570**, 591
    INCLUDE_REGULAR_EXPRESSION, **570**
    INTERPROCEDURAL_OPTIMIZATION, **571**
    INTERPROCEDURAL_OPTIMIZATION_<CONFIG>, **571**
    LINK_DIRECTORIES, **571**
    LISTFILE_STACK, **571**
    MACROS, **571**
    PARENT_DIRECTORY, **571**
    RULE_LAUNCH_COMPILE, **571**
    RULE_LAUNCH_CUSTOM, **572**
    RULE_LAUNCH_LINK, **572**
    TEST_INCLUDE_FILE, **572**
    VARIABLES, **572**
    VS_GLOBAL_SECTION_POST_<section>, **572**
    VS_GLOBAL_SECTION_PRE_<section>, **573**
directory structure, 8, 95
directory structure
    creating, 98
    properties, 23

E

editing CMakeLists files, 14
Emacs mode, 14
embedded devices, 101
environment variables, 1, 7, 14, 54
escape character, 29
executing programs, 98

F

false, 31
file
    component, 57
    copying, 87
    exists, 32
    globbing, 98
    installing, 55
    optional, 57
    permissions, 56
    properties, 23
    regular expressions, 62
    remove, 88
    rename, 59
filtering errors and warnings, 175
final pass, 21
flags, 14, 23, 54
flow control, 30
FLTK, 40, 117
Fortran, 212
function, 30

G

generator
    Borland Makefiles, **360**
    CodeBlocks, **364**
    CodeLite, **364**
    Eclipse CDT4, **365**
    Kate, **365**
    KDevelop3, **365**
    MinGW Makefiles, **360**, 360, 364–366
    MSYS Makefiles, **360**, 361
    Ninja, 252, **361**, 364–366
    NMake Makefiles, **361**, 364–366
    NMake Makefiles JOM, **361**
    Sublime Text 2, **366**
    Unix Makefiles, **361**, 364–366
    Visual Studio 10 2010, **362**, 635
    Visual Studio 11 2012, **363**
    Visual Studio 12 2013, **363**
    Visual Studio 14 2015, **363**
    Visual Studio 6, **361**, 582, 604, 605, 635
    Visual Studio 7, **361**, 635
    Visual Studio 7 .NET 2003, **362**
    Visual Studio 8 2005, **362**
    Visual Studio 9 2008, **362**
    Watcom WMake, **361**
    Xcode, **364**

global property
    ALLOW_DUPLICATE_CUSTOM_TARGETS, **559**
    AUTOGEN_TARGETS_FOLDER, **559**, 560, 575–577
    AUTOMOC_TARGETS_FOLDER, **559**
    CMAKE_C_KNOWN_FEATURES, 534, **560**, 667
    CMAKE_CXX_KNOWN_FEATURES, 534, **560**, 668
    DEBUG_CONFIGURATIONS, 48, 341, **563**
    DISABLED_FEATURES, **563**
    ECLIPSE_EXTRA_NATURES, **566**
    ENABLED_FEATURES, **564**
    ENABLED_LANGUAGES, **564**
    FIND_LIBRARY_USE_LIB64_PATHS, **564**
    FIND_LIBRARY_USE_OPENBSD_VERSIONING, **564**
    GLOBAL_DEPENDS_DEBUG_MODE, **564**
    GLOBAL_DEPENDS_NO_CYCLES, **565**
    IN_TRY_COMPILE, **565**
    JOB_POOLS, **565**, 565, 595, 596
    PACKAGES_FOUND, **565**
    PACKAGES_NOT_FOUND, **565**
    PREDEFINED_TARGETS_FOLDER, **566**
    REPORT_UNDEFINED_PROPERTIES, **566**
    RULE_LAUNCH_COMPILE, **566**
    RULE_LAUNCH_CUSTOM, **566**
    RULE_LAUNCH_LINK, **566**
    RULE_MESSAGES, **567**
    TARGET_ARCHIVES_MAY_BE_SHARED_LIBS, **567**
    TARGET_SUPPORTS_SHARED_LIBS, **567**
    USE_FOLDERS, **567**

H

header files, configured, 80
hello world, 7, 111
history of CMake, 2

I

in-source build, 8, 96
initial pass, 21
installation scripts, 62
installed file property
    CPACK_NEVER_OVERWRITE, **621**
    CPACK_PERMANENT, **621**
    CPACK_WIX_ACL, **621**
installing CMake
    Mac OS, 5
    UNIX, 5
    Windows, 5
installing files, *see* files

J

JAM, 3

K

KDE, 2

L

languages, 29, 212
LaTeX custom target, 91
lexicographic comparison, 31
libraries, 50
libraries
    API changes, 54
    exporting, 67
    importing, 65
    installing prerequisites, 63
    module, 22
    RPATH, 54
    shared, 22
    shared vs static, 50
    soname, 54
    static, 22
    versions, 54
library configurations, 48
linking
    Windows, 48
linking
    libraries, 46
    system libraries, 47
loaded commands, 218, 221
looping constructs, 30

M

Mac OS X, *see* Xcode
Mac OS X
    drag and drop installer, 147
    Package Maker, 147
    Package Makers, 123
    relocatable applications, 63
macros, 34
MakeFiles, 19, 28
Makefiles
    build configurations, 28
manual
    ccmake(1), **263**
    cmake(1), **235**, 279, 360, 364, 495, 498, 630, 633, 647
    cmake-buildsystem(7), 269, 273–275, 316, 338–340, 342, 343, 569, 570, 580, 581, 591, 593–595, 599, 622
    cmake-commands(7), 238, 245, 259, 262, 265, 266, **269**
    cmake-compile-features(7), 339, 357, 534, 560, 578, 579, 581, 583, 584, 593, 667, 668
    cmake-generator-expressions(7), 88, 269–271, 274, 275, 278, 291, 316, 320, 338–340, 342, 343, **356**, 552, 554, 555, 557, 569, 570, 576, 580, 581, 591–595, 599, 619, 622
    cmake-generators(7), 291, **360**
    cmake-gui(1), **261**, 301, 360
    cmake-language(7), 248, 558
    cmake-modules(7), 77, 78, 239, 245, 246, 259, 262, 266, **366**
    cmake-packages(7), 301, 302
    cmake-policies(7), 37, 239, 246, 259, 262, 266, 280, **537**
    cmake-properties(7), 239, 246, 259, 260, 262, 263, 266, **559**
    cmake-qt(7), 495, 575–577
    cmake-variables(7), 24, 88, 239, 240, 246, 260, 263, 266, 267, **623**
    cpack(1), **257**
    ctest(1), **240**, 277, 630, 675–681
microcontroller, 115
MinGW, 10, 117
module
    AddFileDependencies, **366**
    BundleUtilities, **366**
    CheckCCompilerFlag, **369**
    CheckCSourceCompiles, **369**
    CheckCSourceRuns, **370**
    CheckCXXCompilerFlag, **370**, 526
    CheckCXXSourceCompiles, **371**
    CheckCXXSourceRuns, **371**
    CheckCXXSymbolExists, **371**
    CheckFortranFunctionExists, **372**
    CheckFortranSourceCompiles, **372**
    CheckFunctionExists, **373**
    CheckIncludeFile, **373**
    CheckIncludeFileCXX, **373**
    CheckIncludeFiles, **374**
    CheckLanguage, **374**
    CheckLibraryExists, **375**
    CheckPrototypeDefinition, **375**
    CheckStructHasMember, **376**
    CheckSymbolExists, **376**
    CheckTypeSize, **377**
    CheckVariableExists, **377**
    CMakeAddFortranSubdirectory, **378**
    CMakeBackwardCompatibilityCXX, **378**
    CMakeDependentOption, **379**
    CMakeDetermineVSServicePack, **379**
    CMakeExpandImportedTargets, **380**
    CMakeFindDependencyMacro, **380**
    CMakeFindFrameworks, **380**
    CMakeFindPackageMode, **380**
    CMakeForceCompiler, **381**
    CMakeGraphVizOptions, **381**
    CMakePackageConfigHelpers, 299, **383**
    CMakeParseArguments, **387**
    CMakePrintHelpers, **388**
    CMakePrintSystemInformation, **388**
    CMakePushCheckState, **389**
    CMakeVerifyManifest, **389**
    CPack, **411**
    CPackBundle, **389**
    CPackComponent, **390**
    CPackCygwin, **394**
    CPackDeb, **394**
    CPackDMG, **398**
    CPackIFW, **399**
    CPackNSIS, **404**
    CPackPackageMaker, **405**

CPackRPM, **406**
CPackWIX, **415**
CTest, 248–256, 278, 279, **419**
CTestScriptMode, **420**
CTestUseLaunchers, 252, **420**
Dart, **420**
DeployQt4, **421**
Documentation, **422**
ExternalData, **422**
ExternalProject, **425**
FeatureSummary, **428**
FindALSA, **432**
FindArmadillo, **432**
FindASPELL, **433**
FindAVIFile, **433**
FindBacktrace, **435**
FindBISON, **433**
FindBLAS, **434**
FindBoost, **435**
FindBullet, **438**
FindBZip2, **439**
FindCABLE, **439**
FindCoin3D, **439**
FindCUDA, **440**
FindCups, **445**
FindCURL, **446**
FindCurses, **446**
FindCVS, **446**
FindCxxTest, **447**
FindCygwin, **449**
FindDart, **449**
FindDCMTK, **449**
FindDevIL, **449**
FindDoxygen, **449**
FindEXPAT, **450**
FindFLEX, **450**
FindFLTK, **452**
FindFLTK2, **451**
FindFreetype, **452**
FindGCCXML, **453**
FindGDAL, **453**
FindGettext, **453**
FindGIF, **454**
FindGit, **454**
FindGLEW, **455**
FindGLUT, **455**
FindGnuplot, **455**
FindGnuTLS, **456**
FindGTest, **456**
FindGTK, **458**
FindGTK2, **457**
FindHDF5, **458**
FindHg, **459**
FindHSPELL, **460**
FindHTMLHelp, **460**
FindIce, **460**
FindIcotool, **462**

FindImageMagick, **462**
FindITK, **463**
FindJasper, **463**
FindJava, **463**
FindJNI, **464**
FindJPEG, **465**
FindKDE3, **465**
FindKDE4, **467**
FindLAPACK, **467**
FindLATEX, **467**
FindLibArchive, **468**
FindLibLZMA, **468**
FindLibXml2, **468**
FindLibXslt, **469**
FindLua, **470**
FindLua50, **469**
FindLua51, **469**
FindMatlab, **470**
FindMFC, **470**
FindMotif, **471**
FindMPEG, **471**
FindMPEG2, **471**
FindMPI, **472**
FindOpenAL, **473**
FindOpenCL, **473**
FindOpenGL, **473**
FindOpenMP, **474**
FindOpenSceneGraph, **474**
FindOpenSSL, **476**
FindOpenThreads, **476**
Findosg, **481**
Findosg_functions, **477**
FindosgAnimation, **476**
FindosgDB, **477**
FindosgFX, **477**
FindosgGA, **478**
FindosgIntrospection, **478**
FindosgManipulator, **479**
FindosgParticle, **479**
FindosgPresentation, **480**
FindosgProducer, **480**
FindosgQt, **481**
FindosgShadow, **481**
FindosgSim, **482**
FindosgTerrain, **482**
FindosgText, **483**
FindosgUtil, **483**
FindosgViewer, **484**
FindosgVolume, **484**
FindosgWidget, **485**
FindPackageHandleStandardArgs, **485**
FindPackageMessage, **487**
FindPerl, **488**
FindPerlLibs, **487**
FindPHP4, **488**
FindPhysFS, **488**
FindPike, **488**

FindPkgConfig, **489**
FindPNG, **491**
FindPostgreSQL, **491**
FindProducer, **492**
FindProtobuf, **492**
FindPythonInterp, **493**
FindPythonLibs, **494**
FindQt, **500**
FindQt3, **494**
FindQt4, **495**, 575–577, 615, 616
FindQuickTime, **500**
FindRTI, **500**
FindRuby, **501**
FindSDL, **503**
FindSDL_image, **501**
FindSDL_mixer, **502**
FindSDL_net, **502**
FindSDL_sound, **504**
FindSDL_ttf, **505**
FindSelfPackers, **505**
FindSquish, **505**
FindSubversion, **507**
FindSWIG, **508**
FindTCL, **508**
FindTclsh, **509**
FindTclStub, **509**
FindThreads, **510**
FindTIFF, **510**
FindUnixCommands, **511**
FindVTK, **511**
FindWget, **511**
FindWish, **511**
FindwxWidgets, **511**
FindwxWindows, **513**
FindX11, **514**
FindXercesC, **514**
FindXMLRPC, **515**
FindZLIB, **516**
FortranCInterface, **516**
GenerateExportHeader, 52, **518**
GetPrerequisites, **521**
GNUInstallDirs, **523**, 646
InstallRequiredSystemLibraries, **524**
MacroAddFileDependencies, **525**
ProcessorCount, 352, **525**
SelectLibraryConfigurations, **525**
SquishTestScript, **526**
TestBigEndian, **526**
TestCXXAcceptsFlag, **526**
TestForANSIForScope, **526**
TestForANSIStreamHeaders, **527**
TestForSSTREAM, **527**
TestForSTDNamespace, **527**
Use_wxWindows, **533**
UseEcos, **527**
UseJava, **528**
UseJavaClassFilelist, **527**

UseJavaSymlinks, **531**
UsePkgConfig, **531**
UseSWIG, **532**
UsewxWidgets, **533**
WriteBasicConfigVersionFile, **533**
WriteCompilerDetectionHeader, **534**
modules, 37
modules
    find, 38
    find conventions, 78
    find<Package>Config.cmake, 78
    path, 37
    system introspection, 38, 73
modules utility, 38

N

NMake, 19
not found, 72
NSIS, 123, 126, 128
Nullsoft Installer, 123
numeric comparison, 31

O

operator precedence, 31
operators, 31
out-of-source build, 8, 96

P

package configuration file, 81
platform, 211
platforms, 4
PLEASE FILL OUT, 108
plugins, 50
policies, 40
policies
    setting, 41
    stack, 42
    support multiple versions, 45
policy
    CMP0000, **537**
    CMP0001, **538**, 639
    CMP0002, 42, **538**
    CMP0003, 43, 342, **539**
    CMP0004, 342, **540**
    CMP0005, **540**
    CMP0006, **541**
    CMP0007, **541**
    CMP0008, **541**
    CMP0009, 289, **542**
    CMP0010, **542**, 558
    CMP0011, 281, **542**
    CMP0012, **543**
    CMP0013, **543**
    CMP0014, **543**
    CMP0015, **544**
    CMP0016, **544**

CMP0017, **544**
CMP0018, **545**
CMP0019, **545**
CMP0020, **545**
CMP0021, **546**
CMP0022, 322, 341, 342, **546**, 594
CMP0023, **547**
CMP0024, **547**
CMP0025, **548**, 647
CMP0026, **548**
CMP0027, **548**
CMP0028, **549**
CMP0029, 349, **549**
CMP0030, 350, **550**
CMP0031, 324, **550**
CMP0032, 349, **550**
CMP0033, 347, **550**
CMP0034, 350, **551**
CMP0035, 351, **551**
CMP0036, 346, **551**
CMP0037, **552**
CMP0038, **552**
CMP0039, **552**
CMP0040, **553**
CMP0041, **553**
CMP0042, **553**
CMP0043, **554**, 622, 623
CMP0044, **554**
CMP0045, **555**
CMP0046, **555**
CMP0047, **555**, 647
CMP0048, 327, **556**
CMP0049, **556**
CMP0050, **556**
CMP0051, **557**
CMP0052, **557**
CMP0053, 542, **557**
CMP0054, 315, **558**
portability issues, 87
portability of code, 73
porting CMake, 209
POSIX systems, 211
procedure definitions, 30
project
    languages, 29
    name, 29
prop_cache
    type, 24
prop_dir
    ADDITIONAL_MAKE_CLEAN_FILES, 23
    EXCLUDE_FROM_ALL, 23
    LISTFILE_STACK, 23
prop_test
    PASS_REGULAR_EXPRESSION, 227
proxies, 175
purify, 68, 173, 175

Q
qmake, 3
qt, 1, 39
quoting, 6

R
regression testing, 157
regular expressions, 31, 35, 68, 161
relocatable packages, 63, 123
required package, 83
RPATH, 54, 121
RPM, 123, 155
rule variables, 215
running CMake, 8
    ccmake, 10
    cmake, 13
    cmake-gui, 9
    command line, 13

S
SCons, 3
shell commands, 87
source file property
    ABSTRACT, **615**
    AUTORCC_OPTIONS, 577, **615**
    AUTOUIC_OPTIONS, 576, **615**
    COMPILE_DEFINITIONS, 49, 273, **616**
    COMPILE_DEFINITIONS_<CONFIG>, **623**
    COMPILE_FLAGS, **616**
    EXTERNAL_OBJECT, **616**
    Fortran_FORMAT, **617**
    GENERATED, **617**
    HEADER_FILE_ONLY, **617**
    KEEP_EXTENSION, **617**
    LABELS, **617**
    LANGUAGE, **617**
    LOCATION, **618**
    MACOSX_PACKAGE_LOCATION, **618**
    OBJECT_DEPENDS, **618**
    OBJECT_OUTPUTS, **618**
    SYMBOLIC, 271, **619**
    VS_DEPLOYMENT_CONTENT, **619**, 619
    VS_DEPLOYMENT_LOCATION, **619**
    VS_SHADER_ENTRYPOINT, **619**
    VS_SHADER_MODEL, **619**
    VS_SHADER_TYPE, **619**
    WRAP_EXCLUDE, **619**
    XCODE_EXPLICIT_FILE_TYPE, **620**, 620
    XCODE_LAST_KNOWN_FILE_TYPE, **620**, 620
source files, 23
source files
    generated, 90
source package, 127
source packages, 123
subprojects, 202
SWIG, 1, 38

syntax of CMake, 6, 29

T

target
    ALL_BUILD, 10, 91
target platform, 103
target property
    <CONFIG>_OUTPUT_NAME, **583**
    <CONFIG>_POSTFIX, **583**
    <LANG>_VISIBILITY_PRESET, 519, 521, **596**
    ALIASED_TARGET, **573**
    ANDROID_API, **573**, 656
    ANDROID_GUI, **573**, 656
    ARCHIVE_OUTPUT_DIRECTORY, 275, **574**
    ARCHIVE_OUTPUT_DIRECTORY_<CONFIG>, **574**
    ARCHIVE_OUTPUT_NAME, **574**
    ARCHIVE_OUTPUT_NAME_<CONFIG>, **574**
    AUTOGEN_TARGET_DEPENDS, **574**
    AUTOMOC, 559, 560, **575**, 575, 639, 657
    AUTOMOC_MOC_OPTIONS, **575**, 575, 657
    AUTORCC, **576**, 577, 616, 657
    AUTORCC_OPTIONS, **577**, 616, 657
    AUTOUIC, **576**, 576, 615, 657
    AUTOUIC_OPTIONS, **576**, 592, 615, 640, 658
    BUILD_WITH_INSTALL_RPATH, **577**
    BUNDLE, **577**
    BUNDLE_EXTENSION, **577**
    C_EXTENSIONS, **578**, 667
    C_STANDARD, 357, **578**, 578, 579, 667
    C_STANDARD_REQUIRED, **578**, 578, 667
    COMPATIBLE_INTERFACE_BOOL, **579**
    COMPATIBLE_INTERFACE_NUMBER_MAX, **579**
    COMPATIBLE_INTERFACE_NUMBER_MIN, **579**
    COMPATIBLE_INTERFACE_STRING, **580**, 640
    COMPILE_DEFINITIONS, 273, 338, 356, 554, **580**, 592, 622, 640
    COMPILE_DEFINITIONS_<CONFIG>, 554, 581, **622**
    COMPILE_FEATURES, 338, **581**, 593, 640
    COMPILE_FLAGS, **581**
    COMPILE_OPTIONS, 269, 339, 569, **581**, 593, 640
    COMPILE_PDB_NAME, **581**, 582, 604
    COMPILE_PDB_NAME_<CONFIG>, **582**, 604
    COMPILE_PDB_OUTPUT_DIRECTORY, **582**, 582, 605, 658
    COMPILE_PDB_OUTPUT_DIRECTORY_<CONFIG>, **582**, 605, 658
    CXX_EXTENSIONS, **583**, 668
    CXX_STANDARD, 357, **583**, 584, 668
    CXX_STANDARD_REQUIRED, 583, **584**, 668
    DEBUG_POSTFIX, **584**
    DEFINE_SYMBOL, **584**
    EchoString, **584**
    ENABLE_EXPORTS, **584**
    EXCLUDE_FROM_ALL, 274, 275, 319, **585**
    EXCLUDE_FROM_DEFAULT_BUILD, **585**
    EXCLUDE_FROM_DEFAULT_BUILD_<CONFIG>, **585**

    EXPORT_NAME, **585**
    FOLDER, 559, 560, **585**
    Fortran_FORMAT, **586**
    Fortran_MODULE_DIRECTORY, **586**
    FRAMEWORK, **586**
    GENERATOR_FILE_NAME, **586**
    GNUtoMS, **586**
    HAS_CXX, **587**
    IMPLICIT_DEPENDS_INCLUDE_TRANSFORM, **587**
    IMPORT_PREFIX, **591**
    IMPORT_SUFFIX, **591**
    IMPORTED, 65, 274, 275, 339, 357, 455, 495, 498, 516, 553, **590**
    IMPORTED_CONFIGURATIONS, **587**
    IMPORTED_IMPLIB, **588**
    IMPORTED_IMPLIB_<CONFIG>, **588**
    IMPORTED_LINK_DEPENDENT_LIBRARIES, **588**
    IMPORTED_LINK_DEPENDENT_LIBRARIES_<CONFIG>, **588**
    IMPORTED_LINK_INTERFACE_LANGUAGES, **588**
    IMPORTED_LINK_INTERFACE_LANGUAGES_<CONFIG>, **588**
    IMPORTED_LINK_INTERFACE_LIBRARIES, **589**
    IMPORTED_LINK_INTERFACE_LIBRARIES_<CONFIG>, **589**
    IMPORTED_LINK_INTERFACE_MULTIPLICITY, **589**
    IMPORTED_LINK_INTERFACE_MULTIPLICITY_<CONFIG>, **589**
    IMPORTED_LOCATION, 274, 275, **590**
    IMPORTED_LOCATION_<CONFIG>, 274, 275, **589**
    IMPORTED_NO_SONAME, **590**
    IMPORTED_NO_SONAME_<CONFIG>, **590**
    IMPORTED_SONAME, **591**
    IMPORTED_SONAME_<CONFIG>, **590**
    INCLUDE_DIRECTORIES, 316, 340, 356, 359, 570, **591**, 593, 640
    INSTALL_NAME_DIR, 554, **591**, 602
    INSTALL_RPATH, **592**, 602
    INSTALL_RPATH_USE_LINK_PATH, **592**
    INTERFACE_AUTOUIC_OPTIONS, **592**
    INTERFACE_COMPILE_DEFINITIONS, 49, 338, **592**
    INTERFACE_COMPILE_FEATURES, 338, **593**
    INTERFACE_COMPILE_OPTIONS, 339, **593**
    INTERFACE_INCLUDE_DIRECTORIES, 49, 319, 340, 553, 557, **593**
    INTERFACE_LINK_LIBRARIES, 341, 342, 359, **594**
    INTERFACE_POSITION_INDEPENDENT_CODE, 49, **594**
    INTERFACE_SOURCES, 343, **594**
    INTERFACE_SYSTEM_INCLUDE_DIRECTORIES, 340, **595**
    INTERPROCEDURAL_OPTIMIZATION, **595**
    INTERPROCEDURAL_OPTIMIZATION_<CONFIG>, **595**
    JOB_POOL_COMPILE, 566, **595**, 629

JOB_POOL_LINK, 566, **595**, 629
LABELS, **596**
LIBRARY_OUTPUT_DIRECTORY, 275, **596**
LIBRARY_OUTPUT_DIRECTORY_<CONFIG>, **596**
LIBRARY_OUTPUT_NAME, **597**
LIBRARY_OUTPUT_NAME_<CONFIG>, **597**
LINK_DEPENDS, **597**
LINK_DEPENDS_NO_SHARED, **597**
LINK_FLAGS, 22, **598**
LINK_FLAGS_<CONFIG>, **598**
LINK_INTERFACE_LIBRARIES, 48, 341, 342, 594, **598**
LINK_INTERFACE_LIBRARIES_<CONFIG>, 341, 594, **598**
LINK_INTERFACE_MULTIPLICITY, **599**
LINK_INTERFACE_MULTIPLICITY_<CONFIG>, **599**
LINK_LIBRARIES, 356, **599**
LINK_SEARCH_END_STATIC, **599**
LINK_SEARCH_START_STATIC, **600**
LINKER_LANGUAGE, **597**
LOCATION, **600**
LOCATION_<CONFIG>, **600**
MACOSX_BUNDLE, 274, **601**
MACOSX_BUNDLE_INFO_PLIST, **601**
MACOSX_FRAMEWORK_INFO_PLIST, **601**
MACOSX_RPATH, 553, 554, **602**, 662
MAP_IMPORTED_CONFIG_<CONFIG>, 357, **602**
NAME, **602**
NO_SONAME, **602**
NO_SYSTEM_FROM_IMPORTED, **603**
OSX_ARCHITECTURES, **603**, 603, 663
OSX_ARCHITECTURES_<CONFIG>, **603**, 603
OUTPUT_NAME, 274, 275, **603**
OUTPUT_NAME_<CONFIG>, **603**
PDB_NAME, 358, 581, **604**, 604
PDB_NAME_<CONFIG>, 358, 582, **604**
PDB_OUTPUT_DIRECTORY, 358, 582, **605**, 605, 664
PDB_OUTPUT_DIRECTORY_<CONFIG>, 358, 582, **604**, 664
POSITION_INDEPENDENT_CODE, 275, 594, **605**, 640
POST_INSTALL_SCRIPT, 322, **622**
PRE_INSTALL_SCRIPT, 322, **623**
PREFIX, **605**
PRIVATE_HEADER, 319, **605**
PROJECT_LABEL, **606**
PUBLIC_HEADER, 319, **606**
RESOURCE, 319, **606**
RULE_LAUNCH_COMPILE, **606**
RULE_LAUNCH_CUSTOM, **606**
RULE_LAUNCH_LINK, **607**
RUNTIME_OUTPUT_DIRECTORY, 273, 275, **607**
RUNTIME_OUTPUT_DIRECTORY_<CONFIG>, **607**
RUNTIME_OUTPUT_NAME, **607**
RUNTIME_OUTPUT_NAME_<CONFIG>, **607**
SKIP_BUILD_RPATH, **608**

SOURCES, 343, 557, 594, **608**, 640
SOVERSION, 55, 319, **608**
STATIC_LIBRARY_FLAGS, **608**
STATIC_LIBRARY_FLAGS_<CONFIG>, **608**
SUFFIX, **608**
TYPE, **609**
VERSION, 55, 319, **609**
VISIBILITY_INLINES_HIDDEN, 519, 521, **609**
VS_DOTNET_REFERENCES, **609**
VS_DOTNET_TARGET_FRAMEWORK_VERSION, **609**
VS_GLOBAL_<variable>, **610**
VS_GLOBAL_KEYWORD, **610**, 611
VS_GLOBAL_PROJECT_TYPES, **610**
VS_GLOBAL_ROOTNAMESPACE, **610**
VS_KEYWORD, **610**, 610
VS_SCC_AUXPATH, **611**
VS_SCC_LOCALPATH, **611**
VS_SCC_PROJECTNAME, **611**
VS_SCC_PROVIDER, **611**
VS_WINRT_COMPONENT, **611**, 611
VS_WINRT_EXTENSIONS, **611**
VS_WINRT_REFERENCES, **611**
WIN32_EXECUTABLE, 274, 495, **612**
XCODE_ATTRIBUTE_<an-attribute>, **612**, 666
targets, 21
targets
    custom, 91
    custom commands, 88
    exporting, 66
    importing, 65
    properties, 22
test property
    ATTACHED_FILES, **612**
    ATTACHED_FILES_ON_FAIL, **612**
    COST, **612**
    DEPENDS, **613**
    ENVIRONMENT, **613**
    FAIL_REGULAR_EXPRESSION, 159, **613**
    LABELS, **613**
    MEASUREMENT, **613**
    PASS_REGULAR_EXPRESSION, 159, **613**
    PROCESSORS, **614**
    REQUIRED_FILES, **614**
    RESOURCE_LOCK, **614**
    RUN_SERIAL, **614**
    SKIP_RETURN_CODE, **614**
    TIMEOUT, 253, **614**
    WILL_FAIL, **615**
    WORKING_DIRECTORY, 278, **615**
testing, 155
toolchain file, 103
true, 31
tutorial, 222

U

unit testing, 157

UNIX, *see* MakeFiles
UNIX
    libraries, 53
    symbols, 51

V

valgrind, 173, 175
variable
    <PROJECT-NAME>_BINARY_DIR, 327, **636**
    <PROJECT-NAME>_SOURCE_DIR, 327, **637**
    <PROJECT-NAME>_VERSION, 327, **637**, 637
    <PROJECT-NAME>_VERSION_MAJOR, 327, **637**, 637
    <PROJECT-NAME>_VERSION_MINOR, 327, **637**, 637
    <PROJECT-NAME>_VERSION_PATCH, 327, **637**, 637
    <PROJECT-NAME>_VERSION_TWEAK, 327, **637**, 637
    APPLE, 107, **650**
    BORLAND, **650**
    BUILD_SHARED_LIBS, 275, **638**
    CMAKE_<CONFIG>_POSTFIX, **658**
    CMAKE_<LANG>_ARCHIVE_APPEND, **669**
    CMAKE_<LANG>_ARCHIVE_CREATE, **669**
    CMAKE_<LANG>_ARCHIVE_FINISH, **669**
    CMAKE_<LANG>_COMPILE_OBJECT, **669**
    CMAKE_<LANG>_COMPILER, 552, **670**
    CMAKE_<LANG>_COMPILER_ABI, **670**
    CMAKE_<LANG>_COMPILER_EXTERNAL_TOOLCHAIN, **671**
    CMAKE_<LANG>_COMPILER_ID, 358, 534, 548, 555, 556, **670**
    CMAKE_<LANG>_COMPILER_LOADED, **670**
    CMAKE_<LANG>_COMPILER_TARGET, **671**
    CMAKE_<LANG>_COMPILER_VERSION, 358, 379, **671**
    CMAKE_<LANG>_CREATE_SHARED_LIBRARY, **671**
    CMAKE_<LANG>_CREATE_SHARED_MODULE, **671**
    CMAKE_<LANG>_CREATE_STATIC_LIBRARY, **671**
    CMAKE_<LANG>_FLAGS, 521, **672**
    CMAKE_<LANG>_FLAGS_DEBUG, **672**
    CMAKE_<LANG>_FLAGS_MINSIZEREL, **672**
    CMAKE_<LANG>_FLAGS_RELEASE, **672**
    CMAKE_<LANG>_FLAGS_RELWITHDEBINFO, **672**
    CMAKE_<LANG>_IGNORE_EXTENSIONS, **672**
    CMAKE_<LANG>_IMPLICIT_INCLUDE_DIRECTORIES, **672**
    CMAKE_<LANG>_IMPLICIT_LINK_DIRECTORIES, **673**
    CMAKE_<LANG>_IMPLICIT_LINK_FRAMEWORK_DIRECTORIE **673**

CMAKE_<LANG>_IMPLICIT_LINK_LIBRARIES, **673**
CMAKE_<LANG>_LIBRARY_ARCHITECTURE, **673**
CMAKE_<LANG>_LINK_EXECUTABLE, **674**
CMAKE_<LANG>_LINKER_PREFERENCE, **674**
CMAKE_<LANG>_LINKER_PREFERENCE_PROPAGATES, **673**
CMAKE_<LANG>_OUTPUT_EXTENSION, **674**
CMAKE_<LANG>_PLATFORM_ID, **674**
CMAKE_<LANG>_SIMULATE_ID, **674**
CMAKE_<LANG>_SIMULATE_VERSION, **674**
CMAKE_<LANG>_SIZEOF_DATA_PTR, **675**
CMAKE_<LANG>_SOURCE_FILE_EXTENSIONS, **675**
CMAKE_<LANG>_VISIBILITY_PRESET, 519, **660**
CMAKE_ABSOLUTE_DESTINATION_FILES, **638**
CMAKE_ANDROID_API, 573, **656**
CMAKE_ANDROID_GUI, 573, **656**
CMAKE_APPBUNDLE_PATH, 489, 491, **639**
CMAKE_AR, **624**
CMAKE_ARCHIVE_OUTPUT_DIRECTORY, 97, **656**
CMAKE_ARGC, **623**
CMAKE_ARGV0, **623**
CMAKE_AUTOMOC, 575, **657**, 657
CMAKE_AUTOMOC_MOC_OPTIONS, **657**
CMAKE_AUTOMOC_RELAXED_MODE, 575, **639**
CMAKE_AUTORCC, 577, **657**
CMAKE_AUTORCC_OPTIONS, 577, **657**
CMAKE_AUTOUIC, 576, **657**
CMAKE_AUTOUIC_OPTIONS, 576, **657**
CMAKE_BACKWARDS_COMPATIBILITY, **639**
CMAKE_BINARY_DIR, **624**, 645
CMAKE_BUILD_TOOL, **624**
CMAKE_BUILD_TYPE, 28, **639**
CMAKE_BUILD_WITH_INSTALL_RPATH, **658**
CMAKE_C_COMPILE_FEATURES, 338, 560, **667**
CMAKE_C_EXTENSIONS, 578, **667**
CMAKE_C_STANDARD, 578, **667**
CMAKE_C_STANDARD_REQUIRED, 579, **667**
CMAKE_CACHE_MAJOR_VERSION, **624**
CMAKE_CACHE_MINOR_VERSION, **624**
CMAKE_CACHE_PATCH_VERSION, **624**
CMAKE_CACHEFILE_DIR, **624**
CMAKE_CFG_INTDIR, 28, **625**
CMAKE_CL_64, **650**
CMAKE_COLOR_MAKEFILE, **639**
CMAKE_COMMAND, 88, 252, **625**
CMAKE_COMPILE_PDB_OUTPUT_DIRECTORY, 582, **658**, 658
CMAKE_COMPILE_PDB_OUTPUT_DIRECTORY_<CONFIG>, 582, **658**
CMAKE_COMPILER_2005, **651**
CMAKE_COMPILER_IS_GNU<LANG>, **667**
CMAKE_CONFIGURATION_TYPES, 28, **640**
CMAKE_CROSSCOMPILING, 104, 108, **625**
CMAKE_CTEST_COMMAND, 162, **626**

CMAKE_CURRENT_BINARY_DIR, **626**
CMAKE_CURRENT_LIST_DIR, **626**
CMAKE_CURRENT_LIST_FILE, **626**
CMAKE_CURRENT_LIST_LINE, **626**
CMAKE_CURRENT_SOURCE_DIR, **627**
CMAKE_CXX_COMPILE_FEATURES, 338, 560, 581, **668**
CMAKE_CXX_EXTENSIONS, 583, **668**
CMAKE_CXX_STANDARD, 584, **668**
CMAKE_CXX_STANDARD_REQUIRED, 584, **668**
CMAKE_DEBUG_POSTFIX, **658**
CMAKE_DEBUG_TARGET_PROPERTIES, **640**
CMAKE_DISABLE_FIND_PACKAGE_<PackageName>, 303, **640**
CMAKE_DL_LIBS, **627**
CMAKE_EDIT_COMMAND, **627**
CMAKE_ERROR_DEPRECATED, **640**
CMAKE_ERROR_ON_ABSOLUTE_INSTALL_DESTINATION, **640**
CMAKE_EXE_LINKER_FLAGS, **659**
CMAKE_EXE_LINKER_FLAGS_<CONFIG>, **658**
CMAKE_EXECUTABLE_SUFFIX, 88, **627**
CMAKE_EXPORT_NO_PACKAGE_REGISTRY, 287, **641**, 641
CMAKE_EXTRA_GENERATOR, **627**
CMAKE_EXTRA_SHARED_LIBRARY_SUFFIXES, **627**
CMAKE_FIND_LIBRARY_PREFIXES, **641**
CMAKE_FIND_LIBRARY_SUFFIXES, **641**
CMAKE_FIND_NO_INSTALL_PREFIX, **641**, 642, 648
CMAKE_FIND_PACKAGE_NAME, **628**
CMAKE_FIND_PACKAGE_NO_PACKAGE_REGISTRY, 301, **642**, 642
CMAKE_FIND_PACKAGE_NO_SYSTEM_PACKAGE_REGISTRY, 302, **642**, 642
CMAKE_FIND_PACKAGE_WARN_NO_MODULE, **642**
CMAKE_FIND_ROOT_PATH, 106, 294, 296, 297, 302, 305, 306, 308, **643**, 643, 644
CMAKE_FIND_ROOT_PATH_MODE_INCLUDE, 107, 294, 306, **643**
CMAKE_FIND_ROOT_PATH_MODE_LIBRARY, 106, 297, **643**
CMAKE_FIND_ROOT_PATH_MODE_PACKAGE, 302, **643**
CMAKE_FIND_ROOT_PATH_MODE_PROGRAM, 106, 308, **643**
CMAKE_Fortran_FORMAT, **659**
CMAKE_Fortran_MODDIR_DEFAULT, **668**
CMAKE_Fortran_MODDIR_FLAG, **668**
CMAKE_Fortran_MODOUT_FLAG, **669**
CMAKE_Fortran_MODULE_DIRECTORY, **659**
CMAKE_FRAMEWORK_PATH, 489, 491, **644**
CMAKE_GENERATOR, 163, **628**, 630
CMAKE_GENERATOR_PLATFORM, 362, 363, **628**
CMAKE_GENERATOR_TOOLSET, **628**, 630

CMAKE_GNUtoMS, **659**
CMAKE_HOME_DIRECTORY, **628**
CMAKE_HOST_APPLE, 105, 107, **651**
CMAKE_HOST_SYSTEM, 105, 107, 211, **651**
CMAKE_HOST_SYSTEM_NAME, 105, 107, 211, **651**, 651, 653
CMAKE_HOST_SYSTEM_PROCESSOR, 105, 107, 211, **651**, 653
CMAKE_HOST_SYSTEM_VERSION, 107, 211, **651**, 651, 653
CMAKE_HOST_UNIX, 105, 107, **652**
CMAKE_HOST_WIN32, 105, 107, **652**
CMAKE_IGNORE_PATH, **644**
CMAKE_IMPORT_LIBRARY_PREFIX, **629**
CMAKE_IMPORT_LIBRARY_SUFFIX, **629**
CMAKE_INCLUDE_CURRENT_DIR, **659**
CMAKE_INCLUDE_CURRENT_DIR_IN_INTERFACE, **659**
CMAKE_INCLUDE_DIRECTORIES_BEFORE, 316, **644**
CMAKE_INCLUDE_DIRECTORIES_PROJECT_BEFORE, **644**
CMAKE_INCLUDE_PATH, **644**
CMAKE_INSTALL_DEFAULT_COMPONENT_NAME, 318, **645**
CMAKE_INSTALL_MESSAGE, 292, 318, **645**
CMAKE_INSTALL_NAME_DIR, 554, **660**
CMAKE_INSTALL_PREFIX, 56, 62, 113, 317, 384, 385, 642, **645**, 648
CMAKE_INSTALL_RPATH, 122, **660**
CMAKE_INSTALL_RPATH_USE_LINK_PATH, 122, **660**
CMAKE_INTERNAL_PLATFORM_ABI, **669**
CMAKE_JOB_POOL_COMPILE, 566, 595, **629**
CMAKE_JOB_POOL_LINK, 566, 596, **629**
CMAKE_LIBRARY_ARCHITECTURE, 300, **652**
CMAKE_LIBRARY_ARCHITECTURE_REGEX, **652**
CMAKE_LIBRARY_OUTPUT_DIRECTORY, 97, **660**
CMAKE_LIBRARY_PATH, **646**
CMAKE_LIBRARY_PATH_FLAG, **661**
CMAKE_LINK_DEF_FILE_FLAG, **661**
CMAKE_LINK_DEPENDS_NO_SHARED, **661**
CMAKE_LINK_INTERFACE_LIBRARIES, **661**
CMAKE_LINK_LIBRARY_FILE_FLAG, **661**
CMAKE_LINK_LIBRARY_FLAG, **661**
CMAKE_LINK_LIBRARY_SUFFIX, **629**
CMAKE_MACOSX_BUNDLE, **661**
CMAKE_MACOSX_RPATH, 602, **662**
CMAKE_MAJOR_VERSION, **629**, 634
CMAKE_MAKE_PROGRAM, 162, 624, **629**, 635, 636
CMAKE_MAP_IMPORTED_CONFIG_<CONFIG>, **662**
CMAKE_MFC_FLAG, **646**
CMAKE_MINIMUM_REQUIRED_VERSION, 489, 491, 534, 537, **630**
CMAKE_MINOR_VERSION, **630**, 634
CMAKE_MODULE_LINKER_FLAGS, **662**

CMAKE_MODULE_LINKER_FLAGS_<CONFIG>, **662**
CMAKE_MODULE_PATH, 38, 77, 117, 298, **646**
CMAKE_NO_BUILTIN_CHRPATH, **662**
CMAKE_NO_SYSTEM_FROM_IMPORTED, **662**
CMAKE_NOT_USING_CONFIG_FLAGS, **646**
CMAKE_OBJECT_PATH_MAX, **652**
CMAKE_OSX_ARCHITECTURES, 603, **663**
CMAKE_OSX_DEPLOYMENT_TARGET, **663**, 663
CMAKE_OSX_SYSROOT, **663**, 663
CMAKE_PARENT_LIST_FILE, **631**
CMAKE_PATCH_VERSION, **631**, 634
CMAKE_PDB_OUTPUT_DIRECTORY, 605, **663**, 664
CMAKE_PDB_OUTPUT_DIRECTORY_<CONFIG>, 605, **664**
CMAKE_POLICY_DEFAULT_CMP<NNNN>, 281, 537, **647**
CMAKE_POLICY_WARNING_CMP<NNNN>, 548, 556, **647**
CMAKE_POSITION_INDEPENDENT_CODE, 605, **664**
CMAKE_PREFIX_PATH, 489, 491, **647**
CMAKE_PROGRAM_PATH, **647**
CMAKE_PROJECT_<PROJECT-NAME>_INCLUDE, 327, **648**
CMAKE_PROJECT_NAME, **631**
CMAKE_RANLIB, **631**
CMAKE_ROOT, **631**
CMAKE_RUNTIME_OUTPUT_DIRECTORY, 97, **664**
CMAKE_SCRIPT_MODE_FILE, **631**
CMAKE_SHARED_LIBRARY_PREFIX, 88, **631**
CMAKE_SHARED_LIBRARY_SUFFIX, **632**
CMAKE_SHARED_LINKER_FLAGS, **664**
CMAKE_SHARED_LINKER_FLAGS_<CONFIG>, **664**
CMAKE_SHARED_MODULE_PREFIX, **632**
CMAKE_SHARED_MODULE_SUFFIX, **632**
CMAKE_SIZEOF_VOID_P, **632**
CMAKE_SKIP_BUILD_RPATH, **664**
CMAKE_SKIP_INSTALL_ALL_DEPENDENCY, **648**
CMAKE_SKIP_INSTALL_RPATH, **665**
CMAKE_SKIP_INSTALL_RULES, **632**
CMAKE_SKIP_RPATH, 54, **632**
CMAKE_SOURCE_DIR, **633**, 645
CMAKE_STAGING_PREFIX, 294, 296, 297, 302, 305, 306, 308, 642, **648**, 649
CMAKE_STANDARD_LIBRARIES, **633**
CMAKE_STATIC_LIBRARY_PREFIX, **633**
CMAKE_STATIC_LIBRARY_SUFFIX, **633**
CMAKE_STATIC_LINKER_FLAGS, **665**
CMAKE_STATIC_LINKER_FLAGS_<CONFIG>, **665**
CMAKE_SYSROOT, 294, 296, 297, 302, 305, 306, 308, **641**, 643, 644, 648
CMAKE_SYSTEM, 107, 211, 552, **653**
CMAKE_SYSTEM_IGNORE_PATH, **648**

CMAKE_SYSTEM_INCLUDE_PATH, **648**
CMAKE_SYSTEM_LIBRARY_PATH, **649**
CMAKE_SYSTEM_NAME, 104, 107, 116, 211, 358, 636, **652**, 653, 656
CMAKE_SYSTEM_PREFIX_PATH, 642, **649**
CMAKE_SYSTEM_PROCESSOR, 104, 107, 116, 211, **653**
CMAKE_SYSTEM_PROGRAM_PATH, **649**
CMAKE_SYSTEM_VERSION, 104, 107, 211, **653**, 653
CMAKE_TOOLCHAIN_FILE, 104, 628, **633**, 641, 671
CMAKE_TRY_COMPILE_CONFIGURATION, **665**
CMAKE_TWEAK_VERSION, **633**, 634
CMAKE_USE_RELATIVE_PATHS, **665**
CMAKE_USER_MAKE_RULES_OVERRIDE, **649**
CMAKE_USER_MAKE_RULES_OVERRIDE_<LANG>, **675**
CMAKE_VERBOSE_MAKEFILE, **634**
CMAKE_VERSION, 37, 629, 631, **634**, 634
CMAKE_VISIBILITY_INLINES_HIDDEN, 519, 609, **666**
CMAKE_VS_DEVENV_COMMAND, 630, **635**, 635
CMAKE_VS_INTEL_Fortran_PROJECT_VERSION, **635**
CMAKE_VS_MSBUILD_COMMAND, 630, **635**, 635
CMAKE_VS_MSDEV_COMMAND, 630, **635**
CMAKE_VS_NsightTegra_VERSION, **636**
CMAKE_VS_PLATFORM_NAME, **636**
CMAKE_VS_PLATFORM_TOOLSET, **636**
CMAKE_WARN_DEPRECATED, **650**
CMAKE_WARN_ON_ABSOLUTE_INSTALL_DESTINATION, **650**
CMAKE_WIN32_EXECUTABLE, **666**
CMAKE_XCODE_ATTRIBUTE_<an-attribute>, 612, **666**
CMAKE_XCODE_PLATFORM_TOOLSET, **636**
CPACK_<GENNAME>_COMPONENT_INSTALL, **390**
CPACK_ABSOLUTE_DESTINATION_FILES, **681**
CPACK_BINARY_<GENNAME>, **415**
CPACK_BUNDLE_ICON, **390**
CPACK_BUNDLE_NAME, **390**
CPACK_BUNDLE_PLIST, **390**
CPACK_BUNDLE_STARTUP_COMMAND, **390**
CPACK_CMAKE_GENERATOR, **414**
CPACK_COMMAND_HDIUTIL, **399**
CPACK_COMMAND_REZ, **399**
CPACK_COMMAND_SETFILE, **399**
CPACK_COMPONENT_<compName>_DEPENDS, **391**
CPACK_COMPONENT_<compName>_DESCRIPTION, **391**
CPACK_COMPONENT_<compName>_DISPLAY_NAME, **391**
CPACK_COMPONENT_<compName>_GROUP, **391**
CPACK_COMPONENT_<compName>_REQUIRED, **391**

CPACK_COMPONENT_INCLUDE_TOPLEVEL_DIRECTORY, 681
CPACK_COMPONENTS_ALL, 390
CPACK_COMPONENTS_GROUPING, 391
CPACK_CREATE_DESKTOP_LINKS, 415
CPACK_CYGWIN_BUILD_SCRIPT, 394
CPACK_CYGWIN_PATCH_FILE, 394
CPACK_CYGWIN_PATCH_NUMBER, 394
CPACK_DEBIAN_COMPRESSION_TYPE, 396
CPACK_DEBIAN_PACKAGE_ARCHITECTURE, 395
CPACK_DEBIAN_PACKAGE_BREAKS, 397
CPACK_DEBIAN_PACKAGE_CONFLICTS, 397
CPACK_DEBIAN_PACKAGE_CONTROL_EXTRA, 398
CPACK_DEBIAN_PACKAGE_DEBUG, 396
CPACK_DEBIAN_PACKAGE_DEPENDS, 395
CPACK_DEBIAN_PACKAGE_DESCRIPTION, 395
CPACK_DEBIAN_PACKAGE_ENHANCES, 397
CPACK_DEBIAN_PACKAGE_HOMEPAGE, 396
CPACK_DEBIAN_PACKAGE_MAINTAINER, 395
CPACK_DEBIAN_PACKAGE_NAME, 395
CPACK_DEBIAN_PACKAGE_PREDEPENDS, 396
CPACK_DEBIAN_PACKAGE_PRIORITY, 396
CPACK_DEBIAN_PACKAGE_PROVIDES, 397
CPACK_DEBIAN_PACKAGE_RECOMMENDS, 397
CPACK_DEBIAN_PACKAGE_REPLACES, 397
CPACK_DEBIAN_PACKAGE_SECTION, 396
CPACK_DEBIAN_PACKAGE_SHLIBDEPS, 396
CPACK_DEBIAN_PACKAGE_SUGGESTS, 398
CPACK_DEBIAN_PACKAGE_VERSION, 395
CPACK_DMG_BACKGROUND_IMAGE, 398
CPACK_DMG_DS_STORE, 398
CPACK_DMG_FORMAT, 398
CPACK_DMG_VOLUME_NAME, 398
CPACK_ERROR_ON_ABSOLUTE_INSTALL_DESTINATION, 681
CPACK_GENERATOR, 414
CPACK_IFW_ADMIN_TARGET_DIRECTORY, 400
CPACK_IFW_BINARYCREATOR_EXECUTABLE, 401
CPACK_IFW_DOWNLOAD_ALL, 400, 403
CPACK_IFW_PACKAGE_GROUP, 400
CPACK_IFW_PACKAGE_ICON, 400
CPACK_IFW_PACKAGE_LOGO, 400
CPACK_IFW_PACKAGE_NAME, 400
CPACK_IFW_PACKAGE_PUBLISHER, 400
CPACK_IFW_PACKAGE_TITLE, 400
CPACK_IFW_PACKAGE_WINDOW_ICON, 400
CPACK_IFW_PACKAGES_DIRECTORIES, 401
CPACK_IFW_PRODUCT_URL, 400
CPACK_IFW_REPOGEN_EXECUTABLE, 401
CPACK_IFW_REPOSITORIES_ALL, 400, 402
CPACK_IFW_RESOLVE_DUPLICATE_NAMES, 400
CPACK_IFW_TARGET_DIRECTORY, 400
CPACK_INCLUDE_TOPLEVEL_DIRECTORY, 681
CPACK_INSTALL_CMAKE_PROJECTS, 415

CPACK_INSTALL_COMMANDS, 415
CPACK_INSTALL_SCRIPT, 682
CPACK_INSTALLED_DIRECTORIES, 415
CPACK_MONOLITHIC_INSTALL, 413
CPACK_NSIS_COMPRESSOR, 404
CPACK_NSIS_CONTACT, 405
CPACK_NSIS_CREATE_ICONS_EXTRA, 405
CPACK_NSIS_DELETE_ICONS_EXTRA, 405
CPACK_NSIS_DISPLAY_NAME, 405
CPACK_NSIS_ENABLE_UNINSTALL_BEFORE_INSTALL, 404
CPACK_NSIS_EXECUTABLES_DIRECTORY, 405
CPACK_NSIS_EXTRA_INSTALL_COMMANDS, 404
CPACK_NSIS_EXTRA_PREINSTALL_COMMANDS, 404
CPACK_NSIS_EXTRA_UNINSTALL_COMMANDS, 404
CPACK_NSIS_HELP_LINK, 405
CPACK_NSIS_INSTALL_ROOT, 404
CPACK_NSIS_INSTALLED_ICON_NAME, 405
CPACK_NSIS_INSTALLER_MUI_ICON_CODE, 404
CPACK_NSIS_MENU_LINKS, 405
CPACK_NSIS_MODIFY_PATH, 404
CPACK_NSIS_MUI_FINISHPAGE_RUN, 405
CPACK_NSIS_MUI_ICON, 404
CPACK_NSIS_MUI_UNIICON, 404
CPACK_NSIS_PACKAGE_NAME, 405
CPACK_NSIS_URL_INFO_ABOUT, 405
CPACK_OSX_PACKAGE_VERSION, 405
CPACK_OUTPUT_CONFIG_FILE, 414
CPACK_PACKAGE_DESCRIPTION_FILE, 413
CPACK_PACKAGE_DESCRIPTION_SUMMARY, 400, 413
CPACK_PACKAGE_DIRECTORY, 412
CPACK_PACKAGE_EXECUTABLES, 414, 415
CPACK_PACKAGE_FILE_NAME, 413
CPACK_PACKAGE_ICON, 413
CPACK_PACKAGE_INSTALL_DIRECTORY, 400, 413
CPACK_PACKAGE_INSTALL_REGISTRY_KEY, 415
CPACK_PACKAGE_NAME, 412
CPACK_PACKAGE_VENDOR, 400, 412
CPACK_PACKAGE_VERSION, 401, 402, 415
CPACK_PACKAGE_VERSION_MAJOR, 412
CPACK_PACKAGE_VERSION_MINOR, 413
CPACK_PACKAGE_VERSION_PATCH, 413
CPACK_PACKAGING_INSTALL_PREFIX, 128, 682
CPACK_PROJECT_CONFIG_FILE, 413
CPACK_RESOURCE_FILE_LICENSE, 413
CPACK_RESOURCE_FILE_README, 413
CPACK_RESOURCE_FILE_WELCOME, 413
CPACK_RPM_<COMPONENT>_USER_FILELIST, 410
CPACK_RPM_CHANGELOG_FILE, 411
CPACK_RPM_COMPRESSION_TYPE, 407

CPACK_RPM_EXCLUDE_FROM_AUTO_FILELIST,
411
CPACK_RPM_EXCLUDE_FROM_AUTO_FILELIST_ADDITION,
411
CPACK_RPM_GENERATE_USER_BINARY_SPECFILE_
TEMPLATE   410
CPACK_RPM_PACKAGE_ARCHITECTURE, **407**
CPACK_RPM_PACKAGE_DEBUG, **409**
CPACK_RPM_PACKAGE_DESCRIPTION, **407**
CPACK_RPM_PACKAGE_GROUP, 407
CPACK_RPM_PACKAGE_LICENSE, **407**
CPACK_RPM_PACKAGE_NAME, **406**
CPACK_RPM_PACKAGE_OBSOLETES, **408**
CPACK_RPM_PACKAGE_PROVIDES, **408**
CPACK_RPM_PACKAGE_RELEASE, **407**
CPACK_RPM_PACKAGE_RELOCATABLE, **408**
CPACK_RPM_PACKAGE_REQUIRES, **408**
CPACK_RPM_PACKAGE_SUGGESTS, **408**
CPACK_RPM_PACKAGE_SUMMARY, **406**
CPACK_RPM_PACKAGE_URL, **407**
CPACK_RPM_PACKAGE_VENDOR, **407**
CPACK_RPM_PACKAGE_VERSION, **406**
CPACK_RPM_POST_INSTALL_SCRIPT_FILE, **410**
CPACK_RPM_POST_UNINSTALL_SCRIPT_FILE,
410
CPACK_RPM_PRE_INSTALL_SCRIPT_FILE, **410**
CPACK_RPM_PRE_UNINSTALL_SCRIPT_FILE,
410
CPACK_RPM_SPEC_INSTALL_POST, **409**
CPACK_RPM_SPEC_MORE_DEFINE, **409**
CPACK_RPM_USER_BINARY_SPECFILE, **409**
CPACK_RPM_USER_FILELIST, **410**
CPACK_SET_DESTDIR, 128, **682**
CPACK_SOURCE_GENERATOR, **414**
CPACK_SOURCE_IGNORE_FILES, **414**
CPACK_SOURCE_OUTPUT_CONFIG_FILE, **414**
CPACK_SOURCE_PACKAGE_FILE_NAME, **414**
CPACK_SOURCE_STRIP_FILES, **414**
CPACK_STRIP_FILES, **414**
CPACK_SYSTEM_NAME, **415**
CPACK_TOPLEVEL_TAG, **415**
CPACK_WARN_ON_ABSOLUTE_INSTALL_DESTINATION,
683
CPACK_WIX_<TOOL>_EXTENSIONS, **418**
CPACK_WIX_<TOOL>_EXTRA_FLAGS, **418**
CPACK_WIX_CMAKE_PACKAGE_REGISTRY, **418**
CPACK_WIX_CULTURES, **417**
CPACK_WIX_EXTENSIONS, **418**
CPACK_WIX_EXTRA_OBJECTS, **418**
CPACK_WIX_EXTRA_SOURCES, **418**
CPACK_WIX_LICENSE_RTF, **416**
CPACK_WIX_PATCH_FILE, **417**
CPACK_WIX_PRODUCT_GUID, **416**
CPACK_WIX_PRODUCT_ICON, **416**
CPACK_WIX_PROGRAM_MENU_FOLDER, **417**
CPACK_WIX_PROPERTY_<PROPERTY>, **418**
CPACK_WIX_TEMPLATE, **417**

CPACK_WIX_UI_BANNER, **416**
CPACK_WIX_UI_DIALOG, **417**
CPACK_WIX_UI_REF, **416**
CPACK_WIX_UPGRADE_GUID, **415**
CTEST_BINARY_DIRECTORY, 177, 184, 249, 354,
675
CTEST_BUILD_COMMAND, 184, 252, **675**
CTEST_BUILD_NAME, 184, 255, **675**
CTEST_BZR_COMMAND, 249, **675**
CTEST_BZR_UPDATE_OPTIONS, 249, **676**
CTEST_CHECKOUT_COMMAND, 354, **676**, 677
CTEST_CONFIGURATION_TYPE, 252, **676**
CTEST_CONFIGURE_COMMAND, 184, 252, **676**
CTEST_COVERAGE_COMMAND, 253, **676**
CTEST_COVERAGE_EXTRA_FLAGS, 253, **677**
CTEST_CURL_OPTIONS, 255, **677**
CTEST_CUSTOM_WARNING_EXCEPTION, 175
CTEST_CUSTOM_WARNING_MATCH, 175
CTEST_CVS_CHECKOUT, 179, 354, **677**
CTEST_CVS_COMMAND, 179, 249, **677**
CTEST_CVS_UPDATE_OPTIONS, 249, **677**
CTEST_DROP_LOCATION, 174, 255, **677**
CTEST_DROP_METHOD, 174, 255, **678**
CTEST_DROP_SITE, 174, 256, **678**
CTEST_DROP_SITE_CDASH, 174, 256, **678**
CTEST_DROP_SITE_PASSWORD, 174, 256, **678**
CTEST_DROP_SITE_USER, 174, 256, **678**
CTEST_GIT_COMMAND, 249, **678**
CTEST_GIT_UPDATE_CUSTOM, 250, **678**
CTEST_GIT_UPDATE_OPTIONS, 250, **678**
CTEST_HG_COMMAND, 250, **678**
CTEST_HG_UPDATE_OPTIONS, 250, **678**
CTEST_MEMORYCHECK_COMMAND, 253, **679**
CTEST_MEMORYCHECK_COMMAND_OPTIONS,
253, **679**
CTEST_MEMORYCHECK_SANITIZER_OPTIONS,
254, **679**
CTEST_MEMORYCHECK_SUPPRESSIONS_FILE,
254, **679**
CTEST_MEMORYCHECK_TYPE, 254, **679**
CTEST_NIGHTLY_START_TIME, 251, **679**
CTEST_P4_CLIENT, 250, **679**
CTEST_P4_COMMAND, 250, **679**
CTEST_P4_OPTIONS, 250, **679**
CTEST_P4_UPDATE_OPTIONS, 250, **680**
CTEST_SCP_COMMAND, 256, **680**
CTEST_SITE, 184, 256, **680**
CTEST_SOURCE_DIRECTORY, 177, 184, 249, 354,
680
CTEST_SVN_COMMAND, 251, **680**
CTEST_SVN_OPTIONS, 251, **680**
CTEST_SVN_UPDATE_OPTIONS, 251, **680**
CTEST_TEST_TIMEOUT, 253, **680**
CTEST_TRIGGER_SITE, 256, **680**
CTEST_UPDATE_COMMAND, 184, 251, **680**
CTEST_UPDATE_OPTIONS, 251, **681**
CTEST_UPDATE_VERSION_ONLY, 251, **681**

CTEST_USE_LAUNCHERS, 252, **681**
CYGWIN, **653**
ENV, **653**
EXECUTABLE_OUTPUT_PATH, **666**
GRAPHVIZ_EXECUTABLES, **382**
GRAPHVIZ_EXTERNAL_LIBS, **383**
GRAPHVIZ_GENERATE_DEPENDERS, **383**
GRAPHVIZ_GENERATE_PER_TARGET, **383**
GRAPHVIZ_GRAPH_HEADER, **382**
GRAPHVIZ_GRAPH_NAME, **382**
GRAPHVIZ_GRAPH_TYPE, **382**
GRAPHVIZ_IGNORE_TARGETS, **383**
GRAPHVIZ_MODULE_LIBS, **383**
GRAPHVIZ_NODE_PREFIX, **382**
GRAPHVIZ_SHARED_LIBS, **383**
GRAPHVIZ_STATIC_LIBS, **382**
LIBRARY_OUTPUT_PATH, **666**
MSVC, **655**
MSVC10, **653**
MSVC11, **654**
MSVC12, **654**
MSVC14, **654**
MSVC60, **654**
MSVC70, **654**
MSVC71, **654**
MSVC80, **654**
MSVC90, **655**
MSVC_IDE, **655**
MSVC_VERSION, **655**
PKG_CONFIG_EXECUTABLE, 489, **491**
PKG_CONFIG_USE_CMAKE_PREFIX_PATH, 489,
    491
PROJECT_BINARY_DIR, 249, 327, **636**
PROJECT_NAME, 327, 556, **636**
PROJECT_SOURCE_DIR, 249, 252, 327, **637**
PROJECT_VERSION, 327, 386, 556, **638**, 638
PROJECT_VERSION_MAJOR, 327, **638**, 638
PROJECT_VERSION_MINOR, 327, **638**, 638
PROJECT_VERSION_PATCH, 327, **638**, 638
PROJECT_VERSION_TWEAK, 327, **638**, 638
UNIX, 107, **655**

WIN32, 107, **655**
WINCE, **656**
WINDOWS_PHONE, **656**
WINDOWS_STORE, **656**
XCODE_VERSION, **656**
variable argument list, 35
variable CTEST_CUSTOM_MEMCHECK_IGNORE, 175
variable scope, 25
variables
    cache, 19
versions, 37
vim mode, 14
Visual Studio, 2, 4, 10, 14, 19, 28, 30, 55, 88, 90, 91, 94, 96
Visual Studio
    converting to CMake, 100
    file groups, 100
    header files, 100

W

white space, 29
Windows, *see* NSIS
    linking, 48
Windows
    build directory, 98
    CDash, 178
    dllexport, 51
    executable, 22
    executables, 100
    manifest files, 135
    registry entries, 1, 72
    registry values, 7
    relocatable applications, 63
    run time libraries, 135
    symbols, 51
WinMain, 22, 100
wrapping C/C++, *see* SWIG

X

Xcode, 2

41548838R00393

Made in the USA
San Bernardino, CA
15 November 2016